Volume II
Student-Centered Mathematics Series

D1606994

Teaching Student-Centered Mathematics
Developmentally Appropriate Instruction for Grades 3–5

Third Edition

John A. Van de Walle
Late of Virginia Commonwealth University

Karen S. Karp
Johns Hopkins University

LouAnn H. Lovin
James Madison University

Jennifer M. Bay-Williams
University of Louisville

 Pearson

330 Hudson Street, NY NY 10013

Vice President and Editor in Chief: Kevin M. Davis
Portfolio Manager: Drew Bennett
Content Producer: Yagnesh Jani
Portfolio Management Assistant: Maria Feliberty
Executive Product Marketing Manager: Christopher Barry
Executive Field Marketing Manager: Krista Clark
Procurement Specialist: Deidra Smith
Cover Designer: Cenveo, Carie Keller

Cover Art: TongRo/Getty Images
Media Producer: Linda Bishop
Editorial Production and Composition
  Services: SPi Global
Full-Service Project Manager: Jason Hammond,
  SPi Global
Text Font: 10/13

Library of Congress Cataloging-in-Publication Data:
Names: Van de Walle, John A. | Karp, Karen S. | Lovin, LouAnn H. | Bay-Williams, Jennifer M.
Title: Teaching student-centered mathematics. Developmentally appropriate instruction for grades 3–5.
Other titles: Teaching student-centered mathematics. Grades 3–5
Description: Third edition / John A. Van de Walle, late of Virginia Commonwealth University, Karen S. Karp,
  Johns Hopkins University, LouAnn H. Lovin, James Madison University, Jennifer M. Bay-Williams, University
  of Louisville. | New York : Pearson
  Education, [2018] | Series: Student-centered mathematics series ; volume 2 | Includes bibliographical references
  and index.
Identifiers: LCCN 2016051024 | ISBN 9780134556420
Subjects: LCSH: Mathematics–Study and teaching (Elementary) | Individualized instruction.
Classification: LCC QA13 .V34 2018 | DDC 372.7–dc23
LC record available at **https://lccn.loc.gov/2016051024**

ISBN 10: 0-13-455642-9
ISBN 13: 978-0-13-455642-0

About the Authors

The late **John A. Van de Walle** was a professor emeritus at Virginia Commonwealth University. He was a mathematics education consultant who regularly gave professional development workshops for K–8 teachers in the United States and Canada. He visited and taught in elementary school classrooms and worked with teachers to implement student-centered math lessons. He coauthored the Scott Foresman-Addison Wesley Mathematics K–6 series and contributed to the Pearson School mathematics program, enVisionMATH. In addition, he wrote numerous chapters and articles for the National Council of Teachers of Mathematics (NCTM) books and journals and was very active in NCTM, including serving on the Board of Directors, as the chair of the Educational Materials Committee, and as a frequent speaker at national and regional meetings.

Karen S. Karp is at the School of Education at Johns Hopkins University in Baltimore (Maryland). Previously, she was a professor of mathematics education at the University of Louisville for more than twenty years. Prior to entering the field of teacher education she was an elementary school teacher in New York. She is also coauthor of *Elementary and Middle School Mathematics: Teaching Developmentally, Developing Essential Understanding of Addition and Subtraction for Teaching Mathematics in Pre-K–Grade 2*, and numerous book chapters and articles. She is a former member of the Board of Directors of NCTM and a former president of the Association of Mathematics Teacher Educators (AMTE). She continues to work in classrooms to support teachers of students with disabilities in their mathematics instruction.

LouAnn H. Lovin is a professor of mathematics education at James Madison University (Virginia). She coauthored the first edition of the *Teaching Student-Centered Mathematics* Professional Development Series with John A. Van de Walle as well as *Teaching Mathematics Meaningfully: Solutions for Reaching Struggling Learners* (2nd ed.) with David Allsopp and Sarah Vaningen. LouAnn taught mathematics to middle and high school students before transitioning to preK–grade 8. For almost twenty years, she has worked in pre K through grade 8 classrooms and engaged with teachers in professional development as they implement a student-centered approach to teaching mathematics. She has published articles in *Teaching Children Mathematics, Mathematics Teaching in the Middle School*, and *Teaching Exceptional Children* and has served on NCTM's Educational Materials Committee. LouAnn's research on teachers' mathematical knowledge for teaching has focused most recently on the developmental nature of prospective teachers' fraction knowledge.

Jennifer M. Bay-Williams is a professor of mathematics education at the University of Louisville (Kentucky). Jennifer frequently offers professional development about effective mathematics teaching to K–12 teachers and leaders. She has coauthored numerous books, including *On the Money: Math Activities to Build Financial Literacy*; *Mathematics Coaching: Resources and Tools for Coaches and Leaders, K–12*; *Developing Essential Understanding of Addition and Subtraction for Teaching Mathematics in Pre-K–Grade 2*; *Math and Literature: Grades 6–8*; and *Navigating through Connections in Grades 6–8*. Additionally, she has written dozens of articles on teaching and learning in NCTM journals. Jennifer serves on the NCTM Board of Directors, and has served on the TODOS: Equity for All Board, and president of the Association of Mathematics Teacher Educators (AMTE). Jennifer taught elementary, middle, and high school in Missouri and in Peru, and continues to work in classrooms at all levels with students and with teachers.

Brief Contents

Part 1: Establishing a Student-Centered Environment

1 Setting a Vision for Learning High-Quality Mathematics   1

2 Teaching Mathematics through Problem Solving   14

3 Creating Assessments for Learning   38

4 Differentiating Instruction   53

5 Teaching Culturally and Linguistically Diverse Students   67

6 Teaching and Assessing Students with Exceptionalities   84

7 Collaborating with Families and Other Stakeholders   98

Part 2: Teaching Student-Centered Mathematics

8 Exploring Number and Operation Sense   116

9 Developing Basic Fact Fluency   141

10 Developing Whole-Number Place-Value Concepts   163

11 Building Strategies for Whole-Number Computation   182

12 Exploring Fraction Concepts   217

13 Building Strategies for Fraction Computation   250

14 Developing Decimal and Percent Concepts and Decimal Computation   277

15 Promoting Algebraic Thinking   307

16 Building Measurement Concepts   339

17 Developing Geometric Thinking and Concepts   371

18 Representing and Interpreting Data   404

Appendix A   Common Core State Standards: Standards for Mathematical Practice   A-1

Appendix B   Common Core State Standards: Grades 3–5 Critical Content Areas and Overviews   B-1

Appendix C   Mathematics Teaching Practices: NCTM Principles to Actions (2014)   C-1

Appendix D   Activities at a Glance: Volume II   D-1

Appendix E   Guide to Blackline Masters   E-1

References   R-1

Index   I-1

Expanded Table of Contents

Preface   xiv

Part 1: Establishing a Student-Centered Environment

1 Setting a Vision for Learning High-Quality Mathematics   1

Understanding and Doing Mathematics   2

How Do Students Learn?   5

   Constructivism   5

   Sociocultural Theory   6

Teaching for Understanding   7

   Teaching for Relational Understanding   7

   Teaching for Instrumental Understanding   9

The Importance of Students' Ideas   11

Mathematics Classrooms That Promote Understanding   12

2 Teaching Mathematics through Problem Solving   14

Teaching through Problem Solving: An Upside-Down Approach   14

Mathematics Teaching Practices for Teaching *through* Problem Solving   16

Using Worthwhile Tasks   17

   Level of Cognitive Demand   18

   Multiple Entry and Exit Points   19

   Relevant and Well-Designed Contexts   21

   Evaluating and Adapting Tasks   22

   What Do I Do When a Task Doesn't Work?   23

Orchestrating Classroom Discourse   23

   Classroom Discussions   24

   Aspects of Questioning   26

   How Much to Tell and Not to Tell   27

   Leveraging Mistakes and Misconceptions to Enhance Learning   28

Representations: Tools for Problem Solving, Reasoning, and Communication   29

   Build a Web of Representations   29

   Explore with Tools   30

   Tips for Using Representations in the Classroom   31

Lessons in the Problem-Based Classroom   32

   A Three-Phase Lesson Format   32

   Variations of the Three-Phase Lesson   35

Life-Long Learning: An Invitation to Learn and Grow   36

3 Creating Assessments for Learning   38

Assessment That Informs Instruction   38

Observations   40
    Anecdotal Notes   40
    Checklists   40

Questions   42

Interviews   42

Tasks   45
    Problem-Based Tasks   45
    Translation Tasks   46
    Writing   48

Students' Self-Assessment and Reflection   48

Rubrics and Their Uses   49
    Generic Rubrics   50
    Task-Specific Rubrics   50

4 Differentiating Instruction   53

Differentiation and Teaching Mathematics through Problem Solving   53

The Nuts and Bolts of Differentiating Instruction   55
    Planning Meaningful Content, Grounded in Authenticity   55
    Recognizing Students as Individuals   55
    Connecting Content and Learners   56

Differentiated Tasks for Whole-Class Instruction   58
    Parallel Tasks   58
    Open Questions   60

Tiered Lessons   62

Flexible Grouping   65

5 Teaching Culturally and Linguistically Diverse Students   67

Culturally and Linguistically Diverse Students   67
    Funds of Knowledge   67
    Mathematics as a Language   68

Culturally Responsive Mathematics Instruction   69
    Communicate High Expectations   70
    Make Content Relevant   71
    Attend to Students' Mathematical Identities   72
    Ensure Shared Power   73

Teaching Strategies That Support Culturally and Linguistically Diverse Students   73
    Focus on Academic Vocabulary   75
    Foster Student Participation during Instruction   77
    Plan Cooperative/Interdependent Groups to Support Language Development   79

Assessment Considerations for ELLs   81
    Select Tasks with Multiple Entry and Exit Points   81
    Use Diagnostic Interviews   81

Limit Linguistic Load   82
Provide Accommodations   82

6 Teaching and Assessing Students with Exceptionalities   84

Instructional Principles for Diverse Learners   84
Prevention Models   85
Implementing Interventions   88
Explicit Strategy Instruction   88
Concrete, Semi-Concrete, Abstract (CSA)   89
Peer-Assisted Learning   90
Think-Alouds   90
Teaching and Assessing Students with Learning Disabilities   92
Adapting for Students with Moderate/Severe Disabilities   94
Planning for Students Who Are Mathematically Gifted   94
Acceleration and Pacing   95
Depth   95
Complexity   95
Creativity   96
Strategies to Avoid   96

7 Collaborating with Families and Other Stakeholders   98

Sharing the Message with Stakeholders   98
Why Change?   99
Pedagogy   102
Content   103
Student Learning and Outcomes   105
Administrator Engagement and Support   106
Family Engagement   107
Family Math Nights   108
Classroom Visits   110
Involving ALL Families   110
Homework Practices and Parent Coaching   111
Tips for Helping Parents Help Their Child   111
Resources for Families   113
Seeing and Doing Mathematics at Home   114

Part 2: Teaching Student-Centered Mathematics

8 Exploring Number and Operation Sense   116

Developing Addition and Subtraction Operation Sense   117
Addition and Subtraction Problem Structures   117
Teaching Addition and Subtraction   120
Developing Multiplication and Division Operation Sense   123
Multiplication and Division Problem Structures   123

Equal-Group Problems   125

Comparison Problems   125

Array and Area Problems   126

Combination Problems   126

Teaching Multiplication and Division   126

Contextual Problems   127

Symbolism for Multiplication and Division   127

Choosing Numbers for Problems   128

Remainders   128

Model-Based Problems   129

Properties of Multiplication and Division   132

Commutative and Associative Properties of Multiplication   132

Zero and Identity Properties   133

Distributive Property   133

Why Not Division by Zero?   134

Strategies for Solving Contextual Problems   134

Analyzing Context Problems   134

Multistep Word Problems   137

9   Developing Basic Fact Fluency   141

Developmental Phases for Learning the Basic Fact Combinations   142

Teaching and Assessing the Basic Fact Combinations   143

Different Approaches to Teaching the Basic Facts   143

Teaching Basic Facts Effectively   144

Assessing Basic Facts Effectively   145

Reasoning Strategies for Addition Facts   145

One More Than and Two More Than   146

Combinations of 10   147

Making 10   147

Doubles and Near-Doubles   148

Reasoning Strategies for Subtraction Facts   149

Think-Addition   149

Down Under 10   150

Take from 10   151

Reasoning Strategies for Multiplication and Division Facts   151

Twos   151

Fives   152

Zeros and Ones   152

Nines   153

Derived Multiplication Fact Strategies   153

Division Facts   156

Reinforcing Basic Fact Mastery   156

Games to Support Basic Fact Mastery   156

About Drill   159

Fact Remediation   159

What to Do When Teaching Basic Facts   160

What Not to Do When Teaching Basic Facts   161

10 Developing Whole-Number Place-Value Concepts   163

Extending Number Relationships to Larger Numbers   164

Part–Part–Whole Relationships   165

Relative Magnitude   166

Connections to Real-World Ideas   167

Approximate Numbers and Rounding   167

Important Place-Value Concepts   167

Integration of Base-Ten Grouping with Counting by Ones   168

Integration of Base-Ten Groupings with Words   168

Integration of Base-Ten Grouping with Place-Value Notation   170

Base-Ten Models   170

Extending Base-Ten Concepts   171

Grouping Hundreds to Make 1000   171

Equivalent Representations   172

Oral and Written Names for Numbers   173

Three-Digit Number Names   173

Written Symbols   174

Patterns and Relationships with Multidigit Numbers   174

The Hundreds Chart   175

Relationships with Benchmark Numbers   176

Numbers beyond 1000   176

Extending the Place-Value System   177

Conceptualizing Large Numbers   179

11 Building Strategies for Whole-Number Computation   182

Toward Computational Fluency   183

Direct Modeling   184

Invented Strategies   184

Standard Algorithms   187

Development of Invented Strategies in Addition and Subtraction   189

Models to Support Invented Strategies   189

Adding Multidigit Numbers   190

Subtraction as "Think Addition"   192

Take-Away Subtraction   192

Standard Algorithms for Addition and Subtraction   193

Invented Strategies for Multiplication   193

Useful Representations   193

Multiplication by a One-Digit Multiplier   194

Multiplication of Multidigit Numbers   196

Standard Algorithms for Multiplication   198

Begin with Models   199

Invented Strategies for Division   203
   Missing-Factor Strategies   204
   Cluster Problems   204
Standard Algorithms for Division   205
   Begin with Models   205
   Two-Digit Divisors   209
Computational Estimation   211
   Teaching Computational Estimation   212
   Computational Estimation Strategies   213

12   Exploring Fraction Concepts   217
Meanings of Fractions   218
   Fraction Interpretations   218
   Why Fractions Are Difficult   219
Models for Fractions   221
   Area Models   221
   Length Models   223
   Set Models   224
Fractional Parts of a Whole   226
   Fraction Size Is Relative   226
   Partitioning   227
   Iterating   231
   Fraction Notation   236
   Magnitude of Fractions   237
Equivalent Fractions   239
   Conceptual Focus on Equivalence   239
   Equivalent-Fraction Models   240
   Developing an Equivalent-Fraction Algorithm   244
Comparing Fractions   246
   Using Number Sense   247
   Using Equivalent Fractions   248
Teaching Considerations for Fraction Concepts   249

13   Building Strategies for Fraction Computation   250
Understanding Fraction Operations   250
   A Problem-Based, Number Sense Approach   251
Addition and Subtraction   252
   Contextual Examples and Models   252
   Estimation and Invented Strategies   257
   Developing the Algorithms   258
   Fractions Greater Than One   259
   Addressing Common Errors and Misconceptions   260
Multiplication   262
   Contextual Examples and Models   262
   Estimating and Invented Strategies   267

Developing the Algorithms   267
Factors Greater Than One   267
Addressing Common Errors and Misconceptions   268
Division   269
Contextual Examples and Models   269
Estimating and Invented Strategies   273
Developing the Algorithms   274
Addressing Common Errors and Misconceptions   276

14   Developing Decimal and Percent Concepts and Decimal Computation   277
Developing Concepts of Decimals   278
Extending the Place-Value System   278
Connecting Fractions and Decimals   282
Say Decimal Fractions Correctly   282
Use Visual Models for Decimal Fractions   282
Multiple Names and Formats   285
Developing Decimal Number Sense   287
Familiar Fractions Connected to Decimals   287
Comparing and Ordering Decimal Fractions   291
Computation with Decimals   294
Addition and Subtraction   294
Multiplication   296
Division   300
Introducing Percents   301
Models and Terminology   302
Percent Problems in Context   304
Estimation   305

15   Promoting Algebraic Thinking   307
Strands of Algebraic Thinking   308
Generalized Arithmetic   308
Generalization with Number and Operations   308
Meaningful Use of Symbols   314
The Meaning of Variables   316
Making Structure in the Number System Explicit   326
Making Sense of Properties   327
Making Conjectures Based on Properties   329
Patterns and Functional Thinking   331
Growing Patterns   333
Functional Thinking   335

16   Building Measurement Concepts   339
The Meaning and Process of Measuring   340
Concepts and Skills   341
Introducing Nonstandard Units   343

Introducing Standard Units   343
Important Standard Units and Relationships   345
The Role of Estimation and Approximation   345
Strategies for Estimating Measurements   346
Measurement Estimation Activities   348
Length   348
Conversion   349
Fractional Parts of Units   350
Area   351
Comparison Activities   351
Using Physical Models of Area Units   352
The Relationship between Area and Perimeter   355
Developing Formulas for Perimeter and Area   357
Volume   359
Comparison Activities   359
Using Physical Models of Volume Units   360
Developing Formulas for Volumes of Common Solid Shapes   362
Weight and Mass   363
Comparison Activities   363
Using Physical Models of Weight or Mass Units   363
Angles   364
Comparison Activities   364
Using Physical Models of Angular Measure Units   364
Using Protractors   365
Time   366
Comparison Activities   366
Reading Clocks   366
Elapsed Time   367
Money   368

17   Developing Geometric Thinking and Concepts   371
Geometry Goals for Your Students   372
Spatial Sense   372
Geometric Content   373
Developing Geometric Thinking   373
The van Hiele Levels of Geometric Thought   373
Implications for Instruction   379
Shapes and Properties   380
Sorting and Classifying   380
Composing and Decomposing Shapes   382
Categories of Two-Dimensional Shapes   385
Categories of Three-Dimensional Shapes   388
Construction Activities   390
Investigations, Conjectures, and the Development of Proof   394

Learning about Transformations   396

Learning about Location   398

Learning about Visualizations   401

Three-Dimensional Imagery   401

18   Representing and Interpreting Data   404

What Does It Mean to Do Statistics?   405

Is It Statistics or Is It Mathematics?   405

The Shape of Data   406

The Process of Doing Statistics   407

Formulating Questions   408

Classroom Questions   408

Beyond One Classroom   408

Data Collection   410

Using Existing Data Sources   411

Data Analysis: Classification   411

Data Analysis: Graphical Representations   413

Creating Graphs   414

Bar Graphs   414

Circle Graphs   415

Continuous Data Graphs   416

Line Graphs   418

Interpreting Results   419

Appendix A   Common Core State Standards: Standards for Mathematical Practice   A-1

Appendix B   Common Core State Standards: Grades 3–5 Critical Content Areas and Overviews   B-1

Appendix C   Mathematics Teaching Practices: NCTM Principles to Actions (2014)   C-1

Appendix D   Activities at a Glance: Volume II   D-1

Appendix E   Guide to Blackline Masters   E-1

References   R-1

Index   I-1

Preface

All students can learn mathematics with understanding! We believe that teachers can and must create learning environments in which students have this experience. Effective mathematics instruction involves posing worthwhile tasks that will engage students in the mathematics they are expected to learn. Then, by allowing students to interact with and productively struggle with the mathematics using *their* ideas and *their* strategies—a student-centered approach—students will develop a robust understanding of the mathematics. As they learn to see the connections among mathematical topics and to their world, students will value mathematics and feel empowered to use it. The title of this book, *Teaching Student-Centered Mathematics: Developmentally Appropriate Instruction for Grades 3–5*, reflects this vision. Part 1 of this book is dedicated to addressing how to build a student-centered environment in which students can become mathematically proficient and Part 2 elaborates on how that environment can be realized across all content in the grades 3–5 mathematics curriculum.

What Are Our Goals for the Student-Centered Grade-Band Books?

Creating a classroom in which students design their solution pathways, engage in productive struggle, and connect mathematical ideas is complex. Questions arise, such as, "How do I get students to wrestle with problems if they just want me to show them how to do it? What kinds of tasks lend themselves to this type of engagement? Where can I learn the mathematics content I need in order to be able to teach in this way?" With these and other questions firmly in mind, we have three main objectives for the third edition of this series:

1. Illustrate what it means to teach mathematics using a student-centered, problem-based approach.

2. Serve as a go-to reference for all of the mathematics content suggested for grades 3–5 as recommended in the *Common Core State Standard for Mathematics* (CCSSO, 2010) and in other standards used by various states, as well as research-based strategies that depict how students best learn this content.

3. Present a practical resource of robust, problem-based activities and tasks that can engage students in the mathematics that is important for them to learn.

These are also goals of *Elementary and Middle School Mathematics: Teaching Developmentally*, a comprehensive resource for teachers in grades K–8, which has been widely used in universities and in schools. There is overlap between the comprehensive K–8 book and this Student-Centered Mathematics Series; however, we have adapted the Student-Centered Mathematics Series to be more useful for a practicing classroom teacher by addressing the content for specific grade bands (with more activities!), removing content aimed at preservice teachers, and adding additional information more appropriate for practicing teachers. We hope you will find that this is a valuable resource for teaching and learning mathematics!

What's New to the Third Edition of the Student-Centered Mathematics Series?

The most significant change to the third edition is its availability as an Enhanced Pearson eText. Teachers can now take advantage of eText technology, easily accessing downloadable resources to support many of the math activities offered in the text and linking to videos that demonstrate how to teach certain math concepts. Another big change is that the third edition appears in four-color, so pedagogical features are more easily found and studied. We are hopeful too that the addition of color helps to enhance and clarify the ideas we have intended to convey. We have also included some new features that we briefly describe here. (More detailed information about the new features can be found in the following section.) We then highlight the most substantial changes we have made to specific chapters to reflect the changing landscape of mathematics education.

What Are the New eText Features?

Each volume in the Student-Centered Mathematics Series is also available as an Enhanced Pearson eText* with the following point-of-use features:

- *Downloadable Activity Pages and Blackline Masters.* Hyperlinks provide access to ready-to-use teaching resources including Activity Pages and Blackline Masters to support students' engagement in a large number of math activities.

- *Videos.* Links to videos allow teachers to observe an interview with a child, watch an idea play out in a classroom, or listen to a more in-depth description of an important math concept.

- *Activities Correspond to CCSS-M.* The numerous problem-based tasks presented in activity boxes are now linked to the appropriate *Common Core State Standards for Mathematics.*

- *Immediate Access to Expanded Lessons.* A custom basket located on the navigation bar links teachers to full and expanded lessons and include the Blackline Masters or Activity Pages if needed to execute each lesson. Expanded Lessons are referenced at point-of-use in numbered math activities throughout the eText.

What's New in Part 1?

Part 1 consists of seven chapters that focus on important "hot" topics that address ideas for creating a classroom environment in which all students can succeed. These chapters are, by design, shorter in length than the content chapters in Part 2, but are full of effective strategies and ideas. The intent is that these chapters can be used in professional development workshops, book study, or professional learning community (PLC) discussions. Changes to Part 1 chapters include:

Chapter 1: Setting a Vision for Learning High-Quality Mathematics. Changes to this chapter include a new table that relates CCSS-M's mathematical practices (CCSSO, 2010) to NCTM's process standards (2000), clarification about the difference between modeling mathematics and modeling with mathematics, and an additional emphasis on the characteristics of productive classrooms that promote student understanding.

Chapter 2: Teaching Mathematics through Problem Solving. The eight mathematics teaching practices from *Principles to Actions* (NCTM, 2014) have been added! In addition, several new sections were added: evaluating and adapting tasks to increase their potential for

---

* These features are only available in the Pearson eText, available exclusively from www .pearsonhighered.com/etextbooks or by ordering the Pearson eText plus Vol II Book Package (ISBN: 0134081412) or the Pearson eText Access Code Card (ISBN: 0134556402).

learning, growth versus fixed mindsets (connected to productive struggle and learning from mistakes); and effective aspects of questioning. Finally, more detail pertaining to the three-phases (before, during, and after) is provided.

Chapter 3: Creating Assessments for Learning. Supported by the recent position statement from professional organizations (NCSM and AMTE) about assessment for learning (AFL), this chapter was revised to be more explicit about how to collect evidence from students on their progress, interpret that evidence, make informed decisions about the next instructional steps and provide actionable feedback to students. There is also an expanded section on using writing to learn mathematics.

Chapter 4: Differentiating Instruction. This chapter was revised to better highlight differentiated tasks for whole-classroom instruction. You will also find new team-building activities to enhance your students' interactions with each other when working in groups.

Chapter 5: Teaching Culturally and Linguistically Diverse Students. In this chapter, significant revisions were made to reflect research in the field (twenty-two new references). Among these changes was increased attention to Culturally Responsive Mathematics Instruction (CRMI), developed around four key aspects and an expanded section on nurturing students' mathematical identities.

Chapter 6: Planning, Teaching, and Assessing Students with Exceptionalities. Several new tools were added to this chapter including a printable set of cards, each with a Strategy for Making Math Accessible for learners who struggle. This tool can be used when planning core instruction modifications or interventions for students with special needs. There is also a Mathematics Integration Plan Template to support planning for gifted students or students with a high interest in exploring mathematical topics in relation to other subject areas or perspectives.

Chapter 7: Collaborating with Families and Other Stakeholders. This chapter was significantly reorganized to focus on advocacy across stakeholders. This included increased attention to communicating about CCSS Mathematics. Finally, the homework section was expanded, including new activities and games for families.

What's New to Part 2?

The most noteworthy changes to Volume II, Part 2 are related to the content. The *Common Core State Standards* and other new state standards has shifted attention to particular topics of interest to grades three through five teachers. There is a considerable emphasis on multiplicative thinking, rational numbers and the development of the mathematical practices. The list below highlights significant differences in content coverage in this third edition.

Chapter 9: Basic Facts. In Chapter 9, there is an increased focus on assessing basic facts. This section presents the risks of using timed tests and presents a collection of alternative assessment ideas. Because the emphasis at this grade band is on multiplicative thinking the chapter emphasizes foundational facts prior to supporting students in using derived fact strategies for multiplication and division.

Chapter 11: Whole-Number Computation. Chapter 11 includes an expanded discussion of the written records of computing multiplication and division problems including lattice multiplication, open arrays and partial quotients.

Chapter 13: Fraction Operations. Chapter 13 uses a developmental approach capitalizing on learning trajectories. The discussion of developing meaning for each operation is expanded with more examples and activities.

Chapter 15: Algebra. Chapter 15 carefully bridges the connection between arithmetic and algebra with increased attention to relational thinking and the structure of equations. The chapter includes significant attention to content described in the *Common Core State Standards*, including generalizing arithmetic, use of symbols, structure in the number system, and functional thinking.

Chapter 16: Measurement. In this chapter there is an increased emphasis on converting units in the same measurement system. There is also a new section on perimeter which is a focus in the third grade. Across all measurement topics there are new activities and additional activity sheets.

What Special Features Appear in the Student-Centered Math Series?

Features Found in Parts 1 and 2

- *Teaching Tips.* These brief tips identify practical take-away ideas that can support the teaching and learning of specific chapter content being addressed. These might be an instructional suggestion, a particular point about language use, a common student misconception, or a suggestion about a resource.

- *Stop and Reflect.* Reflective thinking is the key to effective learning. This is true not only for our students but also for ourselves as we continue to learn more about effective mathematics teaching. Keep your eye out for these sections that ask you pause to solve a problem or reflect on some aspect of what you have read. These Stop and Reflect sections do not signal every important idea, but we have tried to place them where it seemed natural and helpful for you to slow down a bit and think deeply about an idea. In addition, every chapter in Part 1 ends with a Stop and Reflect section. Use these for discussions in professional learning communities or for reflection on your own.

- *New! Downloadable Resources including Activity Pages and Expanded Lessons.* Many activities that previously required cards or recording sheets now include these as ready-to-use, downloadable pages. You will also find a variety of downloadable resources that support teaching activities such as formative assessment and team-building activities. You can access these downloadable pages by clicking the blue text in the eText at point of use.

- *New! Videos.* The book now includes a collection of videos that are positioned right when you need them—when a child's misconception during a diagnostic interview will reinforce a point, when a strategy needs a more in-depth description or when it helps to see a teacher carry out an idea in a classroom of children. When accessing the e-book, you can click on the link to see an idea in action. There is also a video of John Van de Walle sharing some of his insights on how to teach a mathematics topic through the perspective of a student-centered, problem-based approach.

Additional Features Found in Part 2

- *New! NCTM Teaching Practices Appendix.* The *Principles to Actions* (NCTM, 2014) eight teaching practices are provided in Appendix C. These describe the actions that teachers do to support student thinking and provide guidance on how to enact student-centered mathematics.

- *New! Blackline Masters Hyperlinked in Chapters.* Blackline Masters are used in some of the activities and Expanded Lessons. Look for the call outs for the hyperlinks embedded in the activities that alert you to the corresponding print-friendly PDF of the Blackline Master. In Appendix E, you will find a list of the Blackline Masters and a thumbnail version of each.

- *New! Activities Correspond to the CCSS-M.* Numerous problem-based tasks are presented in activity boxes that are connected to the appropriate *Common Core State Standards for Mathematics.* Additional ideas are described directly in the text or in the illustrations. They are designed to engage your children in *doing* mathematics (as described in Chapter 2). Most of these activities are presented in the numbered activity boxes and include adaptation and accommodation suggestions for English language learners and children with special needs denoted with icons for easy reference. In addition, activities that incorporate technology are denoted with a technology icon. In Appendix D, you will find *Activities at a Glance.* This table lists all the named and numbered activities with a short statement about the mathematical content goal for each, the CCSS-M standard(s) and the page number where it can be located.

It is important that you see these activities as an integral part of the text that surrounds them. The activities are inserted as examples to support the development of the mathematics being discussed and how your children can be supported in learning that content. Therefore, we hope that you will not use any activity for instruction without reading carefully the full text in which it is embedded.

- *New! Downloadable Expanded Lessons.* In each chapter, one or more activities have been expanded it into a complete lesson plan, following the *before, during, after* structure described in Chapter 2 and are available by clicking on the link in the eText. These Expanded Lessons provide a model for converting an activity description into a full lesson that can engage children in developing a robust understanding of the related concept. In this new edition, all of the Expanded Lessons are now aligned with CCSSO grade-level recommendations and include adaptation suggestions for English language learners and children with disabilities. Many use the new Activity Pages or Blackline Masters.

- *New! Common Errors and Misconceptions.* Each chapter in Part 2 includes a table with common errors and misconceptions for chapter-related mathematical topics. This table includes examples of student work or verbal responses you should look for when a child is exhibiting these errors and ways to help the child move past these mistaken understandings. Using these tables, you can anticipate how you might support children in confronting common barriers so they can be unearthed and debunked. These lists also help you plan for gathering student assessment data that is targeted to catch areas of confusion or misconceptions prior to formally assessing children on a high-stakes evaluation of their performance. These examples were identified through the research literature and from the voices of teachers like yourself, about the common mistakes their children are making.

- *Formative Assessment Notes.* Assessment should be an integral part of instruction. As you read, we want you to think about what to listen and look for (assess) in different areas of content development. Therefore, you will find Formative Assessment Notes that describe ways to assess your children's developing knowledge and understanding. These Formative Assessment Notes can also help improve your understanding about how to help your children through targeted instruction.

- *Technology Notes.* These notes provide practical information about how technology can be used to help your children learn the content in that section. Descriptions include open-source software, interactive applets, and other Web-based resources—all of which are free.

- *Standards for Mathematical Practice Notes.* Connections to the eight Standards of Mathematical Practice from the *Common Core State Standards* are highlighted in the margins. The location of the note indicates an example of the identified practice in the nearby text.

- *Common Core State Standards Appendices.* The *Common Core State Standards* outline eight Standards for Mathematical Practice (Appendix A) that help children develop and demonstrate a deep understanding of and capacity to do mathematics. We initially describe these practices in Chapter 1 and highlight examples of the mathematical practices throughout the content chapters in Part 2 through margin notes. We used the *Common Core State Standards for Mathematics* (CCSSO, 2010) as a guide to determine the content emphasis in each volume of the series. Appendix B provides a list of the critical content areas for each grade level discussed in this volume.

- *Big Ideas.* Much of the research and literature espousing a developmental approach suggests that teachers plan their instruction around "big ideas" rather than isolated skills or concepts. At the beginning of each chapter, you will find a list of the key mathematical ideas associated with the chapter. These lists of learning targets can provide a snapshot of the mathematics you are teaching.

Acknowledgments

We would like to begin by acknowledging *you:* the reader, the teacher, the leader, and the advocate for your students. The strong commitment of teachers and teacher leaders to always strive to improve how we teach mathematics is the reason this book was written in the first place. And, because of ongoing input and feedback, we endeavored to revise this edition to meet your changing needs. We have received thoughtful input from many teachers and reviewers, and all of it has informed the development of this substantially revised third edition!

In preparing the third edition we benefited from the thoughtful input of the following educators who offered comments on the second edition or on the manuscript for the third: Alanna Arenivas, Dallas Independent School District; Josh Costelnock, Kyrene School District; Gwendolyn Lloyd, Penn State. Their comments helped push our thinking on many important topics. Many specific suggestions offered by these reviewers found their way into the pages of this book. We offer our sincere appreciation to these esteemed educators for their valued suggestions and constructive feedback.

As we reviewed standards, research, and teaching articles; visited classrooms; and collected students' work samples, we were continually reminded of the amazing commitment to effective mathematics teaching and learning. From the mathematics educators and mathematicians working on standards documents, to the teachers who facilitate discussions about mathematics in preK–grade 8 classrooms and then share the results with others, we are grateful for the broad and heartfelt commitment to mathematics education for *all* students on the part of so many educators—particularly the teachers with whom we have worked in recent years.

We also want to acknowledge the strong support of our editorial team throughout the process, from the first discussions about what the third edition might include, through the tedious editing at later stages in the development. Without their support, the final product would not be the quality resource we hope you find it to be. Specifically, we thank Meredith Fossil for helping us envision our work, Linda Bishop for seeing this vision through, and both of them for their words of encouragement and wisdom. Working on three volumes of a book simultaneously is quite an undertaking! We are also truly grateful for Miryam Chandler at Pearson and Jason Hammond and the team at SPi Global who helped us wade through the permissions process and the production and editing of our new edition and eText.

Even with the support of so many, researching and writing takes time. Simple words cannot express the gratitude we have to our families for their support, patience, and contributions to the production of these books. Briefly we recognize them by name here: Karen thanks her husband, Bob Ronau, and her children and grandchildren, Matthew, Tammy, Josh, Misty, Matt, Christine, Jeff, Pamela, Jessica, Zane, Madeline, Jack, and Emma. LouAnn thanks her husband, Ramsey, and her two sons, Nathan and Jacob. Jennifer thanks her husband, Mitch, and her children, MacKenna and Nicolas.

The origin of this book began many years ago with the development of *Elementary and Middle School Mathematics: Teaching Developmentally* by John A. Van de Walle. What began as a methods book for pre-service teachers spread enthusiastically throughout the teaching community because it offered content support, activities, and up-to-date best practices for teaching mathematics. The three-volume series was developed as a way to focus on and expand the specific grade-level topics. John was adamant that *all* children can learn to reason and make sense of mathematics. We acknowledge his commitment and his significant contributions to the field of mathematics education. His ideas and enduring vision continue to inspire the work you see in this new edition.

The response to the second edition has been amazing. We hope the third edition will be received with as much interest and enthusiasm as the second and continue to be a valuable support to your mathematics teaching and your children's learning.

1

Setting a Vision for Learning High-Quality Mathematics

In his book *The World Is Flat* (2007) Thomas Friedman discusses how globalization through technology has created the need for people to have lasting, adaptable skills so they can survive the ever-changing landscape of available jobs. He points out that in our digital world, lovers and doers of mathematics will always have career options and opportunities. However, no matter their career choice, given the extent to which our world relies on technology and the processing of massive amounts of information, all students need to develop skillsets that will allow them to be successful in our economy and society. Lynn Arthur Steen, a well-known mathematician and educator, stated, "As information becomes ever more quantitative and as society relies increasingly on computers and the data they produce, an innumerate citizen today is as vulnerable as the illiterate peasant of Gutenberg's time" (1997, p. xv).

To prepare students for an ever-changing world, for jobs that possibly do not even exist today, can't we just pay more attention to the high school curriculum? Certainly what students learn in high school is important. However, a growing number of studies points to a strong association between early gains in mathematical ability and later academic achievement (e.g., Claessens, Duncan, & Engel, 2009; Watts, Greg, Duncan, Siegler, & Davis-Kean, 2014). So we need to begin this preparation early in elementary school and continue to build on this foundation throughout the school years.

Understanding and Doing Mathematics

The changing world influences what should be taught in mathematics classrooms, even in grades 3–5. The dialogue on the best ways to prepare students to be successful in this changing world has involved mathematics educators, researchers, teachers, policymakers, and elected officials and has considered the many National Council of Teachers of Mathematics (NCTM) standards documents, international assessments, and research.

One of the influential documents that added to this dialogue is *Adding It Up* (National Research Council (NRC), 2001). Based on a review of the research on how students learn mathematics, this document identified the following five strands of mathematical proficiency that are seen as indicators of someone who understands (and can do) mathematics.

- *Conceptual understanding:* Having a robust web of connections and relationships within and between ideas, interpretations, and representations of mathematical concepts.
- *Procedural fluency:* Being able to flexibly choose and accurately and efficiently perform an appropriate strategy for a particular problem. For more on fluency, go to the NCTM website and search for the 2014 Annual Meeting Webcast "President's Session—Fluency . . . It's More Than Fast and Accurate."
- *Strategic competence:* Being able to make sense of, represent, and determine solutions to mathematical problems.
- *Adaptive reasoning:* Being able to think about, explain, and justify one's ideas using mathematically sensible reasons coupled with the ability to shift strategies when needed.
- *Productive disposition:* Having an ingrained awareness that mathematics makes sense and is useful, valuable, and rewarding along with the belief that one is capable of being successful in learning and doing mathematics through hard work and perseverance.

Figure 1.1

Interrelated and intertwined strands of mathematical proficiency.

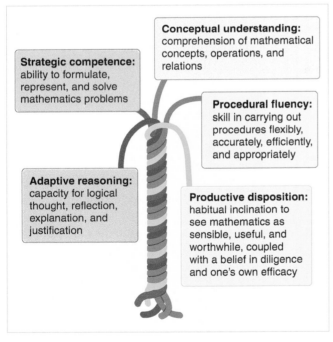

Source: From "The Strands of Mathematical Proficiency" in *Adding It Up: Helping Children Learn Mathematics.* Edited by Jeremy Kilpatrick, Jane Swafford, and Bradford Findell. Published by proceedings of the National Academy of Sciences, © 2001.

Figure 1.1 illustrates the interrelated and interwoven nature of the strands of mathematical proficiency: As one strand develops it builds on and builds up other strands, resulting in a strengthened whole. As an example, consider the ineffective practice of teaching procedures in the absence of conceptual understanding. Often this approach yields a lack of retention and increased errors, rigid approaches, and inefficient strategy use (watch a related video at https://www.youtube.com/watch?v=FVKtQwARe6c). When students are in classrooms where these strands of proficiency are allowed to develop together, they are able to build a stronger understanding of both mathematical concepts and procedures.

Numerous other reports and standards were developed as part of the effort to improve mathematics teaching and learning and prepare students for the ever-changing world. Among these are the *Common Core State Standards* (CCSS-M) (CCSSO, 2010) and other state standards that recognize the need for coherent and rigorous standards that promote college- and career-readiness.

In particular, the CCSS-M articulates an overview of critical areas for each grade from K–8 to provide a coherent curriculum built around big mathematical ideas. At this time, more than 40 states; Washington, D.C.; four territories; and Department of Defense Schools have adopted the CCSS-M.

A few states chose to not adopt these standards from the start and others are still deciding their level of participation or re-evaluating their own standards against CCSS-M. Nonetheless, this represents the largest shift of mathematics content in the United States in more than 100 years.

This effort to develop standards that promote college- and career-readiness has resulted in attention to the *processes* of *doing* mathematics, not just the *content*. Notably, NCTM (2000) identifies the process standards of problem solving, reasoning and proof, representation, communication, and connections as ways in which students acquire and use mathematical knowledge. Students engaged in the process of *problem solving* build mathematical knowledge and understanding by grappling with and solving genuine problems as opposed to completing routine exercises. They use *reasoning and proof* to make sense of mathematical tasks and concepts and to develop, justify, and evaluate mathematical arguments and solutions. Students create and use *representations* (e.g., diagrams, graphs, symbols, and manipulatives) to reason through problems. They also engage in *communication* as they explain their ideas and reasoning verbally, in writing, and through representations. Students develop and use *connections* between mathematical ideas as they learn new mathematical concepts and procedures. They also build *connections* between mathematics and other disciplines by applying mathematics to real-world situations. The process standards should not be regarded as separate content or strands in the mathematics curriculum; rather they are integral components of all mathematics teaching and learning. By engaging in these processes, students *learn* mathematics by *doing* mathematics.

The CCSS-M also includes the Standards for Mathematical Practice (CCSSO, 2010), which are ways in which students can develop and demonstrate a deep understanding of and capacity to do mathematics (see Appendix A). Whether your state has adopted the CCSS, the eight Standards of Mathematical Practice are worthy of attention. These mathematical practices are based on the underlying frameworks of the NCTM process standards and the components of mathematical proficiency identified by the National Research Council's document *Adding It Up* (NRC, 2001). Like the NCTM process standards, these practices are not separate, but integral to all mathematics teaching and learning. Here we provide a brief discussion about each mathematical practice.

1. *Make sense of problems and persevere in solving them.* To make sense of problems, students need to learn how to analyze the given information, the parameters, and the relationships in a problem so that they can understand the situation and identify possible ways to solve it. One way to help students analyze problems is to have them create bar diagrams to make sense of the quantities, relationships, and operations involved. Once students learn various strategies for making sense of problems, encourage them to remain committed to solving them. As they learn to monitor and assess their progress and change course as needed, they will solve the problems they set out to solve!

2. *Reason abstractly and quantitatively.* This practice involves students reasoning with quantities and their relationships in problem situations. You can support students' development of this practice by helping them create representations that correspond to the meanings of the quantities, units, and operations involved. When appropriate, students should also learn to represent and manipulate the situation symbolically. Encourage students to find connections between the abstract symbols and the representation that illustrates the quantities and their relationships. For example, when fourth graders draw a bar diagram showing one tree as being four times the height of another tree, encourage them to connect their representation to the expression $4 \times h$, where h is the height of the shorter tree. Ultimately, students should be able to move flexibly between symbols and other representations.

3. *Construct viable arguments and critique the reasoning of others.* This practice emphasizes the importance of students' using mathematical reasoning to justify their ideas and solutions,

including being able to recognize and use counterexamples. Encourage students to examine each others' arguments to determine whether they make sense and to identify ways to clarify or improve the arguments. This practice emphasizes that mathematics is based on reasoning and should be examined in a community—not carried out in isolation. Tips for supporting students as they learn to justify their ideas can be found in Chapter 2.

4. *Model with mathematics.* This practice encourages students to use the mathematics they know to describe, explain, and solve problems from a real-world context. For third graders, this could mean writing a multiplication or division equation to represent a given situation or using their measurement sense to determine whether a rug advertised in the newspaper would fit in a designated location in their classroom. Be sure to encourage students to determine whether their mathematical results make sense in the context of the given situation. Note that this practice is different from *modeling mathematics*, which involves using representations to illustrate mathematical ideas (e.g., an area model to show one meaning of 4×3).

Teaching Tip

Research suggests that students, in particular girls, may tend to continue to use the same tools because they feel comfortable with the tools and are afraid to take risks (Ambrose, 2002). Look for students who tend to use the same tool or strategy every time they work on a task. Encourage all students to take risks and to try new tools and strategies.

5. *Use appropriate tools strategically.* Students should become familiar with a variety of problem-solving tools and they should learn to choose which ones are most appropriate for a given situation. For example, fifth graders should experience using the following tools for computation with decimals: base-ten manipulatives, decimal grids, pencil and paper, calculators, and number lines. Then, if these students are asked to find the sum of 3.45 and 2.9 and provide their reasoning, they could use base-ten manipulatives or decimal grids to illustrate the meaning of each decimal and how the decimals were combined.

6. *Attend to precision.* In communicating ideas to others, it is imperative that students learn to be explicit about their reasoning. For example, they need to be clear about the meanings of operations and symbols they use, to indicate units involved in a problem, and to clearly label diagrams that accompany their explanations. As students share their ideas, emphasize this expectation and ask clarifying questions that help make the details of their reasoning more apparent. Teachers can further encourage students' attention to precision by introducing, highlighting, and encouraging the use of accurate mathematical terminology in explanations and diagrams.

7. *Look for and make use of structure.* Students who look for and recognize a pattern or structure can experience a shift in their perspective or understanding. Therefore, set the expectation that students will look for patterns and structure and help them reflect on their significance. For example, help students notice that the order in which they multiply two numbers does not change the product—both 4×7 and 7×4 equal 28. Once students recognize this pattern through several experiences with other examples, they will have a new understanding and use of a powerful property of our number system: the commutative property of multiplication.

8. *Look for and express regularity in repeated reasoning.* Encourage students to step back and reflect on any regularity that occurs to help them develop a general idea or method or to identify shortcuts. For example, as students begin multiplying numbers, they will encounter situations in which a number is multiplied by 0. Over time, help them reflect on the results of multiplying any number by 0. Eventually they should be able to express that when any number is multiplied by 0, the product is always 0.

Note that the process standards are embedded the mathematical practices. Table 1.1 shows one way to think about the relationship between the process standards and the eight mathematical practices. For example, ways to engage students in reasoning and proof involve the mathematical practices of reasoning abstractly and quantitatively, constructing viable arguments and critiquing others' reasoning, modeling with mathematics, and looking for and making use of structure. Bleiler, Baxter, Stephens, and Barlow (2015) provide additional ideas to help teachers further their understanding of the eight mathematical practices. Students who learn to use these processes and practices of *doing* mathematics have a greater chance of becoming mathematically proficient.

Table 1.1. Connections between NCTM's process standards and CCSS-M's mathematical practices.

	MP1	MP2	MP3	MP4	MP5	MP6	MP7	MP8
Problem Solving	■	■		■	■		■	■
Reasoning and Proof		■	■	■			■	
Communication			■		■	■		
Representation	■		■	■	■			
Connections				■			■	■

MP1: *Make sense of problems and persevere in solving them.*
MP2: *Reason abstractly and quantitatively.*
MP3: *Construct viable arguments and critique the reasoning of others.*
MP4: *Model with mathematics.*
MP5: *Use appropriate tools strategically.*
MP6: *Attend to precision.*
MP7: *Look for and make use of structure.*
MP8: *Look for and express regularity in repeated reasoning.*

How Do Students Learn?

As noted in NCTM's (2014) *Principles to Actions* document, research in mathematics education as well as in cognitive science supports the notion that learning is an active process in which each student, through personal experiences, interactions with others, and reflective thought, develops his or her own mathematical knowledge. The active nature required in developing the NCTM Process Standards and the CCSS-M Mathematical Practices is what makes them such powerful places for students to learn as they engage in doing mathematics.

Two research-based theories about learning, constructivism and sociocultural theory, provide us with specific insights into the active nature of the learning process. Although one theory focuses on the individual learner and the other emphasizes the social and cultural aspects of the classroom, these theories are not competing and are actually compatible (Norton & D'Ambrosio, 2008).

Constructivism

At the heart of constructivism is the notion that learners are not blank slates but rather creators (constructors) of their own learning (Piaget, 1976; von Glasersfeld, 1995). All people, all of the time, construct or give meaning to things they experience or think about. Whether you are listening passively to a lecture or actively engaging in synthesizing findings in a project, your brain uses your existing knowledge to make sense of the new information.

Through reflective thought, people connect existing ideas to new information and in this way modify their existing knowledge to incorporate new ideas. Making these connections can happen in either of two ways—*assimilation* or *accommodation*. Assimilation occurs when a new concept "fits" with prior knowledge and the new information expands an existing mental network. Accommodation takes place when the new concept does not "fit" with the existing network, thus creating a cognitive conflict or state of confusion that causes what learning theorists call *disequilibrium*. As an example, some students assimilate fractions into their existing knowledge for whole numbers. When they begin to compare fractions, they treat the numerators and denominators separately, as if they represent two whole numbers that have no relationship to each other. Such a student might mentally compare $\frac{2}{3}$ and $\frac{3}{4}$ by explaining that since $2 < 3$ (the numerators) and $3 < 4$ (the denominators), $\frac{2}{3} < \frac{3}{4}$. This student might initially confirm this erroneous thinking by using an area model that corresponds to a part-whole fraction to illustrate that $\frac{2}{3} < \frac{3}{4}$ because $\frac{2}{3}$ has less area than $\frac{3}{4}$. A teacher could then challenge this student to compare the fractions $\frac{1}{2}$ and $\frac{2}{5}$. This student's overgeneralization of whole-number ideas (e.g., $1 < 2$ and $2 < 5$, and so $\frac{1}{2} < \frac{2}{5}$) is then called into question when he or she reflects on the area model illustrating that $\frac{1}{2} > \frac{2}{5}$. To settle the dissonance, the student eventually has to accommodate (i.e., modify) his or her knowledge for comparing fractions. It is through the struggle to resolve the disequilibrium that the brain modifies or replaces the existing knowledge so that the new concept fits and makes sense, resulting in a revision of thought and a deepening of the person's understanding.

For an illustration of what it means to construct an idea, consider Figure 1.2. The blue and red dots represent ideas, and the lines joining the ideas represent the logical connections or relationships that develop between ideas. The red dot is an emerging idea—one that is being constructed. Whatever existing ideas (blue dots) are used in the construction are connected to the new idea (red dot) because those are the ideas that give meaning to the new idea. The more existing ideas that are used to give meaning to the new one, the more connections will be made.

Each student's unique collection of ideas is connected in different ways. Some ideas are well understood and well formed (i.e., connected), while others are less so as they evolve. Students' experiences help them develop connections and ideas about whatever they are learning.

Figure 1.2

How someone constructs a new idea.

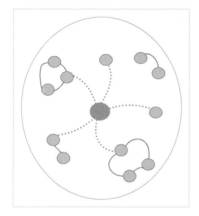

Sociocultural Theory

Like constructivism, sociocultural theory not only positions the learner as actively engaged in seeking meaning during the learning process, but it also suggests that the learner can be assisted by working with others who are "more knowledgeable." According to sociocultural theory, every learner has a unique zone of proximal development, which is a range of knowledge that may be out of reach for the individual to learn alone, but is accessible if the learner has the support of peers or more knowledgeable others (Vygotsky, 1978). For example, when students are learning about perimeter and area, they do not necessarily recognize that two rectangles can have the same perimeter but different areas. A more knowledgeable person (a peer or teacher) will know that if students explore creating different rectangles that have the same perimeter, the examples they generate will suggest this relationship between a rectangle's perimeter and area.

The most effective learning for any given student occurs when classroom activities are within his or her zone of proximal development. Targeting that zone helps teachers provide students with the right amount of challenge while avoiding boredom on the one hand and anxiety on the other when the challenge is beyond the student's current capability. Consequently, classroom discussions based on students' own ideas and solutions are absolutely crucial to their learning (Wood & Turner-Vorbeck, 2001).

Teaching for Understanding

Teachers generally agree that teaching for understanding is a good thing. But what do we mean by *understanding*? Understanding is being able to flexibly think about and use a topic or concept. It goes beyond knowing; it is more than a collection of information, facts, or data. It is more than being able to follow steps in a procedure. One hallmark of mathematical understanding is a student's ability to justify why a given mathematical claim or answer is true or why a mathematical rule makes sense (CCSSO, 2010). Although students might *know* their basic multiplication facts and be able to give you quick answers to questions about these facts, they might not *understand* multiplication. They might not be able to justify how they know an answer is correct or provide an example of when it would make sense to use a particular basic fact. These tasks go beyond simply knowing mathematical facts and procedures. Understanding must be a primary goal for all of the mathematics you teach.

Understanding exists along a continuum (Figure 1.3) from an instrumental understanding—doing or knowing something without meaning—to a relational understanding—knowing what to do and why. These two terms were introduced by Richard Skemp in 1978 and continue to provide an important distinction about what is important for students to know about mathematics. Instrumental understanding, at the left end of the continuum, shows that ideas (e.g., concepts and procedures) are learned, but in isolation (or nearly so) to other ideas. Here you find ideas that have been memorized. Due to their isolation, poorly understood ideas are easily forgotten and are unlikely to be useful for constructing new ideas. At the right end of the continuum is relational understanding. Relational understanding means that each new concept or procedure (red dot) is not only learned, but is also connected to many existing ideas (blue dots), so there is a rich set of connections.

Figure 1.3

Continuum of understanding.

The common notion of quickly "covering the material" and moving on is problematic when trying to help children develop relational understanding. Relational understanding is an end goal—that is, it is developed over time by incorporating active learning through the process standards and mathematical practices and striving toward mathematical proficiency. Therefore, relational understanding must be a goal for both daily and long-term instruction.

Teaching for Relational Understanding

To explore the notion of understanding further, let's look into a learner-centered fourth-grade classroom. In learner-centered classrooms, teachers begin *where the students are*—with *the students'* ideas. Students are allowed to solve problems or to approach tasks in ways that make sense to them. They develop a robust understanding of mathematics because they are the ones who explain, provide evidence or justification, find or create examples, generalize, analyze, make predictions, apply concepts, represent ideas in different ways, and articulate connections or relationships between the given topic and other ideas.

In this particular fourth-grade classroom, students have already reviewed double-digit addition and subtraction computation and have been working on multiplication concepts and facts. They mastered most of their multiplication facts by the end of third grade but as part of an extension, the students have used contexts embedded in story problems. They are also illustrating how repeated addition can be related to the number of rows of square tiles within a rectangle. These students' combined experiences from grades 3 and 4 have resulted in a collection of ideas about tens and ones (from their work with double-digit addition and subtraction), an understanding of the meaning of multiplication as related to unitizing (i.e., a row of six as one six), a variety of number strategies for mastering multiplication facts based on the properties of the operation, and a connection between multiplication and arrays and area.

The teacher sets the following instructional objectives for her students:

1. Begin development of computational strategies for multiplication with multi-digit numbers based on place value and the properties of operations.

2. Illustrate and explain multiplication calculations using equations and arrays and/or area models.

The lesson begins with a task that is designed to set the stage for the main part of the lesson. On a projector, the teacher shows a 6 × 8 rectangle made of square tiles. The bottom row of eight tiles is shaded to draw students' attention to it (see Figure 1.4). The students quickly agree that adding up 6 eights will tell how many squares are in the rectangle. The teacher asks, "But if we didn't remember that 6 rows of 8 is 48, could we slice the rectangle into two parts where we know the multiplication fact and use that to get the total mentally?" Students are given a few minutes to think of at least one way to slice the rectangle, to share the idea with a partner, and to prepare to share with the class. The students offer four ideas:

Figure 1.4

A 6 by 8 rectangle split into 5 by 8 and 1 by 8 rectangles to make it easier to find the number of square tiles.

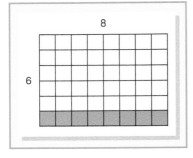

- "We sliced one row off the bottom. The top part is 5 by 8, so 40 tiles. Forty plus the 8 tiles on the bottom row makes 48 tiles."

- "We cut the rectangle in half top to bottom. Each smaller rectangle is 6 by 4; 24 and 24 is 48." The teacher asks, "How did you add the two 24s?" One of the students from the group explained, "We used double 25 and took 2 off." A student from a different group noted, "You could also add 20 and 20 to get 40, and then add on 4 and 4 to get 48."

- "Our strategy was the same idea, but we sliced the rectangle in half the other way and got 3 times 8 or 24, and then we doubled it, which is 48."

- "We used doubles. If you take 2 columns of 6, that's 12. Then double that will give you 4 columns, or 24. And then double 24 is 48."

The teacher passes out centimeter grid paper. On the board she sketches a large rectangle, labels the dimensions 8 and 24, and tells the students that she wants each of them to construct an 8- by 24-cm rectangle on the grid paper. She explains that the students' task is to figure out how many square tiles are in the rectangle without counting them. Instead, they are to slice the rectangle into two or more parts—like they did with the 6 by 8 example—and use the smaller parts to figure out how many tiles are in the entire rectangle. As is the norm in the class, the teacher expects the students to be prepared to explain their reasoning and to support it with words, numbers, and drawings.

Stop and Reflect

Before reading further, solve this problem by finding two or more ways to slice the 8- by 24-cm rectangle into two or more parts. Draw a sketch for each way you can think of. Then check to see if your ways are alike or different from those that follow.

The students work in pairs for about 15 minutes as the teacher circulates. The teacher listens to different students talk about the task and offers a hint to a few students who are stuck: "What multiplication facts related to 8 do you know? How could you use those facts to slice the rectangle?" Soon the teacher begins a discussion by having specific students share their ideas and answers. As the students report, the teacher records their ideas on the board. Sometimes the teacher asks questions to help clarify ideas for others. She makes no evaluative comments, though she asks the students who are listening if they understand or have any questions to ask the presenters. The following solution strategies are common in classes where students are regularly asked to generate their own approaches. Figure 1.5 shows sketches for three of these methods.

Figure 1.5

Three different ways to slice a rectangle into smaller parts to make it easier to find its area.

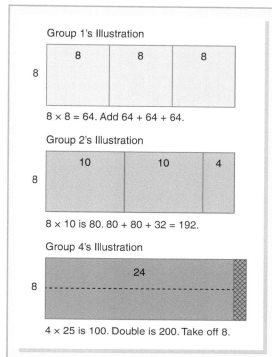

- **Group 1:** "We know that 24, the top dimension, divided by 3 is 8, so we made three 8 by 8 squares. We know 8 times 8 is 64. We added 64 plus 64 plus 64." There is a brief discussion about how the students added the 64s mentally.

- **Group 2:** "We used groups of ten along the side that is 24 cm long. We sliced 2 sections of 10, and then there were 4 left at the end. Eight times 10 is 80. That makes 160 in the 2 big sections, and then the last section is 8 by 4. We added 160 and 32 in our heads."

- **Group 3:** "Our method was sort of like that, but we just used 8 times 20, which is 160. Then you add the 32 at the end."

- **Group 4:** "We didn't really slice the rectangle. Instead, we added an extra column of 8 at the end and made it 8 by 25. Then we knew that 4 rows of 25 is like a dollar, or 100. That makes 200 squares in all. But then we had to take off the 8 from the extra column that we added."

Stop and Reflect   500 ⟨ 250   ⟨? 3x ▱ ⟨850° 8∩ ✗ 2.5

What ideas did you learn from those shared in this example? Try using some of these ideas to find the product of 6 and 38. These numbers may make you think of a method not used in the task just discussed.

This vignette illustrates that when students are encouraged to solve a problem in their own way (using their own particular set of blue dots, or ideas), they are able to make sense of their solution strategies and explain their reasoning. This is evidence of their development of mathematical proficiency.

During the discussions in classes such as this one, ideas continue to grow. The students may hear and immediately understand a clever strategy shared by a classmate that they could have used but that did not occur to them. Others may begin to create new ideas that build from thinking about their classmates' strategies. Some students in the class may hear excellent ideas from their peers that do not make sense to them. These students are simply not ready or do not have the prerequisite concepts (blue dots) to understand these new ideas. In future class sessions there will be similar opportunities for all students to grow at their own pace based on what they already understand.

Teaching for Instrumental Understanding

In contrast to the lesson just described, in which students are developing concepts (understanding multi-digit multiplication) and procedures (the ability to multiply flexibly) and building relationships between these ideas, let's consider how a lesson with the same basic objective (multidigit multiplication) might look if the focus is on instrumental understanding.

In this classroom, the teacher distributes centimeter grid paper and asks students to draw the 8- by 24-cm rectangle on their paper. On the board the teacher draws a rectangle and writes the multiplication problem 8 × 24 beside it. The teacher directs the students to count over to the right 20 squares and to draw a vertical line in the rectangle as she demonstrates the process on the board. Then the teacher uses a series of questions to guide students through each step in the U.S. standard algorithm for multidigit multiplication. Students record the steps on their own paper at the same time.

- The teacher points to the small section of the rectangle and asks, "What is 8 times 4?"
- Students respond, "Thirty-two."
- The teacher notes, "We want to record the 32 in our problem." (She demonstrates how to write a 2 beneath the line in the problem and carry the 3. She also writes "32" in the small portion of the rectangle.)
- The teacher asks, "What is 8 times 2?" (Attention is directed to the 8 by 20 portion of the rectangle.)
- Students respond, "Sixteen."
- The teacher explains, "Because we are multiplying 8 by 20, we just add 0 to get 160 or 16 tens." (The teacher writes "16 tens" in the large portion of the rectangle.)
- The teacher continues the process: "We already have three tens. How much is 16 and 3?"
- Students respond, "Nineteen."
- The teacher continues the algorithm: "We record the 19 tens below the line. The final answer is 192." (See Figure 1.6.)

Figure 1.6

The U.S. standard algorithm is modeled using a rectangle partitioned into tens and ones.

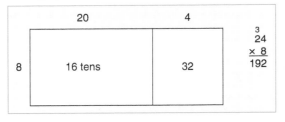

Next, the students are given five similar multiplication problems. For each problem they are to sketch a small rectangle on their paper and show how it is partitioned into tens and ones. Then they record the two products in the rectangle and complete the computation on the side. The teacher helps students who are struggling by guiding them through the steps that were modeled in the first example.

In this lesson, the teacher and students use an area model on centimeter grid paper to illustrate the various partial products in the problem. After engaging in several similar lessons, most students are likely to remember, and possibly understand, how to multiply multidigit numbers by using the standard algorithm. It is important to note that this lesson on the standard algorithm, in combination with other lessons that reinforce other approaches, *can* build relational understanding, as it adds to students' repertoire of strategies. But if this lesson represents the sole approach to multiplying multi-digit numbers, then students are more likely to develop an instrumental understanding of mathematics because the lesson provides few opportunities to build connections between mathematical concepts. For example, students are not provided opportunities to apply other strategies that may help them build connections between multiplication and place value, multiplication and addition, or multiplication and estimation. Building these connections between mathematical ideas and across representations is a fundamental characteristic of relational understanding.

Stop and Reflect

Before reading further, what similarities and differences did you notice between the two classrooms? How do you think these differences might affect the learning that takes place?

The Importance of Students' Ideas

Let's take a minute to compare these two classrooms. By examining them more closely, you can see several important differences. These differences affect what is learned and who learns. Let's consider the first difference: Who determines the procedure to use?

In the first classroom, each student looks at the numbers in the problem, thinks about the relationships between the numbers, and *then* chooses a suitable computational strategy. They are developing several strategies to solve multiplication problems by exploring numbers (taking numbers apart and putting them together differently); using various representations, such as arrays and area models; and thinking about connections between addition and multiplication. The students in the first classroom are being taught mathematics for understanding—*relational* understanding—and are developing the kinds of mathematical proficiency described earlier.

In the second classroom, the teacher provides one strategy for how to multiply—the standard algorithm. Although the standard algorithm is a valid strategy, the entire focus of the lesson is on the steps and procedures that the teacher has outlined. The teacher solicits no ideas from individual students about how to combine the numbers. She can only find out who has or has not been able to follow her directions. And even more problematic is that the teacher shares a commonly taught "rule" that does not always work: when you multiply by 10 you just "add" a zero. (For example, this "rule" does not apply when you multiply 14.5×10.)

When students have more choice in determining which strategies to use, as in the first classroom, there are more opportunities for learners to interact with each other and with the teacher as they share ideas and results, compare and evaluate strategies, challenge results, determine the validity of answers, and negotiate ideas. As a result, they can learn more content and make more connections. In addition, if teachers do not seek out and value students' ideas, students may come to believe that mathematics is a body of rules and procedures that are learned by waiting for the teacher to tell them what to do. This view of mathematics—and what is involved in learning it—is inconsistent with mathematics as a discipline and with the learning theories described previously.

A second difference between the two classrooms is the learning goals. Both teachers might write "understand multidigit multiplication" as the objective for the day. What is captured in the word *understand* is very different in each setting, however. In the first classroom, the teacher's goals are for students to connect multiplication to what they already know and to see that two numbers can be multiplied in many different ways. In the second classroom, understanding is connected to being able to carry out the standard algorithm supported by a singular approach using grid paper. The learning goals and, more specifically, how the teacher interprets the meaning behind the learning goals, impact what students learn.

These lessons also differ in terms of how accessible they are—and this, in turn, affects *who* learns the mathematics. The first lesson is differentiated in that it meets students where they are in their current understanding. When a task is presented as "solve this in your own way," it has multiple entry points, meaning it can be approached in a variety of ways, some more sophisticated than others. Consequently, students with several different levels of prior knowledge or learning strategies can figure out a way to solve the problem. This makes the task accessible to more learners. Then, as students observe strategies that are more efficient than their own, they develop new and better ways to solve the problem. This approach also requires that the students, rather than the teacher, do the *thinking*.

In the second classroom, everyone has to do the problem in the same way. The students do not have the opportunity to apply their own ideas or to see that there are numerous ways to solve the problem. This may deprive students who need to continue working on the development of basic ideas of tens and ones, as well as students who could easily find one or more ways to do the problem if only they were asked to do so. The students in the second classroom are also likely to use the same method to multiply all numbers instead of looking for more efficient ways to multiply numbers based on the relationships between the numbers.

For example, they are likely to multiply 4×51 using the standard algorithm instead of thinking, "That would be 4×50 and then 4 more." Recall the importance of building on prior knowledge and learning from others. In the first classroom, student-generated strategies, multiple approaches, and discussions about the problem represent the kinds of strategies that enhance learning for a range of learners.

Students in both classrooms will eventually succeed at finding products of multidigit numbers, but what they learn about multiplication—and about doing mathematics—is quite different. Understanding and doing mathematics involves generating strategies for solving problems, applying those approaches, seeing if they lead to solutions, and checking to see if answers make sense. These activities were all present in the first classroom but not in the second. Consequently, students in the first classroom, in addition to successfully finding products of multidigit numbers, will develop richer mathematical understanding, become more flexible thinkers and better problem solvers, remain more engaged in learning, and develop more positive attitudes toward learning mathematics.

For more information about relational and instrumental understanding as well as the short-term and the long-term effects of teaching with each type of understanding as your goal, watch this video: https://www.youtube.com/watch?v=TW_RQXWiCFU.

Mathematics Classrooms That Promote Understanding

An important part of helping students develop relational understanding and mathematical proficiency is to ensure the students are the ones doing the thinking, talking, and the mathematics, however, there are other factors that play a role. Based on an extensive review of the literature, Schoenfeld and Floden (2014) identified the following five dimensions of "productive classrooms—classrooms that produce powerful mathematical thinkers" (p. 2). We address each of these dimensions throughout the book, but in particular, in Chapters 1–7.

1. *The Mathematics:* We have discussed in this chapter the importance of coherent and rigorous standards that promote college- and career-readiness. This includes developing procedural proficiency in conjunction with conceptual understanding as well as developing productive habits of minds through the mathematical processes and practices.

2. *Cognitive Demand:* Productive struggle is an important part of the process of learning and doing mathematics. We discuss in Chapter 2 the importance of engaging students in appropriate levels of challenge that allow them to productively struggle. Activities throughout Part 2 of the book are designed to be high cognitive demand tasks.

3. *Access to Mathematical Content:* All students must be actively engaged in learning core mathematical ideas. To make this happen for some students, purposeful and appropriate levels of support must be in place. These ideas are addressed in Chapters 4–6.

4. *Agency, Authority, and Identity:* Learning is enhanced when students are engaged with others who are working on the same ideas. Encouraging student-to-student dialogue that involves making conjectures, explaining, justifying, and building on each other's ideas can help students think of themselves as capable of making sense of and doers of mathematics. This requires that the teacher create a classroom culture in which students can learn from one another, a topic that is addressed in Chapter 2.

5. *Uses of Assessment:* Eliciting students' ideas and reasoning to inform subsequent instruction has the potential to contribute to everyone's learning, especially when common misunderstandings and mistakes are capitalized on and explored. We discuss assessment that supports instruction and learning in Chapter 3.

✐ Teaching Tip

Listen carefully to students as they talk about what they are thinking and doing as they engage in a mathematical task. If they respond in an unexpected way, try to avoid imposing your ideas onto their ideas. Ask clarifying questions to try to make sense of the sense your students are making.

As with most complex phenomena, these dimensions that promote a productive classroom are interrelated. For example, the results of assessment (dimension 5) can help identify an appropriate mathematical task (dimension 1) that can, in turn, affect the potential for cognitive demand (dimension 2). The degree of appropriate support provided (dimension 3) in conjunction with all of the above can influence how a student perceives him or herself as a doer of mathematics (dimension 4). Students have the best chance of becoming powerful mathematical thinkers and doers in classrooms where these five dimensions are implemented well.

Three of the most common types of teaching are direct instruction, facilitative methods (also called a *constructivist approach*), and coaching (Wiggins & McTighe, 2005). With direct instruction, the teacher usually demonstrates or models, lectures, and asks questions that are convergent or closed-ended in nature. With facilitative methods, the teacher might use investigations and inquiry, cooperative learning, discussion, and questions that are more open-ended. In coaching, the teacher provides students with guided practice and feedback that highlights ways to improve their performances. You might wonder, if the goal is to teach mathematics for relational understanding, which type of instructional approach is most appropriate. Unfortunately, there is no definitive answer because there are times when it is appropriate to engage in each of these types of teaching, depending on the instructional goals, the learners, and the situation.

Constructivism, a theory of learning (not a theory of teaching), explains that students learn by developing and modifying ideas and by making connections between these ideas—and each type of instruction can support students' learning when used at the appropriate time. The instructional approach chosen should depend on the ideas and relationships students have already constructed. Assessment can shed light on what and how our students understand, and, in turn, can help us determine which teaching approach may be the most appropriate at a given time. Sometimes students need time to investigate a situation so they can become aware of the different ideas at play and how those ideas relate to one another (facilitative). Sometimes they need to practice a skill and receive feedback on their performance to become more accurate (coaching). Sometimes they are ready to make connections by listening to a lecture (direct instruction). The key to teaching for understanding, no matter which type of teaching you use, is to maintain the expectation for students to reflect on and productively struggle with the situation at hand. In other words, regardless of instructional design, the teacher should not be doing the thinking, reasoning, and connection building—it must be the students who are engaged in these activities.

Most people go into teaching because they want to help students learn. It is hard to think of allowing—much less planning for—the students in your room to struggle. Not showing them a solution when they are experiencing difficulty seems almost counterintuitive. If our goal is relational understanding, however, the struggle is part of the learning, and teaching becomes less about the teacher and more about what the students are doing and thinking.

Keep in mind that you too are a learner. Some ideas in this book may make more sense to you than others. Some ideas may even create dissonance for you. Embrace this feeling of disequilibrium and uneasiness as an opportunity to learn—to revise your perspectives on mathematics and on the teaching and learning of mathematics as you deepen your understanding so that you can help your students deepen theirs.

Stop and Reflect

Look back at the chapter and identify any ideas that challenge your current thinking about mathematics or about teaching and learning mathematics or that simply make you uncomfortable. Try to determine why these ideas challenge or raise questions for you. Write these ideas down and revisit them later as you read and reflect further.

2

Teaching Mathematics through Problem Solving

Preparing students to be quantitatively literate so they can function in today's increasingly complex world will allow them to think more logically, work flexibly with numbers, analyze evidence, and communicate their ideas to others effectively. Unfortunately, as Elizabeth Green points out in her article *Why Do Americans Stink at Math?* (2014, February), many Americans of all ages demonstrate quantitative deficiencies. Green argues that to overcome these quantitative deficiencies we must change our view of mathematics from rules to be memorized to sense-making ways of looking at the world around us. Teaching mathematics through problem solving is a method of teaching mathematics that supports students in developing the kinds of skills and understanding that will serve them well in today's world and beyond. In this chapter, we focus on how to teach through problem solving, including how to select worthwhile tasks and facilitate student engagement in those tasks.

Teaching through Problem Solving: An Upside-Down Approach

For many years and continuing today, mathematics has been taught using an "I-we-you" approach: The teacher presents the mathematics (I), students practice the skill with the teacher (we), and, finally, the students, on their own, continue to practice the skill and solve word problems that require using that skill (you). In this approach—called teaching *for* problem solving—the role of problems is to provide applications for newly learned skills. For example, students learn the algorithm for adding fractions and once that is mastered, solve story problems that involve adding fractions. Unfortunately, this "do-as-I-show-you" approach to mathematics teaching has not been successful in helping many students understand mathematics concepts (e.g., Pesek & Kirshner, 2002; Philipp & Vincent, 2003). Here are a few reasons why:

- It requires that all students have the necessary knowledge to understand the teacher's explanations—which is rarely, if ever, the case.
- It communicates that there is only one way to think about and solve the problem, which is a misrepresentation of mathematics and genuine problems.
- It positions the student as a passive learner who is dependent on the teacher to show them ideas, rather than as an independent thinker who is capable and responsible for solving the problem.
- It decreases the likelihood that a student will attempt a novel problem without explicit instructions on how to solve it.

In the past we assumed that walking students through a procedure or showing a step-by-step method for solving a particular type of problem was the most helpful approach to learning. However, this approach can actually make students worse at solving problems and doing mathematics, not better.

Teaching mathematics *through* problem solving means that students work with problems to learn new mathematics and to extend their current understanding. This is sometimes called learning through *inquiry*. With this approach, problem solving is completely inter-woven with learning. As students do mathematics—make sense of cognitively demanding tasks, provide evidence or justification for strategies and solutions, find examples and con-nections, and receive and provide feedback about ideas—they are simultaneously engaged in the activities of problem solving and learning. Students learn mathematics through real contexts, problems, situations, and models that allow them to build meaning for the concepts (Hiebert et al., 1997). Teaching *through* problem solving acknowledges what we now know about learning and doing mathematics (see Chapter 1). Our understanding is always chang-ing, incomplete, situated in context, and interconnected. What we learn becomes part of our expanding and evolving network of ideas—a network without endpoints.

So teaching *through* problem solving might be described as "upside down" from the traditional approach of teaching *for* problem solving because the problem or task is presented at the beginning of a lesson and related knowledge or skills emerge from exploring the problem. An example of teaching through problem solving might have students explore the following situation before they know the standard algorithm of adding fractions by using common denominators.

Tatyana needs $\frac{1}{2}$ foot and $\frac{1}{3}$ foot of ribbon for a school project. Figure out the total length of ribbon she will need.

The teacher would explain to the class that there is more than one way to solve this prob-lem and that they are to find as many different solution paths as they can. As students work on the problem, they may use fraction strips, they may choose to draw the ribbon lengths, or they may simply use numbers to capture their ideas.

Stop and Reflect

Find a way to determine how long the ribbon will be without using the standard algorithm of finding common denominators to add the fractions.

Through this context and exploration students could be led to develop the standard algorithm for adding fractions. This problem also generates opportunities for students to improve their fraction sense as they find ways to model fractions and their equivalents. The ribbon provides a context for thinking of fraction of a length, expanding on student understanding of fraction of an area. It also emphasizes the meaning of the part–whole fraction relationship as students investigate how they might combine different sized fractional parts.

Teaching *through* problem solving positions students to engage with mathematics to learn important mathematical concepts. With this approach, students:

- Ask questions
- Determine solution paths
- Use mathematical tools
- Make conjectures
- Seek out patterns

- Communicate findings
- Make connections to other content
- Make generalizations
- Reflect on results

Hopefully these student behaviors sound familiar. This list reflects the CCSS Standards for Mathematical Practice and the NCTM process standards as well as components of being mathematically proficient that were discussed in Chapter 1.

Mathematics Teaching Practices for Teaching *through* Problem Solving

Teaching *through* problem solving requires a paradigm shift, which means that teachers are doing more than just tweaking a few things about their teaching; they are changing their philosophy about how they think students learn best and how they can best help them learn. At first glance, it may seem that the teacher's role is less demanding because the students are doing the mathematics, but the teacher's role is actually more demanding in such classrooms.

Classrooms where students are engaging with and making sense of mathematics through inquiry do not happen by accident—they happen because the teacher uses practices and establishes expectations that encourage risk taking, reasoning, the generation and sharing of ideas, and so forth. Table 2.1 lists eight research-informed, high-leverage teaching practices, identified in NCTM's (2014) *Principles to Actions*, that support students to develop a robust understanding of mathematics. These teaching practices are designed to address issues of access and equity so that all students can succeed in learning mathematics. We will refer back to these teaching practices throughout this chapter as we consider how to teach mathematics *through* problem solving.

Table 2.1. Eight mathematical teaching practices that support student learning.

Teaching Practice	What Is the Teacher Doing to Enact the Practice?
1. Establish mathematics goals to focus learning	• Articulates clear learning goals that identify the mathematics students will learn in a lesson or lessons. • Identifies how the learning goals relate to a mathematics learning progression. • Helps students understand how the work they are doing relates to the learning goals. • Uses the articulated goals to inform instructional decisions involved in planning and implementation.

2. Implement tasks that promote reasoning and problem solving	• Selects tasks that:
	  • Have maximum potential to build and extend students' current mathematical understanding.
	  • Have multiple entry points.
	  • Require a high level of cognitive demand.
	• Supports students to make sense of and solve tasks using multiple strategies and representations, without doing the thinking for the students.

3. Use and connect mathematical representations	• Supports students to use and make connections between various representations. • Introduces representations when appropriate. • Expects students to use various representations to support their reasoning and explanations. • Allows students to choose which representations to use in their work. • Helps students attend to the essential features of a mathematical idea represented in a variety of ways.
4. Facilitate meaningful mathematical discourse	• Facilitates productive discussions among students by focusing on reasoning and justification. • Strategically selects and sequences students' strategies for whole class discussion. • Makes explicit connections between students' strategies and ideas.

5. Pose purposeful questions	• Asks questions that
	  • Probe students' thinking and that require explanation and justification.
	  • Build on students' ideas and avoids funneling (i.e., directing to one right answer or idea).
	  • Make students' ideas and the mathematics more visible so learners can examine the ideas more closely.
	• Provides appropriate amounts of wait time to allow students to organize their thoughts.

6. Build procedural fluency from conceptual understanding	• Encourages students to make sense of, use, and explain their own reasoning and strategies to solve tasks. • Makes explicit connections between strategies produced by students and conventional strategies and procedures.
7. Support productive struggle in learning mathematics	• Helps students see mistakes, misconceptions, naïve conceptions, and struggles as opportunities for learning. • Anticipates potential difficulties and prepares questions that will help scaffold and support students' thinking. • Allows students time to struggle with problems. • Praises students for their efforts and perseverance in problem solving.
8. Elicit and use evidence of student thinking	• Decides what will count as evidence of students' understanding. • Gathers evidence of students' understanding at key points during lesson. • Interprets students' thinking to gauge understanding and progress toward learning goals. • Decides during the lesson how to respond to students to probe, scaffold, and extend their thinking. • Uses evidence of students' learning to guide subsequent instruction.

Source: Based on *Principles to Actions: Ensuring Mathematical Success For All* (NCTM), © 2014.

Using Worthwhile Tasks

When teachers teach mathematics *through* problem solving, the teacher needs to use worthwhile or rich tasks that promote reasoning and problem solving. Not surprisingly, this is one of the eight mathematics teaching practices identified in *Principles to Actions* (NCTM, 2014) (see practice #2 in Table 2.1). As a teacher you need to know what constitutes a worthwhile task and where to find, adapt, or create such tasks. A worthwhile task is problematic as this video demonstrates (https://www.youtube.com/watch?v=XI3-52B0V6s). It poses a question for which (1) the students have no prescribed or memorized rules or methods, and (2) there is no perception that there is a specific "correct" solution method (Hiebert et al., 1997). Because the process or solution method is not obvious, justification is central to the task.

A worthwhile task can take many forms. It might be open-ended or clearly defined; it may involve problem solving or problem posing; it may include words or be purely symbolic; it may develop concepts, procedures, or both; it may take only a few minutes to solve or weeks to investigate; or, it may involve a real-life scenario or be abstract. What makes the task worthwhile is that it is problematic as it engages students in figuring out how to solve it. Here are some tasks to try.

CONCEPT: AREA AS RELATED TO MULTIPLICATION AND ADDITION (GRADE 3)

Sam wants to make an outside pen for his dog. He bought 36 square stones, with sides 1-foot long, to use for the floor. If Sam wants to have a rectangular floor in the dog pen, how can he arrange the 36 square stones? Can you find more than one way? How many ways do you think there are? Why?

CONCEPT: EQUALITY (GRADE 5)

$$6 \times p = 3 \times p + 18$$

Find a number p so that the equation is true. Is there more than one number for p that will make the equation true? Why or why not?

PROCEDURE: MULTIPLYING TWO-DIGIT WHOLE NUMBERS (GRADE 4)

Solve this problem in two different ways: 32×17_____

For each way, explain how you solved it.

Note that a task can be problematic at first and then become routine as a student's knowledge and experience grows. For example, the third example above could be a rich task to explore in grade 3 or 4, but would be "routine" for older or more mathematically advanced students. If the task immediately triggers an approach that the student goes directly to use, the task may be appropriate practice, but it is not a task that is likely to provide the students with new mathematical insights or knowledge.

In thinking about the variety of worthwhile tasks that you can pose, it is important to incorporate tasks that develop both procedural fluency and conceptual understanding. Remember that *procedural fluency* and *conceptual understanding* are two of the five intertwined strands of mathematical proficiency discussed in Chapter 1. Both are equally valuable in students' development toward proficiency—so much so that they are included in one of the teaching practices from *Principles to Action* (NCTM. 2014): *build procedural fluency from conceptual understanding* (see Table 2.1). Using worthwhile tasks where students are able to use a variety of methods and strategies that make sense to them, are expected to explain and justify their approaches, and are encouraged to look for connections among strategies is precisely how students build procedural fluency from conceptual understanding.

Level of Cognitive Demand

Engaging students in productive struggle is one of the teaching practices identified in *Principles to Actions* (NCTM, 2014) (see Table 2.1). It is crucial to student's learning mathematics with understanding (Hiebert & Grouws, 2007). Posing worthwhile tasks sets the stage for this productive struggle because such tasks are cognitively demanding, meaning they require higher-level thinking. High-level, cognitively demanding tasks challenge students to make connections, analyze information, and draw conclusions (Smith & Stein, 1998). On the other hand, low-level cognitively demanding tasks (also called *routine problems* or *lower-level tasks*) are straightforward and involve stating facts, following known procedures, and solving routine problems. As an example of different levels of tasks, consider the degree of reasoning required if you ask fourth grade students to find the product of three given numbers versus if you ask them to find three numbers whose product is 108. The first task only requires students to multiply three numbers. The second task requires them to use number sense to generate three reasonable numbers that will result in a given product. As a consequence of working on this second task, students have potential opportunities to think about and use number relationships while they work on their computational skills for multiplication.

Table 2.2 shows a well-known framework that is useful in determining whether a task has the potential to challenge students (Smith & Stein, 1998). As you read through the descriptors for low-level and high-level cognitively demanding tasks, you will notice that the low-level tasks are straightforward and routine, meaning that they do not engage students in productive struggle. Although there are appropriate times to use low-level cognitively demanding tasks, a heavy or sole emphasis on tasks of this type will not lead to a relational understanding of mathematics. When students know that struggle is an expected part of the process of doing mathematics, they embrace the struggle and feel success when they reach a solution (Carter, 2008).

Table 2.2. Levels of cognitive demand.

Low-Level Cognitive Demand Tasks	High-Level Cognitive Demand Tasks
Memorization • Involve either memorizing or producing previously learned facts, rules, formulas, or definitions • Are routine in that they involve exact reproduction of a previously learned procedure • Have no connection to related concepts	**Procedures with Connections** • Focus students' attention on the use of procedures for the purpose of developing deeper levels of understanding of mathematical concepts and ideas • Suggest general procedures that have close connections to underlying conceptual ideas • Are usually represented in multiple ways (e.g., visuals, manipulatives, symbols, problem situations) • Require that students engage with the conceptual ideas that underlie the procedures in order to successfully complete the task
Procedures without Connections • Use of procedures is specifically called for • Are straightforward, with little ambiguity about what needs to be done and how to do it • Have little or no connection to related concepts • Are focused on producing correct answers rather than developing mathematical understanding • Require no explanations, or the explanations only focus on listing or restating the steps of the procedure	**_Doing_ Mathematics** • Require complex and nonalgorithmic thinking (i.e., nonroutine—without a predictable, known approach) • Require students to explore and to understand the nature of mathematical concepts, processes, or relationships • Demand self-monitoring or self-regulation of students' own cognitive processes • Require students to access relevant knowledge in working through the task • Require students to analyze the task and actively examine task constraints • Require considerable cognitive effort

Reprinted with permission from *Mathematics Teaching in the Middle School*, Vol. 03, No. 05, pp. 344–350, copyright 1998, by the National Council of Teachers of Mathematics. All rights reserved.

Multiple Entry and Exit Points

Your students will likely have a wide range of experiences in mathematics, so it is important to use problems that have multiple entry points, meaning that the problems have varying degrees of challenge or can be approached in a variety of ways. Having multiple entry points can help accommodate the diversity of learners in your classroom because students are encouraged to use a strategy that makes sense to them instead of using a predetermined strategy that they may or may not be ready to use successfully. Having a choice of strategies can also lower the anxiety of students, particularly English Language Learners (Murrey, 2008). Some students may initially use less-efficient approaches, such as guess and check, but they will develop more advanced strategies through effective questioning by the teacher and by reflecting on other students' approaches. For example, for the task of finding three numbers whose product is 108, one student may use a guess and check approach, listing three numbers and multiplying them to see if their product is 108, whereas another student may use a more systematic approach, such as dividing 108 by 2 and then splitting the resulting 54 into two factors. Still another student may readily know that 3 is a factor of 108 because of his or her knowledge of divisibility by 3, and use that information and the fact 108 is an even number to find two more factors. Asking students to compare these approaches, and in particular to identify advantages and disadvantages of each, can help students move toward more advanced strategies.

Tasks should also have multiple exit points or various ways that students can express solutions that reveal a range of mathematical sophistication. For example, students might draw a diagram, write an equation, use manipulatives, or act out a problem to demonstrate their understanding. Even though students might initially select an inefficient or less sophisticated approach, as ideas are exchanged during and after the problem is solved, students will have opportunities to understand and try other approaches. As they discuss ideas, draw visuals, use manipulatives, or act out a problem, defend their strategy, critique the reasoning of others, and write about their reasoning, they engage in higher-level thinking. As an added bonus, the teacher is also able to gather useful formative assessment data about students' mathematical understanding.

Consider the opportunities for multiple entry and exit points in the following tasks for third grade.

TASK 1:

(The teacher draws a 4 × 7 inch rectangle on the board and labels the sides.) What is this polygon called? What is the perimeter of this polygon?

TASK 2:

(The teacher gives each student a sheet of grid paper.) On your grid paper, draw, describe, and name a polygon that has the following side lengths: 4 units, 4 units, 7 units, and 7 units. Can you make more than one polygon with these same dimensions?

Stop and Reflect

To what degree do these tasks offer opportunities for multiple entry and exit points?

With the first task students will gain some experience calculating perimeter but they will miss any opportunity to think deeply about the situation or the concept. Although perimeter is more implicit in the second task, it offers more opportunity for students to engage with the notion of perimeter and polygons in a variety of ways, which also offers the teacher more information about each student's level of understanding. For example, if a student initially thinks that only one polygon (a rectangle) can be made, this is informative. As students create new polygons, do they calculate the perimeter each time? Do they think that the area is the same for all the polygons with the same perimeter? Clearly, the second task offers many more opportunities for all students to engage in the task in a variety of ways.

Relevant and Well-Designed Contexts

One of the most powerful ways to teach mathematics through problem solving is to begin the lesson with a problem that can get students excited about learning mathematics. Compare the following fourth-grade introductory tasks on multiplying 2 two-digit numbers. Which one do you think would more exciting to students?

> *Classroom A:* "Today we are going to use grid paper to show the sub-products when we multiply 2 two-digit numbers."

> *Classroom B:* "The school is planning a fall festival and our grade level is in charge of selling drinks. The principal said we had 14 cases of bottled water in the storage closet. I went into the storage closet to see how many bottled waters we have. I could see 4 cases, each having 35 bottles in 7 rows of 5, at the front of the closet, but the others were in the back where I could not see them so I could not count them all. We need to figure out a way to determine how many bottles of water we have."

Familiar and interesting contexts increase students' engagement. Your goal as a teacher is to design problems using familiar and interesting contexts that provide specific parameters, constraints, or structure that will support the development of the mathematical ideas you want students to learn. Note that in solving a worthwhile problem the problematic or engaging aspect of the problem must be a result of the mathematics that the students are to learn. Any context or external constraints used should not overshadow but highlight the mathematics to be learned. In the context used in Classroom B above, the situation involves 14 cases of drinks that are separated into 4 cases and 10 cases. The teacher is aware that some of her students will find it difficult to work with double digits, so she structures the context to subtly suggest a way to partition the numbers into smaller numbers. She is also aware that a few of her students still tend to count large amounts by ones, but the constraint that each case has 5 drinks in 7 rows again subtly suggests skip counting by fives as a way to determine how many bottles are in each case. This constraint begins to incrementally move these students toward more efficient ways of counting (i.e., multiplication). Also, the fact that each case is almost 40 bottles may lead some students to use computational estimation to round the amount to 40 as they grapple with how to determine how many drinks are in 14 cases. For those students who have already mastered their basic facts for multiplication, the two groupings of cases help them move toward multiplying with two-digit numbers. By building in this structure through constraints and parameters, teachers can support students in developing more sophisticated strategies that honor where the students currently are in their understanding (Fosnot & Dolk, 2001).

Children's literature is a rich source for generating high cognitive demand tasks with multiple entry and exit points. For example, the popular fantasy novel *Harry Potter and the Sorcerer's Stone* (Rowling, 1998) offers several possibilities for tasks that can be launched from the story. For example, the author describes Hagrid, one of the characters in the book, as twice as tall and five times as wide as the average man. Students in grades 3–4 can each cut a strip of paper that is as tall as they are and another one that is as wide as their shoulders (you can cut strips from cash register rolls). Then they can figure out how big Hagrid would be if he were twice as tall and five times as wide as they are. In grades 4–5, students can create a table that shows each student's height and width and look for a pattern (it turns out to be about 3 to 1). Then they can figure out Hagrid's height and width and see whether they keep the same ratio (it is 5 to 2).

Evaluating and Adapting Tasks

In a great many places you will find suggestions for tasks that *someone* believes are effective for teaching a particular mathematics concept or skill. Unfortunately, many of these readily available tasks fall short of being worthwhile or rich tasks. Table 2.3 provides some reflective questions you can use to evaluate whether a task you are considering has the maximum potential to help your students learn relevant mathematics. These questions are meant to help you consider to what extent the task meets these criteria, so all the boxes do not need to be checked off. A task could rate very high on the number of problem-solving strategies, but miss the mark for having a relevant context for your students, and therefore you would decide to change the context to something more interesting. Or, the task is complete with worthwhile features and problem-solving strategies but it does not match the mathematical goals for the lesson. You may choose to alter the task to focus on the relevant mathematics or save it for when it is a better match.

Table 2.3. Reflective questions to use in selecting worthwhile tasks.

Task Evaluation and Selection Guide	
Task potential	Try it and ask … ❏ What is problematic about the task? ❏ Is the mathematics interesting? ❏ What mathematical goals does the task address (and are they aligned to what you are seeking)? ❏ What strategies might students use? ❏ What key concepts and/or misconceptions might this task elicit?
Problem-Solving strategies	Will the task elicit more than one problem-solving strategy ❏ Visualize ❏ Look for patterns ❏ Predict and check for reasonableness ❏ Formulate conjectures and justify claims ❏ Create a list, table, or chart ❏ Simplify or change the problem ❏ Write an equation
Worthwhile features	To what extent does the task have these key features: ❏ High cognitive demand ❏ Multiple entry and exit points ❏ Relevant contexts
Assessment	In what ways does the task provide opportunities for you to gain insights into student understanding through: ❏ Using tools or models to represent mathematics ❏ Student reflection, justification, and explanation ❏ Multiple ways to demonstrate understanding

You will find many problems in student textbooks, on the Internet, at workshops you attend, and in articles you read that don't quite meet the mark of a worthwhile task. Boaler (2016) offers the following six suggestions for adapting tasks to increase their potential for learning:

1. *Allow multiple ways:* Modify the task so students can use multiple methods, strategies, and representations to solve.
2. *Make it an exploration:* Change the task so that students must do more than complete a procedure and change it so there is potential to learn by doing the task. For example, rather than ask students to multiply $\frac{4}{5}$ by 3, ask them for various numbers they could multiply to get the fraction $\frac{12}{5}$.

3. *Postpone teaching a solution method:* This way students have the opportunity to use their intuition to think about the situation before learning about conventional methods. For example, prior to teaching students conventional methods for measuring volume, ask them to devise ways to measure the volume of a shoe box.

4. *Add a visual requirement:* Visualization can be a powerful tool for enhancing understanding. You can require students to use color coding to show connections or relationships. Or require that they use two different manipulatives to justify their solution.

5. *Increase the number of entry points:* To lower the floor, simply ask students to write down everything they know about the problem or the given concept. To raise the ceiling, once students have completed a task, have them write their own related questions. Challenge them to write questions that are more difficult than the original question and to justify why they are more difficult.

6. *Reason and convince:* Require students to not only provide their reasoning but to be convincing in their mathematical argument and to require others to be as well. Ask learners to be skeptics and to ask clarifying questions of others. You will need to model the expectations for being a skeptic by asking students follow-up questions when they have not been convincing enough.

Additional strategies for modifying tasks to offer differentiated challenges for students can be found in the chapter on differentiating instruction (Chapter 4).

What Do I Do When a Task Doesn't Work?

Sometimes students may not know what to do with a problem you pose, no matter how many hints and suggestions you offer. Do not give in to the temptation to "tell them." When you sense that a task is not moving forward, don't spend days just hoping that something wonderful may happen. You may need to regroup and offer students a simpler but related task that gets them prepared for the one that proved too difficult. If that does not work, set it aside for the moment. Ask yourself why it didn't work well. Did the students have the prior knowledge they needed? Was the task too advanced? Consider what might be a way to step back or step forward in the content in order to support and challenge the class. Nonetheless, trust that teaching mathematics *through* problem solving offers students the productive struggle that will allow them to develop understanding and become mathematically proficient.

Orchestrating Classroom Discourse

Participating in discussions about mathematics contributes to students' understanding in a multitude of ways. Discussions improve students' ability to reason logically as they learn to share their ideas and listen to the ideas of others. Misconceptions and naïve conceptions are also more likely to be revealed in discussions, providing opportunities for teachers to explicitly address them. As students realize they can learn from each other, they are more motivated and interested in what their classmates have to say.

Learning how to orchestrate an effective classroom discussion is quite complex and requires attention to a number of elements. The goal of productive discourse is to keep the cognitive demand high while students are learning and formalizing mathematical concepts (Breyfogle & Williams,

Teaching Tip

What are misconceptions and naïve conceptions? Consider a misconception as a student understanding that is not mathematically accurate, for example, thinking thirds means three parts regardless of the size of the parts. A naïve conception is a partial and typically less powerful, but mathematically accurate understanding—for example, thinking of 2/3 in terms of part-whole (and not as two one-thirds). In either case, these conceptions are important to diagnose so that a deep understanding can be developed.

2008/2009; Kilic et al., 2010; Smith, Hughes, Engle, & Stein, 2009). The purpose is not for students to state their answers and get validation from the teacher. The aspects involved in orchestrating classroom discourse are so important, they directly involve three out of the eight teaching practices from *Principles to Actions* (NCTM, 2014): Facilitate meaningful mathematical discourse; Pose purposeful questions; and Elicit and use evidence of student thinking.

Classroom Discussions

The value of student talk throughout a mathematics lesson cannot be overemphasized. As students describe and evaluate solutions to tasks, share approaches, and make conjectures, learning will occur in ways that are otherwise unlikely to take place. Questions such as those that ask students if they would do it differently next time, which strategy made sense to them (and why), and what caused problems for them (and how they overcame them), are critical in developing mathematically proficient students. As they listen to other students' ideas, they come to see the varied approaches in how problems can be solved and see mathematics as something that they can do.

Smith and Stein (2011) identified five teacher actions for orchestrating productive mathematics discussions: anticipating, monitoring, selecting, sequencing, and connecting. The first action, *anticipating* responses to the selected worthwhile task, takes place before the lesson even begins. As students work on the task, the teacher *monitors*, observing students' strategies and asking questions such as:

- How did you decide what to do? Did you use more than one strategy?
- What did you do that helped you make sense of the problem?
- Did you find any numbers or information you didn't need? How did you know that the information was not important?
- Did you try something that didn't work? How did you figure out it was not going to work?

These and similar questions are meant to help students reflect on their strategies and help the teacher determine which strategies to *select* for public discussion in the next part of the lesson. Having selected a range of strategies to be shared, the teacher strategically *sequences* the presentations so that particular mathematical ideas can be emphasized. During the presentations, the teacher generates questions and ideas that *connect* strategies and mathematical concepts. These tend to be questions that are specific to the task, but some general questions include:

- How did [Kathy] represent her solution? What mathematical terms, symbols, or tools did she use? How is this like/different from [Colin's] strategy?
- Was there something in the task that reminded you of another problem we've done?
- What might you do the same or differently the next time you encounter a similar problem?

Notice these questions focus on the problem-solving process as well as the answer, and what worked as well as what didn't work. A balanced discussion helps students learn how to do mathematics.

Because of the important benefits of talking about mathematical ideas, you also need to make sure that everyone participates in the classroom discussion. Finding ways to encourage students to share their ideas and to engage with others about their ideas is essential to productive discussions. You may need to explicitly discuss with students why discussions are important and what it means to actively listen and respond to others' ideas. Wagganer (2015) shares some helpful ideas to explicitly teach students how to engage in active listening. For example, students can demonstrate they are listening by making eye contact with the speaker and through nonverbal cues (e.g., nodding); letting the speaker finish before sharing questions or ideas; and responding appropriately and respectfully by asking questions or summarizing the speaker's ideas. Also, Table 2.4 identifies five "talk moves" that help get everyone talking about mathematics (Chapin, O'Connor, & Anderson, 2009).

Table 2.4. Productive talk moves for supporting classroom discussions.

Talk Moves	What It Means and Why	Example Teacher Prompts
1. Revoicing	This move involves restating the statement as a question in order to clarify, apply appropriate language, and involve more students. It is an important strategy to reinforce language and enhance comprehension for ELLs.	"You used the hundreds chart and counted on?" "So, first you recorded your measurements in a table?"
2. Rephrasing	Asking students to restate someone else's ideas in their own words will ensure that ideas are stated in a variety of ways and encourage students to listen to each other.	"Who can share what Ricardo just said, but using your own words?"
3. Reasoning	Rather than restate, as in talk move 2, this move asks the student what they think of the idea proposed by another student.	"Do you agree or disagree with Johanna? Why?"
4. Elaborating	This is a request for students to challenge, add on, elaborate, or give an example. It is intended to get more participation from students, deepen student understanding, and provide extensions.	"Can you give an example?" "Do you see a connection between Julio's idea and Rhonda's idea? What if . . . "
5. Waiting	Ironically, one "talk move" is to not talk. Quiet time should not feel uncomfortable, but should feel like thinking time. If it gets awkward, ask students to pair-share, and then try again.	"This question is important. Let's take some time to think about it."

Source: Based on *Classroom Discussions: Using Math Talk to Help Students Learn, Grades K–6,* by Suzanne H. Chapin, Catherine O'Connor, Nancy Canavan Anderson. Published by Math Solutions, © 2009.

Considerable research into how mathematical communities develop and operate provide additional insight into promoting effective classroom discourse (Chapin, O'Conner, & Anderson, 2009; Rasmussen, Yackel, & King, 2003; Stephan & Whitenack, 2003; Wood, Williams, & McNeal, 2006; Yackel & Cobb, 1996). This collection of research offers the following recommendations:

- Encourage student–student dialogue rather than student–teacher conversations that exclude the rest of the class. "Juanita, can you answer Lora's question?" "Devon, can you explain that so that LaToya and Kevin can understand what you are saying?" When students have differing solutions, have them work these ideas out as a class. "George, I noticed that you got a different answer than Tara. What do you think about her explanation?"

- Encourage students to ask questions. "Pete, did you understand how they did that? Do you want to ask Antonio a question?"

- Ask follow-up questions whether the answer is right or wrong. Your role is to understand students' thinking, not to lead students to the correct answer. So follow up with probes to learn more about their answers. Sometimes you will find that what you assumed they were thinking is not correct. And if you only follow up on wrong answers, students quickly figure this out and get nervous when you ask them to explain their thinking.

- Call on students in such a way that, over time, everyone is able to participate. Use time when students are working in small groups to identify interesting solutions that you will highlight during the sharing time. Be intentional about the order in which the solutions are shared; for example, select two that you would like to compare and have students present them back-to-back. All students should be prepared to share their strategies.

- Demonstrate to students that it is okay to be confused and that asking clarifying questions is appropriate. This confusion, or disequilibrium, just means they are engaged in doing real mathematics and indicates that they are learning. Make a point to tell them this!

- Move students to more conceptually based explanations when appropriate. For example, if a student says that he knows 4.17 is more than 4.163, you can ask him (or another student) to explain why this is so.

- Be sure all students are involved in the discussion. ELLs, in particular, need more than vocabulary support; they need support with mathematical discussions (Moschkovich, 1998). For example, use sentence starters or examples to help students know what kinds of responses you are hoping to hear and to reduce the language demands. Sentence starters can also be helpful for students with disabilities because it adds structure. Have students practice their explanations with a peer. Invite students to use illustrations and actual objects, when appropriate, to support their explanations. These strategies benefit all students, not just students in the class who struggle with language.

- Pay attention to whether you are taking over students' thinking. Jacobs, Martin, Ambrose, and Philipp (2014) identify warning signs of such behavior—for example, interrupting a student's strategy or explanation, manipulating the tools instead of allowing the student to do so, and asking a string of closed questions (i.e., funneling). Taking over students' thinking sends the message that you do not believe they are capable and can inhibit the discourse you are trying to encourage.

Aspects of Questioning

Questions are important in learning about students' thinking, challenging conclusions, and extending the inquiry to help generalize patterns. Questioning is very complex and something that effective teachers continue to improve on throughout their careers. Here are some major considerations related to questioning that influence students' learning.

1. *The "level" of the question asked.* There are numerous models that identify different levels of questions. For example, the Levels of Cognitive Demand in Table 2.2 include two low-level demand categories and two high-level demand categories. Also, Bloom's Taxonomy Revised includes six levels (knowledge, comprehension, application, analysis, synthesis, evaluation), with each level meant to be more cognitively demanding than the previous (Anderson & Krathwohl, 2001). However, you can still ask a low-level cognitively demanding "create" question on Bloom's Taxonomy Revised. For example, brainstorming ideas would be lower-level than say, designing a model, but both could be categorized as "create." Check out Simpson, Mokalled, Ellenburg, and Che (2015) who share a tool that can help analyze the depth of knowledge that can occur across the categories in Bloom's Taxonomy Revised. Regardless of the taxonomy or specific categories, it is critical to ask higher-level, cognitively demanding questions to support students in developing a robust understanding of mathematics.

2. *The type of understanding that is targeted.* Both procedural and conceptual understanding are important, and questions must target both. If questions are limited to procedural ideas, such as "How did you solve this?" or "What are the steps?" then students will think about procedures, but not about related concepts. Questions focused on conceptual knowledge include, "Will this rule always work?" "Why use common denominators to add fractions?" "How does the equation you wrote connect to the picture?" and "How is your strategy like Caroline's?"

3. *The pattern of questioning.* Some patterns of questioning teachers use do not lead to classroom discussions that encourage all students to think (Herbel-Eisenmann & Breyfogle, 2005). One such common pattern of questioning goes like this: teacher asks a question, student answers the question, teacher confirms or challenges answer (called "initiation-response-feedback" or "IRF" pattern). Another ineffective pattern is "funneling," when a teacher continues to probe students in ways to get them to a particular answer. This is different than a "focusing" pattern, which uses probing questions to negotiate a classroom discussion and help students understand the mathematics. The talk moves described previously are intended to help facilitate a focusing discussion.

4. *Who is doing the thinking.* Make sure your questions engage all students! When you ask a great question, and only one student responds, then students will quickly figure out they don't need to think about the answer and all your effort to ask a great question is wasted. Instead, use strategies to be sure everyone is accountable to think about the questions you pose. For example, ask students to "talk to a partner" about the question. Or have students record their ideas on a whiteboard or index card.

5. *How you respond to an answer.* When you confirm a correct solution rather than use one of the talk moves, you lose an opportunity to engage students in meaningful discussions about mathematics and so limit the learning opportunities. Use students' solutions to find out if others think the conclusions made are correct, whether they can justify why, and if there are other strategies or solutions to the problem and how they are connected.

How Much to Tell and Not to Tell

One of the most perplexing dilemmas for teachers is how much information and direction to provide to students during mathematical inquiry. On one hand, telling can diminish what is learned and lower the level of cognitive demand in a lesson by eliminating the productive struggle that is key to conceptual understanding (Hiebert & Grouws, 2007). On the other hand, telling too little can sometimes leave students floundering. Following are suggestions about three things that you need to tell students (Hiebert et al., 1997):

- *Mathematical conventions:* Symbols, such as $\times$ and $\leq$, are conventions. Terminology is also a convention. As a rule of thumb, symbolism and terminology should be introduced after concepts have been developed, and then specifically as a means of expressing or labeling ideas.

- *Alternative methods:* If an important strategy does not emerge naturally from students, then you should propose the strategy, being careful to identify it as "another" way, not the only or the preferred way.

- *Clarification or formalization of students' methods:* You should help students clarify or interpret their ideas. For example, suppose a student explained that she solved 1000–369 by "adding one to 369 to get 631." You might be familiar with this strategy and therefore understand the student's reasoning, although it is incomplete. So that other students will better understand her reasoning, help the student be more explicit about why she added one to 369 and how she ended up with 631. For example, start by simply asking the student why she added 1 to 369. The reason is to make the numbers easier to work with—it's easier to subtract 1000–370 than 1000–369. Ask the student to describe her reasoning after she changed the problem to the easier problem, 1000–370. She may explain it like this: "I subtracted 1000–300 which is 700 and then subtracted 70 to equal 630. Then I added one which is 631." Here again, probe the student for why she added 1 instead of subtracted 1. She may explain, "When I subtracted 370 instead of 369, I subtracted one more than I really needed to. So I needed to add 1 back in which equals 631."

Also look for opportunities to highlight a significant idea in students' methods and point out related concepts. For example, sometimes students are uncertain about what is actually being measured when they measure angles. If you think about moving or rotating through an angle, the movement can help focus students' attention to the attribute of the angle being measured. Suppose, because of the context you have used, a student describes moving or turning through an angle as he is determining its measure. Stop and point out this significant idea. In addition, relate this idea to how you move through an interval on a ruler as you use it to measure the length of an object. The notion of moving through an interval or rotating through an angle is an important measurement concept that highlights the attribute being measured. Drawing everyone's attention to this connection can help students see the connection, which in turn can enhance their understanding.

The key is that you can share information as long as it does not solve the problem, remove the need for students to reflect on what they are doing, or prevent them from developing solution methods that make sense to them (Hiebert et al., 1997).

Leveraging Mistakes and Misconceptions to Enhance Learning

Students inevitably will make mistakes and exhibit misconceptions and naïve conceptions—especially when we pose challenging tasks in our classrooms. You may not want to highlight a student's mistake or misconception because you are concerned that it might embarrass the student or confuse the struggling learners in your classroom. How we choose to treat mistakes and misconceptions in the classroom can have a tremendous effect on students' perceptions about learning and themselves as learners.

When mistakes, misconceptions, and naïve conceptions are perceived and used (explicitly or implicitly) to judge how "smart" someone is, students want to hide their mistakes as well as their lack of understanding. Students can develop a fixed mindset in which they believe their intelligence is set and cannot be further developed through effort (Dweck, 2006), which means they are very unlikely to persevere in solving difficult problems that require productive struggle (Boaler, 2013). To them, difficult tasks are not perceived as opportunities to learn and improve, but rather as spotlights that highlight their inadequacies (Boaler, 2016; Dweck, 2006). On the other hand, students who adopt a growth mindset appreciate, take on, and persist with challenges because they perceive these as opportunities to learn. They also view mistakes as a chance to reconsider, revise, and improve their understanding. An online TED talk of Carol Dweck describing mind-sets (titled "The power of believing you can improve") is worth watching.

We want students to embrace a growth mindset—to see mistakes, misconceptions, and struggles as opportunities for learning. In fact, this is a critical part of the teaching practice *support productive struggle in learning mathematics* (see Table 2.1). Publicly valuing a mistake or misconception in class and having students think about why it is a mistake or misconception reinforces the important message that we all make mistakes and have misconceptions and can improve our understanding by examining them more closely. You can even design lessons around tasks that elicit common misconceptions or mistakes (Bray, 2013; Lim, 2014). For example, Bray (2013) chose a task that required students to create thirds rather than halves or fourths because she knew some students would try to use halving to create the fractional parts. The task also elicited misconceptions about whether thirds meant three parts or three *equal* parts.

Flawed ideas, strategies, and solutions can come from either student's work or from the teacher. If the mistakes or misconceptions come from students in the class, Bray (2013) offers some helpful suggestions for ensuring that the error maker is respected. For example, ask the student for permission to publicly share the mistake or misconception, give the student the choice to explain, acknowledge to the class where there is good reasoning involved in the student's flawed thinking, and express appreciation for the opportunity to analyze the mistake or misconception as a way to improve their classmates' mathematical understanding.

Choosing to publicly treat mistakes and misconceptions in a positive light in your classroom will help students be risk takers and to persevere with challenging tasks. Rather than fearing mistakes and misunderstandings they will appreciate the powerful role these can play in learning.

Representations: Tools for Problem Solving, Reasoning, and Communication

One of the teaching practices identified in *Principles to Actions* (2014) is *use and connect mathematical representations.* The fact that representations made the cut on this short list should give you some sense of its importance in teaching for relational understanding.

Build a Web of Representations

Different representations can illuminate different aspects of a mathematical idea. So to help students build their understanding, they should be encouraged to use, explore, and make connections among multiple representations. Figure 2.1 provides a general Web of Representations that can be applied to any mathematical concept and illustrates the various ways mathematical ideas can be represented. Students who have difficulty translating a concept from one representation to another also have difficulty solving problems and understanding computations (Clement, 2004; Lesh, Cramer,

Teaching Tip

Pay attention to students' choices of representations and use those representations as starting points for dialogues with them about their thinking. What they find important may be surprising and informative at the same time.

Figure 2.1

Mathematical understanding can be demonstrated through these different representations of mathematical ideas. Translations between each can help students develop new concepts and demonstrate a richer understanding.

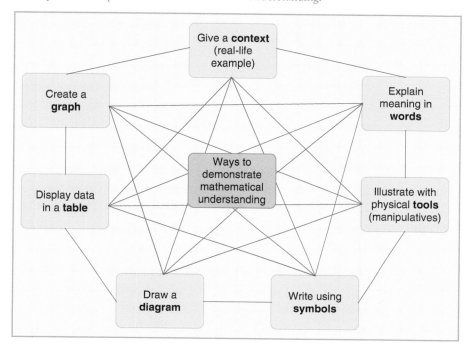

Doerr, Post, & Zawojewski, 2003). Strengthening students' ability to move between and among representations improves their understanding and retention of ideas. For any topic you teach, you can give students the Translation Task to complete. (More information is given regarding the use of the Translation Task in Chapter 3, Creating Assessments for Learning.) Fill out one box and ask students to insert the other representations, or you can invite a group to work on all four representations for a given topic (e.g., multiplication of multidigit numbers).

Explore with Tools

A *tool* is any object, picture, or drawing that can be used to explore a concept. CCSS-M includes calculators and manipulatives as tools for doing mathematics (CCSSO, 2010). Manipulatives are physical objects that, regardless of the age of the students, can be used to illustrate and explore mathematical concepts. Choices for manipulatives (including virtual manipulatives) are plentiful—from common objects such as lima beans to commercially produced materials such as Pattern Blocks. A range of manipulatives (e.g., geoboards, base-ten blocks, spinners, number lines) are available in a virtual format, for example, on the National Library of Virtual Manipulatives (NLVM) website and the NCTM Illuminations website. Changes can usually be made to virtual representations more quickly than with physical manipulatives or student-generated drawings, leaving more time for exploration. For example, dynamic geometry software allows students to explore shapes, making and testing conjectures about their properties by changing the shapes on the computer screen (see, for example, the applet at Illuminations titled "Exploring Properties of Rectangles and Parallelograms Using Dynamic Software").

Some research suggests benefits to incorporating both physical and virtual manipulatives in instruction (Hunt, Nipper, & Nash, 2011). Physical manipulatives can build the foundation for conceptual understanding while subsequent use of virtual manipulatives can assist learners in bridging to the abstract. For example, at some websites, such as the NLVM website, a displayed decimal representing the computerized base-ten blocks changes as the base-ten blocks are modified so that students can see the corresponding results of the changed manipulatives on the numbers.

Figure 2.2

Objects and names of objects are not the same as mathematical ideas and relationships between objects.

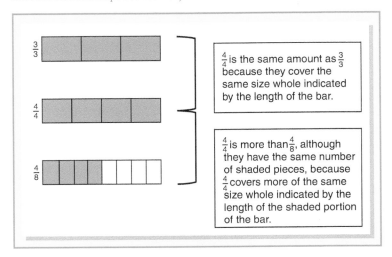

Note a tool does not "illustrate" a concept. While the tool is used to visualize a mathematical concept, an individual has to impose the mathematical relationship on the object (Suh, 2007b; Thompson, 1994). In other words, the manipulative is not the concept but offers a testing ground for emerging ideas. Figure 2.2 shows fraction bars commonly used to represent different fractional quantities. If a student is able to identify the first bar as three-thirds and the second bar as four-fourths, does this mean the student has constructed the concepts of fractions and now can compare fractions using these manipulatives? No, all you know for sure is that the student has learned the names typically assigned to the manipulatives. Some students can identify fractions using fraction manipulatives, but they are not sure what they are supposed to pay attention to when they compare fractions. Is it the size of the pieces, the number of the pieces in the bar, or how much of the bar is shaded? They may be uncertain as to whether the length of the bar (i.e., the size of the whole) is important. Understanding the mathematical concept that four-fourths is larger that four-eighths relies on understanding the relationship between the size of the pieces and the whole in each fraction, and then understanding that when comparing fractions they have to be based on the same size whole. These relationships must be created by students in their own minds and imposed on the manipulative or the model used to represent the concept. For a student who does not yet understand the relationship, the model does not illustrate the concept for that individual. Over time, discussions that explicitly focus on the mathematical concepts can help students make the connections between manipulatives and the related concepts. When you are considering using particular tools in your classroom, take time yourself to try to separate the physical tool from the relationship that you must impose on the tool in order to "see" the concept. This insight will help you support your students as they work with the given tool.

Although tools can be used to support the development of relational understanding, used ineffectively, they do not accomplish this goal. The most widespread misuse of manipulatives occurs when teachers tell students, "Do exactly as I do." There is a natural temptation to get out the materials and show students exactly how to use them. Students mimic the teacher's directions, and it may even look as if they understand, but they could be just following what they see. A rote procedure with a manipulative is still just that—a rote procedure. The converse is to provide no focus or purpose for using the tools. Neither approach promotes thinking or aids in the development of concepts (Ball, 1992; Stein & Bovalino, 2001).

Drawings are another option for students to represent and illustrate mathematical concepts and are important for a number of reasons. First, when students draw, you learn more about what they do or do not understand. For example, when students are comparing $\frac{4}{5}$ and $\frac{2}{3}$ with their own drawings, you can observe whether they understand that the wholes for each of the fractions must be the same size to compare them. Second, manipulatives can sometimes restrict how students can model problems, whereas drawings allow students to use any strategy they want. Figure 2.3 shows an example of a fifth grader's solution for adding $\frac{2}{3}$ and $\frac{3}{5}$. This example illustrates how student-generated drawings can provide significant information about students' understanding. What common misconception does this student's work highlight? Look for opportunities to use students' representations during classroom discussions to help students make sense of the more abstract mathematical symbols and computational procedures. Furthermore, as students use different representations to solve a problem, have them compare and contrast the various ways to facilitate making connections.

Figure 2.3

A fifth grader shows her incorrect thinking about how to add $\frac{2}{3}$ and $\frac{3}{5}$.

Tips for Using Representations in the Classroom

Representations give learners something with which they can explore, reason, and communicate as they engage in problem-based tasks. The goal of using representations is that students are able to manipulate ideas and make connections in a meaningful manner. The following are rules of thumb for using representations in the classroom:

- Introduce new representations or tools by showing how they can represent *the ideas* for which they are intended. But keep in mind that, because the representations are not the concepts, some students may not "see" what you see.
- Encourage students to create their own representations. Look for opportunities to connect these student-created representations to more conventional representations.
- Allow students (in most instances) the opportunity to choose their own representations to reason through a problem and to communicate their ideas to others (Mathematical Practice 5: Use appropriate tools strategically). The representations that students choose to use can provide valuable insight into their ways of interpreting and thinking about the mathematical ideas at hand. Note that it is appropriate to encourage a student who is having difficulty to use a particular representation when you believe it would be helpful.
- Ask students to use representations, such as diagrams and manipulatives, when they explain their thinking. This will help you gather information about students' understanding of the idea and also their understanding of the representations that have been used in the classroom. It can also be helpful to other students in the classroom who may be struggling with the idea or the explanation being offered.
- In creating tasks and when facilitating classroom discussions, look for opportunities to make connections among the different representations used (and make sure each is understood). Helping students make these connections is crucial to their learning.

Lessons in the Problem-Based Classroom

Lessons that engage students in problem solving look quite different from traditional lessons that follow the "I-we-you" or "explain, then practice" pattern. Mathematical practices such as modeling mathematics, reasoning quantitatively, and looking for generalizations and structure are not developed in a lecture-style lesson. In contrast, in classrooms where learning is assumed to be a complex process and where inquiry and problem solving are emphasized, worthwhile tasks are posed to challenge students' thinking and students are expected to communicate and justify their ideas. In these kinds of classrooms, preparing a lesson shifts from preparing an agenda of what will happen to creating a "thought experiment" to consider what might happen (Davis, Sumara, & Luce-Kapler, 2008).

The first teaching practice listed in Table 2.1, *establish mathematics goals to focus learning*, is one of the most important. Being clear about the target mathematics that you want students to learn as a result of a particular lesson or lessons helps you to be intentional as you make instructional choices during planning as well as implementation. For example, in planning the lesson, you need to purposefully select a worthwhile task that has maximum potential to illuminate the target learning goals. Without this intentionality, your lesson can lack focus and consequently, not culminate in the desired results. The three-phase lesson format discussed next is intended to support the creation of intentional lessons that support mathematical inquiry.

A Three-Phase Lesson Format

A lesson format that uses the three phases *before*, *during*, and *after* provides a structure for teaching mathematics through inquiry or problem solving. *Before* refers to what happens in the lesson to set up the inquiry, *during* refers to the time during which the students explore the worthwhile problem, and *after* refers to what happens in the lesson after the problem is solved (e.g., discussion, reflection, and making connections). A lesson may take one or more math sessions, but the three-phase structure can also be applied to shorter tasks, resulting in a 10- to 20-minute mini-lesson. Table 2.5 describes appropriate teacher actions and provides some illustrative examples for each phase of the lesson.

Table 2.5. Teaching mathematics through problem solving lends itself to a three-phase structure for lessons.

Lesson Phase	Teacher Actions in a Teaching Mathematics through Problem-Solving Lesson	
Before	Activate prior knowledge.	Begin with a related but simpler version of the task; connect to students' experiences; brainstorm approaches or solution strategies; estimate or predict whether tasks involve a single computation or are aimed at the development of a computational procedure.
	Be sure the problem is understood.	Have students explain to you what the problem is asking. Go over vocabulary that may be troubling. Caution: This does *not* mean that you are explaining how to *do* the problem, just that students should understand what the problem is about.
	Establish clear expectations.	Tell students whether they will work individually, in pairs, or small groups, or if they will have a choice. Tell them how they will share their solutions and reasoning.
During	Let go!	Although it is tempting to want to step in and "help," hold back and enjoy observing and learning from students.
	Notice students' mathematical thinking.	Base your questions on students' work and their responses to you. Use prompts like: "Tell me what you are doing"; "I see you have started to [multiply] these numbers.";"Can you tell me why you are [multiplying]?" [substitute any process/strategy]; "Can you tell me more about . . . ?"; "Why did you . . . ?";"How does your diagram connect to the problem?"
	Provide appropriate support.	Look for ways to support students' thinking and avoid telling them how to solve the problem. Ensure that students understand the problem ("What do you know about the problem?"); ask the student what he or she has already tried (e.g., "Where did you get stuck?"); suggest that the student use a different strategy ("Can you draw a diagram?"; "What if you used cubes to act out this problem?"; "Is this like another problem we have solved?"); create a parallel problem with simpler values (Jacobs & Ambrose, 2008).
	Provide worthwhile extensions.	Challenge early finishers in some manner that is related to the problem just solved. Possible questions to ask are: "I see you found one way to do this. Are there any other solutions?"; "Are any of the solutions different or more interesting than others?" Some good questions for extending thinking are, "What if . . . ?" or "Would that same idea work for . . . ?"
After	Promote a community of learners.	You must teach your students about your expectations for this part of the lesson and how to interact respectfully with their peers. Role play appropriate (and inappropriate) ways of responding to each other. The "Orchestrating Classroom Discourse" section in this chapter provides strategies and recommendations for how to facilitate discussions that help create a community of learners.
	Listen actively without evaluation.	The goal here is noticing students' mathematical thinking and making that thinking visible to other students. Avoid judging the correctness of an answer so students are more willing to share their ideas. Support students' thinking without evaluation by simply asking what others think about a student's response.
	Summarize main ideas and identify future problems.	Formalize the main ideas of the lesson, helping to highlight connections between strategies or different mathematical ideas. In addition, this is the time to reinforce appropriate terminology, definitions, and symbols. You may also want to lay the groundwork for future tasks and activities.

Before

The essence of the *before* phase of the lesson is to prepare students to work on the worthwhile task you have purposefully selected. What you do in the *before* phase of the lesson will vary depending on the mathematical goals and the selected task. For example, if your students are familiar with solving word problems and know they are expected to use words, diagrams, and equations to explain their reasoning in writing, all that may be required is to read through the problem together and make sure everyone understands it. On the other hand, if the task requires students to model the situation with a new manipulative, more time may be needed to familiarize them with the tool. Or if vocabulary needs to be revisited, a related but simpler task could be used in the *before* phase as a way to activate prior knowledge to ensure students understand the terms used in the focus task.

As you plan for the *before* part of the lesson, it is important to analyze the problems you will give to students in order to anticipate their approaches and possible misinterpretations or misconceptions (Wallace, 2007). This process can inform what you do to prepare the students to work on the selected task, without giving away how to solve the task. The more questions raised and addressed prior to the task, the more engaged students will be in the *during* phase.

During

In the *during* phase of the lesson students engage in mathematical activity (alone, with partners, or in small groups) to explore, gather, and record information; make and test conjectures; and solve the mathematical task. In this phase of the lesson you should be engaged in "professional noticing"—that is, in the moment, trying to understand what students know, how they are thinking and approaching the task at hand, and how to respond appropriately to extend students' thinking (Jacobs, Lamb, & Philipp, 2010). In making instructional decisions in the *during* phase you must ask yourself, "Does my action lead to deeper thinking or does it remove the need to think?" These decisions are based on carefully listening to students' ideas and knowing the learning goals of the lesson. This is very different from listening for or leading students toward an answer. Don't be afraid to say that you don't understand a student's strategy. When you are open to learning, you help students become more comfortable with engaging in the learning process.

Students will look to you for approval of their results or ideas. This is not the time to evaluate or to tell students how to solve the problem. When asked whether a result or method is correct, respond by asking, "How can you decide?" or "Why do you think that might be right?" Asking questions such as "How can we tell if that makes sense?" reminds students that the correctness of the answer lies in the justification, not in the teacher's brain or answer key.

Letting go, one of the teacher actions in this phase, includes allowing students to make mistakes. Ask students to explain their process or approach when they make mistakes as well as when they are correct. As they explain they may catch their mistake. Also, in the *after* portion of the lesson, students will have the opportunity to explain, justify, defend, and challenge solutions and strategies. This process of uncovering and working through misconceptions and computational errors emphasizes the important notion that mistakes and misconceptions are opportunities for learning (Boaler, 2016; Dweck, 2006).

Use this time in the *during* phase to identify different representations and strategies students used, interesting solutions, and any misconceptions that arise that you will highlight and address during the *after* phase of the lesson. As you notice the range of ideas, consider how they are related and in what order you might sequence the sharing of solutions in the *after* phase of the lesson (Smith & Stein, 2011).

After

In the *after* phase of the lesson your students will work as a community of learners, discussing, justifying, and challenging various solutions to the problem that they have just worked on. The *after* phase is where much of the learning will occur as students reflect individually and collectively on the ideas they have explored. As in the *during* phase of the lesson, the goal here is noticing students' mathematical thinking; but additionally, in the *after* phase we want to make this thinking visible to other students. By strategically sequencing which drawings, notations, and ideas are shared, you can create spaces for students to take up, try on, connect, and expand on the ideas of others. This is also the time to reinforce precise terminology, definitions, or symbols. After students have shared their solutions, strategies, and reasoning, formalize the main ideas of the lesson, highlighting connections between strategies or different mathematical ideas.

Because this is the place in the lesson where much of the learning will occur, it is critical to plan for and save ample time for this part of the lesson. Twenty minutes is not at all unreasonable for a good class discussion and sharing of ideas. It is not necessary to wait for every student to finish the task before moving into the *after* portion of the lesson. The time they have engaged with the task should prepare them to share and compare ideas.

Variations of the Three-Phase Lesson

The basic lesson structure we have been discussing assumes that the lesson is developed around a task given to the whole class. However, not every lesson is structured in this way. The three-phase format can be applied to other lesson structures, such as mini-lessons and math stations.

Mini-Lessons

A three-phase lesson that capitalizes on the use of routines can be accomplished in as few as 10 minutes. These mini-lessons are not intended to replace the math curriculum or consume most of the instruction time for math, but like in longer lessons, students are expected to use strategies that make sense to them and to explain their thinking. A routine called *Number Talks*, already embraced in many elementary classrooms, engages students in using number relationships and the structures of numbers to do mental computations, followed by sharing their various strategies (Humphreys & Parker, 2015; Parrish, 2014). These brief routines are praised for developing students' number sense as well as their enthusiasm for thinking about and sharing their strategies (Parrish, 2011). McCoy, Barnett, and Combs (2013) share seven mathematical routines that can be easily used with a variety of mathematical content and at various grade levels. One routine, *Alike and Different*, requires students to consider how two or more numbers, shapes, properties, and so on are similar and different. Having students explain and justify their reasons for the similarities and differences they identify is valuable experience in constructing mathematical arguments. McCoy, Barnett, and Combs (2013) also identify ways to increase the cognitive demand of tasks as students become familiar with a given routine.

Once the routine is introduced and understood by students, the *before* part of the mini-lesson involves posing the task to the students and ensuring they understand the vocabulary and any context used. In the *during* portion of the mini-lesson, students spend time developing their own ideas about the task. You can then have the students pair with a classmate and discuss each other's strategies. You can also have small groups discuss or go straight to the whole class to share and compare strategies. Just keep in mind that think-pair-share provides an opportunity to test out ideas and to practice articulating them. For ELLs, students with learning disabilities, and students who are reluctant to participate in larger groups, this offers both a nonthreatening chance to speak and an opportunity to practice what they might later say to the whole class. Like in longer lessons, the *after* part of the mini-lesson involves students sharing, justifying, questioning, and looking for connections between ideas.

Math Stations

Sometimes a mathematical concept or topic can be explored by having students work on different tasks at various classroom locations or *math stations*. Students can work on concepts or topics at math stations as an initial introduction, as a midway exploration, or as a follow-up task that provides practice or allows extension. Because you can decide which students will be assigned to which stations, you can differentiate the content at each station. For example, each station can use different manipulatives, situations, or technology, require students to use a different approach to solve a problem, or vary in terms of the difficulty of the task (e.g., different stations can use different numbers that change the level of difficulty). (For more information regarding differentiation see Chapter 4.)

For a given topic, you might prepare four to eight different activities (you can also use the same activity at two different math stations). However, be sure to keep the stations focused on the same topic or concept so that you can help students build connections across the stations. Using stations that focus on a variety of topics will more likely result in a disconnected learning experience for students.

When using math stations, it is still important to think about the *before* phase in which you elicit prior knowledge, ensure the task is understood, and establish clear expectations. For example, to ensure greater student success at the stations, model what happens at each station and review any necessary skills and vocabulary. The *during* phase is still the time where students engage in the task, but with math stations, they stop and rotate to new stations within this phase of the lesson. It is still important to interact with and ask students questions as they engage in tasks from the different stations and even more important to keep track of their strategies, including those you will later highlight. In the *after* phase, you may decide to focus on one particular station, begin with the least challenging station and progress to the most challenging one, or instead of discussing each station, ask students to talk about what they learned about the target topic or concept.

A good task for a math station is one that can be repeated multiple times during one visit. This allows students to remain engaged until you are ready for them to transition to another station or activity. For example, at one station students might play a game in which they take turns describing to each other various two-dimensional figures based on the kind and number of angles and the presence or absence of parallel or perpendicular lines. Technology-enhanced tasks on the computer or interactive whiteboard that can be repeated can provide the focus of a station, but these tasks must be carefully selected. Among other aspects, you will want to choose technology-based tasks that require students to engage in reflective thought. For example, the applet at Illuminations titled "Exploring Properties of Rectangles and Parallelograms" offers students opportunities to explore geometric relationships using dynamic software. The dynamic nature of the software allows students to stretch, shrink, and rotate rectangles and parallelograms as they think about what features remain the same even with these changes. Students can also reflect on the commonalities and differences between rectangles and parallelograms. Another Illuminations applet "Playing Fraction Tracks" provides a game setting in which students have opportunities to reason about how various fractions relate to a whole, to compare different fractional quantities, and to work with equivalent fractions. Even if math stations, such as ones that use these applets, are used for independent work, the three-phase model can be implemented by placing a series of reflective questions at each station for students to use as they participate in the tasks.

Life-Long Learning: An Invitation to Learn and Grow

In her book *Building A Better Teacher* (2015), Elizabeth Green attacks the myth of the natural-born teacher—the common notion that good teachers are good because of an innate ability for teaching. Instead she develops the case that teaching is a complex craft that must be taught and developed over time. No matter where you are in your journey as a teacher, there is always more to learn about the content and methodology of teaching mathematics. In fact, the mathematics content and teaching described in this book may not be similar to what you experienced as a student in grades K–8. We know a great deal more about teaching and learning mathematics than we did even five years ago! Just as we would not expect doctors to be using the exact same techniques and medicines that were prevalent when you were a child, teachers' methods should be transformed through the powerful collection of expert knowledge about how to design effective instruction based on such things as how the mind functions and the influence of motivation on learning (Wiggins, 2013).

Planning three-phase inquiry lessons using worthwhile tasks and ensuring that the lesson meets the needs of all students requires intentional and ongoing effort. Questions are likely to surface. You can access responses to seven of the most commonly asked questions about problem-based teaching approaches by clicking here. These questions and responses may help as you contemplate how to plan for your students, or consider ways to advocate for teaching through problem solving with other teachers, families, and/or administrators.

The best teachers are always trying to improve their practice through reading the latest article, reading the newest book, attending the most recent conference, or participating in the next series of professional development opportunities. Highly effective teachers never stop learning—they never exhaust the number of new mental connections that they can make. As a result, they never experience teaching as a stale or stagnant profession.

Stop and Reflect

Describe in your own words what is (and isn't) meant by "teaching mathematics *through problem solving*." What do you foresee to be opportunities and challenges to implementing problem-based mathematics tasks effectively in your classroom?

3

Creating Assessments for Learning

Assessment That Informs Instruction

When using a problem-based approach, teachers might ask, "How do I assess?" NCTM's position statement on formative assessment (2013), and the joint NCSM/AMTE position statement on formative assessment (n.d.) stress several important ideas: (1) assessment should enhance students' learning, (2) assessment is a valuable tool for making instructional decisions, and (3) feedback should help learners progress. This aligns with the distinction between assessment *of* learning, where students are only evaluated on what they know at a given moment in an effort to home in on what they don't know, and assessment *for* learning (AFL), where students are continually evaluated so that instruction can be targeted to gaps and their learning is improved over time (Hattie, 2015; Wiliam & Leahy, 2015).

Assessment is not separate from instruction and should include the critical CCSS mathematical practices and NCTM processes that occur in the course of effective problem-based instructional approaches (Fennell, Kobett, & Wray, 2015). A typical end-of-chapter or end-of-year test of skills may have value, but it rarely reveals the type of data that can fine tune instruction to improve individual students' performance. In fact, Daro, Mosher, and Corcoran (2011) state that "the starting point is the mathematics and thinking the child brings to the lesson, not the deficit of mathematics they do not bring" (p. 48). NCTM's *Principles to Actions* (2014) urges teachers in their mathematical teaching practices to incorporate evidence of children's thinking into an ongoing refinement of their instruction.

Assessments usually fall into one of two major categories: summative or formative. *Summative assessments* are cumulative evaluations that take place usually after instruction is completed. They commonly generate a single score, such as an end-of-unit test or a standardized test that is used in your state or school district. Although the scores are important for schools and teachers, used individually they often do not help shape day-to-day teaching decisions.

On the other hand, *formative assessments* are assessments that are used to check students' development during instructional activities, to preassess, or to attempt to identify students' naïve understandings or misconceptions (Hattie, 2009; Popham, 2008; Wiliam & Leahy, 2015). When implemented well, formative assessment is one of the most powerful influences on achievement (Hattie, 2009). It dramatically increases the speed and amount of a child's learning (Nyquist, 2003; Wiliam, 2007; Wilson & Kenney, 2003) by providing targeted feedback to students and using the results and evidence collected to inform your decision making about next steps in the learning progression.

Wiliam (2010) notes three key processes in formative assessment: (1) Identify where learners are; (2) Identify goals for the learners; and (3) Identify paths to reach the goals. Let's look at an example of this process. For example, a formative assessment for a third-grade class could be to have a group of students solve the following word problem: "If Lindy has 34 shells in her collection and Jesse has 47, how many shells are in both collections? Immediately the teacher observes one student quickly jotting down a straight line on the paper, making a tick mark with a 34 underneath and using small arcs to jump up four times to 74 and then makes one jump of six and another jump of one and indicating 81 with a tick mark (see Figure 3.1). Another student selects from a collection of base-ten materials in the center of the table, models each number, groups the tens together, then combines the ones and trades 10 of the ones for one additional ten piece, getting 81 as an answer. Observing a different student, the teacher notes he is using counters but is counting by ones. First he counts out the 34 counters, then the 47, and then recounts them all to reach 78 (miscounting along the way). The information gathered from observing these students reveals very different paths for the next steps. This teacher is at the first step in Wiliam's three key processes, noting where students are in their learning. Moving into the second step, the teacher notes that one student should move to more challenging tasks while two students need to move closer to the CCSS standard of representing and solving addition and subtraction problems within 100 through more targeted instruction.

Figure 3.1

A student uses an empty number line to add 34 + 47.

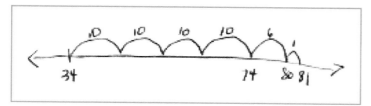

If summative assessment can be described as a digital snapshot, formative assessment is like streaming video. One is a picture of what a student knows that is captured in a single moment of time; the other is a moving picture that demonstrates active student thinking and reasoning. In the following pages and throughout Part 2 of this book in Formative Assessment Notes, we focus on four basic methods for using of formative assessments to evaluate students' understanding: observations, questions, interviews, and tasks. Here we discuss each method in depth.

Observations

All teachers learn useful bits of information about their students every day. When the three-phase lesson format suggested in Chapter 2 is used, the flow of evidence about students' performance increases dramatically, especially in the *During* and *After* portions of lessons. If you have a systematic plan for gathering this information while observing and listening to students during regular classroom instruction, at least two very valuable results occur. First, information that may have gone unnoticed is suddenly visible and important. Second, observation data gathered systematically can be combined with other data and used in planning lessons, providing feedback to students, conducting parent conferences, and determining grades.

Depending on the information you are trying to gather, several days to two weeks may be required to complete a single observation of how a whole class of students is progressing on a standard. Shorter periods of observation will focus on a particular cluster of concepts or skills or on particular students. Over longer periods, you can note growth in mathematical processes or practices, such as developing problem solving, representation, or reasoning. To use observation effectively, take seriously the following maxim: Only try to collect data on a reasonable number of students in a single class period.

Anecdotal Notes

The act of *professional noticing* is a process where you observe learners through a focus on three phases: (1) attending; (2) interpreting; and (3) deciding (Jacobs, Lamb, & Philipp, 2010). You want to collect anecdotal notes on these phases to help understand learners' strategies and thinking as you plan potential next steps. That means you *attend* to everything such as if the child is nodding his head or if she is using her fingers to count, or if she is creating appropriate models, or if he is using strategies that he can clearly describe and defend. Then *interpret* those students' gestures, comments, drawings and actions by making notes of possible strengths and the level of sophistication of their conceptual understanding. Then you can move to noting *decisions* for subsequent instructional actions.

One system for recording your professional noticing is to write these anecdotal notes on an electronic tablet and store them in a spreadsheet or in a multicolumn table that documents such things as students' use of mathematical practices. In any case, focus your observations on approximately five students a day. The students selected may be members of one or two cooperative groups or a group previously identified as needing additional support.

Checklists

To help focus your attention, a checklist with several specific processes, mathematical practices, or content objectives can be devised (see Figure 3.2). As you can see there is a place for comments that should concentrate on big ideas and conceptual understanding. For example, you will probably find a note such as "is beginning to see how multiplication facts can be related, such as using 10×7 to think about 9×7 more useful than "knows easy multiplication facts but not hard ones."

Another Observation Checklist involves listing all students in a class on one to three pages (see Figure 3.3). Across the top of the page are specific abilities or common misconceptions to look for, possibly based on learning progressions. Pluses and minuses, checks, or codes can be entered in the grid. A full-class checklist is more likely to be used for long-term objectives such as problem-solving processes, strategic use of representations or tools, and such skill areas as basic fact fluency or computational estimation. Dating entries or noting specifics about observed performance is also helpful.

Figure 3.2

A focused checklist and rubric that can be printed for each child.

NAME: Sharon V.

PLACE VALUE	NOT THERE YET	ON TARGET	ABOVE AND BEYOND	COMMENTS
Understands numerator/ denominator		✓		
Area models		✓		Used pattern blocks to show $\frac{2}{3}$ and $\frac{3}{6}$
Set models	✓			
Uses fractions in real contexts	✓			
Estimates fraction quantities		✓		Showing greater reasonableness
MATHEMATICAL PRACTICES				
Makes sense of problems and perseveres		✓		Stated problem in own words
Models with mathematics	✓			Reluctant to use abstract models
Uses appropriate tools		✓		

Figure 3.3

A class observation checklist.

Topic: Mental Computation Adding 2-digit numbers Names	Not There Yet Can't do mentally	On Target Has at least one strategy	Above and Beyond Uses different methods with different numbers	Comments
Lalie		✓ 3-18-2017 3-21-2017		
Pete	✓ 3-20-2017	✓ 3-24-2017		Difficulty with problems using 8 and 9
Sid			✓ + 3-20-2017	Flexible approaches used
Lakeshia		✓		Counts by tens, then adds ones
George		✓		
Pam	✓			Beginning to add the group of tens first
Maria		✓ 3-24-2017		Using a posted hundreds chart

Questions

Probing students' thinking through questioning can provide better data and more insights to inform instructional next steps. As you circulate around the classroom to observe and evaluate students' understanding, your use of questions is one of the most important ways to formatively assess in each lesson phase. Have **Question Probes** on a tablet or in print as you move about the classroom to prompt and probe students' thinking.

To make sure you are asking critical thinking questions you may want to consider videotaping yourself and having a friend score how many high-level or how many recall questions you are asking. Use a matrix such as the Cognitive Rigor Matrix (Simpson, Mokalled, Ellenburg, & Che, 2014/2015) which is a blend of Bloom's Taxonomy and Webb's Depth of Knowledge (2002) for additional information.

Getting students used to responding to these questions (as well as accustomed to asking questions about their thinking and the thinking of others) helps prepare them for the more intensive questioning used in interviews.

Interviews

"An assessment system designed to help steer the instruction system must give good information about direction as well as distance to travel. A system that keeps telling us we are not there yet is like a kid in the back seat whining 'are we there yet?' " (Daro et al., 2011, p. 51). Interviews, particularly diagnostic interviews, are a means of getting in-depth information about a child's knowledge of concepts and strategy use to provide needed navigation. The diagnostic interview is usually a one-on-one investigation of a child's thinking about a particular concept, process, or mathematical practice that lasts from three to ten minutes. The challenge of diagnostic interviews is that they are assessment opportunities, not teaching opportunities, making it hard to watch students make errors and not respond immediately. The interviews are used to listen to students' descriptions of their strategies and probe their understanding with the purpose of discovering both strengths and gaps.

To start, select a problem that matches an essential understanding for the topic students are studying and have paper, pencils, and a variety of materials available (particularly manipulatives used during previous instruction). Also, be ready to jot down notes about emerging understandings, common methods you expect students to use, or common misunderstandings that you anticipate. Then ask the child to solve the problem and make sure the child verbalizes his or her thinking at several points. Encourage multiple representations by asking the child to demonstrate his or her thinking using materials or drawings. Fennell, Kobett, and Wray call this the "show me" approach (2015, p. 56).

Sometimes students self-correct a mistake but, more frequently, you can unearth a child's misunderstanding or reveal what strategies are mastered. When you focus on exploring common errors and pitfalls, then you can build greater sophistication in students' conceptual understanding (Bray & Santagata, 2014). Elementary grades diagnostic interviews might include tasks such as counting a group of objects and writing down the number on paper, or asking students to solve a missing addend problem such as $44 + \square = 12 + 50$. Also, see a

✑ *Teaching Tip*

These interviews can be time intensive but they have the potential to provide information that you simply cannot get in any other way. So how can you accomplish this? Think of these interviews as tools to be used for only a few students at a time, not for every child in the class. Briefly interview a single child while others work on a task or are in learning centers. Some teachers work with one child at an interactive whiteboard and record the whole conversation, any written work, or use of virtual manipulatives. Other times a paraprofessional or student teacher can interview.

Sample Interview for Intermediate Grades and/or **Student Observation and Interview: Learning Through Problems**.

After examining hundreds of research studies, Hattie (2009) found that feedback that teachers received from students on what they knew and did not know was critical in improving students' performance. That is precisely what diagnostic interviews are designed to do! For example, are you sure that your students have a good understanding of place value, or are they just doing subtraction exercises according to rote procedures? Remediation will be more successful if you can pinpoint why a child is having difficulty before you try to fix the problem. *Let's look at an actual example of a diagnostic interview.*

Ms. Marsal was working with George, a student with disabilities who was displaying difficulty with calculating multidigit numbers. George also exhibited unreasonable estimates to computations, in some cases thinking the answer to a problem would result in tens when it was in the hundreds. To get feedback from George to reveal what he understood and where some gaps might be, Ms. Marsal planned a diagnostic interview. Using an adaptation of a task (Griffin & Lavelle, 2010), she asked George to write the number that goes with 3 ones, 1 hundred, and 5 tens (see the top of Figure 3.4). Although base-ten materials were available, they went untouched. George responded by writing 315 (writing the number in the left-to-right order he saw the numerals, without attention to place value). As is necessary in these interviews, Ms. Marsal resisted the temptation to immediately correct him, and instead probed further by asking George to take out the amount shown on the paper (3 ones, 1 hundred, and 5 tens) using base-ten materials. Showing fluency with the values of base-ten materials, George took out the correct amounts and placed them on the table, in the order given in the problem, not in place value order. Then when offered a place value mat, George said, "I get it," and placed the materials in the correct positions on the mat. When asked to write the number that corresponded with the materials, George wrote the number (153) as seen in Figure 3.4. Ms. Marsal asked why he got two different numbers and which number he thought was correct. George quietly pondered and then pointed to the second number and said, "This one is right; I think you were trying to trick me."

Figure 3.4

Student's work on a diagnostic interview task.

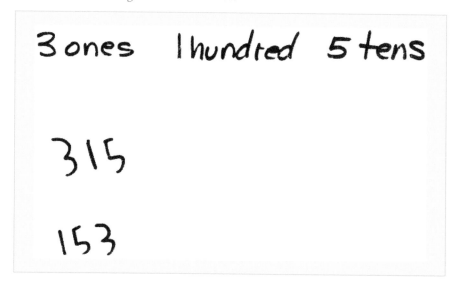

Although this interview revealed that the student had a good grasp of the value of base-ten materials, it did reveal that there were lingering gaps in his understanding place value concepts. Yet, this is a case in which the diagnostic interview was an actual learning experience. Notice that the teacher explicitly linked the assessment to classroom instruction through the use of concrete materials and the structured semiconcrete support of the place value mat. This connection provided a way for the student to think about the number rather than just the individual digits. In addition, the cognitive dissonance caused by getting two different numerical outcomes, one responding to just the written numbers and words and the other with the corresponding concrete materials, enabled more connected ideas to emerge. Planning could then begin for future instruction based on actual evidence from the student.

There is no one right way to plan or structure a diagnostic interview. In fact, flexibility is a key ingredient. You should, however, have an overall plan that includes an easier task and a more challenging task in case you have misjudged your starting point. Also, did you notice that Ms. Marsal had appropriate instructional materials ready for the student to use? Be sure you have materials available that have potential to provide insight into students' understanding. Also be prepared to probe students' thinking with question like these:

- Can you explain what you just did?
- How would you explain this to a second grader (or your younger sister)?
- Can you draw a picture to help you think about this problem?
- What does this [point to something on the paper] stand for?
- Why did you solve it that way?
- Can you show me what you are thinking with [materials such as fraction pieces, counters, hundreds chart, and so on]?
- Why do you think you got two different answers? Which one do you think is correct?
- If you tried to do this problem again, which approach would you try first?

In each case, it is important to explore whether students (1) understand what he or she did, and (2) can use models to connect actions to what he or she wrote or explained earlier.

Consider the following suggestions as you implement your diagnostic interview:

- *Avoid revealing whether the child's answer is right or wrong.* Often facial expressions, tone of voice, or body language can give a child clues. Instead, use a response such as "Can you tell me more?" or "I think I know what you are thinking."
- *Wait silently for the child to give an answer.* Give ample time to allow a child to think and respond. Only then should you move to rephrasing questions or probing for a better understanding of a child's thoughts. After the child gives a response (whether it is accurate or not), wait again! This second wait time is even more important because it encourages the child to elaborate on initial thoughts and provide more information.
- *Avoid interjecting clues or teaching.* The temptation to interrupt is sometimes overwhelming. Watch and listen. Your goal is to use the interview not to teach but to find out where the child is in terms of conceptual understanding and procedural fluency.
- *Give opportunities for students to share their thinking without interruption.* Encourage students to use their own words and ways of writing things down. Correcting language or spelling words can sidetrack the flow of students' explanations.

The benefits of diagnostic interviews become evident as you plan instruction that capitalizes on students' strengths while recognizing possible weaknesses and confusion. Also, unlike large-scale testing, you can always ask another question to find out more when the child is taking an incorrect or unexpected path. You may also discuss results of interviews with colleagues to gain shared insights (Stephan, McManus, & Dehlinger, 2014). These insights are invaluable in moving students to mathematical proficiency, as there is perhaps no better method for developing instruction that supports students' understanding than having them explain their thinking and a team of teachers sharing a conversation about evidence.

Tasks

Tasks refer to products that include performance-based tasks, writing, and students' self-assessments. Good assessment tasks for either instructional or formative assessment purposes should permit every student, regardless of mathematical ability, to demonstrate his or her knowledge, skill, or understanding.

Problem-Based Tasks

Problem-based tasks are tasks that are connected to actual problem-solving activities used in instruction. High-quality tasks permit every child to demonstrate his or her abilities (Rigelman & Petrick, 2014; Smith & Stein, 2011) and include real-world or authentic contexts that interest students or relate to recent classroom events. Of course, be mindful that English language learners may need support with context as challenges with language should not overshadow the attention to their mathematical ability.

Problem-based tasks have several critical components that make them effective. They:

- Focus on an important mathematics concept or skill aligned to valued learning targets.
- Stimulate the connection of students' previous knowledge to new content.
- Allow multiple solution methods or approaches that incorporate a variety of tools.
- Offer opportunities for students to correct themselves along the way.
- Provide occasions for students to confront common misconceptions.
- Encourage students to use reasoning and explain their thinking.
- Create opportunities for observing students' use of mathematical processes and practices.
- Generate data for instructional decision making as you listen to your students' thinking.

Notice that the following examples of problem-based tasks are not elaborate, yet when followed by a discussion, each can engage students for most of a class session (also see Problem-Based Tasks). What mathematical ideas and practices are required to successfully respond to each of these tasks?

THE WHOLE SET (GRADES 3–4):

Learning targets: (1) Determine a whole, given a fractional part (using a set model). (2) Make sense of quantities and their relationships in context.

Mary counted 15 cupcakes left from the whole batch that her mother made for the picnic. "We've already eaten two-fifths," she noticed. How many cupcakes did her mother bake?

IN BETWEEN (GRADES 4–5):

Learning targets: (1) Estimate the products to double-digit multiplication problems. (2) Use reasoning and regularity of patterns to identify a solution.

Write a multiplication problem that has a product that falls between the answers to these two problems:

$$49 \qquad 45$$
$$\times\, 25 \qquad \times\, 30$$

Write an explanation of how you came up with your solution.

CLOSE DECIMALS (GRADES 4–5):

Learning Targets: (1) Compare two decimals by reasoning about their size. (2) Analyze and critique the reasoning of others.

Alan tried to make a decimal number as close to 50 as he could using the digits 1, 4, 5, and 9. He arranged them in this order: 51.49. Jerry thinks he can arrange the same digits to get a number that is even closer to 50. Do you agree or disagree? Explain.

Much can be learned about students' understanding in a discussion that follows students solving the task individually. In particular, it is important for students to compare and make connections between strategies and debate ideas in order to assist them in organizing their thoughts, thinking about their position, and analyzing the ideas of others. This can be developed by forcing students decide whether a conjecture is true (e.g., Does the order of factors affect the answer in a multiplication problem?). The resulting discussions will often reveal students' misconceptions and serve as ways to remember previous discussions (Barlow & McCrory, 2011).

Translation Tasks

One important assessment option is what we refer to as a _translation task_. Using four possible representations for concepts (see Figure 2.3), students are asked to demonstrate understanding using words, models, and numbers for a single problem. As students move between these representations, there is a better chance that a concept will be formed correctly and integrated into a rich web of ideas.

So what is a good way of structuring a translation task? With use of a template based on a format for assessing concept mastery from Frayer, Fredrick, and Klausmeier (1969) (see Figure 3.5) and the Translation Task Template, you can give students a computational equation and ask them to:

- Write a word problem that matches the equation.
- Illustrate the equation with materials or drawings.
- Explain their thinking about the process of arriving at an answer or the meaning of the operation.

In particular, students' ability to communicate how they solved a problem is critical for open-response questions on many summative assessments (Parker & Breyfogle, 2011).

Translation tasks can be used for whole-class lessons or for individual or small-group diagnosis. For example, fifth-grade students may be given a 10×10 grid with 75 squares shaded, as in the section titled "Manipulatives/Illustration" in Figure 3.5. Their

Figure 3.5

Translation task template with example task.

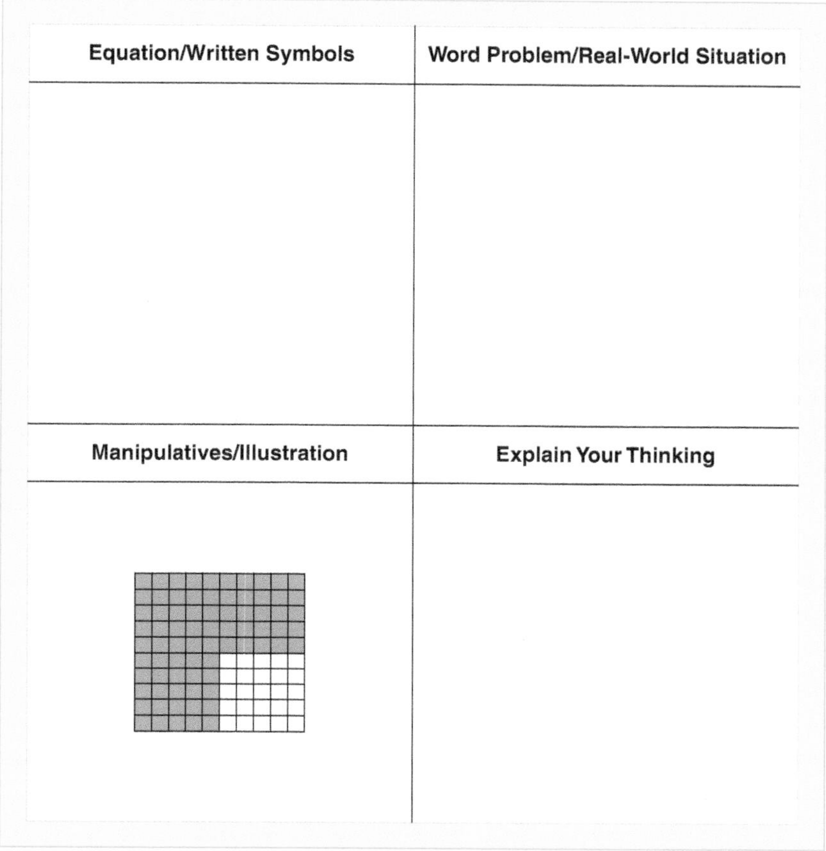

Equation/Written Symbols	Word Problem/Real-World Situation
Manipulatives/Illustration	**Explain Your Thinking**

task could be to write the percent of the square that is shaded in "Equation/Written Symbols" (or write the percentage and corresponding fraction and decimal), describe a real-world situation in which that percentage is used in "Word Problem/Real World Situation," and explain to another person in writing what percent means in "Explain Your Thinking." Think about using translation tasks when you want to find out more about a student's ability to represent ideas and explain how these representations are connected. Depending on the concept, the translation task can start in a different section of the template.

Consider these possible starters.

- In "Word Problem," write "One side of the rectangle is 6 cm. The area is 48 square centimeters. How long is the other side?"

- Students make a corresponding drawing, write an equation (e.g., $6 \times \_\_ = 48$ or $48 \div 6 = \_\_\_$), and explain how they solved the problem.

In "Equation/Written Symbols," write "$3\frac{4}{8} + 2\frac{1}{4}$". Then students should write a corresponding word problem, make an illustration to demonstrate the solution, and explain to a friend how they thought about strategies that would help solve the problem.

Writing

As an assessment tool, writing in journals, exit slips, or other formats provide a unique window to students' perceptions and the way they are thinking about an idea. **Watch this video (https://www.youtube.com/watch?v=dIk0LEmtHl4)** on using exit slips with fifth graders. Students can make sense of problems, express early ideas about concepts, unearth confusion, connect representations, justify a claim with evidence, or even clarify strategy use (Casa, 2015). When students explain their thinking about their solutions to a task in writing prior to class discussions, the written record serves as a rehearsal for the class conversation. Students who otherwise have difficulty thinking on their feet now have a script to support their contributions. Call on more reluctant talkers first so that their ideas are heard and valued. They can also summarize a learning situation through such prompts as:

Concepts and Processes

- "I think the answer is . . . I think this because . . ."
- Write an explanation for a new or younger student of why 4×7 is the same as 7×4 and whether this works for 6×49 and 49×6. If so, why?
- Explain to a student who was absent today what you learned about decimals.
- If you got stuck today in solving a problem, where in the problem did you have trouble?
- After you got the answer to today's problem, what did you do so that you were convinced your answer was reasonable? How sure are you that you got the correct answer?
- Write a story problem that goes with this (equation, graph, diagram, picture).

In Mathematical Practice 3, mathematically proficient students "build a logical progression of statements to explore the truth of their conjectures" and are able to "justify their conclusions, communicate them to others, and respond to the arguments of others" (NGA, 2010, pp. 6–7). Helping students assemble evidence to show how they answered a problem often requires showing them the work of other students. By showing exemplars and counterexamples from real or created peers, students begin to identify elements of a sound argument and cohesive communication (Lepak, 2014).

Additionally, student writing is an excellent form of communication with parents during conferences. Writing shows evidence of students' thinking, telling parents much more than any grade or test score.

Students' Self-Assessment and Reflection

Wiliam (2015) stresses that a key strategy in effectively using formative assessment is the activation of students as "owners of their own learning" (p. 169). Stiggins (2009) suggests that students should be informed partners in understanding their progress in learning and how to enhance their growth in understanding concepts. They should use their own assessment results to move forward as learners as they see that "success is always within reach" (p. 420). Student self-assessments should not be your only measure of students' learning or dispositions, but rather a record of how *students perceive* their strengths and weaknesses as they begin to take responsibility for their learning.

You can gather student self-assessment data in several ways, including preassessments that catch areas of confusion or naïve conceptions prior to formally assessing students on particular content or by regularly using exit slips (paper slips or a web application with a quick question or two) when students are concluding the instructional period (Wieser, 2008).

As you plan for student self-assessment, consider what you need to know to help you find better instructional strategies and revised learning targets. Convey to your students why you are having them do this activity—they need to grasp that they must play a role in their mastery of mathematics rather than just focus on completing a task. Encourage them to be honest and candid. Use open-ended prompts such as:

- How well do you think you understand the work we have been doing on fractions during the last few days? What is still causing you difficulty with fractions?
- Write two important things you learned in class today (or this week).
- Which problem(s) on the activity sheet/quiz did you find most challenging? Which were easiest?

Discussions of how students can improve can start when they analyze their own mistakes or have discussions with other students about which answers they think are correct. When students get back a test—make sure they use the feedback and revisit any errors and confirm that they understand what they need to learn next or how to revise. This attention to using feedback and mistakes to improve one's understanding moves students from a performance orientation to a mastery orientation (Pintrich, 2003).

Although in general, it takes additional time to infuse students' self-assessments and formative assessment into the daily schedule, allowing students to take part in the assessment process is motivating and encourages them to monitor and adapt their approaches to learning. Remember, start the process of incorporating these assessment ideas in this chapter over time building strategy by strategy (Petit & Bouck, 2015) and growing your ability to effectively assess students.

Rubrics and Their Uses

Problem-based tasks tell us a great deal about what students know, but how do we analyze and use this information? These assessments yield an enormous amount of information that must be evaluated by examining more than a simple count of correct answers. A *rubric* is a scale based on predetermined criteria with two important functions: (1) It permits students to see what is central to excellent performance, and (2) it provides you with scoring guidelines that support equitable analysis of students' work.

In a teaching-through-problem-solving approach, you will often want to include criteria and performance indicators on your rubrics such as the following:

- Solved the problem(s) accurately and effectively.
- Persevered and demonstrated resilience when facing a challenging problem.
- Explained strategies they used or justified their answer.
- Used logical reasoning.
- Expressed a grasp of numerical relationships and/or mathematical structure.
- Incorporated multiple representations and/or multiple strategies.
- Demonstrated an ability to appropriately select and use tools and manipulatives.
- Communicated with precise language and accurate units.
- Identified general patterns of ideas that repeat, making connections from one big idea to another.

Generic Rubrics

Generic rubrics identify categories of performance instead of specific criteria for a particular task and therefore can be used for multiple assignments. The generic rubric allows you to score performances by first sorting into two broad categories, as illustrated in the four-point rubric shown in Figure 3.6. Then you to separate each category into two additional levels as shown. A rating of 0 is given for no response, no effort, or for responses that are completely off task. The advantage of this scale is the relatively easy initial sort into "Got It" or "Not There Yet."

Another possibility is to use your three- or four-point generic rubric on a reusable form (see **Four-Point Rubric**), as in Figure 3.6. This method is especially useful for planning purposes. But there are times when generic rubrics do not give enough definition of specific criteria for a particular task. For those instances, try a task-specific rubric.

Figure 3.6

A four-point generic rubric.

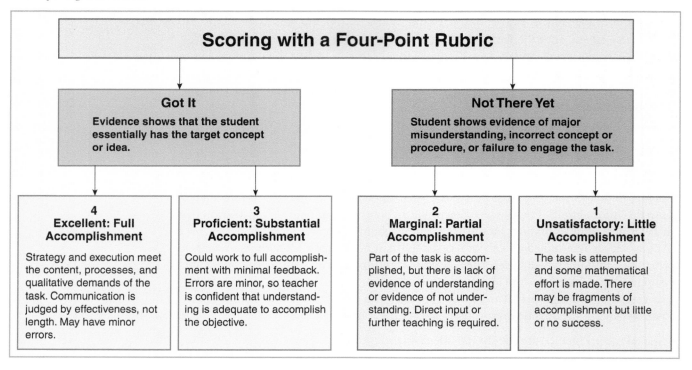

Task-Specific Rubrics

Task-specific rubrics include specific statements, also known as *performance indicators* that describe what students' work should look like at each rubric level and, in so doing, establish criteria for acceptable performance on that particular task (see Figure 3.7 and **Anecdotal Note Rubric**). Initially, it may be difficult to predict what students' performance at different levels will or should look like, but your criteria depend on your knowledge and experience with students at that grade level and your insights about the task or mathematical concept. One important part of setting performance levels is predicting students' common misconceptions or their expected approaches to similar problems.

Figure 3.7

Record names in a rubric used during an activity or for a single topic over a period of several days.

Observation Rubric		
Partition Regions into Equal Shares (3/17)		
Above and Beyond Clear understanding. Communicates concept in multiple representations. Shows evidence of using idea without prompting. *Can partition rectangles and circles into two, four, and eight equal shares. Explains that partitioning the same wholes into more shares makes smaller shares.*	Sally Latania Greg	 Zal
On Target Understands or is developing well. Uses designated models. *Can partition regions into equal shares and describes as "halves" and "fourths." May need prompt to compare halves and fourths.*	Lavant Julie George Maria	Tanisha Lee J.B. John H.
Not There Yet Some confusion or misunderstanding. Only models idea with help. *Needs help to do activity. No confidence.*	John S.	Mary

To facilitate developing performance levels, write out indicators of "proficient" or "on target" performances before using the task (see Figure 3.7). This excellent self-check ensures that the task is likely to accomplish your purpose. If you find yourself writing performance indicators in terms of the number of correct responses, you are most likely looking at drill or practice exercises, not the problem-based tasks for which a rubric is appropriate. Like athletes who continually strive for better performances rather than "good enough," students should always recognize opportunities to excel. When you take into account the total performance (processes, strategies, answers, justifications, extensions, and so on), it is always possible to "go above and beyond."

Early in the year, discuss your rubric (such as Figure 3.7) with the class and post it prominently. Make it a habit to discuss students' performance on tasks in terms of the rubric. For example, if you are using the anecdotal note rubric, rubric language can be used informally: "Tanisha, the rubric states to get an Above and Beyond you need to solve the problem with two different representations and explain your thinking. Is that what you did?" This approach lets students know how well they are doing and encourages them to persevere by giving specific areas for improvement. You might also have students use the rubric to self-assess their work, having them explain reasons for their ratings. Then target follow-up instruction in response to their gaps and misunderstandings building on their identified strengths.

Stop and Reflect 500 ⑨₂²⁵⁰ ⟨?⟩ 3ᵡ ▱ˢ⁵⁰ ∞∩ ✗ 2.5

Consider the task "The Whole Set" on page 45. Assume you are creating a task-specific four-point rubric to share with your fourth graders. What task-specific indicators would you use for level 3 and level 4 performances? Start with a level 3 performance, then think about level 4. Try this before reading further.

Determining performance indicators is always a subjective process based on professional judgment. Here is one possible set of indicators for the "The Whole Set" task:

Level 3: Determines correct answer or uses an approach that would yield a correct answer if not for minor errors. The picture drawn or the explanation does not fully explain the combining and sharing process.

Level 4: Determines the total number of cupcakes and the amount of each equal share using words, pictures, and numbers to explain and justify the result and how it was obtained.

What about level 1 and level 2 performances? Here are suggestions for the same task:

Level 2: Uses some aspect of fractions appropriately (e.g., divides 15 into 5 groups instead of 3) but fails to illustrate an understanding of how to determine the whole. Shows evidence that they don't understand that a fraction is a number (students may suggest it is two whole numbers.)

Level 1: Shows some effort but little or no understanding of addition or how to make equal shares.

Unexpected methods and solutions happen. Don't limit students to demonstrating their understanding only as you thought they would when there is evidence that they are accomplishing your objectives in different ways. Such occurrences can help you revise or refine your rubric for future use.

✐ Teaching Tip

When you return papers, review the indicators with students, including examples of correct answers and successful responses. This will help students understand how they could have done better. Often it is useful to show anonymous students' work. Let students decide on the score for an anonymous child. Importantly, students need to see models of what a level 4 performance looks like.

Stop and Reflect 500 ⑨₂²⁵⁰ ⟨?⟩ 3ᵡ ▱ˢ⁵⁰ ∞∩ ✗ 2.5

How can having students assess peers' work (both strong and weak responses) support their ability to generate more in-depth responses?

4

Differentiating Instruction

Every classroom at every grade level contains a range of students with varying abilities and backgrounds. Perhaps the most important work of teachers today is to be able to plan (and teach) lessons that support and challenge *all* students to learn important mathematics. Designing and implementing instruction in ways that best reach each student is the crux of differentiated instruction. We address differentiation first in a general sense in this chapter. Then in the next two chapters, we focus on differentiation with specific learners, English Language Learners and learners with exceptionalities.

Differentiation and Teaching Mathematics through Problem Solving

Teachers have for some time embraced the notion that students vary in reading ability, but the idea that students can and do vary in mathematical development may be new. Mathematics education research reveals a great deal of evidence demonstrating that students vary in their understanding of specific mathematical ideas. Attending to these differences in students' mathematical development is key to differentiating mathematics instruction for your students.

Interestingly, the problem-based approach to teaching is the best way to teach mathematics while attending to the range of students in your classroom. In a traditional, highly directed lesson, it is often assumed that all students will understand and use the same approach and the same ideas as determined by the teacher. Students not ready to understand the ideas presented by the teacher must focus their attention on following rules or directions without developing a conceptual or relational understanding (Skemp, 1978). This, of course, leads to endless difficulties and can leave students with misunderstandings or in need of significant remediation. In contrast, in a problem-based classroom, students are expected to approach problems in a variety of ways that make sense to *them*, bringing to each problem the skills and ideas that they own. So, with a problem-based approach to teaching mathematics, differentiation is already built in to some degree.

To illustrate, let's consider a third-grade classroom in which the teacher posed the following task to students.

In the school library there are 489 books. 215 of the books are about different kinds of mammals. How many of the books are not about mammals?

She asked the students to be ready to explain how they got their answers. Following are some of the students' explanations:

Edwin: I used an open number line. I started at 215 and counted up 5 to get to 220, then added 80 to get to 300, then 100 to get to 400, and then 89 to get to 489 [see Figure 4.1]. I knew I needed to add 5 + 80 + 100 + 89, but it was easier to add 5 + 80 + 100 + 90 which is 185 + 90, or 275. But since I added one to 89 to make the addition easier, I needed to subtract one from my answer. So my answer is 274.

Jeana: I started at 489 and went backwards to 215, but I did not use a number line. I did it in my head. I knew I needed to subtract 89 from 489, which is 400. Then I jumped down to 300 by subtracting 100. Then I subtracted 80 from 300, which is 220, and then 5 more, equaling 215. So I added 89 + 100 + 80 + 5, which is 274, to find out how much I subtracted.

Carmen: I added 11 to each number in the problem so I had 500 − 226. Then I subtracted 500 − 200 to equal 300 and then 300 − 20 to equal 280. Then all I had to do was subtract 6 more to equal 274.

Sam: My way was like Carmen's, but I subtracted something from each number to make the problem easier. I subtracted 15 from each number so that I had 474 − 200. Then I could see that the answer was 274.

Figure 4.1

Edwin's strategy to find 489–215.

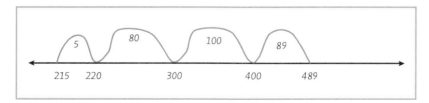

Some students recognized they can add or subtract the same amount to both numbers in a subtraction problem and maintain the difference. Others used an adding up strategy supported with a number line. Still others used mental math and subtracted quantities in chunks that made sense to them. If the teacher had expected all students to use a number line, then many of the students might have used a method that did not make sense to them or a less-efficient method than they would have independently used. Also, the cognitive demand of the task would have been lowered. If the teacher had expected all the students to recognize that you can add or subtract the same quantity from the numbers to create easier numbers to work with while maintaining the original difference, then some students may have been confused because they are not ready for this strategy. Instead, the teacher allowed the students to use their own ideas to determine how many books were about topics other than mammals. This expectation and the recognition that different students will approach and solve the same problem in various ways honors students' varying mathematical development and sets the stage for differentiated mathematics instruction. In addition, by listening to how different students approached the task, the teacher has acquired important information that can be used to plan subsequent instruction that meets a variety of students' needs.

The Nuts and Bolts of Differentiating Instruction

Differentiation is an instructional approach that requires a shift from focusing on the "middle-of-the-road" students to attending to all students. As overwhelming as this may sound, differentiation does not require a teacher to create individualized lessons for each and every student in the classroom. Rather, it requires emphasizing three basic ideas:

- Planning lessons around meaningful content, grounded in authenticity.
- Recognizing each student's readiness, interest, and approach to learning.
- Connecting content and learners by modifying content, process, product, and the learning environment (Sousa & Tomlinson, 2011).

Planning Meaningful Content, Grounded in Authenticity

Before you begin to think about differentiation, you first need to know where you want students to "be" at the end of the learning experience. You must be explicitly aware of the content that students should know, understand, and be able to do after engaging in a given lesson or sequence of lessons. This awareness enables you to effectively guide students' learning by varying or differentiating instruction. If you do not have a clear idea about the specific learning outcomes, identifying how and when to differentiate can be difficult. In fact, Tomlinson (1999) claims that "If the 'stuff' [content] is ill conceived, the 'how' [differentiation] is doomed" (p. 16).

Note that the content must be authentic and grounded in important mathematics that emphasizes the big ideas in ways that require students to develop relational understanding. Authentic content engages students with the heart of mathematics by requiring them to be problem solvers and creators of knowledge. Through this kind of engagement, students also develop a productive disposition toward mathematics and see it as sensible, useful, and worthwhile.

Recognizing Students as Individuals

Knowing each student in the context of learning requires finding out who he or she is as an individual on traits such as readiness, interests, and learning profile. *Readiness* refers to a student's proficiency with the knowledge, understanding, and skills embedded in specific learning goals. *Interest* means a student's attraction to particular topics, ideas, and events. Using contexts that are interesting and familiar to students enhances their attention and motivation to engage and achieve (Sousa & Tomlinson, 2011). A *learning profile* identifies how a student approaches learning—how each student prefers to learn (e.g., in groups, alone); prefers to process and reason about information (e.g., by listening, observing, participating, or through talking; by thinking about details first and then the big picture or vice versa; by doing one task at a time or multitasking); and prefers to use or demonstrate what has been learned (e.g., writing, verbalizing, drawing). When deciding how to structure the environment, tasks, and assessments, consider students' preferences for learning to structure the environment, tasks, and assessments and you will greatly facilitate the learning process. This is not to say that you must narrow learning experiences to only students' preferences all the time. That is simply impossible to do. What is possible is to look for opportunities to provide students some learning choices. Furthermore, knowing students' preferences alerts you to when they may need additional supports or guidance when those preferences are not possible to incorporate.

Information about your students' traits can inform how you might modify different elements of the classroom (Sousa & Tomlinson, 2011; Tomlinson, 2003). You can gather information pertaining to students' readiness by using preassessments several days before a given unit so that you have time to analyze the evidence and assess each student's readiness for the unit. You can also use surveys, typically at the beginning and midpoint of the year, to gather information about students' interests and learning profiles. Interest surveys give students opportunities to share personal interests (e.g., what they like to do after school, on the weekends, and during the summer; what school subjects they find most interesting and why) and information about pets, siblings, and extracurricular activities. Use your students' interests to provide contexts for the mathematics they are learning to increase their motivation and engagement. Learning profile surveys or questionnaires also help students think about what helps them learn and what does not, such as preferring to work in pairs versus alone, being able to work with background noise, and needing to process ideas verbally (see Figure 4.2). Teacher observation can also provide valuable insights into student learning profiles. By recording students' information on index cards, you can quickly refresh your memory by looking through the cards as you plan lessons. You can also sort the cards to help you create groups based on interests or learning profiles.

Figure 4.2

Learning profile inventory.

When working on a task I like to . . .	I like to work . . .	When working I like the room to be . . .	When working I like . . .	When learning about new ideas I like to . . .	When sharing information, I like to . . .
☐ sit at my desk ☐ sit somewhere other than my desk ☐ stand ☐ lie on the floor ☐ other	☐ with a partner ☐ in a small group ☐ alone ☐ other	☐ warm ☐ cool ☐ darker, lights off ☐ brightly lit ☐ other	☐ quiet ☐ noise ☐ music ☐ other	☐ hear about it ☐ read about it ☐ see visuals about it ☐ use materials to explore ☐ talk about it ☐ other	☐ talk ☐ show ☐ write ☐ other

Connecting Content and Learners

A critical component of differentiated lesson planning is determining how to modify four classroom elements to help the learner better connect with the content (Tomlinson, 2003). These four classroom elements are content, process, product, and the learning environment.

Content: What You Want Each Student to Learn

Generally, what is learned (the big ideas) should be relatively the same for all students. However, content can still be differentiated in terms of depth (level of complexity) and breadth (connecting across different topics) (Murray & Jorgensen, 2007; Small, 2012). Students' readiness typically informs the level of complexity or depth at which the content is initially presented for different groups of students. Interest and learning profiles tend to inform differentiation geared toward breadth.

An example of a depth adaptation for developing understanding and skill with organizing, representing, and interpreting data is a mini-lesson in which all students organize and represent data and answer questions based on the data. Some students may have a smaller set of data to deal with or they may be asked to answer given questions about the data, while others, who are ready for more sophisticated content, are asked to generate their own questions about the data. An example of a breadth adaptation for the same objective is to allow students a choice in terms of the kind of data with which they will work. For example, based on their interests, students might choose to work with data pertaining to sports, books, science, gaming, or pets. By working with data from various contexts, students not only learn something about those contexts, but they can also begin to see the broader applications of organizing, representing, and interpreting data.

Process: How Students Engage in Thinking about Content

Although the big ideas of a learning experience remain relatively stable when differentiating, how students engage with and make sense of the content—the *process*—changes. Tomlinson (1999) described the process as students "taking different roads to the same destination" (p. 12). You can use different strategies or encourage students to take different "roads" to increase access to the essential information, ideas, and skills embedded in a lesson (Cassone, 2009; Tomlinson, 2003). For example, the use of manipulatives, games, and relevant and interesting contextual problems provides different ways for students to process their ideas while engaging with content.

The mathematical process standards in the *Principles and Standards for School Mathematics* (NCTM, 2000), which served as a basis for the Standards for Mathematical Practice in the *Common Core State Standards* (CCSSO, 2010), lend themselves well to differentiating how students engage with and make sense of content. In particular, the representation process standard emphasizes the need to think about and use different ways to represent mathematical ideas, which can help students make connections between concepts and skills.

Teaching Tip

Be sure that the differentiated tasks you ask students to do are closely aligned with the learning objectives of the lesson.

With the communication process standard, students can use verbal or written communication as they share their reasoning, depending on their strengths. In addition, the problem-solving process standard allows for differentiation because of the myriad of strategies that students can use—from drawing a diagram or using manipulatives to solving a simpler problem and looking for patterns.

Due to students' different levels of readiness, it is imperative that they be allowed to use a variety of strategies and representations that are grounded in their own ideas to solve problems. You can facilitate students' engagement in thinking about the content through a variety of methods. For example, teachers may

- Use visuals or graphic organizers to help students connect ideas and build a structure for the information in the lesson.
- Provide manipulatives to support students' development of a concept.
- Provide different manipulatives from those previously used with the same content to expand students' understanding.
- Use an appropriate context that helps students build meaning for the concept and that employs purposeful constraints that can highlight the significant mathematical ideas.
- Share examples and nonexamples to help students develop a better understanding of a concept.
- Gather a small group of students to develop foundational knowledge for a new concept.

- Provide text or supplementary material in a student's native language to aid understanding of materials written or delivered in English.
- Set up learning centers or a tiered lesson (a lesson that offers learners different pathways to reach a specific learning goal).

Product: How Students Demonstrate What They Know, Understand, and Are Able to Do after the Lesson Is Over

The term *product* can refer to what a student produces as a result of completing a single task, or to a major assessment after an extended learning experience. The products for a single task are similar to the ways students share their ideas in the *After* portion of a lesson, described in Chapter 2, which could include students explaining their ideas with manipulatives, through a drawing, in writing, or simply verbally. The products related to an extended experience can take the form of a project, portfolio, test, write-up of solutions to several problem-based inquiries, and so on. An important feature of any product is that it allows a variety of ways for students to demonstrate their understanding of essential content.

Learning Environment: The Logistics, Physical Configuration, and Tone of the Classroom

Consider how the physical learning environment might be adapted to meet students' needs. Do you have a student who prefers to work alone? Who prefers to work in a group? Who can or cannot work with background noise? Who prefers to work in a setting with brighter or dimmer lighting? Attending to these students' needs can affect the seating arrangement, specific grouping strategies, access to materials, and other aspects of the classroom environment. In addition to the physical learning space, establishing a classroom culture in which students' ideas and solutions are respected as they explain and justify them is an important aspect of a differentiated classroom. Refer to the recommendations provided in Chapter 2 pertaining to facilitating effective classroom discussions and establishing a supportive and respectful learning environment.

Differentiated Tasks for Whole-Class Instruction

One challenge of differentiation is planning a task focused on a target mathematical concept or skill that can be used for whole-class instruction while meeting a variety of students' needs. Let's consider two different kinds of tasks that can meet this challenge: parallel tasks and open questions (Murray & Jorgensen, 2007; Small, 2012).

Parallel Tasks

Parallel tasks are two or three tasks that focus on the same big idea but offer different levels of difficulty. The tasks should be created so that all students can meaningfully participate in a follow-up discussion with the whole class. You can assign tasks to students based on their readiness, or students can choose which task to work on. If they choose a task that is too difficult, they can always move to another task. Consider how the following parallel tasks emphasize the big idea of division but at different levels of difficulty.

TASK 1:

There are 48 fourth graders on the playground. They want to form 4 teams with an equal number of students on each team. How many students will be on each team?

TASK 2:

There are 1080 fourth graders in our school system. There are an equal number of fourth graders at each of the 5 elementary schools. How many fourth graders would be at each school?

Stop and Reflect   500 ⑨, ²⁵⁰   ③ 3ͳ ▱ ⁸ᵏ₆⁹ ∞ₙ ✓ ₂,₅

Which of the two tasks do you think would be more difficult and why?

Both tasks provide opportunities for students to work with division, but the size of the numbers in the second task increases the level of difficulty. If students need to use manipulatives to fairly share the 48 students among 4 teams, the numbers in the first task still allow for their use. On the other hand, the numbers in the second task would be too cumbersome for students to model using single cubes, but they could use base-ten materials to equally distribute 1080 into 5 groups. If you want to encourage students to move beyond using manipulatives, only offer the single cubes with the second task. Students will then have an incentive to think about using another strategy. Even if students use the long division or partial quotients algorithm with the second task, the size of the numbers and the presence of zeroes in the dividend still make it more challenging.

You can facilitate a whole-class discussion by asking questions that are relevant to both tasks. For example, with respect to the previous two tasks, you could ask the following questions of the whole class:

- How did you determine how many students were in each group?
- Some of you indicated that you split up the total number of students based on place value and then thought about how to share those amounts across your equal groups. Why does that strategy make sense?
- Suppose there was one more fourth grader. How would that change your answer?
- Suppose the number of students in each group increased by one. How many more fourth graders would there be?

Although students work on different tasks, because the tasks are focused on the same big idea, these questions allow them to extend their thinking as they hear others' strategies and ideas.

For many problems involving computation, you can simply insert multiple sets of numbers to vary the difficulty. In the following problem, students are permitted to select the first, second, or third number in each set of brackets. Giving a choice increases motivation and helps students become more self-directed learners (Bray, 2009; Gilbert & Musu, 2008).

LEARNING OBJECTIVE: (CCSS-M: 3.OA.A.1; 3.OA.A.3)
Represent and solve problems involving multiplication.

Task: Mark had [2, 5, 8] markers in [6, 7, 12] boxes. How many markers does Mark have?

The following parallel tasks for fifth graders focus on the big idea of division.

TASK 1:

Create a word problem that can be solved by dividing a whole number by a unit fraction.

TASK 2:
Create a word problem that can be solved by dividing two multi-digit whole numbers.

With the first task, the teacher provides an option for students who are ready to deal with problems that involve division with unit fractions. The parallel task still offers an opportunity for students to think about division, but without them having to deal with the increased challenge of fractions.

In thinking about how to create parallel tasks, once you have identified the big idea you wish to focus on, consider how students might differ in their reasoning about that idea. The size of the numbers involved, the operations students can use, and the degree of structure inherent in the task are just a few things to consider as you create parallel tasks. Start with a task from your textbook and then modify it to make it suitable for a different developmental level. The original task and the modified task will serve as the parallel tasks offered simultaneously to your students. If you number the parallel tasks and allow students to choose the task they will work on, be sure there are instances in which the more difficult task is the first one. This randomness will ensure that students consider both options before they choose their task.

Open Questions

Many questions found in textbooks are closed, meaning there is one answer and often only one way to get there. These kinds of questions cannot meet the needs of the range of learners in your classroom. Alternatively, open questions are broad-based questions that can be solved in a variety of ways or that can have different answers. Because these kinds of questions invite meaningful responses from students who are at varying developmental levels, they more readily meet the needs of a range of learners (Small, 2012). Following are two examples of open questions. Both questions can have different answers and can also be solved in a variety of ways.

- I measured an object in the classroom and found that it weighed 10 grams. What could the object be?

- The product of three numbers is 1200. What could the three numbers be?

Stop and Reflect

How would you solve each of these tasks? Can you think of at least two different strategies and at least two different answers for each task?

Open questions have a high level of cognitive demand, as described in Chapter 2, because students must use more than recall or do more than merely follow steps in a procedure. As such, there are ample opportunities for them to approach the problems at their own level, which means open questions automatically accommodate for student readiness. Consequently, when given an open question, most students can find something appropriate to contribute, which helps to increase their confidence in doing mathematics and can provide you insight into their level of understanding.

You can use a variety of strategies, such as the following, to create open questions (Small, 2012; Sullivan & Lilburn, 2002):

- Give the answer and ask for the problem.
- Replace a number in a given problem with a blank or a question mark.
- Offer two situations or examples and ask for similarities and differences.
- Create a question that can generate a range of possible answers so that students have to make choices.

The two previous examples of open questions illustrate the first strategy of giving an answer and asking for the problem. Here are examples of using the other three strategies to convert standard questions to open questions.

STRATEGY:

Replace a number in a given problem with a blank or question mark.

Standard Question	Open Question
23	?3
× 68	× 6?

STRATEGY:

Offer two situations or examples and ask for similarities and differences.

Standard Question	Open Question
Write the decimal 34.562 in expanded form.	How are the decimals 34.562 and 43.265 similar and how are they different?

STRATEGY:

Create a question that can generate a range of possible answers so that students have to make choices.

Standard Question	Open Question
List two equivalent fractions for $\frac{1}{2}$. Explain why they are equivalent.	The numerator of one fraction is 1 and the numerator of an equivalent fraction is 3. What could the denominators of the equivalent fractions be? Explain why they are equivalent.

Facilitating follow-up discussions is also important when you use open questions. While students work on an open question, walk around and observe the strategies they are using and the answers they are finding. During this time, plan which students will share their ideas during the follow-up discussion, ensuring that a variety of strategies and answers are examined. During the discussion, look for opportunities to help students make connections between different ideas that are shared. For example, in the previous task in which students are looking for similarities and differences between the decimals 34.562 and 43.265, one student might say that the two decimals have the same number of digits and another student might say that both numbers use the same place values. You could ask the class, "If two decimals have the same number of digits, does it always mean they will also use the same place values?" Asking questions that challenge students to clarify similarities or patterns they find can help them build connections, can support those who need additional help to track on significant ideas, and can also challenge students to extend their understanding. You could also do a gallery walk during which students posted their solutions for others to view. With the open question related to creating equivalent fractions, students could go on a gallery walk and use sticky notes to write questions or comments to give feedback to their peers about their examples and the related illustration or explanations.

Tiered Lessons

In a tiered lesson, you set the same learning goals for all students, but different pathways are provided to reach those learning goals, thereby creating the various tiers. First you need to decide which category you wish to tier: content, process, or product. If you are new to preparing tiered lessons, tier only one category until you become more comfortable with the process. Once you decide which category to tier, determine the challenge of each of the defined tiers based on student readiness levels, interests, and learning profiles (Kingore, 2006; Murray & Jorgensen, 2007; Tomlinson, 1999). Murray and Jorgensen (2007) suggest starting with creating three tiers to make the process more manageable: a regular tier or lesson, an extension tier that provides extra challenge, and a scaffolding tier that provides more background or support. Once you have this framework, you can design as many tiers as needed to meet your students' needs. All tiered experiences should have the following characteristics (Sousa & Tomlinson, 2011):

- Address the same learning goals.
- Require students to use reasoning.
- Be equally interesting to students.

Figure 4.3

Problem-solving cue sheet.

Ways to help me think about the problem	$489 - 215 = ?$ $215 + ? = 489$
	Manipulatives 
	Drawing 
	Open number line 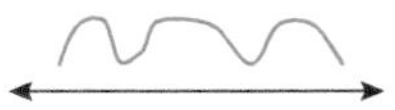
	Mental math 
	Other

We have already considered some ways to tier the content by using parallel tasks and open questions. However, varying the degree of challenge is not just about the content. You can also tier lessons using any of the following four aspects (Kingore, 2006):

- *Degree of assistance:* If some students need additional support, you can partner students, provide examples, help them brainstorm ideas, or provide a cue sheet (Figure 4.3).
- *Structure of the task:* Some students, such as students with disabilities, benefit from highly structured tasks. However, gifted students often benefit from a more open-ended structure.
- *Complexity of the task:* Make tasks more concrete or more abstract and/or include more difficult problems or applications.
- *Complexity of the process:* As you think about your learners, ask yourself these questions: How quickly should I pace this lesson? How many instructions should I give at one time? How many higher-level thinking questions are included as part of the task(s)?

Consider in the following examples how the original task is adapted to change the level of challenge. Assume that the students do not know the standard algorithm for changing mixed numbers to fractions to complete the computation.

ORIGINAL TASK (GRADE 4):

Elliot is making birdhouses. He had $3\frac{1}{4}$ gallons of paint. He used $2\frac{3}{4}$ gallons to paint the birdhouses he has made. How much paint does Elliot have left? Explain how you know.

The teacher has distributed fraction circles to students to model the problem and paper and pencils to illustrate and record how they solved the problem. He asks them to model the problem and be ready to explain their solution.

ADAPTED TASK (GRADE 4):

Elliott had some paint. He used some of it to paint birdhouses. How much paint does Elliot have left? Explain how you know.

The teacher asks students what is happening in this problem and how they might solve the problem and what tools might help them solve the problem. Then he distributes task cards that indicate how much paint Elliot started with and how much he used. The teacher has varied the difficulty of the tasks by considering whether the student will need to break up the first quantity to determine the amount left. He also offers the more advanced students fractional amounts with unlike denominators.

Card 1 (easier)

Elliot starts with $3\frac{3}{4}$ gallons.

He uses $2\frac{1}{4}$ gallons.

Card 2 (middle)

Elliot starts with $3\frac{1}{4}$ gallons.

He uses $2\frac{3}{4}$ gallons.

Card 3 (advanced)

Elliot starts with $3\frac{1}{2}$ gallons.

He uses $2\frac{1}{4}$ gallons.

In each case, students must use words, pictures, models, or numbers to show how they figured out the solution. Various tools are provided (fraction circles, fraction bars, and grid paper) for students' use.

Stop and Reflect

Which of the four aspects that change the challenge of tiered lessons was addressed in the adapted task?

You would preassess your students to determine the best ways to use these task cards. One option is to give students only one card, based on their current academic readiness (e.g., easy cards to those who struggle with subtraction of mixed numbers). A second option is to give out cards 1 and 2 based on readiness, then use card 2 as an extension for those who successfully complete card 1, and card 3 as an extension for those who successfully complete card 2. In each of these cases, you will need to record at the end of the lesson which students were able to model and explain the various levels of the problems so that the next lesson can be appropriately planned. Notice that this tiered lesson addresses both the complexity of the task (difficulty of different cards) and the process (instructions are broken down by first starting with the no-numbers scenario).

The following example illustrates how to tier a lesson based on *structure*. Notice that the different tasks vary in how open-ended the work is, yet all tasks focus on the same learning goal of identifying properties of parallelograms.

LEARNING OBJECTIVE: (CCSS-M: 5.G.B.3)

Classify parallelograms according to their properties

Students are given a collection of parallelograms including squares and rectangles as well as nonrectangular parallelograms. The following tasks are distributed to different groups, based on their learning needs and prior knowledge of quadrilaterals:

- *Group A:* Explore the set of parallelograms. Use your ruler and protractor to measure the parallelograms. Make a list of the defining properties that you think are true for every parallelogram. (open-ended)
- *Group B:* Measure the parallelograms' angles and sides using your ruler and protractor. Record any patterns related to sides, angles, and diagonals that are true for all of the parallelograms. (slightly structured)
- *Group C:* First, sort the parallelograms into rectangles and nonrectangles. Use a ruler to measure the sides and a protractor to measure the angles of the parallelograms. Look for patterns in your measurements that define the shapes as parallelograms. Use the following suggestions and questions to work through the problem:

  1a. What pattern do you notice about the measures of the *sides* of all the parallelograms in the *nonrectangle* set?
  1b. What pattern do you notice about the measures of the *sides* of all the parallelograms in the *rectangle* set?
  2a. What pattern do you notice about the measures of the *angles* of all the parallelograms in the *nonrectangle* set?
  2b. What pattern do you notice about the measures of the *angles* of all the parallelograms in the *rectangle* set? (most structured)

The three tiers in this lesson reflect different degrees of difficulty in terms of task structure. However, all students are working on the same learning objective and they all must engage in reasoning about the properties of two-dimensional shapes to complete their tasks.

In Chapter 6 you will read about response to intervention (RtI), a multitier student-support system that offers struggling students increasing levels of intervention. We want to distinguish between the tiers in RtI and tiered lessons used in differentiation. In RtI the tiers refer to the different degrees of intervention offered to students as needed—from the first tier that occurs in a general education setting and involves the core instruction for all students based on high-quality mathematics curriculum and instructional practices to the upper tier that could involve one-on-one instruction with a special education teacher. Tiered lessons used in differentiation would be an avenue to offer high-quality core instruction for all students in the first tier or level of RtI.

✎ *Teaching Tip*

Make sure students understand the vocabulary used in tasks before they begin working independently. For instance, one of the tasks in the tiered lesson example uses the word *property*. Before they start the task, have a group discussion with students who are assigned that task about the meaning of the term.

Flexible Grouping

Allowing students to collaborate on tasks supports and challenges their thinking and increases their opportunities to communicate about mathematics and build understanding. In addition, many students feel that working in groups improves their confidence, engagement, and understanding (Nebesniak & Heaton, 2010). Even students who prefer to work alone need to learn the life skill of collaboration and should be provided opportunities to work with others.

Determining how to place students in groups is an important decision. Avoid grouping by ability. This kind of grouping, although well-intentioned, perpetuates low levels of learning and actually increases the gap between more and less dependent students. Watch this video (https://www.youtube.com/watch?v=R4iAwShVIBE) that shares some of the negative effects of ability grouping. Instead, consider using *flexible grouping* in which the size and makeup of small groups vary in a purposeful and strategic manner (Murray & Jorgensen, 2007). When coupled with the use of differentiation strategies, flexible grouping gives all students the chance to work successfully in groups.

Flexible groups can vary based on students' readiness, interests, language proficiency, and learning profiles, as well as the nature of the tasks. For example, sometimes students can work with a partner because the nature of the task best suits two people working together. At other times, flexible groups might be created with four students because their assigned task has enough components or roles to warrant a larger team. Note that although it can be tempting to occasionally place struggling learners with more capable students, consistently pairing struggling learners with more capable students is not helpful for either group. The idea behind flexible grouping is that groups can and do easily change in response to all students' readiness, interests, and learning profiles and the nature of the task they will be doing.

Regardless of how you group your students, the first key to successful grouping is individual accountability. Although the group is working together on a task, individuals must be able to explain the content, the process, and the product. Second, and equally important, is building a sense of shared responsibility within a group. At the start of the year, it is important to engage students in Team-Building Activities and to set expectations that all group members will participate in the assigned group tasks and that all group members will be responsible for ensuring that the entire group understands the concept.

Reinforcing individual accountability and shared responsibility may create a shift in your role as the teacher. When a member of a small group asks you a question, pose the question to the whole group to find out what the other members think. Students will soon learn that they must use teammates as their first resource and seek teacher help only when the whole group needs help. Also, when you are observing groups, rather than asking Amanda what she is doing, ask Kyle to explain what Amanda is doing. Having all students participate in the oral report to the whole class also builds individual accountability. Letting students know that you may call on any member to explain what the group did is a good way to ensure that all group members understand what they did. In addition, having students individually write and record their strategies and solutions is important. Using these techniques will increase the effectiveness of grouping, which in turn will help students learn mathematical concepts more successfully.

Stop and Reflect

Why is teaching mathematics through problem solving (i.e., a problem-based approach) a good way to differentiate instruction and reach all students in a classroom?

5

Teaching Culturally and Linguistically Diverse Students

Culturally and Linguistically Diverse Students

We are lucky to be in a country composed of people from all over the world. The percentage of culturally and linguistically diverse children in the United States continues to increase. In 2012–2013, 9.2 percent, or about 4.4 million students, participated in an ELL program in public schools (Kena et al., 2015), and about 24 percent (almost 18 million) of U.S. children are Latino (Annie E. Casey Foundation, 2014). Collectively, our students provide rich diversity in cultural practices and languages, and this must be reflected in our mathematics classrooms. Teaching for access, equity and empowerment requires high expectations for all students and this means that in planning, teaching, and assessing, we are responsive to students' backgrounds, experiences, cultural perspectives, traditions, and knowledge (NCTM, 2014).

Funds of Knowledge

Students from different countries, regions, or experiences, including those who speak different languages, are often viewed as challenges to a teacher or school. Rather, students' varied languages and backgrounds should be seen as a resource in teaching (Gutiérrez, 2009). Valuing a person's cultural background is more than a belief statement; it is a set of intentional actions that communicate to the student, "I want to know about you, I want you to see mathematics as part of your life, and I expect that you can do high-level mathematics." In getting to know students, we access their funds of knowledge—the essential knowledge or information that they use to survive and thrive (Moll et al.,1992; Chao, Murray, & Gutiérrez, 2014). Unfortunately, too many teachers view non-Asian and non-European ELLs as behind academically and socially, and lacking the skills needed to succeed (Chval & Pinnow, 2010; Vollmer, 2000).

Instead of teaching students from a deficit model (i.e., focusing on their lack of knowledge and experience), we can connect students' experiences at home and with family to those of the mathematics classroom. Family and community activities, such as playing games, weaving, cooking, and story-telling, can serve as cultural and linguistic resources in learning mathematics.

Mathematics as a Language

Mathematics is commonly referred to as a "universal language," but this is not the case. Conceptual knowledge (e.g., what division is) is universal. Procedures (e.g., how you divide or factor) and symbols are culturally determined and are not universal. For example, the division process in France, Spain, Honduras, Cuba, and other countries varies from that used in the United States, as does the language and notation that is used to describe the process (Perkins & Flores, 2002; Secada, 1983) (see Figure 5.1).

Figure 5.1

Steps and thought processes of division algorithm common in France, Spain, and Central and South America.

Step in the Algorithm	Explanation or Think Aloud for the Step
2144⌐32	What number times 32 is close to 214? 6 is close because 6 times 2 is twelve and 18 and 1 is 19. 7 is too big since 7 times 2 is 14 and 21 plus 1 is 22, so it must be 6.
2144⌐32 6	6 times 32 is 192.
192 2144⌐32 6	214 minus 192 is 22, and bring down the 4.
192 2144⌐32 224 6	What number times 32 is close to 224? 7. 7 times 32 is 224.
224 192 2144⌐32 224 67	224 minus 224 is 0.
224 192 2144⌐32 224 67 0	The answer is 67.

Another example is simplifying expressions such as $2(8 + 15 - 11)$ (*Common Core State Standards* content for fifth grade). In the United States, students are typically instructed to simplify inside the parentheses first (order of operations). But in Mexican textbooks, the expression is evaluated by using the distributive property,

$2(8 + 15 - 11) = 2 \times 8 + 2 \times 15 - 2 \times 11 = 16 + 30 - 22 = 24$ (Perkins & Flores, 2002). Notice that both ways are equivalent and accurate. Making the connection between these two approaches explicit (1) honors different cultural approaches and (2) aligns with the vision in the *Common Core State Standards*—to teach mathematics with deep understanding.

How we do mathematics is also influenced by culture. For example, mental mathematics is highly valued in many countries, whereas in the United States recording every step is valued. Compare the following two division problems from a fourth-grade classroom (Midobuche, 2001):

Can you follow what the first student did? If you learned division in the United States, this is likely easy to follow. But, if you learned division in another country, you may wonder why the first solution has so many steps. Can you follow the second example? It is, in effect, the same thinking process, only the multiplication and related subtraction are done mentally. The critical equity question, though, is not just whether you can follow an alternative approach, but how will you respond when you encounter a student using such an approach?

- Will you require the students to show their steps (disregarding the way they learned it)?
- Will you ask students to elaborate on how they did it?
- Will you have students show other students their way of thinking?

The latter two responses communicate to students that you are interested in their way of knowing mathematics and that there are many ways in which different people and different cultures approach mathematics. Supporting a range of strategies for algorithms is an important way to show that you value students as individuals and is a good way to gain insights into possible culturally influenced strategies (Gutiérrez, 2015).

> ♪ *Teaching Tip*
>
> Instead of requiring students to write all their steps, ask them to think aloud as they solve a problem, or ask how they did it in their head.

Culturally Responsive Mathematics Instruction

Culturally responsive mathematics instruction includes attention to mathematical thinking, language, and culture, and it applies to all students, including students from different ethnic groups, different socioeconomic levels, and so on. It includes consideration for content, relationships, cultural knowledge, flexibility in approaches, use of accessible learning contexts (i.e., contexts familiar or interesting to students), a responsive learning community, and working in cross-cultural partnerships (Aguirre & del Rosario Zavala, 2013; Averill, Anderson, Easton, Te Maro, Smith, & Hynds, 2009). Culturally responsive mathematics instruction can improve the performance of all students, as well as narrow the academic performance gap (Boaler, 2008; Kisker, Lipka, Adams, Rickard, Andrew-Ihrke, Yanez, & Millard, 2012). Table 5.1 lists four **Aspects of culturally responsive mathematics instruction**, along with questions to guide planning, teaching, and assessing.

Table 5.1 Aspects of culturally responsive mathematics instruction.

Aspect of Culturally Responsive Instruction	Teacher Reflection Questions
Communicate high expectations.	Does teaching focus on understanding big ideas in mathematics? Are students expected to engage in problem solving and generate their own approaches to problems? Are connections made among mathematical representations? Are students justifying their strategies and answers, and are they presenting their work?
Make content relevant.	In what ways is the content related to familiar aspects of students' lives? In what ways is prior knowledge elicited/reviewed so that all students can participate in the lesson? To what extent are students asked to make connections between school mathematics and mathematics in their own lives? How are student interests (events, issues, literature, or pop culture) used to build interest and mathematical meaning?
Attend to students' mathematical identities.	In what ways are students invited to include their own experiences within a lesson? Are story problems generated from students and teachers? Do stories reflect the real experiences of students? Are individual student approaches presented and showcased so that each student sees his or her ideas as important to the teacher and peers? Are alternative algorithms shared as a point of excitement and pride (as appropriate)? Are multiple modes used to demonstrate knowledge (e.g., visuals, explanations, models) valued?
Ensure shared power.	Are students (rather than just the teacher) justifying the correctness of solutions? Are students invited (expected) to engage in whole-class discussions in which they share ideas and respond to one another's ideas? In what ways are roles assigned so that every student feels that he or she is contributing to and learning from other members of the class? Are students given a choice in how they solve a problem? In how they demonstrate knowledge of the concept?

Communicate High Expectations

Too often, our first attempt to help students, in particular ELLs, is to simplify the mathematics and/or remove the language from the lesson. Simplifying or removing language can take away opportunities to learn. Culturally responsive instruction stays focused on the big ideas of mathematics (i.e., is based on standards such as the *Common Core State Standards*) and helps students engage in and stay focused on those big ideas. In addition to focusing on the big ideas, using tasks worthy of groupwork, emphasizing multiple representations, incorporating student justifications and presentations are features of classrooms that support equitable opportunities to learn mathematics (Cabana, Shreve, & Woodbury, 2014; Dunleavy, 2015). For example, in a lesson on perimeter and area of nonstandard shapes, a recording sheet might begin with definitions of each term and then a drawing or photograph added to illustrate the situation (Murrey, 2008). The teacher can incorporate opportunities for students to share their definitions and to discuss the meaning of the task prior to engaging in solving it. In this way, ELLs are able to use appropriate mathematical language and focus on finding a solution.

Make Content Relevant

There are really two components to making content relevant. One is to think about the *mathematics*: Is the mathematics itself presented meaningfully, and is it connected to other content? The second is to select *contexts*: Is the mathematics presented so that it connects to relevant/authentic situations in students' lives?

Mathematical Connections

Helping students see that mathematical ideas are interrelated will fill in or deepen their understanding of and connections to previously taught content. For example, consider the following fifth-grade problem:

Melisa is making braided bracelets. To prepare one she needs six strands of colored rope, each of them $1\frac{1}{4}$ feet long. She wants to make eight, one for each of her friends who are coming to her party. How much rope does she need to have?

You may recognize that this task includes adding and multiplying fractions. Although the mathematics is already presented in a conceptual and meaningful manner, it is important to connect whole number and fraction operations. For example, to find how much rope is needed for eight people ($6 \times 1\frac{1}{4}$ feet, or $7\frac{1}{2}$ feet per person, then $8 \times 7\frac{1}{2}$ to find total amount of rope), a student may use addition because of the fraction, not recognizing that multiplication can be used. Asking questions such as, "How did you solve it?" or "How did you decide to [add/multiply]?" and "Are these ways equivalent?" helps students make meaningful connections between whole numbers and fractions and between addition and multiplication.

Context Connections

Making content relevant is also about contexts. The context of creating bracelets grounds student thinking in something familiar so they can focus on reasoning about the mathematical relationships. Using problems that connect students to developmentally appropriate social or peer connections is one way to contextualize learning. Another is to make connections to historical or cultural contexts. Seeing mathematics from various cultures provides opportunities for students to "put faces" on mathematical contributions. For example, the Mayan place-value system can be introduced as a way to think about the structure of our base-ten system. Students can then apply this understanding to large numbers (grades 3 through 5) and decimal fractions (grade 4). Another is to make connections to historical or cultural contexts. Or you can have students create freedom quilts, which tell stories about the Underground Railroad (Neumann, 2005) and can be used to develop *Common Core State Standards* goals such as discovering that shapes can be partitioned into different shapes that each have the same area (grade 3) or classifying shapes based on properties (grades 3 through 5).

    Analyze existing textbook lessons to see if the contexts used actually help students make sense of the mathematics—if they do not, then adapt the contexts so that they do (Drake et al., 2015). Additionally, sometimes data is provided in textbook tasks that can be replaced with data from your community, making it much more relevant and interesting to students, as

Teaching Tip

When looking at a textbook lesson, consider rearranging and prioritizing those tasks that (1) make connections between students' prior knowledge and experiences, (2) lend to students using their own strategies, and (3) encourage students to explain their thinking (Drake et al., 2015).

well as potentially teaching students something important about their community (Simic-Muller, 2015). Using everyday situations can increase student participation, use of different problem strategies, and consequently help students develop a productive disposition (Tomaz & David, 2015).

Attend to Students' Mathematical Identities

A focus on student's mathematical identities overlaps with the previous category, but it merits its own discussion. A student's *mathematical identity* is their disposition toward mathematics and sense of competence as learner and a contributor in mathematics classrooms (Cobb, Gresalfi, & Hodge, 2009). Whether it is intentional or not, all teaching is identity work, as students are constantly adapting and redefining themselves based on their experiences in mathematics classrooms (Gutiérrez, 2015). Our goal is to develop productive dispositions in all students (i.e., the tendency to believe that steady effort in math learning pays off and to see oneself as an effective learner and doer of mathematics [NRC, 2001]). There are a number of ways that teachers can shape students' mathematical identities. One way to do this is "assigning competence" (Boaler & Staples, 2014, p. 27). As the teacher listens during small group work, they hear different contributions from students. During later discussion, the teacher can attribute ideas to individuals, saying something like, "That relates to the strategy Nicolas used." This strategy recognizes Nicolas as capable in mathematics, influencing how he perceives himself, as well as how other classmates might perceive him.

Additionally, telling stories about their own lives, or asking students to tell stories, makes mathematics relevant to students and can raise student achievement (Turner, Celedón-Pattichis, Marshall, & Tennison, 2009). Table 5.2 provides ideas for making mathematics relevant to a student's home and community.

Table **5.2** Where to find mathematics in students' homes and community.

Where to Look	What You Might Ask Students to Record and Share (and Mathematics That Can Be Explored)
Grocery store or market advertisements	• Cost of an item of which they bought more than one (multiplication) • Cost of an item that came with a quantity (e.g., dozen eggs) (division) • Better buy of two items of different sizes (division) • Shapes of different containers (geometry) • Different types/brands of different foods they select, such as what kind of bread (data)
Photographs	• A person they admire (data) • A favorite scene (geometry, measurement) • 2-D and 3-D shapes in their home or neighborhood geometry • Flowers (multiplication with number of petals, algebraic thinking)
Artifact (game or measuring device) from their culture or that is a favorite	• Mathematics of the game (operations, algebraic thinking) • Measuring devices (fractions, decimals, operations)

Read the following teacher's story to see how she incorporated family history and culture into her class by reading *The Hundred Penny Box* (Mathis, 1986). In Mathis's story, a 100-year-old woman remembers an important event in every year of her life as she turns over each of her 100 pennies. Each penny is more than a coin; it is a "memory trigger" for her life.

Taking a cue from the book, I asked all the students to collect one penny from each year they were alive, starting from the year of their birth and not missing a year. Students were encouraged to bring in additional pennies their classmates might need. Then, the students consulted with family members to create a penny time line of important events in their lives. Using information gathered at home, they started with the year they were born, listing their birthday and then recording first steps, accidents, vacations, pets, births of siblings, and so on.

Students in grades 3 through 5 can prepare fraction or decimal number lines sharing events that happened since their birth. The number line is an important model to use in teaching fractions and this context helps students build meaning of fractions on the number line. For example, you can ask students "What events happened in the first $\frac{1}{4}$ of your life?" or "What has happened in the most recent $\frac{1}{6}$ of your life?" or "If you had a sister born when you were 2, for what fraction of your life have you had that sister?"

Ensure Shared Power

When we think about creating a positive classroom environment, one in which all students feel as if they can participate and learn, we are addressing considerations related to power. The teacher plays a major role in establishing and distributing power, whether intentional or not. In many classrooms, the teacher has the power—telling students whether answers are right or wrong (rather than having students determine correctness through reasoning), dictating processes for how to solve problems (rather than giving choices for how students will engage in the problems), and determining who will solve which problems (rather than allowing flexibility and choice for students). Effective teachers encourage students to make mathematics contributions and validate reasoning, reaching a higher level of rigor (Gresalfi & Cobb, 2006). The way that you assign groups, seat students, and call on students sends clear messages about who has power in the classroom. The "assigning competence" strategy just described in student mathematical identities is a teacher move to distribute power (who knows the math in our class). When teachers position ELLs as contributing in meaningful ELLs in similar ways, eliciting and valuing their ideas (Yoon, 2008). And, when teachers delegate authority to marginalized students, they learn more (Dunleavy, 2015).

 *Teaching Tip*

In reflecting on teaching, focus on student participation. Which students struggled most? Were there multiple entry points? How might certain students have been encouraged to participate more?

Teaching Strategies that Support Culturally and Linguistically Diverse Students

Culture and language are interwoven and interrelated. Therefore, teaching strategies that support diverse learners often attend to a students' background, as well as their language. Creating effective learning opportunities for ELLs involves integrating the principles of bilingual education with those of standards-based mathematics instruction. When learning about mathematics, students may be learning content in English for which they do not know the words in their native language (e.g., *numerator* and *denominator* in the study of fractions).

Story problems may also be difficult for ELLs not just because of the language but also because the sentences in story problems are often structured differently from sentences in conversational English (Janzen, 2008). ELLs need to use both English and their native language to read, write, listen, and speak as they learn appropriate content—a position similarly addressed in NCTM standards documents and position statements. The strategies discussed in this section are the ones that appear most frequently in the literature as critical to increasing the academic achievement of ELLs in mathematics classrooms (e.g., Celedón-Pattichis & Ramirez, 2012; Echevarria, Vogt, & Short, 2008). Table 5.3 **Reflective questions for planning and teaching mathematics lessons for ELLs** offers an "at-a-glance" format of some reflective questions related to instructional planning and teaching to support ELLs.

Teaching Tip

Any one of the categories in Table 5.3 could be the focus of a lesson study, discussions with colleagues, or the basis for individual reflection. The importance lies not in the specific suggestions, but in the concept of having an eye on language development *and* mathematics content.

Table 5.3. Reflective questions for planning and teaching mathematics lessons for ELLs.

Process	Mathematics Content Considerations	Language Considerations
Reflective Questions for Planning		
1. Determine the mathematics.	• What mathematical concepts (aligned to grade-level standards) am I teaching? • What student-friendly learning objectives will I post? • How does this mathematics concept connect to other concepts students have learned?	• What language objectives might I add (e.g., reading, writing, speaking, and listening)? • What visuals or words will I use to communicate the content and language objectives?
2. Consider student needs.	• How can I connect the content to be taught to content that students have learned? Or, how will I fill in gaps if students don't have prerequisite content needed for the lesson?	• What context or models might I select that are a good match to students' social and cultural backgrounds and previously learned vocabulary?
3. Select, design, or adapt a task.	• What task can I use that addresses the content identified in No. 1 and the needs of my students identified in No. 2? • How might I adapt a task so that it has multiple entry and exit points (i.e., is challenging and accessible to a range of students)?	• What context might I use that is meaningful to the students' cultures and backgrounds? • What language pitfalls does the task have? Which of these will I eliminate, and which of these need explicit attention? • Which words or phrases, even if familiar to students, take on new meaning in a mathematics context (e.g., homonyms, homophones, and words such as *product, similar, find*)?

Table 5.3. Reflective questions for planning and teaching mathematics lessons for ELLs. (*continued*)

Process	Mathematics Content Considerations	Language Considerations
Reflective Questions for Teaching		
1. Introduce the task (the *Before* phase).	• How will I introduce the task in a way that elicits prior mathematics knowledge needed for the task? • Is a similar task needed to build background related to the content (or would such a preview take away from the purpose or challenge of the task)?	• How can I connect the task to students' experiences and to familiar contexts? • What key vocabulary do I want to introduce so that the words will be used throughout the lesson? (Post key vocabulary in a prominent location.) • What visuals and real objects can I use that bring meaning to the selected task? • How can I present the task in visual, written, and oral formats? • How will I be sure that students understand what they are to do in the *During* phase?
2. Work on the task (the *During* phase).	• What hints or assists might I give as students work that help them focus without taking away their thinking? • What extensions or challenges will I offer for students who successfully solve the task? • What questions will I pose to push the mathematics identified in the learning goals?	• Have I grouped students for both academic and language support? • Have I encouraged students to draw pictures, make diagrams, and/or use manipulatives? • Have I used strategies to reduce the linguistic demands (e.g., graphic organizers, sentence starters such as, "I solved the problem by . . .," recording tables, and concept maps) without hindering the problem solving?
3. Debrief and discuss the task and the mathematics (the *After* phase).	• How will students report their findings? • How will I format the discussion of the task? • What questions will I pose to push the mathematics identified in the learning goals?	• In what ways can I maximize language use in nonthreatening ways (e.g., think–pair–share)? • How can I encourage and reinforce different formats (multiple exit points) for demonstrating understanding of the lesson content? • How might I provide advance notice, language support, or rehearsal to English language learners so that they will be comfortable speaking to their peers? • Am I using appropriate "wait time"?
Formative Assessment		
Throughout lesson and unit	• What questions will I ask during the lesson, or what will I look for in the students' work as evidence of learning the objectives (*During* and *After* phases)? • What follow-up might I provide to students who are not demonstrating understanding of the mathematics?	• What words will I use in my questions to be sure the questions are understood? How might I use a translator to assist in assessing? • If a student is not succeeding, how might I diagnose whether the problem is with language, content, or both? • What accommodations can I provide to be sure I am accessing what the students know?

Focus on Academic Vocabulary

ELLs enter the mathematics classroom from homes in which English is not the primary language of communication. Although a person may develop conversational English language skills in a few years, it takes as many as seven years to learn *academic language*, which is the language specific to a content area such as mathematics (Cummins, 1994). Academic language is harder to learn because it is not used in a student's everyday world. In addition, there are unique features of the language of mathematics that make it difficult for many students, in particular those who are learning English. Teaching the academic language of mathematics evolves over time and requires thoughtful and reflective instructional planning.

Honor Use of Native Language

Valuing a student's native language is one of the ways you value his or her cultural heritage. In a mathematics classroom, students can communicate in their native languages while continuing their English language development (Haas & Gort, 2009; Moschkovich, 2009; Setati, 2005). For example, a good strategy for students working individually or in small groups is having them think about and discuss the problem in their preferred language. If a student knows enough English, then the presentation in the *After* phase of the lesson can be shared in English. If the student knows little or no English and does not have access to a peer who shares his or her native language, then a translator, the use of a Web-based dictionary, or a self-made mathematics-focused dictionary can be a strong support. Students within the small group can also be coached to use visual aids and pictures to communicate. Bilingual students will often code-switch, moving between two languages. Research indicates that the practice of code-switching supports mathematical reasoning because students select the language in which they can best express their ideas (Moschkovich, 2009).

Certain native languages can support learning mathematical words. Because English, Spanish, French, Portuguese, and Italian all have their roots in Latin, many math words are similar across languages (Celedón-Pattichis, 2009; Gómez, 2010). For example, *aequus* (Latin), *equal* (English), and *igual* (Spanish) are cognates. See if you can figure out the English mathematical terms for the following Spanish words: *división, hexágano, ángulo, triángulo, álgebra, circunferencia,* and *cubo.* Students may not make this connection if you do not point it out, so it is important to explicitly teach students to look for cognates.

Use Content and Language Objectives

If students know the purpose of a lesson, they are better able to make sense of the details when they are challenged by some of the oral or written explanations. When language expectations are explicitly included, students will know that they will be responsible for reaching certain language goals alongside mathematical goals and will be more likely to attempt to learn those skills or words. Here are two examples of dual objectives:

1. Students will analyze properties and attributes of three-dimensional solids. (mathematics)
2. Students will describe in writing and speaking a similarity and a difference between two different solids. (language and mathematics)

Explicitly Teach Vocabulary

Intentional vocabulary instruction must be part of mathematics instruction for all students. There is strong evidence that teaching a set of academic vocabulary words intensively across several days using a variety of instructional activities supports ELLs (Baker et al., 2014). Vocabulary support can happen throughout a lesson, as well as reinforced before or after a lesson. These additional opportunities can reinforce understanding as they help students learn the terminology. Examples include these:

- Self-made math dictionaries that link concepts and terms with drawings or clip art pictures (Kersaint, Thompson, & Petkova, 2009)
- Foldables of key words for a topic (for example, see *Dinah Zike's Teaching Mathematics with Foldables* (Zike, n.d.), a free download)

- Games focused on vocabulary development (e.g., "Pictionary" or "$10,000 Pyramid")
- Interactive word walls, including visuals and translations
- Graphic organizers that look at multiple ways to help define a term (for example, **Vocabulary Reference Card Template**)

All students benefit from an increased focus on language; however, too much emphasis on vocabulary can diminish the focus on mathematics. Importantly, the language support should be *connected* to the mathematics and the selected task or activity (Bay-Williams & Liver, 2009).

As you analyze a lesson, you must identify terms related to the mathematics and to the context that may need explicit attention. Consider the following grade 4 short constructed response item (medium level of difficulty) from the 2009 National Assessment of Educational Progress (NAEP) (National Center for Education Statistics, n.d.):

Sam did the following problem:

$$2 + 1 = 3$$

$$6 + 1 = 7$$

Sam concluded that when he adds 1 to any whole number, his answer will always be odd.

Is Sam correct? _____

Explain your answer.

In order for students to engage in this task, the terms *even* and *odd* must be understood. Both terms may be known for other meanings beyond the mathematics classroom (*even* can mean level and *odd* can mean strange). *Concluded* is not a math word, but also must be understood if an ELL student is to understand the meaning of the problem. Finally, you must give guidance on how students will explain their answers—do they need to use words, or can they use pictures or diagrams?

Stop and Reflect   500 ◠, 250   ⸮ 3✕ ▱ ˢ ⅋ ° ∞∩ ✗ 2.5

> *Odd* and *even* are among hundreds of words whose meanings in mathematics are different from everyday usage. Other terms include *product, mean, sum, factor, acute, foot, division, difference, similar,* and *angle.* Can you name five others?

Foster Student Participation during Instruction

Student participation is important to learning (Tomaz & David, 2015; Wager, 2014). Facilitating discourse that provides access to ELLs is critical. This includes (1) efforts to ensure that ELLs understand and have the background for engaging in the focus task(s), and (2) the need to put structures in place for student participation throughout the lesson.

Build Background Knowledge

Similar to building on prior knowledge, building background also takes into consideration native language and culture as well as content (Echevarria, Vogt, & Short, 2012). If possible, use a context and appropriate visuals to help students understand the task you want them to solve. This is a nonthreatening and engaging way to help students make connections between what they have learned and what they need to learn.

Some aspects of English and mathematics are particularly challenging to ELLs (Whiteford, 2009/2010). For example, teen numbers sound a lot like their decade number—if you say *sixteen* and *sixty* out loud, you can hear how similar they are. And, decimal fractions (e.g., 0.15) sound like whole numbers (e.g., 1500). Emphasizing the *n* in *teen* or the *ths* in decimal fractions helps ELLs hear the difference. Remember, too, that the U.S. measurement system may be unfamiliar to ELLs. When encountering content that may be unfamiliar or difficult for ELLs, devote additional time to building background so that students can engage in the mathematical tasks without also having to navigate language and background knowledge.

Use Comprehensible Input

Comprehensible input means that the message you are communicating is understandable to students. Modifications include simplifying sentence structures and limiting the use of nonessential or confusing vocabulary (Echevarria, Vogt, & Short, 2012). Note that these modifications do not lower expectations for the lesson. Sometimes, teachers put many unnecessary words and phrases into questions, making them less clear to nonnative speakers. Compare the following two sets of teachers' instructions:

NOT MODIFIED:

You have a worksheet in front of you that I just gave out. For every situation, I want you to determine the total area for the shapes. You will be working with your partner, but each of you needs to record your answers on your own paper and explain how you got your answer. If you get stuck on a problem, raise your hand.

MODIFIED:

Please look at your paper. (Holds paper and points to the first picture.) You will find the area of each shape. What does area mean? (Allows wait time.) How can you calculate area? (*Calculate* is more like the Spanish word *calcular,* so it is more accessible to Spanish speakers.) Talk to your partner. (Points to mouth and then to a pair of students as she says this.) Write your answers. (Makes a writing motion over paper.) If you get stuck (shrugs shoulders and looks confused), raise your hand (demonstrates).

Notice that three things have been done: sentences have been shortened, confusing words have been removed, and related gestures and motions have been added to the oral directives. Also, notice the wait time the teacher gives. It is very important to provide extra time after posing a question or giving instructions to allow ELLs time to translate, make sense of the request, and then participate.

Another way to provide comprehensible input is to use a variety of tools to help students visualize and understand what is verbalized. In the preceding example, the teacher models the instructions. Effective tools include manipulatives, real objects, pictures, visuals, multimedia, demonstrations, and literature. When introducing a lesson, include pictures, real objects, and diagrams. For example, if you are teaching volume of rectangular solids, show different kinds of cubes (e.g., 1-inch cubes, 1-centimeter cubes, number cubes). Ask students, "How many same-sized cubes will fill the rectangular container?" And, as you ask, physically move some cubes into the container to illustrate. Review terms for the container (base, length, width, height) and label a container for reference. Students should be expected to include multiple representations of their understandings such as drawing, writing, and explanation of what they have done.

Engage Students in Discourse That Reflects Language Needs

Discourse, or the use of classroom discussion, is essential for *all* learning (Cirillo, Steele, Otten, Herbel-Eisenmann, McAneny, & Riser, 2014), but is particularly important for ELLs, who need to engage in productive language (writing and speaking), not just receptive language (listening and reading) (Baker et al., 2014). As noted in *Application of Common Core State Standards for English Learners*:

> ELLs are capable of participating in mathematical discussions as they learn English. Mathematics instruction for ELL students should draw on multiple resources and modes available in classrooms—such as objects, drawings, inscriptions, and gestures—as well as home languages and mathematical experiences outside of school. Mathematical instruction should address mathematical discourse and academic language (CCSSO, 2011, p. 2).

There are strategies you can use in classroom discourse that help ELLs understand and participate in discussions. Practicing an explanation first with a partner can increase participation. Revoicing, using gestures and visuals, inviting sharing and justification, and asking other students to respond to ELLs' ideas are all ways to support participation (Shein, 2012; Turner, Dominguez, Maldonado, & Empson, 2013). *Revoicing* is a research-based strategy that helps ELLs hear an idea more than once and hear it restated with the appropriate language applied to concepts. Students from other countries often solve or record problems differently, so inviting ELLs to share how they solved a problem can enhance the richness of discussion about a task. Importantly, ELLs cannot always explain their ideas fully, but rather than call on someone else; press for details. This pressing, or expansion move (Choppin, 2014), helps the teacher decide whether the idea makes sense *and* it helps other students make sense of the ideas (Maldonado, Turner, Dominguez, & Empson, 2009). Note that these teacher moves also attribute ideas to students, thereby enhancing their mathematical authority (power), as discussed earlier in this chapter.

 *Teaching Tip*

Making the strategies of ELLs public and connecting their strategies to others supports the learning of all students while building the confidence of the ELLs.

Plan Cooperative/Interdependent Groups to Support Language Development

The use of cooperative groups is a valuable way to support ELLs (Baker et al., 2014). For ELLs, groups provide the opportunity to use language, but only if the groups are carefully formed in a way that considers students' language skills. Placing an ELL with two English-speaking students may result in the ELL being left out. On the other hand, grouping all Spanish speakers together prevents these students from having the opportunity to hear and participate in mathematics in English. Consider placing a bilingual student in a group with a student who has limited English, or place students who have the same first language together with native speakers so that they can help one another understand and participate (Garrison, 1997; Khisty, 1997).

CLASSROOM VIGNETTE

The strategies just described are subtle moves in teaching. As you read the following vignette, look for strategies that the teacher applies to provide support for ELLs while keeping expectations high.

> Ms. Steimer is teaching a third-grade lesson that involves the concepts of estimating length (in inches) and measuring to the nearest half inch. The task asks students to use estimation to find three objects that are about 6 inches long, three objects that are about 1 foot long, and three objects that are about 2 feet long. Once identified, students are to measure the nine objects to the nearest half-inch and compare the measurements with their estimates.
>
> Ms. Steimer has several English language learners in her class, including a student from Korea who knows very little English and a student from Mexico who speaks English well but is new to U.S. schools. These two students are not familiar with the measurement units of feet or inches. Ms. Steimer knows they will likely struggle in trying to estimate or measure in inches and will not have measured using fractions. She takes time to address the language and the increments on the ruler to the entire class. Because the word *foot* has two meanings, Ms. Steimer decides to address that explicitly before launching into the lesson. She begins by asking students what a "foot" is. She allows time for them to discuss the word with a partner and then share their answers with the class. She explains that today they are going to be using the measuring unit of a foot (while holding up the foot ruler). She asks students what other units can be used to measure. In particular, she asks her English language learners to share what units they use in their countries of origin, having metric rulers to show the class. She asks students to study the ruler and compare the centimeter to the inch by posing these questions: "Can you estimate about how many centimeters are in an inch? In 6 inches? In a foot?"
>
> Moving to the lesson objectives, Ms. Steimer draws a large line on the board to represent an inch on the ruler. She marks the halfway point and labels the ends of the giant inch as 18 inches and 19 inches. Below it she draws a snake whose length ends at the $18\frac{1}{2}$ inch mark. Then she asks students how long the snake is and writes the measurement $18\frac{1}{2}$ inches on the board. Next, she asks students to tear a paper strip that they estimate is 6 inches long. Students then measure their paper strips using their rulers, writing down their measurement to the nearest half-inch. Now she has them ready to begin estimating and measuring.

Stop and Reflect   500 ☌ 250   ⮂ ⁇ 3⁎ ▱ ∫⁵⁹° ⁸∩ ⚖ 2.5

What specific strategies to support ELLs can you identify?

There are a number of strategies in the vignette that provide support for ELLs: recognizing the potential language confusion around the word *foot*, as well as lack of familiarity with U.S. measurement; using the think-pair-share technique; and looking at the ruler to compare measurement systems. Using concrete models (the ruler and the torn paper strip) to build on students' prior experiences (use of the metric system in Korea and Mexico) and visuals (illustrating on the board how to read the $\frac{1}{2}$ on the ruler with a giant inch) provide support. Most important, Ms. Steimer did not diminish the challenge of the task with these strategies. If she had altered the task—for example, not expecting the ELLs to estimate since they didn't know how to measure using an inch—she would have lowered her expectations. Conversely, if she had simply posed the problem without taking time to have students study a ruler or provide other visuals, she might have kept her expectations high but failed to provide the support that would enable her students to succeed. Finally, by making a connection for all students to the metric system, she showed respect for the students' cultures and broadened the horizons of other students regarding measurements in other countries.

Assessment Considerations for ELLs

If a teacher wants to understand what a student knows about mathematics, then the student should be able to communicate that understanding in a way that is best for the student, even if the teacher may need a translation. Research shows that ELLs perform better when a test is given in their native language (Robinson, 2010). Several strategies can assist teachers in using formative assessments with ELLs, including tasks with multiple entry and exit points, diagnostic interviews, tasks that limit the linguistic load, accommodations, and self-assessment.

Select Tasks with Multiple Entry and Exit Points

An aspect of teaching mathematics through problem solving that is important, particularly for ELLs, is to select tasks carefully. If a problem can be solved in multiple ways, an ELL is more likely to be able to design a strategy that makes sense and then illustrate that strategy. Inviting students to show and/or explain their strategy provides options for ELLs to use words and pictures to communicate their thinking.

Use Diagnostic Interviews

When ELLs do not get a correct answer or cannot explain a response, it is easy to assume it is a lack of mathematical understanding rather than a language issue. Diagnostic interviews provide a chance to observe what content or language the student does or does not understand. Fernandez, Anhalt, and Civil (2009) describe such an interview experience using the NAEP item presented in Figure 5.2.

Figure 5.2

An NAEP-released item posed to 15 fourth-grade ELL students in an after-school setting.

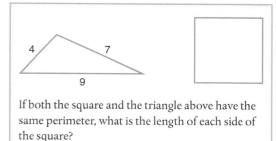

If both the square and the triangle above have the same perimeter, what is the length of each side of the square?

a. 4

b. 5

c. 6

d. 7

Stop and Reflect　500 ◠͵²⁵⁰　🖐 ⏸3ᴌ ▱ ˢ꜀˚ ∞∩ ⤳²·⁵

Before reading further, review Figure 5.2 and consider what you think might have prevented students from answering the problem correctly.

As you reviewed the problem, you may have considered numerous reasons that students might have struggled with this problem, including a lack of understanding the mathematical concept of perimeter, or the terminology of perimeter, square, or triangle. What did the diagnostic interviews reveal? Students struggled with what the question was asking. The word *if* stumped one student because she did not understand the "if . . . then" meaning in mathematics (a challenge for native English speakers as well). Once the word *if* was removed from the sentence, she was able to solve the problem. Most of the students interviewed could solve the problem once they understood it.

This perimeter problem reminds us of how important it is to follow up with students when they are not successful on a task in order to figure out why. The fact that there are many possible reasons why a student might not be able to solve a task, some related to language and others to mathematics, is a strong argument for using diagnostic interviews. If we misdiagnose the reason for a student's struggles, our interventions will be misguided.

Diagnostic interviews also can be used prior to instruction in order to assess the mathematical and language needs of students. Hearing an ELL's interpretation of a problem and seeing how she approaches the problem provide valuable insights that you can incorporate into your planning and teaching.

Limit Linguistic Load

If you are trying to assess student understanding, look for language that can interfere with students' understanding the situation (e.g., unneeded elaboration in a story, difficult or unfamiliar vocabulary). Consider the perimeter problem in Figure 5.2. It is important for students to learn the meaning of "if . . . then" phrases, but it would have been more clear if the problem had been stated as: "The square and the triangle have the same perimeter. What is the length of one side of the square?" Removing pronouns like *they, this, that, his, her,* and using actual names can assist ELLs in understanding some problems. For example, recall the bracelet problem:

Melisa is making braided bracelets. To prepare one she needs six strands of colored rope, each of them $1\frac{1}{4}$ feet long. She wants to make 8, one for each of her friends who are coming to her party. How much rope does she need to have?

Rewritten, it might read:

Melisa is making bracelets. She needs six strands of rope to make one bracelet. Each strand is $1\frac{1}{4}$ feet long. Melisa wants to make 8 bracelets for her friends. How many feet of rope does Melisa need?

Notice that it is not only reducing the language, but also adding specific referents that makes the meaning of the story clearer. Of course, this particular problem could be adapted further by using illustrations and removing even more of the context, which may be more appropriate depending on the language proficiency of the ELLs.

If there are more problems in a lesson or assessment, staying with the same scenario/context allows students to focus their thinking on the mathematics without getting bogged down in different contexts. For example, instead of using a different division of fractions situations, stay with bracelets as a context but change the problem details (what is known, unknown). This reduces the linguistic load but keeps the mathematical challenge high.

 *Teaching Tip*

To reduce the linguistic load for students, pick one scenario/context, and stay with it for an entire lesson or series of lessons.

Provide Accommodations

For assessing, *providing accommodations* refers to strategies for making sure that the assessment itself is accessible to children. This might mean allowing students to hear the question (students often can understand spoken English better than written English), shortening the assessment, or extending the time (Kersaint, Thompson, & Petkova, 2009). In addition, you can refer to word walls and provide sentence starters so that the ELL knows what type of response you want. For example, "My equation fits the story because . . ." In general, the goal with assessment accommodations, like teaching accommodations, is to put structures in place so that ELLs can understand what you want them to learn and you can understand what they have learned.

Stop and Reflect

The goal of equity is to offer every student access to important mathematics. What might you have on a list of things to do (and things not to do) that support equity, access and empowerment?

6

Teaching and Assessing Students with Exceptionalities

Instructional Principles for Diverse Learners

The NCTM position statement on Access and Equity in Mathematics Education states that we should hold the expectation that all children can reach mathematics proficiency and that high levels of performance must be attained regardless of race, ethnicity, gender, socioeconomic status, ability, or linguistic background including those in special education and gifted education (NCTM, 2014). Students need opportunities to advance their knowledge supported by teaching that gives attention to their individual learning needs. Students' backgrounds are not only an important part of who they are as people, but who they are as learners—and this background enriches the classroom.

Many *achievement* gaps are actually *instructional* gaps or *expectation* gaps. It is not helpful when teachers set low expectations for students, as when they say, "I just cannot put this class into groups to work; they are too unruly" or "My students with disabilities can't solve word problems—they don't have the reading skills." Operating under the belief that some students cannot do mathematics ensures that they don't have ample opportunities to prove otherwise. Instead, we suggest you consider Storeygard's (2010) mantra for teachers which proclaims—"My kids can!"

We know that teaching for equity is much more than providing students with an equal opportunity to learn mathematics, instead, it attempts to attain equal outcomes for all students by being sensitive to individual differences. How you will maintain equal outcomes and high expectations while providing for individual differences with strong support can be challenging. Equipping yourself with an ever-growing collection of instructional strategies for a variety of students is critical. A strategy that works for one student may be completely ineffective with another, even for a student with the same exceptionality. Addressing the needs of *all* means providing access and opportunity for:

- Students who are identified as struggling or having a disability.
- Students who are mathematically gifted.
- Students who are unmotivated or need to build resilience.

You may think, "I do not need to read the section in this chapter on mathematically gifted students because they will be pulled out for math enrichment." Students who are mathematically talented need to be challenged in the daily core instruction, not just when they are participating in a gifted program.

One of the basic tenets of education is individualizing the content taught and methods used for students who struggle, particularly those with special needs. Mathematics learning disabilities are best thought of as cognitive differences, not cognitive deficits (Lewis, 2014). Students with disabilities often have mandated individualized education programs (IEPs) that guarantee access to grade-level mathematics content—preferably in a general education classroom. This legislation also implies that educators consider individual learning needs not only in terms of *what* mathematics is taught but also *how* it is taught.

Essential in making decisions about how you can adapt instruction to meet individual learner's needs is the use of accommodations and modifications. An accommodation is a response to the needs of the environment or the learner; it does not alter the task. For example, you might write down directions for a student instead of just saying them orally. A modification changes the task, making it more accessible to the student. For example, if finding the area of a compound shape, you might break the shape up into two rectangles for a student and ask them to find the area of each shape and combine. Then the next shape they will attempt without the modification. When modifications result in an easier or less demanding task, expectations are lowered. Modifications should be made in a way that leads back to the original task, providing scaffolding or support for learners who may need it. Complete an **Accommodation or Modification Needs** table to reflect on how you will plan for students in your classroom who have special needs. Record the evidence that you are adapting the learning situation.

In this chapter, we share research-based strategies that reflect these equity principles while providing appropriate accommodations and modifications for the wide range of students in your classroom.

Prevention Models

In many school systems, a systematic process for achieving higher levels performance for all students often includes a multitiered system of support (MTSS) frequently called response to intervention (RtI). This approach commonly emphasizes ways for struggling students to get immediate assistance and support rather than waiting for students to fail before they receive help or also for identifying students who are far exceeding standards and need additional challenges. Multitiered models are centered on the three interwoven elements: high-quality curriculum, instructional support (interventions), and formative assessments that capture students' strengths and weaknesses. Often this model is used to determine whether low achievement is due to a lack of high-quality mathematics (i.e., "teacher-disabled students") (Baroody, 2011; Ysseldyke, 2002) or due to an actual learning disability. This model can also help determine more intensive, instructional options for students who may need to have additional advanced mathematical challenges beyond what other students study.

Response to Intervention

RtI (**https://www.youtube.com/watch?v=nkK1bT8ls0M**) is a multitiered student support system often represented in a three-tier triangle format. As you might guess, there are a variety of RtI models developed by school systems as they structure their unique approaches to meeting students' needs. As you move up the tiers the number of students involved decreases, the teacher–student ratio decreases, and the level of intervention increases. Each tier in the triangle represents a level of intervention with corresponding monitoring of results and outcomes, as shown in Figure 6.1. The foundational and largest portion of the triangle (Tier 1) represents the core instruction for **all** students based on high-quality mathematics curriculum, highly engaging instructional practices (i.e., manipulatives, conceptual emphasis, etc.) and progress monitoring assessments. For example, if using a graphic organizer in Tier 1 core instruction the following high-quality practices would be expected in the three phases of the lesson—*Before, During,* and *After*:

Before. States purpose, introduces new vocabulary, clarifies concepts from needed prior knowledge in a visual organizer, and defines tasks of group members (if groups are being used).

During. Displays directions in a chart, poster, or list; provides a set of guiding questions in a chart with blank spaces for responses.

After. Facilitates a discussion to highlight or make more explicit the significant concepts or skills and then presents a summary and list of important concepts as they relate to one another.

Tier 2 represents students who did not reach the level of achievement expected during Tier 1 instruction. Students who move to Tier 2 should receive supplemental targeted instruction (interventions) using more explicit strategies with systematic teaching of critical skills and concepts, more intensive and frequent instructional opportunities, and more supportive and precise prompts (Torgesen, 2002). The National Council of Teachers of Mathematics' position statement on Interventions (2011) endorses the use of interventions that increase in intensity as students demonstrate continuing struggle with learning mathematics. Interventions may require "heroic action to preclude serious complications" (Fuchs & Fuchs, 2001, p. 86).

If further assessment reveals students have made favorable progress, the extra interventions are faded and discontinued. But, if difficulties and struggles still remain, the interventions can be adjusted in intensity, and in rare cases, students are referred to the next tier of support. Tier 3 is for students who need more intensive assistance, which may include comprehensive mathematics instruction or a referral for special education evaluation or special education services. Instructional strategies for the three tiers are outlined in Table 6.1.

Figure 6.1

Response to intervention—using effective prevention strategies for all children.

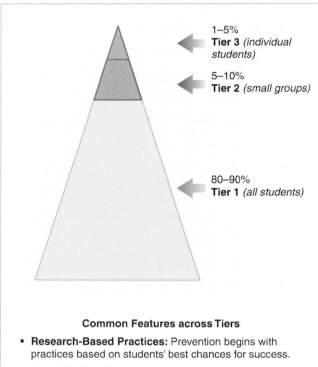

Common Features across Tiers

- **Research-Based Practices:** Prevention begins with practices based on students' best chances for success.
- **Data-Driven:** All decisions are based on clear objectives and formative data collection.
- **Instructional:** Prevention and intervention involve effective instruction, prompts, cues, practice, and environmental arrangements.
- **Context-Specific:** All strategies and measures are selected to fit individual schools, classrooms, or students.

Source: Based on Scott, Terence, and Lane, Holly. (2001). *Multi-Tiered Interventions in Academic and Social Contexts.* Unpublished manuscript, University of Florida, Gainesville.

Table 6.1 Interventions for teaching mathematics in a multitiered model.

Tiers	Interventions
Tier 1	**Highly qualified regular classroom teacher:** • Incorporates high-quality, engaging, and rigorous curriculum • Expects that all students will be challenged • Builds in CCSSO Standards for Mathematical Practice and NCTM process standards • Commits to teaching the curriculum as defined • Uses multiple representations such as manipulatives, visual models, and symbols • Monitors progress to identify struggling students and students who excel at high levels for possible interventions • Uses flexible student grouping • Fosters active student involvement • Communicates high expectations
Tier 2	**Highly qualified regular classroom teacher, with collaboration from other highly qualified educators (i.e., special education teacher):** • Works with students (often in small groups) in engaging, high-quality and rigorous supplemental sessions outside of the core instruction • Conducts individual diagnostic interviews to target a student's strengths and weaknesses to focus next instructional steps • Slices back (Fuchs & Fuchs, 2001) to material from a previous grade to ramp back up to grade-level curriculum • Collaborates with special education, gifted, and/or ELL specialists • Creates lessons that emphasize the big ideas (focal points) or themes • Incorporates CSA (concrete, semi-concrete, abstract) approach • Shares thinking in a think-aloud to demonstrate how to make problem-solving decisions • Incorporates explicit systematic strategy instruction (summarizes key points and reviews key vocabulary or concepts prior to the lesson) • Models specific behaviors and strategies, such as how to handle measuring materials or geoboards • Uses mnemonics or steps written on cards or posters to help students follow, for example, the stages of problem solving • Uses peer-assisted learning, where another student can provide help to a student in need • Supplies families with additional instructional support materials to use at home • Encourages students use of self-regulation and self-instructional strategies such as revising notes, writing summaries, and identifying main ideas • Teaches test-taking strategies and allows the students to use a highlighter on the test to emphasize important information
Tier 3	**Highly qualified special education teacher:** • Works one-on-one with students • Uses tailored instruction based on specific areas of strengths and weaknesses • Modifies instructional methods, motivates students, and adapts curricula • Uses explicit contextualization of skills-based instruction

Progress Monitoring

A key to guiding students' movement within the multitiered prevention model is the monitoring of their progress. One way that you can collect evidence of students' knowledge of concepts through the use of diagnostic interviews (examples are described in Chapter 3 and throughout the book in a feature called Formative Assessment Notes) (Hodges, Rose, & Hicks, 2012). Another approach is to assess students' growth toward fluency in basic facts, an area that is well-documented as a barrier for students with learning disabilities (Mazzocco, Devlin, & McKenney, 2008). Combining instruction with short daily assessments proved to be a way to help students not only be better at remembering the facts but better at generalizing to other facts (Woodward, 2006). The collection of information gathered from these assessments will reveal whether students are making the progress expected or if more intensive instructional approaches need to be put into place.

Implementing Interventions

NCTM has shared a set of effective, research-based strategies (NCTM, 2007b) for teaching the subset of students for whom the initial core instruction was not effective (the students needing Tier 2 or Tier 3 interventions). These strategies include systematic and explicit instruction, think-alouds, concrete and visual representations of problems, peer-assisted learning activities, and formative assessment data provided to students and teachers. These interventions, proven to be effective for students with disabilities, may represent principles different from those used at Tier 1.

Explicit Strategy Instruction

Explicit instruction is characterized by highly structured, teacher-led instruction on a specific strategy. When engaging in this explicit instruction you do not merely model the strategy and have students practice it, instead you try to illuminate the decision-making along the way—a process that may be troublesome for these particular learners without support. In this instructional strategy, after you assess the students so that you know what to target, you use a tightly organized sequence from modeling the strategy to prompting students through the model, to practice. Your instruction uses these teacher-led explanations of concepts and strategies, including the critical connection building and meaning making that help learners relate new knowledge with concepts they know. Let's look at a classroom teacher using explicit instruction:

> *As you enter Mr. Logan's classroom, you see a small group of students seated at a table listening to the teacher's detailed explanation and watching his demonstration of equivalent fraction concepts. The students are using manipulatives, as suggested by Mr. Logan, and moving through carefully selected tasks. He tells the students to take out the red "one-fourth" pieces and asks them to check how many "one-fourths" will exactly cover the blue "one-half" piece. Mr. Logan asks, "Is **equivalent** a word you know?" Then, to make sure they don't allow for any gaps or overlaps in the pieces, he asks them to talk about their reasoning process by asking the question, "What are some things you need to keep in mind as you place the fourths on the half?" Mr. Logan writes their responses on the adjacent board as $\frac{2}{4} = \frac{1}{2}$ and also as "two-fourths is the same as one-half" to connect the ideas that they are looking for how many fourth pieces cover one-half piece. Then he asks them to compare the brown "eighths" and the yellow "sixths" to the piece representing one-half and records their responses. The students take turns answering these questions a loud. During the lesson Mr. Logan frequently stops the group, interjects points of clarification, and directly highlights critical components of the task. For example, he asks, "Are you surprised that it takes more eighths to cover the half than fourths?" Vocabulary words, such as **whole**, **numerator**, **denominator**, and **equivalent**, are written on the "math word wall" nearby and the definitions of these terms are reviewed and reinforced throughout the lesson. At the completion of the lesson, students are given several similar examples of the kind of comparisons discussed in the lesson as independent practice.*

A number of aspects of explicit instruction can be seen in Mr. Logan's approach to teaching fraction concepts. He employs a teacher-directed teaching format, carefully describes the use of manipulatives, and incorporates a model-prompt-practice sequence. This sequence starts with verbal instructions and demonstrations with concrete models, followed by prompting, questioning, and then independent practice. The students are deriving mathematical knowledge from Mr. Logan's oral, written, and visual clues.

As students with disabilities solve problems, explicit strategy instruction can help guide them in carrying out tasks. First ask them to read and restate the problem, draw a picture or make a model with materials, develop a plan by linking this problem to previous problems, write the problem in a mathematical sentence, break the problem into smaller pieces, carry out operations, and check answers using a calculator, hundreds chart or other appropriate tools. These self-instructive prompts, or self-questions, structure the entire learning process from beginning to end. Unlike more inquiry-based instruction, the teacher models these steps and explains components using terminology that is easily understood by students who struggle—students who did not discover them independently through initial Tier 1 or 2 activities. Yet, consistent with what we know about how all students learn, students are still doing problem solving (not just skill development).

Concrete models can support explicit strategy instruction. For example, a teacher demonstrating a multiplication array with cubes might say, "Watch me. Now make a rectangle with the cubes that looks just like mine." In contrast, a teacher with a more inquiry-oriented approach might say, "Using these cubes, how can you show me a representation for 4 × 5?" Although initially more structured, the use of concrete models in this fashion will provide students with disabilities with greater access to abstract concepts.

There are a number of possible advantages to using explicit strategy instruction for students with disabilities. This approach helps you make more explicit for these students the covert thinking strategies that others use in mathematical problem solving. Although students with disabilities hear other students' thinking strategies in the *After* phase of each lesson, they frequently cannot keep up with the rapid pace of the sharing. Without extra time to reprocess the conversation, students with disabilities may not have access to these strategies. More explicit approaches are also less dependent on the student's ability to draw ideas from past experience or to operate in a self-directed manner.

There are some aspects of explicit strategy instruction that have distinct disadvantages for students with special needs, particularly the times students must rely on memory—often one of their weakest skills. There is also the concern that highly teacher-controlled approaches promote prolonged student dependency on teacher assistance. This is of particular concern for students with disabilities because many are described as passive learners.

Students learn what they have the opportunity to practice. Students who are never given opportunities to engage in self-directed learning (based on the assumption that this is not an area of strength) will be deprived of the opportunity to develop skills in this area. In fact, the best explicit instruction is scaffolded, meaning it moves from a highly structured, single-strategy approach to multiple models, including examples, and nonexamples. It also includes immediate error correction followed by the fading of prompts to help students move to independence. To be effective, explicit instruction must include making mathematical relationships explicit (so that students, rather than only learning how to do that day's mathematics, make connections to other mathematical ideas). Because making connections is a major component in how students learn, it must be central to learning strategies for students with disabilities.

Concrete, Semi-Concrete, Abstract (CSA)

The CSA (concrete, semi-concrete, abstract) intervention has been used in mathematics education for a variety of topics for years (Dobbins, Gagnon, & Ulrich, 2014; Griffin, Jossi, & van Garderen, 2012; Heddens, 1964; Hunter, Bush, & Karp, 2014). Based on Bruner and Kennedy's stages of representation (1965), this model reflects concrete representations such as manipulative materials that encourage learning through movement or action (enactive stage) to semi-concrete representations of drawings or pictures (iconic stage) and learning through abstract symbols (symbolic stage). Built into this approach is the return to visual models and concrete representations as students need or as students begin to explore new concepts or extensions of concepts learned previously. As students share reasoning that shows they are beginning to understand the mathematical concept, there can be a shift to semi-concrete representations. This is not to say that this is a rigid approach that only moves to abstraction after the other phases. Instead, it is essential that there is parallel modeling of number symbols throughout this approach to explicitly relate the concrete models and visual representations to the corresponding numerals and equations. CSA also includes modeling the mental conversations that go on in your mind as you help students articulate their own thinking. Used particularly in a combination with explicit strategy instruction, this approach has met with high levels of success for students with disabilities (Flores, Hinton, & Strozier, 2014; Mancl, Miller, & Kennedy, 2012, Miller & Kaffar, 2011).

Peer-Assisted Learning

Students with special needs also benefit from other students' modeling and support (McMaster & Fuchs, 2016). The basic notion is that students learn best when they are placed in the role of an apprentice working with a more skilled peer or "expert." Although the peer-assisted learning approach shares some of the characteristics of the explicit strategy instruction model, it is distinct because knowledge is presented on an "as-needed" basis as opposed to a predetermined sequence. The students can be paired with older students or peers who have more sophisticated understandings of a concept. At other times, tutors and tutees can reverse roles during the tasks. Having students with disabilities "teach" others is an important part of the learning process, so giving students with special needs a chance to explain their thinking to a peer or younger student is a valuable learning tool.

Think-Alouds

When you use a "think-aloud" as an instructional strategy you demonstrate the steps to accomplish a task while verbalizing the thinking process and reasoning that accompany the actions. Remember, don't start with where your thinking is; assess and start where the student's thinking is. Let's look at an example. Consider a problem in which fourth-grade students are given the task of determining how much paint will be needed to cover the walls of their classroom. Rather than merely demonstrating, for example, how to use a ruler to measure the distance across a wall, the think-aloud strategy would involve talking through the steps and identifying the reasons for each step while measuring the space. As you place a tick mark on the wall to indicate where the ruler ended in the first measurement, you might state, "I used this line to mark off where the ruler ends. How should I use this line as I measure the next section of the wall? I know I have to move the ruler, but should I repeat what I did the first time?" All of this dialogue occurs prior to placing the ruler for a second measurement.

Often teachers share alternatives about how else they could have carried out the task. When using this metacognitive strategy, try to talk about and model possible approaches (and the reasons behind these approaches) in an effort to make your invisible thinking processes visible to students.

Although you will choose any of these strategies as needed for interventions, your goal is always to work toward high student responsibility for learning. Movement to higher levels of understanding of content can be likened to moving up a hill. For some, formal stair steps with support along the way is necessary (explicit strategy instruction); for others, ramps with encouragement at the top of the hill will work (peer-assisted learning). Other students can find a path up the hill on their own with some guidance from visual representations (CSA approach). All people can relate to the need to have different support during different times of their lives or under different circumstances, and it is no different for students with special needs (see Table 6.2). Yet students with special needs must eventually learn to create a path to new learning on their own, as that is what will be required in the real world after formal education ends. Leaving students with only knowing how to climb steps with support and then later in life having them face hills without constant assistance and encouragement from others will not help them attain their life goals.

Table 6.2 Common stumbling blocks for students with disabilities.

Stumbling Blocks for Students	What Will I Notice?	What Should I Do?
Trouble forming mental representations of mathematical concepts	• Can't interpret a number line with fractional intervals • Has difficulty going from a story about a garden plot (finding area) to a graph or dot paper representation	• Explicitly teach the representation—for example, demonstrate exactly how to draw a diagram (e.g., partition the number line) • Use larger versions of the representation (e.g., number line or grid paper) so that students can move on or interact with the model
Difficulty accessing numerical meanings from symbols (issues with number sense)	• Has difficulty with basic facts; for example, doesn't recognize that 3×5 is equal to 5×3 • Does not understand the meaning of the equal sign • Can't interpret if an answer is reasonable	• Explicitly teach multiple ways of representing a number showing the variations at the same time • Use a number balance to support understanding of the equal sign • Use multiple representations for a single problem to show how it would be carried out in a variety of ways (base-ten blocks, illustrations, and numbers) rather than using multiple problems
Difficulty keeping numbers and information in working memory	• Gets confused when multiple strategies are shared by other students during the *After* portion of the lesson • Forgets how to start the problem-solving process	• Record in writing the ideas of other students during discussions • Incorporate a chart that lists the main steps in problem solving as an independent guide or make bookmarks with questions the students can ask themselves as self-prompts
Lacks organizational skills and the ability to self regulate	• Misses steps in a process • Writes computations in a way that is random and hard to follow	• Use routines as often as possible or provide self-monitoring checklists to prompt steps along the way • Use graph paper to record problems or numbers • Create math walls as a reference
Misapplies rules or overgeneralizes	• Applies rules such as "Always add a zero on the end of a number when you multiply it by ten" too literally, resulting in errors such as $2.5 \times 10 = 2.50$ • Mechanically applies algorithms—for example, adds $\frac{7}{8}$ and $\frac{12}{13}$ and generates the answer $\frac{19}{21}$.	• Always give examples as well as counter examples to show how and when "rules" should be used and when they should not. • Tie all rules into conceptual understanding, don't emphasize memorizing rote procedures or practices

Teaching and Assessing Students with Learning Disabilities

Students with learning disabilities often have very specific difficulties with perceptual or cognitive processing that may affect memory; general strategy use; attention; the ability to speak or express ideas in writing; the ability to perceive auditory, visual, or written information; or the ability to integrate abstract ideas (Berch & Mazzocco, 2007). Although specific learning needs and strategies that work for one child may not work for another, there are some general ideas that can help as you plan instruction for students with special needs. The following questions should guide your planning:

1. What organizational, behavioral, and cognitive skills are necessary for the students with special needs to derive meaning from this activity?
2. Which students have significant weaknesses in any of these skills or concepts?
3. What are the children's strengths?
4. How can I provide additional support in these areas of weakness so that students with special needs can focus on the conceptual task in the activity? (Karp & Howell, 2004, p. 119)

Each phase of the lesson evokes specific planning considerations for students with disabilities. Some strategies apply throughout a lesson. The following discussion is based on Karp and Howell (2004) and although not exhaustive provides some specific suggestions for offering support throughout the lesson while maintaining the challenge.

1. *Structure the Environment*
   - *Centralize attention.* Move the student close to the board or teacher. Face students when you speak to them and use gestures. Remove competing stimuli.
   - *Avoid confusion.* Word directions carefully and ask the student to repeat them. Give one direction at a time. Use the same language for consistency. For example, talk about base-ten materials as ones, tens, and hundreds rather than interchanging those names with "flats," "rods," and other words about their shape rather than their value.
   - *Create smooth transitions.* Ensure that transitions between activities have clear directions and there are limited chances to get off task.

2. *Identify and Remove Potential Barriers*
   - *Help students remember.* Recognize that memory is often not a strong suit for students with disabilities and therefore develop mnemonics (memory aids) for familiar steps or write directions that can be referred to throughout the lesson. For example, **STAR** is a mnemonic for problem solving: **S**earch the word problem for important information; **T**ranslate the words into models, pictures, or symbols; **A**nswer the problem; **R**eview your solution for reasonableness (Gagnon & Maccini, 2001).

   - *Provide vocabulary and concept support.* Explicit attention to vocabulary and symbols is critical throughout the lesson. Preview essential terms and related prior knowledge/concepts, create a "math wall" of words and symbols to provide visual cues, and connect symbols to their precise meanings.

✐ Teaching Tip

Note that searching the word problem for important information is different from identifying "key words" as the use of a "key word approach" is not effective.

- *Use "friendly" numbers.* Instead of using $6.13 use $6.00 to emphasize conceptual understanding rather than mixing computation and conceptual goals. Incorporate this technique when computation and operation skills are *not* the lesson objective.

- *Vary the task size.* Assign students with special needs fewer problems to solve. Some students can become frustrated by the enormity of the task.

- *Adjust the visual display.* Design assessments and tasks so that there is not too much on a single page. The density of words, illustrations, and numbers on a page can overload students. Find ways to put one problem on a page, increase font size, or reduce the visual display.

3. *Provide Clarity*
    - *Repeat the timeframe.* Give students additional reminders about the time left for exploring materials, completing tasks, or finishing assessments. This helps students with time management.

    - *Ask students to share their thinking.* Use the think-aloud method or think-pair-share strategy.

    - *Emphasize connections.* Provide concrete representations, pictorial representations, and numerical representations. Have students connect them through carefully phrased questions. Also, connect visuals, meanings and words. For example, as you fold a strip of paper into fourths, point out the part-whole relationship with gestures as you pose a question about the relationship between $\frac{2}{4}$ and $\frac{1}{2}$.

    - *Adapt delivery modes.* Incorporate a variety of materials, images, examples, and models for visual learners. Some students may need to have the problem or assessment read to them or generated with voice creation software. Provide written instructions in addition to oral instructions.

    - *Emphasize the relevant points.* Some students with disabilities may inappropriately focus on the color of a cube instead of the quantity of cubes when filling a prism to measure volume.

    - *Support the organization of written work.* Provide tools and templates so students can focus on the mathematics rather than the creation of a table or chart. Also use graphic organizers, picture-based models, and paper with columns or grids.

    - *Provide examples and nonexamples.* Give examples of acute angles as well as angles that are not acute. Help students focus on the characteristics that differentiate the examples from those that are not examples.

4. *Consider Alternative Assessments*
    - *Propose alternative products.* Provide options for how to demonstrate understanding (e.g., a verbal response that is written by someone else, voice recorded, or modeled with a manipulative). Use voice recognition software or word prediction software that can generate a whole menu of word choices when students type a few letters.

    - *Encourage self-monitoring and self-assessment.* Students with learning disabilities often need support in self-reflection. Asking them to review an assignment or assessment to explain what was difficult and what they think they got right, can help them be more independent and take greater responsible for their learning.

    - *Consider feedback charts.* Help students monitor their growth by charting progress over time.

5. *Emphasize Practice and Summary*
    - *Consolidate ideas.* Create study guides that summarize the key mathematics concepts and allow for review. Have students develop their own study guides.

    - *Provide extra practice.* Use carefully selected problems (not a large number) and allow the use of familiar physical models.

Not all of these strategies will apply to every lesson or every student with special needs, but as you are thinking about a particular lesson and certain individuals in your class, you will find that many of these will allow your students to engage in the task and accomplish the learning goals of the lesson. Explore Strategies for Making Math Accessible for a handy collection of cards that you can use to think about particular students as you plan. The Center for Applied Special Technology (CAST) website contains resources and tools to support the learning of all students, especially those with disabilities, through universal design for learning (UDL).

Adapting for Students with Moderate/Severe Disabilities

Students with moderate/severe disabilities (MSD) often need extensive modifications and individualized supports to learn mathematics. This population of students may include those with severe autism, sensory disorders, limitations affecting movement, cerebral palsy, processing disorders such as intellectual disabilities and combinations of multiple disabilities.

Originally, the curriculum for students with severe disabilities was called "functional," in that it often focused on life-related skills such as managing money, telling time, using a calculator, measuring, and matching numbers to complete such tasks as entering a telephone number or identifying a house number. Now directives and assessments have broadened the curriculum to address the grade-level expectations in the *Common Core State Standards* (CCSSO, 2010) or other curriculum policy documents.

At a beginning level, develop number sense, use measuring tools, compare graphs, explore place-value concepts (often linked to money use), use the number line, and compare quantities. When possible, the content should be connected to life skills and features of jobs. Shopping skills or activities in which food is prepared are both options for mathematical problem solving. At other times, link mathematical learning objectives to everyday events in a practical way. For example, when the operation of division is studied, figuring how candy can be equally shared at Halloween or how game cards can be dealt would be appropriate. Students can also undertake a small project such as constructing a box to store different items as a way to explore shapes and both length and volume measurements.

Do not believe that all basic facts must be mastered before students with moderate or severe disabilities can move forward in the curriculum; students can learn geometric or measuring concepts without having mastered all basic facts. Geometry for students with moderate and severe disabilities is more than merely identifying shapes, but is in fact critical for orienting in the real world. Concepts such as parallel and perpendicular lines and curves and straight sides become helpful for interpreting maps of the local area. Students who learn to count bus stops and judge time can be helped to successfully navigate their world.

The handout Math Activities for Students with Moderate or Severe Disabilities offers ideas across the curriculum appropriate for teaching students with moderate to severe disabilities. Also, look at the Additional Strategies for Supporting Students with Moderate/Severe Disabilities handout for more ideas on how you can modify grade-level instruction.

Planning for Students Who Are Mathematically Gifted

Students who are mathematically gifted include those who have high ability or high interest. Some may be gifted with an intuitive knowledge of mathematical concepts, whereas others have a passion for the subject even though they may work hard to learn it. Many students' giftedness becomes apparent to parents and teachers when they grasp and articulate mathematics concepts at an age earlier than expected. They are often found to easily make connections between topics of study and frequently are unable to explain how they quickly got an answer (Rotigel & Fello, 2005).

Many teachers have a keen ability to spot talent when they note students who have strong number sense or visual/spatial sense (Gavin & Sheffield, 2010). Note that these teachers are not pointing to students who are fast and speedy with their basic facts, but those who have the ability to reason and make sense of mathematics.

Do not wait for students to demonstrate their mathematical talent; instead develop it through a challenging set of tasks and inquiry-based instruction (VanTassel-Baska & Brown 2007). Generally, as described in the RtI model, high-quality core instruction is able to respond to the varying needs of diverse learners, including the talented and gifted. Yet for some of your gifted students, the core instruction may prove not to be enough of a challenge.

Pre-assessing students by curriculum-based tests and also other measures such as concept maps prior to instruction allows the evaluation of what the student already knows and in some cases identifies how many grade levels ahead they might be (Rakow, 2012). Without this information the possibility of targeting the next steps and adaptations becomes guess work.

There are four basic categories for adapting mathematics content for gifted mathematics students: *acceleration and pacing*, *depth*, *complexity*, and *creativity* (Johnsen, Ryser, & Assouline, 2014). In each category, your students should apply, rather than just acquire, information. The emphasis on applying, implementing, and extending ideas must overshadow the mental collection of facts and concepts.

Acceleration and Pacing

Acceleration recognizes that your students may already understand the mathematics content that you plan to teach. Some teachers use "curriculum compacting" (Reis & Renzulli, 2005) to give a short overview of the content and assess students' ability to respond to mathematics tasks that would demonstrate their proficiency. Allowing students to increase the pace of their own learning can give them access to curriculum different from their grade level while demanding more independent study. But, moving students to higher mathematics (by moving them up a grade, for example) will not succeed in engaging them as learners if the instruction is still at a slow pace. Research reveals that when gifted students are accelerated through the curriculum they are more likely to explore STEM (science, technology, engineering, and mathematics) fields (Sadler & Tai, 2007).

Depth

Enrichment activities go into depth beyond the topic of study to content that is not specifically a part of your grade-level curriculum but is an extension of the original mathematical tasks. For example, while studying place value both to very large numbers and decimals, mathematically gifted students can stretch their knowledge to study other bases such as base five, base eight, or base twelve. This provides an extended view of how our base-ten numeration system fits within the broader system of number theory. Other times the format of enrichment can involve studying the same topic as the rest of the class while differing on the means and outcomes of the work. Examples include group investigations, solving real problems in the community, writing data-based letters to outside audiences, or identifying applications of the mathematics learned.

Complexity

Another strategy is to increase the sophistication of a topic by raising the level of complexity or pursuing greater depth to content, possibly outside of the regular curriculum or by making interdisciplinary connections. For example, while studying a unit on place value, mathematically gifted students can deepen their knowledge to study other numeration systems such as Roman, Mayan, Egyptian, Babylonian, Chinese, and Zulu. This provides a multicultural view of how our numeration system fits within the historical number systems (Mack 2011). In the algebraic thinking strand, when studying sequences or patterns of numbers, mathematically gifted students can learn about Fibonacci sequences and their appearances in the natural world in shells and plant life. See the **Mathematics Integration Plan** that can be used to help plan ways to integrate core content for a gifted student or depending on the student's ability can be used by students to create independent explorations or research. Using this approach, students can think about a mathematics topic through another perspective or through an historic or even futuristic viewpoint.

Creativity

By presenting open-ended problems and investigations students can use divergent thinking to examine mathematical ideas—often in collaboration with others. These collaborative experiences could include students from a variety of grades and classes volunteering for special mathematics projects, with a classroom teacher, principal, or resource teacher taking the lead. Their creativity can be stimulated through the exploration of mathematical "tricks" using binary numbers to guess classmates' birthdays or design large-scale investigations of the amount of food thrown away at lunchtime (Karp, K. & Ronau, R., 1997). A group might create tetrahedron kites or find mathematics in art (Bush, Karp, Lenz, & Nadler, 2016). Another aspect of creativity provides different options for students in culminating performances of their understanding, such as demonstrating their knowledge through inventions, experiments, simulations, dramatizations, visual displays, and oral presentations.

Noted researcher on the mathematically gifted, Benbow (Read, 2014), states that acceleration combined with depth through enrichment is best practice. Then learning is not only sped up but the learning is deeper and at more complex levels.

Strategies to Avoid

There are a number of ineffective approaches for gifted students, including the following:

1. *Assigning more of the same work.* This is the least appropriate way to respond to mathematically gifted students and the most likely to result in students hiding their ability.

2. *Giving free time to early finishers.* Although students find this rewarding, it does not maximize their intellectual growth and can lead to students hurrying to finish a task.

3. *Assigning gifted students to help struggling learners.* Routinely assigning gifted students to teach other students who are not meeting expectations does not stimulate their intellectual growth and can place them in socially uncomfortable or sometimes undesirable situations.

4. *Providing gifted pull-out opportunities.* Unfortunately, generalized gifted programs are often unrelated to the regular mathematics curriculum (Assouline & Lupkowski-Shoplik, 2011). Disconnected, add-on experiences are not enough to build more complex and sophisticated understanding of mathematics.

5. *Offering independent enrichment on the computer.* Although there are excellent enrichment opportunities to be found on the Internet and terrific apps, the practice of having gifted students use a computer program that focuses on skills does not engage them in a way

that will enhance conceptual understanding, critical thinking or support students' ability to justify their thinking.

Sheffield writes that gifted students should be introduced to the "joys and frustrations of thinking deeply about a wide range of original, open-ended, or complex problems that encourage them to respond creatively in ways that are original, fluent, flexible, and elegant" (1999, p. 46). Accommodations, modifications, and interventions for mathematically gifted students must strive for this goal.

Stop and Reflect

How is equity in the classroom different from teaching all students equitably?

7

Collaborating with Families and Other Stakeholders

Sharing the Message with Stakeholders

Teaching mathematics developmentally, addressing the increased content demands articulated in the *Common Core State Standards* initiative (CCSSO, 2010), and ensuring that students are mathematically proficient requires *everyone's* commitment. We often hear educators make statements such as, "You must have the principal's support" and "You need to get parents on board," and we nod our heads in agreement. As educators it is not enough to know what the changes are; we must also understand *why* change in mathematics content and teaching strategies is needed and be able to share this message in jargon-free ways with families, administrators, politicians, and other stakeholders. And, involving stakeholders is not only about getting support for your mathematics program—it is about supporting student learning! Parental involvement at school results in higher levels of student academic achievement (Barnard, 2004; Lee & Bowen, 2006).

In this chapter, we discuss ideas for developing a collaborative community that understands and is able to support high-quality mathematics teaching and learning for every student. Also, we hope that this chapter (and the rest of this book) is helpful in presenting a strong case for why we need to teach developmentally-appropriate, student-centered mathematics.

Changes to the mathematics curriculum—new textbooks, content topics, technologies, teaching philosophies, instructional strategies, and routines—warrant communication with parents, principals, and community leaders. Communicating with families is one of the most important components of successfully implementing a new mathematics curriculum (Bay, Reys, & Reys, 1999). Without such opportunities for communication, people may draw their own conclusions about the effectiveness of the mathematics curriculum, develop frustrations and negative opinions about what is happening in their child's classroom or school, and communicate this apprehension to other parents and community leaders. This has certainly been the case in states that initially adopted the *Common Core State Standards for Mathematics* (CCSS-M), and then had it voted out again. The reasons people opposed the standards (or support them) are sometimes not actually characteristics of the CCSS-M, but rather characteristics that have been assigned to the CCSS-M.

Rather than hope that there will be support for changes in mathematics teaching and learning, it is important to anticipate possible questions and concerns and develop a plan to address them (Bay-Williams & Meyer, 2003). Table 7.1 highlights common questions parents and other stakeholders ask about mathematics programs.

Table 7.1 Questions related to change in mathematics teaching and learning.

Category	Types of Questions
Why Change?	• Why is mathematics teaching changing? • Is there evidence that this approach or curriculum is effective? • What are the *Common Core State Standards* and why do we have national standards? • Where can I learn more about the *Common Core State Standards*?
Pedagogy	• Why isn't the teacher teaching? (And what is the point of reinventing the wheel?) • Why is my child struggling more than in previous years? • Are students doing their own work when they are in groups? Is my child doing the work of other students? • Are calculators and other technology interfering with my child's fluency?
Content	• Is my child learning the basic skills? • Why is my child learning different algorithms/strategies (than I learned) for doing the operations? • Why are there less skills and more story problems?
Student Learning and Outcomes	• Will these standards prepare my child for middle school, high school, college, and beyond (e.g., ready for ACT, SAT, Algebra in eighth or ninth grade)? • Why is my child struggling more than in previous years? • How can I help my child with their homework; to be successful?

Be proactive! Don't wait for concerns or questions to percolate. Providing a forum for parents, administrators, and community leaders around mathematics highlights the importance of the subject and gives stakeholders confidence that your school is a great place for preparing children for college and beyond. In the sections that follow, we share possible responses to the four areas of concern's in Table 7.1.

Why Change?

Change in many domains is considered a good thing. Why, then, is any change in mathematics teaching met with resistance? Additionally, the same people who claim to not be good at math or to not like math, are often the ones most concerned about changes in mathematics teaching and learning. Navigating through change in mathematics requires strong justification for why the change is occurring, and the justification must resonate with the particular stakeholders' concerns and experiences.

Changes in Content

Reflecting on how other professions—from doctors to mechanics to dentists to bankers to hair stylists—have changed their practices over the past 25-plus years can make for an interesting comparison. Many fields have changed based on changes in society, different desired outcomes, available tools and technologies, research on what works, and new requirements within the job.

Another approach is to share research on the *ineffectiveness* of the traditional U.S. approach to teaching mathematics. The Trends in International Mathematics and Science Study (TIMSS), an international study conducted regularly that includes many countries, continues to find that U.S. students achieve at an average level in fourth grade, then below average in mathematics than international students in eighth grade and high school. Discuss the implications of unpreparedness for students who want to seek higher-paying jobs on what is now an international playing field.

Evidence for Change

Just as research and advancements have changed procedures doctors and mechanics use, research and advancements have informed alterations in procedures used in mathematics. In teaching mathematics, this can be what we have learned about teaching (e.g., to start with concrete tools or to make connections explicit) or what we have learned about specific content (e.g., that writing equations in nontraditional ways improves student understanding of equivalence [McNeil, Fyfe, Petersen, Dunwiddie, & Brletic-Shipley, 2011]). Also, in nearly all careers, certain mathematical proficiencies are essential: being able to select appropriate tools, determine and implement a strategy or algorithm, communicate and compare approaches, and reflect on the result of a procedure or solution. In other words, preparing students to be college and career ready, means addressing the mathematical proficiencies described in the CCSS Mathematical Practices and NCTM Process Standards.

CCSS Mathematics

Chapter 1 addressed the CCSS. Here we focus on advocating with stakeholders related to the standards. If you are teaching in a "Common Core" state, then you may have encountered a number of questions about the CCSS and/or heard various incorrect facts communicated about the CCSS-Mathematics. CCSSI provides a list of myths and facts (see http://www.corestandards.org/about-the-standards/myths-vs-facts/). Here we summarize six common (and detrimental) myths related to mathematics (with facts in *italics* afterward):

Myth 1.   CCSS are national standards. *Fact: CCSS was designed by Governor's and State School Officers. They were adopted by states, and states can add to the core as they see fit. States are in charge of implementation and assessment of students.*

Myth 2.   CCSS-Mathematics lowers existing state standards. *Fact: An analysis of state standards shows that the common core sets higher expectations than any individual state standards (and states can add more rigor if they choose).*

Myth 3.   CCSS are not internationally benchmarked. *Fact: This was a significant purpose in creating the standards.*

Myth 4.   CCSS do not prepare students for algebra in grade 8. *Fact: Those that complete CCSS-M through grade 7 can take algebra in grade 8.*

Myth 5. CCSS content is not in the right place. *Fact: Content was placed based on learning trajectories and research on student learning.*

Myth 6. CCSS dictates how teachers should teach. *Fact: The standards simply list what mathematics should be learned at what level. The Mathematical Practices describe what a mathematically proficient student can do. How to reach these outcomes for what a student should know and do are not addressed in the standards.*

Whether your state is or is not using the CCSS-M, there are no doubt times when change in mathematics teaching and learning need to be communicated to various stakeholders. These messages must be carefully composed! We sometimes say things that, although well intentioned, increase the concerns of stakeholders rather than reassure them. Table 7.2 provides three such examples.

Stop and Reflect

Consider a statement you have heard or used with families. Ask yourself, "How might a parent (or other stakeholder) respond if he or she heard this statement?" "What might the parent misinterpret?" "How might my principal respond?" Then, read the responses in the table to see whether they represent stakeholders like those in your setting.

Table 7.2 Statements and possible (unintended) interpretations of the statements.

Original Statement	What a Stakeholder Might Think	A Stronger, Carefully Composed Statement
"The [mathematics program] still addresses skills, but it also includes concepts."	"Why are they bringing skills up? They must be taking those away. My child/U.S. children have to know basics. How can I put a stop to this?"	"The skills in the [mathematics program] are expanding from what we once learned and now include . . ."
"It is important for students to learn from one another, so I will be more in the role of facilitator."	"The teacher is not teaching? My child does better when things are explained clearly. When I come to see you teach, what am I looking for if you are just letting the kids learn on their own?"	"In our classroom, we learn from one another. I give carefully selected tasks for students to discuss, and then we talk about them together so that everyone has a chance to learn the mathematics we are doing, and that approach gives me the chance to work one-on-one as needed."
"This year, we are doing a whole new mathematics program that the state has adopted."	"My worst nightmare—an experiment of something new during the years my child is in elementary school. This will cause problems for the rest of his life."	"We are doing some new things in order to make sure your child is well prepared for . . . [or that our program is the best available]. You might have noticed that last year we [added writing as a component to our math program]. This year, here are the big things we hope to accomplish . . ."

Initially, these statements may not seem harmful, but they can set off alarms from the lens of a stakeholder. Consider these reactions, and then review the shifted language in the third column, which communicates a stronger (and less potentially disconcerting) message. It is very important to convey to stakeholders an excitement for and pride in your mathematics program. Being tentative, reserved, vague, or silent on the mathematics program can only raise concerns in the community. Help parents and administrators to understand that the mathematics program students are experiencing aligns with best practices in education, represents what students need to know in today's world, and prepares students for mathematics at the next level as well as the mathematics they need for life.

Pedagogy

When stakeholders ask questions that point to their belief that mathematics is best learned through direct instruction—just as they learned it—it is important to provide a rationale for why mathematics teaching and learning might be different now.

Teacher as Facilitator

Recall that two important findings about how children develop conceptual understanding is through (1) engaging in productive struggle and (2) making connections explicit (Hiebert & Grouws, 2007). Related to these two important research findings, compare the difference between being *shown* how to do something (e.g., "This is how you find perimeter; now practice this") and *developing* an understanding of something (e.g., "What different fence options do you have when trying to enclose 12 square meters for a garden and *how* did you calculate the perimeter?"). You can help parents identify the skills and concepts that are developed through these two experiences. Ask, "Where do you see the concept of perimeter? Where do you see the development of the procedure?" Point out that skills are (still) important, and students benefit by generating their own procedures and connecting those procedures to a solid understanding. As students explore carefully selected tasks they engage in productive struggle and have the opportunity to make connections among mathematical ideas and strategies.

Address the role of the teacher as *organizer* (organizes a worthwhile mathematical task), *facilitator* (facilitates student interaction), and *questioner* (asks questions to help students make connections or to deepen their understanding). Remind parents that just because the teacher is not *telling* their child what to do does not mean that the teacher is not teaching. The teacher is orchestrating the class so that each student develops the appropriate connections, understands the mathematics, has the ability to solve problems and is developing a disposition that they can do mathematics.

Cooperative Groups

Parents and other stakeholders may also wonder about how frequently their child works in cooperative groups because this may differ from their own mathematics learning experiences. Help parents see the role of others in their learning as they solved the problems and as they heard solutions from those who were working at other tables. Connect that experience to the value of cooperative learning. You can do this in a variety of ways:

1. *Share the one-page parent overview from the NCTM Families Ask department titled "Cooperative Learning" (Coates & Mayfield, 2009).* "Families Ask," a feature posted on the NCTM website and published in *Mathematics Teaching in the School*, provides over 20 excellent, written-for-parents discussions on a range of topics appropriate for Grades 3 through 5.

2. *Include a feature in your parent newsletter.* Early in the year, you can feature cooperative learning and address its importance across content areas. In mathematics, this can include the following benefits: hearing different strategies, building meaning, designing solution strategies, and justifying approaches—all of which are essential to building a strong understanding of mathematics and important life skills.

3. *Send home letters introducing math units.* If you are about to teach a unit on adding and subtracting fractions, a letter can help parents know the important aspects of the content. This is a great time to mention that students will work in groups so that they can see different ways to illustrate fractions with pictures, and explain the meaning of the procedure.

4. *Do a cooperative learning mathematics activity at a family math night or back-to-school event.* Use a task that lends itself to assigning roles to different members of the group and won't take long to solve. Have parents work with two to three others to solve the task.

Parents may initially worry that students working in groups are simply copying from other students and not learning. Share strategies you use to build in individual accountability and shared responsibility. For example, teachers may ask each student to record explanations in his or her notebook. At other times, you may assign specific roles to each member of the group.

> ### Teaching Tip
>
> Being proactive about communicating the *benefits* of cooperative learning, as well as how you build in *individual accountability* and *shared responsibility*, will go a long way toward converting parent concerns into parent support.

Use of Technology

Parents may be avid users of technology yet still have concerns about their child using calculators and computers in grades 3 through 5 when children haven't yet mastered their basic facts for multiplication or learned procedures for fractions and decimal computation. Even though research overwhelmingly finds that students using calculators achieve at least as much as those not using calculators, calculators are widely blamed for students' lack of reasoning and sense making. Reassure parents that students will learn the basic facts and procedures, and the calculator can support that learning.

The calculator is used when it is appropriate to support the mathematical goals of the day. For example, when the learning goal is understanding and developing formulas for volume, a calculator is appropriate. Share an example task. In a lesson on volume (fifth grade), students might bring boxes from home and measure them two ways. First, they see how many centimeter cubes fit in the box. Second, they measure the length, width, and height to the nearest centimeter and calculate the volume. These two ways are compared. In this case, the calculator helps keep the focus on volume, rather than on calculations with decimals.

An important message to parents is that mastery of basic facts should *not* be a prerequisite to using a calculator. Instead, students (and teachers) should be making good decisions about whether a calculator supports or detracts from solving a particular problem (and learning the intended mathematics).

Content

Basic Facts and Standard Algorithms

A common concern of parents is that their children are not learning standard algorithms or the procedures they remember using when they were in elementary or middle school. You must address (at least) two points related to this critical issue. First, the skills that parents are looking for (e.g., invert and multiply for dividing fractions) are still in the curriculum—they just may look different because they are presented in a way based on understanding, not just memorization. Standard algorithms are still taught but they are taught *along with* alternative (or invented) strategies that build on students' number sense and reasoning. Let parents experience that both invented and standard algorithms are important in being mathematically proficient by inviting them to solve the following problems:

$$1399 + 547 = \underline{\hspace{2cm}} \qquad 5009 - 998 = \underline{\hspace{1.5cm}}$$
$$487 + 345 = \underline{\hspace{2cm}} + 355$$

Ask for volunteers to share the ways that they thought about the problems. For the subtraction problem, for example, the following might be shared:

5000 take away 1000 is 4000, then add the 9 and 2 back on to get 4011.

998 up to 1000 is 2, up to 5000 is 4002, and up 9 more is 4011.

5009 to 5000 is 9, then down to 1000 is 4000 more (4009), and then down to 998 is 2 more (4011).

These invented strategies, over numerous problems, reinforce place-value concepts and the relationship between addition and subtraction. Noticing that these values are both near 1000 helps to select a strategy. The standard algorithm for this problem is very messy, and one that frequently results in computational errors. The best choice for solving this problem is one of the ways described above. The key to procedural fluency is to first assess the values in the problem and then decide how to solve it. This bird's-eye view of the problem is important in doing mathematics—rather than always doing the same thing regardless of the numbers. This is very evident in the third example, which can be solved with no computation if the relationships among the numbers are first noticed.

Second, what is "basic" in the 21st century is much more than computation. Many topics in upper elementary were not a part of the curriculum a generation ago (e.g., fraction multiplication and division). Looking together through the essential concepts in the *Common Core State Standards* or the NCTM *Curriculum Focal Points* helps parents see that the curriculum is not just an idea generated at their child's school but the national consensus on what upper elementary-school students need to learn.

Practice and Problem Solving

Parents may also wonder why there are fewer skill/practice problems and more story problems in the curriculum. Effective mathematics learning environments are rich in language. Real mathematics involves more "word" problems and far fewer "naked number" skill problems. In contrast to when the parents went to school, skills are now less needed in the workplace because of available technology, but the importance of number sense, reasoning, and being able to solve real problems has increased. Because some students struggle with reading and/or writing, share strategies you use to help them understand and solve story problems (Figure 7.1).

Figure 7.1

Share with parents how you support reading and problem solving.

Reading Strategies for Mathematics Problems

- Read aloud (whole class)

- Read a math problem with a friend

- Find and write the question

- Draw a picture of the problem

- Act out the problem

- Use a graphic organizer (recording page with problem-solving prompts)

- Discuss math vocabulary

- Play math vocabulary games

Student Learning and Outcomes

At the heart of parents' interest in school mathematics is wanting their child to be successful, not only in the current classroom but also at the next level of school and later on in the high-stakes assessments like the ACT or SAT for college entrance or to enter the workforce.

Preparation for College and Career

If your state has implemented the *Common Core State Standards*, you can share that the standards are for K–12 and designed to prepare students for college and future careers. The *Common Core State Standards* website has an increasing number of resources for parents (http://corestandards.org) to help them ensure that their child is college- and career-ready. Because the standards are at least as rigorous as prior state standards, and have an increased focus on student reasoning and sense making, they better prepare students for high-stakes assessments such as the ACT or SAT, which over the years have adapted to reflect changes in content expectations in high school curriculum, such as the increased focus on statistics (Jaschik, 2014; Peterson's, 2015). As noted in the CCSS myths and facts, these standards are more rigorous, and therefore better prepare students for high-stakes assessments, and still prepare students to take algebra in eighth or ninth grade.

Parents may be more interested in how your specific school is doing in preparing students for the future. Share evidence from your school of mathematics success, including stories about an individual student (no name given) or the success of a particular classroom, like the following one received by a principal:

> I was worried at the start of the year because my son has never liked math and was coming home with pretty complicated problems to solve. But, now he is coming home telling me all about the math problems he is doing at school (more like projects than practice!). As an aside, I am also learning a lot—I didn't learn this way, but I am finding the homework problems are really interesting as we figure them out. I wish I could have learned math this way when I was in school! I am just curious if this is something he will get to do again in fourth grade, or if this is just something the teacher is doing just for this year.

Such communications help parents see that there is a transition period and that, in the end, a standards-based approach helps engage students and build their understanding over time.

Productive Struggle

Parents may worry when they see their child struggle with a single mathematics problem because they may believe that fast means successful. But faster isn't smarter. The book *Faster isn't Smarter* (Seeley, 2009) is a great read on this topic written for families, educators, and policy makers. Seeley offers 41 brief messages, many of which can address parent questions about mathematics (e.g., "A Math Message to Families: Helping Students Prepare for the Future," "Putting Calculators in their Place: The Role of Calculators and Computation in the Classroom," and "Do It in Your Head: The Power of Mental Math"). As noted above, engaging students in productive struggle is one of the two most effective ways teachers can help students develop conceptual understanding (the other is making connections among mathematical ideas) (Bay-Williams, 2010; Hiebert & Grouws, 2007). Rather than presenting a series of simpler problems for students to practice, standards-based curricula characteristically focus on fewer tasks, each of which provides students with an opportunity for higher-level thinking, multiple strategy solutions, and more time focused on math learning.

Share the first Standard for Mathematical Practice (Figure 7.2), and ask the parents what they notice. Focus on the importance of *perseverance*. This is true in mathematics and in life. Reassure parents that some tasks take longer because of the nature of the tasks, not because their child lacks understanding. Mathematics is not nearly as much about speed and memorization as it is about being able to grapple with a novel problem, try various approaches from a variety of options, and finally reach an accurate answer.

Figure 7.2

Standard 1 from the Standards for Mathematical Practice.

---

1. Make sense of problems and persevere in solving them.

Mathematically proficient students start by explaining to themselves the meaning of a problem and looking for entry points to its solution. They analyze givens, constraints, relationships, and goals. They make conjectures about the form and meaning of the solution and plan a solution pathway rather than simply jumping into a solution attempt. They consider analogous problems, and try special cases and simpler forms of the original problem in order to gain insight into its solution. They monitor and evaluate their progress and change course if necessary. Older students might, depending on the context of the problem, transform algebraic expressions or change the viewing window on their graphing calculator to get the information they need. Mathematically proficient students can explain correspondences between equations, verbal descriptions, tables, and graphs or draw diagrams of important features and relationships, graph data, and search for regularity or trends. Younger students might rely on using concrete objects or pictures to help conceptualize and solve a problem. Mathematically proficient students check their answers to problems using a different method, and they continually ask themselves, "Does this make sense?" They can understand the approaches of others to solving complex problems and identify correspondences between different approaches.

Source: From Common Core State Standards for Mathematics. Published by *Common Core State Standards Initiative,* © 2010.

Administrator Engagement and Support

Teachers cite a supportive principal as one of the most essential components in successfully implementing a standards-based curriculum (Bay, Reys, & Reys, 1999). Principals play pivotal roles in establishing a shared vision for a problem-based mathematics program. Principals, however, often cannot take the time to attend the professional development workshops that are designed for teachers who will be teaching the mathematics program. And what they need to know is qualitatively different from what a classroom teacher needs to know.

Since the launch of the *Common Core State Standards,* school administrators, parents, and community members are more aware than ever about mathematics standards. If your state has not adopted the *Common Core State Standards,* there are still state-level standards that are the focus of mathematics goals and assessments. Even though principals are hearing more about mathematics standards, higher standards, and the need to ensure that all students are successful, it does not mean they understand what standards-based mathematics curriculum *is* in terms of the content or the related CCSS Standards for Mathematical Practice or NCTM Process Standards.

Administrators are likely to get bombarded with broad or specific questions from parents: "Is 'New Math' back?" "Why isn't the teacher teaching the procedures for multiplying and dividing?" "What are the Standards for Mathematical Practice?" or any of the other questions offered earlier in this chapter. When a principal is asked these questions, he or she needs to give a convincing response that is accurate and that also addresses the heart of the parents' concerns—that their child is going to get a sound math experience that will prepare him or her for college and career.

Meyer and Arbaugh (2008) suggest professional development specifically for principals. Although their focus is on the adoption of standards-based textbooks, the plan they outline applies to all principals who are seeking to be knowledgeable and effective advocates for implementing new standards or mathematics curricula. The following ideas are adapted from their suggested professional development to focus on one-on-one conversations.

1. *Contrast old and new curriculum.* As a first step, it is important to know what is new and different in the mathematics program. One way to start is to provide a set of materials that represent typical *Common Core State Standards*–aligned tasks alongside the previous curriculum. Point out the noticeable similarities and differences or the key features of the curriculum. (Note: It is important to focus on *both* similarities *and* differences—not *everything* is being replaced, and this is an important message.)

2. *Discuss how parents and students will respond.* Anticipate what will be noticed by parents (or their children): Which changes might be welcomed? Which changes might be worrisome? How will the welcome aspects be promoted and the worrisome aspects be explained?

3. *Experience the curriculum.* Invite the principal to visit your classroom or other classrooms where the Standards for Mathematical Practice or the NCTM Process Standards are being infused. Ask the principal to join a group of students and listen to their discussion of how they are solving a problem. Or organize a lesson when, in the *After* phase, the students actually present their solutions to the principal. For example, in fourth grade, have students show their different ways for multiplying fractions using visuals and explanations. If possible, ask the principal to solve one of the problems the students are doing and share his or her strategy with the class. This firsthand experience can provide the principal with a wonderful story to share with parents and with insights that won't be gained from reviewing standards documents.

4. *Discuss emerging issues.* Plan a regular time to meet with the principal to discuss what he or she has heard from families about the mathematics program. Discuss what you might do to respond to questions (some of the anticipated issues may already have been described in the preceding section on parents' concerns). If there is a question about a problem-based approach, Chapter 2 should be a great read for a principal, and contains talking points to share with others.

Finally, keep your principal apprised of successes and breakthroughs. These stories provide the principal with stories and evidence to share when pressed by parents or community members. Principals are very often your strongest advocates and are in a position to serve as buffers between school mathematics and the community.

Stop and Reflect

What do you think the parents of your students would most value about "teaching mathematics *through* problem solving," and how will you use your response to this question to build strong family support and engagement? (Repeat the question for other stakeholders, such as your principal.)

Family Engagement

Parents know the importance of mathematics for their child's future. They participate in their child's learning by supporting homework, attending back-to-school nights or PTA meetings, and by meeting with teachers, even if they may recall unpleasant experiences or difficulties with school mathematics from their own schooling. Understanding that memories of mathematics classes are not always pleasant for parents and appreciating parental support prepare us to suitably identify for parents the mathematics goals that students should be experiencing in the 21st century.

Communication with families is key to encouraging their support and involves using one-way, two-way, and three-way communication strategies (Figure 7.3).

Figure 7.3

Ways to communicate with families.

One-way communication strategies	Letters sharing the goals of a unit	Websites where resources and curriculum information are posted	Newsletters
Two-way communication strategies	Log of student work (signed or commented on by parent)	PTA meetings/open houses	One-on-one meetings, class or home visits
Three (or more)–way communication strategies	Family math nights	Conferences (with parent and child)	Log/journal of student learning with input from student, parent, and teacher

Numerous studies have found a positive relationship between the level of parental involvement and their child's achievement in school (e.g., Aspiazu, Bauer, & Spillett, 1998; Henderson et al., 2002). Parents need frequent opportunities to get information directly from the school leaders and teachers about their child's mathematics program, including the kind of instruction that might differ from what they experienced in their own schooling. Even if your school has been engaged in implementing a mathematics program for a decade that reflects the NCTM *Principles and Standards for School Mathematics* and now the *Common Core State Standards*, the program will still be new to the parents of your students.

Family Math Nights

There are many ways to conduct a family or community mathematics event, such as including a math component in a back-to-school night, discussing it in a PTA meeting, or hosting a showcase for a new mathematics program. One idea is to host a Math Orientation Workshop (Ernst & Ryan, 2014). The purpose of this event is to develop consistency between the way math is taught in school and the way parents help at home. Beyond a focus on the content, parents can learn about *dispositions* of effective problem solvers, including the importance of asking questions; developing persistence; using multiple ways to solve problems; learning from mistakes; and reflecting on whether solutions make sense (see Ernst and Ryan [2014] for more details on designing and implementing this event). Providing opportunities to parents to learn about specific mathematics topics prior to their children learning the topics can lead to increased relationships with parents and increased student achievement (Knapp, Jefferson, & Landers, 2013).

Critical to any plan is providing opportunities for parents to be learners of mathematics so that they can experience what it means to *do mathematics* (just like their children). When choosing mathematical tasks to use with parents, be sure the tasks focus on content that really matters to them and relates to what they already know is a part of the grades 3 through 5 curriculum (e.g., a task about fractions and a measurement activity are good ideas). Tasks throughout this book are ideal for a math night. Figure 7.4 contrasts two third-grade problems for learning about perimeter—one that is straightforward and lends to a procedural approach (add up the sides), and one that is designed for a teaching-through-problem-solving experience (explore and find different perimeters for a given area).

Teaching Tip

Welcome back or family math nights are a great time to have parent–child teams experience doing math tasks together.

Stop and Reflect   500 ⟳ 250   ⟲ ? 3% ▱ 8 ؟° ∞∩ ⤳ 2.5

What distinctions do you notice between the two tasks in Figure 7.2? What is valued as "doing mathematics" in both of the problems?

Figure 7.4

Problems to explore at a parent or community night.

Problem 1: Find the perimeter of this rectangle.

5 ft.

12 ft.

Problem 2: You want to put up a fence around a rectangular garden. You are enclosing an area of 36 square feet. What will be the dimensions of your garden and what amount of fencing will you need to buy? Is there more than one way to build your garden? If so, select the one you think is best and be ready to justify your choice.

The contrasting perimeter problems are ideal for discussing with parents what it means to do mathematics because they (1) offer a familiar context, (2) require minimum prior knowledge, (3) have multiple solution strategies, (4) involve using manipulatives (color tiles and/or grid paper), and (5) (in the second example) connect the mathematical ideas of area, perimeter, rectangles, and squares, as well as addition and multiplication. Another good choice is a fraction problem because not only are they central to the curriculum for grades 3 through 5, but also because understanding fractions is essential to be successful in algebra in middle school. They also bring to the forefront how teaching conceptually is better than the procedural approach the parents had when they were students. See Chapters 12 and 13 for more excellent activities related to fractions.

The potential each of these problems has to support and challenge students in making sense of mathematics should be made explicit during a discussion with parents. After giving parents time to do both tasks and discussing solution strategies (as you would with students), ask participants to consider the learning opportunities in the two contrasting tasks. Ask questions such as the following:

- What skills are being developed in each problem?
- Which problem gives more opportunity to make connections between mathematics and the real world?
- Which task would your child be more motivated to solve? Why?

Help parents identify the depth of the mathematics in the teaching-through-problem-solving task. Remind them that in grades 3 through 5, students are building important foundations for algebraic thinking—looking for patterns, reasoning, and generalizing. Help parents see these aspects in this measurement problem. Share the *Common Core State Standards* and the NCTM standards (in parent-friendly language), and focus on the goal of having students becoming mathematically proficient as described in those standards. Ask parents, "Where do you see these proficiencies being supported in the two tasks we did?"

Address any or all of the questions in Table 7.1 that apply to your setting. One way to do this is to have parents write their questions on note cards and collect them so you can identify common questions and decide the order in which to discuss each one.

Teaching Tip

Provide copies of the appropriate *Common Core State Standards* Introduction and Overview pages (the first two pages for each grade), and allow parents time to think about each "Critical Area."

Classroom Visits

Invite parents to engage in your mathematics lessons, observing or interacting with students. An invitation to come to a mathematics lesson or a math event (e.g., family math night) gives parents the chance to witness firsthand such things as how you ask questions, how problems can be solved in many ways, and how calculators can be used to support reasoning. They may notice that you encourage students to select their own strategy and explain how they know it works. Parents will also pick up on the language that you are using and will be able to reinforce that language at home. You can even provide a note-taking template that includes categories such as the following:

- What is the big idea of the lesson?
- What illustrations or tools are being used to help students (your child) understand?
- What are some questions the teacher is asking that I could also ask?
- What does the teacher do when a student (my child) is stuck or needs challenged?

Involving ALL Families

Some families are at all school events and conferences; others rarely participate. However, all families want their children to be successful in school. Parents who do not come to school events may have anxiety related to their own school experiences, or they may feel completely confident that the school and its teachers are doing well by their child and that they do not need to participate. In some cultures, questioning a teacher may be perceived as disrespectful. Rodríguez-Brown (2010, p. 352), a researcher on Hispanic families, writes, "It is not that Latino parents do not want to support their children's learning. . . . [They] believe that it is disrespectful to usurp the teacher's role."

Try to find ways to build a strong rapport with all families. Some strategies to consider include the following:

1. *Honor different strategies for doing mathematics.* While this is a recommendation in standards documents, it is particularly important for students from other countries because they may have learned different ways to do the operations (Civil & Planas, 2010).

2. *Communicate with positive notes and phone calls.* Be sure to find a way to compliment each student's mathematical thinking (not just a good score on quiz) at some point early in the school year.

3. *Host informal gatherings to discuss mathematics teaching and learning.* Having regular opportunities to meet with the parents allows the development of rapport and trust. Consider hosting events in out-of-school facilities. Schools in communities with a high level of poverty have found that having parent events at a community center or religious institution brings in families that are reluctant to come into a school.

4. *Incorporate homework that involves the family.* When a student brings in homework that tells about his or her family and you provide positive feedback or a personal comment, then you are establishing a two-way communication with the family via homework.

5. *Translate letters that are sent home.* If you are doing a class newsletter (for families) or a letter describing the next mathematics unit, make an effort to translate the letter into the native language of the families represented in your class. If you cannot do this, consider having the first class session include a component in which students write to their families about what they are about to do. Ask them to write in their parents' first language and to include visuals to support their writing. Ask parents to respond (in their language of choice). This is a great practice for helping students know what they need to learn, and it communicates to families that they are an important part of that learning.

6. *Post homework on your webpage.* For parents who are not native speakers of English, posting problems on your site makes it easier to take advantage of online translations. While these translations may not be perfectly accurate, they can help parents and students understand the language in the problems.

For more suggestions on ensuring that your mathematics tasks and homework are meeting the needs of culturally and linguistically diverse students, see Chapter 5 and read "NCTM Research Brief: Involving Latino and Latina Parents in Their Children's Mathematics Education" (Civil & Menéndez, 2010). For suggestions on students with special needs, see Chapter 6.

Homework Practices and Parent Coaching

You may have heard parents say, "I am not good at math" or "I don't like solving math problems." While parents may feel this way, such messages to their child can impede their success in mathematics. In fact, a parent's emotions are connected to the student's emotions, and these positive emotions are connected to better performance (Else-Quest, Hyde, & Hejmadi, 2008). It is our responsibility as educators to figure out ways to redirect parents to portray mathematics in a positive light.

Tips for Helping Parents Help Their Child

Explicitly teaching parents *how to* help their children has also been found to make a difference in supporting student achievement and student attitudes (Cooper, 2007; Else-Quest et al., 2008; Patall, Cooper, & Robinson, 2008). Take the following recommendations into consideration when thinking about the homework that you will assign to your students.

1. *Mimic the three-phase lesson model.* Table 2.5 describes the three-phase lesson model. Homework can reflect these general phases. Complete a brief version of the *Before* phase of a lesson to be sure the homework is understood before students go home. At home, students complete the *During* phase. When they return with the work completed, apply the sharing techniques of the *After* phase of the homework. Students can even practice the *After* phase with their family if you encourage this through parent or guardian communications. Some form of written work must be required so that students are held responsible for the task and are prepared for the class discussion.

2. *Use a distributed-content approach.* Homework can address content that has been taught earlier in the year as practice, that day's content as reinforcement, or upcoming content as groundwork. Interestingly, research has found that distributed homework (homework that combines all three components) is more effective in supporting student learning (Cooper, 2007). The exception is students with learning disabilities, who perform better when homework focuses on reinforcement of skills and current class lessons.

3. *Promote an "ask-before-tell" approach with parents.* Parents may not know how best to support their child when he or she is stuck or has gotten a wrong answer. One important thing you can do is to ask parents to implement an "ask-before-tell" approach (Kliman, 1999). This means that before parents explain something, they should ask their child to explain how he or she did it. The child may self-correct (a life skill), and if not, at least the parents can use what they heard from their child to provide targeted assistance. Teach successful homework strategies to students, and share these strategies with parents. For example, the following ideas, suggested by Wieman and Arbaugh (2014), can be posted in your classroom and sent home:

   - Look for examples in our notes or daily work. Try those problems again.
   - If you are stuck, take a break, then come back and try again.
   - If you are confused, write a statement or question describing what is confusing.
   - Ask for help using specific questions (from parents, peers, or online support sites)

4. *Provide good questioning prompts for parents.* Providing guiding questions for parents or guardians supports a problem-based approach to instruction as they help their children. Figure 7.5 provides guiding questions that can be included in the students' notebooks and shared with families. Translating questions for parents who are not native speakers of English is important. Often, a student can help you with this task.

Figure 7.5

Questions for families to help their children with homework.

These guiding questions are designed to help your child think through his or her math homework problems. When your child gets stuck, ask the following:

- What do you need to figure out? What is the problem about?
- What words are confusing? What words are familiar?
- Do you have similar problems to look at?
- What math words or steps do you use in class?
- Where do you think you should begin?
- What have you tried so far? What else can you try?
- Can you describe where you are stuck or what is confusing?
- Can you make a drawing or chart to help you think about the problem?
- Does your answer make sense?
- Is there more than one answer?

5. *Use Games and Interactives.* Find opportunities to assign games or interactives for homework. The intent is that the student plays with family members (e.g., parent, sibling). The game can be played as part of a lesson and then sent home to play two to three times, with a written summary of what happened as they played due the next day. Games can be assigned to develop fluency with such concepts as reinforcing basic

facts, order of operations, using symbolic notation for expressions and equations, and so on. Fixed-Factor War (Britt, 2015), is one such engaging activity that can be offered as a homework option at various times throughout the year.

Teaching Tip

Providing specific guidance to families makes a big difference in what to do (and *not* do) to help their children learn mathematics and be confident in doing mathematics.

GAME: FIXED FACTOR WAR

Use a deck of cards, removing face cards. Identify a factor (e.g., 5) and place one of those cards in the middle. Deal the rest of the cards to the two players, face down. Each player turns up a card, says the product, followed by the multiplication sentence, taking turns with who goes first. The player with the larger product gets the cards.

Example: Fixed Factor is 5. Player one turns up a 2 and says "Ten—Five times two equals ten (or two times five equals ten)." Player 2 two turns up a 6 and says, "30—Five times six equals thirty." If there is a tie—it is a 'war' and they repeat the process, but the winner of the next round wins both sets of cards.

Several features of this game make it a great choice for homework: It only requires a deck of cards. The student can choose the fixed product, or the parent can pick one for which they think their child needs practice. Finally, it sets up opportunities for mathematical discussion. For example, asking "How did you solve it?" and "What reasoning strategy might you use?" help the student to develop and practice strategies and parents to hear those strategies.

Many interactives and applets are available across content strands(some of which are shared throughout Part 2 of this book). Asking students to explore, play, or solve on an applet can be another way to engage families with students. A favorite is the *Factor Game* or *Factor Dazzle*, which can be found in Classroom Resources on the NCTM website, and other places. This is a fun strategy game that helps students practice factors and multiples, a skill for which they need to be fluent in order to solve operations involving rational numbers.

Homework of this nature communicates to families the problem-based or sense-making nature of your classroom and might help them see the value in this approach. A final note: A little bit goes a long way—if students are to spend time solving meaningful problems, then just a few engaging problems a night can accomplish more than a long set of practice problems.

Resources for Families

Parents will be better able to help to their child if they know where to find resources. The Internet can either provide a wealth of information or be an overwhelming distraction. Help parents locate the good places to find math support. First, check whether your textbook provides websites with online resources for homework, including tutorials, video tutoring, videos, connections to careers and real-world applications, multilingual glossaries, audio podcasts, and more. Second, post websites that are good general resources. Here are some examples:

- *Figure This! Math Challenges for Families.* This NCTM website has a teacher corner and a family corner. It offers outstanding resources to help parents understand standards-based mathematics, help with homework, and engage in *doing* mathematics with their children. It is also available in Spanish.

- *Math Forum*@NCTM. This very popular and useful site includes many features for teachers and families. For example, "Ask Dr. Math" is a great homework resource because students can write in their questions and get answers fairly quickly. Parents may also want to read or participate in math discussion groups, read about key issues for the mathematics community, or download some of the very interesting problems posted here.

- *National Library of Virtual Manipulatives* (NLVM) This site has numerous applets and virtual tools for learning about many mathematics topics, appropriate for the classroom and the home.

There are also great websites for specific content. For example, Conceptua Math has excellent applets for exploring fraction operations. Finally, print books can be important resources for teachers. Here are a couple that we recommend:

- *It's Elementary: A Parent's Guide to K5 Mathematics* (Whitenack, Cavey, & Henney, 2015). This book explains current teaching practices and fundamental math concepts, with many examples and student work.
- *What's Math Got to Do with It?: How Parents and Teachers Can Help Children Learn to Love Their Least Favorite Subject* (Boaler, 2009). Jo Boaler describes how math can be understandable and fun, how children can excel in math, and how parents and schools can help.

Teaching Tip

Don't forget the value of your own website as the first site for parents to visit for support. Post your unit letters to families, newsletters, access to homework assignments, possible strategies for doing the homework, and even successful student solutions.

Seeing and Doing Mathematics at Home

In the same way that families support literacy by reading and talking about books with their children, families can and should support numeracy. Because this has not been the practice in many homes, it means you, as the teacher, have the responsibility to help parents see the connection between numeracy and everyday life. Consider asking families to make the *Math Promise* (Legnard & Austin, 2014). Family members make this promise to one another, which means they explicitly agree they will do math together—get to know each other's mathematical reasoning, play math games, and notice mathematics in their daily lives. In her article "Beyond Helping with Homework: Parents and Children Doing Mathematics at Home," Kliman (1999) offers some excellent suggestions, which include asking parents to share anecdotes, find mathematics in the books they read, and create opportunities during household chores. Figure 7.6 provides a sample letter home that suggests these ideas to parents.

Trips in the car can include informal and fun mathematics explorations. For example, license plates can be noted and family members can try to use the numbers on the plate to create a true mathematics equation or someone can select a target number, and the values from the plate are used to try to reach that target number (Hildebrandt, Biglan, & Budd, 2013). Today's Date (Mistretta, 2013) is another activity that can be a part of informal family discussions. Today's Date involves taking the date (e.g., 18) and thinking of different expressions, ways to write it, and connections to personal interests (e.g., a favorite athletes number or the age of a cousin). These tasks have many possible solutions and can be used repeatedly at any time of the year.

Figure 7.6

Sample letter to parents regarding ways to infuse mathematics into their interactions with their child.

Making Math Moments Matter (M⁴)

Dear Families:

As a fifth grader, your child is increasingly aware of what is going on in the world. In that world is a lot of math! In our class this year we are working on **fractions** and **decimals**, as well as learning about **volume** of different containers. It will really help your child to <u>understand</u> and <u>see the importance</u> of math, if you find ways to talk about "math moments" (on any math topic, but especially fractions, decimals, and volume). We call it Making Math Moments Matter (M⁴ for short). Here are some ways to have fun with M⁴ at home.

Share stories. Share a math moment at dinner (or in the car). When have you used mathematics today (shopping, laundry, budgets, etc.)? Think of the many things you might have estimated—how long it will take to get to work, or to run a series of errands. Take turns sharing stories. We will share family math moments in class!

Connecting to reading. As they tell you about the book they are reading, ask quantity-type questions: What fractions (or percent) of the time is the main character at school? What fraction of the book have you read? What fraction will you read tonight?

Chores. Yes, chores! If it takes $\frac{3}{4}$ of an hour to do a load of laundry, how long will 3 loads take? If you walk the dog for 0.25 hour twice each day, how many hours is the dog walked in a week? A month? If you earn $5 an hour walking dogs, what might you earn in a week?

Scavenger hunts. Riding in the car can be more interesting if there are things to look for. Consider challenging your fifth grader to look for fractions, decimals, or percents on signs. Search for as many 3-D shapes as you can (e.g., a train car is a rectangular solid, a trash can is a cylinder, etc.).

8

Exploring Number and Operation Sense

BIG IDEAS

1 Addition and subtraction are connected. Addition names the whole in terms of the parts and subtraction names a missing part. This structure holds true whether students are considering whole numbers or other numbers such as fractions and decimals.

2 Multiplication involves counting groups of equal size and determining how many there are in all (multiplicative thinking) or using a representative set as a unit in a multiplicative comparison.

3 Multiplication and division are related. Division names a missing factor in terms of the known factor and the product. Division can be interpreted as fair sharing or as repeated subtraction.

4 Models can be used to solve contextual problems for all operations and to figure out what operation is involved in a problem, regardless of the size of the numbers. Models can also be used to give meaning to number sentences. Representing contextual situations with equations is at the heart of algebraic thinking.

Helping students learn to connect different meanings, interpretations, and relationships to the four operations of addition, subtraction, multiplication, and division can assist them in accurately and fluently applying these operations in real-world settings. This is the goal of this chapter and the Operations Core (National Research Council [NRC], 2009)—in which students learn to see mathematical situations in their day-to-day lives or in story problems and begin to make models of these situations in words, pictures, models, and/or numbers (e.g., equations).

The Operations Core builds and expands on the NRC's Number Core and Relations Core that are developed in the primary grades and will be extended in the discussion of number sense and place value in Chapter 10. As children learn to connect the big ideas listed earlier, they can and should simultaneously be developing more sophisticated ideas about number, recognizing ways to think about basic fact combinations, and accurately and fluently applying these operations in real-world situations. This develops *operation sense*.

In third grade students solve problems (including two-step problems) using all four operations and they develop an understanding of the relationship between multiplication and division including applying the properties of multiplication. In the fourth grade students expand the interpretation of multiplicative situations as a comparison and continue to solve multistep word problems including the interpretation of remainders. Fifth graders are expected to perform fluently with all operations using multi-digit whole numbers using algorithms, strategies that consider place value and the application of the properties of the operations (CCSSO, 2010).

As in earlier grades, contextual problems are the primary teaching tool that you can use to help children activate problem-solving strategies (Jong & Magruder, 2014; Schwartz, 2013) and gain a rich understanding of the operations. What might a good lesson that is built around contextual problems look like? The answer comes more easily if you think about children not just solving the problems but also using multiple representations to explain how they went about solving the problem and why they think they are correct. If they are recording these ideas on paper, whatever they put on their paper, whether a written explanation or a drawing they used to help them solve the problem, it should explain what they did well enough to allow someone else to understand it. With the emphasis on children explaining their thinking and reasoning, lessons should focus on two or three problems and the related discussions of strategies.

Developing Addition and Subtraction Operation Sense

Although students begin learning about addition and subtraction prior to third grade, which is where this book begins, there are structures that support the learning of additive situations that don't expire (Karp, Bush, & Dougherty, 2014). Instead, these same structures can support students' thinking about addition and subtraction with larger whole numbers as well as with fractions and decimals.

Addition and Subtraction Problem Structures

Let's begin with a look at three categories of problem structures for additive situations (which include both addition and subtraction), and later explore four problem structures for multiplicative situations (which include both multiplication and division). These categories help students develop a schema to separate important information and to structure their thinking. In particular, researchers suggest that students with disabilities should be explicitly taught these underlying structures so that they can identify important characteristics of the situations and determine when to add or subtract (Fagnant & Vlassis, 2013; Fuchs et al., 2004; Xin, Jitendra, & Deatline-Buchman, 2005). When students are exposed to new problems, the familiar characteristics will assist them in generalizing from similar problems on which they have practiced. Furthermore, teachers who are not aware of the variety of situations and corresponding structures may randomly offer problems to students without the proper sequencing that can support students' full grasp of the meaning of the operations. By knowing the logical structure of these problems, you will be able to

Standards for
Mathematical Practice

┌─────────────────────────┐
│ **7** **Look for and make** │
│ **use of structure.** ▶ │
└─────────────────────────┘

help children interpret a variety of real-world contexts. More importantly, you will need to present a variety of problem types (within each structure) as well as recognize which structures produce the greatest challenges for students.

Researchers have separated addition and subtraction problems into structures based on the kinds of relationships involved (Verschaffel, Greer, & DeCorte, 2007). These include change problems (*join* and *separate*), *part–part–whole* problems, and *compare* problems (Carpenter, Fennema, Franke, Levi, & Empson, 2014). The basic structure for each of these three categories of problems is illustrated in Figure 8.1.

Figure 8.1

Basic structures for addition and subtraction story problem types. Each structure has three numbers and any one of the three numbers can be the unknown.

Problem Type and Structure with Physical Action Involved: Change Problems

	Result Unknown	Change Unknown	Start Unknown
Join (add to) **(a)** 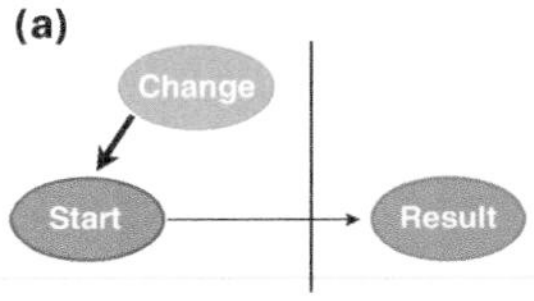	Sandra had 8 pennies. George gave her 4 more. How many pennies does Sandra have altogether? $8 + 4 = \square$	Sandra had 8 pennies. George gave her some more. Now Sandra has 12 pennies. How many did George give her? $8 + \square = 12$	Sandra had some pennies. George gave her 4 more. Now Sandra has 12 pennies. How many pennies did Sandra have to begin with? $\square + 4 = 12$
Separate (take from) **(b)** 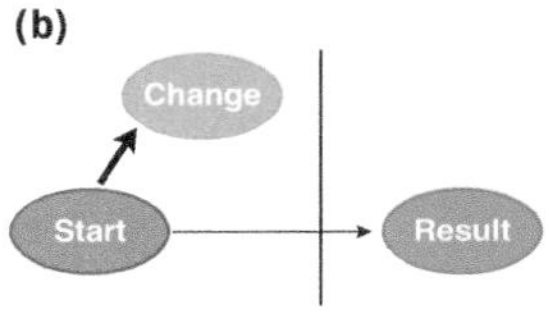	Sandra had 12 pennies. She gave 4 pennies to George. How many pennies does Sandra have now? $12 - 4 = \square$	Sandra had 12 pennies. She gave some to George. Now she has 8 pennies. How many did she give to George? $12 - \square = 8$	Sandra had some pennies. She gave 4 to George. Now Sandra has 8 pennies left. How many pennies did Sandra have to begin with? $\square - 4 = 8$

Problem Type and Structure with No Physical Action Involved: Part-Part-Whole and Compare Problems

	Whole Unknown	One Part Unknown	Both Parts Unknown
Part-Part-Whole **(c)** 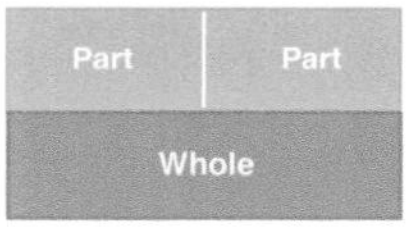	George has 4 pennies and 8 nickels. How many coins does he have? $4 + 8 =$	George has 12 coins. Eight of his coins are pennies, and the rest are nickels. How many nickels does George have? $12 = 4 + \square$ or $12 - 4 = \square$	George has 12 coins. Some are pennies and some are nickels. How many of each coin could he have? $12 = \square + \square$

	Difference Unknown	Larger Quantity Unknown	Smaller Quantity Unknown
	Situations of - How many more?		
Compare **(d)** 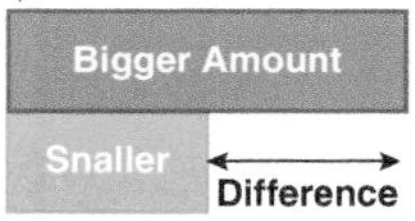	George has 12 pennies, and Sandra has 8 pennies. How many more pennies does George have than Sandra? $8 + \square = 12$	George has 4 more pennies than Sandra. Sandra has 8 pennies. How many pennies does George have? $8 + 4 = \square$	George has 4 more pennies than Sandra. George has 12 pennies. How many pennies does Sandra have? $\square + 4 = 12$
	Situations of - How many fewer?		
	George has 12 pennies. Sandra has 8 pennies. How many fewer pennies does Sandra have than George? $12 - 8 = \square$	Sandra has 4 fewer pennies than George. Sandra has 8 pennies. How many pennies does George have? $\square - 4 = 8$	Sandra has 4 fewer pennies than George. George has 12 pennies. How many pennies does Sandra have? $12 - 4 = \square$

Depending of which of the three quantities is unknown, a different problem type results. Each of the problem structures is illustrated with the story problems that follow using the number family 40, 80, 120. Note that the problems are described in terms of their structure and interpretation and not as addition or subtraction problems. Contrary to what you may have thought, a joining action does not always mean addition, nor do separate or remove actions always mean subtraction.

Examples of Change Problems

Join/Add To Problems.   For the action of joining, there are three quantities involved: an initial or *start amount*, a *change amount* (the part being added or joined), and the *result amount* (the total amount after the change takes place). In Figure 8.1(a) this is illustrated by the change being "added to" the start amount. See the Join Story Activity Page. Students can work with base-ten materials and model the problem on the graphic organizer. Any one of these three quantities can be unknown in a problem as shown in Figure 8.1(a).

Separate/Take From Problems.   In *separate problems*, the start amount is the whole or the largest amount, whereas in the *join problems*, the result is the largest amount (whole). In separate problems, the change represents an action where an amount is being removed or taken away from the start value (Figure 8.1(b)). See the Separate Story Activity Page for a useful graphic organizer.

Part–Part–Whole Problems.   *Part–part–whole* problems also known as *put together* and *take apart* problems in the *Common Core State Standards* (CCSSO, 2010), involve two parts that are conceptually or mentally combined into one collection or whole, as in Figure 8.1(c). In these situations, either the missing whole (total unknown), one of the missing parts (one addend unknown), or both parts (two addends unknown) must be found. There is no meaningful distinction between the two parts in a part-part-whole situation, so there is no need to have a different problem for each part as the unknown. The third situation in which the whole or total is known and the two parts are unknown creates opportunities to think about all the possible decompositions of the whole as, instead of having one answer, this situation usually produces a set of correct answers (Caldwell, Kobett, & Karp, 2014; Champagne, Schoen, & Riddell, 2014). This structure links directly to the idea that numbers are embedded in other numbers. Students can break apart 75 into 50 and 25. Each of the addends (or parts) were embedded in the 75 (whole). See Part-Part-Whole Story, an Activity Page for the corresponding graphic organizer.

Compare Problems.   *Compare problems* involve the comparison of two quantities. The third amount in these problems does not actually exist but is the difference between the two amounts. Figure 8.1(d) illustrates the compare problem structure and the Compare Story Activity Page can help students model the situation. There are three ways to present compare problems, corresponding to which quantity is unknown (smaller, larger, or difference). For each of these, two examples are given in Figure 8.1(d): One problem in which the difference is stated in terms of "how many more" and another in terms of "how much less?" Note that the language of "more" will often confuse students and thus presents a challenge in interpretation.

You can find more examples of compare problems as well as the other problem types in the *Common Core State Standards* (see Table 1 in the CCSS Mathematics Standards Glossary; CCSSO, 2010, p. 88).

Stop and Reflect

Go back through all of these examples and match the numbers in the problems with the components of the structures in Figure 8.1. First, print off a copy of the graphic organizer Activity Page that corresponds to that problem structure and then use base-ten materials to model (solve) the problem as you think children might do. Then, for example, which numbers in the Join Problems match to start, change, and result on your graphic organizer? Finally, for each problem, write either an addition or subtraction equation that you think best represents the problem as you did it with the materials and compare your equation to those in Figure 8.1.

In most curricula, the overwhelming emphasis is on the easiest problem types: join and separate with the result unknown. These become the de facto definitions of addition and subtraction: Addition is "put together" and subtraction is "take away." The fact is, these are not the only meanings of addition and subtraction and the subtraction symbol should not be read as "take away."

Problem Difficulty

Some of the problem types are more difficult than other problem types. The join or separate problems in which the start part is unknown (e.g., Sandra had some stickers) are often the most difficult, probably because as students try to model the problem they do not know how many materials to put down to begin. Problems in which the change amounts are unknown are also difficult. As mentioned, compare problems are often challenging because the language "how many more" often confuses students into adding instead of finding the difference. Students also need to recognize that the quantities in comparison problems come from different wholes and the quantities in part–part–whole problems come from the same whole.

> **✎ Teaching Tip**
>
> Remember that students often mistakenly think of the equal sign as an operation sign (meaning to do a computation) rather than a relational sign (indicating a relationship between quantities). When you read an equation at the point of the equal sign say "equals" or "is the same as." This reinforces the meaning of the symbol.

As students begin to translate a story problem into an equation, they may be challenged to create a matching equation that depicts the corresponding operation. This is particularly important as students move into explorations that develop algebraic thinking. The structure of the equations also may cause difficulty for English language learners, who may not initially have the flexibility in creating equivalent equations due to reading comprehension issues with the story situation.

Teaching Addition and Subtraction

So far you have seen a variety of story problem structures for addition and subtraction, and you have used base-ten materials to help you understand how these problems can be solved by your students. Combining the use of situations and models (base-ten materials, drawings, bar diagrams, number lines) is important in helping students construct a deep understanding of these two operations. Let's examine how each approach can be used in the classroom. As you read this section, note that addition and subtraction are taught at the same time to reinforce their inverse relationship.

Contextual Problems

There is more to think about than simply giving students word problems to solve. In contrast to the rather straightforward and brief contextual problems given in the primary grades, you need to set the problems you give in meaningful contexts.

Fosnot and Dolk (2001) point out that in story problems, students tend to focus on getting the answer. "Context problems, on the other hand, are connected as closely as possible to children's lives, rather than to 'school mathematics.' They are designed to anticipate and to develop children's mathematical modeling of the real world" (p. 24). Contextual problems might derive from recent events in the classroom, a field trip, a discussion in art, science, or social studies, or from children's literature. Because contextual problems connect to relevant life experiences, they are important for English language learners, too, even though it may seem that the language initially presents a challenge to ELLs. Some strategies to support comprehension of problems include using a noun-verb word order, replacing terms such as "his/her" and "it" with a name, and removing unnecessary vocabulary words. Also visual aids, gestures, or actual students modeling the scenario would assist ELLs and students with disabilities.

You may wish to stay with a particular context, which is particularly important for ELLs and students with disabilities, but at the same time allow for variety and differentiation. For example, it might be interesting to combine or compare the populations of cities or counties in your region. Place the names of the cities on cards and either write the population directly on the card or have a corresponding chart for students to refer to. Then give students two cards and use the **City Population Word Problem** Activity Page, or you can have students create their own word problems. Students who can handle the larger numbers can work with densely populated locations, while students needing a gentler ramp up to the content can start with two sparsely populated areas.

Lessons Built on Context or Story Problems.   What might a good lesson built around word problems look like? The answer comes more naturally if you think about students not just solving the problems but also using words, pictures, and numbers to explain how they went about solving the problem and justifying why they are correct. In a single class period, try to focus on a few problems with an in-depth discussion, rather than a lot of problems with little elaboration. Students should be allowed to use whatever physical materials or drawings they feel they need to help them. Whatever they put on their paper should explain what they did well enough to allow someone else to understand their thinking.

A particularly effective approach is having students correct other students' written solutions. For example, you can give the class a set of fictitious students' work with calculations related to a recent school event or other interesting context. By using anonymous work, the students in your class can analyze the reasoning used, assess the selection of the operation, find any mistakes in computation, and identify possible errors in copying numbers from the problem.

Standards for
Mathematical Practice

**3 Construct
viable arguments
and critique the
reasoning of others.**

Choosing Numbers for Problems.   When adding and subtracting in grades 3 through 5, it is best to use relevant real-world data to link to students' interests or other subject areas, such as science. One advantage of using this kind of information is that you can differentiate problems in accordance with students' number development, giving them numbers as large as they can conceptually grasp. Word problems can serve as an opportunity to learn about number and computation at the same time. For example, a problem involving the combination of 315 and 420 has the potential to help students focus on sets of hundreds, then sets of tens or ones. They might think "add 300 and 400, and then add 35 more." You can learn more about *invented strategies* for computation in addition and subtraction in Chapter 11.

Model-Based Problems

Many students will use base ten materials, bar diagrams, or number lines (models) to solve story problems. These models are thinking tools that help them understand what is happening in the problem and keep track of the numbers and steps in solving the problem. Problems can also be posed using models when there is no context involved.

When the parts of a set are known, addition is used to name the whole in terms of the parts. This simple definition of addition serves both *action situations* (join and separate) and static or *no-action situations* (part–part–whole). If base-ten materials are used as models, the two parts should be in different piles or on different sections of a place value mat. For students to see a relationship between the two parts and the whole, the image must be kept as two separate sets. This helps students reflect on the action after it has occurred. "These 35 base-ten blocks are the ones I started with. Then I added 55 base-ten blocks, and now I have 90 altogether."

The use of *bar diagrams* (also called *strip* or *tape diagrams*) as semi-concrete visual representations is a central fixture in both Japanese curriculum and what is known as *Singapore mathematics*. As with other tools, they support students' mathematical thinking by generating "meaning making space" (Murata, 2008, p. 399) and are a precursor to the use of number lines (including empty or minimally notated number lines). Murata states, "Tape diagrams are designed to bring forward the relational meanings of the quantities in a problem by showing the connections in context" (2008, p. 396). Here is an example. Note how the matching bar diagram (see Figure 8.2) visually connects to the part–part–whole diagram students have been using since the primary grades.

Mary made 686 biscuits. She sold some of them. If 298 were left over, how many biscuits did she sell? (Beckmann, 2004).

Figure 8.2

A bar diagram that supports students' thinking about the problem.

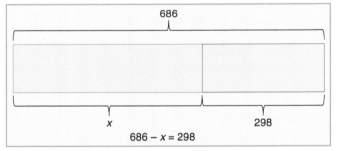

You can find online bar diagram tools called "Thinking Blocks" at Math Playground's website and as a free app in the iTunes Store. Thinking Blocks can be used to help students model and solve contextual problems involving operations with whole numbers and fractions.

A *number line* is an essential model, but it can initially present conceptual difficulties for children below second grade and students with disabilities (National Research Council Committee, 2009). This is partially due to students' difficulty in seeing the unit, which is a challenge when it appears in a continuous line. A number line is also a shift from counting a number of individual objects in a collection to continuous length units. There are, however, ways to introduce and model number lines that support young learners as they learn to use this representation. Familiarity with a number line is essential because third graders will use number lines to locate fractions and add and subtract time intervals, fourth graders will locate decimals on number lines and use them for measurement, and fifth graders will use perpendicular number lines in coordinate grids (CCSSO, 2010).

A number line measures distances from zero the same way a ruler does. If you don't actually teach the use of the number line through an emphasis on the unit (length), students may focus on the tick marks or numerals instead of the spaces (a misunderstanding that becomes apparent when students' answers are consistently off by one). At first students can build a number path by using a given length, such as a set of Cuisenaire rods of the same color to make a straight line of multiple single units. This will show each length unit is "one unit" and that same unit is repeated over and over (iterated) to form the number line (Dougherty, 2008). Furthermore, if arrows (hops) are drawn for each number in an expression, the length concept is more clearly illustrated. Number lines also scaffold the process as they can show which part of the operation has been carried out and what still needs to be acted upon. Eventually, the use of a ruler or a scale in a bar graph or coordinate grid will reinforce this model.

There's an interactive number line at the Math Learning Center that helps students visualize number sequences and model strategies for addition, subtraction, multiplication and division. It can be used to represent sequences of numbers, including whole numbers and multiples of a variety of numbers. An app version of this and other free tools are available for use on a variety of digital devices.

Developing Multiplication and Division Operation Sense

A key component of the third-grade curriculum is to help students develop *operation sense* with respect to multiplication and division. This means facilitating students' connections of the different meanings of multiplication and division to each other, as well as connections to addition and subtraction. Operation sense supports students' effective application of these operations in real-world settings.

Standards for
Mathematical Practice

◀ **8 Look for and express regularity in repeated reasoning.**

Multiplication and Division Problem Structures

Like addition and subtraction, there are problem structures that will help you as the teacher in formulating and assigning multiplication and division tasks. They will also help your students with generalizing as they solve familiar situations.

Most researchers identify four different classes of multiplicative structures: equal groups, comparison, area (CCSS-M includes arrays with area), and combinations (see Figure 8.3).

Figure 8.3   The four problem structures for multiplication and division story problems.

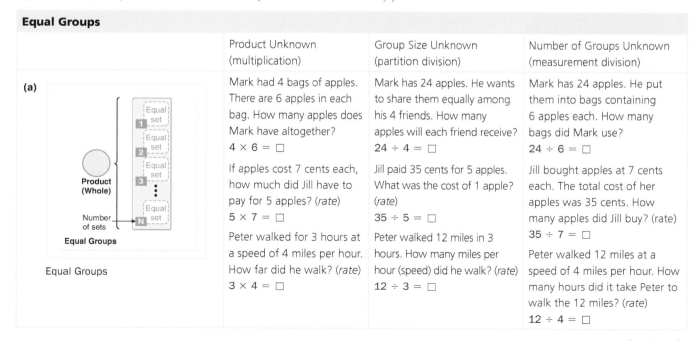

Equal Groups

(a)	Product Unknown (multiplication)	Group Size Unknown (partition division)	Number of Groups Unknown (measurement division)
Equal Groups	Mark had 4 bags of apples. There are 6 apples in each bag. How many apples does Mark have altogether? $4 \times 6 = \square$	Mark has 24 apples. He wants to share them equally among his 4 friends. How many apples will each friend receive? $24 \div 4 = \square$	Mark has 24 apples. He put them into bags containing 6 apples each. How many bags did Mark use? $24 \div 6 = \square$
	If apples cost 7 cents each, how much did Jill have to pay for 5 apples? (*rate*) $5 \times 7 = \square$	Jill paid 35 cents for 5 apples. What was the cost of 1 apple? (*rate*) $35 \div 5 = \square$	Jill bought apples at 7 cents each. The total cost of her apples was 35 cents. How many apples did Jill buy? (rate) $35 \div 7 = \square$
	Peter walked for 3 hours at a speed of 4 miles per hour. How far did he walk? (*rate*) $3 \times 4 = \square$	Peter walked 12 miles in 3 hours. How many miles per hour (speed) did he walk? (*rate*) $12 \div 3 = \square$	Peter walked 12 miles at a speed of 4 miles per hour. How many hours did it take Peter to walk the 12 miles? (*rate*) $12 \div 4 = \square$

Figure 8.3   The four problem structures for multiplication and division story problems. (*continued*)

Comparison Problems

	Product Unknown (multiplication)	Group Size Unknown (partition division)	Multiplier Unknown (measurement division)
(b) Multiplicative Comparison	Jill picked 6 apples. Mark picked 4 times as many apples as Jill. How many apples did Mark pick? $6 \times 4 = \square$ This month, Mark saved 5 times as much money as last month. Last month, he saved $7. How much money did Mark save this month? $5 \times 7 = \square$	Mark picked 24 apples. He picked 4 times as many apples as Jill. How many apples did Jill pick? $24 \div 4 = \square$ This month Mark saved 5 times as much money as he did last month. If he saved $35 this month, how much did he save last month? $35 \div 5 = \square$	Mark picked 24 apples, and Jill picked only 6. How many times as many apples did Mark pick as Jill did? $24 \div 6 = \square$ This month Mark saved $35. Last month, he saved $7. How many times as much money did he save this month as last? $35 \div 7 = \square$

Array and Area Problems

	Product Unknown	Group Size Unknown	Number of Groups Unknown
(c) Array	A carton has 3 rows of soup cans with 5 cans in each row. How many soup cans are there? $3 \times 5 = \square$	There are 15 soup cans placed in a carton in 3 equal rows. How many soup cans are in each row? $15 \div 3 = \square$	There are 15 soup cans placed in a carton in equal rows of 5 cans. How many rows are there? $15 \div 5 = \square$
(d) Area	A garden is 4 feet by 7 feet. What is the area of the garden? $4 \times 7 = \square$ sq. feet	A garden has an area of 28 square feet. If one side is 4 feet long, how long is the side next to it? $28 \div 4 = \square$ feet	A garden has an area of 28 square feet. If one side is 7 feet long, how long is the side next to it? $28 \div 7 = \square$ feet

Combination Problems

(e) Combinations	Sam bought 4 pairs of pants and 3 jackets, and they all can be worn together. How many different outfits consisting of a pair of pants and a jacket does Sam have? $4 \times 3 = \square$	The combination structure is rarely used to divide.

Of these the two structures *equal groups* (the focus in the CCSS-M third-grade standards) and *multiplicative comparison* (the focus in the CCSS-M fourth-grade standards), are by far the most prevalent in the elementary school (CCSSO, 2010). Arrays begin to be considered in second grade in the CCSS-M as addition situations with equal groups, and area problems are introduced in the third grade under the CCSS-M domain of Measurement and Data. Problems with combinations are found in seventh grade in the CCSS-M when students identify all of the possible outcomes in situations exploring probability.

Equal-Group Problems

In multiplicative problems, one number or *factor* counts how many sets, groups, or parts of equal size are involved. The other factor tells the size of each set, group, or part. The third number in this structure is the *whole* or *product* and is the total of all of the parts. The parts and wholes terminology is useful in making the connection to addition. When the number and size of groups are known, the problem is a multiplication situation with an *unknown product* (How many in all?). When either the *group size is unknown* (How many in each group?) or the *number of groups is unknown* (How many groups?), then the problem is a division situation. But note that these division situations are not alike. Problems in which the size of the group is unknown are called *fair-sharing* or *partition* division problems. The whole is shared or distributed among a known number of groups to determine the size of each. If the number of groups is unknown but the size of the equal group is known, the problems are called *measurement division* or sometimes *repeated-subtraction* problems. The whole is "measured off" in groups of the given size. Use the illustrations in Figure 8.3(a) as a reference. Watch this video clip and you will observe a student demonstrating measurement division as he uses information about the total amount and the size of each equal group to find the number of groups (unknown). Older students tend to prefer the partition model to the measurement models saying they find it easier (Kinda, 2013), but it is important to emphasize both as the context of the problem leads to the corresponding structure!

Sometimes equal-group problems have been called *repeated-addition* problems, as the equal group is being added over and over. And in fact, multiplication is an efficient way to carry out a repeated-addition situation with small whole numbers. This may be an important initial connection for young learners to make, as the multiplication and the repeated addition produce the same results for positive whole numbers. But by the time students are multiplying fractions, this notion falls apart. Additionally, repeated addition is not an efficient way to carry out multiplication with larger whole numbers—it is just the opposite (try 23×57). So, move away from additive thinking to thinking of a multiplier and equal sets as soon as you are able to do so. There is also a subtle difference between equal-group problems and those that might be termed *rate* problems (e.g., If there are 4 apples per child, how many apples would 3 children have?). In a rate problem, students are working with a composed unit (in this case, apples per child).

Comparison Problems

In multiplicative comparison problems there are really two different sets or groups, as there were with comparison situations for addition and subtraction. In additive situations, the comparison is an amount or quantity difference between the two groups. In multiplicative situations, the comparison is based on one group being a particular multiple of the other (multiple copies). With multiplication comparison, there are three possibilities for the unknown: The product, the group size, and the number of groups (see Figure 8.3(b)).

Stop and Reflect

What you just read is complex yet important. Stop now and get a collection of about 35 counters and a set of paper plates to model the equal-group examples starring Mark. Match each story with one of the structures modeled in Figure 8.3(a). How are these problems alike and how are they different? Repeat the exercise for the Jill problems.

Repeat the same process with the multiplicative comparison problems (see Figure 8.3(b)) using one colored plate different from your other plates to represent the reference set. Again, start with the first problem in each set and then try the second problems. Reflect on how these problems are the same and different.

Array and Area Problems

The array is a model for an equal-group situation (Figure 8.3(c)). It is shown as a rectangular grouping with the first factor (the number of groups) representing the number of rows and the second factor (the number of items in each equal group) representing the number found in each row (this is the U.S. convention for what each factor represents). CCSS-M groups the topic of arrays with area rather than with the equal-group problems because the array can be thought of as a logical lead-in to the row-and-column structure of an area problem. But remember an array can be modeled with circular counters or any items as you see in the sample problems in 8.3(c) (also using dots [Matney & Daugherty, 2013]). Yet, if you begin to use the small square tiles for the array and move the tiles tightly together, the result can be recorded on grid paper and connected more easily to the area problem structure. Using the discrete items first prepares students for the more sophisticated use of continuous units with measuring area.

What distinguishes *area* problems from the others is that the product is literally a different type of unit from the two factors. In a rectangular shape, the product of two lengths (length × width) is an area, usually square units. Note in Figure 8.3(d) how different the square units are from the two factors of length: 4 feet times 7 feet is not 28 feet, but 28 square feet. The factors are each one-dimensional units, but the product consists of two-dimensional units. The study of area will be considered in great depth in Chapter 16 on measurement.

Combination Problems

This structure is more complex and therefore not a good introductory point, but it is important that you recognize it as another category of multiplicative problem structures. *Combination* problems involve counting the number of possible pairings that can be made between two or more sets. Figure 8.3(e) shows one common method of modeling combination problems with two sets—using rows and columns in a matrix format. Counting how many combinations of two or more things or events are possible is important in determining probabilities. The combinations concept is most often found in the statistics and probability domain in grade 7.

Teaching Multiplication and Division

Multiplication and division are often taught separately, with multiplication preceding division. It is important, however, to combine multiplication and division soon after multiplication has been introduced in order to help students see how these operations have an inverse relationship. These topics are first presented in grade 2 (CCSSO, 2010) and then become a major focus in third grade, with continued development in the fourth and fifth grades. "In grades 3–5, students should focus on the meanings of, and relationship between, multiplication and division. It is important that students understand what each number in a multiplication or division expression represents. . . . Modeling multiplication problems with pictures, diagrams, or concrete materials helps students learn what the factors and their product represent in various contexts" (NCTM, 2000, p. 151).

A major conceptual hurdle in working with multiplicative structures is understanding groups of items as single entities while also understanding that a group contains a given number of objects (Blote, Lieffering, & Ouewhand, 2006; Clark & Kamii, 1996). Students can solve the problem "How many apples are in 4 baskets of 8 apples each?" by counting out four sets of eight counters and then skip counting them all. To think multiplicatively about this problem as four sets of eight requires students to conceptualize each group of eight as a single entity to be counted. Experiences with making and counting equal groups, especially in contextual situations, are extremely useful.

Contextual Problems

When teaching multiplication and division, it is essential to use interesting contextual problems instead of more sterile story problems (or "naked numbers")—and yes, assessments focus on these contextual problems! However, as with addition and subtraction, there is more to think about than simply giving students word problems to solve. Consider the following problem.

Yesterday, we discovered that it took 7 yards of paper to cover the bulletin board in the school's front lobby. There are 25 more bulletin boards of the same size in the hallways around the school. How many yards of paper will we need if we cover all the bulletin boards in the school hallways?

This problem is based on students' experiences and builds on that known context that all can access. When such a familiar and relevant context is used, students are more likely to demonstrate spontaneous and meaningful approaches to solving a problem, as they are connected to it.

What might a good lesson look like for a third-, fourth-, or fifth-grade class that is built around problems? The tendency in the United States is to have students solve many problems in a single class period with a focus on getting the answers. But if you change the focus to sense making, solving only a few problems using multiple representations strategically such as physical materials, drawings, as well as equations partnered with a discussion of strategies can be a better approach. Whatever students write on paper they should explain it in enough detail for another person to follow their thinking. Leave enough space on an activity sheet to encourage multiple strategies—it is amazing how leaving only a small space will just prompt an answer and nothing more. Watch this video (**https://www.youtube.com/watch?v=VW-XpG6u3Dk**) of a third-grade classroom to see how a graphic organizer can support this process with a technique called "Choose Three Ways!"

 ## Formative Assessment Note

Observing the techniques students use to solve problems will provide you with important information, therefore, it is essential that you look at more than the answers students get. For example, suppose you asked a student to figure out 7 times 26. In response the student adds 26 seven times on paper. The student's use of an additive approach informs you that it might be fruitful to focus on the idea of taking numbers apart in useful ways—part–part–whole ideas. For example, working with the factor 25 instead of 26 can be easier, especially if the student thinks in terms of quarters: 4 quarters equals one dollar (or 100 cents) and 8 quarters equals two dollars (or 200 cents). Because only seven 25s are needed, that would equal 175. Taking care of the one remaining 7 left from thinking about the 26 as 25, the student can add 175 and 7. If you have been working on benchmarks of 5 and 10, you can observe the student's use of these ideas in adding 175 and 7. Does the student count up from 175 or decompose 7 into 5 and 2 to add more efficiently?

Symbolism for Multiplication and Division

When students solve simple multiplication story problems before learning about multiplication symbolism, they will most likely begin by writing repeated-addition equations to represent what they did. This is your opportunity to introduce the multiplication sign and explain what the two factors mean.

 ## Teaching Tip

To ease the language demands on ELLs, you may want to build lessons around only two or three problem contexts.

The convention in the United States is that 4×8 refers to four sets of eight, not eight sets of four. There is no reason to be so rigid about this convention that you would mark a student as incorrect (particularly because the convention is just the opposite in some countries where they would say four taken eight times). The important thing is that the students can tell you what each factor in their equations represents. These conventions about translating a multiplicative situation into numbers allow us to communicate clearly about the problem with each other. It also helps to build toward the commutative property of multiplication.

The quotient 24 divided by 6 is represented in three different ways: $24 \div 6$, $6\overline{)24}$, and $\frac{24}{6}$. Students should understand that these representations are equivalent. Students often mistakenly read $6\overline{)24}$, as "6 divided by 24," due to the left to right order of the numerals. Generally, this error does not match what they are thinking.

Compounding the difficulty of division notation is the unfortunate phrase "goes in to" as in "6 goes in to 24." This phrase carries little meaning about division, especially in connection with a fair-sharing or partitioning context. The "goes in to" terminology is simply engrained in adult parlance; it has not been in textbooks for years. Instead of this phrase, you can use appropriate terminology with students, such as "How many groups of 6 are in 24?"

Choosing Numbers for Problems

When selecting numbers for multiplicative story problems or activities, there is a tendency to think that large numbers pose a burden to students, or that 3×4 is somehow easier to understand than 4×17. An understanding of products or quotients is not affected by the size of the numbers, as long as the numbers are within your students' grasp. A contextual problem involving 14×8 is very appropriate for third graders. When given the challenge of using larger numbers, students are likely to invent computational strategies (e.g., ten 8s and then four more 8s) or model the problem with manipulatives.

Remainders

More often than not in real-world situations, division does not result in a whole number. For example, problems with 6 as a divisor will result in a whole number answer only one time out of six. In the absence of a context, a remainder can be dealt with in only two ways: It can either remain a quantity left over, or it can be partitioned into fractions. In Figure 8.4, the problem $11 \div 4$ is modeled to show a remainder as a fraction.

In the CCSS students begin to interpret remainders in the fourth grade. In real contexts, remainders sometimes have three additional effects on answers:

- The remainder is discarded, leaving a smaller whole-number answer.
- The remainder can "force" the answer to the next highest whole number.
- The answer is rounded to the nearest whole number for an approximate result.

The following problems illustrate all five possibilities.

1. You have 30 pieces of candy to share fairly with 7 friends. How many pieces of candy will each friend receive?

   Answer: 4 pieces of candy and 2 left over. (left over)

2. Each jar holds 8 ounces of liquid. If there are 46 ounces in the pitcher, how many jars will that be?

   Answer: 5 and $\frac{6}{8}$ jars. (partitioned as a fraction)

Figure 8.4

Remainders expressed as fractions.

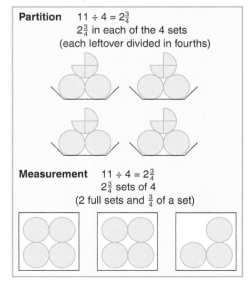

Partition $11 \div 4 = 2\frac{3}{4}$
   $2\frac{3}{4}$ in each of the 4 sets
   (each leftover divided in fourths)

Measurement $11 \div 4 = 2\frac{3}{4}$
   $2\frac{3}{4}$ sets of 4
   (2 full sets and $\frac{3}{4}$ of a set)

3. The rope is 25 feet long. How many 7-foot jump ropes can be made?

   Answer: 3 jump ropes. (discarded)

4. The ferry can hold 8 cars. How many trips will it have to make to carry 25 cars across the river?

   Answer: 4 trips. (forced to next whole number)

5. Six children are planning to share a bag of 50 pieces of bubble gum. About how many pieces will each child get?

   Answer: About 8 pieces for each child. (rounded, approximate result)

Students should not just think of remainders as "R 3" or "left over." Addressing what to do with remainders must be central to teaching about division. In fact, one of the most common errors students make on high-stakes assessments is to divide, get an answer with a remainder, and then no pay attention to the context when selecting their answer. For example, in problem 3 above, answering with $3\frac{4}{7}$ ropes doesn't make any sense. Rest assured that this incorrect response will be a multiple choice option on the major assessment because common errors are used to create possible answers!

Stop and Reflect

It is useful for you to create problems using different contexts. See if you can create division problems for which the contexts would result in remainders dealt with as fractions, "forced" or rounded up, and rounded down.

Model-Based Problems

In the beginning, students will be able to use the same models—sets, bar diagrams, and number lines—for all four operations. A model not generally used for addition, but that is extremely important and widely used for multiplication and division, is the array. An *array* is any arrangement of things in equal groups of rows and columns, such as a rectangle of square tiles, blocks, or circular counters (see the 10 × 10 array).

To make clear the connection to addition, very early multiplication activities with equal-group problems can also include writing an addition sentence for the same model. A variety of models are shown in Figure 8.5. Notice that the products are not included—only addition and multiplication expressions or equations are written. This is another way to avoid the tedious counting of large sets. A similar approach is to write one sentence that expresses both concepts at once, for example, $9 + 9 + 9 + 9 = 4 \times 9$.

As with additive problems, students benefit from activities with models to focus on the meaning of the operation and the associated symbolism such as Activity 8.1.

Activity 8.1

CCSS-M: 4.OA.B.4

Factor Quest

Start by having students think about a context that involves arrays, such as parade formations, seats in a classroom, or patches of a quilt. Then, assign a number that has several factors—for example, 12, 18, 24, 30, or 36. Have students find as many arrays as they can (perhaps made from square tiles or cubes). Then have them record their arrays by drawing them on grid paper—see the Factor Quest Activity Page. For each, write the corresponding multiplication equations. For students with physical disabilities who may have limited motor skills to manipulate the materials, you can use the Factorize applet on the NCTM Illuminations website.

Figure 8.5

Models for equal-group multiplication.

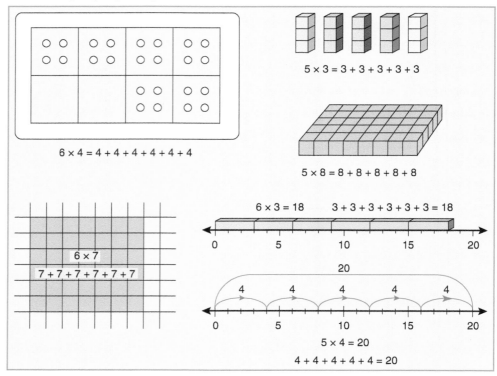

$6 \times 4 = 4 + 4 + 4 + 4 + 4 + 4$

$5 \times 3 = 3 + 3 + 3 + 3 + 3$

$5 \times 8 = 8 + 8 + 8 + 8 + 8$

$6 \times 3 = 18$ $3 + 3 + 3 + 3 + 3 + 3 = 18$

6×7

$7 + 7 + 7 + 7 + 7 + 7$

$5 \times 4 = 20$

$4 + 4 + 4 + 4 + 4 = 20$

Standards for
Mathematical Practice

7 Look for and make
use of structure.

Draw students' attention to the dimensions of the arrays, having them make the connection between the factors in the multiplication expression to the number of rows and columns (the dimensions of the rectangle). Your class will undoubtedly want to decide whether a rectangle that is 3 by 8 should be counted differently from one that is 8 by 3. Leave the decision to the class, but take advantage of the opportunity to discuss how 3 rows of 8 are the same amount as 8 rows of 3. Note that if equal groups are made on paper plates rather than arrays, 3 sets of 8 look very different from 8 sets of 3. So, as students begin to think about the commutative property of multiplication, array models provide a helpful representation.

The next activity is an extension of "Factor Quest," in that students look for patterns in the factors they find for numbers, such as the number of factors, the type of factors, the shape of the resulting array, and so on. Rather than always assigning numbers that have several factors, this activity suggests including numbers that have only a few factors so that differences between numbers become more distinct.

Activity 8.2

CCSS-M: 4.OA.B.4

Factor Patterns

Tell students that their task is to find all the multiplication expressions and the corresponding rectangular array(s) for several numbers (e.g., 1 through 16 or 10 through 25). Have enough square tiles available that students can use them to explore possible arrays. For example, for the number 12, they can build 12 × 1, 6 × 2, 4 × 3, and the three matching pairs using the commutative property. Then they can record their rectangles on **1-Centimeter Grid Paper** and label each rectangle with the corresponding multiplication expression (e.g., 6 × 2). This organization helps when students are comparing arrays across different numbers. After identifying the multiplication expressions and the rectangular arrays, students are to look for patterns in the factors and rectangular arrays. For example, which numbers have the fewest number of arrays and, therefore, the fewest number of factors? Which numbers have only a factor of 1 and itself? Which numbers have arrays that form a square? What can you say about the factors for even numbers? Do even numbers always have two even factors? What about odd numbers? Encourage students to think about why different patterns occur.

Use this activity to explore the positive whole numbers that are *prime* (numbers greater than 1 that only have a factor of itself and 1) and those that are *composites* (numbers that can be made with two or more different arrays—has factors other than 1 and itself). Have students continue to consider the patterns that they notice as they classify different numbers into these categories.

Activities 8.1 and 8.2 can also include division concepts. When students have learned that 3 and 6 are factors of 18, they can write the equations $18 \div 3 = 6$ and $18 \div 6 = 3$, along with $3 \times 6 = 18$ and $6 + 6 + 6 = 18$ (assuming that three sets of six were modeled). Activity 8.3 is a variation of these activities but focuses instead on division. Having students create word problems to fit what they did with the tiles, cubes, or counters is another excellent elaboration of this activity. Connecting the situation to the models and to the equation is important in demonstrating understanding.

◢▶ Activity 8.3

CCSS-M: 3.OA.A.2

Divide and Conquer

Using the context of a story about sharing such as *Bean Thirteen* (McElligott, 2007), provide students with an ample supply of counters (beans) and some way to place them into small groups (small paper cups). Have students count out a number of counters to be the whole or total amount and then record this number: Next specify either the number of equal groups to be made or the size of the groups: "Separate your counters into four equal-sized groups" or "Make as many groups of four as is possible." Have students write the corresponding multiplication equation for what their materials show; under that, have them write the division equation. For ELLs, be sure they know what *groups, equal-sized groups,* and *groups of four* mean. For students with disabilities, consider having them start with a partition approach (i.e., separate your counters into three groups), in which they share the counters by placing one at a time into each cup. Explore the **Expanded Lesson: Divide and Conquer** for additional details about this activity.

Be sure to have the class do both types of exercises: number of equal groups unknown and group size unknown. Discuss with the class how these two situations are different, yet each is related to multiplication and each is written as a division equation. You can show the different ways to write division equations at this time, such as $31 \div 4$, $4\overline{)31}$, and $\frac{31}{4}$. Do Activity 8.3 several times. Make sure to include whole quantities that are multiples of the divisor (no remainders) and situations with remainders. Note that it is technically incorrect to write the answer to a problem like $31 \div 4$ as 7 R 3 because this is not a number (a quotient should be a number). As written, the 3 is not well defined because it is really $\frac{3}{4}$. However, in the beginning, the form 7 R 3 may be the most appropriate.

note

Explore the applet "Rectangle Division" from the National Library of Virtual Manipulatives for an interactive illustration of division with remainders that demonstrates vividly how division is related to multiplication. A division problem is presented with an array and the dimensions of the array can be modified, but the number of squares (product) stays constant. If, for example, you model the problem $52 \div 8$, it will show an 8 by 6 array with 4 remaining squares in a different color ($8 \times 6 + 4$), as well as any other variation of 52 squares in a rectangular array plus a shorter column for the extra squares.

The activity can be varied by changing the model. Have students build arrays using square tiles or blocks or by having them draw arrays on square grid paper and present the exercises by specifying how many squares are to be in the array. You can then specify the number of rows that should be made (partition) or the length of each row (measurement). How could students model the remainder using drawings of arrays on grid paper?

When modeling multiplicative comparison problems, consider exploring them with the use of a bar diagram. See Figure 8.6 for a bar diagram related to the following situation:

Figure 8.6

A student's work shows a model for multiplicative comparisons.

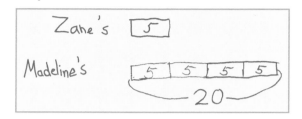

> Zane has 5 small toy cars. Madeline has four times as many cars. How many cars does Madeline have?

Activity 8.4

CCSS-M: 4.NBT.B.6

The Broken Division Key

 Have students find methods of using a calculator to solve division exercises without using the divide key. "Find at least two ways to figure out 61 ÷ 14 without pressing the divide key." If the problem is put in a story context, one method may actually match the problem better than another. Good discussions can follow different solutions with the same answers. Are they both correct? Why or why not?

Consider ways to explore a broken multiplication key as well.

---

t e c h n o l o g y ⏻

note

There are several Broken Calculators apps that can be found on the web that allow for problems at different levels of difficulty.

Stop and Reflect

Can you find three ways to solve 61 ÷ 14 on a calculator without using the divide key? For hints, see the footnote.*

Properties of Multiplication and Division

There are multiplicative properties that are useful and, thus, worthy of attention. The emphasis should be on the ideas, not merely the terminology or definitions.

Commutative and Associative Properties of Multiplication

It is not obvious that 3×8 is the same as 8×3 or that, in general, the order of the factors makes no difference (the *commutative property*). A picture of 3 sets of 8 objects cannot

---

*There are two measurement approaches to find out how many 14s are in 61 (by repeatedly adding or subtracting 14). A third way is essentially related to partitioning or finding 14 times what number is close to 61.

immediately be seen as equal to 8 piles of 3 objects. Nor on a number line is 8 hops of 3 noticeably the same as 3 hops of 8. The array, by contrast, is quite powerful in illustrating the commutative property, as shown in Figure 8.7(a). Students should build or draw arrays and use them to demonstrate why each array represents two equivalent multiplication expressions.

As in addition, there is an *associative property* of multiplication that is fundamental in flexibly solving problems (Ding, Li, Capraro, & Capraro, 2012). This property allows that when you multiply three numbers in an expression you can multiply either the first pair of numbers and then multiply that answer by the third number or multiply the last pair of numbers and then multiply that answer by the first number. Either way the product remains the same. A context is helpful, so here is an example that could be shared with students: "Each tennis ball costs $2. Each can has 3 tennis balls. How much will it cost if we need to buy 6 cans?" After analyzing the problem by showing actual cans of tennis balls or illustrations, students should try to consider the problem two ways: (1) find out the cost for each can and then the total cost $6 \times (3 \times 2)$; and (2) find out how many balls in total and then the total cost $(6 \times 3) \times 2$ (Ding, 2010). See Figure 8.7(b)).

Figure 8.7

A model for the commutative property for multiplication (a) and an illustration of a problem showing the associative property of multiplication (b).

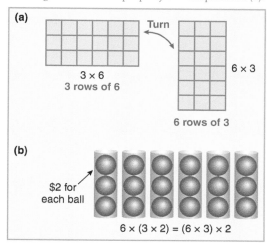

Zero and Identity Properties

Factors of 0 and, to a lesser extent, 1 often cause conceptual challenges for students. In textbooks, you may find that a lesson on factors of 0 and 1 has students use a calculator to examine a wide range of products involving 0 or 1 (423×0, 0×28, 1536×1, etc.) and look for patterns. The pattern suggests the rules for factors of 0 and 1, but not a reason. In another lesson, a word problem might ask how many grams of fat there are in 7 servings of celery, with 0 grams of fat in each serving. This contextual approach is far preferable to an arbitrary rule because it asks students to reason. Make up interesting word problems involving factors of 0 or 1, and discuss the results. Problems with 0 as a first factor are really strange. Note that on a number line, 5 hops of 0 lands at 0 (5×0). What would 0 hops of 5 be? Another fun activity is to try to model 6×0 or 0×8 with an array. (Try it!) Arrays for factors of 1 are also worth investigating. (Numbers that can only be made with an array with dimensions of 1 and the number itself are prime numbers!)

Distributive Property

The *distributive property of multiplication over addition* refers to the powerful idea that you can split (decompose) either of the two factors in a multiplication problem into two or more parts and then multiply each of the parts by the other factor and add the results. The final product is the same as when the original factors are multiplied. The concept involved is very useful in relating one basic fact to another, and it is also involved in the development of two-digit computation. But concrete representations and the use of real contexts are essential for students to make sense of this critically important property (Ding & Li, 2014). For example, word problems are an option, such as if you want to find the number of yogurts in 9 six-packs, use the logic that 9×6 is equal to $(5 \times 6) + (4 \times 6)$. The 9 packs have been split into 5 six-packs and 4 six-packs. Figure 8.8 illustrates how the array model (with square tiles or grid paper) can be used to demonstrate that a product can be broken up into two parts. The next activity is designed to help students discover how to partition factors or, in other words, learn about the distributive property of multiplication over addition.

Figure 8.8

Models for the distributive property of multiplication over addition.

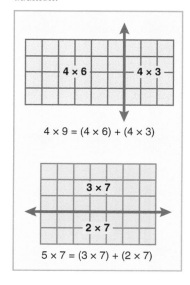

> ◣▶ **Activity 8.5**
>
> CCSS-M: 3.OA.B.5; 5.OA.A.1
>
> ### Divide It Up
>
> Supply students with several sheets of **1-Centimeter Grid Paper** or color tiles to represent a small garden that will be planted with two different kinds of vegetables. Assign each pair of students a garden plot size, such as 6 × 8. Garden sizes (products) can vary across the class to differentiate for varying skill levels or they can all be the same. Ask students to find all of the different ways to make a single slice or cut through the garden to divide the plot for the two different vegetables. For each slice, students write an equation. For a slice that results in one row of 8, students would write 6 × 8 = (5 × 8) + (1 × 8). The individual products can be written in the arrays as is shown in Figure 8.8. Although the CCSS-M suggests that grade five students learn about the use of grouping symbols such as parentheses, the full discussion of the order of operations is not until sixth grade.

Why Not Division by Zero?

Sometimes students are simply told "Division by zero is not allowed," sometimes because teachers do not fully know how to explain this concept (Quinn, Lamberg, & Perrin, 2008). Some students harbor misconceptions that the answer should be either zero or the number itself. To avoid merely sharing an arbitrary rule, pose problems to be modeled that involve zero: "Take 30 counters. How many groups of 0 can be made?" or "Put 12 blocks in 0 equal groups. How many in each group?" or "Can you show me how to share 5 oranges with 0 children?" Then move students toward reasoned explanations (Crespo & Nicol, 2006) that consider the inverse relationship of multiplication and division and take the answer and put it back into a multiplication problem as a check. Then, with the orange problem, you would ask, "What, when multiplied by 0, produces an answer of 5?" There is no answer. Therefore, division by zero is undefined; it just doesn't make sense when we use our definition of division and its inverse relationship to multiplication.

Strategies for Solving Contextual Problems

We have suggested the use of contextual problems or story problems to help students develop meanings for multiplication and division. But often students in grades 3 through 5 (although not exclusively so) are at a loss for what to do. Also, struggling readers or ELLs may need support in understanding the problem. In this section you will learn some techniques for helping them.

Analyzing Context Problems

Consider the following problem:

In building a road through a neighborhood, workers filled large holes in the ground with dirt brought in by trucks. 638 truckloads of dirt were required to completely fill the holes. The average truck carried $6\frac{1}{4}$ cubic yards of dirt, which weighed 7.3 tons. How many tons of dirt were used to fill the holes?

Typically, in fifth-grade books, problems of this type are found as part of a series of problems revolving around a single context or theme. Data may be found in a graph or chart, or perhaps a short news item or story. Students have difficulty deciding on the correct operation and are often challenged to identify the appropriate data for solving the problem. Sometimes students will find two numbers in the problem and guess at the correct operation. Instead, students need tools for analyzing problems. At least two strategies can be very helpful: (1) thinking about the answer before solving the problem, or (2) working a simpler problem.

 Formative Assessment Note

What do you do if a student is having difficulty solving word problems? Use the **Multiplicative Word Problem** Activity Page and give each child a collection of these problems. Provide appropriate physical materials (e.g., counters, square tiles, grid paper), for testing ideas. Have students select two or three of the problems that they think are similar. Then they should use a glue stick to paste the problems they choose onto the top of the **Word Problem Sort** Activity Page. Direct students to use the bottom of the page to write an explanation of their thinking and tell how they decided the problems are alike. This sorting process (based on Caldwell, Kobett, & Karp, 2014) helps students analyze the meaning of the story problem sentence by sentence and look for structure.

Think about the Answer before Solving the Problem

Students who struggle with solving word problems need to spend adequate time thinking about the problem and what it is about. In addition, ELLs need to comprehend both the contextual words (like *dirt*, *filled*, and *road*) and the mathematical terminology (*cubic yards, weighted, tons, how many*). Instead of rushing in and beginning to do calculations, believing that "number crunching" is what solves problems, they should spend time talking about (and later thinking about) what the answer might be. In fact, one great strategy for differentiation is to pose the problem with the numbers missing or covered up (Holbert & Barlow, 2012/2013). This eliminates the tendency to number crunch. For our sample problem, it might look like this:

- *What is happening in this problem?* Some trucks were bringing dirt to fill up holes.
- *Is there any extra information we don't need?* We don't need to know how many cubic yards are in each truck.
- *What will the answer tell us?* How many tons of dirt were needed to fill the holes. My answer will be some number of tons.
- *Will that be a small number of tons or a large number of tons?* Well, there were 7.3 tons on each truck, but there were a lot of trucks, not just one. The answer is probably going to be a lot of tons.
- *About how many do you think it will be?* If there were 1000 trucks, it would be 7300 tons. So it will be less than that. But it will be more than half of 7300, so the answer is more than 3650 tons.

Standards for Mathematical Practice

◄ **1** Make sense of problems and persevere in solving them.

7 Look for structure.

In this type of discussion, three things are happening. First, students are focusing on the problem and the meaning of the answer, instead of on numbers. The numbers are not important in thinking about the structure of the problem. Second, with a focus on the structure of the problem, students identify the numbers that are important as well as the numbers that are not important. Third, the thinking leads to a rough estimate of the answer and the unit of the answer (tons, in this case). In any event, thinking about what the answer tells and about how large it might be is a useful starting point.

Figure 8.9

Two ways students created a simpler problem.

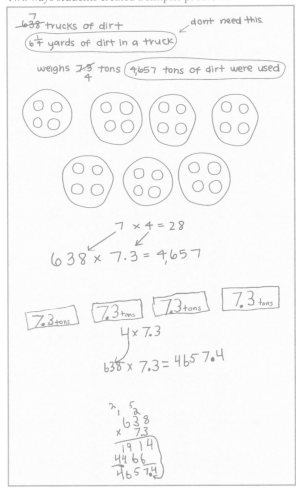

Work a Simpler Problem

The reason that models are rarely used with problems such as the dirt problem is that the large numbers are very challenging to model. Distances in thousands of miles, and time in minutes and seconds—data likely to be found in the upper elementary grades—are difficult to model. The general problem-solving strategy of "try a simpler problem" can almost always be applied to problems with unwieldy numbers.

A simpler-problem strategy has the following steps:

1. Substitute small whole numbers for all relevant numbers in the problem.
2. Model the problem (with base-ten materials, drawings, number lines, arrays) using the new numbers.
3. Write an equation that solves the simpler version of the problem.
4. Write the corresponding equation substituting back the original numbers.
5. Calculate!
6. Write the answer in a complete sentence, and decide whether it makes sense.

Figure 8.9 shows how the dirt problem might be made simpler. It also shows an alternative, in which only one of the numbers is made smaller and the other number is illustrated symbolically. Both methods are effective.

The idea is to provide strategies students can consistently use to analyze a problem and not just guess at what computation to use. It is much more useful to have students do a few problems for which they must use a model of a drawing to justify their solution than to give them a lot of problems for which they guess at a solution but don't use reasoning and sense making.

Caution: Avoid the Key Word Strategy!

In the past, it was often suggested that students should be taught to find "key words" in story problems to use to decide which operation to use. Some students are encouraged to use lists of key words with their corresponding operation linked to the word. For example, this strategy suggests that if you see the words *altogether* and *in all* in a story problem that means you should add, and *left* and *fewer* indicates that you should subtract. The word *each* suggests multiplication. To some extent, the overly simple and formulaic story problems often found in textbooks reinforce this approach (Sulentic-Dowell, Beal, & Capraro, 2006). When problems are written in this way, it may appear that the key word strategy is effective.

In contrast with this belief, researchers and mathematics educators have long cautioned against the strategy of key words (e.g., Clement & Bernhard, 2005; Heng & Sudarshan, 2013; Karp, Bush, & Dougherty, 2014; Sowder, 1988). Here are four arguments against the key word approach:

1. The key word strategy sends a terribly wrong message about doing mathematics. The most important approach to solving any contextual problem is to analyze it and make sense of it using all the words. The key word approach encourages students to ignore

the meaning and structure of the problem and look for an easy way out. Mathematics is about reasoning and making sense of situations. Sense-making strategies always work!

2. Key words are often misleading. Many times the key word or phrase in a problem suggests an operation that is incorrect. The following problem shared by Drake and Barlow (2007) demonstrates this possibility.

There are three boxes of chicken nuggets on the table. Each box contains six chicken nuggets. How many chicken nuggets are there in all? (p. 272)

Drake and Barlow found that one student generated the answer of 9, using the words "how many in all" as a suggestion to add 3 + 6. Instead of making sense of the situation, the student used the key word approach as a shortcut in making a decision about which operation to select.

3. Many problems have no key words. A student who has been taught to rely on key words is then left with no strategy.

Here's an example:

Aidan has 28 goldfish. 12 are orange and the rest are yellow. How many goldfish are yellow?

---

4. Key words don't work with two-step problems or more advanced problems, so using this approach on simpler problems sets students up for failure with more complex problems because they are not learning how to read for meaning.

Multistep Word Problems

Two-step word problems appear for the first time in the CCSS-M when second graders are expected to solve two-step addition and subtraction word problems. Then two-step problems in all four operations are a part of the third-grade standards and in fourth grade they add to those standards by including problems resulting in remainders that must be interpreted. Fifth graders solve multi-step problems with measurement scenarios and of course, multistep problems continue with a variety of numbers and contexts in middles school and beyond. Yet, students often have difficulty with the multistep problems with more than one step, particularly students with learning disabilities (Hord & Marita, 2014). First, be sure they can analyze the structure of one-step problems in the way that we have discussed.

The following ideas, adapted from suggestions by Huinker (1994), are designed to help students see how two problems can be linked together to help think about multistep problems.

1. Give students a one-step problem and have them solve it. Before discussing the answer, have the students use the answer to the first problem to create a second problem. The rest of the class can then be asked to solve the second problem. Here is an example:

Given problem: It took 3 hours for the Morgan family to drive the 195 miles to Washington, D.C. What was their average speed?

Second problem: The Morgan children remember crossing the river at about 10:30 a.m., or 2 hours after they left home. About how many miles from home is the river?

2. Make a "hidden question." Repeat the approach above by giving groups of students a one-step problem. Give different problems to different groups. Have them solve the first problem and write a second problem. Then they should write a single combined problem that leaves out the question from the first problem. That question from the first problem is the "hidden question." Here is a simple example:

Given problem: Toby bought three dozen eggs for 89 cents a dozen. How much was the total cost?

Second problem: How much change did Toby get back from $5?

Hidden-question problem: Toby bought three dozen eggs for 89 cents a dozen. How much change did Tony get back from $5?

Have other students identify the hidden question. Because all students are working on a similar task but with different problems (be sure to mix the operations), they will be more likely to understand what is meant by a hidden question.

3. Pose standard multistep problems, and have the students identify and answer the hidden question. Consider the following problem:

The Marsal Company bought 275 widgets wholesale for $3.69 each. In the first month, the company sold 205 widgets at $4.99 each. How much did the company make or lose on the widgets? Do you think the Marsal Company should continue to sell widgets?

4. Begin by considering the questions that were suggested earlier: "What's happening in this problem?" (*Something is being bought and sold at two different prices.*) "What will the answer tell us?" (*How much profit or loss there was.*) These questions will get you started. If students are stuck, you can ask, "Is there a hidden question in this problem?" Although the examples given here provide a range of contexts, for ELLs, using the *same* (relevant and familiar) context across this three-step process would reduce the linguistic demands and therefore make the stories more comprehensible—and the mathematics more accessible.

Another approach is to use a table to help students support their working memory (Hord & Marita, 2014). By assisting students in organizing information into such sequential categories as What is the question? What is the important information? and What is the first thing you should do?, students can get a start on making sense of the problem. Then they can repeat this process until all of the problem's multiple steps have been accomplished.

Formative Assessment Note

One of the best ways to assess students' knowledge of the meaning of the operations is to have them generate story problems for a given equation, result, or operation (Lannin, Chval, & Jones, 2013; Whitin & Whitin, 2008). Use a diagnostic interview to see whether your student can flexibly think about an operation using the **Translation Task** Activity Page based on the work of Sheild and Swinson (1996). Give students an expression, such as 5 × 7, ask that they record and answer it in the upper-left-hand quarter, write a story problem representing the expression in the upper-right-hand quarter of the paper, draw a picture (or model) in the lower left section, and describe how they would tell a younger student how to solve this problem in the last section. (Students with disabilities could dictate the story problem and the description of the solving process while the teacher transcribes.) Students who can ably match scenarios, models, and explanations to the computation will demonstrate their understanding, whereas struggling students will reveal areas of weakness. This assessment can be adapted by giving students the result (e.g., "24 cents") and asking them to write a multiplication problem (or a division problem, or any other appropriate type of problem) that will generate that answer, along with models and word problems written in the remaining quarters. Another option is to use a piece of children's literature to write a word problem that emphasizes the meaning of one of the four operations. The student then has to complete the other three sections.

Common misconceptions and how to help students move beyond them are presented in Table 8.1, as well as at the conclusion of each chapter in Part 2.

Teaching Tip

Anticipating student misconceptions is a critical part of planning—it can greatly influence how the lesson is structured.

Table 8.1. Common errors and misconceptions about the operations and how to help.

Common Error or Misconception	What It Looks Like	How to Help
1. There is no relationship between addition and subtraction and/or multiplication and division (they do not see the inverse relationship)	Students don't use addition to solve subtraction situations Students don't use multiplication to solve division problems (Ding, 2016).	• Avoid the rote use of fact families to teach the inverse relationship as that emphasizes procedures without having students see the relationship. • Use concrete materials and have students act out a series of problems with the same three numbers—showing how the part-part-whole or the number in each group, the number of groups and the product relate to each other. • Explicitly point out the inverse relationship.
2. Addition or multiplication make numbers bigger (and the corollary that the factors in a multiplication problems are always smaller than the product)	Students believe that they should always get a larger answer in an addition or multiplication problem. They use this idea to check for a reasonable answer or to justify their thinking.	• When students point out these patterns say that these ideas are only true for some numbers (Karp, Bush, & Dougherty, 2014). • Point out counterexamples that are within their reach such as that 54 + 0 = 54 or that 15 × 0 = 0.

(continued)

Table 8.1. Common errors and misconceptions about the operations and how to help. *(continued)*

Common Error or Misconception	What It Looks Like	How to Help
3. Division makes numbers smaller and the divisor must be less than the dividend	Students believe that they should always get a smaller answer in a subtraction or division problem. Students use this idea to check for a reasonable answer or to justify their thinking.	• Provide examples as well as counterexamples such as $8 \div 1 = 8$. Have students discuss when this "rule" works and when it does not. • Have students find ways to share 3 cookies with 5 friends. This will help them act out the division and see that the divisor can be greater than the dividend. • Avoid using generalizations that may appear to be "rules" unless the students are clear of the circumstances in which they will always work.
4. Students choose the wrong operation in word problems	Students add or use the operation you've been studying all week to answer all word problems	• Focus on the structure of the problems using graphic organizers or the story problem sorting activities discussed in this chapter.
5. Students think the remainder is left over and not part of the answer	Students write 9 R 2 and do not use the remainder in deciding how to answer the question Students forget about the remainder and do not include it in their answer at all.	• Give students the multiple problems shared in this chapter that show the various ways remainders need to be interpreted and how that interpretation affects the answer. • Give students problems from anonymous students that have the remainder interpreted improperly. Have students "grade" the problems and share the findings in a class discussion.
6. Students write the wrong division equation from the word problem	When given the problem 120 divided by 5 in a problem they write $5 \div 120$ or $120 \div 5$	• Ask students to create a story using the correct equation. See if the equation accurately matches the original problem.
7. Division by zero	Students write: $5 \div 0 = 0$	• Students must focus on division as having an inverse relationship with multiplication. What number when you multiply it by zero will equal 5? • Ask students to take out 5 counters. How many sets of 0 can be made? Or put 5 blocks in 0 equal groups. How many blocks are in each group?

9

Developing Basic
Fact Fluency

BIG IDEAS

1   Students move through three phases in developing fluency with basic fact combinations: counting, reasoning strategies and mastery (Baroody, 2006). Instruction and formative assessment must help students through these three phases without rushing them to know their facts only through memorization.

2   Number relationships provide the basis for strategies that help students remember basic facts. For example, when solving 7×8 you can help students think about decomposing the 7 into $2 + 5$. Then $(2 + 5) \times 8$ is the same as $2 \times 8 + 5 \times 8$. Using the distributive property and building off the benchmark of 5 allows students to use the structure and number relationships that continue to help them with larger numbers.

3   All of the facts are conceptually related so students can figure out new or unknown facts using those they already know. In the case of multiplication, 6×8 can be thought of as five 8s (40) and one more 8. It might also be three 8s doubled.

4   When students struggle with developing basic fact fluency, they may need to return to the use of strategies and number relationships, more drill is not the answer.

Basic facts for addition and multiplication are the number combinations for which both *addends*, or both *factors*, are less than 10. Basic facts for subtraction and division are the corresponding combinations. Therefore, $15 - 8 = 7$ is a basic subtraction fact because the corresponding addends are each less than 10. The goal with basic facts is to develop fluency.

The *Common Core State Standards* (CCSSO, 201) describe this as students being able to (1) flexibly, (2) accurately, (3) efficiently, and (4) appropriately solve problems.

Developmental Phases for Learning the Basic Fact Combinations

Mastery of a basic fact means that a student can give a quick and accurate response (in about 3–5 seconds) without resorting to inefficient means, such as counting by ones. According to the *Common Core State Standards for Mathematics* (CCSSO, 2010), addition and subtraction concepts should be learned in first grade, with quick recall of basic addition and subtraction facts mastered by the end of grade 2. Also in second grade, multiplication begins with knowledge of equal groups of objects which is the foundation for the one-digit multiplication facts which must be known by the end of grade 3.

Developing fluency with basic facts is a developmental process—just like every topic in this book! Flash cards and timed tests are not the best way to foster fluency. Instead, focus on number sense! Research indicates that early number sense predicts school mathematics success more than other measures of cognition like verbal, spatial, or memory skills (Jordan, Kaplan, Locuniak, & Ramineni, 2007; Locuniak & Jordan, 2008; Mazzocco & Thompson, 2005).

Students progress from counting by ones to eventually "just knowing" that $2 + 7$ is 9 or that 5×4 is 20. This developmental progression takes time and students must experience many opportunities to learn a variety of reasoning strategies. Arthur Baroody, a mathematics educator who does research on basic facts, describes three phases in the process of learning facts (2006, p. 22):

1. *Counting strategies*—using object counting (e.g., blocks or fingers) or verbal counting to determine the answer. Example: $4 + 7 =$ _____. Student starts with 7 and counts on verbally (8, 9, 10, 11), or the student counts 4, counts 7, and then "counts all" over again to reach 11.

2. *Reasoning strategies*—using known information to logically determine an unknown combination. Example: 6×6. Student knows that 6×5 equals 30, so one more group of 6 is 36.

3. *Mastery*—producing answers efficiently (fast and accurately). Example: 5×5. Student quickly responds, "It's 25; I just know it."

Over many years, research supports the notion that basic fact mastery is dependent on the development of reasoning strategies (Baroody, 2003, 2006; Brownell & Chazal, 1935; Carpenter & Moser, 1984; Fuson, 1992; Henry & Brown, 2008). We align with this research by focusing on effective ways to teach students in grades 3 through 5 to use reasoning strategies and sense making to master the basic facts (Baroody's phases 2 and 3).

 Formative Assessment Note

When are students ready to work on reasoning strategies? Based on the research, when they are able to (1) efficiently use counting strategies (start with the largest number and count up, or in the case of multiplication, start with a known fact and count up one more group) and (2) when they are able to decompose numbers (e.g., that 6 can be decomposed into $5 + 1$). Interview students by posing one-digit multiplication problems and ask how they solved it. For example, 3×8—do they know this represents 3 groups of 8? Do they see it as 2 eights and one more group of 8?

Teaching and Assessing the Basic Fact Combinations

This section describes the different ways that basic fact instruction has been implemented in schools followed by a section describing effective strategies.

Different Approaches to Teaching the Basic Facts

Over the last century, three main approaches have been used to teach the basic facts. The pros and cons of each approach are briefly described here.

Memorization

This approach moves from presenting concepts of addition and multiplication straight to the memorization of each fact, without devoting time to developing strategies (Baroody, Bajwa, & Eiland, 2009). This approach requires students to memorize 100 separate addition facts (just for the combinations of 0 through 9) and 100 separate multiplication facts (0–9). Students may even have to memorize subtraction and division facts separately, bringing the total to more than 300 individual facts! There is strong evidence that this method simply does not work. You may be tempted to respond that you learned your facts in this manner, however, as long ago as 1935 studies concluded that students actually develop a **variety of strategies** for learning basic facts in spite of the large amounts of isolated drill they experience (Brownell & Chazal, 1935). Moreover, Baroody (2006, p. 27) points out three limitations with memorization:

- *Inefficiency.* There are too many facts to memorize.
- *Inappropriate applications.* Students misapply the facts and don't check their work for reasonableness.
- *Inflexibility.* Students don't learn flexible strategies for finding the sums or products and therefore continue to count by ones.

Notice that a memorization approach works against the development of *fluency* (which includes being able to flexibly, accurately, efficiently, and appropriately solve problems).

Struggling learners and students with disabilities often have difficulty memorizing so many isolated facts and are trapped in phase 1, relying on the use of counting strategies instead of developing more complex mathematical thinking (Mazzocco et al., 2008). Instead, they need explicit instruction on reasoning strategies. In addition, drill can cause unnecessary anxiety and undermine student interest and confidence in mathematics. Connecting new knowledge to what students already know allows all students to master the basic facts.

Explicit Strategy Instruction

For more than three decades, explicit strategy instruction has been used in many classrooms. Students learn a strategy, then explore and practice the strategy. Research supports the use of explicit strategy instruction as effective in helping all students learn (and remember) their basic facts (e.g., Baroody, 1985; Bley & Thornton, 1995; Fuson, 1984, 1992; Rathmell, 1978).

Explicitly teaching strategies supports student reasoning in choosing strategies that help them get solutions rather than give the students something new to memorize. It is not effective to just memorize strategies (for the same reason that memorizing isolated facts doesn't work). A heavy focus on memorizing basic fact strategies, results in students who lack number-sense (Henry & Brown, 2008). The key is to help students experience the possible strategies and then choose one that helps them solve the particular problem.

Guided Invention

Standards for
Mathematical Practice

7 Look for and make use of structure. ▶

Guided invention also focuses on strategies, but in a more open-ended manner. It emphasizes having students select a strategy based on their knowledge of number relationships (Gravemeijer & van Galen, 2003). For example, a student may think of 9×4 as "9 times 2 is 18 and double that equals 36." Another student notes that 10×4 equals 40, so you take 4 from the 40 to get 36. Still another student may know 9×5 equals 45 and you subtract 9 from that to get 36. What is important is that students use number combinations and relationships that make sense to them.

Gravemeijer and van Galen call this approach *guided invention* because many of the efficient strategies will not be developed by all students without teacher guidance. That is, the teacher designs sequenced tasks and problems that will promote students' noticing of number relationships. Then, students articulate these strategies and share them with peers where they talk through the decisions they made and share counterexamples.

Teaching Basic Facts Effectively

Plan experiences that help students move on a trajectory through the three phases. One effective approach is to use story problems with numbers selected in such a manner that students are most likely to develop a particular strategy as they solve them.

Use Story Problems

Research reveals that when a strong emphasis is placed on solving problems, students not only become better problem solvers but also master more basic facts than students in a drill-based program (National Research Council, 2001). Story problems provide a context that can help students understand the situation and apply flexible strategies for doing computation.

Some teachers are hesitant to use story problems with ELLs or students with disabilities because of the additional language or reading required, but because language supports understanding, story problems are important for all students. But contexts selected must be relevant and understood.

Multiplication stories can focus on array situations. Arrays help students see how to decompose a fact (splitting the rows) and see the commutative property (e.g., $3 \times 7 = 7 \times 3$). For example, consider that a class is working on the 7s facts. The teacher points to the calendar (an array) and poses the following question:

In 3 weeks we will be going to the zoo. How many days until we go to the zoo?

Standards for
Mathematical Practice

3 Construct viable arguments and critique the reasoning of others. ▶

Suppose that Aidan explains how he figured out 3×7 by starting with double 7 (14) and then adding 7 more. Ask students to explain why Aidan's approach worked.

This requires students to attend to ideas that come from their classmates. Now explore with the class if doubling could be used for other 7s facts. Ask, "How might doubling help us find how many days in 4 weeks (4×7)? Students may discuss that this problem can be thought of as a combination of facts (e.g., that 4×7 equals $2 \times (2 \times 7)$ or 7 doubled and doubled again), applying important properties of multiplication.

With other multiplication story problems, students may notice that all of the facts with a 3 as a factor will work for the "double and add one more set" strategy. Others may say that you can always add one more group on if you know the next smaller fact. For example, for 6×8, you can start with 5×8 and add 8. Students with disabilities may be challenged to keep all of their peers' ideas in working memory, so recording the ideas and strategies where they are visible as a reference is an effective support.

Explicitly Teach Reasoning Strategies

Standards for
Mathematical Practice

◀ **2 Reason abstractly
and quantitatively.**

A second approach is to explicitly teach reasoning strategies. A lesson may be designed to have students examine collections of facts for which a particular type of strategy is appropriate. The "big idea" behind teaching reasoning strategies is for student to make use of *known facts* and relationships to *derive unknown facts*.

Don't expect to introduce a strategy and have it understood by students in just one lesson or activity. Just as when using story problems, students need lots of opportunities to make strategies their own, or to use new strategies that classmates have shared. Many students will simply not be ready to use an idea in the first few days, and then suddenly something will connect and the idea has meaning! No student should be forced to adopt someone else's strategy, but every student should be required to understand strategies that are presented in discussions.

To help students recall possible strategy options, it is a good idea to display reasoning strategies so they can be used as a reference. Give strategies names that make sense to students with corresponding examples (e.g., "Strategy for $\times$ 3: Double and add one more set. Ex: $3 \times 7 = (2 \times 7) + 7 = 14 + 7 = 21$").

Assessing Basic Facts Effectively

A glance back at Chapter 3 will illustrate many formative assessment strategies: observations, questions, interviews, and tasks. Why do we use these strategies? To identify what students know and what they do not know so that we can design instruction. Why, then, is assessment of basic facts often limited to timed tests? We must do better if we are going to ensure that all students learn their basic facts.

What Is Wrong with Timed Tests?

First, timed tests do not assess the four elements of fluency: (1) flexibility, (2) appropriate strategy use, (3) efficiency, and (4) accuracy (Kling & Bay-Williams, 2014). You gain no insights into which strategies students are using, nor if they are flexible in using those strategies. You have a little insight into how efficient they are, but you don't really know much here either, because they might have used very inefficient strategies for some facts while going quickly through others. So, at best, you get a sense of which facts they are getting correct (accuracy). Second, timed tests negatively affect students' number sense and recall of facts (Boaler, 2012, 2014; Henry & Brown, 2008; Ramirez, Gunderson, Levine, & Beilock, 2013). Third, timed tests are not needed for students to master their facts (Kling, 2011), so they take up time that could be used in meaningful and more engaging learning experiences.

How Might I Assess Basic Fact Fluency?

As you assess, remember there is no one "best" strategy for any fact. For example, $7 + 8$ could be solved using Making 10 or Near-Doubles. The more you emphasize choice, the more students will be able to find strategies that work for them, and that will lead to their own fact fluency.

Think about each of the four elements of fluency (appropriate strategy selection, flexibility, efficiency, and accuracy) and ask yourself, "How can I determine if each of my students is able to do that for this set of facts?" Table 9.1 offers a few ideas for each element of fluency (based on Kling & Bay-Williams, 2014).

Reasoning Strategies for Addition Facts

Addition facts—the sums through 20—are considered mastery items in the second-grade curriculum (CCSSO, 2010). However, very few third-grade teachers will ever see a new class that

Table 9.1 Effective strategies for assessing basic fact fluency.

Aspect of Fluency	Observation	Interview Probes	Tasks
Appropriate strategy selection	As they play a game, are they selecting a strategy that makes sense for that fact? For example, for 9 × 5 they might skip count by fives.	Tell a student that Nicolas solved 6 × 8 by changing it in his mind to 5 × 8 and adding one more group of 8. What did he do? Did he use a good strategy? Tell why or why not.	Review the multiplication table. Write which facts are your "toughies." Next to each one, tell a strategy that would help you find that product.
Flexibility	Listen as students discuss their strategies. Do they notice that 8 × 3 is equal to 3 × 8?	Ask a student to solve 6 × 7 using one strategy. Then ask him to try solving it using a different strategy.	Explain how you think about these two problems: 11 × 3 = 11 × 9 =
Efficiency	How long does it take students to select a strategy? Are they quick to use doubles? Does efficiency vary with certain facts, like multiplication facts with easy skip counts like 5s or ones that have more challenging skip counts like the 7s facts?	Ask a student to sort the fact cards in this collection by the ones you *just know* and the ones where you *use a strategy*.	Here are 10 basic fact problems. If you *just know* the answer, circle it. If you *used a strategy*, write the strategy's name (e.g., Double and Double again).
Accuracy	Notice which facts are students consistently getting correct.	Ask: What is the answer to 7 × 8? How do you know it is correct? How can you check your answer?	Review your [3s facts] with your partner using these fact cards. Sort them into the ones when you were correct and those that were not correct. Record which facts you are sure of and which you are still learning.

has mastered all addition facts, and many teachers of fourth and fifth graders find students who still have gaps. For teachers in grades 3 through 5, the following ideas are important:

- Addition facts can be connected to one or more very important number relationships. For students who have not reached fluency, devote attention to those relationships rather than spending time on drill.
- Students rarely reach fluency with a subtraction fact if they don't know the corresponding addition fact. That is, if a student knows 12 − 8, it is almost certain that he or she knows 8 + 4. Therefore, addition fact fluency should be considered a prerequisite to subtraction fact fluency.
- Diagnosis of what facts students have mastered and where gaps remain will help you develop a targeted instructional plan. Time invested in this analysis will save time!

The following sections provide a brief look at key strategies for addition facts that will help you plan effective activities to help students in grades 3 through 5 reach fact fluency with addition and subtraction.

One More Than and Two More Than

As students enter third grade there is an expectation that some strategy use and facts are mastered. Because 51 of the 100 addition facts involve a 0, 1, or a 2, these are likely facts that are known. Students who are missing facts with a zero are often holding on to the faulty notion that "addition makes bigger." Therefore, they might answer 8 to 7 + 0. These facts do not require any strategy, but rather a good understanding of the meaning of zero and the meaning of addition.

Many students use a counting-on strategy for facts with addends of 1 or 2, as well as those involving a 3. However, we strongly suggest that you discourage the use of counting on for all facts. It is difficult for some students to separate counting on for some facts and not for others. Students in grades 3 through 5 who have not yet mastered addition facts are often using counting on for facts such as 8 + 5, for which that strategy is not efficient. Try Activity 9.1 for students who need additional practice.

Activity 9.1

CCSS-M: 2.OA.B.2

One More Than and Two More Than with Dice and Spinners

Make a die with sides labeled + 1, + 2, + 1, + 2, "one more," and "two more" (or higher numbers if other practice is needed). Use with another die labeled 3, 4, 5, 6, 7, and 8 (or whatever values students need to practice). After each roll of the dice, students should say the complete fact: "Four and two more equals six." Alternatively, roll one die and use a spinner with + 1 on one half and + 2 on the other half. For students with disabilities, you may want to start with a die that just has + 2 on every side and then another day move on to a + 3 die and so on. This will help emphasize and practice one approach. Similarly, in Expanded Lesson: Two More Than/Two Less Than, students use dot cards to connect the idea of more and less to adding and subtracting.

Combinations of 10

Perhaps the most important strategy for students to know is using the combinations that add to 10 (Kling, 2011). Starting with story problems using two numbers that add to 10, or that ask how many are needed to equal 10, can assist this process.

The ten-frame is a very useful tool for creating a visual image for students developing this strategy. Place six counters starting on the upper left corner on one ten-frame and ask, "How many more to equal 10?" This activity can be repeated frequently with counters or the little ten-frame cards until all combinations that equal 10 are mastered. Knowing number combinations that equal 10 not only helps with basic fact mastery but also builds the foundations for working on addition with higher numbers and understanding place-value concepts. Consider, for example, 28 + 7. Using the Combinations of 10 strategy, students can add 2 up to 30 and then 5 more. This strategy can be extended to Combinations of 100.

Making 10

Thirty-six facts have sums greater than 10, and all of those facts can be solved by using the Making 10 strategy; making this a very useful approach. Before using this strategy, be sure that students have learned to think of the numbers 11 to 18 as 10 and some more. Surprisingly, many third-grade students have not constructed this relationship.

Students use their known facts that equal 10 and then add the rest of the remaining addend on to the 10. For example, to solve 6 + 8, students can start with the larger number and see that 8 is 2 away from 10; therefore, they take 2 from the 6 to equal 10 and then add on the remaining 4 to get the answer 14. This process is also called Break Apart to Make Ten (or BAMT) (Sarama & Clements, 2009) and Up Over 10 (CCSS-M uses the name Making 10). Activities 9.2, 9.3, and 9.4 are additional ways to support students who still need to practice strategies for addition.

Activity 9.2

CCSS-M: 2.OA.B.2

Move It, Move It

This activity is designed to help students focus on the strategy of Making 10. Access the Move It, Move It Activity Page and a Double Ten-Frame. Place flash cards next to the ten-frames or a fact can be given orally. The students should first model each number in the two ten-frames with counters to represent the problem (9 + 6 would mean covering nine places on one frame and six on the other). Ask students to move it—that is, to decide a way to group the counters to show (without counting) what the total is. Ask students to explain what they did and connect it to the new equation. For example, 9 + 6 may become 10 + 5 by moving one counter up to the first ten-frame. Emphasize strategies that are working for students, such as Combinations of 10 or Making 10 (See Blackline Master 1). After students have found a total, have students share and record the equations. Students who are still using counting strategies or students with disabilities may need additional experience or one-on-one time working on this process.

The Making 10 strategy is heavily emphasized in high-performing countries (Korea, China, Taiwan, and Japan) in which students learn facts sooner and more accurately than U.S. students (Henry & Brown, 2008). Henry and Brown found that the Making 10 strategy contributed more to developing fluency with facts (e.g., 7 + 8) than using doubles (even though doubles had been emphasized by teachers and textbooks). Moreover, this strategy can be later applied to adding "up over" 20, 50, or other benchmark numbers. For example, for 28 + 7, students can make 30, seeing that 28 + 7 = 30 + 5. Thus, the long-term utility of this reasoning strategy deserves significant attention.

Activity 9.3

CCSS-M: 2.OA.B.2

Frames and Facts

Make little ten-frame cards and display them to the class on a projector. Show an 8 (or 9) card. Place other cards beneath it one at a time as students respond with the total. Have students say what they are doing. For 8 + 4, they might say, "Take 2 from the 4 and put it with 8 to equal 10. Then 10 and the 2 more left over equals 12." Move to harder cards, like 7 + 6. Ask students to record each equation. Especially for students with disabilities, highlight how they should explicitly think about filling in the little ten-frame starting with the higher number. Show and talk about how it is more challenging to start with the lower number as a counterexample.

+	0	1	2	3	4	5	6	7	8	9
0	0	1								
1	1	2	3							
2		3	4	5						
3			5	6	7					
4				7	8	9				
5					9	10	11			
6						11	12	13		
7							13	14	15	
8								15	16	17
9									17	18

Doubles and Near-Doubles

There are only 10 doubles facts, and only seven of these have addends of 3 or greater. However, these seven facts provide useful anchors for other facts often referred to as the *near-doubles:* facts such as 6 + 7 or 5 + 4, for which the addends are only one apart (plus one or minus one). This is a strategy that uses a known fact to drive an unknown fact. The strategy is to double the smaller number and add 1, or to double the larger number and then subtract 1. Therefore, students must know the doubles before you focus on this strategy.

Some students find it easy to extend the idea of the near-doubles to double-plus-two.

Activity 9.4

CCSS-M: 2.OA.B.2

On the Double!

Create a display of the doubles or use the **On the Double** Activity Page (see Figure 9.1). Then cut out the cards with **Near-Doubles Cards** (e.g., 4 + 5). Ask students to find the doubles fact that could help them solve the fact they have on the card and place it on that spot. Ask students if there are other doubles that could help.

Reasoning Strategies for Subtraction Facts

Subtraction facts prove to be more difficult than addition. This is especially true when students have been taught subtraction through a *count-count-count* approach—that is, for 13 – 5, *count* 13, *count* off 5, *count* what's left. Counting is the first phase in reaching basic fact mastery, but unfortunately many fourth, fifth, and sixth graders are still counting.

Without opportunities to learn and use reasoning strategies, students will continue to rely on inefficient counting strategies, which is a slow and often inaccurate approach. Therefore, spend sufficient time working on the reasoning strategies outlined here to help students move to phase 2 and to mastery (phase 3).

Figure 9.1

Near-doubles facts.

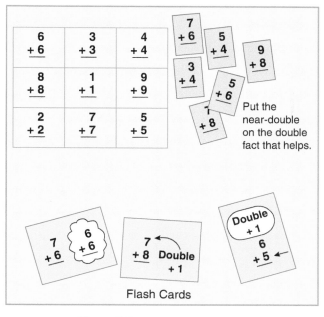

Think-Addition

As the name of this strategy implies, students use known addition facts to produce the unknown quantity or part of the whole (subtraction). In Figure 9.2, subtraction is modeled in such a way that students are encouraged to think, "What adds to this part to make the total?" thus using the inverse relationship of addition to subtraction to produce the answer. If this important relationship between parts and wholes—between addition and subtraction—can be made, subtraction facts and two- and three-digit subtraction problems will be much easier (Peltenburg, van den Heuvel-Panhuizen, & Robitzsch, 2012). When students see 9 − 4, you want them to think spontaneously, "Four and what number adds to nine?" By contrast, observe a third-grade student who struggles with this fact. The idea of thinking addition never occurs to the student. Instead, the student counts back from 9 and may or may not end up with 5 as the answer. The value of think-addition to solve subtraction problems cannot be overstated. This means that it is essential that addition facts be mastered first.

Story problems that promote think-addition are those that sound like addition but have a missing addend: join–start unknown; join–change unknown; and part–part–whole–part unknown (see Chapter 8 for more on these problem structures). Consider this problem:

Figure 9.2

Using a think-addition model for subtraction.

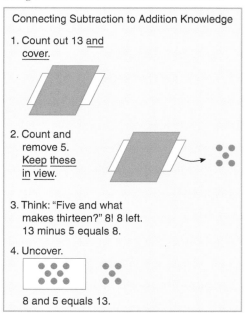

Jack had 5 fish in his aquarium. Grandma gave him some more fish. Then he had 12 fish. How many fish did Grandma give Jack?

Standards for
Mathematical Practice

> **7** **Look for and make use of structure.** ▶

Notice that the action is join, which suggests addition. Students should think, "*Five and how many more adds up to 12?*" In the discussion in which you use problems such as this, your task is to connect this thought process with the subtraction fact 12 − 5. Students may use a Making 10 strategy to solve this problem, just as they did with addition facts ("It takes 5 to get to 10 and 2 more to 12 . . . . Equals 7").

 ## Formative Assessment Note

For third graders and beyond, you may need to assess another aspect of the addition and subtraction relationship—two expressions on either side of the equal sign. This is a format that your students should be able to solve using sense making. For example, in an interview try 8 + 4 = □ + 5. If students are reasoning that this, too, is a "think-addition" situation, that will give you important information that they are on the right track. By contrast, if they put a 12 (added the 8 + 4) or 17 (added all the numbers) in the box, you can suspect that your student is not using think-addition and may even have a misconception about the meaning of the equal sign (see Chapter 15 for additional information).

Stop and Reflect 500 ୨,²⁵⁰   ⁇3⅗ ▱⁸⅚° ∞∩ ✘ 2.5

Look at the three subtraction facts shown here and try to reflect on what thought process you use to get the answers. Even if you "just know them," think about what a possible approach might be.

14	12	15
−9	−7	−6

Down Under 10

You may have applied a think-addition strategy the problems in the Stop and Reflect. Or, in the first problem you may have started with the 14 and take away to 10 (4) and then take away 1 more to 9, for a total difference of 5. This reasoning strategy is called Down Under 10. If you didn't already use this strategy, try it with one of the examples.

This reasoning strategy is a derived fact strategy because students use what they know (that 14 minus 4 equals 10) to figure out a related fact (14 − 5). Like the Combinations of 10 and Making 10 strategies, this strategy is also emphasized in high-performing countries (Fuson & Kwon, 1992) and not emphasized enough in the United States. One reason this strategy is so useful is that it supports students' number sense while moving them to fact fluency.

Reinforce the Down Under 10 strategy, by posing story problems such as the following:

Becky has 16 stuffed animals. She gave 7 to a friend. How many does Becky have left?
(separate problem)

Becky walks 16 blocks to school. Corwin walks 9 blocks. How many more blocks does Becky
walk?
(comparison problem)

Take from 10

This excellent strategy is also consistently used in high-performing countries but not commonly used in the United States. It takes advantage of students' knowledge of the combinations that equal 10, and it works for all subtraction problems in which the starting value (minuend) is greater than 10. For example, take the problem $16 - 8$. Students decompose the 16 into $10 + 6$. Subtracting from the 10 (because they know this fact), $10 - 8$ equals 2. Then they add the 6 back on $(2 + 6)$ to get 8. Try it on these examples:

$$15 - 8 = \quad 17 - 9 = \quad 14 - 8 =$$

Reasoning Strategies for Multiplication and Division Facts

Using a problem-based approach and focusing on reasoning strategies are just as important, if not more so, for developing fluency with multiplication and related division facts (Baroody, 2006; Wallace & Gurganus, 2005). As with addition and subtraction facts, start with story problems and concrete materials as you develop reasoning strategies. Watch this video of John A. Van de Walle as he discusses reasoning strategies for **multiplication.**

Understanding the commutative property reduces the number of basic facts to be learned in half! This can be visualized by using arrays. For example, a 2×8 array is described as 2 rows of 8 or can be turned to show 8 rows of 2. In both cases, the answer is 16.

Twos

Multiplication facts should not be presented in numerical order starting with 0s, 1s, and so on up though the 9s. Instead, build on students' strengths and prior knowledge and begin with a more conceptually sound approach. Facts that have 2 as a factor are equivalent to the addition doubles and should already be known by students. Help students realize that 2×7 is the same as $7 + 7$. One way to begin developing the doubles is by using a children's literature connection, *Two of Everything* (Hong, 1993). This Chinese folktale is the story of a couple (the Haktaks) who find a magic pot that doubles everything that is put inside. Using that story as a context, a simple doubling machine in the shape of a pot can be drawn, or students can use a mat with a pot shape. First, concrete items of a given number are deposited in the pot with the question "What amount comes out?" Then cards can be made with an input number on one card and the students

Teaching Tip

Although the numerical answers to 2×8 and 8×2 are the same, the calculations they mean are different: the convention in the United States is that 2×8 means 2 groups of 8; 8×2 means 8 groups of 2. The model you use should help explain the calculation. Although you shouldn't mark a student as incorrect for missing this distinction, you need to be precise in your language and models as you demonstrate representations of the problem in class.

×	0	1	2	3	4	5	6	7	8	9
0			0							
1			2							
2	0	2	4	6	8	10	12	14	16	18
3			6							
4			8							
5			10							
6			12							
7			14							
8			16							
9			18							

have to write the output on another card as it goes through the doubling pot or function machine. A pair of students or a small group can use input/output machines, with one student suggesting the input and the other(s) stating the output. Use this **Double Magic** Activity Page to help students record their ideas.

Also try story problems in which 2 is the number of sets. For example, have a calendar available and ask, "Our field trip is in 2 weeks. How many days will we need to wait?" (2 groups of 7 or 2 × 7) Later, use problems in which 2 is the size of the sets. For example, have buttons available and ask, "George was making sock puppets. Each puppet needed 2 buttons for eyes. If George makes 7 puppets, how many buttons will he need for the eyes?" (7 groups of 2 or 7 × 2).

Fives

×	0	1	2	3	4	5	6	7	8	9
0						0				
1						5				
2						10				
3						15				
4						20				
5	0	5	10	15	20	25	30	35	40	45
6						30				
7						35				
8						40				
9						45				

Practice skip counting by fives to 100. Keep track of how many groups of five have been counted (If we jump by 5s four times on the number line, where will we land?). Use arrays that have rows of 5 dots (see Figure 9.3). Point out that such an array with six rows is a model for 6 × 5, eight rows is 8 × 5, and so on. Time to the minute is also a good context for fives because of the structure of an analog clock.

Activity 9.5　　　CCSS-M: 3.OA.A.1; 3.OA.C.7

Clock Facts

Focus on the minute hand of the clock. When it points to a number, how many minutes after the hour is it? See Figure 9.3. Connect this idea to multiplication facts with 5. Hold up a **Clock Fact Card**, and then point to the number on the clock corresponding to the other factor. In this way, the fives facts become the "clock facts."

Figure 9.3

Fives facts.

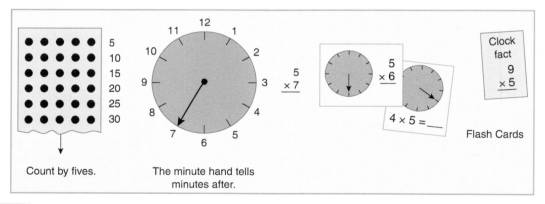

Count by fives.　　The minute hand tells minutes after.

×	0	1	2	3	4	5	6	7	8	9
0	0	0	0	0	0	0	0	0	0	0
1	0	1	2	3	4	5	6	7	8	9
2	0	2								
3	0	3								
4	0	4								
5	0	5								
6	0	6								
7	0	7								
8	0	8								
9	0	9								

Zeros and Ones

Thirty-six facts have at least one factor that is either 0 or 1. These facts, although seemingly easy on a procedural level, sometimes confuse students with "rules" they may have learned for addition. For example, when you add zero to a number (6 + 0), it does not change the number, but 6 × 0 is always zero or that 1 + n is the next counting number, but 1 × n does not change the number (equals n). The concepts behind these facts can be developed best through story problems. For example, invite students to tell stories to match a problem.

Avoid rules that aren't conceptually based, such as "Any number multiplied by zero is zero."

$6 \times 0 =$ ___. There are six rows of chairs with no people in each. How many people?

$0 \times 6 =$ ___. You worked 0 hours babysitting at $6 an hour. How much money did you make?

Nines

Facts with a factor of 9 include the largest products but can be among the easiest to learn due to several reasoning strategies and patterns that support students' learning. For example, 9s can be derived from 10s. First, 9×7 is the same as 10×7 less one set of 7, or $70 - 7$. Because students can often easily multiply by 10 and subtract from a decade value, this strategy makes sense. You might introduce a related idea by showing a set of connecting cubes (see Figure 9.4) with only the end cube a different color. After explaining that every bar has 10 cubes, ask students to find a way to figure out how many cubes are pink.

Nines facts have interesting patterns that lead to finding the products: (1) the tens digit of the product is one less than the "other" factor (the factor other than 9), and (2) the sum of the two digits in the product equals 9. For 7×9, 1 less than 7 is 6, and 6 and 3 equals 9, so the answer is 63. Ask students to record each fact for nines in order ($9 \times 1 = 9, 9 \times 2 = 18 \ldots 9 \times 9 = 81$) and write down patterns they notice. After discussing all the patterns, ask students how these patterns can be used to figure out a product to a nines fact. Challenge students to think about why this pattern works. (*Warning:* This strategy, grounded in the base-ten system, can be useful, but it also can cause confusion because the conceptual connection is not easy to see.) The nine pattern illustrates one of the values of pattern and regularity in mathematics.

A tactile way to help students remember the nifty nines is to use fingers—but not for counting! Here's how: Hold up both hands. Starting with the pinky on your left hand, count over to the finger that matches the factor (other than nine). For example, for 4×9, you move to the fourth finger (see Figure 9.5). Bend it down. Now look at the fingers— those fingers to the left of the folded finger represent tens; those to the right represent ones. You have three tens to the left of the folded finger and six ones to the right—36 (Barney, 1970).

×	0	1	2	3	4	5	6	7	8	9
0										0
1										9
2										18
3										27
4										36
5										45
6										54
7										63
8										72
9	0	9	18	27	36	45	54	63	72	81

Figure 9.4

Another way to think of the nines.

$4 \times 10 = 40$

4×9 is 4 less, 36

Standards for Mathematical Practice

8 **Look for and express regularity in repeated reasoning.**

Derived Multiplication Fact Strategies

Only 25 multiplication facts remain (actually only 15 if students use the commutative property). These remaining facts can be learned by relating each to an already known fact. Again, students must first know their foundational facts of 0s, 1s, 2s, 5s, and 10s.

Decomposing a Factor

This strategy involves the partitioning of one of the factors into a sum that will generate easier facts and then the products are joined for the total. So, for example, 8×6 can have the factor of 6 decomposed into $4 + 2$. Then I know 8×4 equals 32 and 8×2 equals 16. The sum of 32 and 16 equals 48.

Figure 9.5

Nifty nines using fingers to show 4×9.

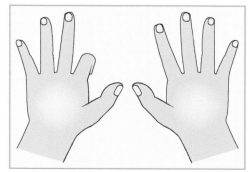

×	0	1	2	3	4	5	6	7	8	9
0										
1										
2										
3				9	12		18	21	24	
4				12	16		24	28	32	
5										
6				18	24		36	42	48	
7				21	28		42	49	56	
8				24	32		48	56	64	
9										

Figure 9.6

An array is a useful model for developing strategies for the hard multiplication facts.

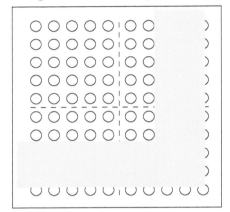

Arrays are powerful models for deriving multiplication facts using this strategy. Provide students with copies of the 10×10 **dot array** (Figure 9.6). The lines in the array make counting the dots easier and often suggest the use of the easier fives facts as helpers. For example, 7×7 equals 5×7 plus 2×7, or $35 + 14$.

Activity 9.6 is an example of a game that helps students derive the facts using arrays.

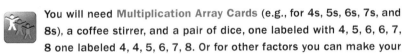

Activity 9.6

CCSS-M: 3.OA.A.1; 3.OA.B.5; 3.OA.C.7

Strive to Derive

You will need **Multiplication Array Cards** (e.g., for 4s, 5s, 6s, 7s, and 8s), a coffee stirrer, and a pair of dice, one labeled with 4, 5, 6, 6, 7, 8 one labeled 4, 4, 5, 6, 7, 8. Or for other factors you can make your own cards (and corresponding dice) using **1-Centimeter Grid Paper** and cut out each possible size and label the multiplication fact on the card.). Spread the cards on the table so they can be seen. Player 1 rolls the dice and selects the related array card. Player 1 then places the coffee stirrer to partition the array into known facts. If Player 1 rolled a 4 and a 6, she would pick the 4-by-6 array. She can partition it as 2×6 and 2×6 or as 3×6 and 1×6. If Player 1 can solve the fact using derived facts in this way, she scores 1 point. Return array card to the collection. Player 2 repeats the process. Continue to 10 points. Initially, or to modify for students who struggle, focus on one set of facts, for example, Strive to Derive from 5 where one die has all 5s on it.

Doubling and Halving

Doubling is very effective in helping students learn difficult facts (Flowers & Rubenstein, 2010–2011). The Double and Double Again strategy shown in Figure 9.7(a) is applicable to all facts with 4 as a factor. To multiply by 4, you can double and double again. For example, 4×6 is the same as 2×6 doubled. Doubling has been found to be very effective in helping middle school students master multiplication facts, increasing their reasoning skills as well as their confidence (Flowers & Rubenstein, 2010/2011).

Note, though, that for 4×8, double 16 is also a difficult addition. Help students with this by discussing, for example, that $15 + 15$ is 30, and $16 + 16$ is 2 more, or 32. Adding $16 + 16$ on paper defeats the development of efficient reasoning.

The Double and One More Set strategy shown in Figure 9.7(b) is a way to think of facts with 3 as one factor. With an array or a set picture, the double part can be circled, and it is clear that there is one more set. Two facts in this group involve difficult mental additions: 3×8 and 3×9. Using doubling and one more, you can generate any fact.

If either factor is even, a Half Then Double strategy as shown in Figure 9.7(c) can be used. Select the even factor, and cut it in half. If the smaller fact is known, that product is doubled to get the new fact.

Figure 9.7

Reasoning strategies of doubling, halving, and adding or subtracting a group to derive an unknown fact.

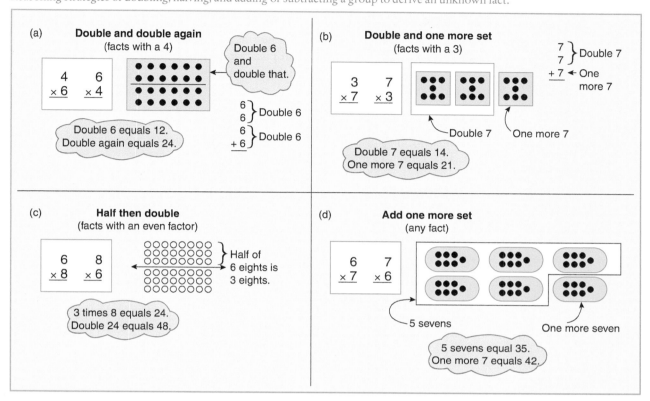

Adding or Subtracting a Group

This strategy builds off known foundational facts and then adds or subtracts the remaining group (see Figure 9.7(d)). For example, 3×8 is connected to 2×8 (double 8 and add 8 more). The fact 9×8 might be a challenge, but the student can think 10×8 equals 80 and subtract one group of 8 and get 72.

When using 5×8 to help with 6×8, the language "6 groups of eight" or "6 eights" is very helpful in remembering to add *8 more and not 6 more*. This Adding or Subtracting a Group reasoning strategy reinforces students' number sense and relationships between numbers and can be used to derive any unknown fact.

Standards for
Mathematical Practice

7
**Look for and
express regularity in
repeated reasoning.**

 Formative Assessment Note

Use word problems as a vehicle for assessing harder facts in a one-on-one diagnostic interview. Consider this problem: *Connie put her old crayons into bags of 7. She was able to make 8 bags with 3 crayons left over. How many crayons did she have?* Or *Carlos and Jack kept their baseball cards in albums with 6 cards on each page. Carlos had 4 pages filled, and Jack had 8 pages filled. How many cards did each boy have?* (Do you see the opportunity for the Half Then Double strategy?)

As the student works to get an answer, encourage her to talk about the strategies she is using. Ask her if she can solve it another way. This push adds to the benefit of the assessment by seeing what methods your student can draw from. Remember, students with disabilities may need arrays and pictures of sets or groups to help interpret the information from the problems and support their thinking about multiplication facts and relationships.

Division Facts

Division fact mastery is dependent on the inverse relationship of multiplication and division. For example, to solve $36 \div 9$, we tend to think, "Nine times what number equals thirty-six?" In fact, because of this relationship, the reasoning strategies for division are to (1) think multiplication and then (2) apply a known multiplication fact, as needed. Story problems with missing factors can be a vehicle to develop this connection.

Exercises such as $50 \div 6$ might be called *near facts*. Divisions with remainders are much more prevalent in real-life situations than division facts or division without remainders. To determine the answer to $50 \div 6$, most people mentally review a short sequence of multiplication facts, comparing each product to 50: 6 times 7 (low), 6 times 8 (close), 6 times 9 (high). It must be 8. That's 48 and 2 left over. Students should be able to do these near-fact problems mentally and with reasonable speed.

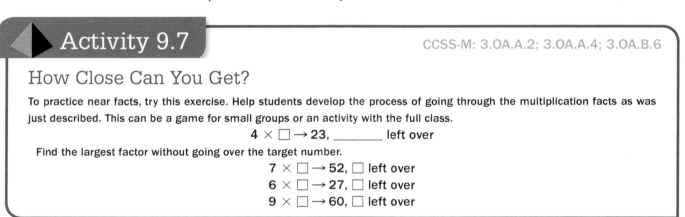

◀▲ Activity 9.7   CCSS-M: 3.OA.A.2; 3.OA.A.4; 3.OA.B.6

How Close Can You Get?

To practice near facts, try this exercise. Help students develop the process of going through the multiplication facts as was just described. This can be a game for small groups or an activity with the full class.

$4 \times \square \rightarrow 23,$ _____ left over

Find the largest factor without going over the target number.

$7 \times \square \rightarrow 52, \square$ left over
$6 \times \square \rightarrow 27, \square$ left over
$9 \times \square \rightarrow 60, \square$ left over

Reinforcing Basic Fact Mastery

When students "just know" a fact, or can apply a reasoning strategy so quickly they almost don't realize they've done it (e.g., doubling) they have reached phase 3: mastery. The *Common Core State Standards* precisely state that students will "know from memory" (CCSSO, 2010, pp. 19, 23). Repeated experiences with reasoning strategies are effective in committing facts to memory; memorizing is not. Therefore, games or activities that focus on reasoning strategies are more effective than drilling with flash cards or computer programs.

Drill in the absence of accomplishing success at previous phases has repeatedly been demonstrated as ineffective. Students must be fluent with the basic facts, as students who continue to struggle with the facts often fail to understand higher mathematics concepts. Their cognitive energy gets pulled into computation when it should be focusing on the more sophisticated concepts being developed (Forbringer & Fahsl, 2010).

Games to Support Basic Fact Mastery

Games are fun to play over and over again and therefore are an excellent way to provide repeated experiences for students to learn their facts. Playing games that infuse reasoning strategies helps students be able to flexibly select strategies, decide which strategy is most appropriate for the given problem, and become more efficient and accurate in finding the answer. This is what it takes to become *fluent* with the basic facts! In addition, games increase student involvement, encourage student-to-student interaction, and improve communication—all of which are related to improved academic achievement (Bay-Williams & Kling, 2014; Forbringer & Fahsl, 2010; Kamii & Anderson, 2003; Lewis, 2005). Look at these ideas in a **Collection of Classic Games** that are adapted to help students with basic fact mastery.

As you use games, remember to focus on related clusters of facts and on what individual students need to practice. Also, encourage students to self-monitor—they can create their own game/board/game, including the facts they are working on.

Activity 9.8

What's under My Thumb?

Create a deck of circle cards with fact families (either addition or multiplication) for each pair of students or have students create their own based on the facts they need to be practicing (see Figure 9.8(a)). You can begin this activity as a whole class and ask students why they think the numbers go together and why one number is circled. Then hold up a card with your thumb over one number. Ask, "What is under my thumb?" Call on a student to share the answer and how they reasoned to get the answer. Place students in partners with their sets of cards and play. Groups can switch decks with other groups for more experiences. Individuals can explore cards like the ones in Figure 9.8(b), with the answer on the back. Alternatively, you can use **Missing Number Cards** rather than circles (see Figure 9.8(c)) or the **Missing Part Worksheet**. Differentiate for students with disabilities by strategically selecting a cluster that emphasizes a particular strategy.

As a follow up to Activity 9.8, you can create a set of your own cards using the blank **Missing Number Cards template** (see Figure 9.9) can be used to fill in any sets of facts you wish to emphasize.

Figure 9.8

Introducing missing number cards. Note: These are shown for addition/subtraction but work well for multiplication/division, too.

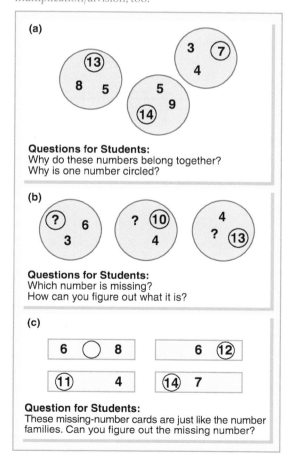

Figure 9.9

Example of a missing number activity page. Although shown here with addition, this page can also be used with multiplication.

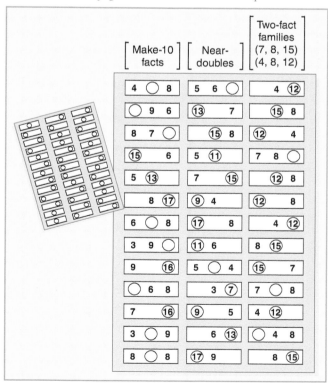

Consider Activity 9.9 for a way to engage students in creatively applying all four operations.

Activity 9.9

CCSS-M: 2.OA.B.2; 3.OA.C.7; 5.OA.A.1

Bowl a Fact

In this activity (suggested by Shoecraft, 1982), you draw circles placed in a triangular fashion to look like bowling pins, with the front circle labeled 1 and the others labeled consecutively through 10. Use the **Bowl a Fact** Activity Page that includes lines for recording equations. For culturally diverse classrooms, be sure that students are familiar with bowling. (If they are not, consider showing an online video clip.)

Take three dice and roll them. Students use all three numbers on the three dice to come up with equations that result in answers that are on the pins. For example, if you roll 4, 2, and 3, they can "knock down" the 5 pin with $4 \times 2 - 3$. If they can produce equations using these three numbers to knock down all 10 pins, they get a strike. If not, they roll again and see whether the three new numbers used in equations can knock the rest of the pins down for a spare. The pins that are left standing are added to get a score. Low score wins. After demonstrating the game, students can play in small groups.

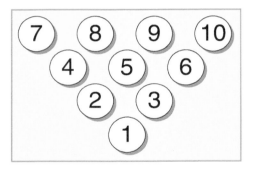

Activity 9.10

CCSS-M: 2.OA.B.2;
3.OA.B.5; 3.OA.B.6; 3.OA.C.7

Salute!

Place students in groups of three and give each group a deck of cards (omitting face cards and use aces as ones). Two students draw a card without looking at it and place it on their foreheads facing outward so the others can see it. The student without a card tells the product (or the sum) of the two cards. The first of the other two students to correctly say the factor (or addend) on their forehead wins the round and the set of cards. For ELLs, students with disabilities, or reluctant learners, speed can increase anxiety and inhibit participation. You can remove speed of response by having the two students write down the card they think they have (within five seconds) and rewarding them one point if they are correct. This activity can be differentiated by including only certain cards (e.g., multiplication facts using only the numbers 1 through 5).

About Drill

Drill—repetitive nonproblem-based activity—in the absence of reasoning has repeatedly been demonstrated as ineffective. However, drill can strengthen memory and retrieval capabilities (Ashcraft & Christy, 1995). Drill is only appropriate after students know strategies and have moved from phase 2 to phase 3. Drill should also be low-stress and engaging. The many games and activities in this chapter can continued to be played even after students know the facts from memory. Students will smile when they see cards coming out for another game of *Salute*!

Too often, drill includes too many facts too quickly, and students become frustrated and overwhelmed. Also, students progress at different paces—gifted students tend to be good memorizers, whereas students with intellectual disabilities have difficulty memorizing (Forbringer & Fahsl, 2010). Rather than work on all facts, identify a group of facts (e.g., 3s) and look at patterns within that set. Students can create their own cards with each fact written both ways (e.g., 3×7 and 7×3), create a dot array, and record the answer on the back. They can work on these at home, with a partner, and keep track of the ones they "just know" and the ones for which they use a strategy.

A plethora of **Online Resources for Basic Fact Mastery** provide opportunities to drill on the basic facts. One disadvantage of most of these sites is that they focus on all the facts at one time. Two exceptions (sites that organize drill by fact family) are *Fun 4 the Brain* and *Math Fact Café*.

Fact Remediation

Students who have not mastered their basic addition facts by third grade or their multiplication facts by the fourth grade (or beyond) are in need of interventions that will help them master the facts. More drill is not an intervention!

Students who do not know their facts may be stuck back in phase 1 (counting strategies) and likely lack number sense and reasoning strategies (phase 2). Effective remediation first requires figuring out which facts a student knows and which ones he or she does not. Second, effective remediation requires a focus on the three phases—determining where a student is and explicitly teaching reasoning strategies (phase 2) in order to reach mastery (phase 3). Review the ideas offered in the Assessing Basic Facts section to figure out what students do and do not know. Then, use these ideas to help students master all of their facts.

1. *Explicitly teach reasoning strategies.* Students' fact difficulties are due to a failure to develop or to connect concepts and relationships. They need instruction focused at phase 2, not phase 3. Because in an intervention a student may not have the benefit of class discussions of strategies, share strategies that "other students have used." Be certain students have a conceptual understanding of the strategy and are able to use it.

   For example, if a third grader knows his addition facts within 10, but struggles with the ones that sum to 11 through 19, then you know which facts to target. Determine if he knows the Combinations of 10 strategy. Practice it until he is fluent with it. Then, explicitly teach the Making 10 strategy. For multiplication, you might notice that a student is good at doubling. Help her write the way to solve her "toughies" using doubles.

2. *Provide hope.* As noted in the discussion of timed tests, students' confidence can be affected. Students may feel they are destined to use finger counting forever. Let those students know that they will explore strategies that will help them be successful with learning their facts. Shorten quizzes and turn off the timers.

3. *Inventory the known and unknown facts for each student.* Find out which facts are known quickly and comfortably and which are not. Invite students to do this for themselves as well. Provide sheets of all facts for one operation in random order and have the students circle the facts they must pause to answer using a strategy or counting and answer the ones they immediately "just know." Review the results with them and discuss which strategies and facts you will work on.

4. *Diagnose strengths and weaknesses.* Find out what students are thinking when they encounter an unknown fact. Do they count on their fingers? Add up tick marks or numbers in the margins? Guess? Try to use a related fact? Write down times tables? Are they able to use any of the relationships or strategies suggested in this chapter? Conduct a 10-minute diagnostic interview with each student in need. Pose unknown facts and ask the student how he or she approaches them. Note the connections that are already there.

5. *Build in success.* Begin with easier and more useful strategies, and point out how one strategy can be used to learn many facts. Success builds success! Have students use fact charts to show which set of facts are mastered. It is surprising how the chart quickly fills up.

6. *Provide engaging activities.* Use the many games and activities in this chapter to work on phase 2 and phase 3. As students play, ask which strategies they are using. Deemphasize competition and emphasize collaboration. Prepare take-home versions of a game and assign students to play the game at home at least once. Invite parents in for a Math Night and teach them games that they can enjoy (e.g., *Salute!*) and teach families to focus on reasoning strategies over memorization as they play the games.

As you begin a well-designed fact program for a student who has experienced failure, be sure that successes come quickly and easily. Exposure to five facts in a three-day period will provide more success than introducing 15 facts in a week. Success builds success! Keep reviewing newly learned facts and those that were already known.

With efficient strategies and individual effort, success will come. Believe!

What to Do When Teaching Basic Facts

Here are some important reminders about effectively teaching the basic facts. This is such an important life skill for all learners that it is essential we, as teachers, use what research suggests are the most effective practices. The following list of recommendations support the development of quick recall of the basic facts.

1. *Ask students to self-monitor.* The importance of this recommendation cannot be overstated. Across all learning, having a sense of what you don't know and what you need to learn is important. It certainly holds true with memorizing facts. Students should be able to identify which facts are difficult for them and continue to work on reasoning strategies to help them derive those facts.

2. *Focus on self-improvement.* Help students notice that they are getting quicker or more accurate. For example, students can keep track of how long it took them to go through their "fact stack," for example, and then, two days later, pull the same stack and see whether they are quicker (or more accurate) compared to the last time.

3. *Limit practice to short time segments.* You can project numerous examples of arrays or areas on a grid in relatively little time. Or you can share a story problem a day—taking five minutes to have students discuss strategies. You can also have each student pull a set of flash cards, pair with another student, and go through each other's set in two minutes. Long periods (10 minutes or more) are not effective. Using the first 5 to 10 minutes of the

day, or extra time just before lunch, can provide continued support on fact development without taking up mathematics instructional time better devoted to other topics.

4. *Work on facts over time.* Rather than do a unit on fact memorization, work on facts over months and months, working on one reasoning strategy or set of facts until it is learned, then moving on. Be sure that foundational facts come first and are committed to memory before teaching derived fact strategies.

5. *Involve families.* Share the big plan of how you will work on the students learning basic facts with students' families. One idea is to have one or two "Take Home Facts of the Week." Ask family members to help students by using reasoning strategies when they don't know a fact.

6. *Make fact practice enjoyable.* There are many games (including those shared in this chapter and many on the web) designed to reinforce facts that are not competitive or anxiety inducing.

7. *Use technology.* When students work with technology, they get immediate feedback and reinforcement, helping them to self-monitor.

8. *Emphasize the importance of knowing their facts.* Without creating pressure or anxiety, highlight to students that in real life and in the rest of their studying of mathematics, they will be using these facts all the time—they really must learn them and learn them well.

What Not to Do When Teaching Basic Facts

The following list describes strategies that may have been designed with good intentions but work against student recall of the basic facts.

1. *Don't use timed tests.* Little insight is gained from times tests and they can potentially affect students negatively. When under the pressure of time, students get distracted and abandon their reasoning strategies. Turn the timers off!

2. *Don't use public comparisons of mastery.* You may have experienced the bulletin board that shows which students are on which step of a staircase to mastering their multiplication facts. Imagine how the student who is on the step 3 feels when others are on step 6. Or imagine the negative emotional reaction to public competition with flash cards for students who don't win. Adults often refer to the competitions with flash cards as the moment they started to dislike mathematics. It is great to celebrate student successes, but avoid public comparisons between students.

3. *Don't proceed through facts in order from 0 to 9.* Work on foundational facts first, then move to the more challenging facts.

4. *Don't work on all facts all at once.* Select a strategy (starting with easier ones) and then work on memorization of that set of facts (e.g., doubles). Be sure these are really learned well before moving on. Differentiation is needed!

5. *Don't expect quick recall too soon.* This has been addressed throughout the chapter, but is worth repeating. Quick recall or mastery can be attained only after students are ready, meaning they have a robust collection of reasoning strategies to apply as needed.

6. *Don't use facts as a barrier to important mathematics.* Mathematics is not solely about computation. Mathematics is about reasoning and using patterns and making sense of things. Mathematics is problem solving. There is no reason that a student who has not yet mastered all basic facts should be excluded from more advanced mathematical experiences.

7. *Don't use fact mastery as a prerequisite for calculator use.* Requiring that students master the basic facts before they can use a calculator has no foundation. Calculator use should

be based on the instructional goals for the day. For example, if your lesson goal is for students to discover the pattern (formula) for the perimeter of rectangles, then a good lesson would have students building and exploring different-shaped rectangles, recording the length, width, and perimeter, and looking for patterns. With a calculator students can quicken the computation and keep the focus on measurement.

Table 9.2 Common errors and misconceptions about basic facts and how to help.

Common Error or Misconception	What it Looks Like	How To Help
1. There is no relationship between addition and subtraction and/or multiplication and division (they do not see the inverse relationship)	Students see $12 - 4$ as unrelated to $4 + 8 = 12$. Students don't use multiplication to solve division problems (Ding, 2016) and therefore don't see how $27 \div 3$ is related to 3×9.	• Use concrete materials and have student act out a series of problems with the same three numbers. For example, for addition show how the part–part–whole model connects addition and subtraction. In multiplication show how the number in each group, the number of group's and the product relate to each other. • Explicitly point out the inverse relationship.
2. Students neglect to use the commutative property of addition and multiplication to support their fact fluency.	Students see $5 + 7$ and $7 + 5$ as two separate addition facts and calculate each individually. Students also see 8×4 and 4×8 as two different problems to solve.	• For addition, show the two groups and then have students reverse the group's position, pointing out that the amount did not change. • For multiplication, show the multiplication fact in the form of an array. Have students rotate the array. Is it the same amount?
3. When using the derived strategy in multiplication to add or subtract a group—students lose track of the group size.	When students try to solve 9×8, they may use 10×8 to derive the answer. But instead of subtracting a group of 8, they think they are to subtract one group and subtract 1 getting the answer of 79.	• Provide examples of the problems using an array. Show how the known fact is used to add or subtract a row (or column) from the array. It is a group not just one counter.
4. When given an unknown to solve for the student treats the unknown as "the answer."	Given the addition problem $8 + 4 = \square + 5$ students put 12 or 17 in the box representing the unknown.	• Focus on the meaning of the equal sign. Students need to be familiar with various equation formats so they can interpret the equal sign as indicating a relationship between quantities.
5. Students' addition answers are always one less than the correct answer	For $7 + 7$ students will say 13. Students who are still using their fingers, or those sometimes using a number line will either count the last finger twice or count the tick marks on a number line starting with the zero. In each case this will consistently result in a sum that is one less than the correct answer.	• Go back to the manipulative materials or the number line and either count the objects again to point out the difference between their answer and the correct one—or in the case of the number line lay down units so the student can see the "step" or unit is counted rather than the tick mark. • By grades 3–5 students should be phasing out the use of any concrete representations and moving toward reasoning strategies to produce addition answers.

10

Developing Whole-Number Place-Value Concepts

BIG IDEAS

1 Number sense is flexibly thinking about numbers and their relationships.

2 Sets of 10 (and tens of tens) can be perceived as single entities or units; for example, three sets of 10 and two ones is a base-ten method of describing 32 single objects. This is the major principle of base-ten numeration.

3 The positions of digits in numbers determine what they represent and which size group they count. This is the major organizing principle of place-value numeration and is central for developing number sense.

4 There are patterns to the way that numbers are formed. For example, each decade has a symbolic pattern reflective of the 0-to-9 sequence (e.g., 20, 21, 22 . . . 29).

5 The groupings of ones, tens, and hundreds can be taken apart in different but equivalent ways. For example, beyond the typical way to decompose 256 into 2 hundreds, 5 tens, and 6 ones, it can be represented as 1 hundred, 14 tens, and 16 ones, or 250 and 6. Decomposing and composing multidigit numbers in flexible ways is a necessary foundation for computational estimation and exact computation.

6 "Really big" numbers are best understood in terms of familiar real-world referents. It is difficult to conceptualize quantities as large as 1000 or more. However, the number of people who will fill the local sports arena is, for example, a meaningful referent for those who have experienced that crowd.

Number sense, a rich, relational understanding of number, involves many different ideas, relationships, and skills. Number sense in grades 3 through 5 should start with larger whole numbers but also be developed beyond whole numbers as other types of numbers—fractions, decimals, and percents—are added to students' repertoire of number ideas. This chapter focuses on number sense with respect to larger whole numbers, whereas future chapters will focus on fraction sense, fraction operations, and decimal and percent concepts. In grades 3 and 4, students extend their understanding to numbers up to 10,000 in a variety of contexts (CCSSO, 2010). Number sense is linked to a complete understanding of place value which is a focus of grade 2 instruction as per the *Common Core State Standards*. In grade 3, students take their knowledge of place value and put it to use to perform multidigit arithmetic including rounding numbers as a means of computational estimation. In fourth and fifth grade, students continue to expand their application of place value to multidigit computations. They also generalize place value understanding to see the relationship of the value of the positions of the digits in a number as ten times the value of the previous digit as they move to the left which will soon be linked to decimals as digits in a number are one-tenth the value of the position as they move to the right. This relationship is critical as students consider the powers of ten (CCSSO, 2010).

A significant part of this development includes students' putting numbers together (composing) and taking them apart (decomposing) in a wide variety of ways as they solve addition and subtraction problems with two- and three-digit numbers. Place value is a way for students to think about larger quantities (Mix, Prather, Smith, & Stockton, 2013) and to enhance their ability to invent their own computation strategies. Without a firm foundation and understanding of place value, students may face chronic low levels of mathematics performance (Chan & Ho, 2010; Moeller, Martignon, Wessolowski, Engel, & Nuerk, 2011). The following big ideas are the foundational concepts that will lead students to a full understanding of place value.

Extending Number Relationships to Larger Numbers

After students learn to count meaningfully, number relationships must become the emphasis to move students away from merely counting and toward developing number sense, a flexible concept of number not completely tied to counting. Students' knowledge of the early number relationships can be built on to extend them to numbers up to and greater than 100. The following three ideas can be demonstrated using the little ten-frames as shown in Figure 10.1(a). First refresh prior knowledge and briefly ask students about the relationships of one more than and one less than. Then, in a similar manner, ask them to consider 10 more than and 10 less than a given number. For example, 70 is 10 more than 60 (that is, one more ten-frame) and 50 is 10 less than 60 (one fewer ten-frame). The second idea is connected to fact strategies. If a student uses the Making 10 addition strategy when thinking about adding on to 8 or 9 by first adding up to 10 and then adding the rest, the extension to similar two-digit numbers is quite simple (see Figure 10.1(b)). Finally, it is a very useful idea to take apart or decompose larger numbers to begin to develop flexibility. Students can think of ways to decompose a multiple of 10 such as 80—into 50 and 30 or into 40 and 40. Once they decompose multiples of 10, the challenge is to think of ways to break apart multidigit numbers that have a 5 in the ones place, such as 25 or 35.

Being able to recognize and generate *equivalent representations* of the same number is the component of number sense that will serve students well during tasks that require estimation, comparison, or computation. This ability, linked to place-value understanding, increases students' flexibility in dealing with numbers because they can easily generate equivalent representations that will make their work easier. Challenge students to find as many different ways to represent a given number as possible. The number 67, for example, is 65 and 2 more, 3 less than 70, and composed of 60 and 7, as well as 50 and 17 or 40 and 27. Each of these forms of 67 may be useful in a variety of computational situations. For instance, if you are adding 67 and 56, thinking of 67 as 50 and 17 allows you to add 50 and 50 (from the 56) to get 100. Now add the 17 and 6 to get 23. Combine the 100 and 23 to get 123. Once students are able to think flexibly like this, they will be able to mentally do additions such as 67 and 56 faster than using an algorithm.

Figure 10.1

Extending early number relationships to mental computation activities.

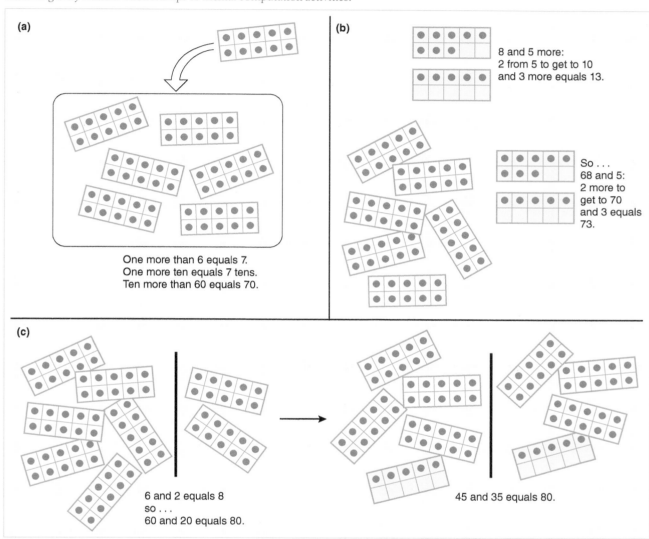

(a)
One more than 6 equals 7.
One more ten equals 7 tens.
Ten more than 60 equals 70.

(b)
8 and 5 more:
2 from 5 to get to 10
and 3 more equals 13.

So . . .
68 and 5:
2 more to
get to 70
and 3 equals
73.

(c)
6 and 2 equals 8
so . . .
60 and 20 equals 80.

45 and 35 equals 80.

Stop and Reflect   500 ⟳ 250   ⚡ ? 3⅀ ▱ ⟍ ♭ ° ∞ ∩ ⟋ 2.5

Before reading on, get some counters or coins. Count out a set of 18 counters in front of you as if you were a child counting them.

Part–Part–Whole Relationships

Any student who has learned how to count meaningfully can count out 18 objects as you just did. What is significant about the experience is what it did *not* cause you to think about. Nothing in counting a set of 18 objects will cause a student to focus on the fact that the amount could be made of two parts. For example, separate the counters you just set out into two piles and reflect on the combination. It might be 12 and 6, 7 and 11, or 14 and 4. Make a change in your two piles of counters and say the new combination to yourself. Focusing on a quantity in terms of its parts (*decomposing numbers*) has important implications for developing number sense as well as operation sense.

Relative Magnitude

Number sense also includes having a grasp on the size of numbers. *Relative magnitude* refers to the size relationship one number has with another—is it much larger, much smaller, close, or about the same? The next activity uses a number line to help students see how one number is related to another.

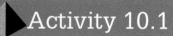

Activity 10.1
CCSS-M: 2.NBT.S.1; 2.NBT.A.2; 2.NBT.A.4

Who Am I?

Sketch a long line (or use cash register tape) and label 0 and 200 at opposite ends. Mark a point with a ? that corresponds to your secret number. (Estimate the position the best you can.) Have students try to guess your secret number. For each guess, place and label a mark on the line with a sticky note until your secret number is discovered. As a variation, the endpoints can be different—for example, try 0 and 1000, 200 and 300, or 500 and 800. For students with disabilities, it is important to mark the guesses that have occurred and where they are located. Labeling those numbers at their actual locations will support students' reasoning in the process of identifying the secret number.

Activity 10.2
CCSS-M: 2.NBT.A.1; 2.NBT.A.2; 2.NBT.A.4; 3.NBT.A.2; 4.NBT.A.2

Close, Far, and In-Between

Put any three numbers on the board. If appropriate, use larger numbers. With these three numbers as referents, ask questions such as the following, and encourage discussion of all responses:

- Which two are closest? How do you know?
- Which is closest to 300? To 250?
- Name a number between 457 and 364.
- Name a multiple of 25 between 219 and 364.
- Name a number that is more than all of these three numbers.
- About how far apart are 219 and 500? 219 and 5000?
- If these are "big numbers," what are some small numbers? Numbers about the same? Numbers that make these seem small?

219 364 457

For ELLs, this activity can be modified by using prompts that are similar to each other (rather than changing the prompts each time, which increases the linguistic demand.) Also, ELLs (and students with disabilities) will benefit from using a visual, such as a number line and from writing the numbers rather than just hearing or saying them.

Look at the corresponding **Expanded Lesson: Close, Far and In-Between**, where students estimate the relative size of numbers between 0 and 1000, and strengthen their conceptual understanding of number size and place value.

Connections to Real-World Ideas

We should not permit students to study place-value concepts without encouraging them to see large numbers in the world around them. You do not need a prescribed activity to bring real numbers into the classroom. First, look for numbers around your school: the number of students in third, fourth, and fifth grade combined, the number of minutes devoted to mathematics throughout the school day (and then each week or year), the number of hours (or minutes) school has been in session since the beginning of the year, or how many hours they've spent in school since kindergarten. Then, there are measurements, numbers at home, numbers on a field trip, and so on. What do you do with these numbers? Turn them into interesting graphs, write stories using the data, and make up problems to solve. For example, how many cartons of chocolate and plain milk are served in the cafeteria each month? Can students estimate how many cartons will be sold in a year? Collecting data and then grouping into tens, hundreds, or thousands will help cement the value of grouping in situations where you need to count and compare.

Approximate Numbers and Rounding

The most familiar form of computational estimation is rounding, which is a way of changing the numbers in a problem to others that are easier to compute mentally. The *Common Core State Standards* say that students in grade 3 are expected to use place-value understanding to round numbers to the nearest 10 or 100 and students in grades 4 should be able to round any multidigit whole number to any place value. At grades 3 and 4 students use rounding to assess the reasonableness of answers. Fifth graders will be using place value understanding to round decimals to any place.

To be useful in estimation, rounding should be flexible and conceptually well-understood. To round a number simply means to select a compatible number. (Note that the term *compatible* is not a mathematical term. It refers to numbers that would make the problem easier to compute mentally.) The compatible number can be any close number and need not be a multiple of 10 or 100, but in many cases students are asked to round to one of these places.

A number line with benchmark numbers highlighted can be useful in helping students select compatible numbers. An empty number line like the one shown in Figure 10.2 can be made using strips of poster board (or cash register tape) taped end to end. Labels are written above the line. The ends can be labeled 0 and 100, 100 and 200, . . . 900 and 1000. Indicate the location of a number above the line that you want to round. Discuss the locations of compatible numbers that are close. Teach students the convention that if a number that is being rounded has a 5 in the place being considered, although it is halfway between two numbers, they round up. The number line is a powerful tool for these discussions.

Figure 10.2

An empty number line can be labeled in different ways to help students round numbers.

Important Place-Value Concepts

Place-value understanding requires an integration of new and sometimes difficult-to-construct concepts of grouping by tens (the base-ten concept) with procedural knowledge of how groups are recorded in our place-value scheme, how numbers are written, and how they are spoken. Importantly, learners must understand the word *grouping* especially English language learners (ELLs) who may become confused because the root word *group* is frequently used for instructing students to work together.

Figure 10.3

Three stages of the grouping of 53 objects.

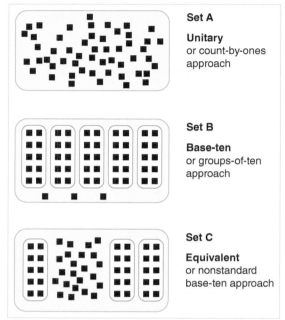

Set A

Unitary
or count-by-ones
approach

Set B

Base-ten
or groups-of-ten
approach

Set C

Equivalent
or nonstandard
base-ten approach

Integration of Base-Ten Grouping with Counting by Ones

Once students can count out a set of 53 by ones, we want to help them see that making groupings of tens and leftovers is a way of counting that same quantity. Each of the sets in Figure 10.3 has 53 tiles, and students can count those sets using three distinct grouping stages to construct the idea that all of these sets are the same.

Your foremost objective should be helping students integrate the grouping-by-tens concept with what they know about numbers from counting by ones. If they only count by ones, ask them, "What will happen if we count these by groups and singles (or by tens and ones)?" If a set has been grouped into tens and ones and counted, then ask, "How can we be really certain that there are 53 things here?" or "How many do you think we will get if we count by ones?" You cannot *tell* students that these counts will all be the same and hope that will make sense to them—it is a relationship they must construct themselves.

Stop and Reflect 500 ⌒ 250 ⟍ ? 3⟋ ▱ ♪ ♭ ° ∞ ∩ ⟋ 2.5

What are some defining characteristics of pre-place-value students and those who understand place value?

There is a subtle yet profound difference between students at these three stages. Some know that the Base-Ten Stage of Figure 10.3 is 53 because they understand the idea that five groups of 10 and 3 more is the same amount as 53 counted by ones; others simply say, "It's 53," because they have been told that when things are grouped this way, it's called 53. The students who understand place value will not need to count base-ten grouping by ones. They understand the "fifty-threeness" of the Unitary Stage and the Base-Ten Stage to be the same. The students in the pre-place-value stage may not be sure how many they will get if they count the tiles in Base-Ten Stage by ones, or if the groups were "ungrouped" how many there would be.

Groupings with fewer than the maximum number of tens are referred to as *equivalent groupings* or *equivalent representations*. Understanding the equivalence of the Base-Ten grouping and Equivalent grouping indicates that grouping by tens is not just a rule that is followed, but also that any grouping by tens, including all or some of the singles, can help tell how many. Many computational techniques (e.g., regrouping in addition and subtraction) are based on equivalent representations of numbers.

Integration of Base-Ten Groupings with Words

The way we say a number, such as "fifty-three" must also be connected with the grouping-by-tens concept. The counting methods provide a connection. The count by tens and ones results in saying the number of groups and singles separately: "five tens and three." Saying the number of tens and ones separately in this fashion can be called *base-ten language*. Students can associate the base-ten language with the standard language: "five tens and three—or fifty-three."

There are several variations of the base-ten language for 53: 5 tens and 3, 5 tens and 3 ones, 5 groups of ten and 3 singles, and so on. Each may be used interchangeably with the standard name "fifty-three." If you have ELLs, it is best to select one base-ten approach (e.g., 5 tens and 3 ones) and consistently connect it to the standard approach. Other languages often use the base-ten format (e.g., 17 in Spanish is *diecisiete*, literally meaning "ten and seven"), so this can be a good cultural connection for students.

 ## Formative Assessment Note

As a third-, fourth-, or fifth-grade teacher, you may not know how much your students understand about place-value concepts. Students are often able to disguise their lack of understanding of place value by following directions, using the base-ten materials in prescribed ways, and using the language of place value.

The diagnostic tasks presented here are designed to help you look more closely at students' understanding of the integration of the three components of place value (concepts, oral names, and written names). Designed as diagnostic interviews rather than full-class activities, these tasks have been used by several researchers and are adapted primarily from Labinowicz (1985), Kamii (1985), and Ross (1986).

The first interview is referred to as the **Digit Correspondence Task.** Take out 36 cubes. Ask the student to count the cubes, and then have the student write the number that tells how many there are. Circle the 6 in 36 and ask, "Does this part of your number have anything to do with how many cubes there are?" Then circle the 3 and repeat the question. As with all diagnostic interviews, do not give clues. Based on responses to the task, Ross (1986, 2002) has identified five distinct levels of place-value understanding:

1. *Single numeral.* The student writes 36 but views it as a single numeral. The individual digits 3 and 6 have no meaning by themselves.
2. *Position names.* The student correctly identifies the tens and ones positions, but still makes no connections between the individual digits and the cubes.
3. *Face value.* The student matches six cubes with the 6 and three cubes with the 3.
4. *Transition to place value.* The 6 is matched with six cubes and the 3 with the remaining 30 cubes but not as three groups of 10.
5. *Full understanding.* The 3 is matched with three groups of 10 cubes and the 6 with six single cubes.

For the second interview, write the number 342. Have the student read the number. Then have the student write the number that is 1 more. Next, ask for the number that is 10 more. You may wish to explore further with models. One less and 10 less can be checked the same way. Observe whether the student is counting on or counting back by ones, or if the student immediately knows that ten more is 352.

A third interview can also provide interesting evidence of depth of understanding. Ask the student to write the number that represents 5 tens, 2 ones, and 3 hundreds (written on paper). Note that the task does not give the places in order. What do you think will be a common misunderstanding? If the student doesn't write 352, then ask the student to show you the number with base-ten materials. Ask them what number they have with the materials. Compare that number to what they wrote previously, if different. What information can you get from the results of this interview?

Teaching Tip

It is important to be precise in your language. Whenever you refer to a number in the tens, hundreds, or thousands (or beyond), make sure you do not just say "six," but instead refer to it with its place value location, such as 6 tens (or 60). Students are often confused when numbers are discussed as single digits rather than describing their actual value.

Figure 10.4

Relational understanding of place value integrates three components shown as the corners of the triangle.

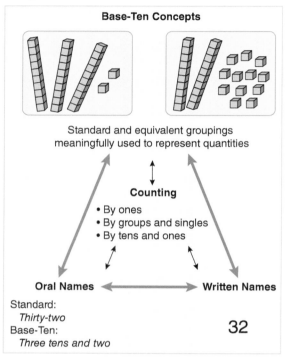

Base-Ten Concepts

Standard and equivalent groupings meaningfully used to represent quantities

Counting
• By ones
• By groups and singles
• By tens and ones

Oral Names ⟷ Written Names

Standard:
Thirty-two
Base-Ten:
Three tens and two

32

Watch this **video clip** and think about what this third grade student knows about place value.

Integration of Base-Ten Grouping with Place-Value Notation

The symbolic scheme that we use for writing numbers (ones on the right, tens to the left of ones, and so on) must be coordinated with the grouping scheme.

Language again plays a key role in making these connections. The explicit count by groups and singles (i.e., 3 tens and 2) matches the individual digits as the number is written in the usual left-to-right manner. A similar coordination is necessary for hundreds and other place values. But keep in mind that having students see "hundred" as ten tens and 100 ones may be a challenge.

Figure 10.4 summarizes the ideas of an integrated place-value understanding that have been discussed so far. Note that all three methods of counting are coordinated as the principal method of integrating the base-ten concepts, the written names, and the oral names.

Base-Ten Models

Physical models for base-ten concepts play a key role in helping students develop the idea of "a ten" as both a single entity and as a set of 10 units. Remember, though, that the models do not "show" the concept to the students; the students must mentally construct the "ten-makes-one relationship" and impose it on the model.

An effective base-ten model for ones, tens, and hundreds is one that is proportional. That is, a model for ten should be physically 10 times larger than the model for a one, and a hundred model should be 10 times larger than the ten model. Proportional materials allow students to check that ten of any given piece is equivalent to one piece in the column to the left (10 tens equals 1 hundred, and so on). Base-ten models can be categorized as *groupable* or *pregrouped*.

Groupable Models

Models that most clearly reflect the relationships of ones, tens, and hundreds are those for which the ten can actually be made or grouped from the single pieces or units. When students put 10 beans in a small cup, the cup of 10 beans literally *is the same as* the 10 single beans. Plastic connecting cubes also provide a good transition to pregrouped ten rods because they form a similar shape. Bundles of wooden craft sticks or coffee stirrers can be grouped with rubber bands. Examples of these groupable models are shown in Figure 10.5(a). These materials provide a good transition to the pregrouped models described next.

Pregrouped Models

Models that are pregrouped are commonly shown in textbooks and are often used in instructional activities. Pregrouped models, such as those in Figure 10.5(b), and the **Base-Ten Materials**, cannot be taken apart or put together. When 10 single pieces are accumulated, they must be exchanged or traded for a ten, and likewise, tens must be traded for hundreds. With pregrouped models, make an extra effort to confirm that students understand that a ten piece really is the same as 10 ones. Students combine multiplicative understanding (each place is 10 times the value of the place to the right) with a positional system (each place has a value). Although there is a pregrouped cube to represent 1000, it is important to group 10 hundred pieces together and attach them together as a cube with an elastic band to show how it is formed. Otherwise, some students may only count the square units they see on the surface of the six faces and may think the cube represents 600.

The **little ten-frame cards** effectively link to the familiar ten frames students used as primary students to think about numbers and, as such, may initially be more meaningful than the concrete versions or paper strips and squares of base-ten materials. This model has the distinct advantage of always showing the distance to the next decade. For example, when 47 is shown with 4 ten cards and a seven card, a student can see that three more units will make five full ten cards, or 50.

Nonproportional Models

Nonproportional models, or models where the ten is not physically 10 times larger than the one, are not used for introducing place-value concepts. They are used when students already have a conceptual understanding of the numeration system and may need additional reinforcement. Examples of nonproportional models include an abacus that has same-sized beads in different columns (on wires), money, or chips that are given different values by color.

Extending Base-Ten Concepts

Now that you have a sense of the important place-value concepts, we turn to activities that assist students in developing and expanding these concepts. This section starts with a focus on the top of the triangle of ideas in Figure 10.3. The connections of this most important component with writing numbers and with the way we say numbers—the bottom two corners of the triangle in the same figure—are discussed separately. However, in the classroom, the oral and written names for numbers can and should be developed in concert with conceptual ideas.

Grouping Hundreds to Make 1000

As students enter third grade, they are expected to know numbers up to 1000 (CCSSO, 2010). Here the issue is not one of

Figure 10.5

Groupable and pregrouped base-ten models.

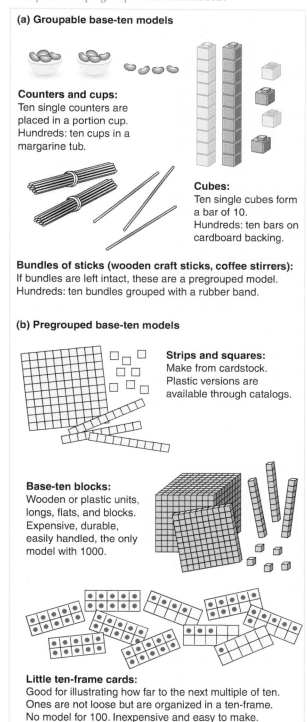

(a) Groupable base-ten models

Counters and cups:
Ten single counters are placed in a portion cup. Hundreds: ten cups in a margarine tub.

Cubes:
Ten single cubes form a bar of 10. Hundreds: ten bars on cardboard backing.

Bundles of sticks (wooden craft sticks, coffee stirrers):
If bundles are left intact, these are a pregrouped model. Hundreds: ten bundles grouped with a rubber band.

(b) Pregrouped base-ten models

Strips and squares:
Make from cardstock. Plastic versions are available through catalogs.

Base-ten blocks:
Wooden or plastic units, longs, flats, and blocks. Expensive, durable, easily handled, the only model with 1000.

Little ten-frame cards:
Good for illustrating how far to the next multiple of ten. Ones are not loose but are organized in a ten-frame. No model for 100. Inexpensive and easy to make. See Blackline Masters 2 and 3.

connecting a count-by-ones concept to a group of 1000, but rather seeing how a group of 1000 can be understood as a group of 10 hundreds as well as 100 tens and 1000 single ones. As a means of introducing thousands as groups of 10 hundreds and also 100 tens, consider the following estimation activity.

Activity 10.3

CCSS-M: 2.NBT.A.1

Too Many to Count?

Show students any quantity with 1,000 to 3,000 items. For example, you might show a garbage bag with a set of wrapped straws or Styrofoam packing peanuts. First, have students make and record estimates of how many straws, for example, are in the bag (they need not put their name on their estimates). Discuss how students determined their estimates. Then distribute portions of the straws to pairs or tables of students to count. Suggest early on that they may want to use rubber bands to create bundles of 10 or 100. If they bundle by 10, then ask, "How can we use these groups of 10 to tell how many straws we have? Can we make new groups from the groups of 10? What is 10 groups of ten called?" Once they see a bundle of 100, let them change their estimates if they wish (limit them to a time period to make this change to emphasize that this is an estimate and not an exact count). When all bundles or groups are made, count the thousands, hundreds, tens, and ones separately. Record on the board as 1 thousand + 4 hundreds + 7 tens + 8 ones.

In this activity, it is important to use a groupable model so that students can see how the 10 groups of 100 are the same as the 1000 individual items. This connection is often lost in the rather simple display of a 1000 in a cube in the pregrouped base-ten models.

Standards for Mathematical Practice

8 Look for and express regularity in repeated reasoning.

note

Electronic versions of pregrouped base-ten manipulatives (such as the *Base Blocks* applet at the National Library of Virtual Manipulatives) are computer representations of the three-dimensional base-ten blocks, including the thousands piece. With simple mouse clicks, students (including those with disabilities) can place ones, tens, hundreds, or thousands on a virtual place-value mat. If 10 of one type are lassoed by a rectangle, they snap together; if a piece is dragged one column to the right, the piece breaks apart into 10 of that unit. Scott Foresman's *eTools* has a similar place value tool with a bit more flexibility. Select the base-ten blocks of your choice and add ones, tens, or hundreds. Place-value columns can be turned on and off, and the "odometer" option can show the number 523 as 5 *hundreds* + 2 *tens* + 3 *ones*, as 500 + 20 + 3, or as *five hundred twenty-three*. A hammer icon will break a piece into 10 smaller pieces, and a glue bottle icon is used to group 10 pieces together.

Compared to real base-ten blocks, these digital materials are free, easily grouped and ungrouped, available in endless supply (even the thousands blocks), and can be manipulated by students and displayed and discussed on a smart board. Research suggests that students' interactions with these materials are just as beneficial as the concrete base-ten blocks (Burris, 2013). Remember though, digital models are no more conceptual than physical models and as such are only a representation for students who understand the relationships involved.

Equivalent Representations

An important variation of the grouping activities is aimed at the equivalent representations of numbers. For example, pose the following task to students who have just completed Activity 10.3.

What is another way you can show 1,478 besides 1 group of a thousand, 4 groups of a hundred, 7 tens, and 8 singles? Let's see how many ways you can find.

Interestingly, most students will go next to 1,478 ones. The following activities focus on creating equivalent representations.

Activity 10.4

CCSS-M: 2.NBT.A.1; 2.NBT.A.3

Three Other Ways

Students work in groups or pairs. First, they show 463 on their desks with base-ten materials in the standard representation. Next, they find and record at least three other ways of representing this quantity. A variation of this activity is to challenge students to find a way to show an amount with a specific number of pieces. "Can you show 463 with 31 pieces?" (There is more than one way to do this.) Students in grade 3 can get quite involved with finding all the ways to show a three-digit number.

Activity 10.5

CCSS-M: 2.NBT.A.1; 2.NBT.A.3

Base-Ten Riddles

Base-ten riddles can be presented orally or in written form (see Base-Ten Riddle Cards). In either case, students should use base-ten materials to help solve them. The examples here illustrate a variety of different levels of difficulty. Have students write new riddles when they complete these.

- I have 23 ones and 4 tens. Who am I?
- I have 4 hundreds, 12 tens, and 6 ones. Who am I?
- I have 30 ones and 3 hundreds. Who am I?
- I am 45. I have 25 ones. How many tens do I have?
- I am 341. I have 22 tens. How many hundreds do I have?
- I have 13 tens, 2 hundreds, and 21 ones. Who am I?
- If you put 3 more hundreds with me, I would be 1150. Who am I?
- I have 23 hundreds, 16 tens, and 2 ones. Who am I?

Oral and Written Names for Numbers

In this section, we focus on helping students connect oral and written names for numbers (see the bottom two corners of the triangle in Figure 10.3) with their use of groups of 10 or 100 or 1000 as efficient methods of counting. Note that the ways we say and write numbers are conventions rather than concepts. Students must learn these conventions by being told rather than through problem-based activities. It is also worth remembering that for ELL students, the convention or pattern in our English number words is probably not the same as it is in their native language. This is especially true of the numbers 11 to 19.

Three-Digit Number Names

The approach to three-digit number names starts with showing mixed arrangements of base-ten materials and having students give the base-ten name (4 hundreds, 3 tens, and 8 ones) and the standard name (438). Vary the arrangement from one example to the next by

Standards for
Mathematical Practice

3 Construct
viable arguments
and critique the
reasoning of others. ▶

changing only one type of piece, that is, add or remove only ones or only tens or only hundreds. It is important for students with disabilities to see counterexamples, so actively point out that some students wrote 200803 for two hundred eighty-three, and ask them whether that is correct. This incorrect version of the number is aptly called "expanded number writing" (Byrge, Smith, & Mix, 2013). The connection between oral and written numbers is not straightforward, with some researchers suggesting these early expanded number writing attempts are an early milestone on the route to full understanding of numbers (Byrge, Smith, & Mix, 2013). These conversations allow students to explore their misunderstandings and focus on the place-value system more explicitly.

The major challenge with three digit numbers is with numbers involving no tens, such as 702, or no hundreds, such as 1046. As noted earlier, the use of base-ten language is quite helpful here. The difficulty of zero-tens (or more generally the internal zero) is more pronounced when writing numerals. Students frequently incorrectly write 7002 for 702. The emphasis on the meaning in the oral base-ten language will be a significant help. At first, students do not see the importance of zero in place value and do not understand that zero helps us distinguish between such numbers as 203, 23, and 230 (Dougherty, Flores, Louis, & Sophian, 2010). Carefully avoid calling zero a "placeholder," as it is a number with a value. ELLs may need additional time to think about how to say and write the numerals, because they are translating all the terms within the number.

Researchers note that there are significantly more errors with four-digit number names than three-digit numbers, so do not think that students will easily generalize to larger numbers without actually exploring examples and tasks (Cayton & Brizuela, 2007).

Written Symbols

To show how the numbers are built, have a set of 27 **Place Value Cards**—one for each of the hundreds (100–900), one for each of the tens (10–90), and ones cards for 1 through 9 (see Figure 10.6). Notice that the cards are made so that the tens card is two times as long as the ones card, and the hundreds card is three times as long as the ones card (you can add thousands cards too, just make them proportionally four times longer than the ones card). As students place base-ten materials for a number (e.g., 457) on a **Place Value Mat**, have them also place the matching cards (e.g., 400, 50, and 7) below the materials in the correct columns. Then starting with the hundreds card, layer the others on top, right aligned. This approach will show how the number is built while allowing the student to see the individual components of the number. This is especially helpful if there are zero tens or other internal zeros in larger numbers. The place-value mat and the matching cards demonstrate the important link between the base-ten models and the written form of the numbers.

The next two activities are designed to help students make connections models, oral language, and written forms. The activities can be done with any multidigit numbers, depending on students' needs.

Figure 10.6

Building numbers with a set of place value cards.

Patterns and Relationships with Multidigit Numbers

In grades 3 through 5, create tasks that require the use of place-value ideas and place-value models with the goal to promote what is sometimes called *ten-structured thinking*, that is, flexibility in using the structure of tens and hundreds in the number system.

Activity 10.6

CCSS-M: 2.NBT.A.1a;
2.NBT.A.1b; 2.NBT.A.3

Say It/Press It

Display models of ones, tens, hundreds (and thousands if appropriate) in a mixed arrangement. Use virtual manipulatives (they come in endless quantities) or simply project a drawing using a cube-square-stick-dot method (use cubes for thousands, squares for hundreds, sticks for tens, and dots for ones) to represent the base-ten materials. Students say the amount shown in base-ten language ("2 thousands, 4 hundreds, 1 ten, and 5 ones") and then in standard language ("two thousand, four hundred fifteen"). Next, students enter the number into their calculators (or they can use paper to respond). Have someone share his or her display and defend it. Make a change in the materials and repeat. You can also do this activity by saying the standard name for a number. Pay special attention to numbers that have components in the teens (e.g., 317) and those with internal zeros (e.g., 408). English Language Learners (ELLs) may need additional time to think of the words that go with the numbers, especially as the numbers get larger.

Activity 10.7

CCSS-M: 2.NBT.A.1; 2.NBT.A.3;
2.NBT.B.5; 2.NBT.B.8; 3.NBT.A.2

Digit Change

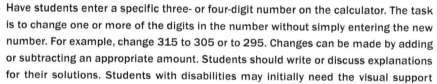

Have students enter a specific three- or four-digit number on the calculator. The task is to change one or more of the digits in the number without simply entering the new number. For example, change 315 to 305 or to 295. Changes can be made by adding or subtracting an appropriate amount. Students should write or discuss explanations for their solutions. Students with disabilities may initially need the visual support of having cards that say "add 10" or "add 100" to explore how the number changes. They may also need base-ten materials to be able to conceptualize the number and then move to more abstract work using only the calculator.

The Hundreds Chart

The **Hundreds Chart** is such an important tool for developing ten-structured thinking that it deserves special attention. The hundreds chart should not be abandoned after grade 2, as is often the case. When students are exploring invented strategies for addition and subtraction, the hundreds chart can be used as a model to support students' thinking and to support the communication of their ideas. The rows of 10 encourage students to think about using strategies based on place value and benchmark numbers—in this case, working with multiples of 10. For example, in adding 47 + 25, students might locate the number 47 on the chart and see that three more counts get them to 50 and then 22 more is easy to compute. Similarly, students might begin with 47 and move down two rows—adding 20—and then count on five more. What is important is not the particular methods that are used, but rather the use of multiples of 10 that is encouraged by the chart.

The hundreds chart is especially useful for exploring patterns created by skip counting. Patterns in skip counts can be observed both in the numbers and in the way that the numbers appear on the chart. For example, skip counts by 3 form diagonal patterns. These patterns point to the regularity of using equal groupings. You may want to see how familiar your students are with these and other hundreds-chart patterns.

In the following activity, number relationships on the hundreds chart are made more explicit by connecting the chart numbers to representations using base-ten models.

As a first step in moving to higher numbers, continue your hundreds charts to 200. Then a more powerful idea is to extend the hundreds chart to 1000.

Activity 10.8

CCSS-M: 2.NBT.A.1; 2.NBT.A.2; 2.NBT.A.3; 2.NBT.B.8; 3NBT.A.2

The Thousands Chart

Provide students with **Blank Hundreds Charts**. Assign groups of three or four students the task of creating a 1-to-1000 chart. The chart is to be made by taping 10 hundreds charts together in a long vertical strip. Students should decide how they are going to divide up the task with different students completing different parts of the 1000 chart (401 through 500 for example). The thousands chart should be discussed as a class to examine how numbers change as you count from one hundred to the next, what the patterns are, and so on. In fact, the hundreds chart activities can all be extended to a thousands chart.

Relationships with Benchmark Numbers

Often in computations it is useful to recognize that a number can be composed of a "familiar" number and some more—as an extension of part–part–whole thinking. The familiar numbers part (maybe a multiple of 50 or 100) is dealt with first, and then the smaller leftover pieces can be considered.

These familiar numbers also are often broken apart (decomposed) in computations. The next activity is useful for developing "think-addition" approaches to multidigit subtraction. Have students share their thinking strategies.

Activity 10.9

CCSS-M: 3.NBT.A.2

200 and Some More

Say a number between 300 and 1000. Students respond with "200 and ___." For 630, the response is "200 and 430." Play using other numbers including those that end in 50 for the first part, such as "450 and some more."

The following activities can be done independently or in pairs, but it is good to do them with the full class so that strategies can be discussed. These activities develop place-value concepts, number sense, or flexible strategies for computation.

Numbers beyond 1000

For students to have good concepts of numbers beyond 1000, the place-value ideas that have been carefully developed must be extended. This is sometimes difficult to do because physical models for thousands are not readily available, or you may just have one large cube to show. At the same time, number-sense ideas must also be developed. In many ways, connecting very large numbers to real amounts is just as important as connecting smaller numbers to real quantities.

Activity 10.10

CCSS-M: 3.NBT.A.2

Calculator Challenge Counting

Students press any three-digit number on the calculator (e.g., 770), then [+] 20. Have them say the sum before they press [=]. Then they continue to add 20 mentally, challenging themselves to say the number before they press [=]. They should see how far they can go before making a mistake.

The constant addend in this activity can be any number, even a three- or four-digit number. After using 20 as your constant, try 25. Try 400 and then 480. As an added challenge, after a student has progressed through eight or ten counts, have the student reverse the process by pressing [−] followed by the same number, and then pressing [=] several times. Have students share their strategies for determining the sum or difference and discuss patterns that appear.

Extending the Place-Value System

Two important ideas developed for three-digit numbers should be extended to larger numbers as students move to thinking about 1,000,000 in fourth grade (CCSSO, 2010). First, the multiplicative structure of the number system should be generalized. That is, ten in any position makes a single thing (group) in the next position, and vice versa. Second, the oral and written patterns for numbers in three digits are duplicated in a clever way for every three digits to the left. These two related ideas are not as easy for students to understand as adults seem to believe. Because models for large numbers are often difficult to demonstrate or visualize, textbooks frequently deal with these ideas in a predominantly symbolic manner. That is not sufficient!

Activity 10.11

CCSS-M: 4.NBT.A.1;
4.NBT.A.3; 5.NBT.A.1

What Comes Next?

Use paper models of **Base-Ten Materials**. The unit or ones piece is a **1** cm square. The tens piece is a **10** cm × **1** cm strip. The hundreds piece is a square, 10 cm × 10 cm. What is next? Ten hundreds is called a thousand. What shape would a thousand be? Tape together a long strip made of **10** paper hundreds squares. What comes next? (Reinforce the idea of "10 makes 1" that has progressed to this point.) Ten thousand strips would make a square measuring 1 meter on each side, making a paper 10,000 model. Once the class has figured out the shape of each piece, the problem posed to them is "What comes next?" Let small groups work on the dimensions of a 100,000 piece. Ten ten-thousand squares (100,000) go together to make a huge strip. Draw this strip on a long sheet or roll of paper, and mark off the **10** squares that make it up. You will have to go out in the hall.

How far you want to extend this square-strip-square-strip sequence depends on your class. The idea that 10 in one place makes 1 in the next can be brought home dramatically. It is quite possible with older students to make the next 10 m × 10 m square using chalk lines on the playground. The next strip is 100 m × 10 m. This can be measured out on a large playground with four students standing in positions to mark the corners. By this point, the

Figure 10.7

With every three places, the shapes repeat.

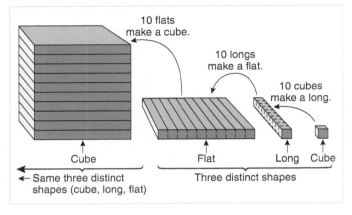

payoff includes an appreciation of both the increase in size of each successive amount as well as the 10-makes-1 progression (powers of ten). The 10 m × 10 m square models 1 million and the 100 m × 10 m strip is the model for 10 million. The difference between 1 million and 10 million is dramatic. Even the concept of 1 million tiny centimeter squares is impressive.

Try the "What Comes Next?" discussion in the context of the three-dimensional base-ten models. The first three shapes are distinct: a cube, a long, and a flat. What comes next? Stack 10 flats and they make a cube, the same shape as the first one, only 1000 times larger. What comes next? (See Figure 10.7.) Ten cubes make another long. What comes next? Ten big longs make a big flat. The first three shapes have now repeated! Ten big flats

Standards for Mathematical Practice

> **7 Look for and make use of structure.** ▶

will make an even bigger cube, and the trio of shapes begins again. The pattern of "10 of these makes 1 of those" is infinitely extendable" (Thomas, 2004, p. 305). Note that students with disabilities often have difficulty interpreting spatial information, which plays into their challenges with interpreting the progression of place-value materials (Geary & Hoard, 2005).

Each cube has a name. The first one is the unit cube; the next is a thousand, the next a million, then a billion, and so on. Each long is 10 cubes: 10 units, 10 thousands, 10 millions. Similarly, each flat shape is 100 cubes.

✑ Teaching Tip

Although we are using the terms *cube, long,* and *flat* to describe the shape of the materials, students will see the shape pattern made as each gets 10 times larger. In fact, it is still critical to call these materials "ones, tens, and hundreds," particularly for students with disabilities. We need to consistently name them by the number they represent rather than their shape. This reinforces conceptual understanding and is less confusing for students who may struggle with these concepts.

To read a number, first mark it off in triples from the right. The triples are then read, stopping at the end of each to name the unit for that triple (see Figure 10.8). Leading zeros in each triple are ignored. If students can learn to read numbers like 059 (fifty-nine) or 009 (nine), they should be able to read any number. To write a number, use the same scheme. If first mastered orally, the system is quite easy. Remind students **not** to use the word "and" when reading a whole number. For example, 106 should be read as "one hundred six," not "one hundred and six." The word "and" will be needed to signify a decimal point. Please make sure you read numbers accurately.

Figure 10.8

The triples system for naming large numbers.

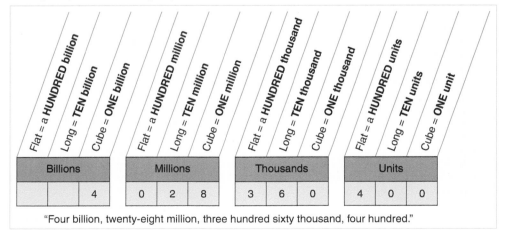

"Four billion, twenty-eight million, three hundred sixty thousand, four hundred."

It is important for students to realize that the system does have a logical structure, is not totally arbitrary, and can be understood.

Conceptualizing Large Numbers

The ideas just discussed are only partially helpful in thinking about the actual quantities involved in very large numbers. For example, in extending the paper square-strip-square-strip sequence, some appreciation for the quantities of 1000 or of 100,000 is acquired. But it is hard for students to translate quantities of small squares into quantities of other items, distances, or time.

Explore this video clip of a teacher discussing with her students how 192,000 is also 19,200 tens. These are important discussions to consider and you will see how they link to computation skills.

Stop and Reflect

How do you think about 1000 or 100,000? Do you have any real concept of a million?

In the following activities, numbers like 1000, 10,000 (see 10,000 Grid paper), or even 1 million are translated literally or imaginatively into something that is easy or fun to think about. Interesting quantities become lasting reference points for large numbers and thereby add meaning to numbers encountered in real life.

Activity 10.12

CCSS-M: 4.NBT.A.1; 4.NBT.A.3; 5.NBT.A.1

Collecting 1,000,000

As a class or grade-level project, collect some type of object with the objective of reaching some specific quantity—for example, 1000 or 10,000 bread tabs or bottle caps to help students begin to see how large these numbers are. If you begin aiming for 100,000 or 1 million, be sure to think it through. One teacher spent nearly 10 years with her classes before amassing a million bottle caps. It takes a small dump truck to hold that many!

Activity 10.13

CCSS-M: 4.NBT.A.1; 4.NBT.A.3; 5.NBT.A.1

How Long?/How Far?

In this activity, talk about real or imagined distances with students by posing investigations for them to consider such as, "How long is a million baby steps?" Other ideas that explore the length of a million objects or people include estimating a line of toothpicks, dollar bills, or candy bars end to end; students holding hands in a line; blocks or bricks stacked up; students lying down head to toe. Standard measures—feet, centimeters, meters—can also be used, with students noting that larger numbers emerge when the smallest units are used. Explore the children's book *How Much Is a Million?* (Schwartz, 1985) for more ideas.

Activity 10.14

CCSS-M: 4.NBT.A.1; 4.NBT.A.3; 5.NBT.A.1

A Long Time

 How long is 1000 seconds? How long is a million seconds? A billion? How long would it take to count to 10,000 or 1 million? (To make the counts all the same, use your calculator to do the counting. Just press the =.) How long would it take to do some task like buttoning and unbuttoning a button 1000 times?

Activity 10.15

CCSS-M: 2.MD.A.3; 3.MD.A.1; 3.MD.C.5

Really Large Quantities

Ask how many:

• energy bars would cover the floor of your classroom.

• steps an ant would take to walk around the school building.

• grains of rice would fill a cup or a gallon jug.

• quarters could be stacked in one stack from floor to ceiling.

• pennies could be laid side by side down the entire hallway.

• pieces of notebook paper would cover the gym floor.

• seconds you have lived.

Big-number projects need not take up large amounts of class time. They can be explored over several weeks as take-home projects, done as group projects or, perhaps best of all, be translated into great school-wide estimation contests. All these and similar activities help students build number sense with larger numbers so they can flexibly think about these numbers and their relationships.

Table 10.1 Common errors and misconceptions and how to help.

Common Error or Misconception	What it Looks Like	How To Help
1. Students lose track of the fact that each digit in a multidigit numeral carries a value dependent on its position in the number.	When students are asked to compare the numbers bolded in the two amounts that follow they will say they are the same. **2**,357 and 49,99**2**.	• Use concrete materials and have student show with materials the value of these two numbers. The constant reading of numbers in addition or subtraction problems as digits (saying 5 instead of 5 tens or fifty) confuses students. • Use the place value cards discussed previously to reinforce how numbers are built. • Students hear numbers like 2,357 read as two, three, five, seven—when they should always be read two thousand, three hundred, fifty-seven. • Use the digit correspondence task described in this chapter to identify which of the five levels of understanding matches your student's performance. • Reinforce that the value of an individual digit in a multidigit number is the product of that digit multiplied by the value assigned to its position in the number.

Table 10.1 Common errors and misconceptions and how to help.

Common Error or Misconception	What it Looks Like	How To Help
2. Students put the word "and" in a number when they read it aloud.	When reading 1,016 students will say "one thousand and sixteen."	• Students must practice reading numbers without using the word "and." The only time the word "and" is used is to represent a decimal point.
3. Students use a form of "expanded number writing" (Byrge, Smith, & Mix, 2013).	Students write "three hundred eighty-five" as something like 300805, 310085 or 3085.	• Provide examples of the actual materials on a place value mat and use the place value cards to show how the matching number is built.
4. When shown a collection of base-ten materials where there is an internal zero the students ignore the zero or misunderstand the zero.	Given five hundreds and 8 units in base-ten materials, students will write that number as 85. The student believes that 802 and 8002 represent the same amount.	• Focus on the meaning of a zero in any number by starting with a number like 408 and asking how that would be shown with materials. Explicitly discuss the role of an internal 0 in the number. • Never refer to 0 as a "placeholder." This terminology gives the impression that it is not a numerical value and it is there just as a way to fill a space. • Never read or refer to 0 as oh or zip. Say "zero" as it is a number.
5. If students are given the place values of numbers out of order they write the number as given left to right regardless of the place value.	When students are asked to write the number that represents: 7 ones, 4 tens, 1 thousand and 3 hundreds. They write 7,413.	• Go back to the base-ten materials and use the place value mat to take out the same amount of base-ten blocks as in the number. Then have the student write the number of base-ten blocks. Have them compare the two answers to consider which one is accurate.
6. Students misinterpret the value of the base-ten materials.	Students think the value of the large 1000 place value block is actually 600 by just calculating the number of squares on each face of the cube.	• Particularly with the 1,000 place value block, if students don't see the building of the block (grouping into a unit), they may confuse the value. So, explicitly show the building of the cube by taking ten of the hundreds blocks and forming a cube with them (holding them together with elastic bands.)

11

Building Strategies for Whole-Number Computation

BIG IDEAS

1 Flexible methods of computation for all four operations involve taking apart (decomposing) and combining (composing) numbers in a variety of ways.

2 Flexible methods for computation require a deep understanding of the properties of the operations (commutative property, associative property, and distributive property of multiplication over addition). How addition and subtraction, as well as multiplication and division, are related as inverse operations is also important.

3 Invented strategies provide flexible methods of computing that vary with the numbers and the situation. Successful use of invented strategies requires that they be understood by the one who is using them, hence the term invented.

4 Standard algorithms are elegant computation strategies based on performing the operation on one place value at a time with transitions to an adjacent position (trades or regrouping). Standard algorithms tend to make students think in terms of digits rather than the composite number, so students often lose sight of the actual place value of a digit.

5 Multidigit numbers can be built up or taken apart in a variety of ways to make them easier to work with. These parts can be used to estimate answer in calculations rather than using the exact numbers.

6 Computational estimations involve using easier-to-handle parts of numbers or substituting difficult-to-handle numbers with close compatible numbers so that computations can be done mentally.

Toward Computational Fluency

Much of the public sees computational skill as the hallmark of what it means to know mathematics in grades 3 through 5. Although that is far from the whole story, learning computational skills with whole numbers is, in fact, a critical component of the curriculum.

As students enter the intermediate grades, they continue working with addition and subtraction of large numbers as they fluently solve problems within 1000 using a variety of strategies (CCSSO, 2010). But the emphasis starting at grade 3 is on computation strategies with multiplication and division. In fact, approximately half of the grade 3 *Common Core State Standards* involve understanding multiplication (Kinzer & Stanford, 2013/2014). However, researchers suggest that invented strategies for multiplication and division are less well documented (Verschaffel et al., 2007) and the relationship between the operations more difficult to grasp than addition and subtraction (Robinson & LeFevre, 2012).

The *Common Core State Standards* for Mathematics (CCSS-M) describes procedural fluency as "skill in carrying out procedures flexibly, accurately, efficiently, and appropriately" (CCSSO 2010, p. 6). To reach procedural fluency, teachers must create an instructional environment that rewards flexibility in solving problems so that students can successfully explore and test new ideas (Verschaffel et al., 2007). Students who only have knowledge of the standard algorithm often have difficulty following procedural steps they do not fully understand (Biddlecomb & Carr, 2011). When students can compute multidigit addition, subtraction, multiplication, and division problems in a variety of ways, complete written records of their work, explain their thinking, and discuss merits of one strategy over another, they are developing as independent learners. Watch this **video (https://www.youtube.com/watch?v=ZFUAV00bTwA)** in which William McCallum and Jason Zimba, lead writers of the *Common Core State Standards* for Mathematics, describe the relationship between developing understanding and fluency in computation.

Consider the following problem.

The school auditorium has 24 rows of seats. There are 39 seats in each row. How many students can be seated in the auditorium?

Stop and Reflect

Try solving this problem using some method other than the algorithm you were taught in school. If you are drawn to begin by multiplying 9 and 4, try a different approach. Can you solve the problem mentally by thinking of the place values of the numbers? What is another way you can solve the problem? Work on this before reading further.

Here are three ways students thought about solving this computation:

Standards for Mathematical Practice

2 Reason abstractly and quantitatively.

- "24 is close to 25, and 25 × 4 equals 100, so 25 × 39 is 25 less than 25 × 40 or 1000 (975) and because I rounded 24 up, the answer is 39 less or 936."
- "39 is close to 40, and if I multiply 20 rows by 40 seats that equals 800. Then I have 4 more rows for 160 more seats. That's 960. Then I have to take 24 away to fix the bump up to 40 from 39, so the answer is 936."
- "20 × 30 equals 600, 20 × 9 equals 180, so together that equals 780. Then, 30 × 4 equals 120, so that's 900. And 9 × 4 equals 36 more so the answer is 936."

Every day students and adults use these more meaningful methods, which can be done mentally, are often faster than the standard algorithm, and make more sense to the person using them and therefore are less susceptible to error.

Direct Modeling

The developmental step that usually precedes invented strategies is called *direct modeling*. This is the use of manipulatives or drawings along with counting to directly represent the meaning of an operation or story problem. Students in grade 3 who consistently count by ones in additive situations most likely have not developed base-ten grouping concepts. As you work with students who are still struggling with seeing ten as a unit (or in multiplication seeing a factor as a unit), suggest that they use a tool to help them think, such as grouping counters. Some students may need to write down the corresponding numbers for memory support (perhaps as they complete intermediate steps).

Students will soon move from direct modeling to invented strategies derived from number sense and the properties of the operations. Invented strategies no longer rely on materials or counting. However, some students may need encouragement to move away from direct modeling. Here are some ideas to foster the fading of direct modeling:

- Record students' verbal explanations in ways that they and others can follow.
- Ask students who have just solved a problem with manipulatives to see whether they can do it mentally.
- Ask students to make a written numeric record of how they solved the problem with physical models. Then have them try to use the same written method on a new problem without the physical models.

Invented Strategies

Carpenter and colleagues (1998) refer to a strategy other than the standard algorithm that does not involve the use of physical materials or counting by ones as an *invented strategy*. In the *Common Core State Standards* (CCSSO, 2010) *invented strategies* are described as "strategies based on place value, properties of operations and or the relationship between addition and subtraction" (or multiplication and division) (pp. 16, 19, 24, 29, 35). More specifically, students are expected to "develop, discuss, and use efficient, accurate, and generalizable methods to compute sums and differences of whole numbers in base-ten notation, using their understanding of place value and the properties of operations" (p. 17) and the same expectation is for products of multidigit whole numbers (p. 27). At times, invented strategies become mental methods after the ideas have been explored, used, and understood. For example, 847 + 256 can be done mentally (850 + 250 equals 1100, add 3 more equals 1103). Some students may write down intermediate steps (such as adding 6 more and then taking 3 less to compensate) to aid in memory as they work through problems. In the classroom, written support is often encouraged as strategies develop because they are more easily shared and help students focus on the ideas.

A number of research studies have focused attention on how learners of a variety of ages handle computational situations when they have been given options for multiple strategies (Ambrose, Baek, & Carpenter, 2003; Carpenter et al., 1998; Csikos, 2016; Fosnot & Dolk, 2001; Keiser, 2010; Lynch & Star, 2014; Rittle-Johnson, Star, & Durkin, 2010; Van Putten, van den Brom-Snijders, & Beishuizen, 2005; Verschaffel, Greer, & De Corte, 2007). These methods strengthen your students' understanding of the properties of numbers, such as in multiplication in which the ability to flexibly break numbers apart hinges on using the distributive property of multiplication over addition.

One of the best ways for students to grow their repertoire is to listen to strategies invented by other class members as they are shared, explored, and tried out. However, students should not be permitted to use any strategy without understanding it (Campbell, Rowan, & Suarez, 1998).

Creating an Environment for Inventing Strategies

Invented strategies are developed from a strong understanding of numbers especially the fundamental knowledge of place-value concepts. For example, the *Common Core State Standards* (CCSSO, 2010, p. 27) suggest that fourth graders should be able to "develop fluency with efficient procedures for multiplying whole numbers; understand and explain why the procedures work based on place value and properties of operations." This standard calls for learners to publicly share emerging ideas. Therefore, students need a classroom environment where they can act like mathematicians and explore ideas without fear.

When students in your classroom attempt to investigate new ideas in mathematics, they should find your classroom a safe and nurturing place for expressing naïve or rudimentary thoughts. Some characteristics described earlier in this book regarding developing a problem-solving environment need to be reiterated here to establish the climate for taking risks, testing conjectures, and trying new approaches. Students also need to know that they will need to persevere and be ready for productive struggle; as that is when learning takes place. Hiebert and Grouws (2007) stated, "We use the word struggle to mean that students expend effort to make sense of mathematics, to figure something out that is not immediately apparent. . . . We do not mean the feelings of despair that some students can experience when little of the material makes sense" (p. 387). We need to encourage students to persevere with material that is challenging but within their grasp and understandable. Consider ways to question, encourage, give time, and acknowledge as part of this process (Warshauer, 2015).

Here are some factors to keep in mind:

- Avoid immediately identifying the right answer when a student states it. Give other students a chance to consider whether the answer and approach are correct.
- Expect and encourage student-to-student dialog, questions, debate, and conjectures. Allow plenty of time for discussion.
- Encourage students to clarify previous knowledge and make attempts to construct new ideas.
- Promote curiosity and openness to trying new things.
- Talk about both right and wrong ideas in a nonevaluative and nonthreatening way.
- Move unsophisticated ideas to more sophisticated thinking through coaching and strategic questioning.
- Use familiar contexts and story problems to build background and connect to students' experiences. Avoid using "naked numbers" as a starting point, as they do not encourage strategy development.
- Show samples of anonymous students' work and allow students to analyze other's thinking.

Standards for Mathematical Practice

◀ **3 Construct viable arguments and critique the reasoning of others.**

When first encouraging students to develop their own methods, select numbers in your problems with care. For example, with subtraction tasks such as $417 - 103$ or $417 - 98$, the numbers used may encourage students to subtract 100 and then adjust. For multiplication, multiples of 5, 10, and 25 are good starting points. Even 325×4 may be easier than 86×7, even though there are three digits in the former example. For division, it is the divisor that requires attention. For example, $483 \div 75$ is easier than $483 \div 67$, and not much harder than $327 \div 6$.

Contrasts with Standard Algorithms

There are significant differences between invented strategies and standard algorithms.

Teaching Tip

Note that the first product is 60 × 7,not 7 times 6, as would be the focus in the standard algorithm. Make sure you use language that recognizes place value (e.g., sixty or six tens).

1. *Invented strategies are number-oriented rather than digit-oriented.* For example, one invented strategy for 68 × 7 begins 60 × 7 equals 420 and 56 more equals 476.

   Using the standard algorithm for 416 + 329, students think of 4 + 3 rather than 400 + 300. Kamii, a longtime advocate for invented strategies, claims that standard algorithms "unteach" place value (Kamii & Dominick, 1998).

2. *Invented strategies are left-handed rather than right-handed.* Invented strategies often begin with the largest parts of numbers (left-most digits) because they focus on the entire number. For 26 × 47, many invented strategies begin with 20 × 40 equals 800, providing some sense of the size of the eventual answer in just one step. In contrast, the standard algorithm begins with 7 × 6 equals 42. By beginning on the right with a digit orientation, the result is hidden until the end. The exception is the standard long-division algorithm.

3. *Invented strategies are a range of flexible options, rather than "one right way."* Invented strategies are dependent on the numbers involved so that students can make the computation easier. Try each of these mentally: 465 + 230 and 526 + 98. Did you use the same method? The standard algorithm suggests using the same tool on all problems. The standard algorithm for the problem 7000 − 25 typically leads to student errors, yet a mental strategy is relatively straightforward.

Benefits of Invented Strategies

The development of invented strategies delivers more than computational proficiency. Positive benefits are:

- *Students make fewer errors.* Research reveals that students using methods they understand make many fewer errors than when they use strategies that they just memorized (Gravemeijer & van Galen, 2003). Not only do students using poorly understood algorithms make errors but the errors are also often systematic and difficult to remediate. Errors with invented strategies are less frequent and rarely systematic.

- *Less reteaching is required.* You may initially be concerned when you find students' early efforts with invented strategies are slow and time consuming. But productive struggle in these early stages builds a meaningful and well-integrated network of ideas that is robust and long lasting and significantly **decreases** the time required for reteaching.

- *Students develop number sense.* Students' development and use of number-oriented, flexible algorithms offers them a rich comprehension of the number system through strategies they understand. In contrast, students using standard algorithms are often unable to explain why they work.

- *Invented strategies are the basis for mental computation and estimation.* When invented strategies are the norm for computation, there is little need to talk about mental computation as if it were a separate skill. As students become more proficient with these flexible methods, they find they are able to do them mentally or sometimes only need to jot down intermediate steps.

- *Flexible methods are often faster than standard algorithms.* Consider 761 + 467. A simple invented strategy might involve 700 + 400 = 1100 and 60 + 60 = 120. The sum of 1100 and 120 equals 1220 and add 8 more for 1228. This is easily done mentally, or even with some recording, in much less time than the steps of the standard algorithm.

- *Algorithm invention is itself a significantly important process of "doing mathematics."* Students who select from a variety of strategies for computing, or who adopt a meaningful strategy shared by a classmate, are both involved in the process of sense making and building confidence. This development of a procedure is a process that was often hidden from students (possibly yourself included). By engaging in this aspect of mathematics, a significantly different and valuable view of "doing mathematics" is revealed to learners.

- *Invented strategies serve students well on standardized tests.* Evidence suggests that students using invented strategies do as well or better than students using standard algorithms in computation on standardized tests (Fleischman, Hopstock, Pelczar, & Shelley, 2010; Fuson, 2003). As an added bonus, students tend to increase their ability to solve word problems because they are the principal vehicle for developing invented strategies. Also, oftentimes students' abilities to estimate with invented strategies help them eliminate unreasonable multiple-choice items and move more rapidly through tests.

Mental Computation

A *mental computation strategy* is simply any invented strategy that is done mentally. What may be a mental strategy for one student may require written support by another. Initially, students may not be ready to do computations mentally, as they may still need direct modeling or to notate parts of the problem as they think it through. As your students become more adept, they can and should be challenged to do computations mentally.

Try mental computation with this example:

$$342 + 153 + 481$$

Stop and Reflect

For this addition task, try the following method: Begin by adding the hundreds, saying the totals as you go—3 hundred, 4 hundred, 8 hundred. Then add on to this the tens in a successive manner and finally the ones. Give it a try.

Standard Algorithms

The focus in teaching standard algorithms should not be as a memorized series of steps, but as making sense of the procedure as a process. Algorithms should have the characteristics of certainty (precise procedures), reliability (always a correct answer if carried out properly), transparency (the process is understood), efficiency (effective approach) and generalizability (solves a collection of similar problems) (Fan & Bokhove, 2014). The *Common Core State Standards* (CCSSO, 2010) require that students eventually have knowledge of standard algorithms (addition and subtraction with multidigit whole numbers in grade 4, multiplication with multidigit whole numbers in grade 5, and division of multidigit whole numbers in grade 6). Notice that the grades in which this knowledge of standard algorithms is required is long after the time when the topic is introduced. This timeline points to the need for full conceptual development to take place first. Importantly, the *Common Core State Standards* recognize that starting by teaching only the standard algorithm doesn't allow students to explore other useful approaches. Understanding how algorithms work and when they are the best choice (over an invented approach) is central to development of procedural proficiency.

Standard Algorithms Must Be Understood

Students may pick up standard algorithms from siblings and other family members while you are still trying to teach a variety of invented strategies. Some of these students may resist learning more flexible strategies thinking that they already know the "right" approach. What do you do then?

First and foremost, apply the same rule to standard algorithms as to all strategies: *If you use it, you must understand why it works and be able to explain it.* In an atmosphere that says, "Let's figure out why this works," students can profit from making sense of standard algorithms just as they should be able to reason about other approaches. But the responsibility for explanations should be theirs, not yours. Remember, "Never say anything a kid can say!" (Reinhart, 2000, p. 478).

The standard algorithm (once it is understood), is a one more strategy to put in students' toolbox of methods. They are a significant part of the development of deep understanding of mathematics (Fan & Bokhove, 2014). But, reinforce the idea that, just like the other strategies, it may be more useful in some instances than in others. For example, point out that for a problem such as 4568 + 12,813, the standard algorithm has distinct advantages. Also, pose problems in which a mental strategy is much more useful than the standard algorithm, such as 504 − 498. Discuss which method seems best in a variety of situations. Watch this video clip of third-grader Estephania, who compares the use of a mental strategy with the standard subtraction algorithm.

Standards for
Mathematical Practice

7 **Look for and make use of structure.**

Delay! Delay! Delay!

Students are unlikely to invent standard algorithms. You will need to introduce and explain them, and help students understand how and why algorithms work. No matter how carefully you introduce these algorithms into your classroom as simply another alternative, students are likely to sense that this is the "right way." So, first, spend a significant time with invented strategies—months, not weeks. Again, note that the *Common Core State Standards* (CCSSO, 2010) require that students learn a variety of strategies based on place value and properties of operations one or two years before the standard algorithms are expected to be mastered. The understanding students gain from working with invented strategies will make it easier for you to meaningfully teach the standard algorithms. If you think you are wasting precious time by delaying, just be reminded of how many years you and others teach the same standard algorithms over and over to students who still make errors with them and are still unable to explain them.

Cultural Differences in Algorithms

Some people falsely assume that mathematics is universal and is easier than other subjects for students who are not native English speakers. In fact, there are many international differences in notation, conventions, and algorithms. Knowing more about the diverse algorithms students might bring to the classroom and their ways of recording symbols for "doing mathematics" will assist you in supporting students and responding to families. What the United States calls the "standard algorithm" may not be customary in other countries, so encouraging a variety of algorithms is important in valuing experiences of all students.

For example, *equal addition* is a subtraction algorithm used in many Latin and European countries. It is based on the knowledge that adding the same amount to both the minuend and the subtrahend will not change the difference (answer). Let's start with a simple example. If the expression to be solved is 15 − 5, the answer (or the difference) doesn't change if you add 10 to the minuend and subtrahend and solve 25 − 15. There is still a difference of 10. Let's look at $62 - 27$ to think about this. Using the familiar algorithm that you may think of as "standard," you would likely regroup by crossing out 6 tens, adding the 10 with a small 1 to the 2 in the ones column (making 12), and then subtracting 7 from the 12 and so forth. In the equal addition approach (see Figure 11.1), you can add 10 to 62 by just mentally adding a 1 (to represent 10) to the 2 in the ones column and thereby having 12, and then you counteract the addition of 10 to the minuend by mentally adding 10 to the 27 (subtrahend), by increasing the tens column by one and subtracting 37. This may sound confusing—but try it. Especially when there are zeros in the minuend (e.g., $302 - 178$), you may find this is a productive option. More important, your possible confusion can give you the sense of how your students (and their families) may react to a completely different procedure from the one they know and find successful.

Figure 11.1

The equal addition algorithm.

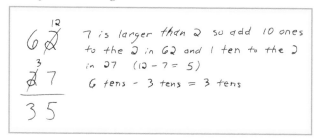

Teaching Tip

Mental mathematics is emphasized in other countries (Perkins & Flores, 2002). In fact, students pride themselves on their ability to do math mentally. Don't be surprised if students from other countries can produce answers without showing work.

Development of Invented Strategies in Addition and Subtraction

You will not be surprised to hear that students do not spontaneously invent wonderful computational methods while you sit back and watch. Here we discuss pedagogical methods that support students' development of invented strategies for multidigit addition and subtraction.

Models to Support Invented Strategies

Common Core State Standards require that third grade students "fluently add and subtract within 1000" using strategies based on "place value, properties of operations and the relationship between addition and subtraction" (CCSSO, 2010, p. 24). Try seeing how you would do these problems without using standard algorithms: $487 + 235$ and $623 - 247$. For subtraction, a think-addition strategy is usually easiest. Occasionally, other strategies appear with larger numbers. For example, "chunking off" multiples of 50 or 25 is often a useful method. For $462 + 257$, pull out 450 and 250 to equal 700. That leaves 12 and 7 more, for 719.

There are three common types of invented strategies to solve addition and subtraction situations that can be extended to higher numbers: *split strategy* (https://www.youtube.com/watch?v=XjRiQpMMI-k) (also called decomposition), *jump strategy* (https://www.youtube.com/watch?v=w9haFFL-AMs) (similar to counting on or counting back), and *shortcut strategy* (https://www.youtube.com/watch?v=_v9Kb-qFVxY) (sometimes known as compensation) (Torbeyns, De Smedt, Ghesquiere, & Verschaffel, 2009). The notion of "splitting" a number into parts (often by place value) is a useful strategy for all operations. Both the word *split* and the use of a visual diagram help students develop strategies (Verschaffel et al., 2007). When recording students' ideas, try using arrows or lines to indicate how two computations are joined together, as shown in Figure 11.2(a).

Figure 11.2

Two methods of recording students' thought processes so that the class can follow the strategy.

(a) How much is 86 and 47?

S: I know that 80 and 20 more is 100.

T: Where do the 80 and the 20 come from?

S: I split the 47 into 20 and 20 and 7 and the 86 into 80 and 6.

T: (illustrates the splitting with lines)
So then you added one of the 20s to 80?

S: Yes, 80 and 20 is 100. Then I added the other 20 and got 120.

T: (writes the equations on the board)

S: Then I added the 6 and the 7 and got 13.

T: (writes this equation)

S: Then I added the 120 to the 13 and got 133.

T: Indicates with joining lines.

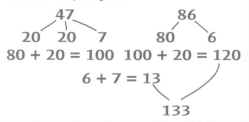

$$80 + 20 = 100 \quad 100 + 20 = 120$$
$$6 + 7 = 13$$
$$133$$

(b) What is 84 minus 68?

S: I started at 84. First, I jumped back 4 to get to 80.

T: Why did you subtract 4 first? Why not 8?

S: It was easier to think about 80 than 84. I will save the other part of 8 until later. Then I jumped back 60 to get to 20.

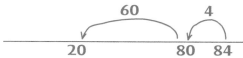

S: Then I jumped back 4.

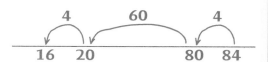

T: Why 4?

S: That was how much I still had left over from 68.

Empty Number Line

The empty number line (also known as an open number line) shown in Figure 11.2(b) is a number line with no prewritten numbers or tick marks. Students can use an empty number line to incorporate a sequential jump strategy that is effective for thinking about addition and subtraction situations (Caldwell, Kobett, & Karp, 2014; Gravemeijer & van Galen, 2003; Verschaffel et al., 2007). The empty number line is more flexible than the usual number line because it can be jotted down anywhere, works with any numbers, and eliminates confusion with tick marks and the spaces between them. It is also found less prone to computational errors (Gravemeijer & van Galen, 2003).

Initially, the empty number line is a good way to help you model a student's thinking for the class, especially when you link to their early understanding of a unit. They need to be reminded that the number line is a length marked off into particular units—and in this case, they are creating their own units with jumps. Students determine the start and result numbers based on the problem they are solving. Then they often use "friendly numbers" to make their jumps and then calculate the total of the jumps (Barker, 2009). The jumps on the line can be recorded as students share or explain each step of their solution counting up or down from an initial number. With time and practice, students will find the empty number line to be a valuable tool to use in supporting their thinking.

Bar Diagrams

Bar diagrams can also be used to support students' thinking and help them explain their ideas to others. Bar diagrams work particularly well for contexts that fit a subtraction comparison situation and a part–part–whole model. See Figure 11.3 for a sample of each. The *shortcut strategy* involves the flexible adjustment of numbers. For example, just as students used 10 as an anchor in learning their facts, they can move from numbers such as 38 or 69 to the nearest 10 (in this case 40 or 70) and then take the 2 or 1 off to compensate later. As another example, $51 - 37$ can be thought of as $37 + 10 = 47$ and $47 + 4$ more equals 51.

In each case, as these examples suggest, the numbers in the problem and the type of problem will influence the strategies students use. Therefore, it is important to think carefully about the type of story problem you pose as well as the numbers you use!

Adding Multidigit Numbers

Although double-digit addition is taught in second grade, students in grades 3 and 4 may still be challenged by these computations. Problems involving the sum of 2 two-digit numbers will usually produce a wide variety of strategies, and it is these strategies that

Figure 11.3

Using bar diagrams to help think about two problems.

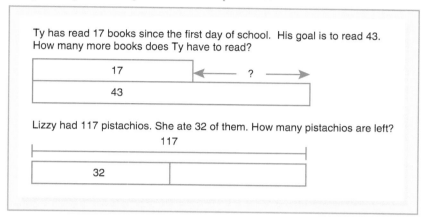

are the foundation for adding three-digit numbers. Some strategies will involve starting with one or the other number and working from that point, either by adding on to the next ten or by adding tens from one number to the other.

Figure 11.4 illustrates four different strategies for addition of 2 two-digit numbers, all of which can be adapted for three-digit numbers. The ways the solutions are recorded are suggestions, but note the frequent use of empty number lines.

Figure 11.4

Four different invented strategies for addition with two-digit numbers.

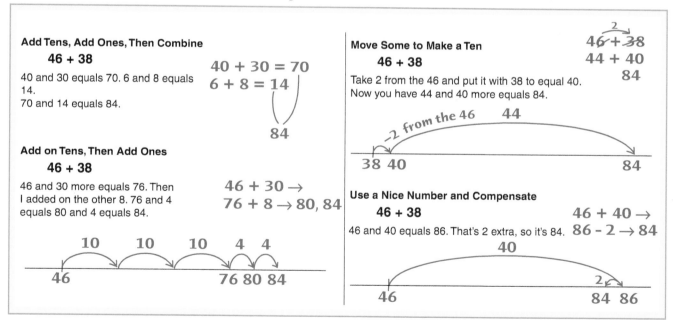

The move to the shortcut or compensation strategies focusing on making a hundred is useful when one of the numbers is close to a multiple of 100. To promote that strategy, present problems with addends like 397 or 508. Note that it is only necessary to adjust one of the two numbers.

Formative Assessment Note

Periodically you will want to focus on a student to determine his or her strategy use. Try the following problem with a student in a diagnostic interview: 46 + 35. See if the student begins by splitting the numbers. That is, for 46 + 35, a student may add on 4 to 46 to get to 50 and then add 31 more, or first add 30 to 46 and then add 4 to get to 80 and then add the remaining 1. In either case, see if they are taking advantage of the utilization of tens. Some students may use an open number line and count up "46, 56, 66, 76," as they draw corresponding arcs and numbers such as +10 and so on. In each case, be mindful of how flexibly students use place-value units because if they are not seeing the ten as a unit, you may need to present more instruction on place value.

Stop and Reflect

Try adding 367 + 155 in as many different ways as you can. How many of your ways are like those in Figure 11.4?

Subtraction as "Think-Addition"

Students who know the think-addition strategy for their basic facts can also use this strategy to solve problems with multidigit numbers. This is an amazingly powerful way to subtract and is particularly successful for students with disabilities (Peltenburg, van den Heuvel-Panhuizen, & Robitzsch, 2011). For example, for 382 − 195, the idea is to think, "How much do I add to 195 to get 382?" Using join with *change unknown* problems or *missing-part* problems (discussed in Chapter 8) will encourage using the think-addition strategy. Here are examples of each.

Sam had 467 baseball cards in his collection. A year later he had 735 cards. How many cards did Sam add to his collection that year?

Juanita counted all of the teacher's pencils. Some were sharpened and some not. She counted 343 pencils in all; 260 pencils were not sharpened. How many were sharpened?

The numbers in these problems encourage the use of multiple strategies that emphasize place value. Students can add hundreds to get close, then add tens and ones. They can add hundreds and overshoot, then come back by tens. You can emphasize the value of using place-value concepts by posing problems involving multiples of 10 or 100.

Take-Away Subtraction

Using a take-away method (particularly with three digits) is more difficult to do mentally. Exceptions involve problems such as 423 − 8 or 576 − 300 (subtracting a number less than 10 or a multiple of 10 or 100). Take away is very likely the strategy that will come to mind first for students who have previously been taught the standard algorithm. We suggest, however, that you emphasize think-addition whenever possible.

Try computing 823 − 579. Use both take-away and think-addition methods. Which is easier for you?

Standard Algorithms for Addition and Subtraction

Standard algorithms for multidigit addition and subtraction are significantly different from nearly every invented method. In addition to starting with the right-most digits and being digit oriented (as already noted), the traditional approaches involve the concept referred to as *trading* or *regrouping*—exchanging 10 in one place-value position for 1 in the position to the left, or the reverse, exchanging 1 for 10 in the position to the right. The terms *borrowing* and *carrying* are obsolete and conceptually misleading. Preferable language is "10 ones are traded for a ten" or "a hundred is traded for 10 tens." Notice that none of the invented strategies involves regrouping. Take a look at Talecia, a third grader, as she loses her connection to the real value of the numbers she is recording when she adds 34 + 57. Students must be able to know the value of the numbers as well as understand the process behind the algorithm.

Invented Strategies for Multiplication

For multiplication, students' ability to break numbers apart in flexible ways is even more important than in addition or subtraction. This skill hinges on the full understanding of the distributive property of multiplication over addition. For example, to multiply 43 × 5, one might think about breaking 43 into 40 and 3, multiplying each by 5, and then adding the results. Students require ample opportunities to develop these concepts by making sense of their own ideas and those of their classmates. Watch Andrew as he uses the distributive property to solve 7 × 12.

Useful Representations

The problem 6 × 34 may be represented in a number of ways, as illustrated in Figure 11.5. Often the choice of a model is influenced by a story problem. To determine how many oranges six classes would need if there are 34 students in each class, students may model 6 sets of 34. If the problem is about a rectangle's area (6 cm × 34 cm), then some form of an array is likely. But each representation is appropriate for thinking about 6 × 34 regardless of the context, and students should get to a point at which they select meaningful ways to think about multiplication and use tools strategically.

How students represent a product is directly related to their methods for determining answers. At first, the equal groups of 34 students in a class might suggest repeated additions—perhaps taking sets two at a time. Double 34 equals 68 and there are three sets of those, so 68 + 68 + 68 = 204. Remember, you want to move them away from repeated addition to thinking multiplicatively. Another option is to think about how the six groups of base-ten materials might be broken into tens and ones: 6 times 3 tens or 6 × 30 and 6 × 4. Or some students use the tens individually: 6 tens equals 60. So that's 60 + 60 + 60 (180); then add on 24 more to equal 204.

All of these ideas should be part of students' repertoire of models for multidigit multiplication computation. The NCTM *Principles and Standards for School Mathematics* suggest,

Figure 11.5

Different ways to model 34×6 may support different computational strategies.

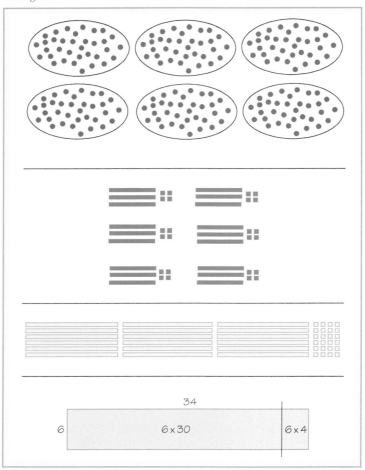

Teaching Tip

Although you may worry that presenting multiple methods to solve problems will overwhelm and confuse your students, researchers found that comparing a variety of methods from the start helped students gain flexibility and enhanced learning (Rittle-Johnson et al., 2010)!

"Having access to more than one method for each operation allows students to choose an approach that best fits the numbers in a particular problem" (NCTM, 2000, p. 155).

Multiplication by a One-Digit Multiplier

As with addition and subtraction, it is helpful to place multiplication tasks in context. Let students model problems in ways that make sense to them. The types of strategies that students use for multiplication are more varied than for addition and subtraction. The three categories described here are strategies grounded in student reasoning, as described in research on multiplicative reasoning (Baek, 2006; Confrey, 2008; Petit, 2009).

Complete-Number Strategies (Including Doubling)

Students who are not yet comfortable decomposing numbers into parts will approach the numbers in the sets as single groups. Often, these early strategies will be based on repeated addition, which in the long term is neither efficient (234×78) nor useful (think about multiplication of fractions (Devlin, 2011). Initially, students may list long columns of the same number and add them up. In an attempt to fade this process, encourage students to recognize that if they add two numbers, the next two will have the same sum, and so on. This doubling can become the principal approach for many students (Flowers & Rubenstein, 2010–2011). Doubling capitalizes on the *distributive property*, whereby doubling 47 is double 40 + double 7, and the *associative property*, in which doubling 7 tens or $2 \times (7 \times 10)$ is the same as doubling 7 and then multiplying by 10 or $(2 \times 7) \times 10$. Figure 11.6 illustrates two methods students may use.

Partitioning Strategies

Students decompose numbers in a variety of ways that reflect an understanding of place value, at least four of which are illustrated in Figure 11.7. The "by decades" partitioning strategy (which can be extended to by hundreds, by thousands, etc.) is the same as the standard algorithm except that students always begin with the largest values. This is a very powerful mental math strategy. Another valuable strategy is to compute mentally with multiples of 25 and 50 and then add or subtract a small adjustment. All partitioning strategies rely on knowledge of the distributive property. Watch Rachel in this **video** as she uses partitioning to solve 45×36.

Figure 11.6

Students who use a complete-number strategy do not break numbers apart into decades or tens and ones.

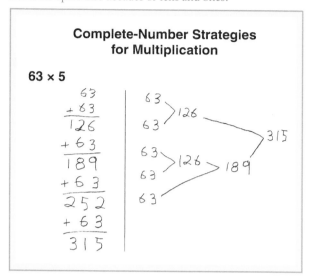

Figure 11.7

Four different ways to make easier partial products.

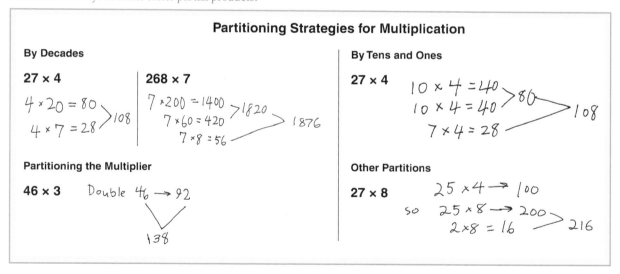

Compensation Strategies

Students and adults look for ways to manipulate numbers so that calculations are easy. In Figure 11.8, the problem 27×4 is changed to an easier one, and then an adjustment or compensation is made. The second example uses the "half-then-double strategy," in which one factor is cut in half and the other is doubled. This is often used when a 5 or a 50 is involved. Because these strategies are so dependent on the numbers involved, they can't be used for all computations. However, they are valuable approaches, especially for mental math and estimation.

Figure 11.8

A compensation is made in the answer, or one factor is
changed to compensate for a change in the other factor.

Compensation Strategies for Multiplication

27 × 4

$27 + 3 \rightarrow 30 \times 4 \rightarrow 120$

$3 \times 4 = 12 \rightarrow -12$

$\overline{108}$

250 × 5

I can split 250 in half and multiply by 10.

$125 \times 10 = 1250$

17 × 70

$20 \times 70 \rightarrow 1400 - 210 \rightarrow 1190$ (3×70)

Multiplication of Multidigit Numbers

As students move from one-digit to two-digit factors, there is value in exposing them to products involving multiples of 10 and 100. This supports the importance of place value and an emphasis on the number rather than separate digits. Consider the following problem.

The Scout troop wanted to make 400 battery packs as a fundraising project. If each pack will have 12 batteries inside, how many batteries are the Scouts going to need?

Students can use $4 \times 12 = 48$ to figure out that 400×12 equals 4800. Make sure you discuss how to say and write "forty-eight hundred." Be alert to students who simply tack on zeros without understanding why. Many students will say "to multiply a number by 10, just put a zero on the end of the number." But very soon this rule will "expire" (Karp, Bush, & Dougherty, 2014) as students try to solve 2.5×10, a problem for which this rule will not work. Try problems in which tens are multiplied by tens, such as 30×60 or 210×40.

Then students should move to problems that involve any two-digit numbers, not just those that are multiples of 10. A problem such as the following one can be solved in many different ways.

The parade had 23 clowns. Each clown carried 18 balloons. How many balloons were there altogether?

Some students might look for smaller products, such as 6×23, and then add that result three times. Another method is to find the answer to 20×23 and then subtract 2×23. Others will calculate and add four separate partial products: $10 \times 20 = 200$, $8 \times 20 = 160$, $10 \times 3 = 30$, and $8 \times 3 = 24$. Two-digit multiplication is both complex and challenging. But, students can solve these problems in a variety of interesting ways, many of which will contribute to the development of the standard algorithm. Figure 11.9 illustrates three fourth-grade students' work prior to instruction on the standard algorithm. Kenneth's work shows how he is *partitioning* the factor 12 into 3 × 2 × 2. Briannon is using a *complete-number strategy*. She may need to see and hear about strategies other classmates developed to move toward a more efficient approach. Nick's method is conceptually very similar to the standard algorithm. As students like Nick begin partitioning numbers by place value, the strategies are often the same as the standard algorithm but without the traditional recording schemes.

Figure 11.9

Three students solve a multiplication problem using invented strategies.

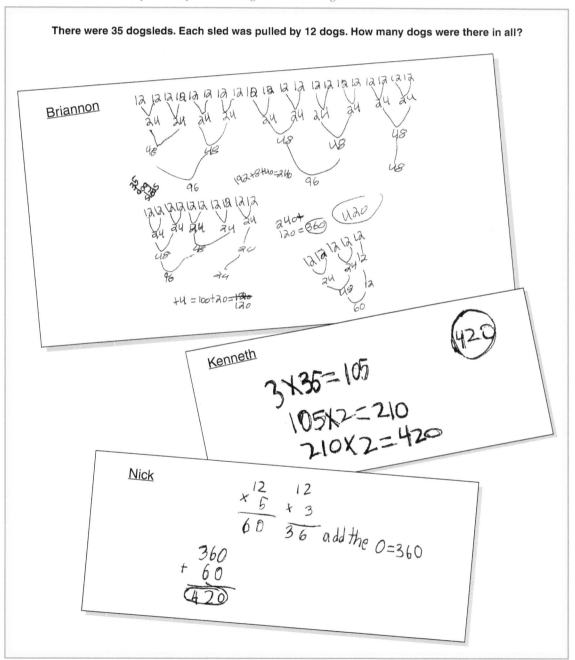

Cluster Problems

One approach to multidigit multiplication is called *cluster problems*. This strategy encourages students to use facts and combinations they already know to figure out more complex computations. For example, to find 34 × 50, students might record the following cluster of known facts:

$$3 \times 50$$

$$10 \times 50$$

$$34 \times 25$$

$$30 \times 50$$

Using these problems as support, students can analyze to see which ones can be used to find the product (there are multiple options). They can also consider adding other problems that might be helpful. In this case, have students make an estimate of the final product before doing any of the problems in the cluster. For example, in the cluster for 34 × 50, 3 × 50 and 10 × 50 may be helpful in thinking about 30 × 50. The results of 30 × 50 and 4 × 50 combine to give you 34 × 50. It may seem that 34 × 25 is harder than 34 × 50. However, if you know 34 × 25, it need only be doubled to get the desired product. At first, you may want to brainstorm clusters together as a class, but when students become familiar with the approach, they should make up their own cluster of problems for a given product.

Cluster problems help students think about ways that they can decompose numbers into easier parts. The strategy of breaking the numbers apart and multiplying the parts—using place-value knowledge coupled with the distributive property—is an extremely valuable technique for flexible computation and prepares students for understanding the standard algorithm. The *Common Core State Standards* state that students do not have to use the formal term *distributive property*, but they expect students to understand why this property works because that knowledge is critical to understanding multiplication (and its ties to algebraic thinking).

Stop and Reflect

Try making up a cluster of problems for 86 × 42. Include all problems that you think might be helpful. Use your cluster to find the product. Is there more than one way?

Were these problems in your cluster? Did you use others?

$$2 \times 80 \qquad 4 \times 80 \qquad 2 \times 86 \qquad 40 \times 80$$

$$6 \times 40 \qquad 10 \times 86 \qquad 40 \times 86$$

All that is required to begin the cluster-problem approach is that your cluster eventually leads to an accurate solution.

Standard Algorithms for Multiplication

The standard multiplication algorithm is probably the most difficult of the four algorithms when students have not had numerous opportunities to explore their own strategies first. As with other algorithms, as much time as necessary should be devoted to the conceptual development of the multiplication algorithm using concrete- or semiconcrete models, with the recording or written part coming later.

Begin with Models

The multiplication algorithm can be developed with a variety of models but when you move to two-digit multipliers, models like the area model have distinct advantages.

Area Model

Start with a context and give students a drawing of a rectangular garden 6 cm × 47 cm. What is the area of the garden? Let students solve the problem in groups using base-ten materials before discussing it as a class.

As shown in Figure 11.10, the rectangle can be sliced or separated into two parts so that one part will be 6 ones by 7 ones, or 42 ones, and the other will be 6 ones by 4 tens, or 24 tens. Notice that the base-ten language "6 ones times 4 tens equals 24 tens" tells how many tens pieces are in the big section. To say "6 times 40 equals 240" is also correct and tells how many units or square centimeters are in the section. What you wish to avoid is saying "6 times 4" when the 4 actually represents 40. Each section is referred to as a partial product. By adding the two partial products, you get the total product or area of the rectangle.

Figure 11.10

A rectangle covered with base-ten pieces is a useful model for two-digit by one-digit multiplication.

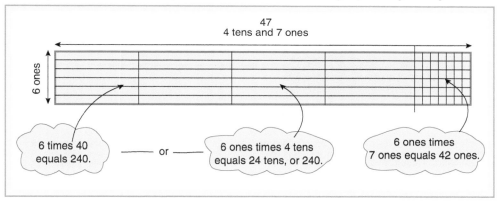

This is called the *area model*, which can be thought about as a connected array. It is an important visual representation that can support students' multiplicative understanding and reasoning (Barmby, Harries, Higgins, & Suggate, 2009; Iszák, 2004). The area model uses a row and column structure to automatically organize equal groups and offers a visual demonstration of the commutative and distributive properties (unlike the number line). The area model can also be linked to successful representations of the standard multiplication algorithm and future topics such as multiplication of fractions (Lannin, Chval, & Jones, 2013) and multiplication of algebraic terms (Benson, Wall, & Malm, 2013).

A valuable exploration with the **area model (https://www.youtube.com/watch? v=mjYYbwuued0)** uses large rectangles that have been precisely prepared with dimensions between 25 cm and 60 cm and square corners. Each group of students uses one of these rectangles to determine how many small ones pieces (base-ten materials) will fit inside. Later, students can simply be given a tracing of a rectangle on grid paper or be asked, "What is the area of a rectangle that is 36 cm × 47 cm?"

Standards for
Mathematical Practice

◀ **5** Use appropriate tools strategically.

For a rectangle that is 36 cm × 47 cm, most students will fill the rectangle with as many hundreds pieces as possible. One obvious approach is to put the 12 hundreds in one corner. This will leave narrow regions on two sides that can be filled with tens pieces and a final small rectangle that will hold ones. Especially if students have had earlier experiences with finding products in arrays, figuring out the size of each subrectangle and combining them to find the size of the whole rectangle is relatively straightforward. Figure 11.11 shows the four regions.

Figure 11.11

Ones, tens, and hundreds pieces fit exactly into the four sections of this 36 cm × 47 cm rectangle.

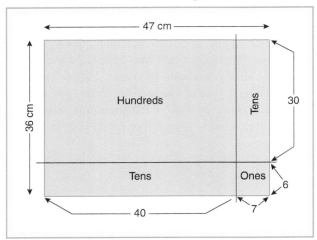

Activity 11.1

CCSS-M: 4.NBT.B.5

Build It and Break It

Select a problem such as **23 × 18.** Use base-ten blocks or 0.5cm grid paper to build the corresponding area model. Then, have students show and record as many ways as possible to "slice" the array into pieces. For example, they could cut the array into **23 × 10 + 23 × 8.** What other vertical or horizontal slices can be made? What property does this link to? Before launching the activity, provide students, particularly ELLs and students with disabilities, a labeled visual of an array (or area model) that includes the terms *array, area model, slice, vertical,* and *horizontal.* In a wrap-up discussion, be sure to focus on the vocabulary of the key concepts (*distributive property, decompose, strategy,* etc.).

Open Array Open arrays (Fosnot & Dolk, 2001; NCTM, 2014) are semiconcrete representations of the area model and can be successfully used after students actually experience several constructions of area models with base-ten materials. Starting with a blank rectangle, students mark off areas (the number of subdivisions depends on the digits in the factors) that align with the distributive property. Students record partial products inside each subdivision. Note that the dimensions of the open array are not necessarily drawn to scale and therefore are often not precisely proportional. But the model can be productively used to think about the multiplication as an area of a rectangle, which aligns to the standard algorithm. The open array will also connect to future work with multiplication of fractions and two polynomials, and also to mathematics history through looks at Egyptian and Russian peasant multiplication

(Lee, 2014). Figure 11.12 shows four steps in the process of developing an open array for the problem 72 × 36: Create an array according to the number of digits in the problem, label the sides with the factors broken down by place value, multiply, and then add the partial products.

Research analyzed sixth graders' varied strategies for solving multiplication problems on the criteria of flexibility, accuracy, and efficiency. Given the problem 13 × 7, only 11 percent of the students used the standard algorithm. When multiplying 2 two-digit numbers, only 20 percent used the standard algorithm, with less than half of that 20 percent reaching the correct answer (Keiser, 2010). Interestingly, the array or area model was most often selected and the most accurate (the selection of the cluster problem strategy was second in accuracy and frequency).

Figure 11.12

The open array is a means to record multidigit multiplication.

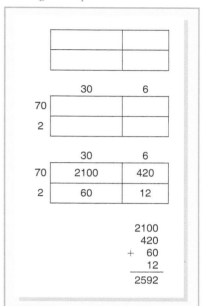

Activity 11.2

CCSS-M: 4.NBT.B.5

Make It Easy

Computer versions of area models can ease some of the difficulties of physically covering rectangular grids with base-ten blocks. Go to the NLVM website and find the Rectangle Multiplication applet. Model a multiplication problem of your choice up to 30 × 30. See how the rectangle is split into two parts rather than four, corresponding to the tens and ones digits in the multiplier. How does this representation correlate to the standard algorithm? For students with disabilities, you may need to initially have a set of base-ten blocks nearby to show how the concrete version corresponds to the computer illustration.

Move from having students draw large rectangles and arrange base-ten pieces, to using **base-ten grid paper**. On the grid paper, students can draw accurate rectangles showing the pieces. Do not impose any recording technique on students until they understand how to use the two dimensions of a rectangle to get a product.

Develop the Written Record

To help students develop a recording scheme, provide **Multiplication Recording** sheets with base-ten columns on which they can record problems. When partial products are written separately and added together, there is little new to learn. But, as illustrated in Figure 11.13(a), it is possible to teach students how to write the first product with a regrouped digit so that the combined product is written on one line. This recording scheme is known to be a source of errors. The little digit representing the regrouping is often the difficulty—it gets added in before the subsequent multiplication or is forgotten. Instead, to avoid errors, encourage students to record partial products. Then it makes no difference in which order the products are written. Figure 11.13(b) shows how students can record partial products, which mirrors how this computation can be done mentally.

Figure 11.13

In the standard form, the product of ones is recorded first. (a) The tens digit of this first product is written as a "regrouped" digit above the tens column. (b) Partial products can be recorded in any order.

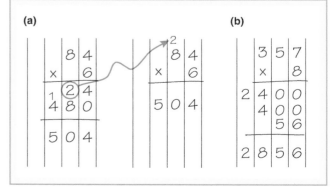

Partial Products. From the area model, the progression to record partial products with a two-digit multiplier is relatively straightforward. Rectangles can be drawn on base-ten grid paper, full-sized rectangles can be filled in with base-ten pieces, or an open array can be used. Now there will be four partial products, corresponding to four different sections of the rectangle.

Several variations in language might be used. Consider 36 × 47 as illustrated in Figure 11.14. In the partial product 30 × 40, if base-ten language is used—*3 tens times 4 tens equals 12 hundreds*—the result tells how many hundreds pieces are in that section. Avoid saying "three times four," which promotes thinking about digits rather than numbers. It is important to stress that a product of *tens times tens is hundreds*.

Figure 11.14 also shows the recording of four partial products in the order of the standard algorithm and how these can be collapsed to two lines if small digits are used

Figure 11.14

A 36 × 47 rectangle filled with base-ten pieces. Base-ten language connects the four partial products to the standard algorithm.

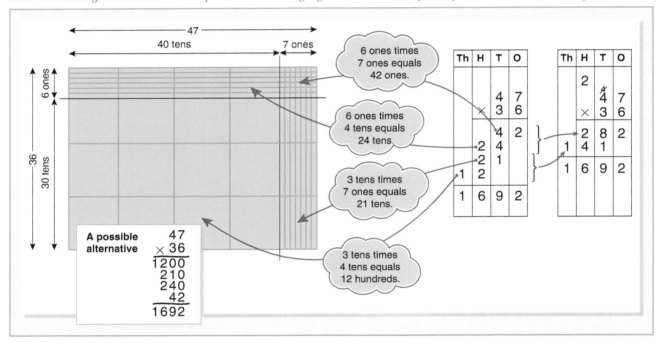

Figure 11.15

36 × 72 shown using a lattice multiplication technique.

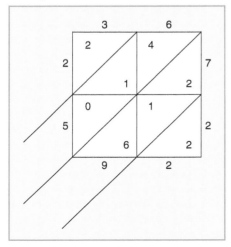

to record the trade. Here the second exchange technically belongs in the hundreds column, but it is often written elsewhere, which again is a source of errors. The lower left of the figure shows another alternative with all four partial products written. Using this approach, multiplying numbers such as 538 × 29 results in six partial products, but far fewer errors!

Lattice Multiplication. Another approach for recording multi-digit multiplication is known as lattice multiplication. Historically, this method has been used in a variety of cultures. Students use a grid with squares split by diagonal lines to organize their thinking along diagonally organized place-value columns. Watch this **video** (**https://www.youtube.com/watch?v=Z3T_NhFlpB0**) to see how the lattice model is set up, filled in, and calculated. Look at Figure 11.15 to see the final recording for the problem 36 × 72.

Invented Strategies for Division

Even though many adults think division is the most onerous of the computational operations, students may find it easier than multiplication. Division computation strategies with whole numbers are developed in third through fifth grades (CCSSO, 2010).

Recall that there are two concepts of division. First, there is partition, or fair sharing, illustrated by the following story problem.

The bag has 783 jelly beans, and Aidan and his four friends want to share them equally. How many jelly beans will Aidan and each of his friends get?

Then there is the measurement, or repeated subtraction:

Jumbo the elephant loves peanuts. His trainer has 625 peanuts. If he gives Jumbo 20 peanuts each day, how many days will the peanuts last?

Students should be challenged to solve both types of problems. However, fair share problems are often easier to solve with base-ten pieces, and they mirror the idea of partitioning that is used in the standard algorithm. Eventually, students will develop strategies that apply to both types of problems.

Figure 11.16 shows strategies that three fourth graders used to solve division problems. The first example (a) illustrates 72 ÷ 3 using base-ten blocks and a sharing process. When no more tens can be distributed, a ten is traded for ones. Then the 12 ones are grouped and distributed, resulting in 24 in each set. This direct modeling approach with base-ten pieces is easy to understand and use.

Figure 11.16

Students use both models and symbols to solve division tasks.

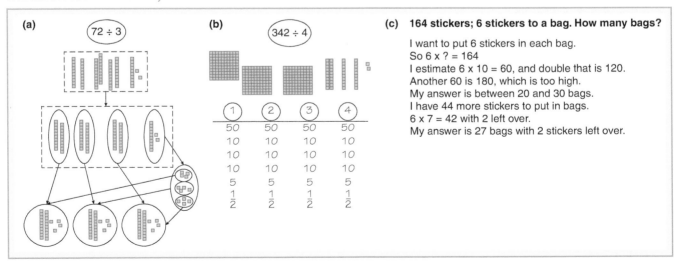

The student work in Figure 11.16(b) shows that for the problem 342 ÷ 4, she sets out base-ten blocks and draws a four-column recording chart to match the divisor and the image of paper plates that had been used previously as an organizational tool for sharing. After noticing that there are not enough hundreds for each child, she splits 2 of the 3 hundreds in half, putting 50 in each of the four columns. That leaves her with 1 hundred, 4 tens, and 2 ones. After trading the hundred for tens (now she has 14 tens), she gives 3 tens to each person, recording 30 in each column. Now she is left with 2 tens and 2 ones, or 22. She knows that 4×5 equals 20, so she gives each child 5, leaving 2. Then she splits the 2 into halves and writes $\frac{1}{2}$ in each column.

The student in Figure 11.16(c) solves a division problem that involves a measurement situation: How many bags with 6 stickers in each can be made if there are 164 stickers? She wants to find out how many groups of six are in 164. As a first step she estimates and tries 6×20. She actually does this by multiplying 6×10 and doubling the answer. Then she tries adding another group of 10 and recognizes that is too high. So she knows the answer is more than 20 and less than 30. Then she thinks about how many sixes in 44, which she knows is 7 with 2 left over. So her answer is 27 bags with 2 stickers left over.

Missing-Factor Strategies

In Figure 11.16(c), notice that the student is using a multiplicative approach. She is trying to find out "What number times 6 will be close to 164 with less than 6 remaining?"

Stop and Reflect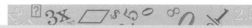

Before reading further, think about the quotient of $318 \div 7$ by trying to figure out what number times 7 (or 7 times what number) is close to 318 without going over. Do not use the standard algorithm.

There are several places to begin solving this problem. For instance, because 10×7 equals 70 and 100×7 equals 700, the answer is between 10 and 100. You might start with multiples of 10. Forty sevens are 280. Fifty sevens are 350. So 40 is not enough, and 50 is too many. The answer has to be forty-something. At this point, you could test numbers between 40 and 50 or add on groups of seven. Or you could notice that 40 sevens (280) leaves you with $20 + 18$ or 38. Five sevens will be 35 of the 38 with 3 remaining. In all, that's $40 + 5$ or 45 with a remainder of 3.

This missing-factor approach is likely to be an invented strategy used by some students if they are solving measurement problems such as the following.

Grace can put 6 pictures on one page of her photo album. If she has 82 pictures, how many pages will she need?

Alternatively, you can simply pose a task such as $82 \div 6$ and ask students, "What number times 6 would be close to 82?" Notice that the missing-factor strategy is equally good for one-digit divisors as two-digit divisors

Cluster Problems

Another approach to developing missing factor strategies is to use cluster problems, as discussed for multiplication. Following are examples of two clusters for two different division problems (written in bold at the bottom of the columns).

Cluster 1	Cluster 2
4 × 100	10 × 72
500 ÷ 4	5 × 70
4 × 25	2 × 72
4 × 6	4 × 72
527 ÷ 4	5 × 72
	381 ÷ 72

Notice that it is useful to include division problems in the cluster. In the first example, $400 \div 4$ could easily replace 4×100 and 4×125 could replace $50 \div 4$. The idea is to capitalize on the inverse relationship between multiplication and division.

Cluster problems provide students with a sense that problems can be solved in different ways and with different starting points. Therefore, rather than cluster problems you can provide students with a variety of first steps for solving the problem.

Stop and Reflect

Solve $514 \div 8$ in two different ways beginning with different first steps. Do your approaches converge before the solution?

For example, here are four possible starting points for $514 \div 8$.

$$8 \times 10 \qquad 400 \div 8 \qquad 8 \times 60 \qquad 80 \div 8$$

When you first ask students to solve problems using two different strategies, they often use an inefficient method for their second approach (or revert to a standard algorithm). For example, to solve $514 \div 8$, a student might perform a very long string of subtractions ($514 - 8 = 506, 506 - 8 = 498, 498 - 8 = 490$, and so on) and count how many times 8 was subtracted. Others will actually draw 514 tally marks and loop groups of 8. These students have not developed sufficient flexibility to think of more efficient methods. Posing a variety of starting points can nudge students into more profitable alternatives. Watch this **video** of a class discussion describing strategies for solving 251×12. What questions does the teacher ask that encourage students to share their thinking? Why do you think the teacher asks students to describe how the strategies are different and how they are the same?

Standard Algorithms for Division

The *Common Core State Standards* (CCSSO, 2010) suggest that the division algorithm with one-digit divisors is developed in the fourth grade, and it should provide the basis for the extension to two-digit divisors in the fifth grade. Students who are still struggling in grade 5 with single-digit divisors can also benefit from the following conceptual development.

Begin with Models

Long division is the one standard algorithm that starts with the left-hand, or biggest, pieces. The conceptual basis for the algorithm most often taught is the partition or fair-share method, the method we will explore in detail here.

Partition or Fair Share Model

Traditionally, if the problem $4\overline{)583}$, was posed, we might hear someone say, "4 goes into 5 one time." Initially, this is quite mysterious to students. How can you just ignore the "83" and keep changing the problem? Preferably, you want students to think of 583 as 5 hundreds, 8 tens, and 3 ones, not as the independent digits 5, 8, and 3. One idea is to use a context such as energy bars bundled in boxes of 10, with 10 boxes (100 pieces) to a carton. Then the problem becomes as follows: "*We have 5 cartons, 8 boxes, and 3 energy bars to share evenly between 4 schools.*" In this context, it is reasonable to share the largest cartons first until no more can be shared. Those remaining cartons are "unpacked," and the boxes shared, and so on.

Stop and Reflect

Try the distributing or sharing process yourself using base-ten pieces, four paper plates, and the problem 583 ÷ 4. Try to talk through the process without using "goes into." Think about sharing equally.

Language plays an enormous role in thinking conceptually about the standard division algorithm. Most adults are so accustomed to the "goes into" language that it is hard to let it go. For the problem 583 ÷ 4, here is some suggested language:

- I want to share 5 hundreds, 8 tens, and 3 ones among these 4 sets. There are enough hundreds for each set to get 1 hundred. That leaves 1 hundred remaining.

- I'll trade the remaining hundred for 10 tens. That gives me a total of 18 tens. I can give each set 4 tens and have 2 tens left over. Two tens are not enough to go around the four sets.

- I can trade the 2 tens for 20 ones and add them to the 3 ones I already had. That equals a total of 23 ones. I can give 5 ones to each of the four sets. That leaves me with 3 ones as a remainder. In all, I gave each group 1 hundred, 4 tens, and 5 ones, with 3 ones left over.

▶ Activity 11.3

CCSS-M: 4.NBT.B.6

Left Overs

Use the **Left Over Game Board** and have students work in pairs and place their game pieces at the "start" point of the path. The first player uses the **Left Over Spinner** and spins. The amount on the spinner is used as the divisor for the number on the start square. If there are left overs after the division, the player moves the number of spaces that equals the remainder. If there is no remainder, the player stays in the same position. If they move the amount of the remainder, they get a bonus turn. The winner is the first to reach the end of the path. You can differentiate the game by using easier (or harder) divisors (see blank spinners on the **Left Over Spinner** Activity Page).

Partial Quotients Using a Visual Model

You can look at division with an eye to partial quotients by using a version of a bar diagram model blended with the repeated subtraction approach. Take a look at the problem 1506 ÷ 3. If multiplication facts we know are used as a guide, then we can repeatedly subtract partial products and record them through an approach that uses measurement division (see Figure 11.17).

Figure 11.17

Using a bar diagram to show partial quotients.

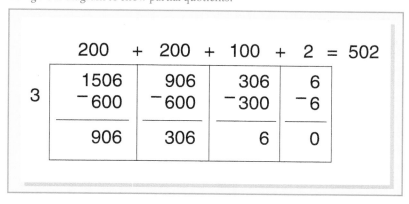

Develop the Written Record

The recording scheme for the long-division algorithm is not completely intuitive. You will need to be explicit in helping students learn to record the fair sharing with models. There are essentially four steps:

1. *Share* and record the number of pieces put in each group.
2. *Record* the number of pieces shared in all. Multiply to find this number.
3. *Record* the number of pieces remaining. Subtract to find this number.
4. *Trade* (if necessary) for smaller pieces, and combine with any same-sized pieces that are there already. Record the new total number in the next column.

When students model problems with a one-digit divisor with physical materials, steps 2 and 3 seem unnecessary. Explain that these steps really help when you don't have the base ten pieces there to count.

Explicit-Trade Method.   Figure 11.18 details each step of the recording process just described. On the left, is the standard algorithm. To the right is an explicit-trade method that matches the actual action with physical models by explicitly recording the trades. Instead of the "bring-down" step of the standard algorithm, traded pieces are crossed out, as is the number of existing pieces in the next column. The combined number of pieces is written in this column using, in this case, a two-digit number. In the example, 2 hundreds are traded for 20 tens, combined with the 6 that were there, for a total of 26 tens. The 26 is, therefore, written in the tens column.

Students often find this **explicit-trade method (https://www.youtube.com/watch?v=33CYjd1zx7g)** invented by John Van de Walle and tested with students in grades 3 to 8, easier to follow. Blank **Multiplication and Division Recording Sheets** with wide place-value columns are highly recommended for this method. By spreading out the digits in the dividend when writing down the problem, you help students avoid the common problem of leaving out a middle zero (see Figure 11.19).

Repeated Subtraction.   A well-known way to record an algorithm is based on repeated subtraction and the measurement model of division. This approach may be viewed as a good way to record the missing-factor approach with partial products recorded in a column to the right of the division computation (see Figure 11.20 and the **Repeated Subtraction Recording Sheet**). Students may prefer this strategy, especially students who bring that approach from other countries and students with learning disabilities

Figure 11.18

The standard algorithm and explicit-trade methods are connected to each step of the division process.

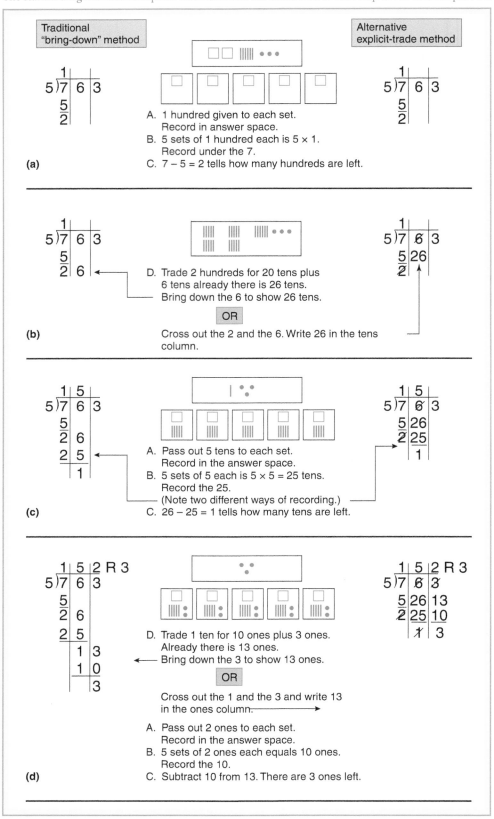

Figure 11.19

Using lines to mark place-value columns helps avoid forgetting to record zeros.

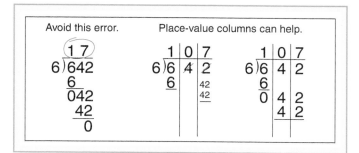

Figure 11.20

The numbers down the right side indicate the quantity of the divisor being subtracted from the dividend. The divisor can be subtracted from the dividend in groups of any amount.

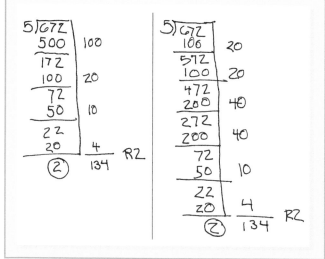

who can select facts they already know and work from that point. This method is also useful with multidigit divisors. Explore Quotient Café on the NCTM Illuminations website for a way to explore a repeated subtraction approach using a variety of story situations.

Two-Digit Divisors

The *Common Core State Standards* state that fifth-grade students should be able to find "whole-number quotients of whole numbers with up to four-digit dividends and two-digit divisors using strategies based on place value, the properties of operations, and/or the relationship between multiplication and division." The CCSS-M goes on to state that the student should "[i]llustrate and explain the calculation by using equations, rectangular arrays, and/or area models" (CCSSO, 2010, p. 35). In the past, a large part of fourth, fifth, and sometimes sixth grade was spent on "long division," with the result that many students did not master the skill and instead came away with negative attitudes toward mathematics. This is particularly worrisome as knowledge and understanding of long division is a predictor of mathematical success in high school (Siegler et al., 2012).

An Intuitive Idea

Suppose that you were sharing a large collection of shells with 36 classmates. Instead of passing them out one at a time, you conservatively estimate that each person could get at least 6 shells. So you give 6 to each person. Now you find there are more than 36 shells left. Do you have everyone give back the 6 shells so you can then give them 7 or 8? That would be silly! You simply pass out more.

The shell example provides two good ideas for sharing in long division. First, always underestimate how much can be shared. You can always pass out more. To avoid overestimating, always pretend there are more sets to share than there really are. For example, if you are dividing 312 by 43 (sharing among 43 sets or "friends"), pretend you have 50 instead. Round *up* to the next multiple of 10. You can determine that 6 pieces can be shared among 50 sets because 6 × 50 is an easy product. Therefore, because there are really only 43 sets, you can give *at least* 6 to each.

Using the Idea Symbolically.

Using these ideas, both the standard algorithm and the explicit-trade method of recording are illustrated in Figure 11.21. The rounded-up divisor,

Figure 11.21

Round the divisor up to 70 to estimate, but multiply what you share by 63. In the ones column, share 8 with each set. Oops! There are 88 left over, so just give 1 more to each set.

Standard algorithm "bring down" method

$$
\begin{array}{r}
58 = 59 \text{ R25} \\
63 \overline{\smash{)}3742} \\
315 \\
\hline
592 \\
504 \\
\hline
88 \\
63 \\
\hline
25
\end{array}
$$

Alternative explicit-trade method

70, is written in a little "think bubble." Rounding up has another advantage: It is easy to use multiples of 70 and compare them to 374. Think about sharing base-ten pieces (thousands, hundreds, tens, and ones). Work through the problem one step at a time, saying exactly what each recorded step stands for.

This approach has proved successful with students who are learning division for the first time, in middle school needing remediation, and students with disabilities. It reduces the mental strain of making choices and essentially eliminates the need to erase. If an estimate is too low, that's okay. And if you always round up, the estimate will never be too high.

A Low-Stress Approach

With a two-digit divisor, it is harder to estimate the right amount to share at each step. First, start by thinking about place value by asking students to consider whether their answer will be in the thousands, hundreds, tens, and so on. Then create a "doubling" sidebar chart (Martin, 2009) that starts with a benchmark multiple of the divisor and then doubles each subsequent product. So, for 3842 ÷ 14, decide first whether the answer is in the thousands, hundreds, or tens. Selecting hundreds in this case, students will then develop a chart of 100, 200, 400, and 800 times 14 (see Figure 11.22). Can you see how knowing 100 times 14 can help you figure out 200 times 14 and other products? Using this doubling chart helps students with products of the divisor multiplied by 100 through 900 by adding the products in various combinations. For example, to know 300 times 14, add the products of 100 times and 200 times the divisor or subtract 100 times 14 from 400 times 14. Knowing these products will logically help students know what 10 through 90 times the divisor is! Then the division becomes focused on the equal groups within the dividend and, as such, lowers stress. This scaffolding will

Figure 11.22

A student uses doubling to generate useful estimates in a sidebar chart.

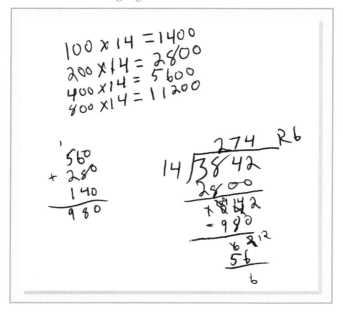

help students (particularly students who are struggling) estimate more successfully while allowing them to concentrate on the division process.

Activity 11.4

CCSS-M: 5.NBT.B.6

Double, Double—No Toil or Trouble!

 Select a division problem with a two-digit divisor such as 936 ÷ 18. Display a corresponding sidebar chart (Martin, 2009) of the products of the divisor (in this case, 10, 20, 40, and 80 times 18). Then think about the division using a missing factor approach and repeated subtraction. See if this helps in the estimation process. When working with students with disabilities, you may need to progress in a structured way by first supplying them with a sidebar chart with the products filled in. Then, on the next day, supply them with the chart and have them fill in the products, moving toward their independent creation and completion of the chart. This "fading" of support moves students in an organized and systematic way to more responsibility for their learning.

Research analyzed students' strategies for solving division problems both within a context and as naked numbers (Keiser, 2012). Given two problems with double-digit divisors, only 4 of 91 students used the standard algorithm and of those 4 students only 2 were correct. Largely, students relied on the repeated subtraction approach or the missing-factor strategy. Errors often occurred when students misapplied mathematical properties. For example, students solving $95 \div 16$ broke it into $95 \div 10 + 95 \div 6$, demonstrating a common misunderstanding. Students thought that when using the distributive property you could break apart the divisor, when instead you need to split the dividend into components.

 ## Formative Assessment Note

To assess understanding of algorithms, call on different students to explain individual steps using the appropriate terminology that connects to the concept of division. Use a **checklist** to record students' responses, indicating how well they seem to understand the algorithm. For students who struggle, conduct a short diagnostic interview to explore their level of understanding in more detail. Begin by having the student complete $115 \div 9$ and ask about what they are thinking as they carry out specific steps in the process. If there is difficulty explaining, have the student use base-ten blocks to perform the computation. Then ask the student to make connections between what was done with the physical models and what was done symbolically.

Computational Estimation

Whenever we are faced with a computation in real life, we have a variety of choices to make concerning how we will find a reasonable answer. A first decision is: "Do we need an exact answer, or will an approximation be okay?" If precision is called for, we can use an invented strategy, a standard algorithm, or a calculator. How close an estimate must be to the actual computation is a matter of context, as was the original decision to use an estimate.

The goal of computational estimation is to be able to flexibly and quickly produce an approximate result that will work for the situation and be reasonable. The *Common Core State Standards* in Mathematical Practice 5 states that students should "detect possible errors by strategically using estimation and other mathematical knowledge" (CCSSO, 2010, p. 7).

Teaching Computational Estimation

Here are some general principles that are worth keeping in mind as you help your students develop computational estimation skills:

- **Use Real Examples**. Use common examples that include comparative shopping (which store has the item for less); adding up distances in planning a trip; determining approximate monthly totals (school supplies, haircuts, lawn-mowing income, time playing video games); and figuring the cost of going to a sporting event or movie including transportation, tickets, and snacks.

- **Use Estimation Language**. Words and phrases such as *about*, *close*, *just about*, *a little more (or less) than*, and *between* are part of the language of estimation. Avoid the word *guess*.

- **Use a Context**. For example, it is important to know whether the cost of a car would likely be $2500 or $25000. Could attendance at the school play be 30 or 300 or 3000? Knowledge of the context can provide information to judge a reasonable range.

- **Accept a Range of Estimates, or Offer a Range As an Option**. Because estimates are based on computation, how can there be different answers? What estimate would you give for 270 + 325? If you use 200 + 300, you might say 500. Or you might use 250 for 270 and 350 for 325, equaling 600. You could also use 300 for 270 and add 325, getting 625. Is only one of these "right"? By sharing students' estimates and letting them discuss how and why different estimates resulted, they can see that estimates fall in a range around the exact answer. Another option is to offer a range of answers. For example, ask students whether the answer will be between 300 and 400, 450 and 550, or 600 and 700.

- **Do Not Reward or Emphasize the One Student's Estimate That is Closest**. It is already very difficult for students to handle "approximate" answers; worrying about accuracy and pushing for the closest answer only exacerbates this problem. Instead, focus on whether answers given are reasonable for the situation or problem at hand.

- **Focus on Flexible Methods, Not Answers**. Remember that having students reflect on the strategies used by classmates will lead to strategy development.

- **Ask for Information, But No Answer**. Consider the risk a student perceives when you ask for an estimate of the product 7 × $89.99. Students commonly try to quickly calculate an exact answer and then round it (Hanson & Hogan, 2000). To counter this, ask questions that provide a focus on the result, using prompts like "Is it more than or less than 1000?" or "Will $500 be enough to pay for the tickets?" The question "About how much?" is quite different from "Is it more than $600?" Another option is to ask students to choose if the answer is between $100 and $400, $500 and $800, or $900 and $1200. Narrow your ranges as students become more adept.

Each activity that follows suggests a format for estimation in which a specific numeric response is not required.

ACTIVITY 11.5   CCSS-M: 3.OA.C.8

Over or Under?

Distribute or project the **Over or Under** Activity Page. In this case, each is either over or under **$1.50**, but the number need not be the same for each task. You can add an interesting context to make the activity accessible to more learners, but remember that using multiple contexts can be difficult for ELLs. Consider playing "Over or Under?" by picking one context (e.g., the price of energy bars or fruit) and then varying the values (5 at 43 cents each, then 6 at 37 cents each, etc.).

Here is an activity in which a specific number is not required to answer the questions.

ACTIVITY 11.6

CCSS-M: 4.OA.A.3

That's Good Enough

Present students with a computation that is reasonably difficult. For example: T-shirts with the school logo cost $9 wholesale. The Spirit Club has saved $257. How many shirts can the club buy for a fundraiser? The task is to describe the steps they would take to get an exact answer but not do them. For students with disabilities, you may give them a series of examples of steps (and counterexamples of steps) that they must choose from and put in order. Share students' ideas. Next, have students actually do one or two steps. Stop and see whether they come up with good estimates.

Activity 11.7

CCSS-M: 4.NBT.A.3; 4.NBT.B.5

High or Low?

Display a computation and three or more possible computations that might be used to create an estimate. The students' task is to decide whether the estimation will be higher or lower than the actual computation. For example, display 736 × 18. For each of the following, decide whether the result will be higher or lower than the exact result and explain why you think so.

$$750 \times 10 \qquad 730 \times 15$$
$$700 \times 20 \qquad 750 \times 20$$

Also explore the High or Low Activity Page for additional problems and the Expanded Lesson: High or Low for an instructional plan for this activity.

Computational Estimation Strategies

Mental calculations using estimations are more complex than just the application of a procedure in that they require a deep knowledge of how numbers work (Hartnett, 2007). The CCSS-M suggest that for all four operations students in grades 3 and 4 (and beyond) should "assess the reasonableness of answers using mental computation and estimation strategies including rounding" (CCSSO, 2010, pp. 23, 29). See Table 11.1 for more information on estimation strategies.

Table 11.1. Estimation strategies.

Estimation Strategy	Description and Strategies	Examples
Front End	• This method focuses on the leading, or left-most, digits in numbers. Once the first digit it identified, then students think about the rest of the number as if there were zeros in the other positions. Adjustments are made to correct for the digits or numbers that were ignored. This method has been shown to be one of the easiest for students to learn (Star & Rittle-Johnson, 2009). • When estimating, avoid presenting division problems using the computational form 7)$\overline{3482}$ because this format suggests a computation rather than an estimate. Present problems in context or use the algebraic form: 3482 ÷ 7.	• 480 × 7 is 400 × 7, or 2800. • 452 × 23, consider 400 × 20, or 8000. Adjust in a second step to 9000. • 3482 ÷ 7, first decide the correct place value of the estimate (100 × 7 is too low, 1000 × 7 is too high, so the estimate will be in the hundreds). There are 34 hundreds in the dividend, so because 34 ÷ 7 is between 4 and 5, the front-end estimate is 400 or 500. In this example, because 34÷7 is almost 5, the more precise estimate is 500.
Rounding	• This method is a way of changing the numbers in the problem to others that are easier to compute mentally. In multiplication, students can either round one number or both. • Use a number line marked by a scale of 5, 10, 100, etc. The ends can be labeled 0 and 100, 100 and 200, 100 and 1000, or a range of your choice. If given a factor such as 463 and asked to round to the nearest 100, the answer is 500; if rounding to the nearest 50 then 450 would be a possible estimate.	• If one factor can be rounded to 10, 100, or 1000, the resulting product is easy to determine without adjusting the other factor (see Figure 11.23(a)). • When one factor is a single digit, round the other factor— so for 7 × 485, round 485 to 500, and the estimate is 3500. That is too high by the amount of 7 × 15 so, if more precision is required, subtract about 100 (an estimate of 7 × 15) (see Figure 11.23(b)). • Another option is to round one factor up and the other down. So for 86 × 28, 86 is between 80 and 90, but 28 is very close to 30. Round 86 down to 80 and 28 up to 30. The estimate of 2400 is only slightly off from the actual product of 2408 (see Figure 11.23(c) for another example).
Compatible Numbers	• This method refers to changing the number to one that would make the problem easier to compute mentally. This is usually used in division by adjusting the divisor or dividend (or both) to close numbers. Many percent, fraction, and rate situations involve division, and the compatible numbers strategy is quite useful.	• 413 × 24 can be thought of as 400 × 25. Because 4 × 25 equals 100, a good estimate is 10,000. • 497 ÷ 48 is approximately 500 ÷ 50, so 10 is a reasonable estimate. • See other examples in Figure 11.24.

Figure 11.23
Rounding in multiplication.

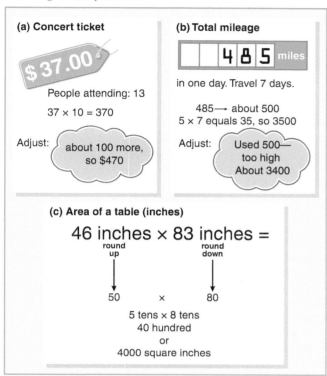

Figure 11.24
Using compatible numbers in division.

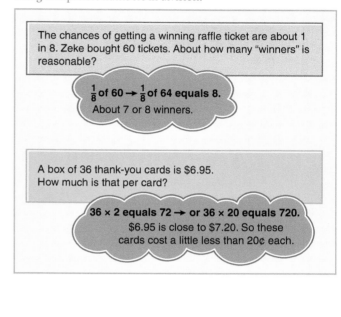

Table 11.2. Common errors and misconceptions and how to help.

Common Error or Misconception	What It Looks Like	How to Help
1. Students incorrectly record the algorithm for addition by not regrouping and ignoring place value.	When students add: 56 + 97 1413	• Use concrete materials and have student show with base-ten materials the value of these two numbers. • Avoid reading numbers in addition or subtraction problems as digits (for example, saying 5 instead of 5 tens or fifty) as this confuses students and they can put down the individual sums rather than regrouping. • Have students estimate the answer first. Do they expect the answer will be in the hundreds? Thousands? Then ask, "Is this answer reasonable?"

2. Reverse regouping.	When students add:
	
	   63
	 + 52
	  16
	
	Students start in the tens place and add backwards, disregarding place value. So in this case when they add 6 + 5 and get the answer of 11, they put down the one and regroup the "one" back to the ones column. 1 + 3 + 2 = 6
		• Ask students to check their answer for reasonableness—if we start with 63 items and add more can we end up with only 16 items?
		• Then go back to modeling the problem using base-ten materials with a place-value mat to carry out the computation. Show how the actions are recorded so that they match the standard algorithm.

(continued)

216 | CHAPTER 11 Building Strategies for Whole-Number Computation

Table 11.2. Common errors and misconceptions and how to help. (continued)

Common Error or Misconception	What It Looks Like	How to Help
3. Confusing the algorithm for multiplication with the algorithm for addition.	For the problem: $\overset{1}{67}$ $+ 7$ $\overline{144}$ Students say, "7 + 7 equals 14, put down the 4 and regroup the 1 above the 6." Then using the 7 as would be done in multiplication says, "7 + 6 equals 13 plus one more is 14. The answer is 144."	• Again it is back to two key strategies—estimating the answer before calculating to see what a reasonable answer might be and returning to act out the situation with the base ten materials.
4. When subtracting two digit numbers, students start in the ones column and take the smaller number from the larger number rather than regroup.	For the problem: 70 $- 23$ $\overline{53}$ Students say "0 from 3 equals 3 and 2 from 7 equals 5. The answer is 53."	• Start with a reminder about subtracting from 0 or other smaller numbers. Show 3 cubes in your hand and ask, "Can you take away 5?" Reinforce the situation by asking for more than you have. • Provide the actual materials on a place-value mat that correspond with the minuend. Then subtract the amount and highlight the need for regrouping when there are not enough of the units needed.
5. When multiplying students ignore internal zeros.	When students are given the problem: 4005 $\times \quad 9$ $\overline{3645}$ The student just writes the products of 9×5 and then 9×4, ignoring the multiplications of 0 tens and 0 hundreds.	• Focus on the meaning of a zero in any number by starting with a number like 4005 and asking how that would be shown with materials. Explicitly discuss the role of a 0 in the number. • Never refer to 0 as a "placeholder." This terminology gives the impression that it is not a numerical value and it is there just as a way to fill a space. • Discuss whether this answer is reasonable by thinking about 4000×10.
6. Students misinterpret the regrouped number in a multiplication problem.	When students are given the problem: $\overset{3}{37}$ $\times \quad 5$ $\overline{305}$ The student uses the regrouped 3 above the tens column by adding it BEFORE they multiply. So instead of multiplying 5×7 and then 5×30, the student is multiplying 5×7, adding the 3 to the "3" in the tens column and then multiplying 5×60, for an answer of 305.	• Go back to the base-ten materials and use an area model to show what the partial products look like. Then consider using the open array model so the actual amounts the student should be multiplying are apparent. • Have the student move away from just using the algorithm until he or she can explain it.
7. Students misuse the distributive property in division.	Students solving $95 \div 16$ broke the problem into $95 \div 10 + 95 \div 6$. Students thought that when using the distributive property you can break apart the divisor, when instead you need to split the dividend into components.	• Go back to using smaller numbers and show either with paper plates to represent the groups—that the number of groups remains stable, it is the quantity of items that need to be "distributed equally" that can be broken up into different collections to reach the correct answer. • This is a rather persistent misconception, be ready for it by presenting the possible confusion early for class discussion. Don't wait for students to demonstrate this misunderstanding.
8. When dividing students ignore internal zeros.	When students given the problem: $8002 \div 2$ they will say the answer equals 41.	• Have students estimate the answer before starting—will the answer be in the tens? Hundreds? Thousands? • Start with a smaller number such as $202 \div 2$ and model the problem with base-ten materials and two paper plates. Then link the action to the algorithm.

12

Exploring Fraction Concepts

BIG IDEAS

1. Fractions are equal shares or parts of a whole or unit. The whole must be specified because it can be continuous (area or a measure) or discrete (collection of a set of objects). Examples of these are area (e.g., $\frac{1}{3}$ of a garden), measure (e.g., $\frac{3}{4}$ of an inch), and set (e.g., $\frac{1}{2}$ of the students in the class).

2. Fractions are numbers with special names that tell how many parts of that size are needed to make the whole, written in the form $\frac{a}{b}$ (when b is not zero). For example, *thirds* require 3 parts to make a whole. And one of those parts would be *one-third*. By partitioning (thirds) and iterating the unit fraction ($\frac{1}{3}$, $\frac{2}{3}$, $\frac{3}{3}$, etc.) students understand the meaning of fractions, especially the role of the numerator and denominator in the number.

3. When partitioning a whole into more equal shares the parts become smaller. For example, eighths are smaller than fifths.

4. Estimating with fractions is critical to understanding their magnitude or position on the number line.

5. Equivalent fractions are ways of describing the same amount by using different-sized fractional parts.

6. Fractions must be experienced using many interpretations, including part of a whole, ratios, and division.

One of the major changes in emphasis in the *Common Core State Standards for Mathematics* is in the increased prominence of fractions in grades 3 through 5. In third grade students develop the idea that a fraction is a number that includes representing its location on a number line, using fraction symbols, and comparing fractions—including finding those which are equivalent. In fourth grade they refine their ability to put fractions in order according to size and generate equivalent fractions. Then, as in fifth grade, fourth graders use this knowledge to support their understanding of fraction operations (CCSSO, 2010).

Fractions present a considerable challenge, and when they are not learned well that can result in shortcomings. This is noted in the IES practice guide *Developing Effective Fractions Instruction for Kindergarten through 8th Grade* (http://ies.ed.gov/ncee/wwc/practiceguide.aspx?sid=15), in which the authors state, "A high percentage of U.S. students lack conceptual understanding of fractions, even after studying fractions for several years; this, in turn, limits students' ability to solve problems" (Siegler et al., 2010, p. 6). This lack of understanding is then translated into difficulties with fraction computation, decimal and percent concepts, algebra and overall success in high school mathematics (Bailey, Hoard, Nugent, & Geary, 2012; National Mathematics Advisory Panel, 2008; Siegler et al., 2012). The topic of fractions is where students often stop trying to understand mathematics and instead resort to rules. Instead, fractions should be taught using multiple experiences with an emphasis on deep conceptual understanding as described in the next sections.

Meanings of Fractions

The first goal in the development of fractions should be to help students construct the idea of *fractional parts of the whole*—the parts which result when the whole or unit has been partitioned into equal-sized portions or equal shares. This, too, is the progression established in the *Common Core State Standards* (CCSSO, 2010) when first and second graders begin to partition circular and rectangular shapes into equal parts as they use the language of fractions, such as halves, fourths, and thirds to describe those subdivisions. Students eventually make connections between the idea of partitioning into fair shares and fractional parts.

Fraction Interpretations

"The concept of unit is fundamental to the interpretation of rational numbers" (Barnett-Clarke, Fisher, Marks, & Ross, 2010, p. 19). Sometimes the words *whole* and *unit* are used interchangeably in discussing fractions, but the unit must be thought about to interpret all the possible concepts that fractions can represent. These interpretations appear to be developmental in nature.

One of the basic interpretations people immediately visualize is the part–whole relationship, including mental examples of part of a whole as shaded. Although the part–whole model is the one most often used in textbooks, researchers suggest that students would understand fractions better with emphasis across the different interpretations of fractions (Clarke, Roche, & Mitchell, 2008; Lamon, 2012).

Stop and Reflect

Other than shading a region of a shape, what are other ways fractions are represented? Name three ideas.

Part–Whole

Using the part–whole interpretation is an effective starting point for building meaning of fractions (Cramer & Whitney, 2010). But remember that part–whole goes beyond shading a region. Part–whole can be part of a group of people ($\frac{3}{5}$ of the class went on the field trip), or part of a length (we walked $3\frac{3}{5}$ of a 5-mile hike). Cramer, Wyberg, and Leavitt (2008) note that the circle model is particularly effective in illustrating the part–whole relationship.

Measurement

Measurement involves identifying an amount of a continuous unit (length, area, volume, or time), and then comparing that amount to a whole unit that is equal to 1. For example, in the fraction $\frac{1}{2}$ of a mile, you can use the amount as the subdivision and compare it to 1 mile. This concept focuses on how much rather than how many parts, which is the case in part–whole situations (Behr, Lesh, Post, & Silver, 1983; Martinie, 2007). The number line models a length unit and is subdivided into equal amounts with the length between 0 and 1 as the unit.

Division

This interpretation links directly to equal shares. Consider the idea of sharing $10 with 4 people. This is not a part–whole scenario, but it still means that each person will receive one-fourth ($\frac{1}{4}$) of the money, or $\frac{10}{4}$ or $2\frac{1}{2}$ dollars. Division is often not connected to fractions, which is unfortunate. Students should understand and feel comfortable with the example written as $\frac{10}{4}$, $4)\overline{10}$, $10 \div 4$, $2\frac{2}{4}$, and $2\frac{1}{2}$ (Flores, Samson, & Yanik, 2006).

Operator

Fractions can be used to indicate an operation, as in $\frac{4}{5}$ of 20 square feet, or $\frac{2}{3}$ of the audience was holding banners. In these situations, the operator (fraction) changes the size or scale (e.g., shrinks, enlarges) through multiplication. This interpretation is not emphasized enough in school curricula (Usiskin, 2007). Just knowing how to represent fractions doesn't mean students will know how to operate with fractions, such as when working in other areas of the mathematics curriculum (Johanning, 2008).

Ratio

The concept of ratio is yet another interpretation that comes into play in grade 6 (CCSSO, 2010). A ratio "expresses a relationship between two (and sometimes more) quantities or parts of quantities and compares their relative measures or counts" (Barnett-Clarke et al., 2010, p. 25). Ratios can be part–part or part–whole. For example, the ratio $\frac{3}{4}$ could be the ratio of those wearing jackets (part) to those not wearing jackets (part), or it could be part–whole, meaning those wearing jackets (part) to all students in the class (whole). Ratios can also be written as a percent.

> **Teaching Tip**
>
> Avoid referring to the "top number" and the "bottom number" when speaking about fractions. This language reinforces the overgeneralization of whole-number thinking. Also, avoid the phrase "three *out* of four" (unless talking about ratios or probability) or "three *over* four" and instead say "three-fourths" (Siebert & Gaskin, 2006).

Were these among the ideas you listed in responding to the Stop and Reflect?

Why Fractions Are Difficult

Although we want students to build on prior knowledge of whole numbers, fractions become more challenging when students misapply whole-number thinking to solve fraction situations. You need to find ways to help students see how fractions are like and different from whole numbers. Table 12.1 shows some common errors and misapplications of whole-number knowledge to fractions that may assist you in heading off problems.

Until students understand fractions meaningfully, they will continue to make errors by over-applying whole-number concepts (Cramer & Whitney, 2010; Lamon, 2012; Siegler et al., 2010). The most effective way to help students reach higher levels of understanding is to use multiple representations, develop multiple approaches, and build in opportunities for them to explain and justify their thinking (Harvey, 2012; Pantziara & Philippou, 2012). This chapter is designed to support you in helping students acquire a deep understanding of fractions.

Table 12.1. Common fraction errors and misconceptions and how to help.

Common Error or Misconception	What It Looks Like	How to Help
1. Numerator and denominator are separate numbers	$\frac{3}{4}$ is seen as the number 3 over the number 4. Students have no concept of the relative size of the fraction.	• Find fraction values on a number line (e.g., an activity each day where students place values on a classroom number line). • Measure with inches to various levels of precision (e.g., to the nearest fourth, or eighth). • Avoid the phrase "three out of four" (unless you are talking about ratios or probability) or "three over four"; instead, say "three-fourths" (Siebert & Gaskin, 2006).
2. Fractional parts do not need to be equal-sized.	$\frac{3}{4}$ (three-fourths) of the figure below is green. 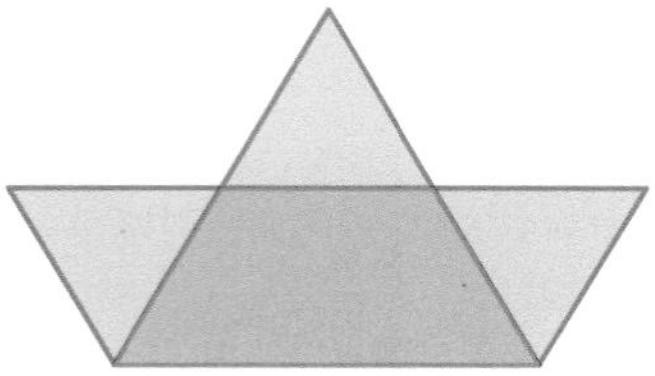	• Have students create their own representations of fractions across various types of models. • Provide problems like the one illustrated here, in which all the partitions are not already drawn and have students draw or show the equal-sized parts.
3. Fractional parts must be same shape.	This square is not showing fourths: 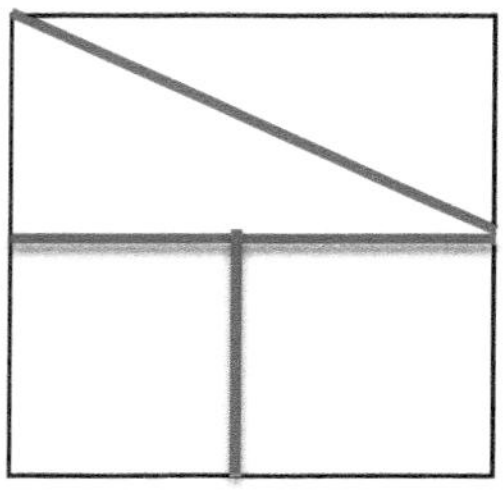	• Provide examples and non examples with partitioned shapes (see Activity 12.4 for example, with the Fourths or Not Fourths or the Sixths or Not Sixths Activity pages). • Ask students to generate as many ways as they can to show fourths (or eighths).
4. Fractions with larger denominators are bigger.	$\frac{1}{5}$ is smaller than $\frac{1}{10}$ because 5 is less than 10.	• Use contexts, for example, ask students whether they would rather go outside for $\frac{1}{2}$ of an hour, $\frac{1}{4}$ of an hour, or $\frac{1}{10}$ of an hour and to explain why. • Use visuals, such as paper strips, number lines, or circles to visualize the approximate size of each fraction. • Teach estimation and benchmark strategies for comparing fractions.
5. Fractions with larger denominators are smaller.	$\frac{1}{5}$ is more than $\frac{7}{10}$ because fifths are bigger than tenths.	
6. Fractions are subtraction.	When students say – If you have $\frac{2}{3}$ you took two pieces *out of* the whole.	• Avoid the use of the language "out of" which supports students' thinking of fractions as subtraction. • Show the connections between the area and length model to help students see the relationships between the parts and wholes.

Models for Fractions

Substantial evidence suggests that effectively using physical models in fraction tasks is important (Cramer & Henry, 2002; Empson & Levi, 2011; Siebert & Gaskin, 2006). Unfortunately, when used, the tendency is to use only area models (Hodges, Cady, & Collins, 2008). This means that students often do not explore fractions with a variety of models or do not have sufficient time to connect the models to the related concepts. In fact, what appears to be critical in learning is that the use of physical tools leads to the use of mental models, which builds students' understanding of fractions (Cramer & Whitney, 2010; Petit, Laird, & Marsden, 2010).

Properly used, tools can help students clarify ideas that are often confused in a purely symbolic form. Sometimes it is useful to do the same activity with two different representations and ask students to make the connections between them. Different representations offer different opportunities to learn. For example, an area model helps students visualize parts of the whole, and a length model shows that there is always another fraction to be found between any two numbers.

Including real-world contexts that are meaningful to students is important (Cramer & Whitney, 2010) because often one representation is more aligned with one context over another. For example, if students are being asked who walked the farthest, a length model is more likely to support their thinking than an area model. Let's look at three categories of models: area, length, and set (see Table 12.2).

Standards for Mathematical Practice

◄ **5** **Use appropriate tools strategically.**

Table 12.2. Models for fraction concepts and related visuals and contexts.

Model Type	Description	Sample Contexts	Sample Manipulatives and Visuals
Area	Fractions are determined based on how a part of a region or area relates to the whole area or region.	Quesadillas (circular food) Pan of Brownies Garden Plot or Playground	Fraction Circles/Rectangles Pattern Blocks Tangrams Geoboards Grid paper regions
Length	Fractions are represented as a subdivision of a length of a paper strip (representing a whole), or as a length/distance between 0 and a point on a number line, subdivided in relation to a given whole unit.	Walking/Distance traveled String lengths Music measures Measuring with inches, fractions of miles, etc.	Cuisenaire Rods Paper strips Number lines
Set	Fractions are determined based on how many discrete items are in the whole set, and how many items are in the part.	Students in the class, school, stadium Type of item in a bag of items	Objects (e.g., pencils, toys) Counters (e.g., two color counters, colored cubes, teddy bears, sea shells)

Area Models

Area is a good place to begin fraction explorations because it lends itself to equal sharing and partitioning. In the discussion of the equal shares, the situations involve something that could be cut into smaller parts. **Circular Fraction Pieces** are the most commonly used as they emphasize the part–whole concept of fractions and the meaning of the relative size of

Teaching Tip

a part to the whole (Cramer et al., 2008). The other models in Figure 12.1 demonstrate how different shapes can be the whole. Various sizes of grid paper (**2-centimeter grid paper**, **1-centimeter grid paper**, **0.5-centimeter grid paper**), or **dot paper** (1-centimeter square dot paper and **1-centimeter dot paper**) provide flexibility in selecting the size of the whole and the size of the parts. Many commercial versions of area manipulatives are available including circles, rectangles, pattern blocks, towers, geoboards and tangrams. Activity 12.1 (adapted from Roddick and Silvas-Centeno, 2007) uses pattern blocks to help students develop the concepts of partitioning and iterating. View this **video** (**https://www.youtube.com/watch?v=uMWFrEx5ZHA**) of a teacher using pattern blocks to explore multiple representations (geometric (pictorial), numeric and verbal).

Figure 12.1

Area or region models for fractions.

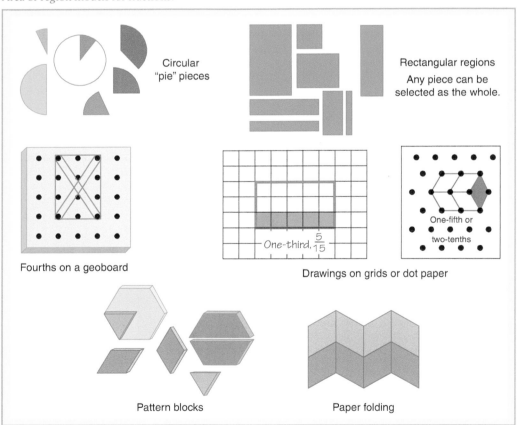

Circular "pie" pieces

Rectangular regions
Any piece can be selected as the whole.

Fourths on a geoboard

One-third, $\frac{5}{15}$

One-fifth or two-tenths

Drawings on grids or dot paper

Pattern blocks

Paper folding

Activity 12.1

CCSS-M: 2.G.A.3; 3.NF.A.2

Playground Fractions

Create this "playground" with your pattern blocks (see **Pattern Block Playground** Activity Page). This playground design represents the whole or unit. For each fraction below, find the pieces of the playground and draw it on your paper:

$\frac{1}{2}$ playground	$\frac{1}{3}$ playground
$1\frac{1}{2}$ playgrounds	$\frac{2}{3}$ playground
2 playgrounds	$\frac{4}{3}$ playgrounds

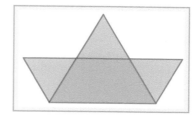

Source: Adapted from Roddick & Silvas-Centeno (2007). Developing understanding of fraction through pattern blocks and fair trade. *Teaching Children Mathematics, 14*(3), 140–141. Reprinted with permission. Copyright 2007, by the National Council Teachers of Mathematics. All rights reserved.

Length Models

With length models, lengths or measurements are compared instead of areas. Either physical materials are compared on the basis of length (i.e., Cuisenaire rods), lines are drawn on paper and subdivided (i.e., number lines), or a measuring tool with a scale is used (i.e., rulers, measuring cups, or thermometers) as shown in Figure 12.2. Length models are very important in developing student understanding of fractions, and need to be used more often in instruction. Siegler and his colleagues (2010) advise teachers to "use number lines as a central representational tool in teaching this and other fraction concepts from the early grades on" (p. 1).

To prepare students for the number line, one length model—Cuisenaire rods—has pieces that are 1 to 10 cm long. Each length is a different color (e.g., the 2 cm rod is red). For example, if you wanted students to work with $\frac{1}{4}$ s and $\frac{1}{8}$ s, you could select the brown Cuisenaire rod, which is 8 cm long. Therefore, the 4-cm rod (purple) becomes $\frac{1}{2}$, the 2-cm rod (red) becomes $\frac{1}{4}$, and the 1-cm rod (white) becomes $\frac{1}{8}$. For exploring twelfths, put the orange rod and red rod together to make a whole that is 12 units long. Virtual Cuisenaire rods can be found at the University of Cambridge's NRICH project and they, just like the physical versions, provide flexibility because any length can represent the whole.

Another linear model can be made from strips of paper or cash register tape which can be folded to produce student-made fraction strips. These paper strips also support the eventual use of the number line and bar diagrams to think about fractional problems.

The number line is a significantly more sophisticated length model and a powerful tool for thinking about fractions (Bright, Behr, Post, & Wachsmuth, 1988). Researchers suggest it is an essential model that should be heavily emphasized in the teaching of fractions (Clarke et al., 2008; Flores et al., 2006; Siegler et al., 2010; Usiskin, 2007). Furthermore, in the *Common Core State Standards* (CCSSO, 2010), third graders are expected to accurately place fractions on the number line. This is one of the few places in the document where a specific instructional model is stipulated. Using the number line helps

Figure 12.2

Length or measurement models for fractions.

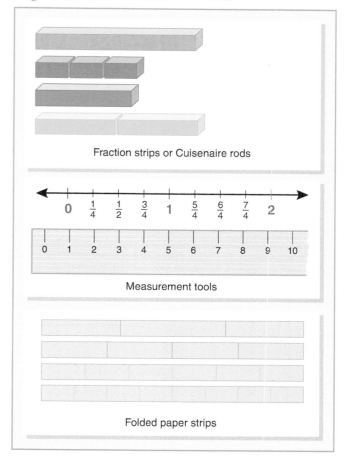

Teaching Tip

Students often have difficulty with positioning fractions on the number line. Make sure they recognize that each number on a line designates the distance of the identified point from zero, not the point itself.

Standards for
Mathematical Practice

▶ **6 Attend to precision.** ▶

students define the unit fraction—particularly the length of the unit (from 0 to the labeled point) on the number line. You will find this model also serves as a bridge that links fractions back to whole numbers while preparing students for integers and algebra.

Length models connect closely to real-world contexts in which fractions are commonly used—measuring. Dougherty, Flores, Louis, & Sophian (2010) emphasize the value of incorporating measurement situations as a way to support student progression from whole numbers to rational numbers.

The number line is used to compare a fraction's relative size to other numbers, which is not as clear when using area models. Importantly, the number line reinforces that there is always one more fraction to be found between two fractions. The following activity (adapted from Bay-Williams & Martinie, 2003) uses a real-world context to engage students in thinking about fractions through a length model.

▶ Activity 12.2　　　　　　CCSS-M: 3.NF.A.2a, b; 3.NF.A.3a, b, d

Who Is Winning?

Use the **Who Is Winning?** Activity Page and give students cash register tape or ask them to draw a number line. The friends below are playing "Red Light, Green Light" and the fractions next to their names represent how far they are from the start line. Who do you think is winning? Can you place these friends on a line to show where they are located between the start and finish?

Mary—$\frac{3}{4}$	Harry—$\frac{1}{2}$	Larry—$\frac{5}{6}$
Han—$\frac{5}{8}$	Miguel—$\frac{5}{9}$	Angela—$\frac{2}{3}$

This game can be differentiated by changing the values of the fractions or the numbers of friends (more fractions). The game "Red Light, Green Light" may not be familiar to ELLs. Modeling the game, with students in the class taking positions on a number line on the floor (clearly mark the starting point) and having the students talk about how they are estimating their location, are good ways to build background and support for students with disabilities.

Set Models

In set models, the whole is understood to be a set of individual (discrete) objects, and subsets of the whole make up fractional parts. For example, 3 objects are one-fourth of a set of 12 objects. The set of 12 objects in this case represents the unit, the whole or 1. The idea of referring to a collection of counters as a single unit makes set models difficult for some students. Putting a piece of yarn in a loop around the objects in the set helps students "see" the whole. Figure 12.3 illustrates several set models for fractions.

A common misconception with set models is to focus on the size of a subset rather than the number of equal sets in the whole. For example, if 12 counters make a whole, then a subset of 4 counters is one-third, not one-fourth, because 3 equal sets make the whole.

Two color counters are an effective manipulative for representing the set model. Counters can be flipped to change their color to model various fractional parts of a whole set. Any set of objects (or people) can be a set model but the whole must be clearly delineated. The following activity can be done as an energizer.

Figure 12.3

Set models for fractions.

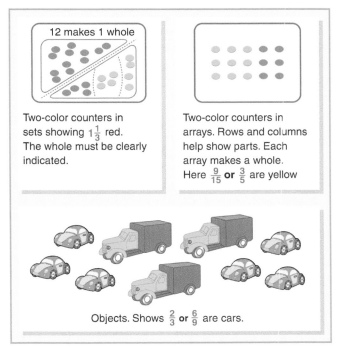

Two-color counters in sets showing $1\frac{1}{3}$ red. The whole must be clearly indicated.

Two-color counters in arrays. Rows and columns help show parts. Each array makes a whole. Here $\frac{9}{15}$ or $\frac{3}{5}$ are yellow

Objects. Shows $\frac{2}{3}$ or $\frac{6}{9}$ are cars.

Activity 12.3

CCSS-M:
3.NF.A.1;
3.NF.A.3b

Class Fractions

Use a group of students as the whole—for example, six students if you want to work on thirds, halves, and sixths. Invite them to the front of the room and ask, "What fraction of our group [are wearing tennis shoes, have brown hair, etc.]?" Have them record the fraction symbols. Over time, change the number of people who represent the whole. Also, consider discussing amounts that represent equivalent fractions such as helping them notice that $\frac{3}{6}$ is equal to $\frac{1}{2}$.

Virtual manipulatives are available for all three models. Virtual manipulatives have been found to positively affect student achievement, especially when they are paired with using the actual manipulatives (Moyer-Packenham, Ulmer, & Anderson, 2012). Recommended sites include:

- **Conceptua Fractions.** This is an excellent free source (although subscription based) that offers area, set, and length models (including the number line). Go to their website to download their free tools and review their other resources. Clicking here (https://www.youtube.com/watch?v=7OJTjYxWCIU) may give you some tips on teaching fractions.

- **Cyberchase (PBS).** Cyberchase is a popular television series. Their website offers videos that model fractions with real-world connections and activities such as "Thirteen Ways of Looking at a Half" (fractions of geometric shapes) and "Make a Match" (concept of equivalent fractions).

- **Illuminations (NCTM) Fractions Model.** Explore all three models of fractions, including fractions greater than one, mixed numbers, decimals, and percentages. Be sure to use NCTM in your search to locate this site and avoid imitators.

- **Math Playground Fraction Bars.** Use this title in a search engine to find fraction bars that allow you or your students to explore fractional parts, concepts of numerator and denominator, and equivalence.

- **National Library of Virtual Manipulatives.** This site offers numerous free models for exploring fractions, including fraction bars and fraction pieces. There is also an applet for comparing and visualizing fractions.

Formative Assessment Note

You will not know whether they really understand the meaning of a fraction unless you have evidence that a student can represent a particular fraction using area, length, and set models. A straightforward way to assess students' knowledge of a fractional amount is to give them a Fraction Assessment paper with *area*, *length*, and *set* written at the top of each section and observe as they draw a picture and write a sentence describing a context or example in all three ways for a selected fraction (e.g., $\frac{3}{4}$).

Fractional Parts of a Whole

The first goal in the development of fractions should be to help students construct the idea of *fractional parts of the whole*—the parts that result when the whole or unit has been partitioned into *equal-sized portions or fair shares*. Recall that Table 12.2 describes the meanings of parts and wholes across each type of model.

Students understand in first and second grade the idea of partitioning a quantity into two or more parts to be shared fairly among friends. Students in grade 3 then make connections between the idea of fair (equal) shares and fractional parts. The next three sections describe ideas foundational to finding equal shares.

Fraction Size Is Relative

A key idea about fractions is that a fraction does not say anything about the size of the whole or the size of the parts. A fraction tells us only about the *relationship between* the part and the whole. Consider the following situation:

Mark is offered the choice of a third of a pizza or a half of a pizza. Because he is hungry and likes pizza, he chooses the half. His friend Jane gets a third of a pizza but ends up with more than Mark. How can that be?

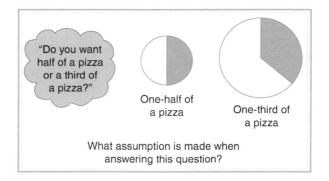

The visual illustrates how Mark was misdirected in his choice. The point of presenting this problem is that whenever two or more fractions are discussed in the same context, one cannot assume (as Mark did) that the fractions are all parts of the same size whole. You can help students understand fractional parts by regularly asking, "What is the whole? Or "What is the unit?"

Comparing two fractions with any representation can be made only if both fractions are parts of the same size whole. For example, if using Cuisenaire rods $\frac{2}{3}$ of a light green rod cannot be compared to $\frac{2}{5}$ of an orange rod.

Partitioning

Sectioning a whole into equal-sized pieces is called *partitioning*, a major part of developing fraction concepts. Again, as students partition a whole we must emphasize that the number of equal parts that make up a whole determines the name of the fractional parts or shares. The words for fractional parts (e.g., halves, thirds, fourths, and so on) are introduced before the symbols are introduced in grade 3 (but it is always good to write the symbols for students in the primary grades so they can begin to make connections). Figure 12.4 illustrates sixths across area, length and set models.

Figure 12.4

Which of these figures are correctly partitioned in sixths? Explain why or why not for each.

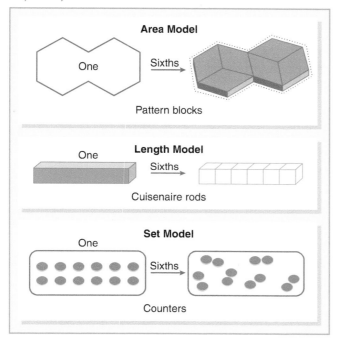

Partitioning with Area Models

When partitioning an area into fractional parts, students need to be aware that (1) the fractional parts must be the same size, though not necessarily the same shape, and (2) the number of equal-sized parts that can be partitioned within the unit determines the fractional amount (e.g., partitioning into 4 equal-sized parts means each part is $\frac{1}{4}$ of the unit). Too often, when students are asked what fraction is shaded, they are shown regions that are partitioned into pieces of the same size and shape. The result is that students think that equal shares need to be the same shape, which is not the case. On the other hand, sometimes visuals do not show all the partitions. For example, consider the following picture:

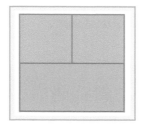

Referring back to the two criteria, a student might think, "If I partitioned the whole so that all pieces are the same size, then there will be four parts; therefore, the smaller partitioned region represents one-fourth" not one-third, as many students without a conceptual understanding might suggest. Activity 12.4 uses partitioned drawings to develop the idea of fractional parts.

Activity 12.4 — CCSS-M: 2.G.A.3; 3.NF.A.1

Fourths or Not Fourths?

Use the **Fourths or Not Fourths** Activity Page, which shows examples and nonexamples (which are very important to use with students with disabilities) of fourths (see Figure 12.5). Ask students to identify the wholes that are correctly partitioned into fourths and those that are not. For each response, have students explain their reasoning. Repeat with other fractional parts such as the **Sixths or Not Sixths** Activity Page.

Figure 12.5

Students should be able to tell (1) which of these figures are correctly partitioned in fourths and (2) why the other figures are not showing fourths.

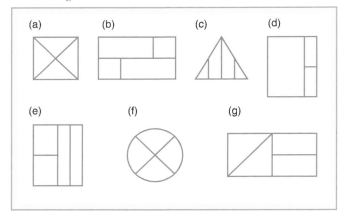

In Activity 12.4, the examples fall in each of the following categories:

1. same shape, same size (equivalent)—shapes a and f
2. different shape, same size (equivalent)—shapes e and g
3. different shape, different size (not equivalent)—shapes b and c
4. same shape, different size (not equivalent)—shape d

Partitioning with Length Models

The explanation of partitioning in the CCSS-M may be difficult to interpret. For example:

3.NF.A.2b: Represent a fraction $\frac{a}{b}$ on a number line diagram by marking off a lengths $\frac{1}{b}$ from 0. Recognize that the resulting interval has size $\frac{a}{b}$ and that its endpoint locates the number $\frac{a}{b}$ on the number line (CCSSO, 2010, p. 24).

Formative Assessment Note

Activity 12.4 is also a useful diagnostic interview to assess whether students understand that it is the *size* of the fraction that matters, not the shape. Have students explain why they do or do not think the shape is partitioned correctly with a focus on the non-examples. If students identify all the wholes that are correctly partitioned except (e) and (g), they hold the misconception that parts should be the same shape. Plan future tasks that focus on equivalence. For example, ask students to take a square on a geoboard or dot paper and partition it into halves, fourths, or other fractional parts.

Put more simply, students need to be able to partition a number line into fourths and realize that each section is one-fourth.

Number lines can be challenging. Students may ignore the size of the interval (the length of each part or unit) (McNamara & Shaughnessy, 2015; Petit, Laird, & Marsden, 2010). Students can develop these skills by folding their own paper strips, rope or a lineup of students (Zhang, Clements, & Ellerton, 2015). Provide examples where the shaded sections are in different positions and where partitioning *isn't* already shown to strengthen their understanding (Sarazen, 2012).

Activity 12.5 provides another option for students to explore number lines that are not fully partitioned.

Activity 12.5

CCSS-M: 3.NF.A.1; 3.NF.A.2a, b

How Far Did Nicole Go?

Give students a copy of **How Far?** or number lines partitioned such that only some of the partitions are showing. Use a context such as walking to school. For each number line, ask, "How far has Nicole gone? How do you know?"

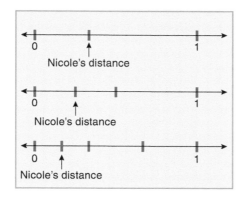

Students can justify their reasoning by measuring the length of each partition. Students with disabilities may need to work on this diagram in a larger scale, such as one made with tape or chalk on the classroom floor. Once the lines are marked and labeled, students can move to the various points to consider the length of the segments from zero.

Shaughnessy (2011) found four common errors students make in working with number lines: (1) use incorrect notation; (2) change the unit (whole); (3) count the tick marks rather than the space between the marks; and (4) count only tick marks that appear without noticing any missing ones. This is evidence that we must use number lines more extensively in exploring fractions (most real-life contexts for fractions are measurement related).

Partitioning with Set Models

Students can partition sets of objects such as coins, counters, or baseball cards. When partitioning sets, students may confuse the number of counters in a share with the name of the share. In the example in Figure 12.6, the 12 counters are partitioned into six sets, or *sixths*. Each share has two counters, but each section should not be mistaken as halves—it is the number of shares that makes the partition show *sixths*. As with the other models, when the equal parts are not already figured out, students may not see how to partition. Students seeing a picture of two cats and four dogs might think $\frac{2}{4}$ are cats (Bamberger, Oberdorf, & Schultz-Ferrell, 2010). Consider the following problem:

Figure 12.6

Given a whole, find fractional parts.

Eloise has 6 trading cards, Andre has 4 trading cards, and Lu has 2 trading cards. What fraction of the trading cards does Lu have?

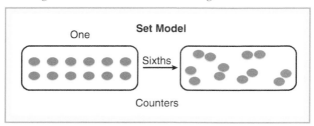

A student who answers "one-third" is not thinking about equal shares but about the number of people with trading cards.

Understanding that parts of a whole must be partitioned into equal-sized shares across different models is an important step in conceptualizing fractions and provides a foundation for exploring equivalence tasks, which are a prerequisite to performing fraction operations (Cramer & Whitney, 2010).

Considerable research has been done with students to determine how they go about the process of forming fair shares and how the tasks and questions posed to students influence their responses (e.g., Empson & Levi, 2011; Lewis, Gibbons, Kazemi, & Lind, 2015; Mack, 2004). To help students build on this research, Siegler and his colleagues state, "Build on students' informal understanding of sharing and proportionality to develop initial fraction concepts" (Siegler et al., 2010, p. 1).

Students in the primary grades partition by thinking about fair shares (division) using circles and rectangles. Sharing tasks are generally posed in the form of a simple story problem: "Four square brownies are being shared among three children so that each child gets the same amount. Show how much each child will get." See how Eduardo reasons about a sharing situation. Task difficulty changes with the numbers involved, the types of things to be shared (regions such as brownies, discrete objects such as pieces of chewing gum), and the presence or use of a physical model.

Students initially perform sharing tasks by distributing items one at a time. When this process leaves leftover pieces, students must figure out how to subdivide so that every group (or person) gets a fair share. Contexts that lend to subdivisions include sandwiches, pizzas, crackers, quesadillas, and even French fries (Tzur & Hunt, 2015). Consider using the book *The Doorbell Rang* (Hutchins, 1986) for a context for sharing activities.

Problem difficulty is determined by the relationship between the number of things to be shared and the number of sharers. Because students' strategies for sharing involve halving, a good place to begin is with two, four, and then eight sharers. For ten brownies and four sharers, many students will deal out two to each child and then halve each of the remaining brownies (see Figure 12.7).

Teaching Tip

Note that when you use the word *equal*, make sure that students realize that it means equal in amount, because the resulting equal shares may not be the same shape (area model).

Figure 12.7

Ten brownies shared with four students.

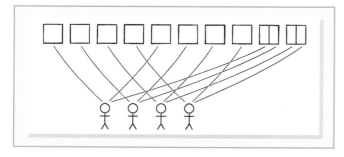

The problems and variations that follow are adapted from Empson (2002).

Consider these variations in numbers (see **Brownie Sharing Cards**):

- 5 brownies shared with 2 children
- 4 brownies shared with 8 children
- 2 brownies shared with 4 children
- 5 brownies shared with 4 children
- 3 brownies shared with 4 children

The last example is significantly more challenging because there are more sharers than items and it involves more than just finding halves. One strategy is to partition each brownie into four parts and give each child one-fourth from each brownie for a total of three-fourths. Students (even adults) are surprised at the relationship between the problem and the answer. **Felisha** explains the fractional amount each of 5 children get when sharing 2 cookies but loses track of what the whole is in determining each person's share.

When you think your students are ready, move them on the progression to three or six sharers. This will force students to confront their halving strategies as it requires an odd number of subdivisions. Several types of sharing solutions are shown in Figure 12.8. Note that some students may need to use paper pieces and physically partition and distribute them.

Because the level of difficulty of these sharing tasks varies, it is useful to create a lesson geared to three ability ranges where all students are challenged. Figure 12.9 shows how one teacher offers these three tiers (easy, middle, and advanced) for her lesson on sharing brownies (adapted from Williams, 2008).

Iterating

In whole-number learning, counting precedes and helps students compare the size of numbers and later to add and subtract. This is also true with fractions. Counting fractional parts, or *iterating*, helps students understand the relationship between the parts (the numerator) and the whole (the denominator). A *unit fraction* is a single fractional part. The fractions $\frac{1}{3}$ and $\frac{1}{8}$ are unit fractions. Students should come to think of counting fractional parts in much the same way as they might count apples or other objects when they first learned about whole numbers. If students know the kind of part they are counting, they can tell with the physical materials

> 🎵 **Teaching Tip**
>
> For all students, and particularly for ELLs, fraction parts often sound like whole numbers (e.g., fourths and fours). Be sure to emphasize the *th* on the end of the word and explicitly discuss the difference between four areas and a *fourth of* an area. Also, write and discuss the meaning of the words *whole* and *hole*.

Figure 12.8

Three different sharing processes.

(a) Four candy bars shared with six children:

Cut all the bars in half.
Cut the last two halves into three parts.
Each child gets a half and sixth.

(b) Four pizzas shared with three children:

Pass out whole pizzas.
Cut the last pizza in three parts.
Each child gets 1 whole and one-third.

(c) Five sandwiches shared with three children:

Cut each sandwich in three parts (thirds).
Each child gets five parts—five-thirds.

Figure 12.9

Examples of differentiating brownie sharing problems.

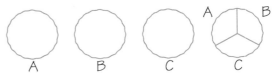

Easy Tasks	Intermediate Tasks	Advanced Tasks
How can 2 people share 3 brownies?	How can 4 people share 3 brownies?	How can 3 people share 2 brownies?
How can 2 people share 5 brownies?	How can 3 people share 5 brownies?	How can 3 people share 7 brownies?
How can 3 people share 4 brownies?	How can 6 people share 4 brownies?	How can 5 people share 4 brownies?

Source: Adapted from Williams, L. (2008). Tiering and Scaffolding: Two Strategies for Providing Access to Important Mathematics. *Teaching Children Mathematics, 14*(6), 324–330.

when they have one whole, two wholes, and so on. After experiences of simultaneously building fraction models and counting fractions aloud students should be able to answer, "How many fifths are in one whole?" just as readily as they know how many ones are in ten. However, in the 2008 National Assessment of Education Progress (NAEP) only 44 percent of fourth graders answered that question correctly (Rampey, Dion, & Donahue, 2009).

Like partitioning, iterating is an important part of being able to understand and use fractions. Understanding that $\frac{3}{4}$ can be thought of as a count of three parts called fourths is an important idea for students to develop (Post, Wachsmuth, Lesh, & Behr, 1985; Siebert & Gaskin, 2006; Tzur, 1999). The iterative concept is clear when focusing on these two ideas about fraction symbols:

- The numerator *counts.* It is the number of repetitions of the unit fraction.
- The denominator tells *what fractional part* is being counted. It is the number of repetitions needed to create the whole.

The fraction symbol is just shorthand for saying *how many* and *what.*

Iterating makes sense with length models because iteration is much like measuring. What if you have $2\frac{1}{2}$ feet of ribbon and are trying to figure out how many fourths of a foot you have? You can draw a strip and start iterating (counting) the fourths:

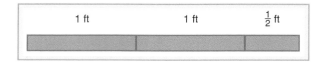

Using a ribbon that is $\frac{1}{4}$ of a foot long as a measuring tool, a student marks off ten fourths:

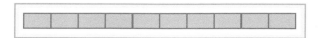

Students should engage in many tasks that involve iterating lengths, progressing in increasing difficulty. For example, give the students a strip of paper and tell them that it is $\frac{3}{4}$ of the whole. Then ask them to find $\frac{1}{2}$, $1\frac{1}{2}$, $2\frac{1}{4}$, and 3. To find these, students should partition the paper strip into three sections to first find $\frac{1}{4}$ and then iterate the $\frac{1}{4}$ to find the fractions listed. Use the **Whole or Part?** Activity Page to explore this in depth. Here is another activity that explores iterating lengths.

Activity 12.6

CCSS-M: 3.NF.A.1; 3.NF.A.2a, b

A Whole Lot of Fun

Use **A Whole Lot of Fun** Activity Page and the **Cutouts for Fraction Strips** Activity Page to give each student a strip of paper like the one here:

Tell students that this strip is three-fourths of one whole (unit). Ask students to sketch strips of the other lengths on their paper (e.g., $\frac{5}{2}$). You can repeat this activity by selecting other values for the starting amount and selecting different fractional values to sketch. A context, such as walking, is effective in helping students make sense of the situation. Be sure to use fractions less than and greater than **1** and mixed numbers.

As noted throughout this text, it is a good idea to create simple story problems or contexts that ask similar questions.

Mr. Samuels has finished $\frac{2}{5}$ of his patio. It looks like this:

Draw a picture like this one on your paper. Then draw another that might be the size of the finished patio.

Iterating can be done with area models. Display some **Circular Fractional Pieces** in groups, as shown in Figure 12.10. For each collection, tell students what type of piece is being shown and simply count them together, "*one*-fourth, *two*-fourths, *three*-fourths, *four*-fourths, *five*-fourths." Pause and ask, "If we have five-fourths, is that greater than one whole, less than one whole, or equal to one whole?" To reinforce the size of the piece you can alter your language to emphasize the unit fraction saying, "One one-fourth, two one-fourths, three one-fourths," and so on.

See Figure 12.10 for some great questions to ask as your students are counting each collection of parts. Also discuss the relationship to one whole. Make informal comparisons

Figure 12.10

Iterating fractional parts using an area model.

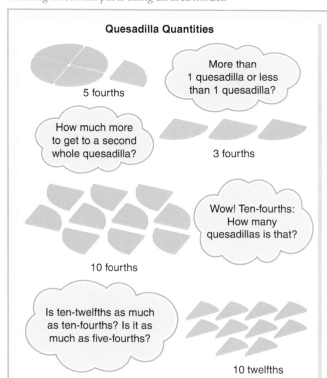

between different collections: "Why did we get more than two wholes with ten-fourths, and yet we don't even have one whole with ten-twelfths?"

Now is the time to lay verbal groundwork for mixed numbers. "What is another way that we could say ten-fourths?" (Two wholes and two more fourths or one whole and six fourths). With this background, students are ready for the following activity.

▶ Activity 12.7

CCSS-M: 3.NF.A.1; 3.NF.A.2a, b

More, Less, or Equal to One Whole

Give students **A Collection of Fractional Parts** Activity Page and a set of Cuisenaire rods. For example, the collection might have seven light green rods and that "each piece is $\frac{1}{8}$." The task is to decide if the collection is less than one whole, equal to one whole, or greater than one whole. Ask students to draw pictures or use symbols to explain their answer. Then try the activity with different fraction models and then with no model, using mental imagery only.

Iteration can also be done with set models. For example, show a collection of two-color counters and ask questions such as, "If 5 counters are one-fourth of the whole collection, how much is 15 counters?" These problems can be framed as engaging puzzles for students. For example: "Three counters represent $\frac{1}{8}$ of my set; how big is my set?" "Twenty counters represent $\frac{2}{3}$ of my set; how big is my set?" **Counting Counters: Find the Part** Activity Page and **Counting Counters: Find the Whole** Activity Page provide such problems for students to solve.

Stop and Reflect

Work through the exercises in Figure 12.11 and 12.12. If you do not have access to Cuisenaire rods or counters, just draw lines or circles. What can you learn about student understanding if they are able to solve problems in Figure 12.11 but not 12.12? If students are having difficulties, what contexts for each model can be used to support their thinking?

📋 Formative Assessment Note

The tasks in Figures 12.11 and 12.12 can be used as performance assessments. If students are able to solve these tasks, they can partition and iterate. That means that they are ready to do comparison and equivalence tasks. If they are not able to solve problems such as these, provide a range of similar tasks, using real-life contexts and involving area, length, and set models.

Figure 12.11

Given the whole, find the part.

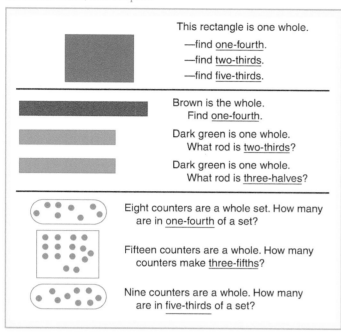

Figure 12.12

Given the part, find the whole.

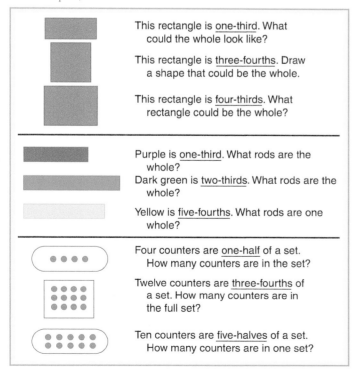

Fraction Notation

The way that we write fractions with a top component and a bottom component and a bar between is a *convention*—an agreement for how to represent fractions. In the CCSS-M, understanding the symbols for fractions is an emphasis in grade 3.

We just need to tell students about conventions. However, understanding of the convention can be clarified by giving explicit attention to the meaning of the numerator and the denominator as part of activities such as those discussed previously for iterating with the ribbon and with quesadillas (Figure 12.10). Always include sets that are more than one, but write them at first as fractions where the numerator is greater than the denominator and not as mixed numbers. After the class has counted and you have written the fraction for at least six sets of different fractional parts, pose the following questions:

- What does the denominator in a fraction tell us?
- What does the numerator in a fraction tell us?
- What might a fraction equal to 1 look like?

Here are some likely explanations from third graders:

- Numerator: This is the counting number. It tells how many shares or parts we have. It tells how many have been counted.
- Denominator: This tells what size piece is being counted. For example, if there are 4 parts in a whole we are counting fourths; if it is 6 parts, we are counting sixths.

This formulation of the meanings of the numerator and denominator may seem unusual to you. It is often said that the numerator tells "how many." (How many *what*?) The denominator is said to tell "how many equal parts it takes to make a whole." This is correct but can also be misleading. For example, a $\frac{1}{6}$ piece can be cut from a cake without making any slices in the remaining $\frac{5}{6}$. That the cake is only in two pieces does not change the fact that the piece taken is $\frac{1}{6}$. Or if a pizza is cut in 12 pieces, two pieces still make $\frac{1}{6}$ of the pizza. So in these two examples, the denominator does not tell how many pieces make the whole.

Smith (2002) points out a slightly more "mathematical" definition of the numerator and denominator. For Smith, it is important to see the denominator as the *divisor* and the numerator as the *multiplier*. That is, $\frac{3}{4}$ is three *times* what you get when you *divide* a whole into 4 parts. This multiplier and divisor idea is especially useful when students are asked later to think of fractions as division; that is, $\frac{3}{4}$ also means $3 \div 4$.

Throughout this chapter, we have included fractions less than one and greater than one. This was done intentionally and should similarly be carried out with students as they are learning fractions. The *Common Core State Standards* state that in third grade, students should be able to write whole numbers as fractions and identify fractions that are equivalent to whole numbers (CCSSO, 2010). Too often, students aren't exposed to fractions greater than one (e.g., $\frac{5}{2}$ or $4\frac{1}{4}$), so when they are, they find them confusing. Note that the term is *mixed number* when $\frac{5}{2}$ is in the form of $2\frac{1}{2}$.

Teaching Tip

Always write fractions with a horizontal bar, not a slanted one. This is a historical convention (an accepted practice that can just be told to students) and is used because the horizontal bar will be the format consistently used in formal algebra. Write $\frac{3}{4}$, not 3/4. Most word processing programs have an equation writing feature that will help you write them in this format.

Teaching Tip

The term *improper* can be a source of confusion because it implies that this representation is not acceptable, which is not the case at all. Instead, it is often the preferred representation in algebra. Avoid using this term and instead use "fraction" or "fraction greater than one." If you must use the term *improper* (due to local standards, for example), then share with students that it is really not improper at all. Note that the word *improper* is not used in the CCSS-M content standards!

Students must understand the many ways to represent fractions greater than one. In the fourth NAEP exam, about 80 percent of seventh graders could change a mixed number to a fraction greater than one fraction, but less than half knew that $5\frac{1}{4}$ was the same as $5 + \frac{1}{4}$ (Kouba et al., 1988). This indicates that many students use procedures without understanding them.

If you have consistently counted fractional parts beyond a whole, as discussed in the previous section, your students already know how to write $\frac{13}{6}$ or $\frac{13}{5}$. Ask students to use a model to illustrate these values and find equivalent representations using wholes and fractions (mixed numbers). Using connecting cubes is an effective way to help students see both forms for recording fractions greater than one (Neumer, 2007) (see Figure 12.13). Students identify one cube as the unit fraction ($\frac{1}{5}$) for the problem ($\frac{12}{5}$). They count out 12 fifths and build wholes. Conversely, they could start with the mixed number, build it, and find out how many total cubes (or fifths) were used. Repeated experiences in building and solving these tasks will lead students to see a pattern of multiplication and division that closely resembles the algorithm for moving between mixed numbers and fractions greater than one.

Context can help students understand the equivalence of these two ways to record fractions, which is the focus of Activity 12.8.

Figure 12.13

Connecting cubes are used to represent the equivalence of $\frac{12}{5}$ and $2\frac{2}{5}$.

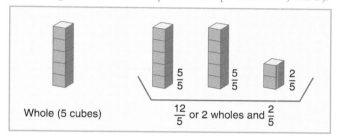

Whole (5 cubes) $\frac{12}{5}$ or 2 wholes and $\frac{2}{5}$

Activity 12.8

CCSS-M: 4.NF.A.3b; 4.NF.B.4a

Pitchers and Cups

Show students a pitcher that holds enough juice to fill six cups. You can even use an actual pitcher and actual cups for sharing with the class. Ask: "If I have $3\frac{1}{2}$ pitchers, how many cups will I be able to fill?" and "If we have 16 students in our class, how many pitchers will I need?" Alter the amount of cups the pitcher can hold to involve other fractions.

Help students move from models to mental images by reminding them of their experiences with iteration. Challenge students to figure out the two equivalent forms without using models. A good explanation for $3\frac{1}{4}$ might be that if there are 4 fourths in one whole, there are 8 fourths in two wholes and 12 fourths in three wholes. The extra fourth makes 13 fourths in all, or $\frac{13}{4}$. Delay presenting the standard algorithm (multiply the denominator by the whole number and add the numerator), because it can interfere with students making sense of the relationship themselves. Watch this **video of Rachel** to see how the procedures can get in the way of understanding.

Magnitude of Fractions

The focus on fractional parts is an important beginning, but number sense with fractions demands more—it requires that students have some intuitive feel of the size (or magnitude) of fractions. They should know "about" how big a particular fraction is and should be able to tell which of two fractions is larger. This requires that students see a fraction as a number, which helps them develop "fraction sense" (Fennell, Kobett, & Wray, 2014).

As with whole numbers, students are often less confident and less capable of estimating than they are at computing exact answers. Therefore, provide many opportunities for students to estimate. Ask questions like "About what fraction of your classmates are wearing sweaters?" Or after tallying survey data about favorite dinners, ask, "About what fraction of our class picked spaghetti?"

The number line is a powerful model for helping students develop a better understanding for the relative size of a fraction (Petit, Laird, & Marsden, 2010). Activity 12.9 offers some examples of visual estimating activities using a rope as a number line.

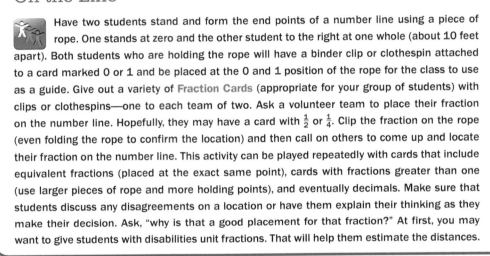

Activity 12.9

CCSS-M: 3.NF.A.2a; 3.NF.A.2b

On the Line

Have two students stand and form the end points of a number line using a piece of rope. One stands at zero and the other student to the right at one whole (about 10 feet apart). Both students who are holding the rope will have a binder clip or clothespin attached to a card marked 0 or 1 and be placed at the 0 and 1 position of the rope for the class to use as a guide. Give out a variety of Fraction Cards (appropriate for your group of students) with clips or clothespins—one to each team of two. Ask a volunteer team to place their fraction on the number line. Hopefully, they may have a card with $\frac{1}{2}$ or $\frac{1}{4}$. Clip the fraction on the rope (even folding the rope to confirm the location) and then call on others to come up and locate their fraction on the number line. This activity can be played repeatedly with cards that include equivalent fractions (placed at the exact same point), cards with fractions greater than one (use larger pieces of rope and more holding points), and eventually decimals. Make sure that students discuss any disagreements on a location or have them explain their thinking as they make their decision. Ask, "why is that a good placement for that fraction?" At first, you may want to give students with disabilities unit fractions. That will help them estimate the distances.

As suggested in Activity 12.9, important reference points or benchmarks for fractions are $0, \frac{1}{2},$ and 1. For fractions less than one, simply comparing them to these three numbers gives quite a lot of information. For example, $\frac{3}{20}$ is small, close to 0, whereas $\frac{3}{4}$ is between $\frac{1}{2}$ and 1. The fraction $\frac{9}{10}$ is quite close to 1. Because any fraction greater than one could be a whole number plus an amount less than one, the same reference points are helpful: $3\frac{3}{7}$ is almost $3\frac{1}{2}$.

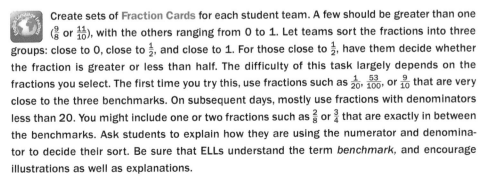

Activity 12.10

CCSS-M: 3.NF.A.3d; 4.NF.A.2

Zero, One-Half, or One

Create sets of Fraction Cards for each student team. A few should be greater than one ($\frac{9}{8}$ or $\frac{11}{10}$), with the others ranging from 0 to 1. Let teams sort the fractions into three groups: close to 0, close to $\frac{1}{2}$, and close to 1. For those close to $\frac{1}{2}$, have them decide whether the fraction is greater or less than half. The difficulty of this task largely depends on the fractions you select. The first time you try this, use fractions such as $\frac{1}{20}, \frac{53}{100},$ or $\frac{9}{10}$ that are very close to the three benchmarks. On subsequent days, mostly use fractions with denominators less than 20. You might include one or two fractions such as $\frac{2}{8}$ or $\frac{3}{4}$ that are exactly in between the benchmarks. Ask students to explain how they are using the numerator and denominator to decide their sort. Be sure that ELLs understand the term *benchmark,* and encourage illustrations as well as explanations.

The next activity is also aimed at developing the same three benchmarks. In "Close Fractions," however, the students must come up with the fractions rather than sort fractions already provided.

This following activity emphasizes the *density of fractions*—that is, there are an infinite number of fractions, so you can always find one in between. This "betweenness property" (Petit, Laird, & Marsden, 2010) links to measurement—there is always a more accurate measurement by using smaller fractional partitions.

▶ Activity 12.11
CCSS-M: 3.NF.A.3d; 4.NF.A.2

Close Fractions

Have students name a fraction that is close to 1 but not more than 1. Next, have them name another fraction that is even closer to 1 than the first. For the second response, they have to explain why they believe the fraction is closer to 1 than the previous fraction. Continue for several fractions in the same manner, each one being closer to 1 than the previous fraction. Similarly, try fractions close to 0 or close to $\frac{1}{2}$ (either under or over). The first several times you try this activity, let the students use models to help with their thinking. Later, have them fade the use of models to see how well their explanations work. Also, consider sharing this Fraction Find Activity Page as a challenge for students who are mathematically gifted or have a high interest in mathematics.

Equivalent Fractions

Equivalent fractions are two different names for the same point on a number line and the same-sized number. Every fraction is equal to an infinite number of other fractions. Students' understanding of equivalent fractions supports their fraction sense because it helps them grasp fraction size (magnitude), relationships (comparing and ordering), and eventually computation (Johanning, 2011).

Conceptual Focus on Equivalence

Stop and Reflect

How do you know that $\frac{4}{6} = \frac{2}{3}$? Before reading further, think of at least two different explanations.

Compare these answers to your answers:

1. They are the same because you can simplify $\frac{4}{6}$ and get $\frac{2}{3}$.

2. If you have a set of 6 items and you take 4 of them, that would be $\frac{4}{6}$. But you can put the 6 items into 3 groups, and the 4 items would then be 2 groups of the 3 groups. That means it's also $\frac{2}{3}$.

3. If you start with $\frac{2}{3}$, you can multiply the numerator and the denominator by 2, and that will give you $\frac{4}{6}$, so they are equal.

4. If you had a square cut into 3 parts and you shaded 2, that's $\frac{2}{3}$ shaded. If you cut all 3 of these parts in half, that would be 6 parts with 4 parts shaded, or $\frac{4}{6}$.

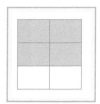

All of these answers are correct, but they reflect different thinking. Responses 2 and 4 are conceptual, although not as efficient. The procedural responses (1 and 3) are efficient, but do not indicate conceptual understanding. Students need a balance with a clear understanding of both the meaning of the concepts and the procedures. Consider how different the concept and the procedure appear to be:

Concept: Two fractions are equivalent if they are representations for the same amount or quantity—if they are the same number.

Procedure: To get an equivalent fraction, multiply (or divide) the numerator and denominator by the same nonzero number.

In a problem-based classroom, students can develop an understanding of equivalent fractions and also develop from that understanding a conceptually based algorithm. As with most algorithms, delay sharing "a rule." Be patient!

Equivalent-Fraction Models

Starting with a context and physical models is a perfect starting point for helping students create an understanding of equivalent fractions. Consider that this is the first time in their mathematics experience that a fixed quantity can have multiple names (actually an infinite number of names). Let's start with area models.

▶ Activity 12.12

CCSS-M: 3.NF.A.3a; 3.NF.A.3b

Different Fillers

Distribute the **Different Fillers** Activity Page or prepare a worksheet with two or three outlines of different fractions, as in Figure 12.14. For example, if the model is circular fraction pieces, start with an outline for $\frac{2}{3}$, $\frac{1}{2}$, and $\frac{3}{4}$. Students use fraction pieces to find as many equivalent fractions for the area as possible (using other pieces of the same size or color). Have students record their findings. After completing the three examples, have students write about patterns they noticed about the fractions that are equivalent to the original outlines.

In the class discussion following the "Different Fillers" activity, ask students, "What equivalent fractions could you find if we had sixteenths in our fraction kit? What other fractions could you find if you could have pieces of any size?"

Figure 12.14

Area models for equivalent fractions.

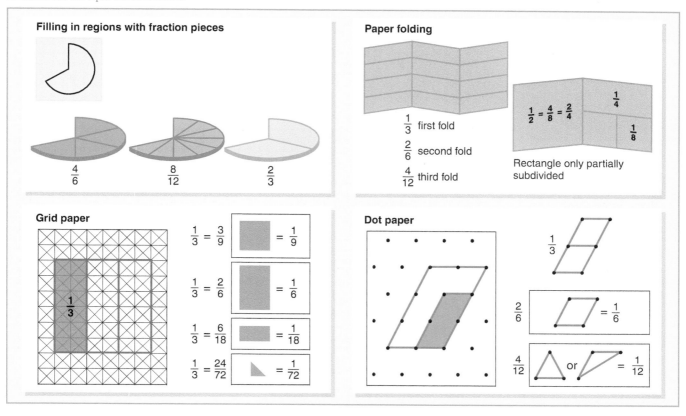

The following activity is a variation using dot paper.

Activity 12.13

CCSS-M: 3.NF.A.1; 3.NF.A.3a, b, c

Dot-Paper Equivalences

Use the **Fraction Names** Activity Page, which includes three different grids with a fraction shaded (each enclosed area represents one whole). Ask students to find fraction names that represent the first shaded region. Then ask them to see how many names they can find (working alone or with a partner). Invite students to share and explain the fraction names they found for problem 1 before moving to the next two problems. Alternatively, cut this page into three task cards, laminate the cards, and place each at a station along with an overhead pen. Have students rotate in partners to a station and see how many fraction names they can find for that shape (using the pen as needed to show their ways). Rotate to the next station. You may also want to refer to the **Dot Paper Equivalences Expanded Lesson**.

To make additional pictures, create your own using grid paper (**2-centimeter grid paper, 1-centimeter grid paper, 0.5 centimeter grid paper, 2-centimeter isometric grid paper,** and **1-centimeter isometric grid paper**) or **1-centimeter square dot paper** and **1-centimeter isometric dot paper**). (See the bottom right side of Figure **12.14**, which is an example drawn on an isometric grid.) The larger the size of the whole, the more names the activity will generate.

Activity 12.13 focuses on what Lamon (2012) calls *unitizing*—that is, given a quantity, finding different ways to chunk the quantity into parts in order to name it. She points out that unitizing requires students to mentally organize the number of pieces and the size of the pieces, which are important components in understanding equivalent fractions or proportional reasoning.

Figure 12.15

Length models for equivalent fractions.

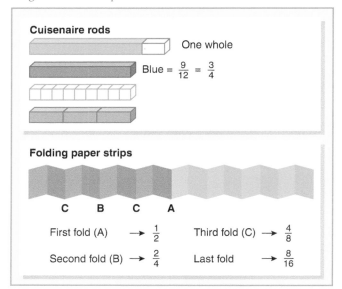

Length models should be used in activities similar to the "On the Line" task. Asking students to locate $\frac{2}{5}$ and $\frac{4}{10}$ on the number line, for example, can help them see that the two fractions are located in the same position and therefore are equivalent (Siegler et al., 2010). Cuisenaire rods or paper strips can be used to designate both a whole and a part, as illustrated in Figure 12.15. Students use smaller rods (or strips) to find fraction names for the given part. To have larger wholes and, thus, more possible parts, use a train of two or three rods for the whole. Folding paper strips is another method of creating equivalent fraction names. In the example shown in Figure 12.15, one-half is subdivided by successive folding in half. If students do not try to fold the strip in an odd number of parts, you should suggest it because these possibilities should be discussed.

Set models can also be used to develop the concept of equivalence. Watch this **video** of John Van de Walle as he discusses fraction equivalencies with two color counters. The following activity highlights unitizing, in which students look for different units or chunks of the whole in order to name a part of the whole in different ways.

Activity 12.14

CCSS-M: 3.NF.A.1; 3.NF.A.3a, b, c

Apples and Bananas

Use the **Apples and Bananas** Activity Page or have students set out a specific number of two-color counters—for example, 24 counters, with 16 of them red (apples) and 8 of them yellow (bananas). The 24 counters make up the whole. The task is to group the counters into different fractional parts of the whole and use the parts to create fraction names for the part of the whole that is apples and the part that is bananas. Ask questions such as, "If we make groups of four, what part of the set is red?" to encourage students to think of different ways to form equal-sized groups. Use Figure 12.16 as a model for how to group the counters in different ways. Students with disabilities might need to start with arrays that can be organized in ways that emphasize the equivalences. ELLs may not know what is meant by the term *group* because, when used in classrooms, the word usually refers to arranging students. Spend time before the activity modeling what it means to group objects.

The following activity moves a step closer to an algorithm for finding equivalent fractions.

Activity 12.15

CCSS-M: 3.NF.A.3a, b, c; 4.NF.A.1

Missing-Number Equivalencies

Use the **Missing-Number Equivalencies** Activity Page or give students an equation expressing an equivalence between two fractions, but with one of the numbers missing. Ask them to draw a picture to solve the equation. Here are four different examples:

$$\frac{5}{3} = \frac{\Box}{6} \qquad \frac{2}{3} = \frac{6}{\Box} \qquad \frac{8}{12} = \frac{\Box}{3} \qquad \frac{9}{12} = \frac{3}{\Box}$$

The missing number can be either a numerator or a denominator or the missing number can either be larger or smaller than the corresponding part of the equivalent fraction. (All four of these possibilities are represented in the examples.) Figure 12.17 illustrates how Zachary represented the equivalences with equations and partitioned rectangles. The examples shown involve simple whole-number multiples between equivalent fractions. Next, consider pairs such as $\frac{6}{8} = \frac{\square}{12}$. In these equivalences, one denominator or numerator is not a whole-number multiple of the other.

When doing "Missing-Number Equivalences" you may want to specify a particular model, such as sets or area. Students with disabilities and other students who struggle may benefit from using clocks to think about equivalence (Chick, Tierney, & Storeygard, 2007). Students were able to use the clocks to find equivalent fractions for $\frac{10}{12}$, $\frac{3}{4}$, $\frac{4}{6}$, and so on.

Figure 12.16

Set models for illustrating equivalent fractions.

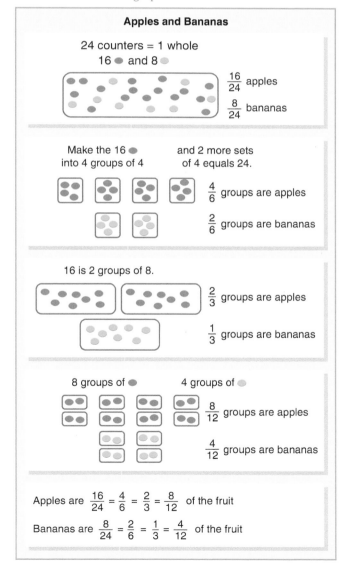

Figure 12.17

A student illustrates equivalent fractions by partitioning rectangles.

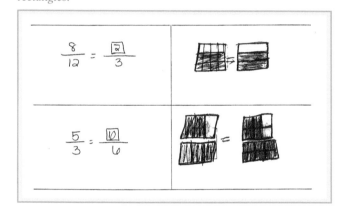

NCTM's Illuminations website offers an excellent set of lessons in units called "Fun with Fra-ctions." Each unit uses one of the model types (area, length, or set) and focuses on comparing and ordering fractions and equivalences using a range of manipulatives and engaging activities to support student learning.

 Formative Assessment Note

Consider using a diagnostic interview to see whether your students are making the connection between equivalence and a variety of models. For example, use Figure 12.18 to see examples of area and set models you might use. Ask, "Which of these fractions are equivalent to $\frac{2}{3}$?" Ask students what they know about the fraction they selected. Students should be able to explain that they are equivalent fractions and that they are fractions that represent the same quantity.

Figure 12.18

Possible figures for diagnostic interviews.

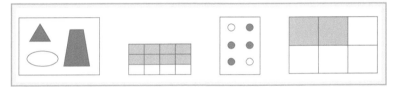

Developing an Equivalent-Fraction Algorithm

When students understand that fractions can have different (but equivalent) names, they are ready to develop a method for finding equivalent names for a particular value. An area model is a helpful visual for connecting the concept of equivalence to the standard algorithm for finding equivalent fractions (multiply both the numerator and the denominator by the same number to get an equivalent fraction). The approach suggested here is to look for a pattern in the way that the fractional parts in both the part and the whole are counted.

▶ Activity 12.16

CCSS-M: 3.NF.A.3b; 4.NF.A.1

Garden Plots

 Give students the **Garden Plots** Activity Page to draw on or have students cut out the squares to fold them. Begin by explaining that the garden is divided into rows of different vegetables. In the first example, you might illustrate four vertical partitions (fourths) and designate $\frac{3}{4}$ as corn. Ask students to partition their square into four rows and shade three-fourths as shown in Jack's work in Figure 12.19. Then explain that the garden will be shared with family and friends in a way that each person's share of the harvest is three-fourths corn. Show how the garden can now be partitioned horizontally to represent two people sharing the corn (i.e., $\frac{6}{8}$). Ask what fraction of the newly partitioned garden is corn. Next, tell students to come up with other ways that other numbers of friends can share the garden (they can choose how many friends, or you can). For each newly partitioned garden, ask students to record an equation showing the equivalent fractions. For students with disabilities, initially prepartition the squares so their efforts focus on shading and the idea of equivalence rather than on partitioning the square accurately.

After students have prepared their own examples, provide time for them to look at their fractions and gardens and notice patterns about the fractions and the diagrams. Once they have time to do this individually, ask students to share. Figure 12.20 provides student explanations that illustrate the range of "noticing."

Figure 12.20

Students explain what they notice about fraction equivalencies based on partitioning gardens in different ways.

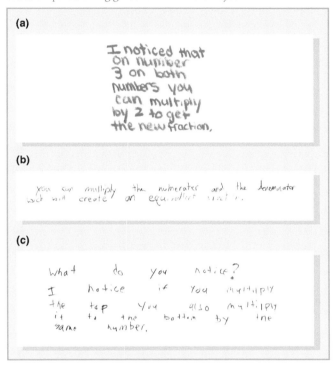

(a)

I noticed that on number 3 on both numbers you can multiply by 2 to get the new fraction.

(b)

you can multiply the numerater and the denominator which will create an equivellent ratio.

(c)

What do you notice?
I notice if you multiply the top you also multiply it to the bottom by the same number.

Figure 12.19

Jack partitions a garden to model equivalent fractions.

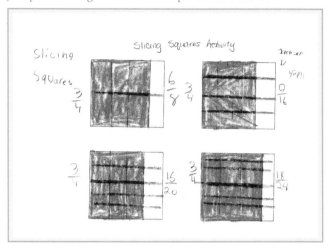

♪ Teaching Tip

Use the language "simplify" or put into "lowest terms." Avoid using the language "reducing fractions" as the fraction is not getting smaller or going on a "diet" as some students will mistakenly explain.

As you can see, for some students more experiences are needed. You can assist in helping students make the connection from the partitioned square to the procedure by displaying a square, for example, partitioned to show $\frac{4}{5}$ (see Figure 12.21). Have another version of the same square with $\frac{4}{5}$ shaded, but adding six equal partitions horizontally. Cover most of the square as shown in the figure. Ask, "What is the new name for my $\frac{4}{5}$?"

The reason for this exercise is that it helps students move away from simply counting the small regions to thinking of the multiplicative relationship. This also helps students develop mental images of models that are critical to understanding equivalence. With the partially covered square, students can see that there are four columns and six rows to the shaded part, so there must be 4×6 parts shaded. Similarly, there must be 5×6 parts in the whole. Therefore, the new name for $\frac{4}{5}$ is $\frac{4 \times 6}{5 \times 6}$, or $\frac{24}{30}$. This thinking lays the groundwork for multiplication of fractions.

Examine examples of equivalent fractions that have been generated with other models, and see if the rule of multiplying the numerator and denominator by the same number holds. If the rule is correct, how can $\frac{6}{8}$ and $\frac{9}{12}$ be equivalent?

Figure 12.21

How can you count the fractional parts if you cannot see them all?

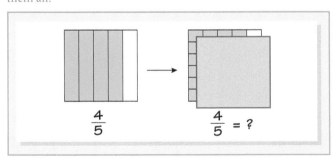

$\frac{4}{5}$ $\frac{4}{5} = ?$

Teaching Tip

Avoid telling students that fraction answers are incorrect if not in simplest or lowest terms. When students add $\frac{1}{6} + \frac{1}{2}$ both $\frac{2}{3}$ and $\frac{4}{6}$ are correct and equivalent answers. Sometimes students will be asked on a test to write their answer in lowest terms, so do share that as a task so they know how to respond.

Figure 12.22

Using the equivalent-fraction algorithm to write fractions in simplest terms.

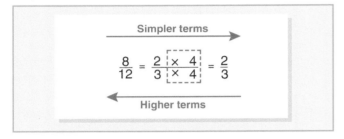

Writing Fractions in Simplest Terms

The multiplication scheme for equivalent fractions produces fractions with larger denominators. To write a fraction in *simplest terms* (or *lowest terms*) means to write it so that numerator and denominator have no common whole-number factors. One meaningful approach to this task of finding simplest terms is to reverse the earlier process, as illustrated in Figure 12.22. The search for a common factor or a simplified fraction should be connected to grouping.

Multiplying by One

Mathematics equivalence is based on the multiplicative identity property of 1 that any number multiplied by 1 remains unchanged. Any fraction of the form $\frac{n}{n}$ can be used as the identity element. Therefore, $\frac{3}{4} = \frac{3}{4} \times 1 = \frac{3}{4} \times \frac{2}{2} = \frac{6}{8}$ Furthermore, the numerator and denominator of the identity element can also be fractions. In this way, $\frac{6}{12} = \frac{6}{12}\left(\dfrac{\frac{1}{6}}{\frac{1}{6}}\right) = \frac{1}{2}$.

Understanding this idea is an expectation of fourth graders (CCSSO, 2010).

Standards for Mathematical Practice

2 Reason abstractly and quantitatively.

Developing the concept of equivalence can be supported with the use of technology. In the NCTM e-Examples, there is a fraction game (Fraction Track Applet 5.1) for two players. The game uses a number line, and knowledge of equivalent fractions plays a significant role. The Equivalent Fractions tool at NCTM's Illuminations website is designed to help students create equivalent fractions by partitioning and shading square or circular areas and then matching each fraction to its location on a number line. Students can use the computer-generated fraction or build their own. Once the rectangular or circular shape is partitioned, the student fills in the parts or fractional region and then builds two models equivalent to the original fraction. The three equivalent fractions are displayed in a table and in the same location on a number line.

Comparing Fractions

When students are examining whether two fractions are equivalent, they are comparing them. If they are not equivalent but are parts of the same whole or unit, there are several ways to find which is greater or smaller. As illustrated in **Ally's Interview** about comparing fractions, students often have misconceptions about fractions and therefore are not able to accurately compare–for example, thinking that larger numbers in the denominator mean the fraction is larger. The ideas described previously for equivalence across area, length, and set models are therefore also appropriate for comparing fractions.

The use of contexts, models, and mental imagery can help students build a strong under-standing of the relative size of fractions (Bray & Abreu-Sanchez, 2010; Petit, Laird, & Marsen, 2010). The next section offers ways to support students' understanding of the relative size of fractions.

Using Number Sense

In the NAEP test, only 21 percent of fourth-grade students could explain why one unit fraction was larger or smaller than another—for example, $\frac{1}{5}$ and $\frac{1}{4}$ (Kloosterman et al., 2004). For eighth graders, only 41 percent were able to correctly put in order three frac-tions given in simplified form (Sowder, Wearne, Martin, & Strutchens, 2004). As these researchers note, "How students can work meaningfully with fractions if they do not have a sense of the relative size of the fractions is difficult to imagine" (p. 116).

Comparing Unit Fractions

As noted earlier, whole-number knowledge can interfere with comparing fractions. Students think, "Twelve is more than three, so twelfths are more than thirds." The inverse relationship between the number of parts and the size of parts cannot be "told" but must be developed in each student through many experiences.

Activity 12.17

CCSS-M: 3.NF.A.3d; 4.NF.A.2

Ordering Unit Fractions

 Use the Fraction Cards and select a set of unit fractions such as $\frac{1}{3}$, $\frac{1}{8}$, $\frac{1}{5}$, and $\frac{1}{10}$. Ask students to use reasoning to put the fraction cards in order from least to greatest. Challenge students to explain their reasoning with an area model (e.g., circles) *and* on a number line. Ask students to connect the two representations with questions such as "What do you notice about $\frac{1}{3}$ of the circle and $\frac{1}{3}$ on the number line?" Students with disabilities may need to place the cards on the number line first. Repeat with fraction cards that have different numerators and different denominators. You can always vary the fractions that are being compared to differentiate the task.

Students may notice that given the same whole, larger denominators mean smaller fractions, but it only holds true when the numerators are the same. But this is not a rule to be memorized. Revisit this basic idea periodically to assess whether students are mistakenly returning to whole-number thinking.

Comparing Any Fractions

You have probably learned rules or algorithms for comparing two fractions. The usual approaches are finding common denominators and using cross-multiplication. These rules can be effective in getting correct answers but require no thought about the size of the fractions. If students are taught these rules before they have had the opportunity to think about the relative sizes of various fractions, they are less likely to develop "fraction sense." The goal is for students to select efficient strategies for determining the larger fraction, not memorizing an algorithmic method of choosing the correct answer.

Assume for a moment that you do not know the common denominator or cross-multiplication techniques. Now examine the pairs of fractions in Figure 12.23 and select the larger of each pair using a reasoning approach that a fourth grader might use.

Figure 12.23

Comparing fractions using concepts.

Which fraction in each pair is greater? Give one or more reasons. Try not to use drawings or models. <u>Do</u> <u>not</u> <u>use</u> common denominators or cross-multiplication. Rely on concepts.

A. $\frac{4}{5}$ or $\frac{4}{9}$ G. $\frac{7}{12}$ or $\frac{5}{12}$

B. $\frac{4}{7}$ or $\frac{5}{7}$ H. $\frac{3}{5}$ or $\frac{3}{7}$

C. $\frac{3}{8}$ or $\frac{4}{10}$ I. $\frac{5}{8}$ or $\frac{6}{10}$

D. $\frac{5}{3}$ or $\frac{5}{8}$ J. $\frac{9}{8}$ or $\frac{4}{3}$

E. $\frac{3}{4}$ or $\frac{9}{10}$ K. $\frac{4}{6}$ or $\frac{7}{12}$

F. $\frac{3}{8}$ or $\frac{4}{7}$ L. $\frac{8}{9}$ or $\frac{7}{8}$

Standards for Mathematical Practice

▶ **7** **Look for and make use of structure.**

The **Which Is Greater?** Activity Page can be used to carry out this activity with students.

The following list summarizes ways that the fractions in Figure 12.23 might be compared.

1. *More of the same sized parts (same denominators).* To compare $\frac{3}{8}$ and $\frac{5}{8}$, think about having 3 parts of something and also 5 parts of the same thing. (This method can be used with problems B and G.)

2. *Same number of parts (same numerators) but parts of different sizes.* Consider the case of $\frac{3}{4}$ and $\frac{3}{7}$. If a whole is partitioned into 7 parts, the parts will certainly be smaller than if partitioned into only 4 parts. (This strategy can be used with problems A, D, and H.)

3. *More than/less than one-half or one whole.* The fraction pairs $\frac{3}{7}$ compared to $\frac{5}{8}$ and $\frac{5}{4}$ compared to $\frac{7}{8}$ do not lend themselves to either of the previous thought processes. In the first pair, $\frac{3}{7}$ is less than one half of the number of sevenths needed to make a whole, and so $\frac{3}{7}$ is less than one half. Similarly, $\frac{5}{8}$ is more than one half. Therefore, $\frac{5}{8}$ is the larger fraction. The second pair is determined by noting that one fraction is greater than one and the other is less than one. (This method could be used with problems A, D, F, G, and H.)

4. *Closeness to one-half or one whole.* Why is $\frac{9}{10}$ greater than $\frac{3}{4}$? Each is one fractional part away from one whole, and tenths are smaller than fourths. Similarly, notice that $\frac{5}{8}$ is smaller than $\frac{4}{6}$ because it is only one-eighth more than one half, while $\frac{4}{6}$ is a sixth more than one half. Can you use this basic idea to compare $\frac{3}{5}$ and $\frac{5}{9}$? (*Hint:* Each is half of a fractional part more than $\frac{1}{2}$.) Also try $\frac{5}{7}$ and $\frac{7}{9}$. (This is a good strategy for problems C, E, I, J, K, and L.)

Did your reasons for choosing fractions in Figure 12.23 match these ideas? It is important that you are comfortable with these comparison strategies as a major component of your own fraction sense, as well as for helping students develop theirs. Notice that some of the comparisons, such as problems D and H, could have been solved using more than one strategy.

Tasks you design for your students should assist them in developing these and possibly other methods of comparing two fractions. The ideas should come from your students' reasoning. To teach "the four ways to compare fractions" merely adds four more mysterious rules and defeats the purpose of encouraging students to apply their own number sense. Instead, select pairs of fractions that will likely elicit the desired comparison strategies.

For students who struggle, you may need to use an area or number-line model so a direct comparison can be made. Place greater emphasis on students' reasoning and connect it to the visual models.

Using Equivalent Fractions

Equivalent-fraction concepts can be used in making comparisons. Ask, "Which of these fractions is greater or are the fractions equal? Smith (2002) points out that this question leaves open the possibility that two fractions that may appear different can, in fact, be equal. In addition to this point, with equivalent-fraction concepts, students can adjust how a fraction looks so that they can use ideas that make sense to them. Burns (1999) describes how fifth graders compared $\frac{6}{8}$ to $\frac{4}{5}$. (You might want to stop for a moment and think how you would compare these fractions.) One student changed the $\frac{4}{5}$ to $\frac{8}{10}$ so that both fractions would be two parts away from the whole and he reasoned from there. Another changed both fractions to a common numerator of 12. Revisit the comparison activities and include pairs such as $\frac{8}{12}$ and $\frac{2}{3}$ in which the fractions are equal but do not appear to be.

Teaching Considerations for Fraction Concepts

Because the teaching of fractions is so important, and because fractions are often not well understood even by adults, a recap of the big ideas is needed. Hopefully you now recognize that one reason fractions are not well understood is that there is a lot to know about them. Another reason is that many people were taught procedures with fractions that are not based on number sense. Clarke and colleagues (2008) and Cramer and Whitney (2010), researchers of fraction teaching and learning, offer several research-based recommendations that provide an effective summary of this chapter and direction for your instruction:

1. Give a greater emphasis to number sense and the meaning of fractions, rather than rote procedures for manipulating them.

2. Provide a variety of physical models and contexts to represent fractions.

3. Emphasize that fractions are numbers, making extensive use of number lines in representing fractions.

4. Spend whatever time is needed for students to understand equivalences (concretely and symbolically), including flexible naming of fractions.

5. Link fractions to key benchmarks and encourage estimation.

13

Building Strategies for Fraction Computation

BIG IDEAS

1   The meanings of the operations on fractions are the same as the meanings for the operations on whole numbers. Operations with fractions should begin by applying these same meanings to fractional parts.

2   For addition and subtraction, an essential understanding is that the numerator counts the number of parts and the denominator the type of part (what unit is being counted). When denominators are different, an equivalent problem can be written.

3   For multiplication by a fraction, an essential understanding is that the denominator is a divisor. This idea allows us to find parts of the other factor.

4   For division by a fraction, there are two ways of thinking about the operation—partition and measurement.

5   Estimation should be an integral part of developing fraction computation to focus students' attention on the meanings of the operations and the expected size of the results.

Understanding Fraction Operations

Success with fractions, in particular computation, is closely related to success in Algebra I. If students enter formal algebra with a weak understanding of fraction computation (in other words, they have only memorized the four procedures but do not understand them), they are at risk of struggling in algebra which in turn can limit college majors and career opportunities (National Mathematics Advisory Panel, 2008).

Building such understanding takes time! The *Common Core State Standards* (CCSSO, 2010) recognize the importance and time commitment required to teach fraction operations well and suggest the following developmental process:

- Grade 3: Students add equal-sized units (in this case unit fractions) to understand that a fraction $\frac{a}{b}$ is the quantity formed by a parts of size $\frac{1}{b}$. This is demonstrated by $\frac{3}{4} = \frac{1}{4} + \frac{1}{4} + \frac{1}{4}$. (This is foundational knowledge for addition of fractions.)

- Grade 4: Students add and subtract fractions with like denominators and multiply fractions with whole numbers.

- Grade 5: Students add and subtract fractions fluently with like and unlike denominators, multiply fractions, divide unit fractions by whole numbers, and divide whole numbers by unit fractions.

- Grade 6: Students divide fractions by fractions.

Students should not immediately start with identifying common denominators and learning procedural rules. As with whole-number operations, sharing standard algorithms early as a quick approach to getting answers leaves students without any means of assessing their results for reasonableness and any grasp of when they should use these procedures. With that procedure-focused approach, the different fraction algorithms soon become a meaningless jumble. Students ask, "Do I need a common denominator, or do I just add the "bottom numbers" like when we multiply the denominators in multiplication?" and "Which fraction do I invert, the first or the second?" and "When can I change the sign in the problem, just in division of fractions or in multiplication of fractions too?" Additionally, students can't adapt to slightly different values, such as mixed numbers. This can be a very confusing experience for even previously strong mathematics students, and could become a point when their confidence in their mathematics abilities may start to falter.

Although incorrect generalizations from whole numbers can confuse students, remember strategically building their understanding about fraction operations from their knowledge of whole-number operations will support their thinking. The properties of the whole number operations align with those for rational numbers (Barnett-Clarke et al., 2010). Using students' prior understanding, combined with a firm grasp of fractions (including relative size and equivalence), provides a strong foundation for fraction computation (Petit, Laird, & Marsden, 2010; Siegler et al., 2010).

In a report that summarizes what works for teaching fraction operations (Siegler et al., 2010), four steps are suggested: (1) use contexts, (2) use a variety of models, (3) include estimation and invented methods, and (4) address misconceptions. These four steps are elaborated for each operation in the sections that follow.

A Problem-Based, Number Sense Approach

Students should understand and have access to a variety of ways to solve fraction computation problems. In many cases, a mental or invented strategy can be applied and a standard algorithm can develop over time. And just as with whole numbers, hurrying to move to the fraction algorithms leaves weaknesses in conceptual understanding that will continue to disadvantage students well into the study of algebra.

In a summary of research on fraction learning, the authors suggest that teachers focus on developing approaches to fraction computation that make sense to learners (Siegler et al., 2010). This research suggests four steps to effective fraction computation instruction:

1. *Use tasks with meaningful contexts.* If this sounds familiar, this recommendation applies to nearly every topic in this book. Huinker (2002) makes an excellent case for using

meaningful contextual problems and for letting students develop their own methods of computation with fractions. Problems or contexts need not be elaborate. What you want is a context that fits both the meaning of the operation and the fractions involved.

2. *Explore each operation incorporating a variety of models.* Have students defend their solutions using models, including simple drawings. Importantly, models must be connected to the symbolic operations. The visuals will help students make sense of the symbols and related operations, but only when they are explicitly connected through repeated experiences and discussions.

3. *Include estimation and invented methods as the foundation for strategy development.* "Estimate $2\frac{1}{2} \times \frac{1}{4}$. Should it be more or less than 1? More or less than 2?" Can you reason to get an exact answer without using the standard algorithm? One way is to apply the distributive property, split the mixed number, and multiply the whole number and the fraction by $\frac{1}{4}$: $(2 \times \frac{1}{4}) + (\frac{1}{2} \times \frac{1}{4})$. Two $\frac{1}{4}$ s are $\frac{2}{4}$ or $\frac{1}{2}$ and a half of a fourth is $\frac{1}{8}$. So add an eighth to a half and you have $\frac{5}{8}$. Estimation and invented methods keep the focus on the magnitude of the numbers and the meaning of the operations, encourage reflective thinking, and build informal number sense with fractions.

4. *Address common misconceptions.* Teachers should present well-known misconceptions to students and discuss openly why some approaches lead to right answers and why other approaches do not (Siegler et al., 2010). For example, students often misapply their prior knowledge—in this case, computation with whole numbers—to their early experiences with operations with fractions. This results in their adding the denominators when combining fractions. In this case you could show students actual physical models to reason and prove the best method to add fractions. But the concepts of the whole number and the fraction operation are the same, and benefits can be had by purposefully connecting these ideas.

In the discussions that follow, estimation and informal exploration is encouraged for each operation. There is also a guided development of each standard algorithm.

Addition and Subtraction

The idea of fostering invented strategies for fractions beginning with contextual problems is similar to the approach described in Chapter 11 for whole-number computation with join, separate, part–part–whole, and compare problem structures (CCSSO, 2010; Chval, Lannin, & Jones, 2013). As with whole numbers, set the expectation that students will use a variety of methods and that these methods will vary widely with the fractions encountered in problems. Students should find ways to solve problems with fractions, and their invented strategies will contribute to the development of the standard algorithms (Huinker, 2002; Schifter, Bastable, & Russell, 1999).

Contextual Examples and Models

In the real world, most students first encounter the need to add or subtract fractions in measurement situations. Whether seeing how much they've grown, adding a half and a quarter hour of time, building a frame for a picture, combining amounts of ribbon needed for a costume, calculating how far they've jogged and how much more they have to run, students naturally see the need to combine and compare portions of units.

One early example emerges from doubling recipes or halving recipes (repeated subtraction). A junior cookbook or a book like *Civil War Recipes* (George, 2010) can provide an authentic problem context with links to social studies. Be sure to have a measuring cup available! Consider these problems based on recipes from the Civil War period: Robert and his brother were eating Northern brown bread. Robert had $\frac{3}{4}$ of his loaf left. His brother had $\frac{7}{8}$ of his loaf left. How much brown bread do the boys have together? Many students will draw a simple rectangle for the two brown bread loaves, as in Figure 13.1. The drawing of $\frac{7}{8}$ suggests that if you had one more eighth it would be a whole. So the combined amount of brown bread it is the same as $1\frac{3}{4}$ with $\frac{1}{8}$ subtracted. Or the drawing might suggest subtracting a fourth (in the form of $\frac{2}{8}$ from $\frac{7}{8}$ and putting it with the $\frac{3}{4}$ to equal a whole. That would leave $\frac{5}{8}$ for a total of $1\frac{5}{8}$.

Here are other problems based on the recipes:

Figure 13.1

How could you combine these two quantities to determine the sum?

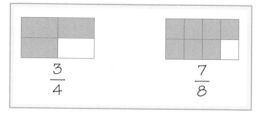

$$\frac{3}{4} \qquad \frac{7}{8}$$

Hardtack is a hard, dry bread often baked in a circular pan. A group of soldiers had $4\frac{1}{2}$ loaves of hardtack. One soldier ate $\frac{7}{8}$ of a loaf. How much was left for others?

Josephine was making gingerbread and cornbread to share with the troops. She needed $2\frac{1}{2}$ cups of buttermilk for the one recipe and $6\frac{1}{4}$ cups for the other recipe. How much buttermilk did she need to prepare both recipes?

Groundnut soup requires $\frac{2}{3}$ of a cup of crushed peanuts for one serving. How much crushed peanuts would be needed if you were going to make two servings (think of using the measuring cup twice)?

Notice that these contextual problems use a mix of models—both area and length or measurement (using a scale on a measuring cup). Encouraging students to model each of these problems is critical to developing the concepts of addition and subtraction of fractions. Notice too that it is sometimes possible to find the sum or difference of two fractions without splitting pieces into smaller parts (common denominators). Often answers are determined by looking at the part left over.

Most of your initial problems should involve fractions with denominators no greater than 12. There is little need in the first phase of instruction to add fifths and sevenths, or even fifths and twelfths. The results involve numbers that cannot be handled easily with any model or drawing. Keep the numbers simple while you are trying to introduce the operations. But, do include mixed numbers and unlike denominators.

Standards for
Mathematical Practice

2 **Make sense of problems and persevere in solving them.**

Formative Assessment Note

Simple problems like

Sammy gathered $\frac{3}{4}$ pounds of walnuts and Chala gathered $\frac{7}{8}$ pounds. Who gathered the most? How much more?

can be used as a formative assessment with an Observation Checklist. On the checklist include concepts such as: (1) Can determine a reasonable estimate; (2) Selects and accurately uses a manipulative or drawing; (3) Recognizes equivalences between fourths and eighths; and (4) Can accurately connect symbols to a model.

Models

Recall that there are area, length, and set models for illustrating fractions. Instruction should initially focus on area and linear models as the use of rectangles and number lines can support how to add and subtract fractions with like denominators.

Area Models.   Cramer, Wyberg, and Leavitt (2008), have found circles to be an effective model for adding and subtracting fractions because circles allow students to develop mental images of the sizes of different pieces (fractions). Figure 13.2 shows how students estimate first (including marking a number line) and then explain with pictures and symbols how they added the fractions. Notice how this student's version of recording what she did with the materials using symbols is very close to the standard algorithm.

Figure 13.2

A student estimates and then adds fractions using fraction pieces.

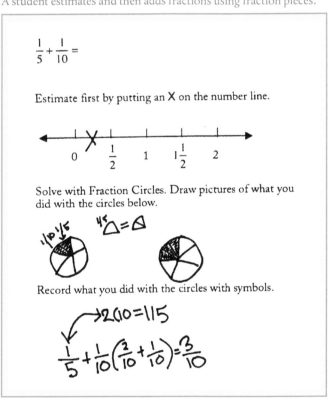

Source: Cramer, K., Wyberg, T., & Leavitt, S. (2008). "The Role of Representations in Fraction Addition and Subtraction." *Mathematics Teaching in the Middle School, 13*(8), p. 495. Reprinted with permission. Copyright 2008 by the National Council of Teachers of Mathematics. All rights reserved.

Consider this problem in which the context is a circular:

Jack and Jill ordered two medium pizzas, one cheese and one pepperoni. Jack ate $\frac{5}{6}$ of a pizza, and Jill ate $\frac{1}{2}$ a pizza. How much pizza did they eat together?

Try to think of two ways that students might solve this problem without using a common-denominator algorithm.

If students draw circles as in the earlier example, some will try to fill in the $\frac{1}{6}$ gap in the pizza to equal one whole. Then they will need to figure out how to get $\frac{1}{6}$ from the $\frac{1}{2}$ they have. If they can think of $\frac{1}{2}$ as $\frac{3}{6}$, they can use one of the sixths to fill in the gap. Another approach, after drawing two pizzas, is to notice that there is a half plus two more sixths in the $\frac{5}{6}$ pizza. Put the two halves together to make one whole, and there are $\frac{2}{6}$ more—$1\frac{2}{6}$. These are two certainly logical solutions that represent the type of reasoning you want to encourage.

There are many other area models that can be used such as rectangles, as shown in Figure 13.3 and pattern blocks. Rectangles can be drawn for any fractional value, depending on how it is partitioned. Pattern blocks have pieces such that the yellow hexagon can be one whole, the blue parallelogram $\frac{1}{3}$, the green triangle $\frac{1}{6}$, and the red trapezoid $\frac{1}{2}$. The following activity adapted from McAnallen and Frye (1995) uses pattern blocks to informally explore ideas about subtraction of fractions.

Figure 13.3

Using area models to subtract fractions.

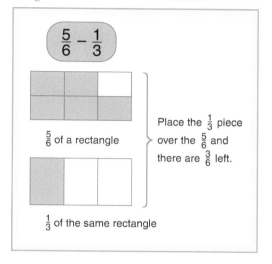

Activity 13.1

CCSS-M: 4.NF.B.3a; 4.NF.B.3b; 4.NF.B.3c; 5.NF.A.1

The Gold Prize

Use pattern blocks to play a game that reinforces subtraction of fractions. All students need a collection of pattern blocks to work with. Start each pair of students with three yellow hexagon pieces and name each yellow as one unit or whole (so they are starting with three wholes). Then roll a die with the following fractions on its faces: $\frac{1}{6}, \frac{1}{3}, \frac{1}{2}, \frac{2}{6}, \frac{2}{3}, \frac{5}{6}$. Let's say one student rolls $\frac{1}{3}$. They must subtract the third from one of the yellow pieces (whole). Students might find trading a yellow for three blue thirds and then removing one of the thirds a useful strategy. Other students may try trading a yellow for two blues and subtracting the third in the process. The idea is to take turns rolling and keep subtracting down to zero. At random points in the game, call "stop" and ask students to note what they have left (such as $2\frac{1}{6}$ and later in the game $1\frac{1}{3}$). This game is actually reinforcing finding common denominators if students make equivalent trades before subtracting a piece.

The key is to select manipulatives that align with the contexts so that students make connections among the situation, the visual, and the symbols. Activity 13.2 works with a rectangular illustration.

 *Teaching Tip*

Notice that we didn't use the set model for introducing these ideas about computation. Set models can initially be confusing and they can accidentally reinforce such mistakes as adding the denominators.

Activity 13.2

CCSS-M: 4.NF.B.3a, d; 5.NF.A.1; 5.NF.A.2

Gardening Together

Give each student an **Empty Garden** Activity Page or make an empty rectangle on paper for them. Ask each student to design a garden to illustrate this situation:

Al, Bill, Carrie, Danielle, Enrique, and Fabio are each given a portion of the school garden for spring planting. Here are the portions you should show on your rectangle (think how you want to organize your divisions before starting):

$$\text{Al} = \tfrac{1}{4} \qquad\qquad \text{Bill} = \tfrac{1}{8} \qquad\qquad \text{Carrie} = \tfrac{3}{16}$$

$$\text{Danielle} = \tfrac{1}{16} \qquad\qquad \text{Enrique} = \tfrac{1}{4} \qquad\qquad \text{Fabio} = \tfrac{1}{8}$$

What fraction of the garden will each of the following groups have if they combine their portions of the garden? Show your work.

Bill and Danielle	Al and Carrie
Fabio and Enrique	Carrie, Fabio, and Al

To challenge students, ask them to solve puzzle-type questions like: "Which two people combined would have the least amount of the garden? The most? Which combinations of friends could combine their portions to work on one-half of the garden?"

 ## Formative Assessment Note

The following can be used with an individual student in a diagnostic interview or with a whole class **Observation Checklist**. Share Kieran's work sample shown here that provides his erroneous justification through words, pictures, and numbers to show that $\tfrac{1}{2} + \tfrac{1}{3} = \tfrac{2}{5}$.

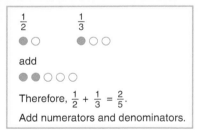

Kieran's work highlights a common misconception that to combine the fractions simply add the numerators and the denominators. And he has provided a picture that seems to support his answer. Ask your students to try the problem on their own first. Then ask, "What do you think of Kieran's answer?" See whether they can talk about how the whole changes with each fraction $(\tfrac{1}{2}, \tfrac{1}{3}, \tfrac{2}{5})$. You will hope they notice the necessity for the wholes (or units) to be the same. But what if they don't see an issue?

Standards for Mathematical Practice

> **1 Construct viable arguments and critique the reasoning of others.**

Students who have naïve understandings of addition of fractions, coupled with Kieran's picture that appears to support this flawed approach, can doubt what they "know for sure." Placing these fractions into a context and using visual models helps students critically examine Kieran's approach. Say, "Suppose you had $\tfrac{1}{2}$ of a small pizza and $\tfrac{1}{3}$ of a large pizza (using a visual of two different sized circles). When you put the two amounts together, you will have part of a pizza. But what is the size of that pizza?" This approach will support their critiquing of the different sized wholes used in Kieran's response.

Length Models.   Cuisenaire rods, rulers, and number lines are all linear or length models. The length model is best, especially in the context of a race or even a submarine sandwich.

An important model for adding and subtracting fractions is the number line (Siegler et al., 2010). One advantage is that it can be easily connected to the ruler, which for students is perhaps one of the most common real contexts for adding or subtracting fractions. The number line requires that students understand $\frac{3}{4}$ as 3 parts of the size one fourth, and also as a value between 0 and 1 (Izsák, Tillema, & Tunc-Pekkam, 2008). Using the number line in addition to area representations can strengthen student understanding (Cramer et al., 2008; Petit, Laird, & Marsden, 2010).

Teaching Tip

Remind students that when given a problem with fractions when no context is used (a "naked number" problem) they should assume the wholes (units) are equal.

▶ **Activity 13.3**

CCSS-M: 4.NF.B.3a, d; 5.NF.A.1; 5.NF.A.2

Jumps on the Ruler

 Use the **Jumps on the Ruler** Activity Page or just provide a ruler and problems such as those below. You can add a linear context such as hair growing or getting cut, and so on. Have students use jumps on the ruler to add and subtract. These jumps encourage students to invent strategies without applying the common denominator algorithm.

$$\frac{3}{4} + \frac{1}{2} \qquad 2\frac{1}{2} - 1\frac{1}{4} \qquad 1\frac{1}{8} + 1\frac{1}{2}$$

When sharing strategies, listen for students iterating (counting) and using fraction equivalencies. In the first problem of Activity 13.3, students might use 1 as a benchmark and use $\frac{1}{4}$ from the $\frac{1}{2}$ to make one whole and then have $\frac{1}{4}$ more to add on to $1\frac{1}{4}$. Similarly, they could use $\frac{1}{2}$ from the $\frac{3}{4}$ to equal a whole and then add on the $\frac{1}{4}$, or they might just know that $\frac{1}{2} = \frac{2}{4}$, then add to get $\frac{5}{4}$ (or $1\frac{1}{4}$). ELLs may not be as familiar with inches because most countries measure in metric units. Spend time prior to the activity discussing how the inch is partitioned and consider adding labels for fourths as a reminder that the inch is different from metric units.

Standards for
Mathematical Practice

◀ **2** Reason abstractly and quantitatively.

Estimation and Invented Strategies

Estimation is a "thinking tool" that should be highlighted as students build meaning for addition and subtraction with fractions (Johanning, 2011). Here, estimation requires that students bring a sense of a fraction's size to the process: estimating the size of the fractions within the problem, and estimating the size of the overall answer. Without that background, they can be asked to estimate the answer to $\frac{8}{9} + \frac{11}{12}$ and, instead of finding an approximate answer, they will make heroic efforts to locate common denominators and identify a precise answer. Even so, they may not grasp how that answer relates to the problem. For example, Petit, Laird, and Marsden (2010, p. xi) looked at a fifth grader's work where the task was to determine which number from a group of answers [20, 8, $\frac{1}{2}$, 1] is closest to the sum of $\frac{1}{12} + \frac{7}{8}$. The student selects a common denominator, creates equivalent fractions and adds to get the correct answer of $\frac{23}{24}$. But, when selecting from multiple options, the student chooses that the answer is closest to 20. The teacher believed this student was going to do well on the test and even stated that there should have been a greater emphasis on the magnitude of the answers. If the student had instead chosen to estimate using benchmarks, the thinking would be "$\frac{1}{12}$ is close to zero and $\frac{7}{8}$ is close to 1, so $0 + 1$ is close to 1" and move to the next assessment item!

Activity 13.4 exemplifies the necessary emphasis on the size of the answer.

Activity 13.4

CCSS-M: 4.NF.B.3a; 5.NF.A.2

More Than or Less Than One?

Tell students that they are going to estimate a sum or difference of two fractions. They are to decide whether the exact answer is greater than 1 or less than 1. Project a problem for about 10 seconds, then hide, cover, or remove it. Ask students to hold up a **Less Than One or More Than One** Card (with "Less Than One" and "More Than One" on either side). Do several problems (Figure 13.4 offers options). Have students discuss how they decided on their estimates. Students with disabilities may need more time and should have a number line marked with benchmark fractions to assist them in visualizing the amounts.

Figure 13.4

Examples for estimating addition and subtraction of fractions.

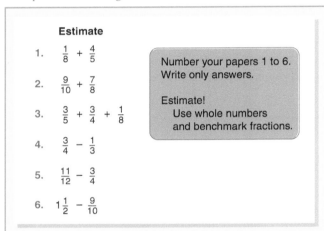

Estimate

1. $\frac{1}{8} + \frac{4}{5}$

2. $\frac{9}{10} + \frac{7}{8}$

3. $\frac{3}{5} + \frac{3}{4} + \frac{1}{8}$

4. $\frac{3}{4} - \frac{1}{3}$

5. $\frac{11}{12} - \frac{3}{4}$

6. $1\frac{1}{2} - \frac{9}{10}$

Number your papers 1 to 6. Write only answers.

Estimate!
Use whole numbers and benchmark fractions.

Here are several variations on the same activity:

- Use a target answer that is different from 1. For example, estimate more than or less than $\frac{1}{2}$, $1\frac{1}{2}$, 2, or 3.
- Adapt to multiplication or division of fractions problems.
- Choose fraction pairs in which both are less than one or both are greater than one. Estimate sums or differences to the nearest half.
- Encourage students to create their own problems and targets. They can trade equations with other students, who in turn need to decide whether the sum or difference is greater than one or less than one (or another value).
- Use the **Estimate, Write, Explain** Activity Page.

Developing the Algorithms

The algorithms develop side by side with the visual models and situations. Students can build on their knowledge of equivalence and invented strategies to develop a meaningful grasp of the common-denominator approach for adding and subtracting fractions. The more fluent students are with exchanging one fractional unit for other equivalent units, the more easily they will be able to adapt problems into equivalent forms, a foundational skill for developing the algorithms.

Like Denominators

The *Common Core State Standards* (CCSSO, 2010) suggest that fourth grade students should add and subtract fractions with like denominators. If students have a good foundation with fraction concepts, they should be able to add or subtract like fractions immediately. Students who are not confident in solving problems such as $\frac{3}{4} + \frac{2}{4}$ or $3\frac{7}{8} - 1\frac{3}{8}$ may lack understanding of the underlying fraction concepts and need additional experiences with concrete materials and relevant contexts. The idea that the numerator counts and the denominator tells what is counted makes addition and subtraction of like fractions the same as adding and subtracting whole numbers. When working on adding with like denominators, it is important to be sure that students are focusing on the key idea—the units are the same, so they can be combined (Mack, 2004).

Formative Assessment Note

Show a student the following problem in a diagnostic interview: $\frac{2}{3} + \frac{1}{2}$. Have a collection of fraction materials available. When your student is convinced that the sum is $1\frac{1}{6}$, substitute $\frac{8}{12}$ for the $\frac{2}{3}$ and $\frac{4}{8}$ for the $\frac{1}{2}$ and ask, "What is this sum ($\frac{8}{12} + \frac{4}{8}$)?" A student who understands that the two problems are equivalent should not hesitate and state that the answer remains the same—$1\frac{1}{6}$. If your student expresses any doubt about the equivalence of the two problems, that should be a clue that the concept of equivalent fractions is not well understood.

Unlike Denominators

Begin by adding and subtracting fractions with unlike denominators, by considering a task such as $\frac{5}{8} + \frac{2}{4}$, in which only one fraction needs to be changed to a common denominator. Let students use fraction pieces and a context about the amount of pizza eaten. Many will note that when they combine the models for the two fractions they make one whole and there is $\frac{1}{8}$ extra. The key question to ask at this point is, "How can we change this problem into one in which the parts are the same sized units?" For this example, it is relatively easy to see that fourths could be changed into eighths. Write the expression $\frac{5}{8} + \frac{4}{8}$, and have students use models (manipulatives or drawings) to explain why the original problem and the converted problem are equivalent. The main idea is to see that $\frac{5}{8} + \frac{2}{4}$ is exactly the same problem as $\frac{5}{8} + \frac{4}{8}$ and that the reason for making the change is so equal-sized units can be combined.

Continue with examples in which both fractions need to be changed—for example, $\frac{2}{3} + \frac{1}{4}$ (or $\frac{2}{3} - \frac{1}{4}$) still using contexts, visuals and student explanations. Focus attention on using models to trade units and show with corresponding symbols how the problem was *rewritten as an equivalent problem* to make it possible to add or subtract equal sized units. This process of finding common denominators is illustrated in Figure 13.5.

Fractions Greater Than One

Include mixed numbers in all of your activities with addition and subtraction, and let students solve these problems in ways that make sense to them. Students will tend to begin with what is familiar and add or subtract the whole numbers first and then deal with the fractions. The challenge arises when the need for regrouping across the whole number and fraction is needed.

Figure 13.5

Rewriting addition and subtraction problems involving fractions.

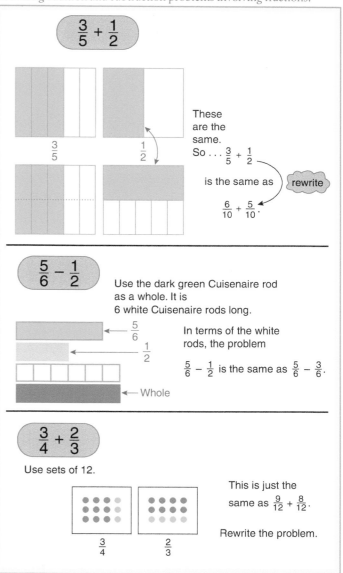

Teaching Tip

> To reinforce equivalences, ask "What equivalent fractions might you use so that you have equal-sized parts?" rather than "What is the common denominator?"

Dealing with whole numbers first makes sense. Consider this problem: You had $5\frac{1}{8}$ yards of fabric and used $3\frac{5}{8}$ yards. How much fabric do you have left? What equation describes this situation? $5\frac{1}{8} - 3\frac{5}{8}$. Ask students to estimate first. Will the answer be greater than 2 or less than 2 yards? It is a length situation, so a number line is a useful way to think about this problem. Given the context students are likely to subtract 3, leaving $2\frac{1}{8}$, and then need to subtract $\frac{5}{8}$. Students may count down (iterate), stopping at $1\frac{1}{2}$. Another approach is to take $\frac{5}{8}$ from the whole part, 2, leaving $1\frac{3}{8}$, and then add the $\frac{1}{8}$ back on to get $1\frac{4}{8}$ or $1\frac{1}{2}$. The "standard" algorithm, which is not as intuitive, is to trade one of the wholes for $\frac{8}{8}$, add them to the $\frac{1}{8}$ to get $1\frac{9}{8}$ and then take away $\frac{5}{8}$.

The National Library of Virtual Manipulatives (NLVM) has three activities that help reinforce fraction addition and subtraction across different models:

- **Fractions—Adding:** Two fractions and an area model for each are given. The user must find a common denominator to rename and then add the fractions.

- **Fraction Bars:** This applet places bars over a number line on which the interval size can be adjusted, providing a flexible model that can be used to illustrate addition and subtraction.

- **Diffy:** This puzzle requires finding the differences between the numbers on the corners of a square, working to a desired difference in the center. This activity encourages students to consider equivalent forms of fractions to solve the puzzle.

Addressing Common Errors and Misconceptions

Explicitly discuss common misconceptions with your students. This is particularly important with fraction operations because students incorrectly generalize rules from whole-number operations (see Table 13.1).

Table 13.1. Common errors and misconceptions in fraction addition and subtraction and how to help.

Common Error or Misconception	What It Looks Like	How to Help
1. Adding both numerators and denominators.	$\frac{3}{4} + \frac{1}{3} = \frac{4}{7}$	• Focus on using a model with a simpler problem. Ask students to combine one fourth and one more fourth with materials and show their answer. Then write $\frac{1}{4} + \frac{1}{4} =$ on the board. Suggest that the answer is $\frac{2}{8}$ and have students match that amount to the models. Have students compare the two models and defend the correct answer. • Use a context and ask, if we are eating eighths of a pizza will we be eating different sized pieces if we combine 3 eighths with 2 eighths? Will our answer be eighths?
2. Failing to identify common denominators.	$\frac{4}{5} + \frac{4}{10} = \frac{8}{10}$ Here students ignore the denominator and just add the numerators (Siegler et al., 2010).	• Use a number line or fraction strip, where students must pay attention to the relative size of the fraction. • Go to NCTM's Illuminations "Making and Using Fraction Strips" to show this idea using a visual.

Table 13.1. Common errors and misconceptions in fraction addition and subtraction and how to help.

Common Error or Misconception	What It Looks Like	How to Help
3. Difficulty finding common multiples.	Students given $\frac{5}{6} + \frac{1}{4} =$ are unsure as to what to use for a denominator.	• Work on having students list a series of multiples for each denominator. Then have them stop when they reach the same number, in this case 12. • Try Activity 13.5.
4. Failing to estimate.	When asked to estimate $\frac{7}{8} + \frac{5}{6}$ students either guess an answer or they carry out the whole calculation finding common denominators and then write down $\frac{41}{24}$.	• Students are sometimes less comfortable with estimation as they believe mathematics is about finding "right" answers. Encourage estimation as part of every fraction computation. • Some students believe estimate means guess, so make sure you avoid using those terms synonymously. • Practice using benchmark fractions and focus on how each of these fractions are close to one whole.

Activity 13.5

CCSS-M: 4.OA.B.4; 5.NF.A.1; 6.NS.B.4

Common Multiple Cards

Give partners a set of **Common Multiple Cards** with pairs of numbers that are potential denominators (see Figure 13.6). First, one student turns over a card and states a common multiple (e.g., for 6 and 8, a student might suggest 48). Then, the partner gets a chance to suggest a smaller common multiple (e.g., 24). Whoever suggests the least common multiple (LCM) keeps the card with the goal to collect the greatest number of cards. Notice that the cards include pairs in which both are prime, where one is a multiple of the other, and those that have a common divisor. Start students with disabilities with the cards on which one number in the pair is a multiple of the other.

A context can help in finding common multiples. The activity **Interference** engages students in determining how often two orbiting satellites will cross paths.

Difficulty with Mixed Numbers

Too often, instruction with mixed numbers is not well integrated into fraction instruction, and therefore students find these values particularly troubling. Here are three misconceptions described in research (Petit, Laird, & Marsden, 2010; Siegler et al., 2010):

1. When given a problem like $3\frac{1}{4} - 1\frac{3}{8}$, students subtract the smaller fraction from the larger. Although this occurs with whole-number subtraction, it is more prevalent with mixed numbers.

2. When given a problem like $4 - \frac{7}{8}$, students don't know what to do with the fact that one number is not a fraction. They will even place an 8 as a denominator for the whole number ($\frac{4}{8} - \frac{7}{8}$) in an attempt to find a solution.

3. When given a problem like $14\frac{1}{2} - 3\frac{1}{8}$, students focus on the whole numbers and don't know what to do with the fractional parts.

One way to avoid and to address these misconceptions, and other misconceptions, is to make them a part of public discussions about whether an approach is correct (or not) and why.

Figure 13.6

Common multiple cards.

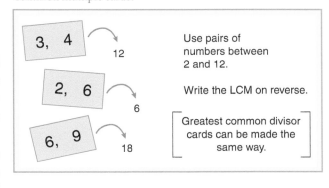

Multiplication

Can you think of a situation that requires using multiplication of whole numbers? Can you think of a situation that requires multiplication of fractions? If not, why might that be? It is not that there are no situations involving fraction multiplication, but the connection between the concept and the procedure is not well understood, so the algorithm is rarely used. Beginning with problems in everyday contexts supports students' ability to gain fluency in not only carrying out the algorithm but also modeling problems, estimating, and seeing where this computation can be applied in a variety of real-world events. As you will see in the sections that follow, the foundational ideas of *iterating* (counting) fractional parts and *partitioning* are at the heart of understanding multiplication of fractions.

Contextual Examples and Models

When working with whole numbers, we would say that 3×5 means "3 sets of 5" (equal sets) or "3 rows of 5" (area or array) or "3 lengths of 5" (number line). The first factor tells how much of the second factor you have or want. One factor is the unit of measure and the other factor is a quantity to be measured (Yeong, Dougherty, & Berkaliev, 2015). Now we connect to this prior knowledge by transition to language such as "$\frac{1}{2}$ of 6" or "$\frac{1}{2}$ of an area or array of 6" or "$\frac{1}{2}$ of a length of 6."

When students move to middle grades, they will learn about ratios and proportional thinking. Therefore, the *Common Core State Standards* expect that fifth graders prepare for these topics by thinking of multiplication of fractions from a perspective of scaling or resizing. Connect the fact that multiplication by the number one leaves the amount unchanged (identity property of multiplication), to multiplying a given number by numbers larger than one produces a larger quantity, and multiplying a given number by numbers smaller than one (fractions, for example) produces smaller quantities. This reasoning about the logical structure of multiplication will enhance students' ability to decide whether their answers are reasonable while providing building blocks for the mathematics ahead. A possible progression of problem difficulty is developed in the sections that follow.

Multiply a Fraction by a Whole Number

The problems in this category include $5 \times \frac{1}{2}$, $6 \times \frac{1}{8}$, $10 \times \frac{3}{4}$, and $3 \times 2\frac{1}{3}$, and are introduced in grade 4 (CCSSO, 2010). Logically, these problems connect to multiplication with whole numbers, so that is where you begin with multiplying fractions. Consider these two problems as a starting point:

Marvin ate 3 pounds of meat every day. How much meat did Marvin eat in one week?

Murphy ate $\frac{1}{3}$ pounds of meat every day. How much meat did Murphy eat in one week?

Stop and Reflect

What expressions represent each situation? What reasoning strategies would you use to solve each problem?

For Marvin, the expression is 7 (groups of) 3 pounds, or 7×3. You can solve this by skip counting 3, 6, 9, 12, 15, 18, 21 to get the answer of 21 pounds (but if you know your facts, you just *multiplied*). Murphy similarly ate $7 \times \frac{1}{3}$ pounds, and it can also be solved by skip counting, this time by his portion size of thirds: $\frac{1}{3}, \frac{2}{3}, \frac{3}{3}, \frac{4}{3}, \frac{5}{3}, \frac{6}{3}, \frac{7}{3}$ to get the answer seven-thirds $\frac{7}{3}$. Notice the skip counting, called *iterating*, is the meaning behind a whole number times a fraction.

Standards for Mathematical Practice

◄ **2** **Reason abstractly and quantitatively.**

Multiply a Whole Number by a Fraction

Students' next experiences with fraction multiplication should involve finding fractions of whole numbers. Although multiplication is commutative, the thinking involved in this type of multiplication involves partitioning (not iterating). The fraction construct is fraction as operator (Lamon, 2012). Examples include $\frac{1}{2} \times 8$, $\frac{1}{2} \times 5$, $\frac{1}{5} \times 8$, $\frac{3}{4} \times 24$, and $2\frac{1}{2} \times 3$. Notice this is a compare or *scaling* situation (think of creating a scale drawing that is $\frac{1}{5}$ of the actual size). In the CCSS-M, this type of fraction multiplication is introduced in grade 5.

These stories can be paired with manipulatives to help students understand this type of fraction operation:

1. The walk from school to the public library takes 25 minutes. When Anna asked her mom how far they had gone, her mom said that they had gone $\frac{1}{2}$ of the way. How many minutes have they walked? (Assume a constant walking rate.)

2. There are 15 cars in Michael's toy car collection. Two-thirds of the cars are red. How many red cars does Michael have?

For a lesson using multiplication stories, use **Expanded Lesson: Multiplication-of-Fraction Stories** and the **Solving Problems Involving Fractions** Activity Page. Notice that the thinking requires partitioning (finding a parts of the whole). How might students think through each problem? For problem 2, students might partition 15 counters into three groups (or partition a line into three parts) and then see how many are in two parts. Recording this thinking in symbols ($\frac{2}{3}$ of 15) gives the following result: $15 \div 3 \times 2$.

Counters (a set model) is an effective tool for finding parts of a whole. Recall that in Chapter 12, counters were used to develop partitioning and iterating with prompts such as, "If the whole is 45, how much is $\frac{1}{5}$ of the whole?" and "If the whole is 24, what is $\frac{3}{8}$ of the whole?" These tasks can be adapted to make an explicit connection to multiplication by having students write the equations that match the question. **Counting Counters: Fraction of a Whole** Activity Page is designed to do this.

An area model, such a rectangle, provides an excellent visual tool for illustrating and making generalizations (Witherspoon, 2014), as can be seen in Activity 13.6.

▶ **Activity 13.6**

CCSS-M: 5.NF.B.4a, b; 5.NF.B.4a, b

How Big Is the Banner?

 Explain to (or show) students that you have a roll of paper for making banners. The roll is one-foot wide (you can also use one-yard or one-meter) and you are going to roll out several feet. The first banner you cut is **1 ft. by 6 ft.**:

(continued)

Ask students, "What is the area of this banner?" (1ft. × 6ft. = 6 square feet). You can ask additional questions about the area of banners of other lengths (with a width of 1 foot). Then, explain to students that you want to cut the banners lengthwise to make additional banners. Ask students to use this rectangle to show banners that are $\frac{1}{2}$ foot × 6 feet. Then ask, "What is the area of each new banner?":

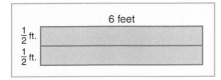

Students fill in the strips to show that there are 3 square feet in each half-strip:

Repeat the process by asking students to find the area of the banners if the original 6 foot banner is now cut lengthwise into three strips (thirds). Repeat with fourths. After exploring this 6-foot banner, use a variety of lengths (e.g., 12 feet, 15 feet) and various widths (e.g., halves, fourths, thirds) to find other areas. Record the matching equations and answers. Encourage students to find patterns that help them determine the area of the banners. Have them consider how the banner is scaled based on the values involved in the problem. For students with disabilities, or students who benefit from using physical materials, cut out paper strips in advance and have them fold the paper to show the partitions.

Fractions of Fractions, without Subdivision

Once students have had experiences with fractions of a whole ($\frac{2}{3}$ of 15) or wholes times fractions (15 groups of $\frac{2}{3}$), a next step is to introduce finding a fraction of a fraction, but to carefully pick tasks in which no additional partitioning is required. See if you can mentally answer the next three problems (again, by using each model type):

You have $\frac{3}{4}$ of a pizza left. If you give $\frac{1}{3}$ of the leftover pizza to your brother, how much of a whole pizza will your brother get?

Someone ate $\frac{1}{10}$ of the bread, leaving only $\frac{9}{10}$. If you use $\frac{2}{3}$ of the bread that is left of the loaf to make sandwiches, how much of a whole loaf will you have used?

Gloria used $2\frac{1}{2}$ tubes of blue paint to paint the sky in her picture. Each tube holds $\frac{4}{5}$ ounce of paint. How many ounces of blue paint did Gloria use?

Figure 13.7 shows how to use different manipulatives to illustrate these three problems. However, there is more than one way to partition. In $\frac{1}{3} \times \frac{3}{4}$, for example, you can find one-third of the three-fourths, or you can find one-third of *each* fourth and then combine the pieces (Izsák, 2008).

Figure 13.7

Connecting representations to the procedure for three problems involving multiplication of fractions.

Task	Finding the starting amount	Showing the fraction of the starting amount	Solution
Pizza Find $\frac{1}{3}$ of $\frac{3}{4}$ (of a pizza) or $\frac{1}{3} \times \frac{3}{4}$			$\frac{1}{3}$ of the $\frac{3}{4}$ is $\frac{1}{4}$ of the original pizza. $\frac{1}{3} \times \frac{3}{4} = \frac{1}{4}$
Bread Find $\frac{2}{3}$ of $\frac{9}{10}$ (of a loaf of bread) or $\frac{2}{3} \times \frac{9}{10}$			$\frac{2}{3}$ of the $\frac{9}{10}$ is 6 slices of the loaf or $\frac{6}{10}$ of the whole. $\frac{2}{3} \times \frac{9}{10} = \frac{6}{10}$
Paint Find $2\frac{1}{2}$ of $\frac{4}{5}$ (ounces of paint) or $2\frac{1}{2} \times \frac{4}{5}$			$2\frac{1}{2}$ of the $\frac{4}{5}$ is $\frac{4}{5} + \frac{4}{5} + \frac{2}{5} = \frac{10}{5}$

Fractions of Fractions: Subdividing the Unit Parts

When the pieces must be subdivided into smaller unit parts, the problems become more challenging.

Zack had $\frac{2}{3}$ of the lawn left to cut. After lunch, he cut $\frac{3}{4}$ of the grass he had left. How much of the whole lawn did Zack cut after lunch?

The zookeeper had a huge bottle of the animals' favorite liquid treat, Zoo Cola. The monkey drank $\frac{1}{5}$ of the bottle. The zebra drank $\frac{2}{3}$ of what was left. How much of the bottle of Zoo Cola did the zebra drink?

In Zack's lawn problem, it is necessary to find fourths of two things, the two-thirds of the grass left to cut. In the Zoo Cola problem, you need thirds of four things, the four-fifths of the cola that remains. Again, the concepts of the numerator counting and the denominator naming what is counted play an important role. Figure 13.8 shows two possible solutions for Zack's lawn problem. Using a paper strip and partitioning is an effective way to solve multiplication of fractions problems, especially when they require additional partitioning (Siebert & Gaskin, 2006). A similar approach can be used for the Zoo Cola problem.

If students use counters to model problems in which the units require subdivision, an added difficulty arises. Figure 13.9 illustrates

Figure 13.8

Solutions to a multiplication problem in which the parts must be subdivided.

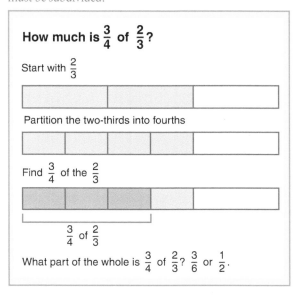

How much is $\frac{3}{4}$ of $\frac{2}{3}$?

Start with $\frac{2}{3}$

Partition the two-thirds into fourths

Find $\frac{3}{4}$ of the $\frac{2}{3}$

$\frac{3}{4}$ of $\frac{2}{3}$

What part of the whole is $\frac{3}{4}$ of $\frac{2}{3}$? $\frac{3}{6}$ or $\frac{1}{2}$.

Figure 13.9

Modeling multiplication of fractions with counters.

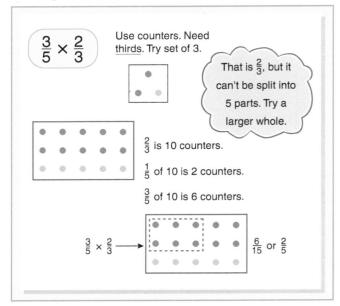

what might happen solving $\frac{3}{5} \times \frac{2}{3}$. (Three-fifths of two-thirds of a whole is how much of a whole?) Here the representation of a whole must be changed so that the thirds can be subdivided. Also, because there is no context to the problem, why not use the commutative property—turn the factors around and consider $\frac{2}{3}$ of $\frac{3}{5}$. Wow! Now it reads as two-thirds of three-fifths! Do you immediately see that the answer equals $\frac{2}{5}$?

Area Model. The area model for modeling fraction multiplication has several advantages. First, it works for problems in which partitioning a length can be challenging. Second, it provides a powerful visual to show that a result can be quite a bit smaller than either of the fractions used or that if the fractions are both close to 1, then the result is also close to one. Third, it is a good model for connecting to the standard algorithm for multiplying fractions. Also it is an CCSS-M expectation that fifth graders are able the use this model to apply and extend previous understandings of fraction multiplication.

To connect these ideas back to multiplication of whole numbers using an array, provide students with a drawing of $\frac{3}{4}$ of a square shaded as shown in Figure 13.10. For example, in $\frac{3}{5} \times \frac{3}{4}$, you are finding $\frac{3}{5}$ of $\frac{3}{4}$, so you must first show $\frac{3}{4}$ (see the first step in Figure 13.10). To find fifths of the $\frac{3}{4}$, draw four horizontal lines through the $\frac{3}{4}$ (see the second step in Figure 13.10), so the whole is partitioned into the same sized pieces (see the third step). Remember, you want to find a fractional part of the *shaded part*. But the *unit*—the way that the parts are measured—must remain the whole square. The shading illustrates three-fifths of three-fourths *of the original whole*, or $\frac{3}{5}$ of $\frac{3}{4}$ of 1. Extending the lines to subpartition the entire whole maintains the relationship between the fractional parts and the whole.

Figure 13.10

Modeling fraction multiplication with the area model.

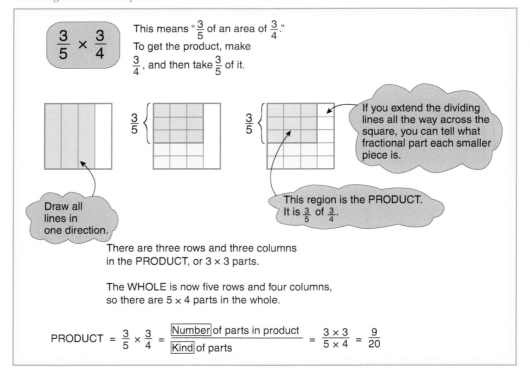

Estimating and Invented Strategies

In the real world, there are many instances when whole numbers and fractions must be multiplied and mental estimates are quite useful. For example, sale items are frequently listed as "half off," or we read of a "one-third increase" in the number of registered voters. To get an estimate of 75 percent of $36.69, it is useful to think of 75 percent as $\frac{3}{4}$, finding one-fourth of the amount (about $9) and then three-fourths (about $27).

With more complex numbers, encourage students to use estimation strategies such as compatible numbers, benchmarks, and relative size of unit fractions:

Teaching Tip

Some textbooks make this sliced-rectangle approach mechanical, such that it actually becomes a meaningless algorithm in itself. Students are told to shade horizontally to show the first factor and shade vertically for the second factor. Without a rationale, they are told that the product is the region that is double-shaded. Such strategies are without meaning and the same as giving students rules to memorize.

- *Compatible numbers:* To estimate $\frac{3}{5}$ of $36.69, a useful compatible number is $35. One-fifth of 35 equals 7, so three-fifths is 3×7, or 21. Then make your adjustment—perhaps add an additional 50 cents, for an estimate of $21.50.
- *Benchmarks:* $\frac{7}{8} \times \frac{5}{12} =$. Think, "$\frac{7}{8}$ is about one, times $\frac{5}{12}$ which is about one-half. But, the answer is a little less, so the answer will be a little less than one-half."
- *Relative size of unit fractions:* $\frac{1}{3} \times 3\frac{4}{5} =$. Think, "I need one third of $3\frac{4}{5}$. One third of 3 equals 1, and $\frac{1}{3}$ of $\frac{4}{5}$ is going to be a little more than $\frac{1}{5}$ (because there are four parts), so the answer is about $1\frac{1}{5}$."

You can mentally calculate products of fractions and whole numbers by thinking of the meanings of the numerator and denominator. For example, $\frac{3}{5}$ is 3 one-fifths. So, if the problem is to find $\frac{3}{5}$ of 350, first think about one-fifth of 350, or 70. If one-fifth equals 70, then three-fifths is 3×70, or 210. Start with compatible numbers, determine the unit fractional part (identify a unit rate), and then multiply by the number of units you want.

Developing the Algorithms

With enough experiences (probably several weeks) using multiple representations, students will begin to notice a pattern. Then, the standard multiplication of fractions algorithm will logically develop from those ideas.

Ask students to solve three examples such as the following, and to illustrate the solution by partitioning a rectangle that represents the whole as was shown in Figure 13.10:

$$\frac{5}{6} \times \frac{1}{2} \qquad \frac{3}{4} \times \frac{1}{5} \qquad \frac{1}{3} \times \frac{9}{10}$$

Ask questions that press students to tell how the computation connects to the illustration, for example, for the first example ask: "How did you figure out how what the unit of the fraction [the denominator] was for the answer?" Or, more specifically, "How did you figure out that the denominator would be twelfths?" "Is this a pattern that is true for the other examples?" Then ask students, "Can you find a similar pattern for the number of parts (the numerator)?"

Teaching Tip

Have students estimate and consider the reasonableness of results so that they can notice the pattern that multiplying a given number by a fraction less than one results in a product smaller than the given number.

Factors Greater Than One

Once students have explored products with both factors less than one, include tasks in which one factor is a mixed number – for example $\frac{3}{4} \times 2\frac{1}{2}$. The more you integrate these problems, students will have opportunities to think about the

Figure 13.11

Using the area model to show multiplication of fractions with factors greater than one.

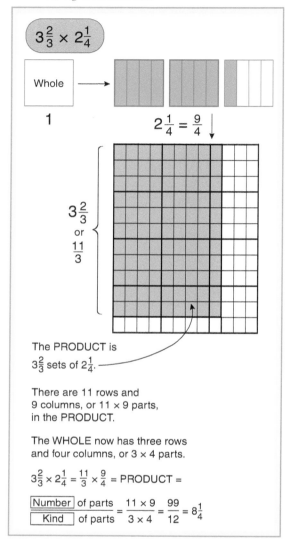

The PRODUCT is
$3\frac{2}{3}$ sets of $2\frac{1}{4}$.

There are 11 rows and
9 columns, or 11 × 9 parts,
in the PRODUCT.

The WHOLE now has three rows
and four columns, or 3 × 4 parts.

$$3\frac{2}{3} \times 2\frac{1}{4} = \frac{11}{3} \times \frac{9}{4} = \text{PRODUCT} =$$

$$\frac{\boxed{\text{Number}} \text{ of parts}}{\boxed{\text{Kind}} \text{ of parts}} = \frac{11 \times 9}{3 \times 4} = \frac{99}{12} = 8\frac{1}{4}$$

Figure 13.12

Partial-product approach to multiplying fractions.

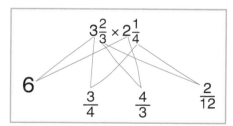

impact of multiplying a number less than one by a number greater than one. Challenging students to see if they can use a similar type of drawing of the area model to explain products with either or both factors greater than one. Figure 13.11 shows how this might look when both factors are mixed numbers. This is an efficient way to solve the problem but not the only approach.

Students can also use the distributive property to find the four partial products, just as they do when multiplying two-digit whole numbers (Figure 13.12). In many cases, the partial products can be solved mentally. Notice that the same four partial products in Figure 13.12 can be found in the rectangle in Figure 13.11. The *Common Core State Standards* expect that fifth graders should be able to explain the impact on a product if one of the factors is a fraction greater than one or if the factor is less than one.

Addressing Common Errors and Misconceptions

Misconceptions can be intensified when students are quickly pressed to memorize rules, such as "multiply both the bottom and the top," and are not given adequate time to explore multiplication of fractions conceptually. The result is an inability to solve multiplication problems, which is a significant barrier for solving proportions and algebraic expressions. Here are some common errors and misconceptions to look for:

Treating the Denominator the Same As in Addition/ Subtraction Problems. Why does the denominator stay the same when adding fractions and get multiplied when fractions are multiplied? What is a conceptual explanation for this? In adding, the process is counting parts of a whole, so those parts must be the same size. In multiplication, you are finding a part of a part, so the part may change size. Compare the two operations with an area model or number line to see how they are conceptually different. Some students *want* to find common denominators to multiply fractions, this will result in the right answer—but it is not an efficient way to solve the problem.

Inability to Estimate Approximate Size of the Answer. Some students think that "multiplication makes bigger," so they have difficulty deciding whether their answers make sense. On the one hand, they may never even think about fraction size, so any answer looks reasonable (e.g., $\frac{1}{2} \times 6\frac{1}{4} = 12\frac{1}{8}$). On the other hand, they might notice the answer ($\frac{1}{2} \times 6\frac{1}{4} = 3\frac{1}{8}$), but become concerned that it can't be right because the answer should be bigger. Estimation, contexts, and visuals help students think about whether answers are reasonable.

Matching Multiplication Situations with Multiplication (and Not Division). Multiplication and division have an inverse relationship, which makes it very important for our language to be precise. In the question, "What is $\frac{1}{3}$ of \$24?" students may correctly decide to divide by 3 or multiply by $\frac{1}{3}$. But they may (incorrectly) divide by $\frac{1}{3}$, confusing the idea that they are finding a fraction of the whole. This is particularly true for ELLs, who may become confused by language such as "divide it *in* half" and "divide it *by* half" (Carr et al., 2009). Estimation can help so ask, "Should the result be larger or smaller than the original amount?"

Using the Deadly Key Word Strategy. When students are deciding which fraction operation is appropriate for solving a word problem, just as was discussed with whole numbers a key word strategy is not useful. In a research study, when students were asked to explain their selection of an operation, 56 percent stated that when dealing with fractions, when you see the word *of*, it always means times. Ironically, 51 percent in explaining their choice of division said *of* means divide, and 33 percent said *of* means subtract (Prediger, 2011)! The best approach is to make meaning of the situation and not just use one or two words in the entire problem to determine a solution strategy. Focus students' attention on the situation qualitatively (without a focus on actual numbers) and continue to ask questions such as, "Should the result be more or less than the initial amount?"

Division

"Invert the divisor and multiply" is probably one of the most mysterious and confusing rules shared in elementary mathematics. To avoid this mystery, students should first examine division with fractions using essential prior knowledge—partitioning and iterating. Division should follow a developmental progression that focuses on four types of problems:

1. A whole number divided by a whole number: $14 \div 5$ OR $22 \div 7$
2. A fraction divided by a whole number: $\frac{1}{2} \div 4$ OR $\frac{7}{8} \div 2$
3. A whole number divided by a fraction: $4 \div \frac{1}{3}$ OR $6 \div \frac{2}{3}$
4. A fraction divided by a fraction: $\frac{7}{8} \div \frac{1}{8}$ OR $2\frac{1}{4} \div \frac{1}{2}$

In the CCSS-M, division involving fractions begins in fifth grade but is limited to the first three types using only unit fractions. In sixth grade, all types are explored.

Contextual Examples and Models

As with whole number division, there are two meanings of division with fractions: partition and measurement (Cramer, Monson, Whitney, Leavitt, & Wyberg, 2010; Kribs-Zaleta, 2008). Although you will present both types of division as you teach, for clarity let's review each meaning separately and look at some story problems for each problem type.

Whole Number Divided by Whole Number

A partition or sharing context is helpful in interpreting division of a whole number by a whole number (Lamon, 2012). Here we limit the discussion to developing a progression for division involving fractions.

Sharing tasks can result in each person receiving a fractional part: 5 sandwiches shared with 4 friends ($5 \div 4$). If you partition each sandwich into fourths, you see that each friend will have five-fourths (friend 1 takes the yellow section from each sandwich, friend 2 takes the red section, and so on):

Notice that $5 \div 4 = \frac{1}{4} \times 5 = \frac{5}{4}$. The first expression means five sandwiches shared with four friends; the second expression means find one-fourth of five sandwiches (that is one person's fair-share); and the final expression means five-fourths is one person's share—a fourth from each of five sandwiches. Students must be able to see the connections and meanings of each of these equivalent expressions. They also need to recognize that division of a whole number by a whole number, is the same as multiplying the number by a unit fraction, which prepares them for the next problem type.

Fraction Divided by a Whole Number

These problem types are introduced in the CCSS-M in grade 5 as unit fractions ($\frac{1}{4} \div 3$) and in sixth grade for nonunit fractions ($\frac{9}{10} \div 3$ OR $2\frac{1}{2} \div 6$). Notice that in partitive (sharing) problems, you are asking, "How much is the share for *one* friend?" Questions could also be "How many miles are walked in *one* hour?" or "How much ribbon for *one* bow?"

There are many situations that can fit this equation. Activity 13.7 provides three different situations for exploring this situation.

Activity 13.7

CCSS-M: 5.NF.B.7a, c

Fractions Divided by Whole Number Stories

Provide students with different situations to explore the same problem. Here are three stories (one area, one linear, and one set):

- **Garden Plots.** Three gardeners are equally sharing $\frac{1}{4}$ of an acre for their plots. What part of an acre is each gardener's plot? The Garden Plots Activity Page provides four "plots" that students can use to illustrate garden sharing problems.

- **Water Bottles.** There is $\frac{1}{4}$ of a gallon of water that is poured equally into three water bottles. How much water is poured into each?

- **Cheese Sticks.** Arlo buys a bag of cheese sticks (24 in the bag). He takes $\frac{1}{4}$ of the cheese sticks to a picnic and shares the cheese sticks equally with 2 friends (and himself). What fraction of the original bag does each person get?

    After they finish, compare the different visuals (area, length and set) and connect the meaning of the operation to the visuals. Ask students to write an expression for each (they should be the same!) Emphasize the notion of "How much for *one*?" After exploring this initial task, students can be challenged to create their own stories to match problems like $\frac{1}{4} \div 3$.

Once students have explored a unit fraction divided by a whole number, they need experiences dividing any fraction (or mixed number) by a whole number, using contexts. Ribbon provides a good linear model:

Cassie has $5\frac{1}{4}$ yards of ribbon to make four bows for birthday packages. How much ribbon should she use for each bow if she wants to use the same length of ribbon for each?

When the $5\frac{1}{4}$ is thought of as fractional parts, there are 21 fourths to share, or 7 fourths for each ribbon. Alternatively, one might think of first allotting 1 yard per bow, leaving $2\frac{1}{4}$ yards, or 9 fourths. These 9 fourths are then shared, 3 fourths per bow, for a total of $1\frac{3}{4}$ yards for each bow. The unit parts required no further partitioning in order to do the division. In the following problem, the parts must be split into smaller parts.

Mark has $1\frac{1}{4}$ hours to finish his three household chores. If he divides his time evenly, how many hours can he give to each chore?

Notice that the question is "How many hours for one chore?" which considers the unit. The five-fourths of an hour that Mark has does not split neatly into three parts. So some or all of the parts must be partitioned. Figure 13.13 shows how to model these with each type of model (area, lengths, and set). In each case, all of the fourths are partitioned into three equal parts, producing twelfths. There are a total of 15 twelfths, or $\frac{5}{12}$ hour for each chore. (Test this answer against the solution in minutes: $1\frac{1}{4}$ hours is 75 minutes, which divided among 3 chores is 25 minutes per chore.) See **Expanded Lesson: Division of Fraction Stories** for a complete lesson using Cassie and Mark's stories.

Whole Numbers Divided by Fractions

This problem type lends to a measurement interpretation (also called *repeated subtraction* or *equal groups*). In these situations, an equal group is taken away from the total repeatedly. For example, if you have 13 quarts of lemonade, how many canteens holding $\frac{1}{3}$ quart each can you fill? Notice that this is not a sharing situation but rather an equal subtraction situation. In this case, the question we ask is "How many thirds are in 13?"

The measurement interpretation is a good way to explore division by a fraction because students can draw illustrations to show the measures (Cramer et al., 2010). And the measurement interpretation will be used to develop an algorithm for dividing fractions, so it is important for students to explore this idea in contextual situations. A good context for a measurement interpretation is counting servings of a particular size.

Notice that the first prompt in Activity 13.8 asks students to compare the impact of unit fraction divisors and then discuss *why* you get more servings when you have smaller fractions as divisors. This helps build the inverse relationship between multiplication and division and

Figure 13.13

Three models of partition division with a whole-number divisor.

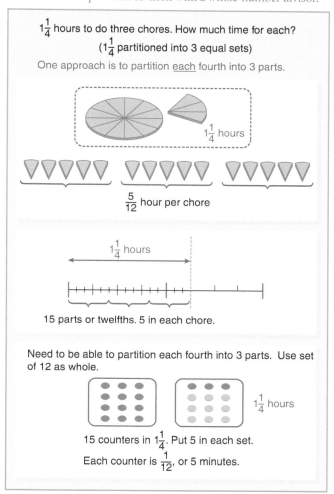

Activity 13.8

CCSS-M: 5.NF.B.7b, c

Sandwich Servings

Super Sub Sandwiches is starting a catering business. A child's serving is $\frac{1}{6}$ of a Super Sub and an adult serving can be either $\frac{1}{3}$ (for a small serving) or $\frac{1}{2}$ (for a medium serving) of a Super Sub. The employees must quickly decide the number of subs for an event based on serving size. See if you can make a decision without computing.

1. Which portion size serves the most people from one Super Sub—child size $\frac{1}{6}$, small $\frac{1}{3}$, or medium $\frac{1}{2}$? Why?

(continued)

$$1 \div \tfrac{1}{6} \qquad 1 \div \tfrac{1}{3} \qquad 1 \div \tfrac{1}{2}$$

2. Describe what is happening in each sandwich situation below (how many sandwiches are ordered and which serving size). Estimate: Which situation serves the most people? Explain your reasoning.

$$8 \div \tfrac{1}{3} \qquad 5 \div \tfrac{1}{2} \qquad 6 \div \tfrac{1}{6}$$

Standards for
Mathematical Practice

8 **Look for and express regularity in repeated reasoning.**

students may notice the general case: $1 \div \tfrac{1}{n} = n$ and, therefore, $a \div \tfrac{1}{n} = a \times n$ (Cavey & Kinzel, 2014). The second prompt provides the opportunity for students to test their conjectures using knowledge from the first prompt on new examples.

After students have explored unit fraction as divisors, students are ready to explore measurement situations with nonunit fraction divisors, such as in this task:

Les & Colin's Smoothies Shop has just bought a machine that blends 6 pints of smoothies for one batch. Their Smoothie Cups hold $\tfrac{3}{4}$ of a pint. How many smoothies can be served from one batch?

A visual that fits this context might be a vertical number line or bar graph, or it could be six rectangles partitioned into fourths. Students may be able to readily count the total number of fourths (24), but not be sure on how to count servings of *three*-fourths. Encourage students to use visuals and to group three of the fourths together as one serving.

A sharing or partitioning interpretation can (and should) be used in working with whole numbers divided by fractions. Remember that the focus question in sharing is "How much for one (e.g., person)?" or "How many for one?"

Fractions Divided by Fractions

Over time, using various contexts and numbers that vary in difficulty, students will be able to take on problems that are more complex both in the context and in the numbers involved. Using the measurement concept of serving size, Gregg and Gregg (2007) use a cookie serving size of $\tfrac{1}{2}$ to bridge from a whole number divided by a fraction to a fraction divided by a fraction. Examples of how you might develop this in a logical sequence are illustrated in Figure 13.14.

As you will note, students build on their whole-number understandings to move to more complex tasks such as the following problem:

Farmer Brown found that he had $2\tfrac{1}{4}$ gallons of liquid fertilizer concentrate. It takes $\tfrac{3}{4}$ gallon to make one tank of mixed fertilizer. How many tankfuls can he mix?

Teaching Tip

Always emphasize units with students as it is easy to forget what whole (unit) the fraction describes.

Try solving this problem yourself. Use any model or drawing you wish to help explain what you are doing. Notice that you are trying to find out how many sets of three-fourths are in a set of nine-fourths. Your answer should be three tankfuls (not three-fourths).

Many problems are not going to result in a whole number answer and it becomes very important to make sense of what is left over or the remainder. If Cassie has 5 yards of ribbon to make bows and each bow needs $1\frac{1}{6}$ yards, she can make only four bows because a part of a bow does not make sense. But if Farmer Brown begins with 4 gallons of concentrate, after making five tanks of mix, he will have used $\frac{15}{4}$, or $3\frac{3}{4}$, gallons of the concentrate. With the $\frac{1}{4}$ gallon remaining, he can make a partial tank of mix. He can make $\frac{1}{3}$ tank of mix because it takes 3 fourths to make a whole, and he has 1 fourth of a gallon (he has one of the three parts he needs for a tank).

As numbers increase in difficulty, students will begin to change all of the numbers to the same fractional unit. That is, both the dividend or given quantity and the divisor are expressed in the same type of fractional parts. This, in essence, results in a whole-number division problem, as you will find when we discuss the common denominator algorithm later.

Estimating and Invented Strategies

Use estimation to support understanding of division of fractions. Because the problem $12 \div 4$. means "How many fours in 12?" Similarly, $12 \div \frac{1}{4}$ means "How many fourths in 12?" There are 48 fourths in 12. With this basic idea in mind, students should be able to estimate problems like $4\frac{1}{3} \div \frac{1}{2}$. Ask students to first use words to describe what these equations are asking (e.g., "How many halves in $4\frac{1}{3}$?"). This can help them think about the meaning of division and then develop a reasonable estimate.

Figure 13.14

Tasks that use the measurement interpretation of "How many servings?" to develop the concept of division of fractions.

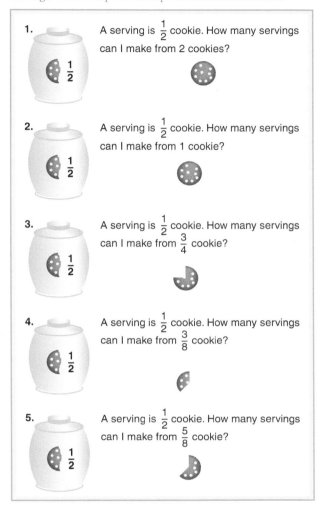

Source: Gregg, J., & Gregg, D. U. (2007). Measurement and fair-sharing models for dividing fractions. *Mathematics Teaching in the Middle School, 12*(9), p. 491. Reprinted with permission. Copyright © 2007 by the National Council of Teachers of Mathematics. All rights reserved.

Activity 13.9

CCSS-M: 5.NF.B.7a, b, c; 6.NS.A.1

The Size Is Right: Division

  Start with either fractions divided by whole numbers OR whole numbers divided by fractions, but then mix up the tasks. Flash for a few seconds and then cover or remove one of the Size Is Right Division Cards. Ask students to pick one of the options from the Dashboard Activity Page. Then invite students to pair-compare their selections and decide if they are reasonable.

Fractions divided by whole numbers

| Less than $\frac{1}{8}$ | Less than $\frac{1}{4}$ | Less than $\frac{1}{2}$ | Less than 1 | More than 1 | More than 2 |

Examples:

$\frac{1}{2} \div 3$ $\qquad$ $\frac{5}{6} \div 2$ $\qquad$ $\frac{7}{9} \div 3$ $\qquad$ $\frac{9}{2} \div 3$ $\qquad$ $\frac{15}{4} \div 3$

Whole numbers divided by fractions

Dashboard:

| Less than 1 | More than 1 | More than 2 | More than 4 | More than 8 |

Examples:

$3 \div \frac{1}{3}$ $1 \div \frac{2}{3}$ $2 \div \frac{1}{3}$ $4 \div \frac{7}{8}$ $4 \div \frac{3}{8}$

For English language learners, provide sentence starters to support opportunities for discussion: "I think the answer is [dashboard choice] because . . . " For students with disabilities or students who benefit from visuals, have tools available such as Cuisenaire Rods or fraction circles so that they can more readily see the relative size of each fraction.

Developing the Algorithms

There are two different algorithms for division of fractions. Methods of teaching both algorithms are discussed here.

The Common-Denominator Algorithm. The common-denominator algorithm relies on the measurement or repeated subtraction concept of division. Additionally, it links to what students have already learned in adding and subtracting fractions with common denominators and is aligned with whole-number division ($25 \div 5$ is how many groups of 5 are in 25?). "The concept of unit plays a central role in this measurement scenario" (Barnett-Clarke et al., 2010, p. 53).

Start by using problems such as $4 \div \frac{2}{3}$. If you use fraction circles (or mentally imagine the circles) you can trade the 4 wholes into thirds. Then using the measurement approach find how many groups of $\frac{2}{3}$ are in $\frac{12}{3}$. There are 6.

Continue with problems without remainders, such as $1\frac{3}{4} \div \frac{1}{8}$ and try a length model. Look at Figure 13.15 to see a student's use of an empty number line to think about this problem. First, the student labels the number line in fourths and then makes jumps in eighths to count out the number of groups.

After trying other problems like this one, you can transition to problems with remainders, such as the following problem that includes a remainder (see Figure 13.16):

Figure 13.15

A student uses a number line to think about division of fractions.

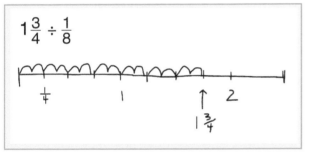

Rory has $\frac{5}{3}$ of a pound of fudge. If she wants to cut the candy into $\frac{1}{2}$-pound pieces for her friends, how many friends will get a piece of fudge?

Standards for
Mathematical Practice

7 Look for and make use of structure. ▶

Cramer and colleagues (2010) discuss the importance of estimation, which also helps support thinking about remainders. They suggest questions such as, "Do you think you will have 2 servings of fudge? Could you have 4 servings?" They also highlight the need to carefully identify the unit; otherwise meaning is lost in interpreting the remainder.

As shown in Figure 13.16, once each number is expressed in terms of the same fractional part, the answer is the same as the whole-number problem $10 \div 3$. Then the problem becomes one of dividing the numerators—but let students notice this pattern. As students begin to observe patterns, connect that discussion to the common denominator algorithm. The resulting algorithm, therefore, is as follows: *To divide fractions, first identify common denominators, and then divide numerators.* For example, if the same amount of fudge would be divided into fourths of a pound, $\frac{5}{3} \div \frac{1}{4} = \frac{20}{12} \div \frac{3}{12} = 20 \div 3 = \frac{20}{3} = 5\frac{2}{3}$.

✎ Teaching Tip

Always discuss what the remainder means. In this case, students should be able to state that the remainder represents a portion of another serving of fudge (not a portion of the whole).

Invert-and-Multiply Algorithm. To invert the divisor and multiply may be one of the most commonly taught, but poorly understood, mathematical procedures in the elementary curriculum. (Were you taught why invert-and-multiply works?)

In an effort to help students see patterns that link to the algorithm, start with a unit fraction as a divisor.

$3 \div \frac{1}{2} =$ (How many servings of $\frac{1}{2}$ in 3 containers?)

$5 \div \frac{1}{4} =$ (How many servings of $\frac{1}{4}$ in 5 containers?)

$3\frac{3}{4} \div \frac{1}{8} =$ (How many servings of $\frac{1}{8}$ in $3\frac{3}{4}$ containers?)

Standards for
Mathematical Practice

8 Look for and
express regularity in
repeated reasoning.

In looking across a collection of these problems, students will notice they are multiplying by the denominator of the second fraction. For example, in the first example, a student might say, "You get two for every whole container, so 2×3 equals 6."

Then move to similar problems, but with a second fraction that is not a unit fraction:

$$8 \div \frac{2}{5} =$$

$$3\frac{3}{4} \div \frac{3}{8} =$$

Have students solve these problems and compare these responses to the problems in the first set. For example, in the first problem, think first of "per unit"—in this case, the unit fraction. Only after identifying that amount should you go back to consider the actual divisor. So, if there are 40 one-fifths in 8, then when you group the fifths in pairs (two-fifths), you will have half as many—20. Stated in servings, if the serving is twice as big, you will have half the number of servings. Similarly, if the divisor is $\frac{3}{4}$, after finding how many fourths, you will group in threes, which means you will get $\frac{1}{3}$ of the number of servings. You can see that this means you must divide by 3 or multiply by $\frac{1}{3}$. This gets at the heart of the definition of division as having an inverse relationship with multiplication; therefore, dividing by a number is equivalent to multiplying by the reciprocal. (Sound familiar?)

Partitioning or sharing examples effectively illustrate the standard algorithm. Consider this example:

You have $1\frac{1}{2}$ oranges, which equals $\frac{3}{5}$ of an adult serving.
How many oranges (and parts of oranges) make up 1 adult
serving? (Kribs-Zaleta, 2008)

You may be thinking that because you know that $1\frac{1}{2}$ oranges equals $\frac{3}{5}$ of a serving, you first need to find what a fifth would be. Logically, that would be one-third of the oranges you have, or $\frac{1}{2}$ an orange (notice you are dividing by the numerator). Then, to get the whole serving, you multiply $\frac{1}{2}$ by 5 (the denominator) to find that there are $2\frac{1}{2}$ oranges in 1 adult serving.

In either measurement or partition interpretations of division, the denominator leads you to find out how many fourths, fifths, or eighths you have, and the numerator tells you the size of the serving, so you group according to how many are in the serving. So the process is *multiply by the denominator and divide by the numerator*. This represents the reasoning behind the well-known

Figure 13.16

Models for the common- denominator method for fraction division.

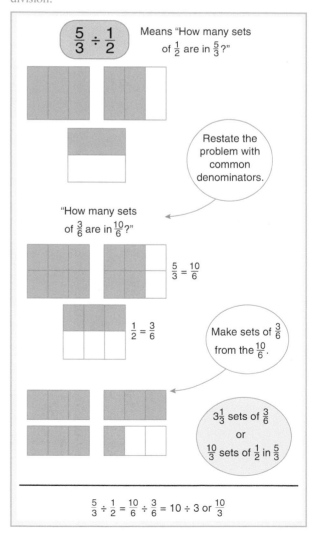

"invert and multiply" algorithm. However, the fraction doesn't need to be inverted; instead just multiply by the denominator and divide by the numerator.

Addressing Common Errors and Misconceptions

The biggest misunderstanding with division of fractions is just not knowing what the algorithm means. Within division of fractions there are some common errors and misconceptions that you need to help students avoid.

Teaching Tip

One way to help students address the misconception that "division always makes smaller" is to ask students to estimate first to help think about a reasonable answer.

Thinking the Answer Should Be Smaller. Based on their experiences with whole-number division, students may think that when dividing by a fraction, the answer should be smaller. For example, Petit, Laird, and Mardsen (2010) describe a student who rules out whole-number answers in a multiple choice for $\frac{1}{2} \div \frac{1}{4}$ because they are "bigger numbers" (p. 164). Although the answers to division with fractions can be smaller if the divisor is a fraction greater than one (e.g., $\frac{5}{3}$), that is not true if the fraction is less than one.

Connecting the Representation with the Answer. Students may understand that $1\frac{1}{2} \div \frac{1}{4}$ means "How many fourths are in $1\frac{1}{2}$?" So they may set out to count how many fourths and get 6. But in recording their answer, they can get confused as to what the 6 refers to and think the answer should be a fraction and thus record it as $\frac{6}{4}$ (Cramer et al., 2010).

Knowing What the Unit Is. Students might get an answer such as $\frac{3}{8}$, but when you say "$\frac{3}{8}$ of what?" they just don't know. To make sense of division, students must know what the unit is. Errors occur less frequently when units (e.g., servings, feet, or quesadillas) are emphasized (Dixon & Tobias, 2013).

Writing Remainders. Knowing what the unit is (the divisor) is critical and must be understood in interpreting the remainder (Cramer et al., 2010; Lamon, 2012; Sharp & Welder, 2014). In the problem $3\frac{3}{8} \div \frac{1}{4}$, students are likely to count 4 fourths for each whole (12 fourths) and one more fourth for $\frac{2}{8}$ but then not know what to do with the remaining eighth. It is important to be sure they understand the measurement concept of division. Ask, "How much of the next piece do you have?" Context can also help—in particular, servings. In this case, if the problem were about pizza servings, there would be 13 full servings and $\frac{1}{2}$ of the next serving.

Another issue with remainders is that students may mistakenly use the original unit (how the whole was divided) instead of using the denominator of the divisor to name the remainder. So, in the case of this last problem with one-eighth as a remaining piece (half of another serving), students might say $\frac{1}{8}$ is the remainder, using the thinking that it must be labeled in terms of the whole. The focus on understanding and stating the unit is critical (Flores & Priewe, 2013/2014; Philipp & Hawthorne, 2015).

Surprisingly, only about 5 percent of mistakes made in fraction computation problems by upper elementary students involve miscalculations (errors in basic fact computations) (Hecht, Vagi, & Torgesen, 2007). Instead, most errors are based on misconceptions and naïve understandings about the size of fractions and how fraction computations must be adapted from whole-number algorithms. Building the "fraction sense" and "fraction operation sense" (Johanning, 2011) that underpins students' thinking is worth the time you spend on these important foundations. Son and Senk (2010) estimate that Korean mathematics curriculum provides five times as many lessons on division of fractions as the United States. We need to provide numerous opportunities for students to experience these ideas using multiple models.

14

Developing Decimal and Percent Concepts and Decimal Computation

BIG IDEAS

1 The base-ten place-value system extends infinitely in two directions: to very small values and to very large values. Between any two place values, the 10-to-1 ratio remains the same.

2 Decimals (also called *decimal fractions*) are a way of writing fractions within the base-ten system (denominators of 10, 100, and so on).

3 The decimal point is a convention that has been developed to indicate the units position. The position to the left of the decimal point marks the location of the units place.

4 Addition and subtraction with decimals are based on the fundamental concept of adding and subtracting the numbers in like position values—an extension from whole numbers.

5 Multiplication and division of two numbers will produce the same digits, regardless of the positions of the decimal point. As a result, multiplicative computations with decimal fractions can be performed as whole numbers with the decimal placed by way of estimation and the identification of patterns.

6 Percents are simply hundredths, and as such are a third way of writing both fractions and decimals.

People need to be able to interpret decimals for such varied needs as reading precise metric measures, calculating distances, interpreting output on a calculator, and understanding sports statistics such as those at the Olympics for which winners and losers are separated by hundredths of a second. Decimals are critically important in many occupations: For nurses, pharmacists, and workers building airplanes, for example, the level of precision affects the safety of the general public. Because students and teachers have been shown to have a greater difficulty understanding decimals than fractions (Martinie, 2007; Stacey et al., 2001; Lortie-Forgues, Tian, & Siegler, 2014; Vamvakoussi, Van Dooren, & Verschaffel, 2012), conceptual understanding of decimals and their connections to fractions must be carefully developed. There is a strong relationship between teachers' content knowledge of decimals, including computation with decimals, and their pedagogical knowledge of the ways to teach these ideas to students (Depaepe et al., 2015)— they go hand in hand.

Developing Concepts of Decimals

In the *Common Core State Standards*, students in fourth grade should "understand decimal notation [to hundredths] for fractions and compare decimal fractions" (CCSSO, 2010, p. 31). In the fifth grade the document highlights one of the critical areas as perform operations with decimals (to hundredths), expand comparisons of decimals to thousandths and round decimals. In the sixth grade, students will extend this work with tenths and hundredths to all decimals, as they develop standard algorithms for all four operations. In the seventh grade, they will develop a "unified understanding of number" (CCSSO, 2010, p. 46) so as to be able to move fluently between decimals, fractions, and percents.

Fractions with denominators of 10, 100, 1000, and so on will be referred to as *decimal fractions*. Fractions such as $\frac{7}{10}$ or $\frac{63}{100}$ can also be written as 0.7 and 0.63 and are examples of decimal fractions. The phrase *decimal fractions* is often shortened to *decimals*, and in this chapter we will use these terms interchangeably.

Explicitly linking the ideas of fractions to decimals can be extremely useful, both from a pedagogical view as well as a practical view. Much of this chapter focuses on that connection.

Extending the Place-Value System

Before exploring decimal numerals with students, it is advisable to review ideas of whole-number place value. One of the most basic of these ideas is the 10-to-1 multiplicative relationship between the values of any two adjacent positions. In terms of a base-ten model, such as paper strips and squares, 10 of any one piece will make 1 of the next larger (to the immediate left), and movement of a piece to the immediate right involves division by 10 (1 divided by 10 is one-tenth).

The 10-to-1 Relationship—Now in Two Directions!

As you learned with the study of place value, the 10-makes-1 relationship continues indefinitely to larger and larger pieces or positional values. If you are using the paper strip-and-square base-ten models, for example, the strip and square shapes alternate in an infinite progression as they get larger. Likewise, each piece to the right in this continuum gets smaller by one-tenth. The critical question becomes, "Is there ever a smallest piece?" In the students' prior experience, the smallest piece is the centimeter square or unit piece. But couldn't that piece be divided into 10 small strips? And couldn't those small strips be divided into 10 very small squares, and so on?

The goal of this discussion is to help students see that a 10-to-1 relationship can extend infinitely in two directions. There is no smallest piece and no largest piece. The symmetry of the system is around the ones place (tens to the left of the ones place, tenths to the right, and so on)—not the common misconception that it is symmetrical around the decimal point. The relationship between adjacent pieces is the same regardless of which two adjacent pieces are being considered. Figure 14.1 illustrates this idea.

Figure 14.1

Theoretically, the strips and squares extend infinitely in both directions.

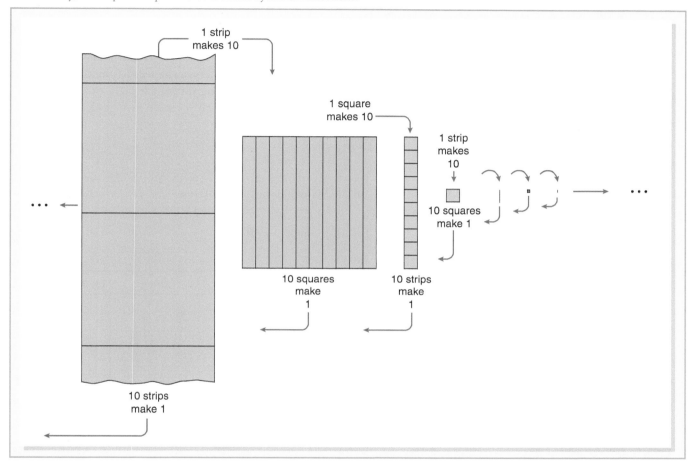

Regrouping

Even at this stage, students need to be reminded of the powerful concept of regrouping. Flexible thinking about place values should be practiced prior to exploring decimals. Having students revisit not only making one 10 from ten units (transforming a smaller unit to a larger unit), but thinking about regrouping 2,451 into 24 hundreds, 5 tens, and 1 unit; or 245 tens and 1 unit; or 2,451 units (transforming a larger unit to a smaller unit). As you can see, this process of reunitizing decimals will be essential in thinking about 0.6 as 6 tenths, as well as 60 hundredths and so on.

The Role of the Decimal Point

Students must know that the decimal point marks the location of the ones (or units) place. That is why on a calculator, when there is a whole number answer, no decimal point appears. Only when the ones place needs to be identified will the decimal point show in the display. Students also need to see that adding zeros to the left of a whole number will have no consequence and adding zeros to the right of a decimal fraction will not change the number.

🎵 *Teaching Tip*

The decimal notation of a 0 in the ones place, such as 0.60, is the accepted way to write decimal fractions less than 1. This is a convention and a way to indicate that there are no units in the number.

Standards for
Mathematical Practice

6 Attend to precision. ▶

An important idea to be realized is that there is no built-in reason why any one position (or base-ten piece) should be chosen to be the unit or ones position. In terms of strips and squares, for example, which piece is the unit piece? The small centimeter square? Why? Why not a larger or a smaller square? Why not a strip? *Any piece of the base ten materials could effectively be chosen as the unit piece.* As shown in Figure 14.2, a given quantity can be written in different ways, depending on the choice of the unit or what piece is used to count the entire collection.

The decimal point is placed between two positions with the convention that the position to the left of the decimal is the units or ones position. Thus, the role of the decimal point is to designate the units position, and it does so by sitting just to the right of that position. A reminder to help students think about the decimal point is shown in Figure 14.3 with the "eyes" focusing up at the name of the units or ones.

Figure 14.2

The decimal point indicates which position is the units.

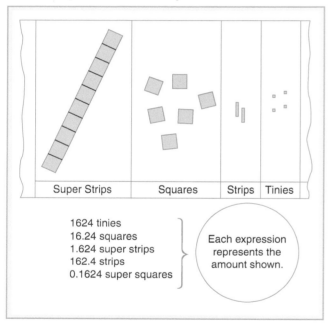

1624 tinies
16.24 squares
1.624 super strips
162.4 strips
0.1624 super squares

Each expression represents the amount shown.

Figure 14.3

The decimal point always "looks up at" the name of the units position. In this case, we have 16.24.

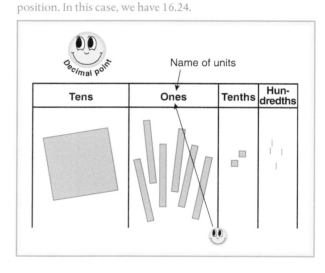

Activity 14.1 illustrates the convention that the decimal indicates the named unit and that the unit can change without changing the quantity.

The Decimal Point Names the Unit

CCSS-M: 4.NF.C.6; 5.NBT.A.3a

Have students display a certain number of base-ten pieces on their desks. For example, put out six squares, two strips, and four tinies, as in Figure 14.2. For this activity, refer to the pieces as *squares, strips,* and *tinies,* and reach an agreement on names for the theoretical pieces both smaller and larger. To the right of tinies can be *tiny strips* and then *tiny squares*. To the left of squares can be *super strips* and *super squares*. For ELLs and students with disabilities, it is particularly important that you write these labels with the corresponding visuals in a prominent place in the classroom (and in student notebooks), so they can refer to this terminology as they participate in the activity. Each student should also have a "smiling" decimal point. Now ask students to write and say how many squares they have, how many super strips, and so on. The students position their decimal point accordingly and both write and say the amounts.

Measurement and Monetary Units. The notion that the decimal identifies the units place is useful in a variety of contexts. For example, in the metric system, seven place values have special names. As shown in Figure 14.4, the decimal point can be used to designate any of these places as the unit without changing the actual measure. The *Common Core State Standards* Mathematical Practice "Attend to Precision" state, "Mathematically proficient students express numerical answers with a degree of precision appropriate for the problem context" (CCSSO, 2010, p. 7). Consider the two measurements 0.06 and 0.060. They are equivalent in terms of numerical value, but the latter communicates a greater level of precision. By adding the additional zero, it signals that the measurement was done to the nearest thousandth and that there were 60 thousandths. In the first case, the measurement was completed only to the nearest hundredth so it might have been 0.058 or 0.063 but not necessarily exactly 0.060.

Standards for
Mathematical Practice

◄ **6** Attend to precision.

Figure 14.4

In the metric system, each place-value position has a name. The decimal point can be placed to designate which length is the unit length. Any of the metric positions can be the unit length, as illustrated here.

	kilometer	hectometer	dekameter	meter	decimeter	centimeter	millimeter	
				3	8	5		

3 meters, 8 decimeters,
and 5 centimeters =

3.85 meters
3850 millimeters
0.00385 kilometers
385 centimeters

Unit names

Our monetary system is also a decimal system. In the amount $172.95, the decimal point designates the dollars position as the unit. There are 1 hundred (dollars), 7 tens, 2 singles, 9 dimes (one-tenth of a dollar), and 5 pennies (one-hundredth of a dollar) in this amount of money, regardless of how it is written. If pennies were the designated unit, the same amount would be written as 17,295 cents or 17,295.0 cents. It could just as correctly be 0.17295 thousands of dollars or 1729.5 dimes.

Teaching Tip

Note that it is incorrect to write .50¢, as that would indicate $\frac{1}{2}$ of a cent! Instead write $0.50 or 50¢.

In the case of measures such as metric lengths or weights or the U.S. monetary system, the name of the unit is written after the number rather than above the digit as on a place-value chart. In the newspaper, we may read about Congress spending $7.3 billion. Here the units are billions of dollars, not dollars. A city may have a population of 2.4 million people. That is the same as 2,400,000 individuals.

Connecting Fractions and Decimals

The symbols 3.75 and $3\frac{3}{4}$ represent the same quantity, yet on the surface the two appear quite different. For students, the world of fractions and the world of decimals are very distinct. Even adults tend to think of fractions as sets or areas (e.g., three-fourths of something), whereas we think of decimals as values or numbers (e.g., weight). When we tell students that 0.75 is the same as $\frac{3}{4}$, this can be especially confusing because the denominators are hidden in decimal fractions. Even though these are different ways of writing the numbers, the amounts are equal. A significant goal of instruction in decimal and fraction numeration should be to help students see that both systems represent the same concepts.

There are two important ways to help students see the connection between fractions and decimals. First, use familiar fraction concepts and models that are easily represented by decimals: tenths, hundredths, and thousandths. Then, help students use models to make meaningful translations between fractions and decimals. These components are discussed in turn.

Say Decimal Fractions Correctly

You must make sure you are reading and saying decimals in ways that support students' understanding. Always say "five and two tenths" instead of "five point two." Using the *point* terminology results in a disconnect to the fractional part that exists in every decimal. This is not unlike the ill-advised reading of fractions as "two over ten" instead of correctly saying "two-tenths." This level of precision in language will provide your students with the opportunity to *hear* the connections between decimals and fractions, so that when they hear "two-tenths," they think of both 0.2 and $\frac{2}{10}$.

Highlight the "ths" at the end of the words as both you and the students talk about decimal fractions. Exaggerate the "ths" in your pronunciations, as initially students are not accustomed to the small differences in such word as tens and tenths.

Standards for
Mathematical Practice

6 Attend to precision. ▶

Use Visual Models for Decimal Fractions

Many previously used fraction manipulatives do not lend themselves to depicting decimal fractions because they cannot show hundredths or thousandths. And research suggests that the connection of decimal numbers to pictorial representations can be challenging (Cramer et al., 2009). Provide models for decimal fractions using the same conceptual approaches that were used previously for fractions—that using multiple representations will help address misunderstandings (Cramer, 2003).

Area Models

Three area models that can be used as representations of decimal fractions are base-ten materials, a rational number wheel and a square 10 × 10 grid.

The base-ten materials have been mentioned previously, but explicitly link them to the decimal number using the **Building Decimal-Number Cards**. Place the correct card under each amount of base-ten materials, for example, tenths, hundredths, and so on, so that students can see how the decimal number is built (make sure you left justify the cards).

A digital version of "Base Blocks—Decimals" is available at the National Library of Virtual Manipulative's website. These blocks can be placed on a place-value chart to represent decimals so that you can designate any of the four blocks as the unit. Later, when students work on decimal computation with addition and subtraction, problems can be created or generated randomly.

Because students may be accustomed to a particular piece being used as the unit (e.g., the small square or cube being 1), they can benefit from activities in which the unit changes, such as Activity 14.2. Remember to call the pieces by their place value name (e.g., hundredths) rather than by their shape (e.g., rod or strip) to reinforce the precise language and the value of the materials.

♩ *Teaching Tip*

Note that some students may be confused by the switch from the values of the base-ten blocks from what they have used for years. Another approach is to switch to paper models from the blocks to help them "rethink" the values of the materials as decimals.

▶ Activity 14.2

CCSS-M: 4.NF.C.6; 5.NBT.A.1; 5.NBT.A.3a

Shifting Units

Give students a collection of paper Base-Ten Materials or base-ten blocks. Ask them to pull out a particular mix; for example, a student might have three squares, seven strips, and four "tinies." Tell students that you have the unit hidden behind your back; when you show it to them, they are to figure out how much they have and to record the value. Hold up one of the units, like the strip. Observe what students record as their value. Ask students to accurately say their quantity aloud. For ELLs and students with disabilities, write labels with the visuals for reference. Repeat several times. Be sure to include examples in which a piece is not represented so that students will understand decimal values like 3.07. Continue playing in partners with one student selecting a mix of base-ten pieces and the other student deciding on the unit and writing and saying the number.

Each circular disk in the **Rational Number Wheel** (see Figure 14.5) is marked with 100 equal intervals around the edge and is cut along one radius. Two disks of different colors, slipped together as shown, can be used to model any fraction less than one. Fractions modeled on this rational number wheel can be read as decimal fractions by noting the spaces around the circumference, but can also be stated as fractions (e.g., $\frac{3}{4}$) helping students further make the connection between fractions and decimals.

The most common area model and the one that research shows provides strong visual images for decimal fractions is a **10×10 grid** (see Figure 14.6) (Cramer et al., 2015; Wyberg, Whitney, Cramer, Monson, & Leavitt, 2011). Another variation is to use base-ten place-value strips and squares. Base-ten blocks are often used for this with a shift in units. Now the 10-cm square that was used as the "hundreds" model for whole numbers is representing the whole or 1. Each ten rod (strip) is then one-tenth, and each small cube (square) (now referred to as a *tiny*) is one-hundredth. With base-ten blocks, the thousands

Figure 14.5

A rational number wheel. For example, rotate the disks to show $\frac{25}{100}$ of the blue plate (also $\frac{1}{4}$ of the circle).

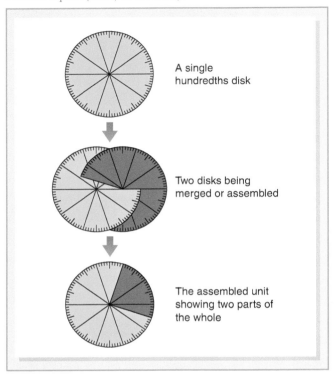

A single
hundredths disk

Two disks being
merged or assembled

The assembled unit
showing two parts of
the whole

Figure 14.6

These 10×10 grids and base-ten materials model tenths and hundredths.

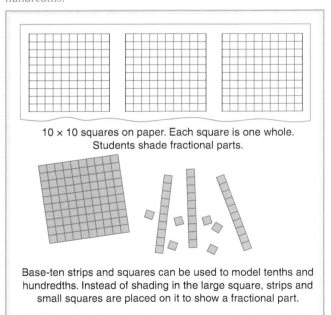

10 × 10 squares on paper. Each square is one whole.
Students shade fractional parts.

Base-ten strips and squares can be used to model tenths and
hundredths. Instead of shading in the large square, strips and
small squares are placed on it to show a fractional part.

block can also represent the whole, and consequently the flats (squares) are then tenths, the rods hundredths, and small cubes thousandths. The **10,000 Grid Paper**, provides a large square that is subdivided into 10,000 tiny squares. Students can identify how many squares are needed for 0.1, 0.01, 0.001, and 0.0001, using appropriate names for the values. Notice that any one of the base-ten pieces can be assigned the value of 1, and that affects the values of the other pieces.

▶ Activity 14.3

CCSS-M: 4.NF.C.5; 4.NF.C.6; 5.NBT.A.1; 5.NBT.A.3a

Decimal Roll and Cover

Give pairs of students a 10×10 grid and a die with faces marked with $\frac{1}{10}, \frac{1}{100}, \frac{5}{100}, \frac{1}{1000}, \frac{5}{1000}, \frac{10}{1000}$, or 0.1, 0.01, 0.05, 0.001, 0.005, and 0.010 (or a combination of fractions and decimals. One student rolls the die and uses a marker to shade the amount on the 10×10 grid. If one tenth is rolled on the die it is marked by shading a whole column of ten small squares on the grid. Each hundredth rolled results in one small square getting shaded and each thousandth rolled requires that a small square be first divided into half and then five more divisions made in the other direction to create ten small equal-sized pieces. Students will eventually note that the $\frac{10}{1000}$ is equivalent to $\frac{1}{100}$. If your students are only working on tenths and hundredths, adjust the faces of the die to reflect appropriate amounts. Together the team should try to cover the whole or 1. This will give them a very dramatic experience with the difference in size of each of these decimal fractions.

Length Models

One of the best length models for decimal fractions is a meter stick. Each decimeter is one-tenth of the whole stick, each centimeter is one-hundredth, and each millimeter is one-thousandth. Any number-line model broken into 100 subparts is likewise a useful model for hundredths.

Empty number lines like those used with whole-number computation are also useful in helping students compare decimals and think about scale and place value (Martinie, 2014). Given two or more decimals, students can use number lines to position the values, revealing what they know about the magnitude of these decimals by using zero, one, other whole numbers, or other decimal values as benchmarks. The number line can effectively uncover students' grasp of the size of decimal values—which summarizes an important unifying principle across whole and rational numbers—that they can be put into order from least to greatest by their magnitude (Durkin & Rittle-Johnson, 2015; Siegler, Thompson, & Schneider, 2011).

Set Models

Many teachers use money as a model for decimals, and to some extent this is helpful. However, for students, money is almost exclusively a two-place decimal system and the physical models are nonproportional (e.g., one-tenth, a dime, does not physically compare to a dollar in that proportion). Numbers like 3.2 or 12.1389 do not relate to money and can cause confusion (Martinie, 2007). Students' initial contact with decimals should be more flexible, so money is not recommended as an initial model for decimals, although it is certainly an important *application* of decimal numeration.

Multiple Names and Formats

We acquaint students with the visual models to help them flexibly think of quantities in terms of tenths and hundredths, and to learn to read and write decimal fractions in different ways. Have students model a fraction, say $\frac{65}{100}$, and then explore the following ideas:

- Is this fraction more or less than $\frac{1}{2}$? Than $\frac{2}{3}$? Than $\frac{3}{4}$? Some familiarity with decimal fractions can be developed by comparison with fractions that are easy to think about.
- What are some different ways to say this fraction using tenths and hundredths? ("6 tenths and 5 hundredths" or "65 hundredths") Include thousandths when appropriate.
- Show two ways to write this fraction ($\frac{65}{100}$ or $\frac{6}{10} + \frac{5}{100}$).

Note that decimals are usually read as a single value. That is, 0.65 is read "sixty-five hundredths." But to understand them in terms of place value, the same number should be decomposed into their place value components—6 tenths and 5 hundredths. A mixed number such as $5\frac{13}{100}$ is usually read the same way as a decimal: 5.13 is "five and thirteen-hundredths." For purposes of place value, it should also be decomposed as $5 + \frac{1}{10} + \frac{3}{100}$.

Turn this into a task by asking students to write the number that has *3 tenths, 6 hundredths and 7 ones*. This will assess students' grasp of decimal place value or whether they become confused by the common left-to-right order in which numbers are written. Making these expanded forms with base-ten materials will be helpful in translating fractions to decimals, which is the focus of Activity 14.4.

Teaching Tip

Please note that it is accurate to use the word *and* when reading the decimal, which represents the decimal point.

Activity 14.4   CCSS-M: 4.NF.C.6; 5.NBT.A.1

Build It, Name It

For this activity, have students use paper Base-Ten Materials. Agree that the large square represents one. Have students cover a decimal fractional amount of the square using their strips and tinies (remember to call the pieces "tenths" and "hundredths"). For example, have them cover $2\frac{35}{100}$ of the square. Whole numbers will require additional squares. The task is to decide how to write and say this fraction as a decimal and demonstrate this connection using their physical models. For students with disabilities, you may want to have the amount shaded rather than have the students try to cover the exact amount, and then ask them to name and write the decimal fraction.

In this last activity, a reason why $2\frac{35}{100}$ is the same as 2.35 is that there are 2 wholes, 3 tenths, and 5 hundredths. It is important to see this physically. The same materials that are used to represent $2\frac{35}{100}$ of the square can be rearranged or placed on a place-value chart with a paper decimal point used to designate the units position as shown in Figure 14.7.

The calculator can also play a significant role in developing decimal concepts.

Activity 14.5   CCSS-M: 4.NF.C.6; 5.NBT.A.1

Calculator Decimal Counting

Recall how to make the calculator "count" by pressing ⊞ 1 ⊜ ⊜ and so on. Now have students press ⊞ 0.1 ⊜ ⊜ and so on. When the display shows 0.9, stop and discuss what this means and what the display will look like with the next count. Many students will reveal a common misconception by predicting 0.10 (thinking that 10 comes after 9). This prediction is even more interesting if, with each press, the students have been accumulating base-ten materials as models for tenths. One more press would mean one more tenth, or 10 tenths. Why doesn't the calculator show 0.10? When the tenth press produces a display of 1 (calculators are not usually set to display trailing zeros to the right of the decimal), the discussion should revolve around trading 10 tenths for one whole. Continue to count to 4 or 5 by tenths.

How many presses to get from one whole number to the next? For students with disabilities and for ELLs, counting out loud along with the calculator "one tenth, two tenths . . ." supports the concept (e.g., ten-tenths being the same as one whole) while reinforcing appropriate mathematical language. Students may need to be reminded that a place is "full" when it has 9 of any unit and the addition of another unit will push to the position that is one place to the left (like the mileage in a car). Once students are working well with tenths, try counting by 0.01 or by 0.001. These counts illustrate dramatically how small one-hundredth and one-thousandth really are. It requires 10 counts by 0.001 to get to 0.01 and 1000 counts to reach 1.

Calculators that permit entry of fractions also have a fraction–decimal conversion key making them valuable tools for connecting fraction and decimal symbolism. Some calculators will convert a decimal such as 0.25 to the fraction $\frac{25}{100}$ and allow for either manual or automatic simplification. But, challenge students to explain why 0.25 and $\frac{25}{100}$ are equivalent and not simply rely on the calculator to do the conversion.

Figure 14.7

Translation of a fraction to a decimal using physical models.

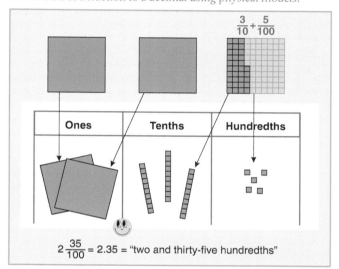

$2\frac{35}{100} = 2.35 =$ "two and thirty-five hundredths"

Developing Decimal Number Sense

So far, the discussion has largely focused on the connection of decimals to fractions with denominators related to 10 and 100. Number sense with decimals implies more—having intuition about, or a flexible understanding of, decimal numbers. To this end, it is useful to connect decimals to the fractions with which students are familiar, to be able to compare and order decimals, and to approximate decimals using benchmarks.

Results of NAEP exams reveal that students have difficulties with the fraction–decimal relationship. In 2004, fewer than 30 percent of high school students were able to translate 0.029 as $\frac{29}{1000}$ (Kloosterman, 2010). In 2009, Shaughnessy found that more than 46 percent of the sixth graders she studied could not write $\frac{3}{5}$ as a decimal. Instead, many wrote $\frac{3}{5}$ as 3.5, 0.35 or 0.3. She also found that more than 25 percent could not write $\frac{3}{10}$ as a decimal. This misconception was also reversed when students wrote the decimal 4.5 as the fraction $\frac{4}{5}$. Division of the numerator by the denominator may be a means of converting fractions to decimals, but it contributes little to understanding the resulting equivalence.

Familiar Fractions Connected to Decimals

Students should extend their conceptual familiarity with common fractions, especially halves, thirds, fourths, fifths, and eighths to the same concepts expressed as decimal fractions. One way to do this is to have students translate familiar fractions to decimals in a conceptual manner, which is the focus of the next two activities.

Activity 14.6

CCSS-M: 4.NF.C.7

Familiar Fractions to Decimals

Give students a "familiar" or commonly used fraction (e.g., $\frac{3}{5}$) to convert to a decimal. Ask students to shade the 10×10 grid to illustrate the value (or build it with **Base-Ten Materials**). Referring to their shaded grid or the base-ten pieces, ask students to write the decimal equivalent. A logical sequence is to start with halves and fifths, then fourths, and possibly eighths. Thirds are a possibility for a student who needs a challenge, as they will result in a repeating decimal. For ELLs,

(continued)

connect the word decimal to the fact that *deci-* means tens. For students with disabilities have some preshaded 10 × 10 grids with different fractions shaded and ask the student to find the grid that shows $\frac{1}{2}$. Have them skip count the squares that are shaded to identify the equivalent of $\frac{50}{100}$. Explore an Expanded Lesson: Familiar Fractions to Decimals for this activity.

Standards for
Mathematical Practice

2 Reason abstractly
and quantitatively.

Figure 14.8 shows how translations in the last activity might work with a 10 × 10 grid. For fourths, students will often shade a 5 × 5 section (half of a half). The question then becomes how to translate this to a decimal. Ask these students how they could think about each half strip as 0.05 and then use the models to reason that 2 of the half strips (0.05 + 0.05 = 0.1). Then you would have 0.1 + 0.1 + 0.05, or 0.25 is they counted shaded squares they would find $\frac{25}{100}$. This approach would start where the students' prior knowledge is and work from there toward a solution. The fraction $\frac{3}{8}$ represents a wonderful challenge. A hint might be to find $\frac{1}{4}$ first and then notice that $\frac{1}{8}$ is half of a fourth. Remember that the next smaller pieces are tenths of the tinies (or thousands). Therefore, half of a tiny is $\frac{5}{1000}$. Note how the student found that $\frac{2}{8} + \frac{1}{8} = \frac{37}{100} + \frac{5}{1000} = 0.375$.

Figure 14.8

A student uses a 10 × 10 grid to convert $\frac{3}{8}$ to a decimal.

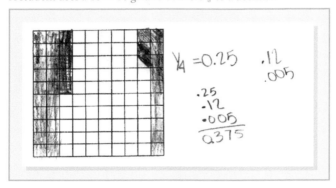

Because the circular model carries such a strong mental link to fractions, it is worth the time to do some fraction-to-decimal conversions with the rational number wheel shown in Figure 14.5 and used in the next activity.

Activity 14.7

CCSS-M: 4.NF.C.7

Estimate, Then Verify

With the blank side of the Rational Number Wheel facing them, have students adjust the wheel to show a given fraction, for example $\frac{3}{4}$ (see Figure 14.5). Next, ask students to estimate how many hundredths they think are equivalent. Then, ask students to justify how they decided their estimate and the corresponding decimal equivalent. Repeat with other fractions.

✎ Teaching Tip

If students struggle to find a decimal equivalent for their rational number wheel fraction, cut up some wheels into tenths and hundredths so that these parts of the fraction could be placed on a chart (see Figure 14.9).

The number line is another good model to connect decimals and fractions. The following activity continues the development of fraction–decimal equivalences.

Activity 14.8

CCSS-M: 4.NF.C.6

Decimals and Fractions on a Double Number Line

Give students five decimal numbers that have familiar fraction equivalents. Keep the numbers between two consecutive whole numbers. For example, use 3.5, 3.125, 3.4, 3.75, and 3.66. Show a number line starting at 3.0 and going to 4.0 as either an empty number line or with subdivisions of only fourths, only thirds, or only fifths, but without labels. The students' task is to locate each of the decimal numbers on the fraction number line and to provide the fraction equivalent for each.

Figure 14.9

Fraction models could be decimal models.

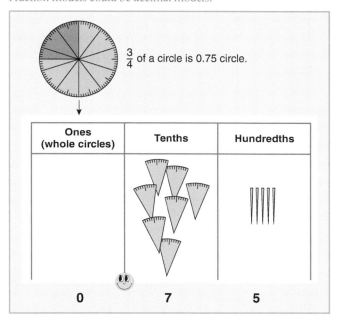

$\frac{3}{4}$ of a circle is 0.75 circle.

Ones (whole circles)	Tenths	Hundredths
0	7	5

📋 Formative Assessment Note

A simple, yet powerful, performance assessment to evaluate decimal understanding has students represent two related decimal numbers, such as 0.7 and 0.07, by using multiple representations: an empty number line, a **10 × 10 Grid**, and **Base-Ten Materials** (Martinie, 2014). Ask students to describe their representations. If students have significantly more difficulty with one model over another this may mean that they have not developed full conceptual understanding of decimal fractions. Placement of decimals on an empty number line is perhaps the most interesting task—and it provides the most revealing information (see Figure 14.10).

Approximation with a Compatible Fraction

In the real world, decimal fractions are rarely those with exact equivalents to common fractions. What fraction would you say approximates the decimal 0.52? In the sixth NAEP exam, only 51 percent of eighth graders selected $\frac{1}{2}$. The other choices were

Figure 14.10

Three different students attempt to draw a number line and show the numbers 0.7 and 0.07.

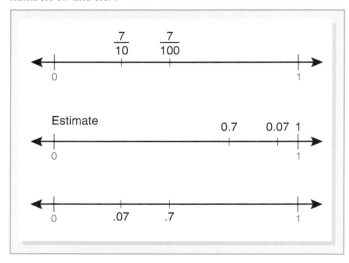

$\frac{1}{50}$ (29 percent), $\frac{1}{5}$ (11 percent), $\frac{1}{4}$ (6 percent), and $\frac{1}{3}$ (4 percent) (Kouba, Zawojewski, & Strutchens, 1997). Again, students need to wrestle with thinking about the size of decimal fractions and begin to develop a sense of familiarity with them.

As with fractions, the first benchmarks that should be developed are 0, $\frac{1}{2}$, and 1. For example, is 7.3962 closer to 7, $7\frac{1}{2}$ or 8? Why? How would you respond to these answers: "Closer to 7 because 3 is less than 5"? or "It is closer to $7\frac{1}{2}$ than 7? Often the 0, $\frac{1}{2}$, or 1 benchmarks work well to make sense of a situation. If more precision is required, encourage students to consider other common fractions (thirds, fourths, fifths, and eighths). In this example, 7.3962 is close to 7.4, which is $7\frac{2}{5}$. Good number sense with decimals entails the ability to quickly think of a fraction that is a close equivalent a skill needed in this next activity.

Activity 14.9

CCSS-M: 4.NF.C.6

Best Match

 Give students a deck of **Fraction-Decimal Cards** of familiar fractions on half of the deck of cards and the decimals that are close to the fractions, but not exact, on the other half. In this game students pair each fraction with the decimal that best matches it in a memory-like game. The difficulty is determined by how close the various fractions are to one another. Some students might select one pairing, then realize there is a better match. For students with disabilities, you may need to have them reflect whether the card they've turned over is close to 0, close to $\frac{1}{2}$, or close to 1, to help support their match-making. Have students share their thinking as the rationales they communicate can provide strategies that other peers will find useful. As a follow-up have students try the **Close to a Familiar Fraction** Activity Page to find out more about the reasoning strategies that they are using.

📋 Formative Assessment Note

You can find out if your students have a flexible understanding of the connections between models and the two-symbol systems for rational numbers—fractions and decimals—with a diagnostic interview. Provide students with a number represented as a fraction, a decimal, or a physical model and have them provide the other two representations along with an explanation. Here are a few examples:

- Write the fraction $\frac{5}{8}$ as a decimal. Use a drawing or a physical model (meter stick or 10 × 10 grid) and explain why your decimal equivalent is correct.

- What fraction is represented by the decimal 2.6? Use an example and a physical model and words to explain your thinking.

- Use both a fraction and a decimal to tell what point might be indicated by this position on the number line. Explain your reasoning.

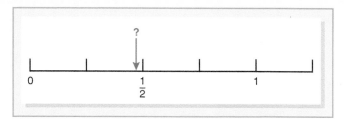

In the last example, it is especially interesting to see which representation students select first—fraction or decimal. Furthermore, do they then translate this number to the other representation or make a second independent estimate?

Other Fraction–Decimal Equivalents

Recall that the denominator is a divisor and the numerator is a multiplier. For example, $\frac{3}{4}$ means the same as $3 \times (1 \div 4)$ or $3 \div 4$. So how would you express $\frac{3}{4}$ on a simple four-function calculator? Simply enter $3 \div 4$. The display will read 0.75.

Too often, students think that dividing the denominator into the numerator is simply an algorithm for converting fractions to decimals, and they have no understanding of why this might work. Use the opportunity to help students develop the idea that in general $\frac{a}{b} = a \div b$, where b is not 0.

Comparing and Ordering Decimal Fractions

Comparing decimal fractions and putting them in order from least to greatest is a skill closely related to comparing fractions and decimals. But comparing decimal fractions, particularly "ragged" decimals of unequal length, has important distinctions from comparing whole numbers. These differences can be initially confusing and cause student errors.

 ## Formative Assessment Note

Consider the following list: 0.36, 0.05, 0.375, 0.97, 0, 2.0, and 0.4. Ask students to order these decimals from least to greatest. Use the chart in Table 14.1 to identify if the students are exhibiting any of the common errors and misconceptions that students exhibit when comparing and ordering decimals (Desmet, Gregoire, & Mussolin, 2010; Nuir & Livy, 2012; Steinle & Stacey, 2004a; 2004b). Knowing these confusions in advance will help you pinpoint ways to improve students' conceptual understanding as they overcome these misconceptions.

All of these common errors and misconceptions reflect a lack of conceptual understanding of how decimal fractions are constructed. Watch these two videos of **Vanessa** and **Sean** comparing decimals. Which of the common errors or misconceptions do you think they are exhibiting? Note that Sean can correctly add, but do you think he fully understands what he is adding? Why or why not?

Table 14.1. Common errors and misconceptions in comparing decimals and how to help.

Common Error or Misconception	What It Looks Like	How to Help
1. Longer is larger.	0.375 is greater than 0.97. 0.44 is less than 0.440.	• Students are using whole number reasoning and selecting the number with more digits as being larger. Have students use decimal models to show each number and compare. Two 10 × 10 grids with each number shaded will help students make the accurate comparison.
2. Shorter is larger.	0.4 is greater than 0.97 because "a tenth is larger than a hundredth."	• Have students create representations of these two decimals focusing on the quantities. Ask. for example, "Is any amount of tenths larger than any amount of hundredths?"
3. Internal zero.	0.58 is less than 0.078 thinking that "zero has no impact." Also, suggesting that 34.08 and 34.8 have the same value.	• When students are confused by a zero in the tenths position for example, have them build the number using Decimal Number Cards. Match this numerical value to a physical model if needed or match it to a number line.
4. Less than zero.	0.36 is less than 0 because zero is a whole number positioned in the ones column (to the left of the decimal point) and therefore is greater than a decimal fraction (to the right of the decimal point).	• Use contexts, for example, ask students whether they would rather have 0 or 0.50 of a dollar. • Use decimal representations on grid paper to visualize the size of each decimal as compared to zero.
5. Reciprocal thinking.	When students compare 0.4 and 0.6, they select 0.4 as larger because they connect 0.4 to $\frac{1}{4}$ and 0.6 to $\frac{1}{6}$ and erroneously decide 0.4 is greater.	• Use decimal materials such as shading 10 × 10 grids to visualize the size of each decimal.
6. Equality.	Students think that 0.4 is not close to 0.375 and/or that 0.3 is smaller than 0.30.	• Show the connections between these values through area models or placing these values on the number line to help students see if the amounts are close in size or as in the case of 0.3 and 0.30 are the same size.

The following activities helps promote discussion about the relative sizes of decimal fractions and are useful in helping students who are challenged by the mistaken thinking described in Table 14.1.

Activity 14.10   CCSS-M: 4.NF.C.6; 4.NF.C.7; 5.NBT.A.1; 5.NBT.A.3a; 5.NBT.A.3b

Line 'Em Up

Prepare a list of four or five decimal fractions that students might be challenged to put in order between the same two consecutive whole numbers. Another option is to use the Line 'Em Up Activity page that uses a context of the height of five plants. First, have students predict the order of the numbers, from least to greatest. Then, require students to use models of their choice to defend their ordering. As students wrestle with representing the numbers with a physical model (perhaps a number line with 100 subdivisions or 10,000 Grid Paper, they will necessarily confront which digits contribute the most to the size of a decimal. For students who are struggling, some explicit instruction might be helpful. Show one of the decimals—3.091, for example. Start with the whole numbers: *Is it closer to 3 or 4?* Then go to the tenths: *Is it closer to 3.0 or to 3.1?"* Repeat with hundredths and thousandths. At each place value position, challenge students to defend their choices with the use of a physical model or other conceptual explanation. A large, empty number line, shown in Figure 14.11, is also useful.

Figure 14.11

Decimal fractions on an empty number line.

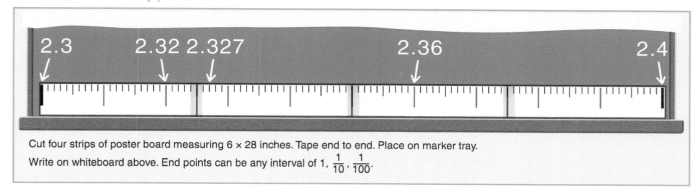

Cut four strips of poster board measuring 6 × 28 inches. Tape end to end. Place on marker tray.

Write on whiteboard above. End points can be any interval of 1, $\frac{1}{10}$, $\frac{1}{100}$.

Density of Decimals

When students only see decimals rounded to two places, this may reinforce the notion that there are no numbers between 2.37 and 2.38 (Steinle & Stacey, 2004b). But an important concept is that there is always another number between any two numbers. Finding a decimal located between any two decimals requires that students understand the density of decimals. Using a linear model helps to show that there is always another decimal to be found between any two decimals as emphasized in the following activities.

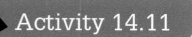

Activity 14.11

CCSS-M: 5.NBT.A.3b

Close Decimals

 Have students name a decimal between 0 and 1.0. Next, have them name another decimal that is even closer to 1.0 than the first. Continue for several more decimals in the same manner, each one being closer to 1.0 than the previous decimal. Similarly, try other benchmarks such as close to 0 or close to 0.5. For students with disabilities, let them use physical models or a number line to help them with their decision making. Later, confirm if they can explain their thinking without representations. Another option is to provide them with two decimals to choose between. Then after time transition back to having them independently generate the decimal.

Activity 14.12

CCSS-M: 5.NBT.C3b; 6.NS.C.6

Zoom

 Stretch a number line (e.g., clothes line or cash register tape) across the front of the room. Ask students to mark where 0.75 and 1.0 are on the line. Then ask students to "zoom in" to find and record three more values between those two values. Ask students to share their thinking strategies. For ELLs make sure they are clear of the meaning of the word between, even demonstrating this relationship with students in the front of the room. For students with disabilities, consider providing them with a set of choices of decimals and ask them to select three that are between 0.75 and 1.0. See the Expanded Lesson: Zoom: Finding Rational Numbers on the Number Line for a full set of procedures, assessment ideas and questions to pose.

Confusion over the density of decimals also plays out when students try to find the nearest decimal (Ubuz & Yayan, 2010). Many times when students are asked to find which decimal is closer to a given decimal, they revert to thinking that tenths are only comparable to tenths and that there are no hundredths between. So, given the question which decimal is closer to 0.19—0.2 or 0.21—they are likely to incorrectly select 0.21 (ignoring that 0.2 is the same as 0.20). They also are not sure that 0.513 is near 0.51, but just a little larger. They may also think that 0.3 is near 0.4 but far away from 0.317. These examples provide evidence that students are in need of additional experiences and probably not yet ready for operations with decimals.

Computation with Decimals

In the past, decimal computation was dominated by the following rules: Line up the decimal points (addition and subtraction), count the decimal places (multiplication), and shift the decimal point in the divisor and dividend so that the divisor is a whole number (division). Some textbooks continue to emphasize these rules, but specific rules for decimal computation are not always necessary if computation is built on a firm understanding of place value and a connection between decimals and fractions.

The *Common Core State Standards* expect that students will understand and be able to explain why procedures make sense (CCSSO, 2010, p. 33). When students who were having difficulty with decimal computation were only taught strictly procedural approaches, initial levels of improved understanding declined rapidly. In only ten days, students' average daily performance levels that were at first approximately 80 percent dropped to a mean of 34 percent (Woodward, Baxter, & Robinson, 1999).

Addition and Subtraction

There is much more to adding and subtracting decimals than knowing to "line up the decimal points." The *Common Core State Standards* (CCSSO, 2010, p. 33) say that fifth graders should "apply their understandings of models for decimals, decimal notation, and properties of operations to add and subtract decimals to hundredths. They develop fluency in these computations, and make reasonable estimates of their results."

But, as you might expect, students may inappropriately use whole number thinking, which can cause confusion. For example, they might add 0.26 + 0.3 and get the answer 0.29. Let's look at ways to avoid that misunderstanding.

Estimating Decimal Sums and Differences

Estimation is important—as often an estimate is all that is needed. Students should become adept at estimating decimal computations before they learn to compute with the standard algorithm. This thinking aligns with the CCSS-M (2010) where fifth graders start to focus on decimal computation but not until the sixth grade is the standard algorithm required. As with fractions, until students have a sound understanding of place value, equivalence and relative size of decimals, they are not ready to develop understanding of decimal operations (Cramer & Whitney, 2010). An emphasis on estimation is particularly important for students who have learned the rules for decimal computation yet cannot decide whether their answers are reasonable. An initial minimum goal should be to have the estimate contain the correct number of digits to the left of the decimal—the whole-number part.

Stop and Reflect

Before continuing, try making whole-number estimates of the following computations:

1. $4.907 + 123.01 + 56.123$
2. $459.8 - 12.345$
3. $0.607 + 0.18$
4. $89.1 - 0.998$

Your estimates might be:

1. Between 175 and 200
2. A little less than 450
3. Close to 0.8
4. About 88

In these examples, an understanding of decimal numeration and basic whole-number estimation skills (e.g., front end, rounding, and compatibles) can produce reasonable estimates. When encouraging students to estimate, do not use rigid rules; instead focus on the size of the numbers, the meaning of the operations, and the use of a variety of strategies.

Developing Addition and Subtraction Algorithms

Invented strategies receive significant attention when developing whole-number computation skills, but there is often less focus on them with decimal computation. Yet, invented strategies are grounded in place value, are efficient, and are often more conceptual for students than standard algorithms. This is certainly true for adding and subtracting decimal fractions. Even after the standard algorithm is learned and understood, students should be encouraged to pick the best method given the situation. This is what mathematically proficient students do.

Consider this problem:

Jessica and Sumiko each timed their own quarter-mile run with a stopwatch. Jessica says that she ran the quarter mile in 74.5 seconds. Sumiko was more precise in her timing, reporting that she ran the quarter mile in 81.34 seconds. Who ran it the fastest and how much faster was she?

Students who understand decimal numeration should be able to estimate approximately what the difference is—close to 7 seconds. Only then should they be challenged to figure out the exact difference using a variety of strategies. The estimate will help them avoid the common error of lining up the 5 under the 4. Instead, students might note that 74.5 and 7 more is 81.5, then figure out how much extra that is (0.16) and subtract the extra to get the difference of 6.34. Other students may count on from 74.5 by adding 0.5 and then add 6 more seconds to get to 81, and finally add on the remaining 0.34 second. This strategy can be effectively represented on an empty number line which aligns with the context of the

Standards for
Mathematical Practices

> **1** **Make sense of problems and persevere in solving them.**

problem. Another strategy is to change 74.5 to 74.50 and subtract using their prior knowledge regarding regrouping with whole numbers. Similar story problems for addition and subtraction, some involving different numbers of decimal places, will help develop students' understanding.

After students have had several opportunities to solve addition and subtraction story problems, see if they can flexibly think about a problem through multiple representations, as in the next activity.

As students become proficient in adding and subtracting with the standard algorithm, continue to provide opportunities for them to estimate, illustrate by using models discussed

Activity 14.13

CCSS-M: 5.NBT.B.7

Representing Sums and Differences

Give students a copy of the Translation Task Activity Page with a problem in the upper left quadrant involving adding decimals with different numbers of places, such as: 73.46 + 6.2 + 0.582. Students should estimate and then calculate the answer. The second task is to write a description of a situation that fits the problem. In the third quadrant they can illustrate the operation using, for example, an empty number line or base-ten pieces. Finally, students explain their thinking by describing how they estimated and what strategies they used to add decimal numbers. The same task can be done with subtraction.

Formative Assessment Note

As students complete Activity 14.13, use a checklist to record whether they are showing evidence of having an understanding of decimal concepts and the role of the decimal point in computation. Note whether students get a correct sum by using a rule they learned, but then are challenged to give an explanation of their thinking. Or are they unable to describe a situation that matches the computation or create a corresponding illustration. If there are difficulties in several areas of the task, rather than continue to focus on how to add or subtract decimals, shift attention back to the foundational decimal concepts until those are understood.

here, use invented strategies, and explain a context to fit the situation. For example, the game on the NLVM website "Circle 3" is a great reasoning experience that challenges students to use logic as they combine decimals to add to 3 (it is not as easy as it sounds!). These types of continued experiences will ensure that students develop procedural proficiency for decimal addition and subtraction.

Multiplication

Multiplication of decimals tends to be poorly understood. Students (and adults) blindly count over how many decimal places they have in the problem to decide where the decimal point will be placed in the answer. Often little attempt is made to assess if the answer is reasonable. Yet, being mathematically proficient means having a much deeper understanding of multiplication of decimals. Students need to be able to use concrete models or drawings, strategies based on place value (invented strategies), and properties of operations, and must be able to explain the reasoning used (CCSSO, 2010). Estimation is essential in building that understanding.

Estimating Products

It might be argued that much of the estimation in the real world involves fractions, decimals, and percents. A key consideration in estimating is using whole numbers to estimate rational numbers.

Decide what numbers you would use in each case as you estimate the problems listed below. Which ones were easy to estimate? Difficult?

1. 5.91×6.1
2. 145.33×0.109
3. 0.58×9.681

A student's reasoning might be similar to the following:

1. This is about 6 times 6, so the answer is about 36.
2. This is like 145 dimes, so divide by 10 and it is about 14.50. Or this is about one-tenth of 145, so 14.5.
3. The first value is about one-half, so half of about 10 is about 5.

When problems involve two very small decimals, estimation is difficult, but it is still possible to look at the answer to see if it is relatively smaller than what the initial factor was (taking a small part of a small part results in an even smaller part).

▶ Activity 14.14
CCSS-M: 5.NBT.B.7; 6.NS.B.3

Hit the Target: Continuous Input

Select a target range. Next, enter the starting number in the calculator, and hand it to the first player. For multiplication or division, only one operation is used through the whole game. After the first or second turn, decimal factors are usually required. This variation develops an excellent understanding of multiplication or division by decimals. A sequence for a target range of 262 to 265 might be like this:

Start with 63.

Player 1	$\times$ 5 $=$ ⟶ 315 (too high)
Player 2	$\times$ 0.7 $=$ ⟶ 220.5 (too low)
Player 1	$\times$ 1.3 $=$ ⟶ 286.65 (too high)
Player 2	$\times$ 0.9 $=$ ⟶ 257.985 (too low)
Player 1	$\times$ 1.03 $=$ ⟶ 265.72455 (very close!)

(What would you press next?)

This game can also be played using division. Adapt the game for addition and subtraction; the first player then presses either $+$ or $-$ followed by a number and then $=$.

Developing Multiplication Algorithms

Explore multiplication of decimals by using problems in a context and by returning to physical models that were useful in thinking about whole number multiplication. Estimation should play a significant role in developing a multiplication algorithm. As a beginning, consider this problem:

The farmer fills each jug with 3.7 liters of cider. If you buy 4 jugs, how many liters of cider is that?

Ask students, "Is the answer more than 12 liters? What is the most it could be?" Once an estimate of the result is decided on, let students use their own methods for determining an exact answer (based on place value and properties). One strategy might be to double 3.7 (which equals 7.4), double it again, and total. Another is to multiply 3×4, then count on 0.7 four times. Or, students may double 3.7 (getting 7.4) and double it again. Eventually, students will agree on the exact result of 14.8 liters. Connect these strategies to the number line, showing how jumps on the decimal number line match the invented strategies.

The area model is particularly useful in illustrating decimal multiplication (Rathouz, 2011). Use a scenario such as this one that aligns with a rectangular array:

Figure 14.12

A student's use of 10×10 grids to reason about 1.5×0.6.

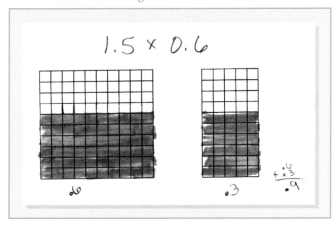

A gardener has 1.5 m² of her garden where she can plant flowers. She decides to plant bluebells on an area that is 0.6 of the garden. On how many total square meters can she plant bluebells?

See a student's solution (Figure 14.12) using a grid diagram to model the problem 0.6×1.5. Each large square represents an area of 1 m² with each row of 10 small squares as 0.1 m² and each small square as 0.01 m². The shaded section shows 0.6 m² + 0.3 m² = 0.9 m². Notice that this is a proportional model allowing students to "see" the values of the factors.

Also use problems that can be illustrated with an empty number line such as:

A frog hops 4.2 inches on each hop. How far away is she from her starting point after 5 hops?

Figure 14.13 provides illustrations of a line to illustrate the frog hops. This illustration should remind students of the multiplication strategies they already know and this connection can be used in developing meaning for the standard algorithm for decimal multiplication.

Figure 14.13

A number line is used to illustrate multiplication of decimals.

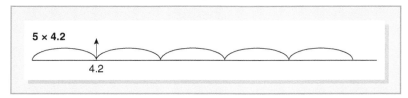

Ask students to compare a decimal product with one involving the same digits but no decimal. For example, how are 23.4×6.5 and 234×65 alike? Interestingly, both products have exactly the same digits: 15210. (The zero may be missing from the decimal product.) Have students use a calculator to explore other products that are alike except for the location of the decimals points involved. The digits in the answer are always alike. After seeing how the digits remain the same for these related products, try the following activity.

Activity 14.15

CCSS-M: 5.NBT.B.7; 6.NS.B.3

Where Does the Decimal Go? Multiplication

Have students compute the following product: 24 × 63. Using the result of this computation (1512) and estimation, have them give the exact answer to each of the following:

0.24 × 6.3   24 × 0.63   2.4 × 63   0.24 × 0.63

For each computation, they should write a rationale for how they decided to place the decimal point. For example, on the first one a student might explain that 0.24 is close to one-fourth and one-fourth of 6 is less than two, so the answer must be 1.512. They can check their results with a calculator. ELLs may apply a different mental strategy that is common in their country of origin. Even if they have trouble articulating their reasoning, it is important to consider alternative ways to reason through the problem. Discussing errors and how to avoid them is also an important class discussion.

Stop and Reflect

What is the value in having students explain how they placed the decimal point in the product? How does that compare to having students count over the number of places?

Another way to support full understanding of the algorithm is to rewrite the decimals in their fraction equivalents. So, if you are multiplying 3.4 × 1.7, that is the same as $\frac{34}{10} \times \frac{17}{10}$. When multiplied, the answer equals $\frac{578}{100}$, which when rewritten as a decimal is 5.78, which corresponds to moving the decimal two places to the left (Rathouz, 2011).

The method of placing the decimal point in a product by way of estimation is more challenging as the product gets smaller. For example, knowing that 37 × 83 is 3071 does not make it easy to place the decimal in the product 0.037 × 0.083. But the standard algorithm can be developed from this problem, all the while helping students understand the properties of multiplication.

Here is the process:

$$0.037 \times 0.83 = \left(37 \times \frac{1}{1000}\right) \times \left(83 \times \frac{1}{100}\right)$$

$$\left(37 \times \frac{1}{1000}\right) \times \left(83 \times \frac{1}{100}\right) = 37 \times 83 \times \frac{1}{1000} \times \frac{1}{100}$$

$$37 \times 83 \times \frac{1}{1000} \times \frac{1}{100} = (37 \times 83) \times \left(\frac{1}{1000} \times \frac{1}{100}\right)$$

$$(37 \times 83) \times \left(\frac{1}{1000} \times \frac{1}{100}\right) = 3071 \times \left(\frac{1}{100,000}\right) = 0.03071$$

This may look complicated, but if you just follow what is happening with the decimal fractions, you can see why you count the number of values to the right of each factor, and then place the decimal in the product so that it has the same number of decimal places. The standard algorithm for decimal multiplication is: Do the computation as if all numbers were whole numbers. When finished, place the decimal point

Standards for Mathematical Practice

2 Reason abstractly and quantitatively.

by reasoning or estimation if possible. If not possible to estimate, count the decimal places as illustrated. Even if students have already learned the standard algorithm, they need to know the conceptual rationale for the algorithm that is centered on place value and the powers of ten for "counting" and shifting the decimal places. By focusing on rote applications of rules, students lose out on opportunities to understand the meaning and effects of operations and are more prone to misapply procedures (Martinie & Bay-Williams, 2003).

Questions such as the following keep the focus on number sense and provide useful information about your students' understanding.

Standards for
Mathematical Practice

3 Construct
viable arguments
and critique the
reasoning of others.

1. Consider these two computations: $3\frac{1}{2} \times 2\frac{1}{4}$ and 2.276×3.18. Without doing the calculations, which product do you think is larger? Provide a reason for your answer that can be understood by someone else in this class.

2. How much larger is 0.26×8 than 0.25×8? How can you tell without doing the computation?

Students' discussions and explanations as they work on these or similar questions can provide insights into their decimal and fraction number sense and the connections between the two representations.

Division

In the same way, multiplication of decimals is often carried out rotely, division of decimals can be poorly understood. Returning to whole number understanding of the meaning of the operation of division can help students make sense of decimal division. Watch this video of John A. Van de Walle as he discusses teaching division of decimals using patterns and a problem-based approach.

Estimating Quotients

Estimation and concrete experiences are both needed to build a strong understanding of division of decimals. In fact, the best approach to estimating in division generally comes from thinking about multiplication rather than division. Consider the following problem:

The trip to Washington was 282 miles. It took exactly 4.5 hours to drive. What were the average miles per hour?

To make an estimate of this quotient, think about what times 4 or 5 is close to 280. You might think $60 \times 4.5 = 240 + 30 = 270$, so maybe about 61 or 62 miles per hour.

Here is a second example without a context.

Make an estimate of $45.7 \div 1.83$. Think only of what times $1\frac{8}{10}$ is close to 46.

Stop and Reflect

Will the answer be more or less than 46? Why? Will it be more or less than 20? Now think about 1.8 being close to 2. What times 2 is close to 46? Use "think multiplication" to produce an estimate.

Because 1.83 is close to 2, the estimate is near 23. And because 1.83 is less than 2, the answer must be greater than 23—say 25 or 26. (The actual answer is 24.972677.)

Developing the Division Algorithm

Although estimation can produce a reasonable result, you may still require a standard algorithm to produce an exact answer in the same way it was done for multiplication. Figure 14.14 shows division by a whole number and how that can be carried out to as many places as you wish. (The explicit-trade method described in Chapter 11 is shown on the right.) Through reasoning, you are placing the decimal point—that is, trade 2 tens for 20 ones, then put 2 ones in each group—so you know the 2 in the quotient is in the ones place.

An algorithm for division is parallel to that for multiplication: Do the computation as if all numbers were whole numbers and then place the decimal by estimation. This is reasonable for divisors greater than 1 or close to a familiar value (e.g., 0.1, 0.5, 0.01). If students have a method for dividing by 45, they can divide by 0.45 and 4.5. So, for example, if the students were solving $24 \div 0.45$, they might think, "I can think of the 45 as 50, or the 45 hundredths as 50 hundredths or five-tenths. So how many halves (rounding the 0.45) are in 24? About 48."

Figure 14.14

Extension of the division algorithm.

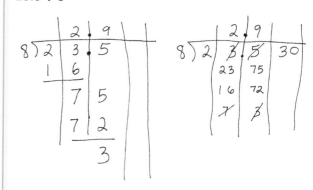

23.5 ÷ 8

Trade 2 tens for 20 ones, making 23 ones.
Put 2 ones in each group, or 16 in all.
That leaves 7 ones.

Trade 7 ones for 70 tenths, making 75 tenths.
Put 9 tenths in each group, or 72 tenths in all.
That leaves 3 tenths.

Trade the 3 tenths for 30 hundredths.

(Continue trading for smaller pieces as long as you wish.)

Activity 14.16

CCSS-M: 5.NBT.B.7; 6.NS.B.3

Where Does the Decimal Go? Division

Provide a quotient such as 146 ÷ 7 = 20857, correct to five digits but without the decimal point. The task is to use only this information and estimation to give a fairly precise answer to each of the following:

146 ÷ 0.7   1.46 ÷ 7   14.6 ÷ 0.7   1460 ÷ 70

For each computation students should write a rationale for their answers and then check their results with a calculator. Any errors should be acknowledged, and the rationale that produced the error adjusted. As noted in multiplication, ELLs may apply a different mental strategy they learned previously, and it is important to value alternative approaches. Again, engage students in explicit discussions of common errors or misconceptions and how to fix them.

Introducing Percents

The term *percent* is simply another name for hundredths and, as such, is a standardized ratio with a denominator of 100. If students can express fractions and decimals as hundredths, the term *percent* can be substituted for the term *hundredth*. Consider the fraction $\frac{3}{4}$. As a fraction expressed in hundredths, it is $\frac{75}{100}$. When $\frac{3}{4}$ is written in decimal form, it is 0.75. Both 0.75 and $\frac{75}{100}$ are read in exactly the same way: "seventy-five hundredths."

When used as operators, $\frac{3}{4}$ of something is the same as 0.75 or 75 percent of that same thing. Thus, percent is merely a new notation and terminology, not a new concept.

The results of the 2005 NAEP exam revealed that only 30 percent of eighth graders could accurately calculate the percent of the tip when given the cost of the meal and the amount of the tip left by the diners. A reason for this weak performance is a failure to meaningfully develop percent concepts.

Models and Terminology

Models are critical in building students' understanding of percent. A common confusion for some students is that they think that $\frac{4}{7}$ is equal to $\frac{4}{7}$ percent (Olson, Zengami, & Slovin, 2010). But, physical models can support understanding by providing the main link among fractions, decimals, and percents, as shown in Figure 14.15 using the **Rational Number Wheel** and the **10 × 10 Grids**. Base-ten models are also suitable for illustrating fractions, decimals, and percents, because they all represent the same idea. The rational number wheel (Figure 14.5) with 100 markings around the edge is a model for percents as well as a fraction model for hundredths. The same is true of a 10 × 10 grid in which each small square inside is 1 percent of the area of the grid. Each row or strip of 10 squares is not only a tenth of the area of the grid, but also 10 percent of the grid.

Zambo (2008) suggests linking fractions to percent with a 10 × 10 grid. By marking one out of every four squares or shading a 5 × 5 region in the corner of the grid, students can discover the link between $\frac{1}{4}$ and $\frac{25}{100}$ or 25 percent. Zambo goes on to suggest that even more complex representations such as $\frac{1}{8}$ can lead to interesting discussions about the remaining squares left at the end, resulting in $12\frac{1}{2}$ out of 100 squares or $12\frac{1}{2}$ percent (or 12.5 percent). Similarly, the common fractions (halves, thirds, fourths, fifths, and eighths) should become familiar in terms of percents as well as decimals. Three-fifths, for example, is 60 percent as well as 0.6. One-eighth of an amount is $12\frac{1}{2}$ percent or 12.5 percent of the quantity. These ideas should be explored with base-ten models and with contexts rather than with poorly understood rules about moving decimal points.

Figure 14.15

Models connect three different notations.

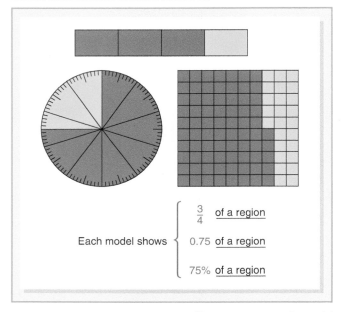

Each model shows $\begin{cases} \frac{3}{4} & \text{of a region} \\ 0.75 & \text{of a region} \\ 75\% & \text{of a region} \end{cases}$

Data representation with circle graphs provides a meaningful opportunity for percent explorations (Whitin & Whitin, 2012). One tool that can be used to link percentages with data collection is a percent necklace. Using fishing cord or sturdy string, link 100 same-sized beads and knot them tightly in a circular "necklace." Anytime a circle graph is displayed in class, the percent necklace can provide an estimation tool. Given any circle graph, place the necklace in a circle so that its center coincides with the center of the circle graph (don't try to align the necklace with the outside edge of the circle graph). If the necklace makes a wider concentric circle, to distinguish the different categories, students use a straight edge to extend the lines straight out to meet the necklace. If the circle graph is larger than the necklace, as it would be in Figure 18.5, merely use the radial lines to denote the categories. Have students count the number of beads between any two lines that represent a category. For example, they might find 24 beads are in the section of the circle graph that shows how many students selected the Grand Canyon as their favorite vacation destination. That becomes an estimate that approximately 24 percent of the students favor the Grand Canyon as a vacation. Counting the beads in a given category gives students an informal approach to estimating percent, while investigating a meaningful physical model for thinking about the per-100 concept.

The activity "Fraction Models," on the NCTM Illuminations website, explores equivalence of fractions, mixed numbers, decimals, and percents. You select the fraction and choose the type of model (length, area [rectangle or circle], or set), and it shows the corresponding visual and all the equivalences.

Here's another activity that focuses just on representations of percent:

Activity 14.17

CCSS-M: 6.RP.A.3c

Percent Memory Match

Use the deck of **Percent Cards** that includes circle graphs with a percentage shaded in and matching percents (such as a card showing a circle with $\frac{1}{2}$ shaded and another card with 50% written on it). Students are to pair each circle graph with the percent that best matches it in a memory game in which they must flip over matching cards to make a pair. For students with disabilities, you may need to have rational number wheels available as a moveable representation to help support their match-making.

Percent concepts can be developed through other powerful visual representations that link to proportional thinking. One option is the use of a three-part model to represent the original amount, the decrease/increase, and the final amount (Lo & Ko, 2013; Parker, 2004). Using three rectangles that can be positioned and divided, students can analyze aspects of a situation and then consider each component of the model. The rectangles can be a particularly useful representation for the often confusing problems that include a percentage increase to find an amount greater than the original. In a 2005 NAEP item, students were asked to calculate how many employees there were at a company whose workforce increased by 10 percent over the previous level of 90. Using Parker's approach of representing the components of the problem (2004), you can see in Figure 14.16 how a student used the proportional rectangle model to come up with a correct solution to this problem.

Another helpful approach to grasping the terminology of percent is through the role of the decimal point. Recall that the decimal point identifies the units position. When the unit is ones, a number such as 0.659 means a little more than 6 tenths of 1. The word *ones* is understood (6 tenths of 1 *one* or one *whole*). But 0.659 is also 6.59 tenths and 65.9 hundredths and 659 thousandths. The name of the unit must be explicitly identified. Because *percent* is another

Figure 14.16

A student uses a model for reasoning about percent.

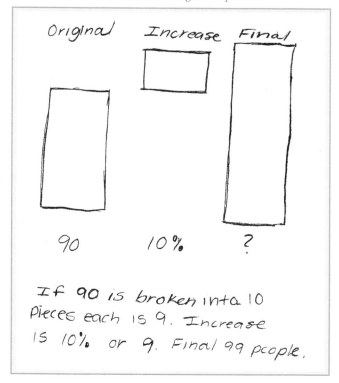

name for *hundredths*, when the decimal point identifies the hundredths position as the units, the word *percent* can be specified as a synonym for *hundredths*. Thus, 0.659 (of some

Figure 14.17

Hundredths are also known as percents.

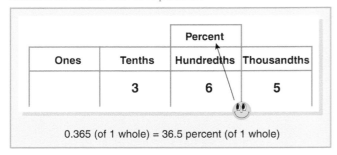

0.365 (of 1 whole) = 36.5 percent (of 1 whole)

whole or 1) is 65.9 hundredths or 65.9 percent of that same whole. As illustrated in Figure 14.17, the notion of placing the decimal point to identify the percent position (i.e., hundredths) is conceptually more meaningful than the rule: "To change a decimal to a percent, move the decimal two places to the right." A more conceptually focused idea is to equate hundredths with percent both orally and in notation.

Percent Problems in Context

Some teachers may talk about "the three percent problems." The sentence "_____ is _____ percent of _____ " has three spaces for numbers. For example, "20 is 25 percent of 80." The classic three percent problems come from this bare expression; two of the numbers are given, and the students are asked to produce the third. Students tend to set up proportions, but are not quite sure which numbers to put where. In other words, they are not connecting understanding with the procedure. Furthermore, commonly encountered percent situations, such as sales figures, taxes, food composition (percent of fat), sport reporting, and economic trends, are almost never in the "_____ is _____ percent of _____" format. Instead of these short, decontextualized prompts, engage students in more realistic contextual problems.

Chapter 12 explored equivalent fractions in which one part was unknown. Developmentally, then, it makes sense to help students make the connection between the exercises done with fraction equivalencies and percents. How? Emphasize equivalency, but add on that you are seeking the equivalency for hundredths. Connect hundredths to percent and replace fraction language with percent language. In Figure 14.18, the three part-whole fraction exercises demonstrate the link between fractions and percents.

Figure 14.18

Part–whole fraction exercises can be translated into percent exercises.

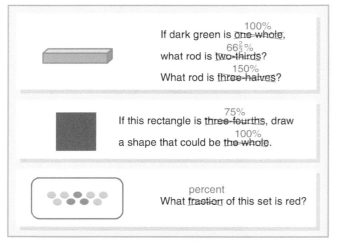

Although students must have some experience with the noncontextual situations in Figure 14.18, it is important to have them explore percent relationships in real contexts. Find or create percent problems, and present them in the same way that they appear in newspapers, on television, and in other real contexts. In addition, follow these guidelines for your instruction:

- Limit the percents to familiar fractions (halves, thirds, fourths, fifths, and eighths) or familiar percents ($\frac{25}{100}$ (25%), $\frac{50}{100}$ (50%)), and use numbers compatible with these fractions. The focus of these exercises is the relationships involved, not complex computations.

- Require students to use physical models, drawings, and contexts to explain their solutions. It is wiser to assign three problems requiring a drawing and an explanation than to give 15 problems requiring only computation and answers. Remember that the purpose is the exploration of relationships, not computational skill.

- Do not rush to developing rules or procedures for different types of problems—encourage students to notice patterns.

- Use the terms *part*, *whole*, and *percent* (or *fraction*). Help students see these percent exercises as the same types of exercises they did with fractions.

- Encourage mental computation.

The following problems meet these criteria for familiar fractions and compatible numbers. Try working each problem, identifying each number as a part, a whole, or a fraction. Draw bar diagrams to help you explain or work through your thought process. Examples of student reasoning using bar diagrams are illustrated in Figure 14.19.

1. The PTA reported that 75 percent of the total number of families were represented at the meeting. If students from 320 families go to the school, how many families were represented at the meeting?

2. The baseball team won 80 percent of the 25 games it played this year. How many games were lost?

3. In Mrs. Carter's class, 20 students, or $66\frac{2}{3}$ percent of the class, were on the honor roll. How many students are in her class?

4. Zane bought his new computer at a $12\frac{1}{2}$ percent discount. He paid $700. How many dollars did he save by buying it at a discount?

5. If Nicolas has read 60 of the 180 pages in his library book, what percent of the book has he read so far?

6. The hardware store bought widgets at 80 cents each and sold them for $1 each. What percent did the store mark up the price of each widget?

Figure 14.19

Students use bar diagrams to solve percent problems.

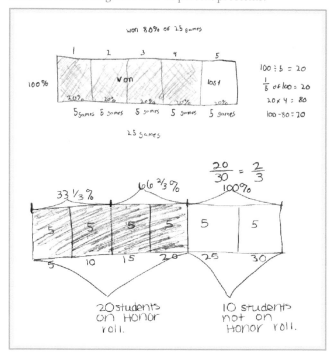

Stop and Reflect

Look at the examples in Figure 14.19. Notice how each problem is solved with simple fractions and mental math. Then try each of the six problems just listed using familiar fraction equivalents? What are some models or drawings that you think your students might use?

 ## Formative Assessment Note

These context-based percent problems can be an effective performance assessment to evaluate students' understanding. Assign one or two, and have students explain why they think their answer makes sense. You might take a percent problem and substitute fractions for percents (e.g., use $\frac{1}{8}$ instead of 12.5 percent) to see how students handle these problems with fractions compared to percents.

If your focus is on reasoning and justification rather than number of problems correct, you will be able to collect all the assessment information you need to plan next instructional steps.

Estimation

Many percent problems do not have simple (familiar) numbers. Frequently, in real life, an approximation or estimate in percent situations is enough to help one think through the situation. An estimate based on an understanding of the relationship confirms that a correct operation has been performed or that the decimal point is positioned correctly.

To help students with estimation in percent situations, two ideas that have already been discussed can be applied. First, when the percent is not a simple one, substitute a close percent that is easy to work with. Second, select numbers that are compatible with the percent involved, to make the calculation easy to do mentally. Here are some examples.

1. The 83,000-seat stadium was 73 percent full. How many people were at the game?

2. The treasurer reported that 68.3 percent of the dues had been collected, for a total of $385. How much more money can the club expect to collect if all dues are paid?

3. Max McStrike had 217 hits in 842 at-bats. What was his batting average?

Stop and Reflect

Use familiar percents, fractions, and compatible numbers to estimate solutions to each of these last three problems. Do this before reading on.

Here are some possible estimates:

1. (Use $\frac{3}{4}$ and 80,000) → about 60,000
2. (Use $\frac{2}{3}$ and $380; will collect $\frac{1}{3}$ more) → about $190
3. (4 × 217 > 842; $\frac{1}{4}$ is 25 percent, or 0.250) → a bit more than 0.250

There are several common uses for estimating percentages in real-world situations. As students gain full conceptual understanding and flexibility, there are ways to think about percents that are useful in a variety of situations:

• *Tips:* To figure a tip, you can find 10 percent of the amount and then half of that again to make a 15 percent tip or double the 10% for a 20% tip!

• *Taxes:* The same approach for finding tips is used for figuring sales tax. Depending on the amount, you can find 10 percent, take half of that, and then find 1 percent and add or subtract that amount as needed. Students should also realize that finding percents is a process of multiplication; therefore, finding 8 percent (tax) of $50 will generate the same result as finding 50 percent (half) of 8, or $4.

• *Discounts:* A 30 percent discount is the same as 70 percent of the original amount, and depending on the original amount, using one of those percents may be easier to use in mental calculations than the other. If a $48 outfit is 30 percent off, for example, you are paying 70 percent. Round $48 to $50. And you have 0.70 × 50 (think 7 × 5) and your cost is less than $35.

Again, these are not rules to be taught; they are real-world reasoning activities to be developed that require a full understanding of percent concepts and the commutative property.

15

Promoting Algebraic Thinking

BIG IDEAS

1 Algebra is a useful tool for generalizing arithmetic and representing patterns and relationships in the world. Explaining the regularities and consistencies across many problems gives students the chance to generalize.

2 Methods we use to compute and the structures in our number system can and should be generalized. For example, the generalization that $a + b = b + a$ tells us that $83 + 27 = 27 + 83$ without computing the sums on each side of the equal sign.

3 Variables as experienced in elementary school are symbols that take the place of numbers or sets of numbers. They have different meanings depending on whether they are being used as representations of quantities that vary or change, representations of specific unknown values, or in a generalized expression or formula.

4 Equations and inequalities are used to express relationships between two quantities. Symbolism on either side of an equation or inequality represents a quantity. Thus, $3 + 8$ and $5n + 2$ are both expressions for numbers, not something "to do."

5 Patterns, both repeating and growing, can be recognized as having common elements, extended to subsequent elements through shared characteristics, and generalized through the identification of rules and relationships.

6 Functional thinking explores relationships that uniquely associate members of one set with members of another set. For every input, there is a unique output.

It is human to try to make sense of the world (and to see how things are related) (Fosnot & Jacob, 2010). Algebraic thinking is sometimes referred to as *generalized arithmetic*, where learners notice patterns that hold true in algorithms and with mathematical properties, and reason quantitatively about such things as whether expressions are equivalent or not. Algebra must be presented in ways that emphasize its usefulness as a tool for making sense of all areas of mathematics and real-world situations.

Algebra is an established content strand in kindergarten through grade 12. Although the level of sophistication changes across grade levels, one thing is clear: The algebra envisioned for grades 3 through 5—and for middle and high school as well—is not the algebra that you most likely experienced. Therefore, the elementary grades become the launching pad for important algebra ideas. Let's look at the critical topics suggested by the *Common Core State Standards* (CCSSO, 2010), at grades 3 through 5:

Grade 3: Students determine unknowns in multiplication and division equations, apply properties of operations (i.e., commutative, associative, and distributive), represent problems with equations including those with variables and identify arithmetic patterns as they solve problems.

Grade 4: Students use symbols to represent the unknown quantity and they generate patterns that follow a rule using both numbers and shapes that follow a rule.

Grade 5: Students write, interpret, and evaluate expressions using symbols (including grouping symbols) and generate and analyze patterns.

Strands of Algebraic Thinking

These expectations illustrate the explicit infusion of algebraic thinking in the four operations as a way to develop students who are not only mathematically proficient in addition, subtraction, multiplication, and division with whole and rational numbers, but who are also able to experience the beginnings of algebraic thinking. Algebraic thinking involves forming generalizations from these experiences with number and computation and formalizing these ideas with the use of a meaningful symbol system. Far from being a topic with little real-world use, algebraic thinking pervades all of mathematics and is essential for making mathematics useful in daily life (Knuth, Stephens, Blanton, & Gardiner, 2016). Although algebra is a separate strand of the curriculum, it is also embedded in all areas of mathematics.

Algebraic reasoning includes three major components that infuse the central notions of generalization and symbolization (Blanton, 2008; Kaput, 2008):

1. Study of structures in the number system, including those arising in arithmetic
2. Study of patterns, relations, and functions
3. Process of mathematical modeling, including the meaningful use of symbols

These three strands provide the organization for this chapter. In each section, we share developmentally appropriate tasks and effective instructional activities across grades 3 through 5.

Generalized Arithmetic

As students explore all aspects of number and computation, including basic facts and behaviors of the four major operations, the central process of creating generalizations helps students gain insights into the structure of the number system (Russell, Schifter, & Bastable, 2011).

Generalization with Number and Operations

Even the most basic arithmetic situations can be extended to look at generalizations about numbers and operations. Exploring patterns in numerical situations, rather than just computing with standard algorithms, is algebraic thinking, and it strengthens understanding of numbers in all the operations (and with all types of numbers)! Here students use what they know about how to decompose and recompose numbers to perform operations and, while doing so, identify generalizable characteristics or behaviors of the process. Using a context such as the story in *Guinea Pigs Add Up* (Cuyler, 2010) consider the following example.

Ten guinea pigs are housed in two different cages in the classroom. What are all the different ways the 10 guinea pigs can be in the two cages?

Stop and Reflect

Can you list all the ways for this to occur? If there were only 8 guinea pigs, how many different ways would be possible? What if there were 25 guinea pigs? Is there a generalizable rule for how many different ways the guinea pigs could be arranged in the two cages?

The significant algebraic thinking comes when you ask students, "How do you know that you've found all the different ways?" They should find that in this situation there are 11 ways to put 10 guinea pigs in two cages, 9 ways for 8 guinea pigs, and 26 ways for 25 guinea pigs. Have students explain this pattern. Can they begin to generalize and suggest why this is the case?

Generalizing can be described using symbols, something that students should do in grades 4 and 5. To move them to that thinking, you might ask, "If I have ten guinea pigs in one cage, how might you describe how many guinea pigs are in the other cage?" Students might answer "Subtract from 10 what is in the first cage and you get what is in the second cage." Record this for the students as 10 – amount of pigs in the first cage = amount of pigs in the second cage. Then you can move from an equation in words to a more generalizable equation like $10 - n = ?$

 Formative Assessment Note

Although younger students can use materials to figure out the guinea pig problem, this is a good performance assessment to use with the whole class or small groups to see to what extent students notice patterns. In this problem, students are trying to identify multiple solutions. As stated, the significant algebra lies in deciding when all of the solutions have been found, so notice how students explain their reasoning. At the most basic level, students will just say they cannot think of any more ways. At the next level, students will strategically use each number from 0 to 10 for one addend (and the corresponding number for the other addend). The final level is reached when a student explains that for each number there is one and only one solution based on reasoning rather than on finding possible solutions. At this final level, the student is making a *generalization* for how to determine the number of possible solutions. The student might say, "There is always one more way to put the guinea pigs in the two cages than the number of guinea pigs."

You can help students begin to understand symbols by asking how they might represent the generalizations by using the letter n to be the number of guinea pigs. The number of ways to be in the two cages will be $n + 1$ because there can be 0, 1, 2 . . . n guinea pigs in the first cage. Finding that there is always one more way to arrange the pets in the cages than there are guinea pigs is a *generalization* for how to determine the number of solutions without listing them. Starting with a problem that is concrete and begins with

Standards for Mathematical Practice

◀ **8** Look for and express regularity in repeated reasoning.

listing numeric possibilities is a way to help students learn to generalize and use variables. To extend the discussion, ask students questions such as, "What if there were 120 guinea pigs—would the rule still be true? How do you know? What if you knew there were 34 different ways the guinea pigs could be in the cages; could you figure out how many guinea pigs there were? Is there a rule for that?"

Slight shifts in how arithmetic problems are presented can open up opportunities for generalizations (Blanton, 2008). For example, instead of a series of unrelated two-digit multiplication problems, consider the following:

$$\begin{array}{cccc} 35 & 52 & 23 & 46 \\ \times\ 52 & \times\ 35 & \times\ 46 & \times\ 23 \end{array}$$

Standards for Mathematical Practice

> **7 Look for and make use of structure.** ▶

Once students have solved these problems, you can focus attention on the factors, asking questions like "What do you notice?" and "Will this always be true?" and "How could we write the pattern you notice using symbols?" In their own words, students will explain that the numbers can be multiplied in any order. Although students may already understand the commutative property from learning their basic facts, they may not recognize the generalizability of the property, and this interaction can help them recognize the power of this important property.

When working on multiplication concepts and related facts, ask students to decide whether the following conjectures are true or false: "If you multiply any whole number by 2, the answer will be an even number" or "If you multiply any whole number by 9, the answer has digits that add up to 9."

Encourage students to make their own generalizations. For example, Figure 15.1 is the work of a fourth grade student who is trying to convince others of her conjecture that if you take half of one factor and you double the other factor, you will get the same answer. Notice how she illustrates this conjecture by sketching rectangular arrays to show why it

Figure 15.1

Examples of a student's work on supporting a conjecture with a representation.

worked. This proof without words shows how this doubling and halving strategy will be true for $D \times H$ by moving the bottom row of squares in the rectangular array and moving that row to a position at the end of the top row of the array. This shows through a representation that $D \times H = \frac{1}{2}D \times 2H$ using a powerful image. This proof can also be then linked to the associative property, in which students can compose or decompose numbers to find solutions. To demonstrate this first with simple numbers such as 4×16, we can show $4 \times 16 = 4 \times (2 \times 8) = (4 \times 2) \times 8 = 8 \times 8 = 64$. Then this can be eventually modeled for $D \times H$ where $D \times H = D \times (\frac{1}{2} \times 2)H = (D \times \frac{1}{2}) \times (2 \times H) = \frac{1}{2}D \times 2H$.

If students are to be successful in algebra, which is more abstract and symbolic than other mathematical topics in their curriculum, such discussions must be a part of the daily experience (Mark, Cuoco, Goldenberg, & Sword, 2010). This explicit focus on noticing patterns, seeking generalizations, and identifying structures using symbols is important in supporting the learning of those who struggle, as well as those who excel (Schifter et al., 2009). To do so requires advanced planning for what questions you can ask to help students think about generalized characteristics within the problem they are working, such as representing relationships (e.g., when the number of guinea pigs in one cage goes down by 1, the number in the other cage goes up by 1) and to think about other problems that follow the same pattern. By exploring patterns and noticing the repetition in reasoning, students begin to link the meanings of the operations with whole numbers and be able to transfer that knowledge later to those same operations with decimal fractions, for example.

The next activity is an interesting exploration for students in grades 3 through 5 and encourages students to notice patterns and move to generalizations.

Teaching Tip

You can help students see relationships and think algebraically by using well-planned, strategic questions. Collect the questions suggested throughout this chapter on note cards or on your tablet and keep them handy for lesson planning or classroom discussions.

Activity 15.1

CCSS-M: 3.OA.A.1; 3.OA.D.9

One Up and One Down: Multiplication

Show students that when you begin with $7 \times 7 = 49$ and then increase one factor and decrease the other factor, each by one, the product is one less than the original: $8 \times 6 = 48$. Their task is to explore this for other numbers multiplied by themselves (squares). To help with their exploration, suggest that they cut out the square array from grid paper. How can they change the square array into the new rectangle using scissors and tape? Students should use words, pictures, and numbers to tell what they have found. Does this pattern only work for square numbers? Students with disabilities will benefit from creating the array with 1-inch square tiles and manipulating the rows to match other students' work with grid paper.

The results of this activity are quite interesting and not obvious. The new product will be one less if the original product is a square—a number multiplied by itself. Figure 15.2 illustrates how an array changes in the case of a square. When the original factors are not alike (increase the larger number and decrease the smaller), the difference can be related to the difference in the original factors.

Here is an activity based on Russell, Schifter, and Bastable (2011) that develops the same thinking strategies, this time with decimals.

▶ Activity 15.2

CCSS-M: 5.NBT.B.7

Don't Push the Point

Start with a simple problem involving multiplication of decimals in which students can analyze the answer without computing. Once they agree that it is a true statement, then follow that equation with a series of related problems that can be solved by thinking about relationships between the expressions rather than computing the answers to each. Try a series such as the following:

$$34 \times 1 = 3.4 \times 10$$
$$34 \times 10 = 3.4 \times ?$$
$$34 \times 100 = 0.34 \times ?$$
$$34 \times 0.1 = 3.4 \times ?$$
$$34 \times 0.01 = 0.34 \times ?$$

Standards for
Mathematical Practice

8 Look for and express regularity in repeated reasoning.

Figure 15.2

What happens when you begin with a number times itself (7×7), and then make one factor one greater and the other factor one less?

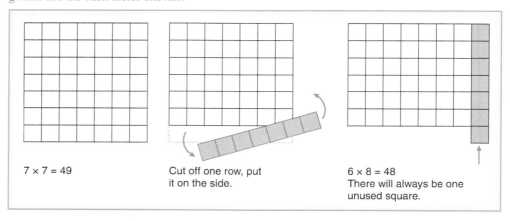

$7 \times 7 = 49$

Cut off one row, put it on the side.

$6 \times 8 = 48$
There will always be one unused square.

Behavior of the Operations

If we look back at previous chapters on operation sense, and whole-number computation to develop algebraic thinking, these ideas need to be infused with identifying the structure and generalizations inherent in the operations. Let's explore the use of the compensation strategy in adding numbers. So, given the problem $67 + 28$, students might suggest adding 3 to 67 to equal 70 and either subtract 3 from 28 to add 25 for a total of 95, or add 28 to 70 to get a total of 98 and then subtract the 3. This "doing and undoing" approach (Cai, Ng, & Moyer, 2011, p. 34) of course also works with multiplication and division, capitalizing on their inverse relationship. These investigations of the operations provide opportunities for conversations that emphasize generalizations. So to think about this addition problem differently, $x + y$ or $67 + 28$ is the same as $(x + a) + (y - a)$ or $(67 + 3) + (28 - 3)$.

For students in grades 3 through 5, these ideas of drawing relationships to algebraic thinking with whole-number operations need to be extended to operations with fractions. As stated by Empson, Levi, and Carpenter (2011), students must begin to anticipate moves they will need to make numerically with fractions that will allow them to transform the numbers (as done previously when they decomposed two-digit whole numbers) into easier numbers with which to operate. For example, in adding $\frac{1}{2} + \frac{7}{8}$, a student can think ahead and say

"$\frac{1}{2} + \frac{7}{8}$ is the same as $\frac{1}{2} + (\frac{4}{8} + \frac{3}{8})$. Then using already known relationships, the student can add using the associative property $(\frac{1}{2} + \frac{4}{8}) + \frac{3}{8}$ for a total of $1\frac{3}{8}$. Empson and colleagues go on to say "to understand arithmetic is to think *relationally* about arithmetic" (p. 412).

Place Value Relationships and Generalizations

Fundamental to mental mathematics is generalizing place-value concepts. Consider the sum $49 + 18$. How would you add it in your head? Many people will try to make a multiple of 10 and think $50 + 17$ (or adjust by two to get $47 + 20$).

There are many interesting patterns in the hundreds chart that can be discovered with a focus on operations and algebraic thinking. To connect arithmetic to algebra in the operations, give students a **Hundreds Chart** and ask, "Without counting, what do we add to get from 72 to 82? From 34 to 44?" When students note the generalized idea that they are adding 10 and moving exactly one row down, they are generalizing the idea of what +10 looks like. In the hundreds chart, moves can be represented with symbols—in this case arrows (for example, $\rightarrow$ means right one column or add 1, and $\uparrow$ means up one row or subtract 10). Consider asking students to complete these problems:

$$14 \rightarrow \rightarrow \leftarrow \leftarrow \qquad 63 \uparrow \uparrow \downarrow \downarrow \qquad 4 \rightarrow \uparrow \leftarrow \downarrow$$

What do you anticipate students will do? They may know to jump 10 (up or down) but still carry out all four arrow moves. Students who are reasoning and moving toward generalizations may recognize that a downward arrow "undoes" an upward arrow (Blanton, 2008). In other words, $+10 - 10$ results in a zero change. Students can write the equations for the arrow moves with numbers or with variables—for example, for the first problem, $n + 1 + 1 - 1 - 1 = n + (1 - 1) + (1 - 1) = n$.

 ## Formative Assessment Note

As students work on these tasks, observe them and record your thoughts using an **Observation Checklist**. Record on the checklist which students are still counting by ones with the use of jumping, or those who are thinking about the relationships and noticing the "doing" and "undoing." What you observe can help focus your discussion as you begin with students sharing the more basic strategies and then have students who have generalized the situation share how they think about it.

 ## Activity 15.3

Diagonal Sums

 Provide each student with a Hundreds Chart. Students select any four numbers in the hundreds chart that form a square. Add the two numbers on each diagonal as in the example shown here.

47	48	49	50
57	58	59	60
67	68	69	70
77	78	79	80

(continued)

Have students explore other squares and share their ideas with a partner of why this pattern works. For students with disabilities, have them use calculators so that they can explore the pattern without getting bogged down in computations. Expand their search to diagonals of any rectangle. For example, the numbers 15, 19, 75, and 79 form four corners of a rectangle. The sums 15 + 79 and 19 + 75 are equal. Challenge students to figure out why this is so.

Stop and Reflect   500 ◌, 250   ⧆ 3𝑥 ▱ ⌁ ⌀ ∞ ∩ ⨯ 2.5

Before reading further, stop and explore why the diagonal sums described in the previous activities are the same. What questions might you ask students to be sure they are noticing the relationship between tens and ones?

Here are some additional tasks you might explore on a hundreds chart. With each task, notice how the first aspect is about number and then questions focus on generalizations (algebraic thinking).

- Skip counting by different numbers (e.g., start with 3, then try 4 or 5) and placing a color marker down on (or shade with a marker) each square on the hundreds chart. Which numbers make diagonal patterns? Which numbers make column patterns? Can you describe a rule for explaining when a number will have a diagonal or column pattern?

- Pick a number. Move down two rows and over one column on the hundreds chart, what is the relationship between the original number and the new number? What algebraic equation describes this movement?

- Find two skip-count patterns where one color marker lands "on top of" the other (that is, all of the shaded values for one pattern are part of the shaded values for the other)? How are these two skip-count numbers related? Is this relationship true for any pair of the numbers you found?

- Pick a number on the chart. Add it to the number to the left of it and to the number to the right; then divide by 3. Try another number. What did you get? Explain what is happening.

These examples extend number concepts to algebraic thinking. Asking questions such as "When will this be true?" and "Why does this work?" require students to generalize and consequently strengthen the number concepts they are learning. Note that when students focus on patterns in skip counting, those identified relationships support their use of invented strategies for multiplication. In fact, the key to exploring patterns in the upper elementary curriculum is not for patterns' sake; it is to strengthen students' understanding of number relationships and properties. The more often you can ask students "Did you notice a pattern?" the more they are considering and making sense of the mathematics they are doing.

Standards for Mathematical Practice

7 Look for and make use of structure. ▶

Meaningful Use of Symbols

One reason that some students are unsuccessful in algebra is that they do not have a strong understanding of the symbols they are using. Symbols represent real situations and values and should be seen as useful tools for solving real-life problems including decision making (e.g., calculating how many boxes of cookies we need to sell to make x dollars or how many employees do we need to finish the project on time).

Looking at equivalent expressions that describe a context while encouraging generalization from a pattern is an effective way to bring meaning to numbers and symbols. The classic task (Boaler & Humphreys, 2005; Burns & McLaughlin, 1990) in Activity 15.4 involves such reasoning.

One method of identifying the pattern is to examine only one growth step and ask students to find a method of determining the number of elements without *counting by one*.

Activity 15.4

CCSS-M: 4.OA.B.4

The Border Tiles Problem

Ask students to build an **8 × 8** square array representing a swimming pool, using square color tiles such that tiles of a different color are used around the border (Figure 15.3). Challenge students to find at least two ways to determine the number of border tiles used without counting them one by one. Students should use their model, words, and number sentences to show how they calculated the number of tiles. Ask students to illustrate their solution on **1-Centimeter Grid Paper**. There are at least five different methods of finding the number of border tiles around a square other than counting them by ones.

Figure15.3

How many different ways can you find to calculate the number of border tiles around an 8 × 8 pool?

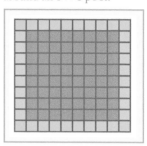

Stop and Reflect   500 ◑ 250   3✗ ▱ ⌓ ° ∞ ⌢ ✗ 2.5

See if you can find four or five different counting schemes for the border tiles problem. Can you see how the different expressions are equivalent? What questions might you pose to students in order to help them focus on the role of the equal sign in recording the equivalent expressions?

A very common solution to the border tiles problem is to notice that there are 10 tiles across the top and also across the bottom, leaving 8 tiles on either side. This might be written as:

$$10 + 10 + 8 + 8 = 36 \text{ or } (2 \times 10) + (2 \times 8) = 36$$

Each of the following expressions can likewise be traced to looking at the tiles in various groupings:

$$4 \times 9$$
$$(4 \times 8) + 4$$
$$(4 \times 10) - 4$$
$$100 - 64$$

More equivalent expressions are possible, because students may use addition instead of multiplication. In any case, once the generalizations are created, students need to justify how the elements in the expression map to the physical representation.

Another approach to the border tiles problem is to have students build a series of pools in growth steps, each with one more tile on the side (3 × 3, 4 × 4, 5 × 5, etc.). Then students can find a way to count the elements of each step using an algorithm that handles the step numbers in the same manner. Students can find, for example, number sentences parallel to what they wrote for the number of tiles in an 8 × 8 to find a 6 × 6 pool and a 7 × 7 pool. Eventually, this can result in a generalized statement, for example, taking the original $(2 \times 10) + (2 \times 8)$ and generalizing it to $2 \times (n + 2) + 2(n)$.

Standards for Mathematical Practice

8 Look for and express regularity in repeated reasoning.

Notice that the task just completed involved numeric expressions—a good place to start. These expressions did not involve the two types of symbols that are perhaps the most important to understand—and, unfortunately, among the least well understood by many students. The first type are relational symbols such as the equal sign (=) and inequality signs (<, >) and variables are the second type. The sections that follow provide strategies for helping students understand these symbols.

The Meaning of Variables

The equal sign is one of the most important symbols in elementary arithmetic, in algebra, and in all mathematics using numbers and operations. At the same time, research dating from 1975 to the present suggest that = is a very poorly understood symbol (Byrd-Hornburg, McNeil, Chesney, & Matthews, 2015; Kieran, 2007; Knuth, Stephens, Blanton, & Gardiner, 2016). The equal sign is rarely represented in textbooks in a way to encourage students to understand the equivalence relationship—an understanding that is critical to understanding algebra (McNeil et al., 2006). Although the *Common Core State Standards* require first graders to "understand the meaning of the equal sign," there are many students in grades 3 through 5 who do not fully understand the relationship that the equal sign describes.

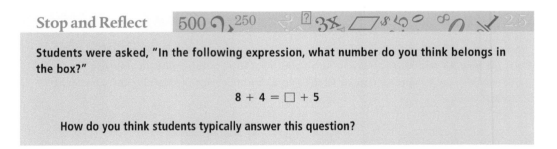

Stop and Reflect

Students were asked, "In the following expression, what number do you think belongs in the box?"

$$8 + 4 = \square + 5$$

How do you think students typically answer this question?

In a classic study, not even one sixth grader out of 145 put a 7 in the box (Falkner, Levi, & Carpenter, 1999). Try it with your students! The most common responses were 12 and 17. (How did students get these answers?)

Where do such misconceptions come from? A large majority of equations that students encounter in elementary school look like this: $5 + 7 = \underline{\quad}$ or $8 \times 45 = \underline{\quad}$. Naturally, students may come to think = as signifying "and the answer is," rather than a symbol to indicate the relationship of equivalence (Carpenter et al., 2003; McNeil & Alibali, 2005; Molina & Ambrose, 2006).

Subtle shifts in the way you approach teaching computation can alleviate this major misconception. For example, rather than always asking students to solve a problem (like $45 + 61$ or 4×26), ask them to find an equivalent expression and use that expression to write an equation (Blanton, 2008). So, for $45 + 61$, students might write $45 + 61 = 40 + 66$. For a multiplication problem, students might write $4 \times 26 = 4 \times 25 + 4$ or $4 \times 26 = 2 \times (2 \times 26)$. Activity 15.5 is a way to apply this idea.

🖋 Teaching Tip

When writing multiple equations in a string of addition, for example, do not attach them with equal signs unless they are equal. For example, when adding 6 and 6 and then adding 3 more to that answer and 7 more to that sum, do *not* write that as $6 + 6 = 12 + 3 = 15 + 7 = 22$. Doing this is incorrect and reinforces that the equal sign means "and the answer is" rather than the correct meaning of only linking quantities that are equal with an equal sign.

Activity 15.5
CCSS-M: 3.OA.A.1; 3.OA.A.2

Equal to the Challenge

 Use the **Equal to the Challenge Cards** or make your own collection of equivalent equations. Have student pairs set the cards out. One student selects a card and then the partners decide which card is equivalent and they put the pair together. You can ask students to verbally state the answer. Students can also play independently. The game can be modified for students with disabilities by creating some easier combinations as a starting point or only using a single operation, such as addition.

Why is it so important that students correctly understand the equal sign? First, it is important for students to understand and symbolize relationships in our number system and the equal sign is a principal method of representing these relationships. For example, $6 \times 7 = 5 \times 7 + 7$ shows a basic fact strategy linked to the distributive property of multiplication over addition. When these ideas, initially developed through arithmetic, are generalized and expressed symbolically, powerful relationships are available for working with other numbers in a generalized manner.

A second reason is that when students fail to understand the equal sign, they typically have difficulty with algebraic expressions (Knuth, Stephens, Blanton, & Gardiner, 2016). The equation $5x - 30 = 70$ requires students to see both sides of the equal sign as equivalent expressions. It is not possible to "do" the left-hand side. However, if both sides are understood as being equivalent, students will see that $5x$ must be 30 more than 70 or $5x = 70 + 30$.

Teaching Tip

When reading equations to students, use the language "equals" or "is the same as" when reading the equal sign. This reinforces that it is a relationship sign, rather than a sign signaling an operation.

Conceptualizing the Equal Sign as a Balance

Helping students understand the idea of equivalence can be developed concretely (Leavy, Hourigan, & McMahon, 2013). The next two activities illustrate how kinesthetic approaches, tactile objects, and visualizations can reinforce the "balancing" notion of the equal sign.

Activity 15.6
CCSS-M: 3.OA.A.1; 3.OA.A.2

Seesaw Students

  Ask students to raise their arms to look like a seesaw (make sure all students, particularly ELLs, know what a seesaw is—use an online video to show how it works). To start, ask students to imagine (or give them cards with a visual) that you have placed nine hamsters (that are of the same weight) in each of their left hands (students should tip to lower the left side). Ask students to imagine that you've placed another nine hamsters on the right side (students level off). Next, with the nine hamsters still there in each hand, ask students to imagine another 5 hamsters added to the left hand.

Now that students have the idea, give them numbers, multiplication facts, or other expressions either verbally or on cards for each side and ask them to show how the

(continued)

Teaching Tip

Remember, this activity can be used for fractions and decimal equivalents, as a way to compare and find equivalencies. Still maintain the emphasis on the equivalence and the equal sign by having students record the equations.

seesaw reacts. This is a particularly important activity for students with disabilities, who may be challenged with the abstract idea of balancing values of expressions, especially in symbolic form such as 15 × 8 = 8 × 15. They show better performance with pictorial or story representations of the equations (Driver & Powell, 2015).

Then use facts that are equal such as 9 × 4 and 6 × 6. When they are in the balanced position, ask students to add an amount such as 5 to one side, then add 5 to the other. How does the seesaw react? Ask, "What if we subtract 5 from each side?"

After acting out the seesaw movement several times, ask students to write Seesaw Findings (e.g., "If you have a balanced seesaw and add more to one side, it will tilt to that side," and "If you subtract the same amount from both sides of the seesaw, it will still be balanced"). These generalizations are critical to developing algebraic thinking.

Formative Assessment Note

You may be surprised at how common it is for students to interpret the equal sign as a symbol separating the problem from the answer. Ask students in a diagnostic interview to tell you what the equal sign means in an equation such as 5 × 8 = 40. Then ask the same question for 8 × 2 = 15 + 1. This equation format, where there is an operation on both sides of the equal sign, is the best to use when evaluating a student's understanding of the meaning of the equal sign (Powell, Kearns, & Driver, 2016). Students often believe that there must be an "answer" or single number on one side of the equal sign. Finally, ask whether it is acceptable to write something such as this: 5 = 5. Here students sometimes believe that there must be an operation involved if there is an equal sign. After the early introduction to the equal sign in first grade, the assumption is that students understand what you mean by "equals." This interview will help uncover any misunderstandings.

Activity 15.7

CCSS-M: 4.NBT.A.1; 5.NBT.A.3a, b

Tilt or Balance?

Give students a copy of **Two-Pan Balances**. In each pan, have them write a numeric expression and ask which pan will tilt down or whether the two sides will balance (see Figure 15.4(a)). They should write either the equation to illustrate the meaning of the equal sign (=) if the expressions balance or when the scale "tilts," indicate the relationship by either a "greater than" or "less than" symbol (> or <). Include examples (like the third and fourth balances in Figure 15.4(a)) for which students can make the determination by analyzing the relationships on both sides rather than doing the computation. For students with disabilities, instead of having them write expressions for each side of the scale, share the **Equal to the Challenge Cards** and have them identify pairs that will make the scale balance.

As an alternative or extension, use missing value expressions. Ask students to find a number that will result in each side tilting, and it being balanced (see Figure 15.4(b)). See the **Expanded Lesson: Tilt or Balance** and the **Tilt or Balance 1 and 2** Activity Pages for more details on teaching this activity.

The balance scale is a concrete tool that can help students understand that if you add or subtract a value from one side, you must add or subtract a like value from the other side to keep the equation balanced.

Figure 15.4

Using expressions and variables in equations and inequalities.
The two-pan balance helps develop the meaning of the equal sign.

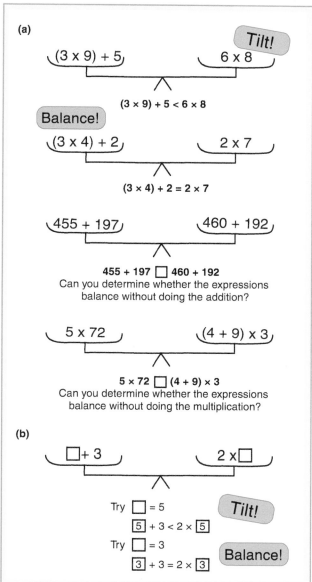

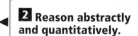

There are several excellent activities online that develop the idea of the balance relationship:

- *PBS Cyberchase Poddle Weigh-In:* Shapes are balanced with numbers between 1 and 4.
- *Agame Monkey Math Balance:* Students select numbers for each side of a balance to make the two sides balance (level of difficulty can be adapted).
- **NCTM Illuminations** *Pan Balance—Numbers* or *Pan Balance—Expressions* provide a virtual balance where students can enter what they believe to be equivalent expressions (with numbers or symbols) each in a separate pan to see whether the expressions balance.

Standards for
Mathematical Practice

◀ **2 Reason abstractly and quantitatively.**

True/False and Open Sentences

Carpenter and colleagues (2003) suggest that a good starting point for helping students with understanding the meaning of the equal sign is to explore equations as either true or false as seen in the following activity.

> ## ▶ Activity 15.8
> CCSS-M: 3.OA.B.5; 4.NBT.B.5; 5.NF.A.1
>
> ### True or False?
>
>
>
> Introduce true/false sentences or equations with simple examples to explain what is meant by a true equation and a false equation. Then put several simple equations on the board, some true and some false. Keep the computations simple so that the focus is on equivalence. Ask students to decide which of the equations are true and which are false. For each response, they must explain their reasoning. Here are some possible examples, but you should fit the problems you use to what your students are studying:
>
> $$120 = 60 \times 2 \qquad 1 = \frac{3}{4} + \frac{4}{3} \qquad 318 = 318$$
>
> $$\frac{1}{2} = \frac{1}{4} + \frac{1}{4} \qquad 345 + 71 = 70 + 344$$
>
> $$210 - 35 = 310 - 45 \qquad 0.4 \times 15 = 0.2 \times 30$$
>
> Listen to the types of reasons that students use to justify their answers and plan additional equations accordingly. ELLs and students with disabilities will benefit from first explaining (or showing) their thinking to a partner (a low-risk speaking opportunity) before sharing with the whole group. For false statements, ask students to rewrite the statement using $>$ or $<$ to make the statement true. *Pan Balance—Numbers* on NCTM's Illuminations website can be used to model and/or verify equivalence.

Standards for Mathematical Practice

> **7** **Look for and make use of structure.** ▶

After students have experienced true/false sentences, introduce an open sentence—one with a box representing an unknown to be filled in or letter used as a variable to represent the unknown. To develop an understanding of open sentences, encourage students to look at the number sentence holistically and discuss in words what the equation represents.

> ## ▶ Activity 15.9
> CCSS-M: 3.OA.A.4; 4.NF.B.3b; 5.OA.A.2
>
> ### What's Missing?
>
>
> Use the set of **Missing Value Equations** or pose several open sentences. Ask students to figure out what is missing and how they know. Notice that the equations encourage students to use relational understanding to figure out how to solve it, and they don't always need to perform the operation. Here is a sampling for operations with fractions and decimals:
>
> $$\frac{1}{2} + \square = 5 \qquad \square + 0.4 = 0.6 \qquad \frac{1}{4} + \frac{1}{2} = \square - 1$$
>
> $$0.3 \times 7 = 7 \times \square \qquad \square \times 4 = 4 \div 2 \qquad 2.4 \div \square = 4.8 \div 6$$
>
> Discuss how students solved the problems. Start with using open boxes, and then use question marks or begin to mix in variables in place of the open box so that students can see the variable as representing a missing value.

Relational Thinking. Students may think about equations in three ways, each developmental in nature (Stephens et al., 2013). First, as noted previously, they may have an operational view, thinking that the equal sign means "do something." Second, they develop a relational–computational view. At this phase, students understand that the equal sign symbolizes a relation between answers to two calculations, but they only see computation as the way to determine if the two sides are equal or not. Finally, students develop a relational–structural view of the equal sign (we will also refer to this as relational thinking). In this thinking, a student uses numeric relationships between the two sides of the equal sign rather than actually computing the amounts. Relational thinking using the third approach is a step toward generalizing from relationships found in arithmetic to relationships used when variables are involved. CCSS-M suggests that students begin to use letters to represent the unknown in third grade.

Consider the following two distinctly different explanations for suggesting $n = 8$ for the open sentence $7 + n = 6 + 9$. Students might explain:

1. Because $6 + 9$ is 15, I need to figure out 7 plus what equals 15. It is 8, so n equals 8.

2. Seven is one more than the 6 on the other side of the equal sign. That means that n should be one less than 9, so it must equal 8.

The first student computes the result on one side and adjusts the result on the other side to make the sentence true (relational–computational approach). The second student uses a relationship between the expressions on either side of the equal sign. This student does not need to compute the values on each side (relational–structural approach). When the numbers are large, relational–structural approach is more efficient and useful.

Stop and Reflect

How are the two students' correct responses for $7 + n = 6 + 9$ different? How would each of these students solve this open sentence?

$$534 + 175 = 174 + n$$

The first student will do the computation and will perhaps have difficulty finding the correct addend. The second student will use relational thinking to reason that 174 is one less than 175, so the variable n must represent one more than 534.

 Formative Assessment Note

You can use these tasks as a diagnostic interview (for those students from whom you need to gather more data). Listen for whether they are using relational thinking. If they are not, ask, "Can you find the answer without doing any computation?" This questioning helps nudge students toward relational thinking and helps you decide what instructional steps are next.

In order to nurture relational thinking and the meaning of the equal sign, explore this series of true/false and open sentences with your class. Select challenging equations designed to elicit relational thinking rather than computation such as using large numbers that make computation difficult (not impossible). Here are some examples.

TRUE/FALSE:

$674 - 389 = 664 - 379$ $5 \times 84 = 10 \times 42$

$37 + 54 = 38 + 53$ $64 \div 14 = 32 \div 28$

OPEN SENTENCES:

$73 + 56 = 71 + n$ $126 - 37 = n - 40$

$20 \times 48 = n \times 24$ $68 + 58 = 57 + 69 + n$

$7.03 + 0.05 = 7.01 + n$ $4800 \div 25 = n \times 48$

Stop and Reflect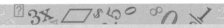

How might you use multistep sentences? Why is it important to have students think about the relationship of these ideas with multistep problems?

▶ Activity 15.10   CCSS-M: 3.OA.A.4; 4.NF.B.3a; 5.OA.A.2

Make a Statement!

 Ask students to write their own true/false and open sentences that they can use to challenge classmates. This works for both equations and inequalities! To support student thinking, provide dice with numerals on them. You can make the dice with different values on the faces to try different possibilities.

Ask students to write three equations (or inequalities) with at least one true and at least

one false sentence. For students who need additional structure, in particular students with disabilities, consider providing frames such as these:

_____ + _____ = _____ + _____   _____ + _____ > _____ + _____

_____ − _____ = _____ − _____   _____ + _____ < _____ − _____

_____ + _____ = _____ − _____   _____ + _____ > _____ − _____

(or use multiplication and division)

Students can trade their set of statements with other students to find the False Statement. Interesting equations/inequalities can be the focus of a follow-up full-class discussion.

The Meaning of Variables

Variables are first mentioned in the CCSS-M standards in grades 3 and 4 when students begin to use letters to stand for unknown quantities. Variables can be used to represent a unique but unknown quantity or represent a quantity that varies. Unfortunately, students often think that the variable is a placeholder for one exact number and not that a variable could represent multiple, even infinite values. Experiences in grades 3–5 should focus on building meaning for variables such as these:

1. *As a specific unknown.* Initially this is the use found in equations such as $8 + \square = 12$. Later, we see exercises such as this: If $3x + 2 = 4 \times 14$, solve for x.

2. *As a pattern generalizer.* Variables are used in statements that are true for all numbers. For example, $a \times b = b \times a$ for all real numbers.

3. *As quantities that vary.* Sometimes two variables are used within an equation to communicate a relationship, such as $y = 3x$ to represent x items that cost $3 each ($y$ would be the total cost). This is called joint variation because when one quantity (x) changes so does another (y). Formulas are also an example of joint variation. In $A = L \times W$, as L (length) and W (width) change, so does A, the area.

Teaching Tip

Variables should be written as lowercase letters in italics. This will also help support students' challenges with seeing the difference between $\times$ as a multiplication operation and the variable x.

Variables as Unknown Values

In the open sentence explorations, the $\square$ or the ? are precursors of a letter variable used as an unknown or missing value. Even in the primary grades, open boxes, as well as question marks or letters, can be used in open sentences or missing value problems. So beginning with boxes and then transitioning to variables helps make this connection explicit. Initial work with finding the value of the variable that makes the sentence true should initially rely on relational thinking (reasoning).

Teaching Tip

Begin to shift your language. Rather than ask students "What number goes in the box?" transition to "What number could the letter represent to make the number sentence true?"

Context can help students develop meaning for variables. Many story problems involve a situation in which the variable is a specific unknown, as in the following basic example:

Gary ate 14 strawberries and Jeremy ate some, too. The container of 25 strawberries was gone! How many did Jeremy eat?

Although students can solve this problem mentally without using algebra, they can begin to learn about variables by expressing it in symbols: $14 + n = 25$, where the n represents the number of strawberries that Jeremy ate. These problems can grow in difficulty over time.

The following activity is a reasonable way for students to experience the meaning of a variable within a context.

Activity 15.11

CCSS-M: 3.OA.D.8; 4.OA.A.3

Story Translations

Read a simple story problem to students but omit the question. Their task is to write an equation that models the situation. For example: "There are 3 full boxes of pencils and 5 extra pencils; there are 41 pencils in all" can be written as $3 \times n + 5 = 41$ in which n represents the number of pencils in a box. Be sure to include stories for all four operations. The activity can be reversed by providing an equation with an unknown and letting students make up a story to go with it. Once equations are agreed on, students should try different strategies to find values that make the sentences true.

Teaching Tip

Avoid using the first letter of the word as a variable in problems (for example, using *s* for strawberries in this example instead of the better choice of *n*). Many students confuse those "first letter in a word" variables with shortened versions of the word (more like a label) instead of thinking of the variable as a quantity (Booth, 1988; Küchemann, 1981). So in the problem above 3*p* could be confused as 3 pencils instead of 3 times the number of pencils in the box (*n*).

Sometimes students will write what may look like different equations. Consider this situation: Al has 3 times as many baseball cards as Mark. If Mark has 75 cards, how many does Al have? Some students may write $x = 3 \times 75$ while others may write $x \div 3 = 75$. Students can then discuss how these equations are alike and different. The result will be a better understanding of the inverse relationship between multiplication and division.

Other times drawings can help represent the ideas and help support the use of variables in equations. Look at the following example.

Roberto has a 54-page book. He wants to read the book in three days. If he wants to read the same number of pages each day, how many pages should he read on the first day?

If you look at Figure 15.5, you will see how two students approached the problem by using drawings to help them decide which operation to use. By representing the unknown amounts with variables they were able to reason about the situation.

Figure 15.5

Drawings that incorporate unknown amounts help students understand what operations to use.

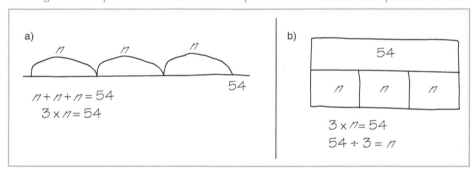

The following activity illustrates how a variable that represents a specific unknown can be manipulated or treated just like a number.

Activity 15.12

CCSS-M: 5.OA.A.2

Solving the Mystery

 Have students do the following sequence of operations:

- Write down any number.
- Add to it the number that comes after it.

- Add 9.

- Divide by 2.

- Subtract the number you began with.

Now you can "read their minds." Everyone ended up with 5! Ask students, "How does this work?" Start with *n*. Add the next number: $n + (n + 1) = 2n + 1$. Adding 9 gives $2n + 10$. Dividing by 2 leaves $n + 5$. Now subtract the number you began with, leaving 5. For students with disabilities or students who are struggling with variables, suggest that instead of using an actual number, they use blocks to begin with and physically build the steps of a problem (see Figure 15.6). See also a second Solving the Mystery Task Activity Page. In this mystery, the result is a two-digit number where the tens place is the first number selected and the ones place is the second number selected (ask students to explain how this works). Also see More Mysteries. Students who need a challenge can generate their own number mysteries!

Figure 15.6

Number mystery sequences can be modeled using a block or a box for the unknown. Additional numbers are shown with counters or base-ten materials.

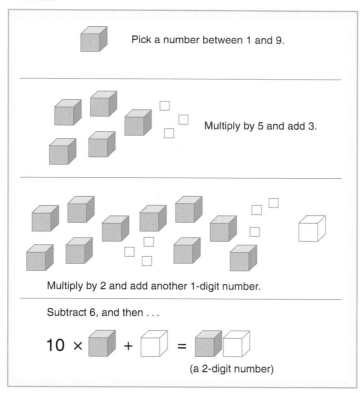

Variables As a Way to Represent Patterns

Variables are often used to illustrate rules or regularities that exist in our number system. We often write down these rules using variables without giving much thought to the fact that students may not understand the variables involved. The next two activities focus on this topic.

Activity 15.13

CCSS-M: 3.OA.B.5; 4.NF.A.3a

What's True for All Numbers?

Ask students how they know that 465 + 137 = 137 + 465 without doing the computation. Students' explanations should show evidence of understanding the commutative property for addition.

How can this be written to show that it's a rule that is true for every number, even fractions and decimals? If students do not suggest it, offer the idea that letters or shapes could be used like this:

$$\Delta + \square = \square + \Delta \quad \text{or} \quad n + m = m + n$$

Be sure students understand that the choice of letter or shape is totally arbitrary, as long as it is understood that each stands for any number and that when the same letter or shape appears in the same equation, it must represent the same value. Try the Missing Numbers Activity Page to have students look for a pattern.

With this introduction, challenge students to find other statements that are true for all numbers. Students with disabilities may need support with some visual examples such as the divided rectangle shown in Figure 15.7. Ask, "What are two ways to calculate the area?" This can lead to the generalized version of the distributive property: $a (b + c) = (a \times b) + (a \times c)$.

Standards for Mathematical Practice

7 Look for and make use of structure. ▶

Figure 15.7

The distributive property of multiplication over addition is just one of many ideas that can be generalized using variables.

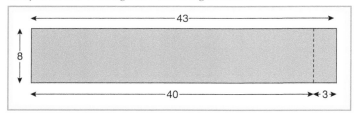

Variables As Quantities That Change Together

Whenever students develop charts that list the corresponding values of two related quantities, they are exploring the idea of joint variation; the value in one column varies according to the value in the other column. Think back to the guinea pigs' problem earlier in this chapter. As one cage gets more guinea pigs, the other gets fewer (joint variation), and as the total number of guinea pigs increases, the different ways they can be placed in the two cages also increases. Students can also make charts relating cost to the number of units purchased or relating miles driven to gallons of gasoline used. In measurement, charts are made that relate perimeter of a square to the length of a side. These are also examples of functions which will be a large part of the middle school experience.

Making Structure in the Number System Explicit

In grades 3 through 5, understanding the properties of the operations are essential to computation (Blanton, Levi, Crites, & Dougherty, 2011). Traditionally, instruction on the properties has been on matching equations to which property they illustrate. That basic pairing is not sufficient and should not be the focus of your instruction on the properties. Instead, emphasize helping students recognize and understand these important generalizations—and more importantly how to use them to generate equivalent expressions in order to solve problems efficiently and flexibly. For example, understanding the commutative property for both addition and multiplication reduces substantially the number of facts to be memorized.

Students should examine these properties explicitly and begin to see they can be written in generalized terms. For example, a student solving $394 + 176 = n + 394$ recognizes the commutative property and uses it to efficiently solve the problem. She may say that n must be 176 because $394 + 176$ is the same as $176 + 394$. To articulate this (and other structural properties of our number system) in a general way, ask students to share the generalization in symbols (e.g., $a + b = b + a$). This makes the connection from number to algebra explicit while using notation that shows that this relationship is true for numbers beyond those in the particular problem. When made explicit and understood, these structures add to students' tools for computation and enrich their understanding of the number system by providing a base for higher levels of abstraction (Blanton et al., 2011; Carpenter et al., 2003).

Just as sets of tasks can be used to generalize an algorithm, sets of tasks can be used to focus on the properties:

35	52	23	46
$\times 52$	$\times 35$	$\times 46$	$\times 23$

$$\frac{1}{6} \times 12 = \qquad 12 \times \frac{1}{6} = \qquad \frac{2}{3} \times 12 = \qquad 12 \times \frac{2}{3} =$$

Although students may understand the commutative property of multiplication with whole numbers, they may not recognize that the property also applies to multiplication of fractions (in fact, all real numbers). Ask students "Is this property true for fractions?" "Is this property true for other types of numbers?" "True for all numbers?"

Making Sense of Properties

Properties of the number system can be built into students' explorations with true/false and open number sentences. Discussing problem sets such as these, and others, helps students to make sense of the properties. In this third-grade vignette, the teacher is helping students to reason about the commutative property.

Teacher: [*Pointing at $5 \times 3 = 3 \times 5$ on the board.*] Is it true or false?

Carmen: True, because 5×3 equals 15 and 3×5 equals 15.

Andy: There are 5 groups of 3 on one side and 3 groups of 5 on the other side. They look different when I show them using counters on paper plates, but they are the same amounts on both sides.

Teacher: [*Writing $6 \times 9 = 9 \times 6$ on the board.*] True or false?

Class: True! It's the same!

Teacher: [*Writing $25 \times 4 = 4 \times 25$ on the board.*] True or false?

Class: True!

Teacher: Who can describe what is going on with these examples?

Rene:	If you are multiplying the same numbers on each side, you get the same amount.
Teacher:	Does it matter what numbers I use?
Class:	No.
Teacher:	[*Writing $a \times 7 = 7 \times a$ on the board.*] What is a?
Michael:	It can be any number because it's on both sides.
Teacher:	[*Writing $a \times b = b \times a$ on the board.*] What are a and b?
Class:	Any number!

Notice how the teacher is developing the generalizable aspects of the commutative property of multiplication in a conceptual manner—focusing on examples to guide students to generalize, rather than asking students to memorize or identify the properties, which can be a meaningless, rote activity.

The structure of numbers can sometimes be illustrated geometrically. For example, as noted previously in Figure 15.7, 8×43 can be illustrated as a rectangular array. That rectangle can be partitioned into two rectangles (e.g., $(8 \times 40) + (8 \times 3)$), preserving the quantity.

Standards for Mathematical Practice

> **7 Look for and make use of structure.** ▶

Challenge students to think about this idea *in general*, first described in words, and then as symbols: $a \times b = (c \times b) + (d \times b)$, where $c + d = a$. Be sure students can connect the examples to general ideas and the general ideas back to examples. This is the distributive property, and it is perhaps the most important central idea in arithmetic (Goldenberg, Mark, & Cuoco, 2010).

Table 15.1. Properties of the operations.

Name of Property	Symbolic Representation	How a Student Might Describe the Pattern or Structure
Addition		
Commutative	$a + b = b + a$	"When you add two numbers in any order, you will get the same answer."
Associative	$(a + b) + c = a + (b + c)$	"When you add three numbers, you can add the first two and then add the third or add the last two numbers and then add the first number. Either way, you will get the same answer."
Additive Identity	$a + 0 = 0 + a = a$	'When you add zero to any number, you get the same number you started with."
	$a - 0 = a$	"When you subtract zero from any number, you get the number you started with."
Additive Inverse	$a - a = 0$ or $a + (-a) = 0$	"When you subtract a number from itself, you get zero."
Inverse Relationship of Addition and Subtraction	If $a + b = c$ then $c - b = a$ and $c - a = b$	"When you have a subtraction problem you can 'think addition' by using the inverse."
Multiplication		
Commutative	$a \times b = b \times a$	"When you multiply two numbers in any order, you will get the same answer."
Associative	$(a \times b) \times c = a \times (b \times c)$	"When you multiply three numbers, you can multiply the first two and then multiply the answer by the third or multiply the last two numbers and then multiply that answer by the first number. Either way, you will get the same answer."
Multiplicative Identity	$a \times 1 = 1 \times a = a$	"When you multiply one by any number, you get the same number you started with."

Table 15.1. Properties of the operations.

Name of Property	Symbolic Representation	How a Student Might Describe the Pattern or Structure
Multiplicative Inverse	$a \times \frac{1}{a} = \frac{1}{a} \times a = 1$	"When you multiply a number by its reciprocal, you will get one."
Inverse Relationship of Multiplication and Division	If $a \times b = c$ then $c \div b = a$ and $c \div a = b$	"When you have a division problem, you can 'think multiplication' by using the inverse operation."
Distributive (Multiplication over Addition)	$a \times (b + c) = a \times b + a \times c$	"When you multiply two numbers, you can split one number into two parts (5 can be *2 + 3*), multiply each part by the other number, and then add them together."

Making Conjectures Based on Properties

A great way to make the properties of the operations explicit is to have students explore ideas on what they notice to be always true. Ask students to try to state an idea in words of something they think is always true. For example, when multiplying a number by a second number, you can decompose the first number and multiply each part by the second number, and you will get the same answer. If a generalization is not clear or entirely correct, have students discuss the wording until all agree and then write this verbal statement of the property on the board. Call it a *conjecture*, and explain that it is not necessarily a true statement just because we think that it is true. Until someone either proves it or finds a counterexample—an instance for which the conjecture is not true—it remains a conjecture.

Noticing generalizable properties and attempting to justify or prove that they are is true is a significant form of algebraic reasoning and is at the heart of what it means to do mathematics (Ball & Bass, 2003; Carpenter et al., 2003; Schifter, Monk, Russell, & Bastable, 2007).

The most common form of justification is the use of examples. Students will try lots of specific numbers in a conjecture. "It works for any number you try." They may try very large numbers as substitutes for "any" number and they may try fractions or decimal values. Proof by example will lead to someone asking, "How do we know there aren't some numbers that it doesn't work for?" Then, students may reason with physical materials or illustrations to show the reasoning behind the conjecture.

The distributive property is central to basic facts and the algorithms for the operations. For example, in learning the multiplication facts, students learn derived fact strategies. For 6×8, they can split up the 6 however they like, multiply its parts by 8, and then put it back together (e.g., $(5 \times 8) + (1 \times 8) = 6 \times 8$). They may justify this with the following rectangles:

Teaching Tip

When students offer the response "I think it is true," make sure you have them elaborate on what "it" is, so that other students can benefit from the thinking and so the student learns to use more precise language.

Standards for Mathematical Practice

◀ **3** Construct viable arguments and critique the reasoning of others.

Teaching Tip

When conjectures are made in class, rather than responding with an answer, ask "Do you think that is always true? How can we find out?" Students need to reason through ideas based on their own thinking rather than simply relying on the word of others.

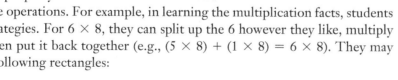

What moves this beyond "proof by example" is an explanation such as, "It would work this way no matter what the numbers are." Activity 15.14 explores properties of odd and even numbers and can lead to proof using physical materials or variables.

Activity 15.14

Broken Calculator: Can You Fix It?

 Distribute calculators to every student. In partners, have them explore one of these two problems. They must decide if it is possible, and either way they must share an example of how to do it (or a counterexample) and prepare a justification or illustration to describe why it does or does not work.

1. If you cannot use any of the even keys (0, 2, 4, 6, 8), can you create an even number in the calculator display? If so, how?

2. If you cannot use any of the odd keys (1, 3, 5, 7, 9), can you create an odd number in the calculator display? If so, how?

Invite early finishers to take on the other problem or to write their justifications using variables. In the follow-up discussion, ask students for other patterns or generalizations they notice about odd and even numbers.

Activity 15.15

Convince Me Conjectures

 Offer students a conjecture to test from the Conjecture Cards Activity Page. For example, "if you add 1 to one addend and subtract 1 from the other addend, the answer will be the same." Ask students to (1) test the conjecture and (2) prove it is true for any number. Point out the difference between testing (just trying it once) and proving. Then invite students to create their own conjecture stated in words. Then they must prepare a visual or verbal explanation to convince others that it is always true. The full class should discuss the various conjectures, asking for clarity or challenging conjectures with counterexamples. All students, but particularly ELLs, may struggle with correct and precise terms. You can "revoice" their ideas using appropriate phrases to help them learn to communicate mathematically, but be careful to not make this the focus—the focus should be on the ideas presented. Students with disabilities benefit from the presentation and discussion of counterexamples.

Odd and even numbers provide an excellent context for exploring structure of the number system. Students will often observe that the sum of two even numbers is even, that the sum of two odd numbers is even, or that the sum of an even and an odd number is always odd. To explain why two odd number addends equal an even number as the answer, a student might explain that when you divide an odd number by two, there will be a leftover. If you do this with the second odd number, it will have a leftover also. The two leftovers will go together when you add the numbers so there won't be a leftover in the sum. Students should also use manipulatives such as connecting cubes to show their reasoning.

Look back as Figure 15.1, which shows a fourth grader's "Convince Me Conjecture" illustration for the conjecture: *For a product, you can take half of the one factor and double the other factor and you will get the same answer.* Although the student's work only shows two examples, the student is illustrating that this process of cutting the array into half and repositioning that piece to create a new array, can be generalized for other numbers. Ask students how they might write the conjecture in symbols. For this example, students might write "If $a \times b = c$, then $\frac{1}{2} a \times 2b = c$.

Using and applying the properties is central to mathematical proficiency as it is not only emphasized in the CCSS-M content standards, but also in the Mathematical Practices (CCSSO, 2010). An explicit focus on looking for structure and making generalizations is also important in supporting the range of learners in the classroom, from those who struggle to those who excel (Schifter, Russell, & Bastable, 2009). Doing so requires planning—deciding what questions you can ask to help students think about generalized characteristics within the problems they are doing—across the mathematical strands.

Patterns and Functional Thinking

Patterns are found in all areas of mathematics. Learning to look for patterns and how to describe, translate, and extend them is part of thinking algebraically. Two of the eight mathematical practices actually begin with the phrase "look for," implying that students who are mathematically proficient pay attention to patterns as they do mathematics.

Identifying and extending patterns is an important process in algebraic thinking. By third grade, students will have had numerous experiences with repeating patterns—patterns that have a core that repeats. In addition to simply extending the patterns using materials or drawings, they should also have translated patterns from one medium to another. For example, a pattern made with triangles and circles can be translated to one involving red and yellow circular counters. The essence of both patterns remains the same. When two patterns made with very different materials are each read in the same manner, how they are mathematically alike becomes obvious—they have the same pattern structure.

Students typically use materials such as color tiles, pattern blocks, toothpicks, or simply drawings to both copy and extend patterns that repeat. A few examples of repeating patterns are shown in Figure 15.8.

Figure 15.8

Examples of repeating patterns using manipulatives.

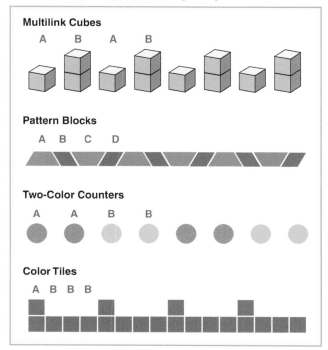

The study of patterns and functions is infused throughout the CCSS-M, and explicitly addressed in these standards:

- *Identify arithmetic patterns.* These may include patterns in the hundreds chart or multiplication table. (grade 3)
- *Generate a number or shape pattern that follows a given rule.* Identify apparent features of the pattern that were not explicit in the rule itself. (grade 4)
- *Generate two numerical patterns using two given rules.* Identify apparent relationships between corresponding terms. (grade 5)

For most repeating patterns, the elements of the pattern can be numbered 1, 2, 3, and so on (often referred to as *terms* or *steps*). The next activity will require consideration of these terms and is a forerunner to looking at the function aspect of patterns.

Activity 15.16   CCSS-M: 4.OA.B.4

Predict down the Line

Provide students with a pattern to extend (e.g., an ABC pattern). Before students begin to extend the pattern, have them predict exactly what element will be in, say, the twelfth step. Students should be required to write an explanation of their thinking regarding the reason for their prediction and support their words with visuals.

Notice in an ABC pattern that the third, sixth, ninth, and twelfth terms are the C element. Students can use their developing concepts of multiplication and division to predict what the 18th and 25th term would be. Ask them to predict what the element will be in the 100th term. Because $100 \div 3 = 33$ remainder 1, it would be the A element in the pattern. If predicting the 100th element, students will not be able to easily check the prediction by extending the pattern.

Students are surrounded by patterns in the world around them and these patterns can be analyzed and used to make predictions. One context is the Olympics. The Summer Olympics are held in 2020, 2024, and every four years after that. The Winter Olympics are held in 2018, 2022, and so on. Ask students to create a way to determine if x year will be an Olympic year (in general), a Summer Olympic year, and/or a Winter Olympic year (Bay-Williams & Martinie, 2004).

Hurricanes also are named in a repeating manner and can be analyzed and generalized as in this next activity.

Activity 15.17   CCSS-M: 4.OA.A.3; 4.OA.B.4; 5.OA.B.3

Hurricane Names

Ask students what they know about hurricanes and hurricane names. Hurricanes are named such that the first one of the year has a name starting with A, then B, and so on. For each letter, there are six names in a six-year cycle using an ABCDEF pattern (except those that are retired after a major hurricane). The gender of the names alternate in an AB pattern. Invite students to select a letter of the alphabet and look up the list of six names on the web. Ask students to answer questions such as these (assume no names are retired):

- Look at the first name on your list. What years will the hurricanes be named after that name? The last name on your list? What years will the hurricanes be a girl's name?
- What will the hurricane's name be in the year 2020? 2030? 2050?
- Can you describe in words how to figure out the name of a hurricane, given the year?

Growing Patterns

Students can explore patterns that involve a progression from step to step (term to term). In technical terms, these are called *sequences*; we will simply call them *growing patterns*. With these patterns, students not only extend or identify the core but also look for a generalization or an algebraic relationship that will tell them what the pattern will be at any point along the way (e.g., the *n*th term). Figure 15.9(a) is a growing pattern in which Step 1 requires three triangles, Step 2 requires six triangles, and so on—so we can say that the number of triangles needed is a function of which numbered step it is (in this case, number of triangles = 3 × step number).

Geometric patterns make good examples because the pattern is easy to see and students can manipulate the objects. Figure 15.9 illustrates three different growing patterns, though the possibilities for visuals are endless. The questions in Activity 15.18, mapped to the pattern in Figure 15.9(a), can be adapted to any growing pattern and help students begin to reason about functional situations.

Analyzing growing patterns should include the developmental progression of reasoning by looking at the visuals, then reasoning about the numerical relationships, and then extending to a larger (or *n*th) case (Friel & Markworth, 2009). Students' experiences with growing patterns should start with fairly straightforward patterns (such as in Figure 15.9) and continue with patterns that are more complicated (such as the Dot Pattern in Figure 15.10).

When discussing a pattern, students should determine how each step in the pattern differs from the preceding step and how to operate on the value of the current step to get to the next step. Examples should encourage students to use both additive and multiplicative strategies.

Growing patterns also have a numeric component—the number of objects in each step. One row of the table or chart is always the number of steps, and the other is for recording how many objects are in that step. This leads to the following activity, based on Figure 15.9(a).

Figure 15.9

Geometric growing patterns using manipulatives.

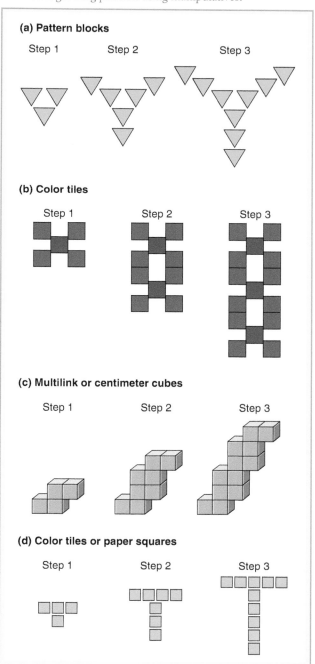

Activity 15.18

CCSS-M: 5.OA.B.3

Predict How Many

Working in pairs or small groups, have students explore the **Predict How Many Triangle Growing Pattern** Activity Page. Or have them complete a table that shows the number of triangles for each step such as this one:

Step Number (Term)	1	2	3	4	5	10	20
Number of Triangles (Element)							

- How many triangles are needed for step 10? Step 20? Step 100? Explain your reasoning.
- Write a rule (in words and/or symbols) that gives the total number of pieces to build any step number (*n*).

ELLs may need clarification on the specialized meanings of *step* and *table* because these words mean something else outside of mathematics.

Analyzing growing patterns should include the developmental progression of reasoning by looking at the visuals, then reasoning about the numerical relationships, and then extending to a larger (or *n*th) case (Friel & Markworth, 2009). Students' experiences with growing patterns should start with fairly straightforward patterns in grade 3 (such as in Figure 15.9) and continue with patterns that are somewhat more complicated (look at Figure 15.10) as they are asked in grades 4 and 5 to generate and analyze patterns. Then students can try **Predict How Many Windows** or **Predict How Many Dot Arrays**.

With the shift to the heavy focus on fractions in grades 3 through 5, including fractions and decimals in working with growing patterns is a crucial algebraic connection to foster.

Figure 15.10

Two different ways to analyze relationships in the "dot pattern."

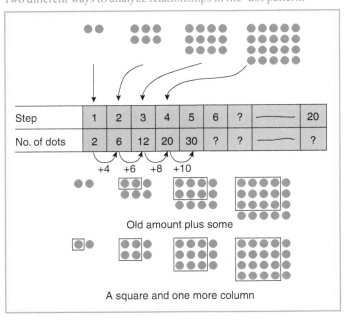

A square and one more column

When looking for relationships, some students will focus on the table and others will focus on the physical pattern. It is important for students to be able to use both representations. If a relationship is found in a table, challenge students to see how that plays out in the physical model, and vice versa.

The patterns discussed so far, repeating and growing patterns, are far from the only patterns in mathematics (not even all the options in growing patterns). Students not only need opportunities to explore patterns, but also to learn to expect, see, and use patterns in all of mathematics.

Standards for
Mathematical Practice

◄ **5** Use appropriate
tools strategically.

Functional Thinking

Functions are relationships that describe situations that demonstrate joint variation (see previous section on variables as quantities that change together) or covariance. Although functions and function notation is the focus of eighth grade (CCSSO, 2010), experiences with functional thinking situations must begin with meaning-making experiences in the elementary grades (Blanton & Kaput 2011; Cañadas, Brizuela, & Blanton, 2016; Stephens, Blanton, Knuth, Isler, & Gardiner, 2015). First, geometric growing patterns provide a concrete and engaging way to introduce functions. Second, contexts build meaning for functions and for the relevance of algebra in general. Third, thinking of functions in an input–output manner helps students develop the meaning of function.

Algebraic thinking also involves learning different ways to represent functions. As we saw with growing patterns, functional relationships can be represented in a real context, in a chart or table, with a graph, with an equation, and with words. Each different representation offers a different way to think about relationships and, thus, helps us to better understand them.

ℒ *Teaching Tip*

Asking questions will help your students analyze specific examples in order to determine the general relationship: What is changing? What is staying the same? What is changing will become the variable.

▶ Activity15.19

CCSS-M: 4.OA.C.5

Two of Everything

Two of Everything: A Chinese Folktale (Hong, 1993) is a story about Mr. and Mrs. Haktak, who discover a pot that doubles whatever goes in it, including Mrs. Haktak! Ask students to explore the doubling pattern in the story by using the Double Magic Activity Page. Students can also make simple tables with "input" and "output" as labels at the top of the two columns to help them generalize and write an equation to describe the pattern. Ask, "What if 200 pencils were dropped in the pot? If 60 tennis balls were pulled out, how many were dropped in the pot?" On the next day, explain that the Magic Pot has been acting up! It is not just doubling, but it is using a different rule. Give students the Magic Pot Mystery Rules Activity Page with partially completed tables that represent different rules. For each, ask students to add examples to the table and explain the rule in words and as an equation. This lesson is good for ELLs because the storyline brings in another culture, it has a concrete situation that is easily acted out or illustrated, completing the tables for the different rules does not involve a great deal of vocabulary, and there are great opportunities for student communication (speaking and listening). This lesson also works well for students with disabilities because using an image of a pot and concrete representations combined with a table of values can support their thinking about an input–output relationship.

Notice the explicit connection in this story to the input–output concept of patterns and relationship. Something goes in the pot, and then something came out of the pot (in-pot, out-pot).

When students examine real-world functions or explore growing patterns, the relationship is found in the context—for example, horses in a race. Students should be engaged in conversations in which they link the multiplicative relationship to the context such as "for every one horse in the race, there are four legs." Another student may say "six legs for every horse if you are counting the jockey."

The students' task is to represent relationships in a variety of ways including words, pictures, numbers, charts, graphs, and equations. Another important type of activity is to determine the relationship or the rule by simply observing the numbers that are paired up without a context involved. This could be done by giving students a partially filled in chart and asking them to determine the rule. A completely equivalent format that is generally more fun is a "function machine" as described in the next activity.

Figure 15.11

A simple function machine is used to play "In and out Machine." Students suggest input numbers and the operator records the output value.

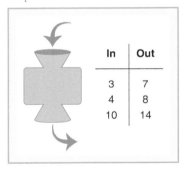

▶ Activity 15.20

CCSS-M: 4.OA.C.5

In and Out Machine

Draw a simple in–out "machine" on the board, as shown in Figure 15.11. The machine "operator" knows the secret rule that is stored in the machine. For example, a rule might be "double the input number and add 1." Students try to guess the rule by putting numbers into the machine and observing what comes out. A list of in–out pairs is kept on the board in a table. Students who think they have guessed the rule raise their hands. As more numbers are put into the machine, those students who think they know the rule are called on to tell what comes out. Continue until most have guessed the rule. Students who need a challenge can create their own rules to try to stump their classmates.

There are numerous websites that offer input–output machine investigations such as those at NLVM, Math Playground, and Shodor Project Interactive, among others.

▶ Activity 15.21

CCSS-M: 5.OA.B.3

Perimeter Patterns

Using a document camera or interactive whiteboard, show rows of same-shape pattern blocks (see Figure 15.12). Working in pairs or small groups, have students build each pattern and explore what patterns they notice about how the perimeter of each row of shapes grows. Ask: "What is the perimeter of a row with 6 squares? 10 squares? Any number of squares?" Repeat the process with trapezoids and hexagons (or have different groups of students working on different shapes). Distribute **Coordinate Graph** paper and ask students to create a graph to illustrate the relationship between the number of pattern blocks in the row and the perimeter.

Figure 15.12

Same-color strings of pattern blocks. Find the perimeter.

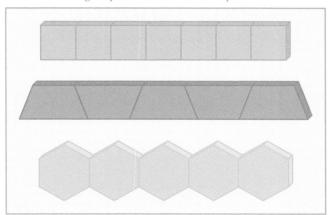

 Formative Assessment Note

Students need to connect the numbers in the tables or charts they build with the actual patterns and with the graphs. After students have constructed a graph for their physical pattern, conduct a diagnostic interview and ask them to select different numbers in the graph and ask them to explain where these numbers came from in the pattern or chart (or both). If your students have been able to find a general rule related to the pattern, they should be able to use the rule to determine the number associated with any set of numbers in the table with any point in the graph.

So far, patterns have been represented by (1) physical materials or drawings, (2) tables, (3) words, and (4) symbols. A graph adds a fifth representation. In the *Common Core State Standards*, coordinate graphs are introduced in fifth grade, in which students represent real-world data and solve mathematical problems in the first quadrant (CCSSO, 2010). Figure 15.13 provides a graph of the border tiles problem and shows a graph for the dot pattern.

Here are some other examples of real-world situations that give rise to graphs for intermediate-grade students.

- The length of a row of students holding arms outstretched. The *x*-axis can represent the number of students; the *y*-axis the length of the row.

- Weight of jellybeans in increments of 10 jellybeans. The weight of jellybeans is a function of the number of jellybeans.

- Height of liquid in a glass determined by the number of units poured in. Liquid is measured into the bottle using a small container, such as a medicine cup. The height of the liquid in the glass is a function of the quantity of liquid poured in.

- Height of bean plants compared to the days since they sprouted. The height of the bean plant is a function of the number of days since it was planted.

Figure 15.13

Graphs of two growing patterns.

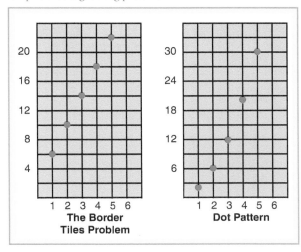

These real-world examples provide opportunities to connect the graphing of points on the coordinate axis with algebra. Ask questions about what students notice about their data on the graph. What might they predict for an x value they did not plot on the graph? Why? How does the graph provide insights into the situation?

Try this with fifth graders who are exploring the volume of solids. Consider the task of creating a tower of 1-inch cubes. The base of the tower is 2 inches by 3 inches. As the height of the tower changes from 1 inch to 10 inches, the volume of the tower will increase in 6-cubic-inch increments for each inch added. The equation would be $V = H \times 6$, and the graph will be a series of points that are in a straight line. The graph or the equation can be used to predict how many cubes would be needed for a tower of any height or, if the number of cubes is known, to be able to determine how tall a tower could be built.

Standards for Mathematical Practice

4 **Model with mathematics.** ▶

Table 15.2. Common errors and misconceptions in Algebra and how to help.

Common Error or Misconception	What It Looks Like	How to Help
1. The equal sign means "give me the answer" or the "answer is coming up next."	$8 + 4 = \boxed{12} + 5$	• Students put an answer such as 12 in the box for the unknown as they are not understanding the equal sign as a relational symbol. Instead of interpreting the equal sign as something they must "do" (in this case add) students need to evaluate each side of the equation to explore the relationship between the quantities. This can be done using a number balance or two-pan balance where the equations are acted out. • Also explore Activities 15.6 and 15.7.
2. Thinking a variable is a label rather than a quantity.	Given a problem about cans of juice in a package, the students might interpret 6c mistakenly as 6 cans when it is instead 6 times the number of cans in the packages.	• Avoid using the same letter for the variable that matches the first letter of the item under consideration.
3. Confusing the variable x for a multiplication symbol or vice versa.	$4x + 5$ yields confusion as students may not know if they should multiply or add the 5.	• Use n as an option instead. • Make sure students know that variables are always italicized and multiplication signs will not be written in italics.
4. Thinking an equation is written "improperly" if it is not in the standard form of $a + b = c$ (for example).	Students are confused by equations such as: $17 = 17$ (identity statements) $5 + 7 = ? \times 2$ (operations on both sides of the equation) $62 = ? - 24$ (operation on the right side of the equation).	• Expose students to a variety of equation formats from the start of the school year. Although familiarity with a variety of formats is a first-grade standard in the CCSS-M there are still many students in grades 3–5 who need consistent exposure to these nonstandard equations using all four operations.

16

Building Measurement Concepts

BIG IDEAS

1 Measurement involves a comparison of an attribute of an item or situation with a unit that has the same attribute. Lengths are compared to units of length, areas to units of area, time to units of time, and so on.

2 Estimation of measures and the development of benchmarks for frequently used units of measure help students increase their familiarity with units, preventing errors and aiding in the meaningful use of measurement.

3 Measurement instruments (e.g., rulers) group multiple units so that you do not have to iterate a single unit multiple times.

4 Area and volume formulas provide a method of measuring these attributes by using only measures of length.

5 Area, perimeter, and volume are related. For example, as the shapes of regions or three-dimensional objects change while maintaining the same areas or volumes, there is an effect on the perimeters and surface areas.

Measurement is the process of describing a continuous quantity with a numerical value. It is one of the most useful mathematics content strands because it is an important component in everything from occupational tasks to life skills for the mathematically literate citizen. From gigabytes that measure amounts of information to font size on computers, to miles per gallon, to recipes for a meal, people are surrounded daily with measurement concepts that apply to a variety of real-world contexts and applications. However, measurement is not an easy topic for students to understand. Data from international studies consistently indicate that

U.S. students are weaker in the area of measurement than any other topic in the mathematics curriculum (Mullis et al., 2004; Thompson & Preston, 2004).

The *Common Core State Standards* (CCSSO, 2010) expect that not only will measurement be an important context for other mathematical ideas such as number and geometry, but there are also other grade-level goals for measurement that are critical:

Grade 3: Students estimate and measure using units of time, liquid volumes, weight in metric units as well as understand area (including its relationship to multiplication and addition) and perimeter.

Grade 4: Students convert measurement units in the same system by expressing a larger unit in the form of a smaller unit, solve problems using the four operations with measurement contexts such as with units of time, liquid volume, weights of objects, money, area (using the formula) and perimeter (using the formula). Students understand the concept of angles and how to measure them in degrees using a protractor.

Grade 5: Students continue to convert measurement units in the same system and use the conversions to solve problems (including multistep problems). They also understand the concept of volume (including its relationship to multiplication and addition) to solve a variety of problems.

In this chapter you will learn how to help students develop a conceptual understanding of the measurement process and the tools of measurement. You will also learn about nonstandard units (what *Common Core State Standards* refers to as *improvised units*) and standard units of measurement, estimation in measurement including the use of benchmarks, and the development of measurement formulas.

The Meaning and Process of Measuring

Suppose that you asked your students to measure an empty bucket, as in Figure 16.1. The first thing they would need to know is *what* about the bucket is to be measured. They might measure the height, depth, diameter (distance across), or perimeter (distance around). All of these are length measures. A bucket also has liquid volume (or capacity) and weight. Each aspect that can be measured is an *attribute* of the bucket. Notice that these are all continuous quantities.

Once students determine the attribute to be measured, they then choose a unit that has the same attribute being measured. Length is measured with units that have length, volume with units that have volume, and so on.

Technically, a *measurement* is a number that indicates a comparison between the attribute of the object (or situation, or event) being measured and the same attribute of a given unit of measure. We commonly use small units of measure to determine a numeric relationship (the measurement) between what is measured and the unit. For example, to measure a length, the comparison can be done by lining up copies of the unit directly against the length being measured. For most attributes measured in schools, we can say that to *measure* means that the attribute being measured is "filled" or "covered" or "matched" with a unit of measure with the same attribute.

In summary, to measure something, one must perform three steps:

1. Decide on the attribute to be measured.
2. Select a unit that has that attribute.
3. Compare the units, by filling, covering, matching, or using some other method, with the attribute of the object being measured. The number of same-sized units required to match the object is the measure.

Measuring instruments, such as rulers, scales, and protractors, are devices that make the filling, covering, or matching process easier. For example, a ruler lines up the units of length and numbers them, and a protractor lines up the unit angles and numbers them.

Figure 16.1

Measuring different attributes of a bucket.

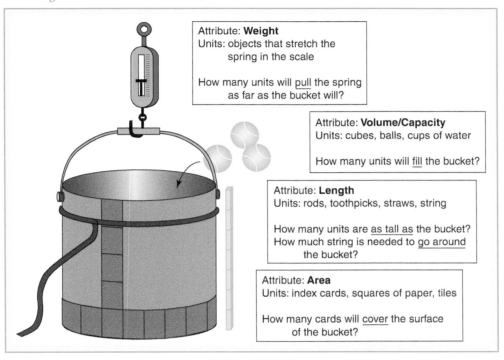

Concepts and Skills

The skill of measuring with a unit must be explicitly linked to the concept of measuring as a process of comparing attributes, using measuring units and using measuring instruments as outlined in Table 16.1.

Table 16.1. Measurement instruction—A sequence of experiences.

Step	Goal	Type of Activity	Notes
1—Making comparisons	Students will understand the attribute to be measured.	Make comparisons based on the attribute. For example, longer/shorter, heavier/lighter. Use direct comparisons whenever possible.	When it is clear that the attribute is understood, there is no further need for comparison activities.
2—Using physical models of measuring units	Students will understand how filling, covering, matching, or making other comparisons of an attribute with measuring units produces a number called a *measure*.	Use physical models of measuring units to fill, cover, match, or make the desired comparison of the attribute with the unit.	Begin with nonstandard units. Progress to the direct use of standard units when appropriate, and certainly before using formulas or measuring tools.
3—Using measuring instruments	Students will use common measuring tools with understanding and flexibility.	Make measuring instruments and use them in comparison with the actual unit models to see how the measurement tool is performing the same function as the individual units. Make direct comparisons between the student-made tools and the standard tools. Standard measuring instruments, such as rulers, scales, and protractors, are devices that make the filling, covering, or matching process easier.	Without a careful comparison with the standard tools, much of the value in making the tools can be lost.

✐ *Teaching Tip*

Remember, when helping students make comparisons you should use precise language in your instruction. Avoid using the phrases "bigger than" and "smaller than" and instead use more precise language such as "longer than" or "holds more than."

Making Comparisons

Sometimes with a measure such as length, a direct comparison can be made in which one object can be lined up and matched to another. But often an indirect method using a third object must be used. For example, if students compare the volume of one box to another, they must devise an indirect way to compare. They may fill one box with beans and then pour the beans into the other box. Another example using length would use a string to compare the height of a wastebasket to the distance around the top. The string is the intermediary, as it is impossible to directly compare these two lengths.

Using Physical Models of Measuring Unit

For most attributes measured in grades 3 through 5, it is possible to have physical models of the units of measure. Time and temperature are exceptions. Many other attributes not commonly measured in school also do not have physical units of measure, such as light intensity, speed, and loudness. Unit models can be found for both nonstandard (sometimes referred to as *informal* or *improvised*) units and standard units. For length, for example, drinking straws (nonstandard) or 1-foot-long paper strips (standard) might be used as units.

To help make the notion of unit explicit, use as many copies of the unit as are needed to fill or match the attribute measured (this is called *tiling* and it involves equal partitioning). To measure the area of the desktop with an index card (nonstandard) as your unit, you can literally cover the entire desk with index cards. Somewhat more difficult is to use a single copy of the unit (this is called *iteration*). That means measuring the same desktop with a single index card by repeatedly moving the card from position to position and keeping track of which areas the card has already covered.

It is useful to measure the same object with units of different size to help students understand that the unit used is important. For each different-sized unit, estimate the measure in advance and discuss the estimate afterward. They also must start to observe that smaller units produce larger numeric measures, and vice versa. This is a concept related to converting units and it is hard for some students to understand. This inverse relationship can only be mentally constructed by estimating, then experimenting, and finally reflecting on the measurements.

Using Measuring Instruments

On the 2003 NAEP exam (Blume, Galindo, & Walcott, 2007), only 20 percent of fourth graders could give the correct measure of an object not aligned with the end of a ruler, as in Figure 16.2. Even at the middle school level, only 56 percent of eighth graders answered the same situation accurately (Kloosterman, Rutledge, & Kenney, 2009). These results point to the difference between using a measuring device and understanding how it works. Students on the same exam also experienced difficulty when the increments on a measuring device were not in one unit increments.

If students construct simple measuring instruments using unit models with which they are familiar, it is more likely that they will understand how an instrument measures. A ruler is a good example. If students line up individual physical units along a strip of cardstock and mark them off, they can see that it is the *spaces* on rulers and not the tick marks or numbers that are important. It is essential that students discuss how measurement with iterating individual units compares with measurement using an instrument. Without this comparison and discussion, students may not understand that these two methods are essentially the

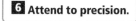
Figure 16.2

"How long is this crayon?"

same. Then they are ready to compare how their "ruler" works with how standard rulers (or other instruments like scales) work.

Introducing Nonstandard Units

It is common in primary grades to use nonstandard units to measure length, but unfortunately, measurement activities in grades 3 through 5, in which other attributes are measured, often do not begin with this important first step. The use of nonstandard units for measurement activities with new units is beneficial at all grade levels for the following reasons:

- Nonstandard units focus directly on the attribute being measured. For example, when discussing how to measure the area of an irregular shape, units such as square tiles or circular counters may be suggested. Each unit covers area and each will give a different result. The discussion can focus on what it means to measure area.

- The use of nonstandard units avoids conflicting objectives in introductory lessons. Is your lesson about what it means to measure area, or about understanding square centimeters?

- Nonstandard units provide a good rationale for using standard units. The need for a standard unit has more meaning when your class has measured the same objects with a collection of nonstandard units and arrived at different and sometimes confusing answers.

The amount of time that should be spent using nonstandard units varies with students' age, level of understanding, and the attributes being measured. Some students need many experiences over multiple days with a variety of nonstandard units of area, weight, and volume. Conversely, fourth graders may only need to work with nonstandard units for a day or two when they learn to measure angles. Transitioning requires movement from discrete to continuous units. When nonstandard units have served their purpose, move on.

Introducing Standard Units

Teaching Tip

Measurement sense demands that students be familiar with standard measurement units, be able to make estimates in terms of these units, and meaningfully interpret measures depicted with standard units.

> Remember as you teach the standard units to review necessary words and symbols and include these on your math word wall.

Perhaps the biggest challenge in measurement instruction is the failure to recognize and separate two types of objectives: (1) understanding the meaning and technique of measuring a particular attribute, and (2) learning about the standard units commonly used to measure that attribute.

Teaching standard units of measure can be organized around three broad goals:

1. *Familiarity with the unit.* Students should have a basic idea of the size of commonly used units and what attribute they measure. Knowing approximately how much 1 liter of water is or being able to estimate a shelf as 5 feet long is as important as measuring either of these accurately.

2. *Ability to select an appropriate unit.* Students should know both what is a reasonable unit of measure in a given situation and the level of precision that is required. (Would you measure your lawn to purchase grass seed with the same precision as you would use in measuring a window to buy a pane of glass?) Students need practice in selecting appropriate standard units and judging the level of precision.

3. *Knowledge of relationships between units.* Students should know the relationships that are commonly used, such as those between inches, feet, and yards, or between milliliters and liters.

Developing Unit Familiarity

Two types of activities can develop familiarity with standard units: (1) comparisons that focus on a single unit, and (2) activities that develop personal referents or benchmarks for single units or easy multiples of units.

Activity 16.1

CCSS-M: 3.MD.B.4

Familiar Measures

Read *Measuring Penny* (Leedy, 2000) to get students interested in the variety of ways familiar items can be measured. In this book, the author bridges between nonstandard units (e.g., dog biscuits, swabs, etc.) and standard units (inches, centimeters, etc.) to measure Penny, the pet dog. Have students use the idea of measuring Penny to find something at home (or in class) to measure in as many ways as they can think using standard units. The measures should include the addition of fractional units to be more precise. Discuss in class the familiar items chosen and their measures so that different ideas and benchmarks are shared.

Of special interest for length are benchmarks found on our bodies. These become quite familiar over time and can be used in many situations as approximate rulers.

Activity 16.2

CCSS-M: 3.MD.B.4; 4.MD.B.4

Personal Benchmarks

Measure your body. About how long is your foot, your stride, your hand span (stretched and with fingers together), the width of your finger, and your arm span (finger to finger and finger to nose)? Compare the distance around your wrist and around your waist, and your height to your waist, shoulder, and your head. Data can be graphed in a line plot. (There are wonderful proportional relationships to be found between these measures, too!) Some of these measures may prove to be useful benchmarks for standard units, and some may be excellent models for single units. (The average child's fingernail width is about 1 cm, and most people can find a 10-cm length somewhere on their hands.)

Choosing Appropriate Units

Should the area of the room be measured in square feet or square inches? Should the concrete blocks be weighed in grams or kilograms? The answers to questions such as these involve more than simply knowing how large units are, although that is certainly required. Another consideration involves the need for precision. If you were measuring your wall in order to cut a piece of molding to fit, you would need to measure it very precisely. The smallest unit would be an inch or a centimeter, and you would also use small fractional parts. But if you were determining how many 8-foot molding strips to buy, the nearest foot would probably be sufficient.

Standards for Mathematical Practice

▶ **6 Attend to precision.** ▶

Activity 16.3

CCSS-M: 3.MD.A.2; 3.MD.C.5; 4.MD.A.1; 5.MD.C.3

Guess the Type of Measurement

Find examples of measurements in newspapers, on signs, or in other everyday situations. Present the context and measures but without units. For example, you may consider ads for carpeting, articles about gas prices, and so forth. You can also use the **Measurement Cards**. The task is to predict what types of measurement were used. Have students discuss their choices. For students with disabilities, you may want to provide the headings for the possible types of measurement so they can sort the real-world measures into groups (i.e., area, volume, weight, time, length).

Important Standard Units and Relationships

Countries worldwide have passed laws stating that international commerce must use metric units. So if U.S. students are going to be prepared for the global workplace, they must be knowledgeable and comfortable with metric units. Results of the 2004 NAEP reveal that only 40 percent of fourth graders were able to identify how many kilograms a bicycle weighed given the choices of 1.5, 15, 150, and 1500 kg. Even among eighth graders, only 37 percent knew how many milliliters were in a liter (Perie, Moran, & Lutkus, 2005). Surprisingly, U.S. students do better on metric units than customary units (Preston & Thompson, 2004).

NCTM's takes a strong position on the metric system (2015) as they point to it being a system used around the world and that all students need to understand metric units and their relationships. Their position statement goes on to say that because we are still using customary measures in day-to-day life, students must work in that system as well. The *Common Core State Standards* state directly in the third, fourth, and fifth grade expectations that units such as meters, centimeters, cubic centimeters, grams, kilograms, and liters are expected.

Stop and Reflect

Why do you think U.S. students are more successful with metric units than the more familiar customary units?

The relationships between units within either the metric or customary systems are conventions. As such, students must simply be told what the relationships are, and instructional experiences must be devised to reinforce them. It can be argued that initially knowing about how much liquid makes a liter, or being able to pace off 3 meters—unit familiarity—is more important than knowing how many cubic centimeters are in a liter. Another approach to unit familiarity is to begin with common items and use their measures as references or benchmarks. A doorway is a bit more than 2 meters high, and a doorknob is about 1 meter from the floor. A bag of flour is a good reference for about 5 pounds. A paper clip weighs about 1 gram, and is about 1 centimeter wide. A gallon of milk weighs a little less than 4 kilograms. However, in the intermediate grades, knowing basic relationships becomes more important as students make conversions between units in the same system.

The customary system has few patterns or generalizable rules to guide students in converting units. In contrast, the metric system was systematically created around powers of ten. Understanding of the role of the decimal point as indicating the units position is a powerful concept for making metric conversions (see Figure 14.4). As students grasp the structure of decimal notation, develop the metric system with all seven places: three prefixes for smaller units (*deci-*, *centi-*, *milli-*) and three for larger units (*deka-*, *hecto-*, *kilo-*). Avoid mechanical rules such as "To change centimeters to meters, move the decimal point two places to the left." Instead, create conceptual, meaningful methods for conversions rather than rules that are often misused, misunderstood, and forgotten.

The Role of Estimation and Approximation

Measurement estimation is the process of using mental and visual information to measure or make comparisons without using measuring instruments. People use this practical skill almost every day. Do I have enough sugar to make cookies? Can you throw the ball 15 meters? Is this suitcase over the weight limit or the size limit for my airplane flight? Will my car fit into that parking space? Here are several reasons for including estimation in measurement activities:

- Estimation helps students focus on the attribute being measured and the measuring process. Think about how you would estimate the area of the cover of a book using playing cards as the unit. To do so, you have to think about what area is and how the units might be placed on the book cover.
- Estimation provides intrinsic motivation to measurement activities. It is interesting to see how close you can come in your estimate to the actual measure.
- When standard units are used, estimation helps develop familiarity with the unit. If you estimate the height of the door in meters before measuring, you must think about the size of a meter.
- The use of a benchmark to make an estimate promotes multiplicative reasoning. The width of the building is about one-fourth of the length of a football field—perhaps 25 yards.

In all measuring activities, emphasize the use of approximate language. The front of the math book is covered by *about* 8 index cards and the area of the sidewalk in front of the school is *about* 15 sheets of newspaper. Approximate language is very useful for students because many measurements do not result in whole numbers. As they become more sophisticated, students will begin to search for smaller units and use fractional units to be more precise, which is an opportunity to develop the idea that all measurements include some error. Acknowledge that each smaller unit or subdivision produces a greater degree of *precision*.

Stop and Reflect

A length measure can never be more than one-half unit in error. Why is this the case?

For example, suppose you are measuring a length of ribbon with a ruler that only shows quarter inches—so the unit is a quarter of an inch. If the length of ribbon falls between $3\frac{3}{4}$ and 4 inches, we would usually round to whichever number is closer to the length of ribbon. If the length of ribbon is more than halfway towards the 4-inch mark, we would say it's 4 inches long. However, if the length of ribbon is less than halfway from $3\frac{3}{4}$, we say it is closer to $3\frac{3}{4}$ inches long. In either case, we are within $\frac{1}{8}$ of an inch or one-half of the unit and are essentially ignoring the difference, and this constitutes our "error." If we need more precision in our measurement, we use smaller units to ensure that our measurement rounding or error is within an acceptable range.

Because mathematically there is no "smallest unit," there is always some error in measurement. The *Common Core Standards for Mathematical Practice* (CCSSO, 2010) include "Attend to Precision." Under that practice, they expect that students "are careful about specifying units of measure" and that they "express numerical answers with a degree of precision appropriate for the problem context" (p. 7).

Strategies for Estimating Measurements

Always begin a measurement activity with students making an estimate. This is true with both nonstandard and standard units. Just as for computational estimation, specific strategies exist for estimating measures. Here are four strategies:

1. *Develop benchmarks or referents.* Research shows that students who acquire mental benchmarks or reference points for measurements *and* practice using them in class

activities are much better estimators than students who have not learned to use benchmarks (Joram, 2003). Students must pay attention to the size of the unit to estimate well (Towers & Hunter, 2010). Referents should be things that are easily envisioned by the student as they must recall an image of a unit that is not present. One example is the height of a child (see Figure 16.3). Students should have a good referent for single units and also useful multiples of standard units.

Figure 16.3

Estimating measures using benchmarks and chunking.

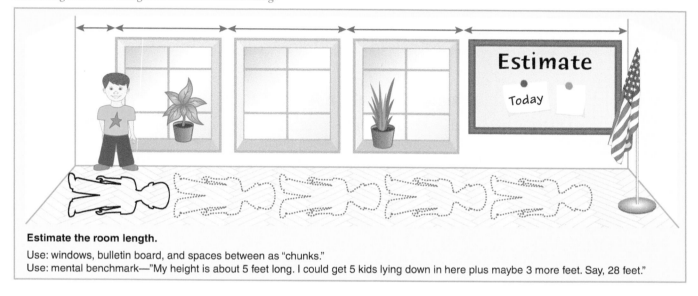

Estimate the room length.
Use: windows, bulletin board, and spaces between as "chunks."
Use: mental benchmark—"My height is about 5 feet long. I could get 5 kids lying down in here plus maybe 3 more feet. Say, 28 feet."

2. *Use "chunking" or subdivisions.* Figure 16.3 shows an example of chunking using windows, bulletin boards and spaces between as chunks. It may be easier to estimate the shorter chunks along the wall than to estimate the whole length. But, if the wall length didn't have useful chunks, it can be mentally subdivided in half and then in fourths or even eighths by repeated subdivisions until a manageable length is found. Length, volume, and area measurements all lend themselves to subdivisions. If considering weight, the weight of a stack of books is easier to estimate if the weight of an "average" book is known.

3. *Iterate units.* For length, area, and volume, it is sometimes easy to mark off single units mentally or physically. You might use your hands or make marks to keep track as you go. If you know, for example, that your stride is about $\frac{3}{4}$ meter, you can walk off a length and then multiply to get an estimate. Hand and finger widths are useful for shorter measures.

Each strategy just listed should be explicitly taught and discussed with students. Suggested benchmarks for useful measures can be developed and recorded on a class chart. Include items found at home. But the best approach to improving estimation skills is to have students do a lot of estimating. Keep the following tips in mind:

1. *Help students learn strategies by having them first try a specified approach.* Later activities should permit students to choose whatever techniques they wish.

2. *Discuss how different students made their estimates.* This will confirm that there is no single right way to estimate while reminding students of other useful approaches.

3. *Accept a range of estimates.* Think in relative terms about what is a good estimate. Within 10 percent for length is quite good. Even 30 percent "off" may be reasonable for weights or volumes.

4. *Encourage students to give a range of estimates that they believe includes the actual measure* (e.g., the door is between 7 and 8 feet tall). This is not only a practical approach in real life, but it also helps focus on the approximate nature of estimation.

5. *Make measurement estimation an ongoing activity.* Post a daily measurement to be estimated. Students can record their estimates and discuss them in a five-minute period. Students can take turns determining the daily measurements to estimate, with individuals or a team of students assigned this task each week.

6. *Be precise with your language.* Do not use the word *measure* interchangeably with the word *estimate* (Towers & Hunter, 2010). Randomly substituting one word for the other will cause uncertainty and possibly confusion in students.

✒ Teaching Tip

Do not promote a "winning" estimate. It discourages estimation and promotes only seeking the exact answer.

Measurement Estimation Activities

Estimation activities need not be elaborate. Any measurement activity can have an "estimate first" component. For more emphasis on the process of estimation itself, simply think of measures that can be estimated, and have students estimate. Here are two suggestions.

▶ Activity 16.4

CCSS-M: 2.MD.A.1; 2.MD.A.3; 4.MD.A.1

Estimation Scavenger Hunt

Conduct estimation scavenger hunts. Give teams a list of either nonstandard or standard measurements, and have them find things that are close to having those measurements. Look at the Estimation Scavenger Hunt Activity Page for some ideas. Do not permit the use of measuring instruments. Create your own scavenger hunt using the units you are studying. Let students suggest how to judge results in terms of accuracy.

Formative Assessment Note

Estimation tasks are a good way to assess students' understanding of both measurement and units. Use an Observation Checklist to take notes about students' estimates and measures of real objects using weight, area, perimeter, and volume. Prompt students to explain how they arrived at their estimates to get a more complete picture of their measurement knowledge. Asking only for a numeric estimate can mask a lack of understanding and will not give you the information you need to provide next instructional steps.

Length

Length is usually the first attribute students learn to measure. Length measurement is not immediately understood by young students, and students in grades 3 through 5 may demonstrate challenges with the concept of length as they begin to investigate problems that include perimeter. Length

✒ Teaching Tip

Remind students that they are counting units, not the lines or tick marks.

is an attribute of an object that is found by locating two endpoints and examining how far it is between those points. We measure lengths by selecting a unit (that has length) and repeatedly matching that unit to the object.

Formative Assessment Note

When considering length instruction in the third or fourth grade, a quick performance assessment may be in order to be sure that students have gained the ideas that are often taken for granted at this level. Here are some ideas that will not take too much time.

- Ask student to draw a line or mark off a distance of a prescribed number of units. Observe whether students know to align equal sized units in a straight line (or on the path being measured) without overlaps or gaps.

- Demonstrate in the classroom how a fictitious second grader used a ruler to measure the length of an object. Make many errors such as using gaps in the placement of the ruler, overlaps, and a wavy line of alignment that doesn't match the quantity being measured. The students' task is to explain why this measurement may be inaccurate.

- Have students measure two different objects. Then ask how much longer the longer object is. Observe whether students can use the measurements to answer or whether they need to make a third measurement to find the difference.

- Have students measure a line with small paper clips and then again with large paper clips. Can they explain the inverse relationship between the measures they find and the size of the units?

If your assessment indicates that there is some confusion about how length is measured, then use the class discussion of these results to help students self-assess and come to deeper understanding.

> **Standards for Mathematical Practice**
>
> ◀ **3** Construct viable arguments and critique the reasoning of others.

Conversion

Linked to the last item of the formative assessment, and as required in the standards (CCSSO, 2010), students must be able to convert measures in the same system to larger or smaller units. Yet, it is a challenge to explain to students that larger units will produce a smaller measure and vice versa. Instead, engage students in activities like the following, in which this issue is emphasized.

▶ Activity 16.5

CCSS-M: 4.MD.A.1; 5.MD.A.1

Changing Units

Have students measure a length with a specified unit. Then provide them with a different unit that is either twice as long or half as long as the original unit. Their task is to predict the measure of the same length using the new unit. Students should write down their estimations and discuss how they made their estimations. Then have them make the actual measurement. Cuisenaire rods are excellent for this activity. Some students can be challenged with units that are more difficult multiples of the original unit.

In "Changing Units," you are looking first for the basic idea that when the unit is longer, the measure is smaller, and when the unit is smaller, the measure is larger. This is a good activity to do just prior to introducing unit conversion with standard units, and is an excellent proportional reasoning task. After completing activities like the one that follows, encourage

> **Standards for Mathematical Practice**
>
> ◀ **2** Reason abstractly and quantitatively.

students to draw conclusions that you multiply to convert a larger unit to a smaller unit. What do you predict is the process to go from a smaller unit to a larger unit?

Activity 16.6
CCSS-M: 4.MD.A.1; 5.MD.A.1

Conversion Please

Give students a copy of the **Two-Column Conversion Table**. Select several items around the classroom and have students measure the items in feet and then again in inches. Only have them complete half of the table. Ask them to describe the relationship between the two measurements. They are likely to notice that the longer the unit chosen the fewer units needed and vice versa. For the second half of the table, give them the item to measure only with feet and have them convert to find how many inches. When complete they can confirm their answers by measuring with inches. Try other units.

Fractional Parts of Units

Students are sometimes initially perplexed when measurements do not result in a whole number, but measurement is an excellent context for students to apply their developing concepts of fractions. Students can relate the idea of unit to the whole, and partition to see half units or other fractional parts. The use of fractional units helps students understand subdivision marks on a ruler.

Students should use their rulers to measure lengths that are longer than their rulers and discuss how that can be done. If they simply read the last mark on the ruler, they may not understand how a ruler is a representation of a continuous row of units. Another challenge is to find more than one way to measure a length with a ruler. Do you have to begin at the end? What if you begin at another unit in the center of the ruler?

Formative Assessment Note

First try having students use a ruler with tick marks but no numbers. This will assess whether students are counting the marks rather than the units. Another good performance assessment of ruler understanding is to have students measure with a ruler that has the first two units broken off. On the 2003 NAEP exam, only 20 percent of fourth graders were able to find the length of a toothpick on a broken ruler (Dietiker, Gonulates, & Smith, 2011). Use an **Observation Checklist** to note whether students say that it is impossible to measure with a broken ruler because there is no starting point. Also note those who match and count the units meaningfully. Here's a **Broken Ruler** Activity Page divided into fractional units that does just that.

All of these ideas can be pulled together in large-scale measuring activities that involve whole and fractional units using rulers, measuring tapes, or even trundle wheels that measure and count meter lengths. Consider an activity described by Kurz (2012), in which different large water shooters were tested to assess whether the manufacturers' claims on how far they can shoot water were actually accurate. Another option is testing the distance paper airplanes can travel (Reeder, 2012). For a site about measuring places, go online to Google Earth's

Measuring Tools where students can measure distances in centimeters, inches, feet, yards, kilometers, and miles.

There are other measures of length, such as perimeter and circumference. Perimeter will be discussed later in this chapter.

Area

Area is the two-dimensional space inside a region. As with other attributes, students must first understand the attribute of area before measuring. Data from the 2011 NAEP suggest that fourth- and eighth-grade students have an incomplete understanding of area with only 24 percent able to find the area of a square given that the square has a perimeter of 12 units and included a drawing of the square with tick marks around the sides. Instead, 44 percent merely counted the eight tick marks around the edge (National Center for Education Statistics, 2014). Estimating and measuring area begins in third grade, as students connect to multiplication using arrays, and continues in fourth grade finding the area of rectangles using formulas and real-world problem. In fifth grade, students explore area problems with fractional measures and use area to find volumes of three-dimensional shapes.

Comparison Activities

Comparing area measures is a bigger conceptual challenge than comparing length measures because areas come in a variety of shapes. Comparison activities with areas should help students distinguish between size (or area) and shape, length, and other dimensions. A long, skinny rectangle may have less area than a triangle with shorter sides. Many students do not understand that rearranging areas into different shapes does not affect the amount of area (although the perimeter can change).

Direct comparison of two areas is frequently impossible, except when the shapes involved have some common dimension or property. For example, two rectangles with the same width can be compared directly as in this Rectangle Comparison Activity Page. Comparison of these special shapes, however, fails to deal with the attribute of area. Instead, activities in which one area is rearranged (conservation of area) are suggested. The following activity can support this purpose.

▶ Activity 16.7

CCSS-M: 3.MD.C.5

Two-Piece Shapes

Cut out a large number of Rectangles of the Same Area, about 3 inches by 5 inches. Each pair of students will need six rectangles. Have students fold and cut the rectangles on the diagonal, making two identical triangles. Next, have them rearrange the triangles into different shapes, including back into the original rectangle. The rule is that only sides of the same length can be matched up and must be matched exactly. Have pairs of students find all the shapes that can be made this way, gluing the triangles on paper as a record (see Figure 16.4). Discuss the area and shape of each response. Does one shape have a greater area than the rest? How do you know? Did one take more paper to make? Help students conclude that although each figure is a different shape, all the figures have the same area.

Figure 16.4

Different shapes, same area.

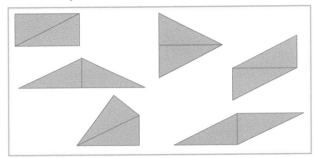

Figure 16.5

Tangrams provide an opportunity to investigate area.

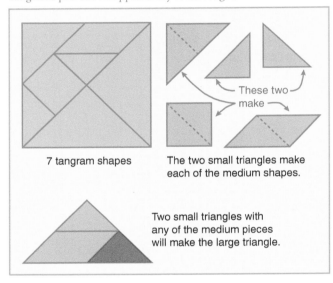

7 tangram shapes

The two small triangles make each of the medium shapes.

These two make

Two small triangles with any of the medium pieces will make the large triangle.

Tangrams, an ancient puzzle, can be used for the same purpose. The standard set of seven **Tangram Pieces** is cut from a square, as shown in Figure 16.5, or an online version can be found at the National Library of Virtual Manipulatives. The two smallest triangles can be used to make the parallelogram, the square, and the medium triangle. This permits a similar discussion about the pieces having the same area but form different shapes.

Using Physical Models of Area Units

Prior to learning any formulas for area, students need multiple opportunities to "cover the surface" of two-dimensional shapes. Although squares are the most common area units, any tile that conveniently covers a plane region can be used such as index cards, sheets of newspaper, or playing cards. Eventually move to models of standard units such as color tiles (1 inch sides) or Cuisenaire rods or base-ten blocks (1 cm sides). Students can use units to measure surfaces in the room such as desktops, bulletin boards, and books. Large regions can be outlined with masking tape on the floor. Small regions can be duplicated on geoboards or grid paper so that students can work at stations. Geoboards are particularly useful when working with students with disabilities (Cass, Cates, Jackson, & Smith, 2002).

In area measurements, there may be lots of units that only partially fit. You may wish to begin with shapes in which the units fit by building a shape with units, and drawing the outline. According to the *Common Core State Standards* (CCSSO, 2010), in third grade, students should begin to wrestle with partial units and mentally put together two or more partial units to count as one unit which prepares them for the use of fractional units in fifth grade. Figure 16.7 shows one possible measurement exercise.

Activity 16.8

CCSS-M: 3.MD.C.5; 3.MD.C.6

Tangram Areas

Give students Outlines of Tangram Shapes and a set of Tangram Pieces, as in Figure 16.6. Ask groups to estimate which one they think has the largest (or smallest) area. Then let students use tangrams to decide which shapes have the same area, which are larger, and which are smaller. Let students explain how they came to their conclusions. Use the animal shapes from *Grandfather Tang's Story* (Tompert, 1997) for additional investigations or look at the Tangram game on PBS Kid's Cyberchase website. Are all the animals or pictures the same area?

Figure 16.6

Compare the area of shapes made of tangram pieces.

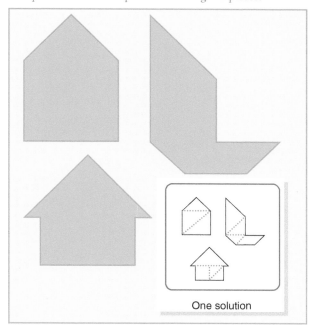

One solution

Figure 16.7

Measuring the area of a large shape drawn with tape on the floor using a cardstock square as the unit.

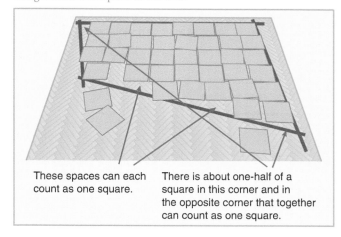

These spaces can each count as one square.

There is about one-half of a square in this corner and in the opposite corner that together can count as one square.

The following activity is a good starting point.

◢ Activity 16.9

CCSS-M: 3.MD.C.5; 3.MD.C.6

Cover and Compare

Draw Two Rectangles, a Parallelogram, a Trapezoid, and a Blob on a sheet of paper. Make it so that the three areas are not the same, but with no area that is clearly largest or smallest. The students' first task is to estimate which of the three shapes has the smallest and the largest area. After recording their estimate, they should trace or glue the same two-dimensional unit on the shapes, overlay a transparency grid, or cut the shapes out and placing them on grid paper. Students should explain their strategy and justification in writing.

Your objective in the beginning is to develop the idea that area is measured by covering or tiling. Do not introduce formulas yet. Groups are likely to come up with different measures for the same region. Discuss these differences with the students and point to the difficulties involved in making estimates around the edges. Avoid the idea that there is one "right" approach.

By fourth grade, students should use spatial reasoning to apply the concept of multiplication using arrays to the area of rectangles. This requires that students develop the ability to see a rectangular region as rows and columns. The following comparison activity is a useful step in that direction.

Activity 16.10

Rectangle Comparison—Square Units

Give students the **Rectangle Comparison** Activity Page that includes four rectangles with a similar area, a physical model of a single square unit and a ruler that measures the appropriate unit. Students are not permitted to cut out the rectangles, but they may draw on them if they wish. The task is to use their rulers to determine, in any way that they can, which rectangle is larger or whether they are the same. They should use words, pictures, and numbers to explain their conclusions. If you want to make your own rectangle comparisons some suggested pairs are:

$$4 \times 10 \text{ and } 5 \times 8 \qquad 5 \times 10 \text{ and } 7 \times 7 \qquad 4 \times 6 \text{ and } 5 \times 5$$

Some students with disabilities may need to have modified worksheets of the figures on grid paper that matches the square units to be used.

The goal of this activity is to apply students' developing concepts of multiplication to the area of rectangles without introducing a formula. In order to count a single row of squares along one edge and then multiply by the length of the other edge, the first row must be thought of as a single unit that is then replicated to cover the rectangle (Outhred & Mitchelmore, 2004). Many students will attempt to draw in all the squares. However, some may use their rulers to determine the number of squares that will fit along each side and, from that, use multiplication to determine the total area (see Figure 16.8). By having students share strategies, more students can be exposed to the use of multiplicative reasoning in this context.

Figure 16.8

Some students use multiplication to tell the total number of square units.

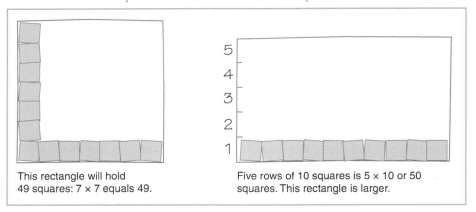

This rectangle will hold 49 squares: 7 × 7 equals 49.

Five rows of 10 squares is 5 × 10 or 50 squares. This rectangle is larger.

Have students try the following example to carry their reasoning to the next level.

A rectangular garden has an area of 120 square feet. If the garden is 8 feet wide, how long is it?

Grids of various types can be thought of as "area rulers." A grid of squares does for area what a ruler does for length. It lays out the units for you. Square grids on transparencies can be made from several kinds of grids (**2-Centimeter Grid Paper, 1-Centimeter Grid Paper, and 0.5-Centimeter Grid Paper**). Have students place the clear grid over a region to be measured and count the units inside. An alternative method is to trace around a region on a paper grid.

The Relationship between Area and Perimeter

Area and perimeter are a continual source of confusion for students. Although perimeter is a content standard (CCSSO, 2010) at grade 3, of the eighth graders given an illustration on the NAEP exam of a rectangle with all side lengths shown, only 71 percent could accurately identify the perimeter. Perhaps confusion emerges because both area and perimeter involve regions to be measured or because students are taught formulas (possibly too soon) for both concepts at about the same time. Teaching these two concepts during a close time frame is particularly challenging for students with disabilities (Parmar, Garrison, Clements, & Sarama, 2011).

Perimeter is a length measure and, as such, it is additive. Students should be able to calculate perimeter given side measures as well as identify missing side lengths.

Teaching Tip

A good hint for helping students remember the concept of perimeter is that the word rim is in perimeter.

What is the perimeter of this figure?

13 cm

5 cm

The perimeter of the rectangle below is 32. What is the length of the side marked A?

12 inches

A

Activity 16.11

CCSS-M: 3.MD.D.8

What's the Rim?

Have students select objects with a perimeter that they would like the whole class to measure (like the cover of a book) or more challenging (the top of a wastebasket). First, students estimate the perimeter on the **What's the Rim?** Activity Page. They also need to choose tools strategically given rulers, cash register tape, or nonstretching string and record their choice. Then they measure the actual amount including the unit. The discussion should include class comparisons of at least one common item that will provide a basis for exploring any measurement errors. Students should describe how they measured objects that were larger than the tool they were using and how they knew when to use a flexible measuring tool (i.e., string or cash register tape). For students with disabilities have them trace the perimeter with their finger prior to measuring.

Even preservice teachers were confused as to whether when you increase the perimeter of a rectangle the area also increases (Livy, Muir, & Maher, 2012). An interesting approach to alleviating this confusion is to contrast area and perimeter as in the next three activities.

Activity 16.12

CCSS-M: 3.MD.D.8; 4.MD.A.3

Fixed Perimeters

Give students a loop of nonstretching string that is **24** centimeters in circumference and **1-Centimeter Grid Paper,** or just use the grid paper alone. The task is to decide what different-sized rectangular gardens can be made with a perimeter of **24 cm**. Each different rectangle can be recorded on the grid paper with the area noted inside the sketch of the garden (A = 20 cm²). Then record all the results on the **Fixed Perimeter Recording Sheet.**

Activity16.13

CCSS-M: 3.MD.C.6; 3.MD.C.7; 4.MD.A.3

Fixed Areas

Provide students with **1-Centimeter Grid Paper.** The task is to see how many rectangular gardens can be made with an area of **36** squared cm—that is, to make filled-in rectangles, not just borders. Each new rectangle should be recorded by sketching the outline of the garden and the dimensions on grid paper. For each rectangle, students should determine and record the perimeter measurement inside the figure (P = **24 cm**). Then record all the results on the **Fixed Area Recording Sheet.** You might also use the **Expanded Lesson: Fixed Areas.**

Stop and Reflect

Let's think about the two previous activities. For "Fixed Areas," will all of the perimeters be the same? If not, what can you say about the shapes with longer or shorter perimeters? Is there a pattern? For "Fixed Perimeters," will the areas be the same? Why or why not? Which rectangle creates the largest area? The smallest area?

Activity 16.14

CCSS-M: 3.MD.C.6; 3.MD.C.7; 4.MD.A.3

Sorting Areas and Perimeters

Students must complete Activities **16.12** and **16.13** first and cut out all of the garden sketches from the grid paper. Then have two charts or locations labeled with "Perimeter" and "Area." Teams should place their figures (left to right) from smallest perimeter (or area) to largest perimeter (or area) on the appropriate chart. Ask students to write down observations, make conjectures, and draw conclusions. Students may be surprised to find out that rectangles having the same areas do not necessarily have the same perimeters and vice versa. And, of course, this fact is not restricted to rectangles.

Standards for Mathematical Practice

2 **Reason abstractly and quantitatively.** ▶

When students complete these activities they will notice an interesting relationship. When the area is fixed, the shape with the shortest perimeter is "square-like," as is the rectangle with the largest area. If you allowed for any shapes whatsoever, the shape with the shortest perimeter and a fixed area is a circle. Students will also notice that the fatter a shape, the shorter its perimeter and the skinnier a shape, the longer its perimeter. (These relationships are also true in three dimensions—replace perimeter with surface area and area with volume.)

Developing Formulas for Perimeter and Area

When students *develop* formulas, rather than just be told the formula, they gain conceptual understanding of the ideas and relationships involved, there is less likelihood that students will confuse area and perimeter, and there is less of a chance they will select the incorrect formula on an assessment.

Formulas for Perimeter

As students move to thinking about formulas, they can consider exploring how the perimeter of rectangles can be put into a general form. Begin by having students generate ways that perimeter problems can be solved. As in the rectangle shown previously, it is common for students to be given a perimeter problem in which only one length and one width are included. So if students are only considering adding these two numbers, discussing the formula $P = l + w + l + w$ will help point out that there are four length dimensions that should be added for a rectangle. This connection to the equation will help avoid the common error of only adding the two given dimensions. An alternative perimeter formula for rectangles that might emerge from the conversations would be $P = 2\,(l + w)$, which will reinforce the multiplication of the pair of sides, or $P = 2l + 2w$, which emphasizes that the perimeter involves combining lengths.

Shodor's Project Interactivate has a tool called "Perimeter Explorer." This online tool allows students to calculate the perimeter of a random shape. A shape is displayed and the student enters a value for the perimeter and the applet then indicates whether or not the value is correct. The student may continue trying until he or she gets the correct answer. An option to compare the perimeters with corresponding areas is given.

Formulas for Area

The results of NAEP testing clearly indicate that students do not have a very good understanding of area formulas. For example, in the 2007 NAEP, only 39 percent of fourth-grade students were able to determine the area of a carpet 15 feet long and 12 feet wide. Such results may be due to an overemphasis on formulas with little or no conceptual background.

Teaching Tip

"Length times width" is not a definition of area.

Two major misconceptions are:

1. *Confusing linear and square units.* The shift in third grade (CCSSO, 2010) to multiplicative thinking may result in students having difficulty as they move from length measurement to the more abstract measurement of area. Putrawangsa, Lukito, Amin, and Wijers (2013) suggest that one of the major issues with area measurement is thinking about area as the length of two lines (length × width), rather than the measure of a surface. A focus on the formula and the use of a ruler to measure the sides confuses the unit as well as the tool for measuring area (as the use of the ruler is indirect). This confusion can cause some students to believe that if there are no sides to measure (no length and width) the shape doesn't have an area (Zacharos, 2006).

   The tasks in Figure 16.9 cannot be solved with simple formulas; they require an understanding of concepts and how area formulas work.

Figure 16.9

Understanding the attribute of area.

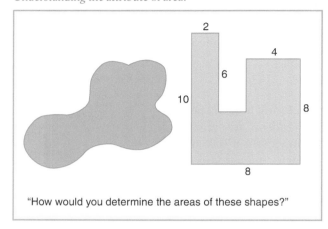

"How would you determine the areas of these shapes?"

Figure 16.10

Heights of two-dimensional figures are not always measured along an edge.

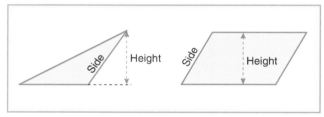

Teaching Tip

A good way to strengthen students' understanding of height is to have them identify the height for every base of a quadrilateral (be sure to vary the shapes so that the height falls inside and outside of the shape).

Standards for
Mathematical Practice

8 Look for and express regularity in repeated reasoning. ▶

2. *Difficulty in conceptualizing the meaning of height and base.* The shapes in Figure 16.10 each have a slanted side and a height given. Students tend to confuse these two. Any side of a figure can be called a *base*. For each base that a figure has, there is a corresponding height. If the figure were to slide into a room on a selected base, the *height* would be the height of the shortest door it could pass through without tipping—that is, the perpendicular distance to the base. The confusion may be because students have a lot of early experiences with the length-times-width formula for rectangles, in which the height is exactly the same as the length of a side.

Area of Rectangles

The formula for the area of a rectangle is one of the first that is developed and is usually given as $A = L \times W$, "area equals length times width." Thinking ahead to other area formulas, an equivalent but more unifying idea might be $A = b \times h$, "area equals *base* times *height*." The base-times-height formulation can be generalized to all parallelograms (not just rectangles) and is useful in developing the area formulas for triangles and trapezoids. Furthermore, the same approach can be extended to three dimensions, in which volumes of cylinders are given in terms of the area of the base times the height. Therefore, base times height connects a large family of formulas that otherwise must be mastered independently.

Research suggests that it is a significant leap for students to move from counting squares inside of a rectangle to a conceptual development of a formula. Battista (2003) found that students often try to cover empty rectangles with drawings of squares and then count the result one square at a time.

An important concept to review is the meaning of multiplication as seen in arrays with an emphasis on the structure of rows and columns of squares. When we multiply a length times a width, we are not multiplying "squares times squares." Rather, the *length* of one side indicates how many squares will fit on that side. If this set of squares is taken as a unit, then the *length* of the other side (not a number of squares) will determine how many of these *rows of squares* can fit in the rectangle. Then the amount of square units covering the rectangle is the product of the number of rows and the length of a row, which is the number of columns (row × columns = area). Revisit Activity 16.10 noting whether students draw in all of the squares and count them. Is so, they have not thought about a row of squares as a single unit that can be replicated.

Now, explain to students that measuring one side to tell how many squares will fit in a row along that side is a useful approach. You would like them to call or think of this side as the *base* of the rectangle, even though some people call it the length or the width. Then the other side you can call the *height*. But which side is the base? Be sure that students conclude that either side could be the base. If you use the formula $A = b \times h$, then the same area will result using either side as the base (see Figure 16.11).

Do you think that students should learn special formulas for the area of a square? Why or why not? Do you think students need specific formulas for the perimeters of squares and rectangles?

Students form general relationships when they move from working with just the rectangle and square to parallelograms, trapezoids and even triangles and see how all these area formulas are related to one idea: length of the base times the height. And students who understand where formulas come from tend to remember them or are able to derive them, and this reinforces the idea that mathematics makes sense.

Volume

Volume is a term for the measure of the "size" of, or the space occupied by, three-dimensional regions—a topic beginning in the fifth grade, according to the *Common Core State Standards* (CCSSO, 2010). The addition of a third dimension challenges students' spatial reasoning. The term *liquid volume* or *capacity* is generally used to refer to the amount of liquid that a container will hold. Standard units of capacity include quarts, gallons, liters, and milliliters. Standard units of the volume of solid figures are expressed in terms of cubic inches or cubic centimeters.

Comparison Activities

Comparing the volumes of solid objects can be challenging. A simple method of comparing liquid volume is to fill one container with something and then pour this amount into the comparison container. By third grade, most students understand the concept of "holds more" with reference to containers. The concept of volume for solid objects may not be as readily understood.

Students should compare the capacities of different containers as in the following activity.

Figure 16.11

Activities leading to the development of the formula for the area of a rectangle.

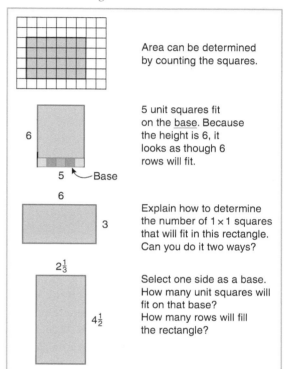

Area can be determined by counting the squares.

5 unit squares fit on the base. Because the height is 6, it looks as though 6 rows will fit.

Explain how to determine the number of 1 × 1 squares that will fit in this rectangle. Can you do it two ways?

Select one side as a base. How many unit squares will fit on that base? How many rows will fill the rectangle?

Activity 16.15

CCSS-M: 3.MD.A.2; 5.MD.C.3

Capacity Sort

Provide a variety of containers, with one marked as the "target." Ask students to sort the collection into those that hold more than, less than, or about the same amount as the target container. Then use the Capacity Sort Activity Page to circle the estimate of "holds more," "holds less," or "holds about the same." Provide a filler (such as water, beans, rice, or Styrofoam peanuts), scoops, and funnels. Working in pairs, have students measure and record results under Actual Measure on the recording sheet. Discuss what students noticed (e.g., that fatter/rounder shapes hold more).

Do not expect students to accurately predict which of two containers holds more because even adults have difficulty making this judgment. Try the following activity.

Activity 16.16

CCSS-M: 5.MD.C.3; 6.G.A.4

Which Silos Holds More?

Give pairs of students two sheets of the same-sized paper. With one sheet they make a tube shape (cylinder) by taping the two long edges together. They make a shorter, fatter tube from the other sheet by taping the short edges together. Then ask, "If these were two silos, would they hold the same amount or would one hold more than the other?" Ask students to write down their predictions. Most student groups will split roughly in thirds: short and fat, tall and skinny, or same volume. To test the conjectures, use a filler such as beans, rice, or pasta. Place the skinny cylinder inside the fat one. Fill the inside tube and then lift it up, allowing the filler to empty into the fat cylinder.

The goal of these activities is for students to realize that surface area (the size of the paper) does not determine the volume, but that there is a relationship between surface area and volume, just as there is between perimeter and area.

The following activity is a three-dimensional adaptation of Activity 16.12, "Fixed Areas."

Activity 16.17

CCSS-M: 5.MD.C.3; 5.MD.C.4; 5.MD.C.5; 6.G.A.2; 6.G.A.4

Fixed Volume: Comparing Prisms

 Give each pair of students a supply of centimeter cubes. Ask students to use 64 cubes (or 36) to build different rectangular prisms with that volume and record the dimensions for each prism formed in Fixed Volume Recording Sheet. If you have ELLs, provide a visual of a rectangular prism, labeling key words such as (*length, width, height, cube, volume,* and *side*). Using the recording page ask students to describe any patterns that they notice as they compare dimensions of each prism to its surface area. What happens as the prism becomes less like a tall, skinny box and more like a cube?

The eventual goal is for students to realize that the dimensions and the volume have a relationship. It is this relationship that leads to the formula for volume.

Using Physical Models of Volume Units

Two types of units can be used to measure volume of solid figures and liquid volume (capacity): solid units and containers. Solid units are objects like wooden cubes that can be used to fill the container being measured. The other unit model is a small container that is filled with liquid and poured repeatedly into the container being measured. The following examples are of units that you might want to collect:

- Liquid medicine cups
- Plastic jars and containers of almost any size

- Wooden cubes or same-sized blocks of any shape
- Styrofoam packing peanuts (produces conceptual measures of volume despite not packing perfectly)

The following activity explores the volume of two boxes.

> ### ▶ Activity 16.18 — CCSS-M: 5.MD.C.3; 5.MD.C.4; 5.MD.C.5
>
> ## Box Comparison—Cubic Units
>
> Provide students with a pair of small boxes that you have made from cardstock (see Figure 16.12). Use unit dimensions that match the cubes that you have for units. Students are given two boxes, exactly one cube, and a corresponding ruler. (If you use 2-cm cubes, make a ruler with the unit equal to 2 cm.) The students' task is to decide which box has the greater volume or if the boxes have the same volume.
>
> Here are some suggested box dimensions ($L \times W \times H$):
>
> $6 \times 3 \times 4$ $5 \times 4 \times 4$ $3 \times 9 \times 3$ $6 \times 6 \times 2$ $5 \times 5 \times 3$
>
> Students should use words, drawings, and numbers to explain their conclusions.

Figure 16.12

Make small boxes by starting with a rectangle and drawing a square on each corner as shown. Cut on the solid lines and fold the box up, wrapping the corner squares to the outside and tape them to the sides.

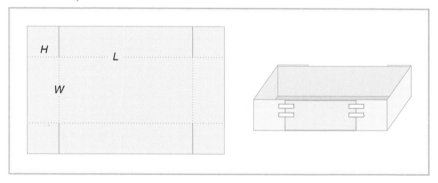

A useful hint for the last activity is to first figure out how many cubes will fit on the bottom of the box. Some students will discover a multiplicative rule for the volume. The boxes can be filled with cubes to confirm conclusions. No formulas should be used unless students can explain them.

Instruments for measuring capacity are generally used for pourable materials such as rice or water. These tools are commonly found in kitchens and laboratories. Students should use measuring cups to explore recipes such as those in the *Better Homes and Gardens New Junior Cookbook* (Better Homes and Gardens, 2012), which provide student-friendly recipes and multiple opportunities to use units of capacity.

The following two activities focus on liquid volume.

Standards for Mathematical Practice

◀ **2** Reason abstractly and quantitatively.

Activity 16.19

CCSS-M: 3.MD.A.2

That's Cool!

Give teams of students beakers marked in milliliters. Tell the students they will receive three ice cubes. First they must estimate how many milliliters of water will be in the beaker when the ice melts. Then the ice is placed in each team's container, and students wait until the ice warms and turns to water. What was the difference between their estimates and their actual answers? Students can use a line plot to record and discuss the different measures.

Activity 16.20

CCSS-M: 3.MD.A.2

Squeeze Play

Students should work in teams, with each team having access to a measuring cup or beaker marked in milliliters. Have several stations set up with buckets and different-sized sponges. Have students first estimate how much water they can squeeze from each sponge using the hand they do not write with. Does a sponge that is two times larger than another sponge provide two times the amount water when squeezed? What do the students notice?

Figure 16.13

Heights of figures are not always measured along an edge or a surface.

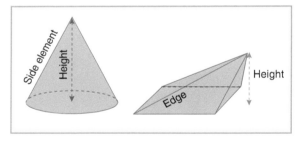

Developing Formulas for Volumes of Common Solid Shapes

A common error that repeats from two- to three-dimensional shapes is when students confuse the meaning of height and base in their use of formulas. Notice that the shapes in Figure 16.13 each have a slanted side and a height given. As mentioned before, the base can be any flat surface of the figure and to visualize the height, have students think of the figure sliding under a doorway and the *height* would be the height of the shortest door it could pass through. Keep this in mind as you work to use precise language to develop formulas for volume.

The relationships between the formulas for volume are completely analogous to those for area. As you read, notice the similarities between rectangles and prisms. Not only are the formulas related, but the process for developing the formulas is similar.

Volumes of Prisms

A *cylinder* is a solid with two congruent parallel bases and sides with parallel elements that join corresponding points on the bases. There are several classes of cylinders, including *prisms* (with polygons for bases), *right prisms, rectangular prisms*, and *cubes* (Zwillinger, 2011). Interestingly, all of these solids have the same volume formula, and that one formula is analogous to the area formula for parallelograms.

The development of the volume formula (see Activity 16.18) is parallel to the development of the formula for the area of a rectangle, as shown in Figure 16.14. The *area* of the base (instead of *length* of the base for rectangles) determines how many *cubes* can be placed on the base forming a single unit—a layer of cubes. The *height* of the box then determines how many of these *layers* will fit in the box just as the height of the rectangle determined how many *rows* of squares would cover the rectangle.

The volume, as just discussed, is $V = A \times h$, with A equal to the *area of the base* and h the *height*. The connectedness of mathematical ideas can hardly be better illustrated than with the connections of all of these formulas to the single concept of *base × height*.

A conceptual approach to the development of formulas helps students understand they are meaningful and efficient ways to measure different attributes of the objects around us. After developing formulas in conceptual ways, students can derive formulas from what they already know. Mathematics does make sense!

Figure 16.14

Volume of a right prism: Area of the base × height.

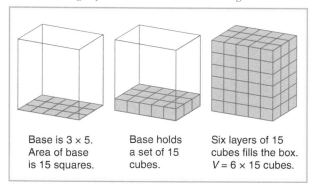

Base is 3 × 5.
Area of base
is 15 squares.

Base holds
a set of 15
cubes.

Six layers of 15
cubes fills the box.
$V = 6 \times 15$ cubes.

Weight and Mass

Weight is a measure of the pull or force of gravity on an object. *Mass* is the amount of matter in an object and a measure of the force needed to accelerate it. On the moon, where gravity is much less than on Earth, an object has a smaller weight than on Earth but the identical mass. For practical purposes, on Earth, the measures of mass and weight will be about the same. In this discussion, the terms *weight* and *mass* will be used interchangeably.

Although the concept of heavier and lighter begins to be explored in kindergarten, the notion of units of weight or mass appears in third-grade standards (CCSSO, 2010). At any grade level, experiences with informal unit weights are good preparation for standard units and scales.

Comparison Activities

The most conceptual way to compare weights of two objects is to hold one in each hand, extend your arms, and experience the relative downward pull on each. Which one weighs more? This personal experience can then be transferred to one of two basic types of scales—balances and spring scales.

When students place the objects in the two pans of a balance, the pan that goes down can be understood to hold the heavier object. Even a relatively simple balance will detect small differences. If two objects are placed one at a time in a spring scale, the heavier object pulls the pan down farther. Both balances and spring scales have real value in the classroom. (Technically, spring scales measure weight and balance scales measure mass. Why?)

Using Physical Models of Weight or Mass Units

Any collection of uniform objects with the same mass can serve as nonstandard weight units. For very light objects, large paper clips, wooden blocks, or plastic cubes work well. Large metal washers found in hardware stores are effective for weighing slightly heavier objects. Coins also can be used (e.g., U.S. nickels weigh 5 grams and pennies weigh 2.5 grams). You will need to rely on standard weights to weigh things as heavy as a kilogram or more.

Weight cannot be measured directly, so either a two-pan balance or a spring scale must be used. In a balance scale, place an object in one pan and weights in the other pan until they balance. In a spring scale, first place the object in the pan and mark the position of the pan on a piece of paper taped behind the pan. Remove the object and place just enough weights in the pan to pull it down to the same level. Discuss how equal weights will pull the spring down with the same force.

Angles

Understanding the concept (or attribute) of angle and measuring angles is one of the standards in the *Common Core State Standards* (CCSSO, 2010), beginning at grade 4 and developing through middle school and high school. Angle measurement can be a challenge for two reasons: The attribute of angle size is often misunderstood, and protractors are commonly introduced and used without understanding how they work.

Comparison Activities

The attribute of angle size might be called the "spread of the angle's rays." Angles are composed of two rays that are infinite in length with a common vertex. The only difference in their size is how widely or narrowly the two rays are spread apart or rotated about the vertex.

To help students conceptualize the attribute of the spread of the rays, two angles can be directly compared by tracing one and placing it over the other (see Figure 16.15). Be sure to have students compare angles with the rays represented with different lengths. A student might think a wide angle with short rays is less than a narrow angle with long rays. This is a common misconception (Munier, Devichi, & Merle, 2008). As soon as students can tell the difference between a large angle and a small angle, regardless of the length of the rays, you can move on to measuring angles.

Using Physical Models of Angular Measure Units

A unit for measuring an angle must be an angle. Nothing else has the same attribute of spread that we want to measure. (Contrary to what many people think, you do not need to use degrees to measure angles.) Measuring an angle involves unit angles that are used to cover the spread of an angle just as length unit cover a length.

> ✍ *Teaching Tip*
>
> Some students think that the length of the rays has an effect on the size of the angle. Explicitly show them that this is not the case, and in fact it is the spread between the rays (be they long or short) that defines the angle.

Figure 16.15

Which angle is larger?

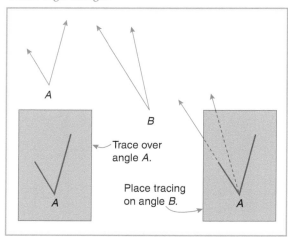

Trace over angle *A*.

Place tracing on angle *B*.

◢ **Activity 16.21**   CCSS-M: 4.MD.C.5

A Unit Angle

Give each student an index card. Have students draw a narrow angle on the card using a straightedge and then cut it out or use Wedges. The resulting wedge can then be used as a unit of angular measure by counting the number of wedges that will fit in a given angle as shown in Figure 16.16. Distribute an Angles Activity Page and have students use their angle unit to measure the angles. Because students made different unit angles, the results will differ and can be discussed and compared in terms of unit size.

Using Protractors

Standards for
Mathematical Practice

◄ **5 Use appropriate
tools strategically.**

The tool commonly used for measuring angles is the protractors (see Figure 16.17). According to the *Common Core State Standards*, fourth-grade students should begin to learn to accurately use protractors. Yet the protractor is one of the most poorly understood measuring instruments. Part of the difficulty arises because the units (degrees) are so small. It would be physically impossible for students to cut out and use a single degree to measure an angle accurately. In addition, the numbers on most protractors run clockwise and counterclockwise along the edge, making the scale hard to interpret without a strong conceptual foundation. Notice that the units of degrees are based on an angle in which the vertex of the rays is located at the midpoint of a circle creating an arc. A "one degree" angle is one in which the arc is $\frac{1}{360}$ of the circle (**degrees**). These small angles are the units used to measure.

Students can make nonstandard waxed-paper protractors (see Figure 16.18) but soon move them to standard instruments. To understand measures on a protractor (see Figure 16.17), students need an approximate mental image of angle size. Then false readings of the protractor scale will be eliminated. One approach is to use an angle maker. You can cut and merge two different colored paper dessert plates in the same way as the rational number wheel in Figure 14.5 on page 261. You can then rotate the plates to match angles observed or to estimate important benchmark angles such as 30, 45, 60, 90, 135, 180, 270, and 360 degrees. If students have a strong grasp of the approximate sizes of angles, this "angle sense" will give them the background needed to move to standard measuring tools.

Figure 16.16

Using a small wedge cut from an index card as a unit angle, this angle measures about $7\frac{1}{2}$ wedges.

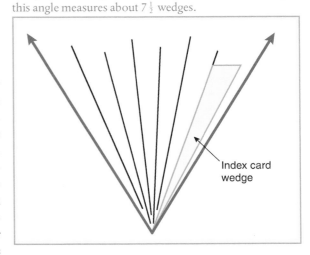

Index card wedge

Figure 16.17

A protractor measures angles.

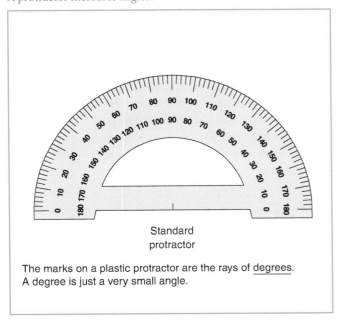

Standard protractor

The marks on a plastic protractor are the rays of <u>degrees</u>. A degree is just a very small angle.

Figure 16.18

Measuring angles in a polygon using a waxed-paper protractor.

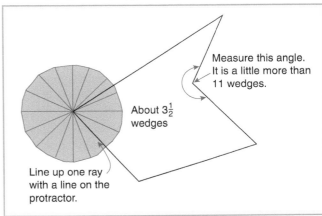

Measure this angle. It is a little more than 11 wedges.

About $3\frac{1}{2}$ wedges

Line up one ray with a line on the protractor.

Have students try their angle measuring skills with pattern blocks. Using one of each piece in the collection of pattern blocks, they answer these questions: What is the measure of each angle? Which angles are equal?

Time

Time is different from most other attributes that are commonly measured in school because it cannot be seen or felt and because it is more difficult for students to comprehend units of time or how they are matched against a given time period or duration.

Comparison Activities

Time can be thought of as the duration of an event from its beginning to its end. As with other attributes, for students to adequately understand the attribute of time, they should make comparisons of events that have different durations. If two events begin at the same time, the shorter duration will end first and the other will last longer. For example, which top spins longer? However, this form of comparison focuses on the ending of the duration rather than the duration itself. In order to think of time as something that can be measured, it is helpful to compare two events that do not start at the same time. This requires that some form of measurement of time be used from the beginning.

Students need to learn about seconds, minutes, and hours and to develop some concept of how long these units are. You can help by making a conscious effort to point out the duration of short and long events during the day. Have students time familiar events in their daily lives: brushing teeth, eating dinner, riding to school, spending time doing homework.

Timing small events of $\frac{1}{2}$ minute to 2 minutes is fun and useful and can be adapted from the following activity.

Activity 16.22

CCSS-M: 3.MD.A.1

Just a Minute!!

Ask students to estimate how long a time period such as a minute is without looking at a clock. Tell them you will give them a starting point and they should stand up when they think a minute is up. Give them a GO and watch a timer to see who stands up and when the students stood up. When the bell rings, students will experience the duration of a minute and be able to compare their estimate to the actual time. You can do this activity with other longer amounts of time.

Also a book such as *Just a Second* (Jenkins, 2011) provides fascinating facts about what can happen in a second, a minute, an hour, a day, a month, and a year. Did you know that a bumblebee beats its wings 200 times a second? Students can use the facts provided to explore and discuss many mathematical problems.

Reading Clocks

The common instrument for measuring time is the clock. However, learning to tell time has little to do with time measurement and more to do with the skills of learning to read a dial-type instrument. Clock reading can be a difficult skill to teach. Starting in first grade, students are usually taught first to read clocks to the hour, then the half hour, and finally to 5- and 1-minute intervals in second and third grades (CCSSO, 2010). In the early stages of this sequence, students are shown clocks set exactly to the hour or half hour. Thus, many students who can read a clock at 7:00 or 2:30 are initially challenged by 6:58 or 2:33.

Digital clocks permit students to read times easily, but do not relate times very well to benchmark times. To know that a digital reading of 7:58 is nearly 8 o'clock, the student must know that there are 60 minutes in an hour, that 58 is close to 60, and that 2 minutes is not a very long time. The analog clock (with hands) shows "close to" times visually without the need for understanding large numbers or even how many minutes are in an hour. On the 2003 NAEP assessment, only 26 percent of fourth graders and 55 percent of eighth grade students could solve a problem involving the conversion of one measure of time to another (Blume, Galindo, & Walcott, 2007).

Elapsed Time

Determining combinations and comparisons of time intervals in minutes is a skill required starting in grade 3 (CCSSO, 2010). If, given the digital time or the time after the hour, students must be able to tell how many minutes to the next hour. This should certainly be a mental process of counting on for multiples of 5 minutes, possibly using an analog clock face as a mental image to support the skip counting. Avoid having students use pencil and paper to subtract 25 from 60. This links to elapsed time, which is a skill that students can find challenging, especially when the period of time includes noon or midnight. The problem is due less to the fact that students don't understand what happens on the clock at noon and midnight as it is that they have trouble counting the interval that spans those times.

Figuring the time from 8:15 a.m. to 11:45 a.m., for example, is a multistep task that requires deciding what to do first and keeping track of the intermediate steps. In this case, you could count hours from 8:15 to 11:15 and add on 30 minutes. But then what do you do if the endpoints are 8:45 and 11:15?

There is also the task of finding the end time given the start time and elapsed time, or finding the start time given the end time and the elapsed time. In keeping with the spirit of problem solving and the use of models, consider having students sketch an empty time line (similar to the empty number line discussed for computation). The number line is also the model suggested in the *Common Core State Standards*. It is important not to be overly prescriptive in telling students how to use the number line because there are various alternatives (Dixon, 2008). For example, in Figure 16.19(a), a student might count by full hours from 10:45, 11:45, 12:45, 1:45, 2:45, 3:45, and then subtract 15 minutes, whereas another student might count 15 minutes to get to 11:00 and then count by full hours 11:00, 12:00, 1:00, 2:00, 3:00, and finally add on 30 minutes. Watch this **video** (**https://www.youtube .com/watch?v=WPvy4knZ_YY**) that uses the Iditarod Sled Dog Race in Alaska as the context for a lesson on elapsed time.

Figure 16.19

A sketch of an empty time line can be useful in solving elapsed time problems.

(a) School began late today at 10:45 a.m. If you get out at 3:30, how much time will you be in school today?

Four hours from 11 to 3. Then 15 minutes in front and 30 minutes at the end—45 minutes. Three hours 45 minutes in all.

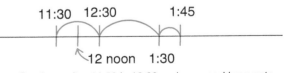

(b) The game begins at 11:30 a.m. If it lasts 2 hours and 15 minutes, when will it be over?

One hour after 11:30 is 12:30 and a second hour gets you to 1:30 and then 15 minutes more is 1:45. It's p.m. because it is after noon.

Also explore What Time Will It Be? at the National Library of Virtual Manipulatives to find elapsed time word problems.

Money

The names of our coins are conventions of our social system. Students learn these names the same way that they learn the names of physical objects in their daily environment—through exposure and repetition.

The value of each coin is also a convention that students must simply be told. For these values to make sense, students must understand 5, 10, and 25, and think of these quantities without seeing countable objects. Where else do we say "this is 5," while pointing to a single item? A student who remains tied to counting objects will be challenged to understand the values of coins. Coin value lessons should focus on purchase power—a dime can *buy the same thing* that 10 pennies can buy.

To name the total value of a group of coins is the same as mentally adding their values. Students should have learned this prior to entering third grade. Make sure students sort their coins and start counting from the highest value. Even though it is actually mental computation, the numbers are fortunately restricted to multiples of 5 and 10 with some 1s added at the end. The next activity is a preparation for counting money.

▶ Activity 16.23

CCSS-M: 2.MD.C.8; 4.MD.A.2

Hundreds Chart Money Count

Have student take out their **Hundreds Chart** and a collection of play money. Begin with only two different amounts, say, a quarter and a dime. Count down using place value to represent the 25 cents in the same way students have used the hundreds chart (two full rows down and over five more spaces). Put the quarter on the place where 25 is located and then count 10 more (down one row) and place the dime on 35. The total is 35 cents. Use other collections of coins (sort like coins together) and what students already know about patterns on the hundreds chart to figure out how to count collections of money. Then create word problems that involve money and have students use the hundreds chart to think about the situations.

When discussing solutions to situations involving counting of coins, give special attention to students who put combinations together utilizing thinking with tens or multiples of five.

Because adding on to find a difference is such a valuable skill, it makes sense to give students experiences with "think addition" as mentioned in Chapter 11, which uses adding on to find differences before asking them to make change. As students become more skillful at adding on, they can see the process of making change as an extension of a skill already acquired.

Table 16.2. Common errors and misconceptions in measurement and how to help.

Common Error or Misconception	What It Looks Like	How to Help
Unsure of the starting point of a ruler.	Students measure at the end of the ruler rather than at the zero.	• Move items along a ruler and ask students if they believe the item has changed size. • Iterate units to show how long the item is and then show how those units match the units on the ruler. • Give students experiences with the broken ruler activity page.
Students count tick marks rather than units.	It's four units. 0 1 2 3 4 5	• Have students iterate units to see how a ruler, for example, is made. Then emphasize the count of the unit and how the number or tick mark indicates the end of the unit.
Students misinterpret the scale of the ruler.	Read the $\frac{1}{2}$ or 1-inch tick marks on a ruler as not another fourth or eighth, when measuring by those units. So, for example, when counting eighths to measure they are consistently one or two units off by ignoring the $\frac{1}{2}$ or 1-inch tick marks.	• Have students use a paper ruler where the units can be shaded one at a time with a marker. They need multiple experiences with iterating units of the same size when measuring.
Measuring perimeter by counting two sides.	7 3 The perimeter is 10.	• This is an artifact of having only two sides labeled with numbers in the problem. Have students draw a line or highlight the sides to show what is being measured for the perimeter of a figure. Then suggest that they label each side before adding the lengths.
Measuring perimeter by counting square units rather than side lengths.	When counting the perimeter on a grid, students count the number of squares around the border of the figure rather than the sides of the squares as a length measure. This will result in a measure that is 4 units less than the actual perimeter.	• Focus on perimeter being a length rather than an area to cover. Show with gestures how the corner needs two units (of fence for example) and that one unit isn't enough. • Have students share strategies as a group, after hearing and seeing other answers, students are likely to self correct. Give students an option to change their answer—but they must give a reason.
You can tell the area of a figure if you know the perimeter and vice versa (Amore and Pinilla, 2006).	Students will say as the area increases so does the perimeter. Students use the formula for area to find the perimeter All shapes with the same perimeter have the same area and all shapes with the same area have the same perimeter	• Avoid teaching the topics of area and perimeter at the same time. • Once taught, focus on the similarities, differences and relationships between the two measurements. • Go back to Activities 16.12, 16.13 and 16.14.
Many students can recite the formula for area but cannot describe what area is in words.	Students state that area is L × W, but cannot give the definition of area. When given a blob shape, students will say it has no area as it doesn't have a length and width.	• Go back to the use of nonstandard units to focus on area as a process of covering two-dimensional space. • Try using Activity 16.9.

(continued)

Table 16.2. Common errors and misconceptions in measurement and how to help. (*continued*)

Common Error or Misconception	What It Looks Like	How to Help
As the side length doubles the area doubles.	When asked what happens to the area of a square if the side of a square doubles, they say the area doubles.	• Actually act this problem out. Because the figure has two dimensions, this is a change in square units, not a change in lengths alone. Students need to place tiles down on the new figure to prove that the area is four times as large–not doubled.
Estimates of measures must be exact and will be graded on how close you are to the "right" answer (Muir, 2005).	Students constantly try to change their estimate to reach the "correct" answer.	• Have students experience activities where there is no prize or "winning" estimate. Instead give a range of estimates that are reasonable. • Avoid using the terms measure and estimate interchangeably. That cuts down on the uncertainty about whether an estimate should be exact.
The larger the rays of the angle, the larger the angle.	Given these two angles, students will say B is the larger angle. Which angle is bigger? A ⟶ B ⟶	• Use the door of the classroom to act out the size of angles. Show how the angle would not be affected by the size of the door—is it only about the spread of the space between the door and the wall of the classroom.
The height of the figure or container indicates its volume.	Students select the tallest as having the greatest volume or capacity.	• Bring a collection of containers (use ones where the tallest is not the largest) and have students estimate the order from smallest liquid volume to largest. Then test each to show the actual outcome.
The length or size of an object is an indication of its weight.	Students select the largest object as the heaviest object.	• Bring a collection of items (use ones where the longest or largest are not the heaviest) and have students estimate the order from lightest weight to heaviest weight. Then test each to show the actual outcome.

17

Developing Geometric Thinking and Concepts

BIG IDEAS

1 What makes shapes alike and different can be determined by geometric properties. Shapes can be classified into a hierarchy of categories according to the properties they share.

2 Transformations provide a significant way to think about the ways properties change or do not change when a shape is moved on the plane. Line symmetry is a component of the transformation called a reflection.

3 Shapes can be described in terms of their location in a plane or in space. Coordinate systems can be used to describe these locations precisely. In turn, the coordinate view of shape offers another way to understand certain properties of shapes.

4 Visualization provides the ability to create mental images that support the identification of properties and help link noticed likenesses to more formal definitions.

Geometry is a "network of concepts, ways of reasoning and representation systems" used to explore and analyze shape and space (Battista, 2007, p. 843). This critical area of mathematics appears in everything from global positioning systems to computer animation. Unique to the *Common Core State Standards*, geometry appears as a domain across grades kindergarten through 8.

Geometry Goals for Your Students

Let's think about the major geometry objectives across the grades in terms of two related frameworks: (1) spatial sense and geometric reasoning about shape and space, and (2) specific geometric content such as knowing about symmetry, triangles, parallel lines, and so forth. These frameworks align with the *Common Core State Standards* (CCSSO, 2010), which suggest the following:

> *Grade 3:* Students understand that shapes in different categories (rectangles, squares, and rhombuses for example) may share attributes (four sides) which sometimes put them in a more inclusive category like quadrilaterals.

> *Grade 4:* Students identify two-dimensional figures based on the types of lines (perpendicular or parallel for example) and size of angles (acute, obtuse, or right). They also can identify line symmetry and draw a line of symmetry in two-dimensional figures.

> *Grade 5:* Students classify two-dimensional figures based on their properties in large categories and subcategories. They also locate points in the first quadrant of the coordinate plane.

Spatial Sense

Spatial sense can be defined as an intuition about shapes and the relationships among shapes. Spatial sense includes the ability to mentally visualize objects and spatial relationships, to turn objects around in one's mind. It also includes a familiarity with geometric descriptions of objects and position. It is a core area of mathematical study, like number (Sarama & Clements, 2009). People with well-developed spatial sense appreciate geometric form in art, nature, and architecture, and they use geometric ideas to describe and analyze their world. When learning mathematics this also includes how students use diagrams and sketches as they develop concepts, the composing and decomposing of shapes, maps and orientation, and visualizing mathematical ideas using mental imagery (Mulligan, 2015).

Interestingly, students who have exceptional ability with spatial relationships such as mentally manipulating two-dimensional and three-dimensional objects have been shown to have greater creative achievements and academic success more than thirty years later especially in STEM fields than students who showed ability with more familiar measures of mathematics and verbal performance (Kell, Lubinski, Benbow, & Steiger, 2013; Wai, Lubinski, & Benbow, 2009).

Some people say that you either are or are not born with spatial sense. This is simply not true! Meaningful experiences with shape and spatial relationships, when provided consistently over time, can and do develop spatial sense. Between 1990 and 2000, NAEP data indicated a steady, continuing improvement in students' geometric reasoning (Sowder & Wearne, 2006). However, students did not just get smarter. Instead, there has been an increasing emphasis on geometry at all grades, particularly in the elementary grades.

Stop and Reflect

Consider your own beliefs concerning an individual's abilities in the area of spatial sense. What do you think causes some people to have better spatial sense than others?

Geometric Content

For too long, the geometry curriculum in the United States emphasized the learning of terminology such as "this is a right triangle." Geometry is much more than vocabulary and naming shapes. Now the attention has shifted to geometric experiences and this heightened importance has led to the creation of a huge assortment of meaningful tasks for students. As with each of the *Common Core State Standards* content standards, the geometry domain has a number of goals that apply to grades 3 through 5:

- *Shapes* and *properties* include a study of the properties of shapes, as well as a study of the relationships built on properties.
- *Transformations* refer to such things as translations, reflections, rotations, and dilations, but in grades 3 through 5, the focus is on reflections through examining line symmetry starting in grade 4.
- *Location* refers to coordinate geometry (fifth grade) and other ways of specifying how objects are located in a plane or in space.
- *Visualization* includes the recognition of shapes in the environment, the development of relationships between two- and three-dimensional objects, and the ability to recognize, construct, and draw figures from different viewpoints.

The content in this chapter is organized around these four categories, with each category beginning with experiences that are foundational and moving toward those that are more challenging. You will notice that more attention is devoted to the topic of shapes and properties because that also aligns with the emphasis of the *Common Core State Standards* for grades 3 through 5.

Developing Geometric Thinking

All learners in your classroom are capable of growing and developing in the ability to think and reason in geometric contexts, but this ability requires ongoing and significant experiences across a developmental progression. Recently there has been an emphasis in mathematics education on identifying learning trajectories as a way to move students forward on different topics (Institute for Mathematics Education, 2013). Fortunately, in geometry such a research-based progression has been well documented. The research of two Dutch educators, Pierre van Hiele and Dina van Hiele-Geldof, provides insights into the differences in individuals' geometric thinking through the description of different levels of thought. The van Hiele (1986) theory significantly influences geometry curricula worldwide and can help all teachers understand developmentally appropriate next steps for their students' geometry instruction.

The van Hiele Levels of Geometric Thought

The van Hiele model is a five-level hierarchy of ways of understanding spatial ideas (see Figure 17.1). Each level describes the thinking processes used in geometric contexts. Specifically, the levels describe what types of geometric ideas we think about (called *objects of thought*) and what students can do (*products of thought*). The levels are developmental and learners of any age begin at level 0 and go through experiences with geometrical ideas to progress to the next level. Characteristics of the van Hiele levels are provided in Table 17.1.

Figure 17.1

At each level of geometric thought, the ideas created become the focus or object of thought at the next level.

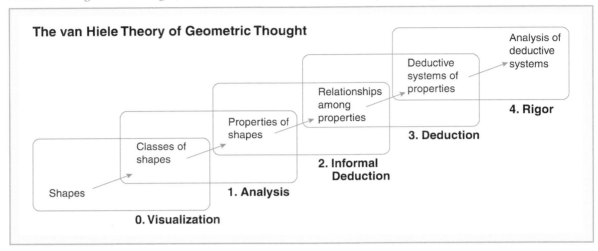

Table 17.1. Characteristics of the van Hiele levels.

Characteristic	Implication
1. Sequential	To arrive at any level above 0, students must move through all prior levels. The products of thought at each level are the same as the objects of thought at the next level, as illustrated in Figure 17.1. The objects (ideas) must be created at one level so that relationships between these objects of thought can become the focus of the next level.
2. Developmental	When instruction or language is at a level higher than that of the students, students will be challenged to understand the concept being developed. A student can, for example, memorize a fact (such as all squares are rectangles) but not mentally construct the actual relationship of how the properties of a square and rectangle are related.
3. Age independent	A third grader or a high school student could be at level 0.
4. Experience dependent	Advancement through the levels requires geometric *experiences.* Students should explore, talk about, and interact with content at the next level while increasing experiences at their current level.

Level 0: Visualization

The objects of thought at level 0 are shapes and what they "look like."

Teaching Tip

Appearance is dominant at level 0 and can therefore overpower students' thinking about the properties of a shape. A level 0 thinker, for example, may see a square with sides that are not horizontal or vertical (it appears tilted) and believe it is a "diamond" (not a mathematical term for a shape) and no longer a square.

Students at level 0 recognize and name figures based on the global visual characteristics of the figure. For example, a square is defined by a level 0 student as a square "because it looks like a square." Although we expect students to demonstrate higher level geometric thinking by grade 3, there are many students in grades 3 through 5 who are still level 0 thinkers. Students at this level will sort and classify shapes based on their appearance: "I put these together because they are all pointy." Students are able to see how shapes are alike and different and as a result, they can create and begin to understand classifications of shapes.

The products of thought at level 0 are classes or groupings of shapes that seem to be "alike."

The emphasis at level 0 is on shapes that students can observe, feel, build (compose), take apart (decompose), or work with in some manner. The general goal is to explore how shapes are alike and different and to use these ideas to create classes of shapes (both physically and mentally). Some of these classes of shapes have names—rectangles, triangles, rhombuses, and so on. Properties of shapes, such as parallel sides, perpendicular lines, line symmetry, right angles, and so on, are included at this level but only in an informal, observational manner.

Although the van Hiele theory applies to students of all ages learning any geometric content, it may be easier to apply the theory to the shapes-and-property category. The following is a good representation of an activity appropriate for level 0 learners who you are trying to move to level 1.

Activity 17.1

CCSS-M: 3.G.A.1

Shape Sorts

Have students work in groups of four with a set of 2-D Shapes (see Figure 17.2) doing the following related activities in order:

- Students each randomly select two shapes and try to find something that is alike about their two shapes and something that is different.

- The group randomly selects one target shape and places it in the center of the workspace. Their task is to find all other shapes that are like the target shape according to the same rule. For example, if they say "This shape is like the target shape because it has a curved side and a straight side," then all other shapes that they put in the collection must have these properties. Challenge them to do a second sort with the same target shape but use a different property.

- Do a "secret sort." You (or one of the students) create a collection of about 3-4 shapes that fit a secret rule. Leave other shapes that belong in your group in the pile. Students try to find additional pieces that belong to the set and/or guess the secret rule.

See the Expanded Lesson: Shape Sorts for more details on this activity.

Figure 17.2

A collection of shapes for sorting.

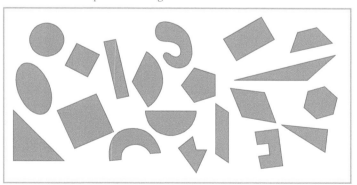

Stop and Reflect

Why might you have students choose their own rules rather than saying, "Find all the pieces with straight sides" or "Find the triangles"?

These find-a-rule activities will elicit a wide variety of ideas as students examine the shapes. They may initially describe shapes with ideas such as "curvy" or "looks like a rocket" rather than geometric properties. But as students notice more sophisticated attributes, you can attach appropriate names to them. For example, students may notice that some shapes have corners "like a square" (explain that those corners are also called *right angles*) or that "these shapes are the same on both sides" (suggest that is called *line symmetry*).

What clearly makes this a level 0 activity is that students are operating on the shapes that they see in front of them and are beginning to see ways they are alike and ways they are different. By forming groups of shapes, students begin to identify shapes belonging to these classes that are not present in their collection.

Level 1: Analysis

Level 1 is where the greatest proportion of grades 3 through 5 content in the *Common Core State Standards* curriculum falls (see list at the beginning of this chapter).

The objects of thought at level 1 are classes of shapes rather than individual shapes.

Students at the analysis level are able to consider all shapes within a class rather than just the single shape on their desk. Instead of talking about *this* particular rectangle, they can talk about general properties of *all* rectangles. By focusing on a class of shapes, students are able to think about what makes a rectangle a rectangle (four sides, opposite sides parallel, opposite sides same length, four right angles, congruent diagonals, etc.). The irrelevant features (e.g., size, color, or orientation) fade into the background and students begin to understand that if a shape belongs to a particular class, such as cubes, it has the corresponding properties of that class. "All cubes have six congruent faces, and each of those faces is a square." These properties were unspoken at level 0. Students operating at level 1 may be able to list all the properties of squares, rectangles, and parallelograms, but may not see that these are subclasses of one another (e.g., that all squares are rectangles and all rectangles are parallelograms). In defining a shape, level 1 thinkers are likely to list as many properties of a shape as they know.

The products of thought at level 1 are the properties of shapes.

While level 1 students continue to use manipulatives and drawings of shapes, they begin to see individual shapes as representatives of classes of shapes. Their understanding of the properties of shapes—such as line symmetry, perpendicular and parallel lines, and so on—continues to be refined. This identification of geometric properties is an important cognitive activity (Yu, Barrett, & Presmeg, 2009).

In the following activity, level 1 students use the properties of shapes, such as line symmetry, angle classification (right, obtuse, acute), parallel and perpendicular, and the concept of equal line segments and angles.

Activity 17.2

CCSS-M: 3.G.A.1; 4.G.A.2; 4.G.A.3

Property Lists for Quadrilaterals

Prepare handouts for **Parallelograms**, **Rhombuses**, **Rectangles**, and **Squares** (see Figure 17.3). Assign groups of three or four students to work with one type of quadrilateral (for ELLs and students with disabilities, post labeled shapes as a reference). Ask students to list as many properties as they can that apply to all of the shapes on their sheet. They will need tools such as index cards (to check right angles, to compare side lengths, and to draw straight lines), mirrors (to check line symmetry), and tracing paper (to see if angles are equal). Encourage students to use the terms "exactly," "at least," "only," and "at most" when describing how many of something: for example, "rectangles have at least two lines of symmetry," because squares—included in the category of rectangles—have four.

Have students prepare their Property Lists under these headings: Sides, Angles, Diagonals, and Symmetries. Groups then share their lists with the class and eventually a class list for each category of shape will be developed. For ELLs, placing emphasis on these words, having students say the words aloud, and having students point to the word as you say it are ways to reinforce meaning and support their participation in discussions.

Figure 17.3

Shapes for "Property Lists for Quadrilaterals."

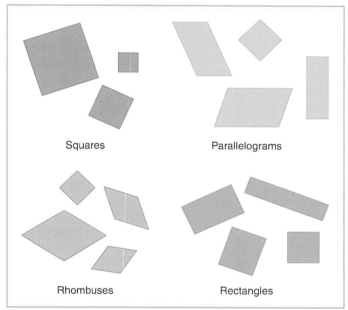

What distinguishes this activity from the earlier level 0 activity is that students must now assess whether the properties apply to all shapes in the category. If they are working on the squares, for example, then their observations must apply to a square mile as well as a square centimeter.

Level 2: Informal Deduction

The objects of thought at level 2 are the properties of shapes.

As students begin to think about properties of geometric objects without focusing on one particular object (shape), they develop relationships between these properties. "If all four angles are right angles, the shape must be a rectangle. If it is a square, all angles are right angles. If it is a square, it must also be a rectangle." Once students have a greater ability to engage in "if–then" reasoning, they can classify shapes using only a minimum set of defining characteristics. For example, four congruent sides and at least one right angle are sufficient to define a square. Rectangles are parallelograms with a right angle. Observations go beyond properties themselves and begin to focus on logical arguments about the properties. Students at level 2 will be able to follow and understand informal deductive arguments about shapes and their properties. "Proofs" may be more intuitive than deductive; however, there is the ability to follow a logical argument. An understanding of a formal deductive system (an agreed on set of rules), however, remains under the surface.

The products of thought at level 2 are relationships among properties of geometric objects.

The signature characteristic of a level 2 activity is the inclusion of informal logical reasoning. Because your students have developed an understanding of the various properties of shapes, it is now time for you to encourage conjecture and to ask "Why?" or "What if?"

Activity 17.3

CCSS-M: 4.G.A.2; 5.G.B.3

Minimal Defining Lists

This activity is a sequel to Activity 17.2, "Property Lists for Quadrilaterals." Once the class has agreed upon property lists for the parallelogram, rhombus, rectangle, and square (and possibly the trapezoid), post the lists, and have students work in groups to find "minimal defining lists," or MDLs, for each shape. An *MDL* is a subset of the properties for a shape that is defining and "minimal." The term *defining* here means that any shape that has all the properties on the MDL must be that shape. *Minimal* means that if any single property is removed from the list, the list is no longer defining. For example, one MDL for a square is a quadrilateral with (1) four congruent sides and (2) one right angle. If a shape has these two properties it must be a square. Another MDL for a square is that is (1) it has four sides of the same length and (2) perpendicular diagonals. Challenge students to find at least two or three MDLs for their shape. A proposed list is not defining if a counterexample—a shape other than one being described—can be produced by using only the properties on the list.

The hallmark of this and other level 2 activities is the emphasis on logical reasoning. "*If* a quadrilateral has these properties, *then* it must be a square." Logic is also involved in proving that a list is faulty—either not minimal or not defining. Here students begin to learn the nature of a definition and the value of counterexamples. In fact, any minimal defining list (MDL) is a potential definition. The other aspect of this activity that clearly involves level 2 thinking is that students focus on analyzing the relationships between properties (for example if a quadrilateral has four right angles, it also has diagonals of the same length.

Level 3: Deduction

The objects of thought at level 3 are relationships between properties of geometric objects.

At level 3, students analyze informal arguments; the structure of a system complete with axioms, definitions, theorems, corollaries, and postulates begins to develop; and they begin to grasp the necessary means of establishing geometric truth. The student at this level is usually in high school and is able to make abstract statements about geometric properties and conclusions based on logic.

The products of thought at level 3 are deductive axiomatic systems for geometry.

Level 4: Rigor

The objects of thought at level 4 are deductive axiomatic systems for geometry.

At the highest level of the van Hiele hierarchy, the objects of attention are axiomatic systems themselves, not just the deductions within a system. This is generally the level of a college mathematics major who is studying geometry as a branch of mathematical science.

The products of thought at level 4 are comparisons and contrasts among different axiomatic systems of geometry.

We have given brief descriptions of all five levels to illustrate the scope of the van Hiele theory. Most students in grades 3 through 5 will be at level 0 or 1, moving to 2 and therefore levels 3 and 4 are beyond the scope of this book.

Formative Assessment Note

How do you discover the van Hiele level of each student? Once you know, how will you select the right activities to match your students' levels? As you conduct an activity, listen to the types of observations that students make and record them on an **Observation Checklist**. Can your students talk about shapes as classes? Do they refer, for example, to "rectangles" rather than talking only about a particular rectangle? Do they generalize that certain properties are attributable to a type of shape or simply the shape at hand? Do they understand that shapes do not change when the orientation changes? With simple observations such as these, you will soon be able to distinguish between levels 0 and 1. By grade 5, if students are not able to understand logical arguments, are not comfortable with conjectures, and are unsure of if–then reasoning, these students are likely still at level 1 or below.

Implications for Instruction

The van Hiele theory and the developmental perspective of this book highlight the necessity of teaching at the student's level of thought. However, almost any activity can be modified to span two levels of thinking, even within the same classroom.

Teaching Tip

The collection of geometric experiences you provide are the single most important factor in moving students up the developmental ladder.

Moving from Level 0 to Level 1

Instructional activities that support students' movement are as follows:

- *Challenge students to test ideas about shapes by using a variety of examples from a particular category.* Say to them, "Let's see if that is true for other rectangles" or "Can you draw a triangle that does *not* have a right angle?" In general, question students to see whether the observations they make about a particular shape apply to other related shapes.

- *Provide ample opportunities to draw, build, make, put together (compose), and take apart (decompose) shapes in both two and three dimensions.* These activities should be built around understanding and using specific attributes or properties.

Teaching Tip

Remember that attributes apply to some of the shapes in a group (e.g., a particular triangle has two equal sides) and properties apply to all shapes in the group (e.g., a triangle has three sides).

- *Apply ideas to entire classes of figure (e.g., all rectangles, all prisms) rather than to individual shapes in a set.* For example, find ways to sort all possible triangles into groups. From these groups, define types of triangles.

Moving from Level 1 to Level 2

Level 2 thinking is expected to begin in grade 5 (CCSSO, 2010), when students are to classify two-dimensional shapes based on their properties (attributes) in categories and subcategories. Instructional considerations that support students moving from level 1 to level 2 are as follows:

- *Challenge students to explore or test examples.* Ask questions that involve reasoning such as "If the sides of a four-sided shape are all equal, will you always have a square?" and "Can you find a counterexample?"

- *Encourage the making and testing of hypotheses or conjectures.* "Do you think that will work all the time?" and "Is that true for all triangles or just equilateral triangles?"

- *Examine the properties of shapes to determine the necessary and sufficient conditions for a shape to be a particular shape.* "What properties must diagonals have to guarantee that a quadrilateral with these diagonals will be a square?"

- *Encourage students to attempt informal proofs.* As an alternative, require them to make sense of informal proofs that you or other students have suggested.

Teaching Tip

Consistently use the language of informal deduction: *all, some, none, if–then, what if,* and so on. Place these words on your math word wall.

The remainder of this chapter offers a sampling of activities organized around four content goals of: shapes and properties, location, transformation, and visualization. Understand that all of these subdivisions are quite fluid; that is, the content areas overlap and build on each other. Activities in one section may help develop geometric thinking in another content area.

Figure 17.4

By sorting shapes, students begin to recognize properties.

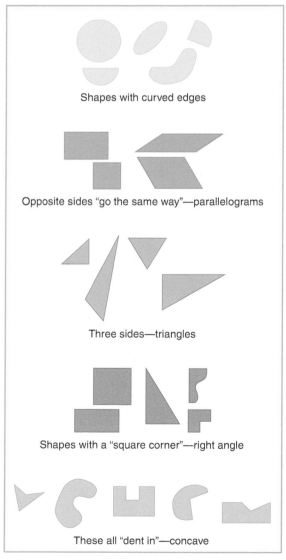

Shapes with curved edges

Opposite sides "go the same way"—parallelograms

Three sides—triangles

Shapes with a "square corner"—right angle

These all "dent in"—concave

Shapes and Properties

This content area is most often associated with geometry in preK through grade 8 classrooms where students are examining, describing, comparing, discussing, and constructing a wide variety of two- and three-dimensional shapes. Triangles should be shown in more than just equilateral forms and not always with the vertex at the top. (If you have students say that a triangle is upside down, it is because they need more experience with triangles in different orientations.) Shapes should have curved sides, straight sides, and combinations of these. Along the way, as students describe the shape or property, the terminology can be introduced.

Sorting and Classifying

In grades 3 through 5, sorting and classifying shapes can be a good formative assessment to see whether students are beginning to notice properties of shapes (level 1) rather than just what the shape "looks like." For variety in two-dimensional shapes, use materials like this set of **Assorted Shapes**. Make multiple copies so that groups of students can all work with the same shapes. Once you have your sets constructed, try Activity 17.1, "Shape Sorts" again.

In any sorting activity, the students—not the teacher—should decide how to group the shapes. By listening to the kinds of attributes that they use in their sorting, you will be able to tell what properties they know and use and how they think about shapes. Figure 17.4 illustrates a few of the many possible ways a set of shapes might be sorted.

The secret sorting activity (in Activity 17.1) is one option for introducing a new property. For example, sort the shapes so that all have at least one right angle or "square corner." When students discover your rule, you have an opportunity to talk more about that property and name the property "right angle."

The following activity is also done with the two-dimensional shapes.

Activity 17.4

CCSS-M: 3.G.A.1; 4.G.A.2

What's My Shape?

Cut out a double set of **2-D Shapes** on cardstock. Glue each shape from one set of the shapes inside a file folder to make "secret shape" folders. The other set should be glued on cards and placed on the table for reference. Designate one student in a group the leader; he or she holds the secret shape folder. The other students are to identify the shape that matches the shape in the folder by asking the leader only yes or no questions. The group can eliminate shapes (turning over the cards) as they ask questions about properties to narrow down the possibilities. They are not allowed to point to a card and ask, "Is it this one?" Rather they must continue to ask questions about properties that reduce the choices to one shape. The final shape card is checked against the shape in the leader's folder. Students with disabilities may need a list of possible properties and characteristics (such as number of sides) to help support their question asking.

The difficulty of Activity 17.4 largely depends on the shape in the folder. The more shapes in the collection that resemble the secret shape, the more difficult the task.

Formative Assessment Note

Adapt "Shape Sorts" (Activity 17.1) for a diagnostic interview. Make sure that you have a collection of solids that has a lot of variation (curved surfaces, etc.). Commercially available collections of three-dimensional shapes or real objects such as cans, boxes, balls and Styrofoam shapes will work. Figure 17.5 illustrates some classifications of solids.

The ways students describe these three-dimensional shapes is useful evidence of their level of geometric thinking. The classifications made by level 0 thinkers are generally limited to the shapes that they have in front of them. Level 1 thinkers will begin to create categories based on properties, and their language will indicate that there are many more shapes in the group than those present. Students may say things like "These shapes have sides with square corners sort of like rectangles" or "These look like boxes. All the boxes have square [rectangular] faces."

Figure 17.5

Classifications of three-dimensional shapes.

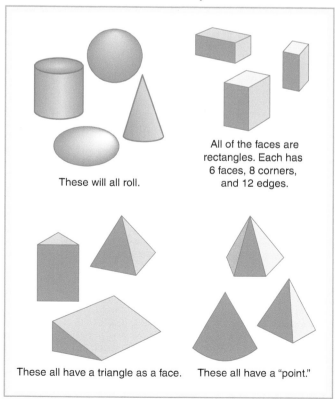

These will all roll.

All of the faces are rectangles. Each has 6 faces, 8 corners, and 12 edges.

These all have a triangle as a face.   These all have a "point."

Activity 17.5

CCSS-M: 3.G.A.1; 4.G.A.2

Can You Make It?

Print out the **Can You Make It?** Activity Page for each student or project one item at a time for the whole class. Students take the descriptions and then create a corresponding shape on the geoboard (note that two of these tasks are impossible). Also encourage students to create challenges for others to try. If the class keeps track of solutions to the challenges in the last activity, there is an added possibility of creating classes of shapes possessing certain properties that may result in definitions of new classes of shapes.

Teaching Tip

If you do this activity in stations with cards, have lots of geoboards available. It is better for two or three students to have 10 or 12 boards at a station than for each to have only one. That way, a variety of shapes can be made and compared before they are changed.

Composing and Decomposing Shapes

Students need to freely explore how shapes fit together to form larger shapes (compose) and how larger shapes can be taken apart into smaller shapes (decompose). This ability to compose and decompose supports geometric measurement such as finding area and volume. Among two-dimensional shapes for these activities, pattern blocks and Tangrams are the best known but Pierre van Hiele (1999) also describes an interesting set of tiles he calls the mosaic puzzle (see Figure 17.6).

Figure 17.6

Materials for composing and decomposing shapes.

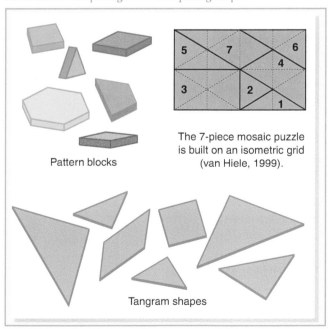

Pattern blocks

The 7-piece mosaic puzzle is built on an isometric grid (van Hiele, 1999).

Tangram shapes

Source: Van Hiele mosaic puzzle reprinted with permission from Developing Geometric Thinking through Activities That Begin with Play, *Teaching Children Mathematics*, 5(6), copyright 1999, by the National Council of Teachers of Mathematics. All rights reserved.

Activity 17.6

CCSS-M: 3.G.A.1; 3.MD.C.5

Tangram Puzzles

Using a set of Tangram Pieces, have students explore the Tangram Puzzles where they compose shapes to create a larger figure (see Figure 17.7). Also notice how the creation of these picture puzzles can also focus on area (if all seven pieces are used, the areas are the same!) and fractional parts. Challenge students to create a puzzle using an illustration that is smaller than the actual tangram pieces. This reduced-size format involves proportional reasoning because the student must mentally enlarge the shape in order to create it with the tangrams.

Figure 17.7

Four tangram puzzles.

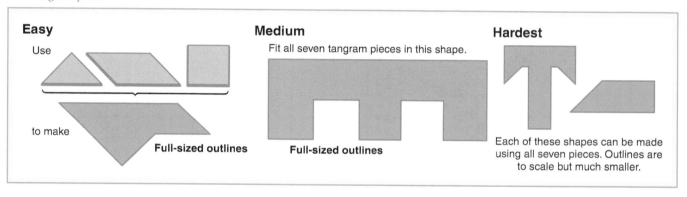

The National Library of Virtual Manipulatives has a tangram applet with a set of 14 puzzle figures that can each be made using all 7 tangram pieces.

Activity 17.7

CCSS-M: 3.G.A.1; 4.G.A.2

Mosaic Puzzle

Give pairs of students a copy of the Mosaic Puzzle. Have them review the Mosaic Puzzle Questions to explore using what they know about a shape's properties to compose and decompose other shapes.

The value of the mosaic puzzle is that it contains five different angles (lending itself to discussions of types of angle measures such as right, acute, and obtuse). Notice that initially students can and should make these geometric distinctions without measuring angles or even mentioning degrees.

The geoboard is one of the best devices for "constructing" two-dimensional shapes. Following are just a few of the many possible activities appropriate for thinking about composing and decomposing shapes using a geoboard.

Activity 17.8

CCSS-M: 4.G.A.1; 4.G.A.2; 4.G.A.3

Geoboard Copy

Prepare **Geoboard Design Cards** (see Figure 17.8). Project the shapes and ask students to copy them on geoboards (or **Geoboard Pattern** or **Geoboard Recording Sheets**). Begin with designs using one band; then create more complex designs with multiple bands that show a shape composed of other smaller shapes. Discuss properties such as number of sides, parallel lines, or line symmetry, depending on the grade level. Students with disabilities may need to have a copy of the card at their desk for closer reference.

Figure 17.8

Shapes on geoboards.

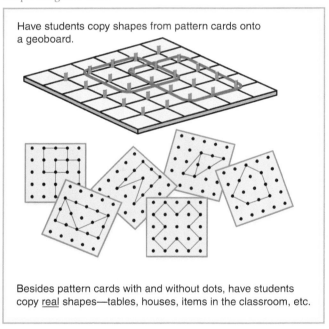

Have students copy shapes from pattern cards onto a geoboard.

Besides pattern cards with and without dots, have students copy <u>real</u> shapes—tables, houses, items in the classroom, etc.

Teach students from the very beginning how to record their designs on geoboard recording sheets. To help students who struggle with this transfer, suggest that they first mark the dots for the corners of their shape ("second row, end peg"). With the corners identified, it is much easier to draw lines between the corners to make the shape. These drawings can be placed in groups for classification and discussion or sent home to families to showcase what students are learning.

Standards for Mathematical Practice

> **5 Use appropriate tools strategically.** ▶

Virtually all of the activities suggested for geoboards can also be done on **dot** or **grid paper**. Allow students to select the tool (geoboard, grid paper, or dot paper) that best supports their thinking for the given problem.

"Geoboard Copy" has an element of proportional thinking in it, just as the tangram puzzles in which students worked from small designs. This concept of scaling (or resizing) is particularly important for fifth graders (CCSSO, 2010). In addition, the use of the geoboard supports the study of area, particularly of compound shapes. Students also begin to understand that rectangles can be decomposed into equal rows or columns, which connects area to multiplication.

With the next activity, the concept of spatial reasoning and fractions can be reinforced.

Activity 17.9

CCSS-M: 3.G.A.2; 3.NF.A.1

Decomposing Shapes

Show students a shape from the Decomposing Shapes Activity Pages and ask them to copy it on their geoboards or Geoboard Recording Sheets. Then specify the number of smaller shapes they should decompose each large shape into, as in Figure 17.9. Also specify whether the smaller shapes are all to be congruent or simply of the same type. You can connect geometry to fractions by discussing the equal parts. Then they can write the fraction of the whole for each part within the composed whole.

Figure 17.9

Subdividing shapes.

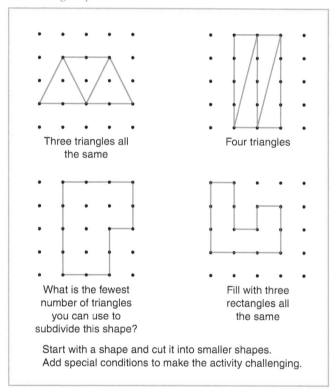

Three triangles all the same

Four triangles

What is the fewest number of triangles you can use to subdivide this shape?

Fill with three rectangles all the same

Start with a shape and cut it into smaller shapes. Add special conditions to make the activity challenging.

One excellent electronic geoboard is found at the National Library of Virtual Manipulatives and includes the instant calculation of perimeter and area of a shape on the geoboard by clicking the "measures" button. Another is the Geoboard applet at the University of Illinois Office for Mathematics, Science, and Technology Education website which has an option that shows the lengths of the sides of the figure.

Categories of Two-Dimensional Shapes

As students' attention shifts to properties of shapes (move to level 1 thinking and beyond), the important definitions of two- and three- dimensional shapes support the exploration of the relationships between shapes. Table 17.2 lists some important categories of two-dimensional shapes. Examples of these shapes can be found in Figure 17.10.

Table 17.2. Categories of two-dimensional shapes.

Shape	Description
Simple Closed Curves	
Concave, convex	An intuitive definition of *concave* might be "having a dent in it." If a simple closed curve is not concave, it is *convex*.
Symmetrical, nonsymmetrical	Shapes may have one or more lines of symmetry.
Regular	All sides and all angles are congruent.
Polygons	Simple closed curves with all straight sides.
Triangles	
Triangles	Polygons with exactly three sides.
Classified by sides	
Equilateral	All sides are congruent.
Isosceles	At least two sides are congruent.
Scalene	No two sides are congruent.
Classified by angles	
Right	One angle is a right angle.
Acute	All angles are smaller than a right angle.
Obtuse	One angle is larger than a right angle.
Convex Quadrilaterals	
Convex quadrilaterals	Convex polygons with exactly four sides.
Kite	Two opposing pairs of congruent adjacent sides.
Trapezoid	At least one pair of parallel sides.
Isosceles trapezoid	A pair of opposite sides is congruent.
Parallelogram	Two pairs of parallel sides.
Rectangle	Parallelogram with a right angle.
Rhombus	Parallelogram with all sides congruent.
Square	Parallelogram with a right angle and all sides congruent.

In the classification of quadrilaterals and parallelograms, some subsets overlap. For example, a square is a rectangle and a rhombus. All parallelograms are trapezoids, but not all trapezoids are parallelograms.* Students often have difficulty seeing this type of subcategory. They may quite correctly list all the properties of a square, a rhombus, and a rectangle and still identify a square as a "nonrhombus" or a "nonrectangle." Encourage your students to be more precise in their classifications. To help learners think about this, suggest that a student can be on two different sports teams. A square is an example of a quadrilateral that belongs to two "teams."

---

* Some definitions of trapezoid specify *only one* pair of parallel sides, in which case parallelograms would not be trapezoids. The University of Chicago School Mathematics Project (UCSMP) uses the "at least one pair" definition, meaning that parallelograms and rectangles are trapezoids. Some regions mandate one definition over another, so consult your local curriculum (Manizade & Mason, 2014).

Figure 17.10

Classification of two-dimensional shapes.

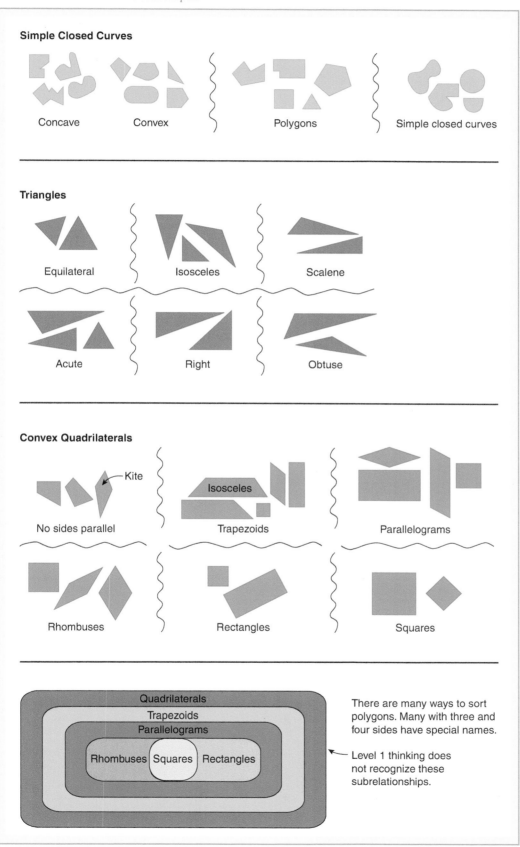

Categories of Three-Dimensional Shapes

Important shapes and relationships also exist in three dimensions, and it is these relationships that will link to students' understanding of how to find the volume of these shapes which is what the *Common Core State Standards* document recommends as part of what fifth graders will explore (CCSSO, 2010). Table 17.3 describes classifications of solids.

Table 17.3. Categories of three-dimensional shapes.

Shape	Description
Sorted by Edges and Vertices	
Sphere and "egglike" shapes	Shapes with no edges and no vertices (corners). Shapes with edges but no vertices (e.g., a flying saucer). Shapes with vertices but no edges (e.g., a football).
Sorted by Faces and Surfaces	
Polyhedron	Shapes made of all faces (a *face* is a flat surface of a solid). If all surfaces are faces, all the edges will be straight lines. Some combination of faces and rounded surfaces (cylinders are examples, but this is not a definition of a cylinder). Shapes with curved surfaces. Shapes with and without edges and with and without vertices. Faces can be parallel. Parallel faces lie in places that never intersect.
Cylinders	
Cylinder	Two congruent, parallel faces called *bases*. Lines joining corresponding points on the two bases are always parallel. These parallel lines are called *elements* of the cylinder.
Right cylinder	A cylinder with elements perpendicular to the bases. A cylinder that is not a right cylinder is an oblique cylinder.
Prism	A cylinder with polygons for bases. All prisms are special cases of cylinders.
Rectangular prism	A cylinder with rectangles for bases.
Cube	A square prism with square sides.
Cones	
Cone	A solid with exactly one face and a vertex that is not on the face. Straight lines (*elements*) can be drawn from any point on the edge of the base to the vertex. The base may be any shape at all. The vertex need not be directly over the base.
Circular cone	Cone with a circular base.
Pyramid	Cone with a polygon for a base. All faces joining the vertex are triangles. Pyramids are named by the shape of the base: *triangular* pyramid, *square* pyramid, *octagonal* pyramid, and so on. All pyramids are special cases of cones.

Figure 17.11 shows examples of cylinders and prisms. Notice that prisms are defined here as a special case of a cylinder with a polygon for a base (Zwillinger, 2011). Figure 17.12 shows a comparable grouping of cones and pyramids.

Stop and Reflect

Explain the following: Prisms are to cylinders as pyramids are to cones. How is this relationship helpful in learning volume formulas?

Figure 17.11

Cylinders and prisms.

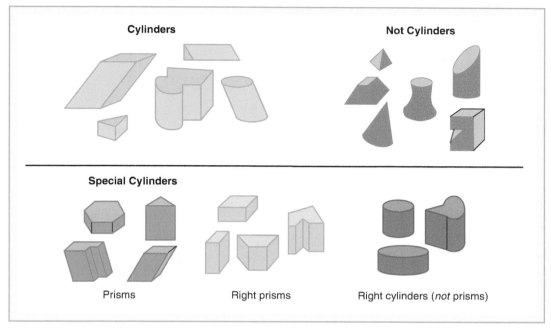

Figure 17.12

Cones and pyramids.

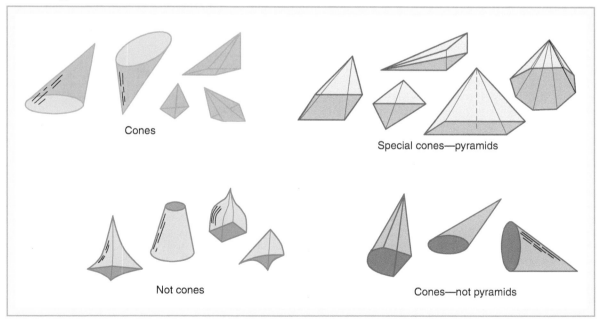

Some textbooks limit the definition of cylinders to just circular cylinders. These books do not have special names for other cylinders. Under that definition, the prism is not a special case of a cylinder. This points to the fact that definitions are conventions, and not all conventions are universally agreed upon. If you return to the development of the volume formulas in Chapter 16, you will see that the more inclusive definition of cylinders and cones allows one formula for any type of cylinder—hence, prisms—with a matching statement that is true for cones and pyramids.

Standards for
Mathematical Practice

◄ **7** **Look for and make use of structure.**

Construction Activities

Building or drawing shapes, lines, and angles is an important activity to help students think about the properties and defining features of shapes (CCSSO, 2010). Through the making of these physical models, students can focus on the properties and components that are central to defining each shape.

Because fifth graders focus a great deal of attention on learning about volume, there is good reason to explore three-dimensional shapes as in the next activity.

▶ Activity 17.10

CCSS-M: 3.G.A.1; 4.G.A.2; 4.G.A.1; 5.MD.C.4

Constructing Three-Dimensional Shapes

As students in grades 3 through 5 make these constructions, they should consider the faces of the solids (whether quadrilaterals or different types of triangles, the angles and the volume of these shapes. Collect one of the following sets of materials for students to use for construction:

1. Plastic coffee stirrers cut into a variety of lengths with twist ties inserted in the ends to use for attaching or modeling clay to connect corners

2. Plastic drinking straws cut lengthwise from the top down to the flexible joint. Insert the slit ends into the uncut bottom ends of other straws, making strong but flexible joints

3. Use rolled newspaper rods with masking or duct tape to create skeletons of three-dimensional solids (see Figure 17.13).

With these handmade models, find the volume of the solids. Also connect to engineering and discuss the strength and rigidity of triangular components in the structures. Point out that triangles are used in many bridges, in the long booms of construction cranes, and in the structural parts of buildings.

Figure 17.13

Large skeletal structures.

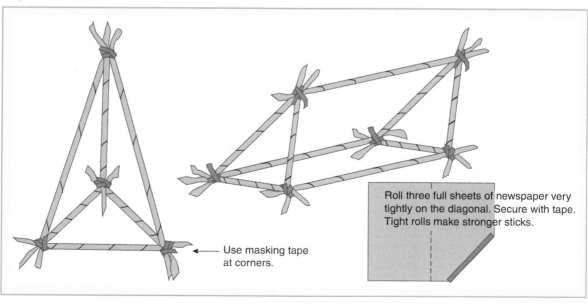

Use masking tape at corners.

Roll three full sheets of newspaper very tightly on the diagonal. Secure with tape. Tight rolls make stronger sticks.

The newspaper rod method is exciting because the structures quickly grow in volume. Let students work in groups of four or five. They will soon discover what makes a structure rigid (triangular components) and ideas of balance and form.

Two of the best-known dynamic geometry programs are *The Geometer's Sketchpad* from Key Curriculum Press and *GeoGebra* (free public domain software). Originally designed for high school students, both can be used starting about fourth grade. To appreciate the potential (and the fun) of dynamic geometry software, you really need to experience it.

In a dynamic geometry program, points, lines, and geometric figures are easily constructed on the computer. Once drawn, the geometric objects can be moved about and manipulated in an endless variety. As the figures are changed, the measurements of distances, lengths, areas, angles, and perimeters update instantly! Additionally, lines can be drawn perpendicular or parallel to other lines or segments. Angles and segments can be drawn congruent to other angles and segments. A figure can be produced that is a reflection of another figure, which can be linked to line symmetry. One of the most significant ideas is that when a geometric object is created with a particular relationship to another, that relationship is maintained no matter how either object is moved or changed. For example, in Figure 17.14, the midpoints of a freely drawn quadrilateral ABCD have been joined to explore the properties of quadrilaterals. The diagonals of the resulting quadrilateral (EFGH) are also drawn and measured. No matter how the points A, B, C, and D are dragged around the screen, even inverting the quadrilateral, the other lines will maintain the same relationships (joining midpoints and diagonals), and the measurements will be instantly updated on the screen.

Figure 17.14

A construction made with dynamic geometry software illustrating an interesting property of quadrilaterals.

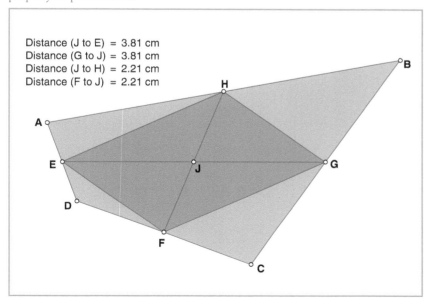

With a dynamic geometry program, if a quadrilateral is drawn, only one shape is observed, as would be the case on paper or on a geoboard (level 1). But now that the quadrilateral can be stretched and altered in endless ways, students actually explore not one shape but an enormous number of examples from that *class* of shapes. If a property does not change when the figure changes on the dynamic geometry program, the property is attributable to the class of shapes (level 2).

Once students are able to describe aspects of shapes, they are ready to explore categories of shapes, moving to higher level geometric thinking. Activity 17.11 targets definitions of two-dimensional shapes.

Activity 17.11

CCSS-M: 3.G.A.2; 4.G.A.2

Mystery Definition

 Give students the **Mystery Definition** Activity Page or project a grade-level-appropriate logic problem (such as the example in Figure **17.15**). At the top of your sheet, for your first collection, be certain that you have allowed for all possible correct options. For example, in the first grouping a square is included in the set of rhombuses. Also, choose nonexamples to be as close to the positive examples as is necessary to help develop a more precise definition. The third or mixed set should also include those nonexamples with which students are most likely to be confused. Students should justify their choices in a class discussion. Note that the use of nonexamples is particularly important for students with disabilities.

Standards for Mathematical Practice

6 Attend to precision. ▶

The value of the "Mystery Definition" activity is that students develop ideas and informal definitions based on their own concept development. After their definitions have been discussed, compared and refined, you can contrast their ideas to the conventional definition for that shape.

Figure 17.15

A mystery definition.

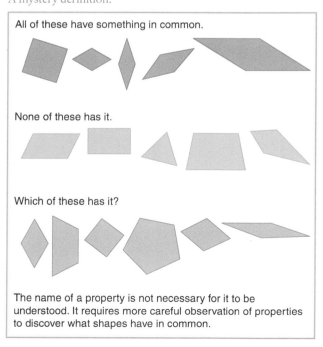

All of these have something in common.

None of these has it.

Which of these has it?

The name of a property is not necessary for it to be understood. It requires more careful observation of properties to discover what shapes have in common.

For defining types or categories of triangles (introduced in grade 4 with the concept of right triangles), the next activity is especially good.

Activity 17.12

CCSS-M: 3.G.A.2; 4.G.A.2; 5.G.B.3; 5.G.B.4

Triangle Sort

Give teams the triangles from the Assorted Triangles Activity Page, which includes right, acute, and obtuse triangles; examples of equilateral, isosceles, and scalene triangles; and triangles that represent every possible combination of these categories. Ask students to cut them out and then sort the entire collection into three discrete groups so that no triangle belongs to two groups. When this is done and descriptions of the groupings are recorded, students should then find a second criterion for creating three different groups. Students with disabilities may need a hint to look only at angle sizes or only at the issue of equal sides, but delay giving these hints if you can. Once the groups have been determined, provide appropriate terminology. For ELLs and other students who may struggle with the vocabulary, it is important to focus on the specialized meaning of the terms (e.g., contrasting *acute pain* and *acute angle*) as well as on root words (e.g., *equi-* meaning equal and *-lateral* meaning side). As a follow-up activity, challenge students to sketch a triangle in each of the nine cells of the Triangle Sort Chart.

Stop and Reflect

Of the nine cells in the chart, two of them are impossible to fill. Can you tell which ones and why?

Quadrilaterals (polygons with four sides) are an especially rich source of investigations. Once students are familiar with the concepts of right, obtuse, and acute angles; equal line segments; and line symmetry, Activity 17.2, "Property Lists for Quadrilaterals," is a good way to bring these ideas together.

The "Property Lists for Quadrilaterals" activity may take several days, but it addresses important geometry content for grade 5 and is worth the time invested. Share property lists beginning with parallelograms, then rhombuses, then rectangles, and finally squares. Have one group present its list. Then others who worked on the same shape should add to or subtract from it. The class must agree with everything placed on the list. Like the "Mystery Definition" activity, it is important to generate definitions and compare them to the common definition for that shape. In addition, students can explore which of these shapes are subcategories of other shapes (e.g., squares are a subset of rectangles).

Standards for
Mathematical Practice

◀ **3** Construct
viable arguments
and critique the
reasoning of others.

As new relationships are presented, introduce proper terminology. For example, if two diagonals intersect in a square corner, then they are *perpendicular*. Other terms such as *parallel*, and terms they will hear in the future such as *congruent*, *bisect*, *midpoint*, and so on can be mentioned and clarified as you help students write their descriptions. This is also an appropriate time to introduce symbols such as ‖ for "parallel."

In the next activity, students examine the diagonals of various classes of quadrilaterals.

Teaching Tip

Vocabulary support can occur in the *After* phase of the lesson, not just in the *Before* phase. This allows vocabulary to grow out of students' meaningful experiences.

Activity 17.13

CCSS-M: 4.G.A.2; 5.G.B.3; 5.G.B.4

Diagonals of Quadrilaterals

Give each student three cardstock Diagonal Strips made from the Activity Page. Punch the nine holes as marked. Use a brass fastener to join two strips. A quadrilateral is formed by joining the four end holes as shown in Figure 17.16. Provide students with the list of possible relationships for angles, lengths and proportional comparisons of parts. Have students use the strips to determine the properties of diagonals that will produce different quadrilaterals. Have students make drawings on 1-Centimeter Dot Paper to test the various hypotheses and record their findings on the Properties of Quadrilateral–Diagonals Activity Page. See the Expanded Lesson: Diagonals of Quadrilaterals for the full description of this instructional experience.

Figure 17.16

Diagonals of quadrilaterals.

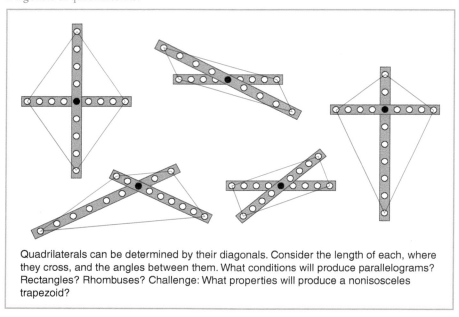

Quadrilaterals can be determined by their diagonals. Consider the length of each, where they cross, and the angles between them. What conditions will produce parallelograms? Rectangles? Rhombuses? Challenge: What properties will produce a nonisosceles trapezoid?

Every type of quadrilateral can be uniquely described in terms of its diagonals using only the conditions of length, proportional comparison of parts, and whether they are perpendicular.

Investigations, Conjectures, and the Development of Proof

As students develop an understanding of various geometric properties and attach these properties to categories of shapes, it is essential to encourage conjecture and to explore informal deductive arguments to develop logical reasoning. Students should begin to attempt—or at least follow—simple proofs and explore ideas that connect directly to algebra.

To understand the difference between levels 1 and 2 of the van Hiele theory, let's revisit the pair of activities "Property Lists for Quadrilaterals" (Activity 17.2) and "Minimal Defining Lists" (Activity 17.3). The parallelogram, rhombus, rectangle, and square all have at least four MDLs. One of the most interesting MDLs for each shape consists only of the properties of its diagonals. For example, a quadrilateral with diagonals that bisect each other and are perpendicular (intersect at right angles) is a rhombus.

Notice that the MDL activity is actually more involved with logical thinking than with examining shapes. Students say, "*If* a quadrilateral has these properties, *then* it must be a square." Logic is also involved in disproving a faulty list. A second feature is the opportunity to discuss what constitutes a definition. In fact, any MDL could be the definition of the shape. We usually choose MDLs based on the ease with which we can understand them. A quadrilateral with diagonals that bisect each other (MDL) does not immediately call to mind a parallelogram, even though that is a defining property.

> ## ♪ *Teaching Tip*
>
> It does little good to simply push students to learn definitions when they are not ready to develop the relationship.

Stop and Reflect

Use the property list for squares and rectangles to prove that "All squares are rectangles." Notice that you must use logical reasoning to understand this statement.

The next activity supports logical reasoning and is a good follow-up to Activities 17.1 and 17.2, because it is not restricted to quadrilaterals and can include three-dimensional shapes as well.

▶ Activity 17.14

CCSS-M: 4.G.A.2; 5.G.B.3; 5.G.B.4

True or False?

Prepare statements such as the following: "If it is a _____, then it is also a _____." "All are _____." "Some are _____" or use the True or False Statements Activity Page. Ask students to determine whether the statements are true or false and present an argument to support the decision (see Figure 17.17). Four or five true-or-false statements will make a good lesson. Once this format is understood, let students challenge their classmates by making their own lists that include a mixture of true and false statements.

Standards for Mathematical Practice

◀ **3** Construct viable arguments and critique the reasoning of others.

Figure 17.17

True or false? A fifth-grade student presents an argument to support her decision.

1. If it is a square, then it is a rhombus.

    TRUE.. A square can be a rhombus Because they are both paralleliograms and all the sides are the exact. Also if you rotate a square than it becums a mombus.

2. If it is a pyramid, then it must have a square base.

    False... To be a pyramid it does not have to have square base. I think this beacuse thair can be tryangular pyramids.

    Net...

> ## ♪ *Teaching Tip*
>
> When a student makes an observation or statement about a geometric concept, it can be written on the board with a question mark as a *conjecture*—a statement the truth of which has not yet been determined. You can ask, "Is it true? Always? Can we prove it? Can we find a counterexample?"

Formative Assessment Note

The "True or False?" activity is also a good diagnostic assessment. Note how the student's response shown in Figure 17.17 gives insights into her fully formed ideas and representations. She also reveals her emerging conceptions as she attempts to make arguments for her choices.

Learning about Transformations

Transformations are changes in position or size of a shape. Traditionally, the study of *translations* (slides), *reflections* (flips), and *rotations* (turns) were initiated in the elementary grades, but in the *Common Core State Standards* these topics have largely moved to middle school (CCSSO, 2010). The study of *line symmetry* is included under the study of transformations due to its link to reflections.

If a shape can be folded on a line so that the two halves match exactly, then it is said to have *line symmetry* (sometimes called *reflectional* or *mirror symmetry*). Notice that the fold line is actually a *line of reflection*—the portion of the shape on one side of the line is reflected onto the other side. Again, that is the connection between line symmetry and transformations.

One way to introduce line symmetry to students is to show examples and nonexamples using an all-of-these/none-of-these approach, as in Figure 17.18. Here's another possibility:

Fold a sheet of paper in half and cut out a shape of your choosing on the side with the fold. When you open the paper, what do you notice?

Another novel approach is to use mirrors. When you place a mirror on a picture or design so that the mirror is perpendicular to the table, you see a shape with symmetry when you look in the mirror. Explore the "Mirror Tool" symmetry activity on the NCTM Illuminations website, where students can investigate symmetry with a virtual mirror.

Figure 17.18

All of these, none of these: a mystery definition.

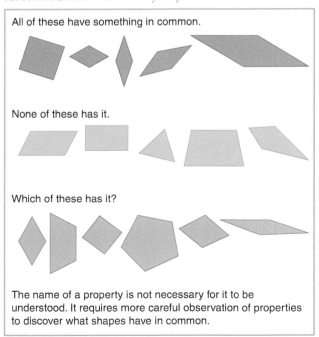

All of these have something in common.

None of these has it.

Which of these has it?

The name of a property is not necessary for it to be understood. It requires more careful observation of properties to discover what shapes have in common.

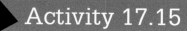

Activity 17.15

CCSS-M: 4.G.A.3

Pattern Block Mirror Symmetry

Give students a plain sheet of paper with a straight line drawn through the middle. Ask students to use about six to eight pattern blocks to make a design completely on one side of the line that touches the line in some way. When the one side is finished, students try to make the mirror image of their design on the other side of the line. After the design is complete, have students use a mirror to check their work. They place the mirror on the line and look into it from the side of the original design. With the mirror in place they should see exactly the same image as they see when they raise the mirror. You can also challenge students to make designs with more than one line of symmetry.

The same task can be done with tangrams or created on a geoboard. If students wish to try the geoboard, first they stretch a band down the center or from corner to corner. Then they make a design on one side of the line and its mirror image on the other. Check with a mirror. This can also be done with dynamic geometry software or on either isometric or rectangular dot grids as described in the following activity.

Teaching Tip

Building symmetrical designs with pattern blocks tends to be easier if the line is "pointing" at the student, that is, with a left and a right side. With the line oriented horizontally or diagonally, the task is harder.

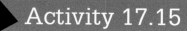

Activity 17.16

CCSS-M: 4.G.A.3

Dot Grid Line Symmetry

Give students a piece of either 1-Centimter Isometric Dot Paper or 1-Centimeter Dot Paper. Students should draw a line through several dots. This line can be horizontal, vertical, or diagonal. Students make a design completely on one side of the drawn line that touches the line, as in the figure shown on the left in Figure 17.19. Have students make the mirror image of their design on the other side of the line or have them exchange their partial design with a peer who must accurately finish it. When finished, they can check their work by placing a mirror on the line and look into it from the side of the original design. They should see exactly the same image as they see when they lift the mirror. You can also challenge them to make designs with more than one line of symmetry.

Have students try these two problems:

A shape with one line of symmetry has exactly 6 sides and two 90 degree angles. Can you draw the shape?

A quadrilateral has diagonals that do not form lines of symmetry, but the quadrilateral is symmetrical (one line). Can you draw the quadrilateral?

These exercises combine several key areas of geometry such as line symmetry, properties of shapes, and visualization with reasoning. Try to have students come up with other problems for their classmates to draw.

Figure 17.19

Exploring line symmetry on dot grids.

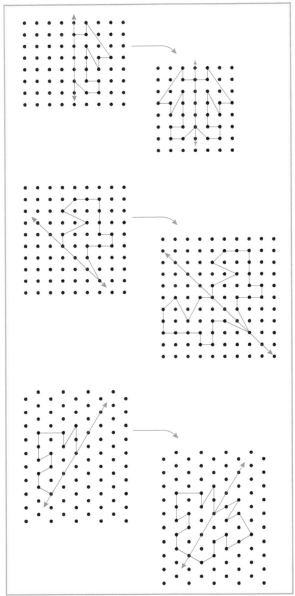

Learning about Location

Location activities begin early, when young children develop positional descriptions for actual events that describe how objects are located with respect to other objects. They say "the ball is under the table," or "that street intersects with the road the school is on." These "place learnings" (Sarama & Clements, 2014) are useful for helping students begin to specify locations. In the same way we use a map to analyze paths from point to point, the use of coordinate systems helps locate places and positions. The *Common Core State Standards* state that fifth-grade students should "[g]raph points on the coordinate plane to solve real-world and mathematical problems" (CCSSO, 2010, p. 34).

Stop and Reflect   500 ☌ 250   ⚹ ⁇ 3☿ ▱ ♄ ♒︎° ♾ ⚔ 2.5

Imagine that a visitor who doesn't know the way wants to walk from our classroom to the gym. What are the exact directions you would give to the visitor? Be specific about distance and turns.

Using coordinate systems helps students refine the way they think and reason about direction, distance, and location while enhancing spatial understanding. Geometry, measurement, and algebra are all supported by the use of a grid system with numbers or coordinates attached that can specify location. As students become more sophisticated thinkers, their use of coordinates progresses.

Activity 17.17

CCSS-M: 5.G.A.1

Hidden Positions

Give each student a **Hidden Positions Gameboard**. Two students sit with a "screen" separating their desktop space so that neither student can see the other's grid (see Figure 17.20). Each student has four different pattern blocks. The first player places a block on four different sections of the 3 × 3 grid. He then tells the other player where to put blocks on her grid to match his own by using directions describing the location of each piece. When all four pieces are positioned, the two grids are checked to see that they are alike. Then the players switch roles. Model the game once by taking the part of the first student. Use words such as *top row, middle row, left, right, above, below, next to* and *beside*. Students can play in pairs as a station activity. For students with disabilities, consider starting with just one shape. Then move to two and so on. For students who need a challenge, extend the grids up to 6 × 6. As the grid size increases, notice how the need for a system of labeling positions increases.

Figure 17.20

The "Hidden Positions" game.

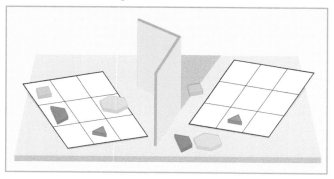

The next activity can serve as a readiness task for coordinates and help students see the value of having a way to specify location without pointing.

Activity 17.18

CCSS-M: 5.G.A.1

What's the Point?

To introduce a coordinate system, give students a Coordinate Grid like the one shown in Figure 17.21 and explain how to use two numbers (positive whole numbers) to designate an intersection point on the grid. The first number tells how far to move to the right. The second number tells how far to move up. In the beginning, use the words along with the numbers: 3 right and 0 up. Be sure to include 0 in your introduction. Then select a point on the grid and have students decide what two numbers name that point. If your point is at (2, 4) and students incorrectly say "four, two," then simply indicate where the point is that they named. Name additional points and then have students suggest options.

 ## Activity 17.19

CCSS-M: 5.G.A.1

Step Right Up

Create a coordinate grid on the floor of the gymnasium using painter's tape, or on the school playground with paint (with permission of course). Give each student a small whiteboard for recording. Select a student and secretly give her a set of coordinates. Then the student moves to that location. Other students write the coordinates for that location and display their answers. This can also be done with Coordinate Grid If you repeatedly call this activity "Step Right Up," that can act as a mnemonic for students with disabilities as they will remember to first step right, then up, to locate the position for coordinates of positive whole numbers. Make sure you tell the students that there are other directions they will be learning for the future and a "right step" will not always be the "right way to go!"

Once a coordinate system has been introduced, students may want to try NCTM's e-Example (applet 4.3). Students move a ladybug by issuing a list of directions to hide the ladybug beneath a leaf. When the directions are complete, the ladybug is set in motion to follow them. The ladybug can also be directed to draw shapes such as a rectangle or to travel through mazes.

The next activity explores the notion of different paths on a grid.

 ## Activity 17.20

CCSS-M: 5.G.A.1; 5.G.A.2

Paths

On a sheet of 2-Centimeter Grid Paper, mark two different points A and B as shown in Figure 17.22. Using a projection display or floor tiles, demonstrate how to describe a path from A to B. For the points in the figure, one path is "up 5 and right 6." Another path might be "right 2, up 3, right 4, up 2." Count the length of each path. As long as you always move toward the target point (in this case either right or up), the path lengths will always be the same. Here they are 11 units long. Students draw three paths on their papers from A to B using different-colored crayons. For each path they write directions that describe their paths. Ask, "What is the greatest number of turns that you can make in your path?" "What is the smallest number?" "Where would A and B have to be in order to get there with no turns?" Then add a coordinate system on the grid and have students describe their paths with coordinates: For example: (1,2), (3,2), (3,5), (7,5), (7,7).

Students who have done this activity should have a general way to describe reflection across an axis in terms of coordinates. Soon fifth graders will be combining this knowledge with their understanding of scaling and resizing to learn about dilations at the middle school level.

Learning about Visualizations

Visualization might be called "geometry done with the mind's eye." It involves being able to create mental images of shapes and then turn them around mentally, thinking about how they look from different viewpoints. It includes the mental coordination of two and three dimensions—predicting the unfolding of a box (called a *net*) by understanding a two-dimensional drawing of a three-dimensional shape. Any activity that requires students to think about, manipulate, or transform a shape mentally or to represent a shape as it is seen visually will contribute to the development of their visualization skills. Visualization activities will have students using a variety of physical shapes and drawings and will challenge them to think about these shapes in different orientations.

Finding out how many different shapes can be made with a given number of simple tiles demands that students mentally flip and turn shapes in their minds and find ways to decide whether they have found them all. That is the focus of the next activity.

Figure 17.21

A simple coordinate grid. The X is at (3,2) and the O is at (1,3). Use the grid to play "Three in a Row" (like Tic-Tac-Toe). Put marks on intersections, not spaces.

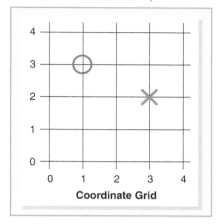
Coordinate Grid

Activity 17.21

CCSS-M: 3.G.A.1

Pentominoes

A pentomino is a shape formed by joining five squares as if cut from a square grid. Each square must have at least one side in common with another. Provide students with five square tiles and a sheet of **1-Centimeter Grid Paper** for recording. Challenge them to see how many different pentomino shapes they can find. Shapes that are flips or turns of other shapes are not considered different. Do not tell students how many pentomino shapes there are. Good discussions will come from deciding whether some shapes are really different and if all shapes have been found. Look at the **Pentominoes** Activity page to see all the possible options.

Figure 17.22

Different paths from A to B on a grid.

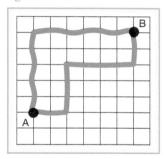

Once students have decided that there are just 12 pentominoes (see Figure 17.23), the 12 pieces can then be used in a variety of activities. For example, try to fit all 12 pieces into a 6 × 10 or 5 × 12 rectangle. Another task is to examine each of the 12 pentominoes and decide which will fold up to make an open box. For those that are "box makers," which square is the bottom?

It is also fun to explore the number of shapes that can be made from six equilateral triangles or from four 45-degree right triangles (halves of squares). With the right triangles, sides that touch must be the same length. How many of each of these "ominoes" do you think there are? These variations work well for a class that has worked previously with pentominoes and wants additional visualization experiences.

Three-Dimensional Imagery

Another aspect of visualization for young students is to be able to think about three-dimensional shapes in terms of their two-dimensional representations: focusing on faces.

Figure 17.23

Pentominoes.

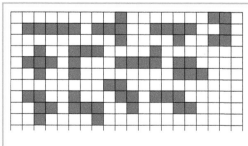

There are 12 pentominoes.

Finding all possible shapes made with five squares—or six squares (called "hexominoes") or six equilateral triangles and so on—is a good exercise in spatial problem solving.

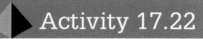

Activity 17.22

CCSS-M: 3.G.A.1; 4.G.A.2

Face Matching

Provide students with **Find a Shape** Activity Page and sets of **Face Matching Cards** (see Figure 17.24). There are two versions of the task: Given a Find a Shape card, find the corresponding solid, or given a solid, identify the matching Find a Shape card. With a collection of individual face matching cards, students can select the cards that go with a particular solid. For another variation, stack all of the single-face cards for one solid face down. Turn the cards up one at a time as clues to identifying the solid. Use the **Face Matching Card Questions** and collect student responses.

Visualization from multiple avenues is explored in this next activity as students must visualize what they are wearing on their back!

Figure 17.24

Matching face cards with solid shapes.

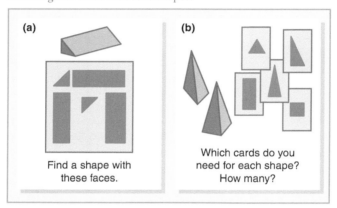

(a) Find a shape with these faces.

(b) Which cards do you need for each shape? How many?

Activity 17.23

CCSS-M: 3.G.A.1; 4.G.A.1; 5.G

Geometry Necklaces

Make necklaces from index cards with two holes punched at the top and a loop of yarn long enough to easily go over all students' heads. Each card should have a two- or three-dimensional shape or any geometric terms appropriate for your students as in **Geometry Necklace Cards**. Put a necklace on each student hanging off their back so they cannot see it. Students should not try to look at their necklace or ask others to tell them what they are wearing. Then students walk around the room and ask only yes/no questions to help them collect information to determine their geometric figure or term. Students may only ask **1 question per person** keeping track of questions and answers on a piece of paper. When students believe they have precisely identified what is on their necklace they should check with the teacher. Then they can assist others (they do not give their peers the answer: instead, they act like a "teacher" and give hints or clues).

Table 17.4. Common errors and misconceptions in geometry and how to help.

Common Error or Misconception	What It Looks Like	How to Help
Unsure of definitions that involve inclusion relations of quadrilaterals –Is a rectangle a square? Rectangle a parallelogram? Square a parallelogram?	When students are asked if this shape is a rectangle, they say no.	• Remind students that they could be in more than one school club or on more than one school team. Shapes are able to be in more than one category in the same way. • Focus on activities where students are able to compare the properties and definitions of shapes such as Activity 17.2 and Activity 17.3.
If four sides are equal the angles must be right angles.	When students are working with the properties alone, with no visual, they will think of the one shape that pops into their mental imaging rather than the whole group of shapes with that definition (four equal sides).	• Focus on the use of counterexamples. This is a particularly helpful way to develop students' ability to prove ideas, and counterexamples are very useful when working with students with disabilities.
Students misname 3D figures by focusing on the 2D face.	Students might call a cube a square or a sphere a circle.	• Give students multiple opportunities to look at 2D and 3D figures together so they can identify the rectangle as a face on a rectangular prism. • Avoid allowing student when they are asked to find a rectangle to say a box (rectangular prism) is a rectangle. Make sure you highlight that the face on one side of the box is a rectangle.
Line of symmetry must be vertical or horizontal.	For example, given a square, students will say there are only two lines of symmetry. In this case, they miss seeing the diagonal lines of symmetry.	• Have students use many different shapes and initially tell them how many lines to look for. Then fade that support so they have to seek out the correct number of lines of symmetry in the figure.
Perpendicular lines must be horizontal and vertical.	Students will say these lines are NOT perpendicular	• This is an artifact of having experience with perpendicular lines shown only as a vertical and a horizontal line. Take the time to show the perpendicular lines in a variety of orientations.
Parallel lines must be horizontal.	Students will say these lines are NOT parallel.	• Like the perpendicular lines, this is an artifact of having experience with the iconic image of parallel lines as two horizontal or two vertical lines. Take the time to show the parallel lines in a variety of orientations.

18

Representing and Interpreting Data

BIG IDEAS

1 Statistics is its own field and different from mathematics; one key difference is the focus on variability of data in statistical reasoning.

2 Doing statistics involves a four-step process: formulating questions, collecting data, analyzing data, and interpreting results.

3 Data are gathered and organized in order to answer questions about the populations from which the data come. With data from only a sample of the population, inferences are made about the population.

4 Different types of graphs and other data representations provide different information about the data and, hence, the population from which the data were taken. The choice of graphical representation can impact how well the data are understood.

5 Graphs can provide a sense of the shape of the data, including how spread out or how clustered the data are. Having a sense of the shape of data is having a big picture of the data rather than the data just being a collection of numbers.

Graphs and statistics bombard the public in areas such as advertising, opinion polls, population trends, health risks, and progress of children in schools. We hear that the average amount of rainfall this summer is more than it was last summer or that the average U.S. family consists of 3.19 people. We read on the U.S. Census website that the median home price in March 2016 was $288,000 and the mean was $356,200. Knowing these statistics should raise an array of questions: How were these data gathered? What was the purpose? What does it indicate to have an average of 3.19 people? Why are the median and the mean for home sales so different? Which statistic makes more sense for communicating the prices of homes?

Statistical literacy is critical to understanding the world around us, essential for effective citizenship, and vital for developing the ability to question information presented in the media (Schaeffer & Jacobbe, 2014; Schield, 2010; Shaughnessy, 2007). Misuse of statistics occurs even in trustworthy sources like newspapers, in which graphs are often designed to exaggerate a finding.

Students in grades 3 through 5 should have meaningful experiences with basic concepts of statistics throughout their school years. The *Common Core State Standards* (CCSSO, 2010) expect the following grade-level goals:

Grade 3: Students represent and interpret data through creating scaled (one-to-many) picture graphs and bar graphs (categorical data) and line plots (numerical data) gathered through measurement activities (with fractional units).

Grade 4: Students make line plots to display numerical data from measurements (with fractional units) and interpret the data to solve problems involving addition and subtraction of fractions.

Grade 5: Students continue to use line plots to display numerical measurement-based data and use operations with fractions to solve problems using information from the graphs.

What Does It Mean to Do Statistics?

Doing statistics is, in fact, a different process from doing mathematics. This is a notion that has received much attention in standards documents and research (Burrill & Elliott, 2006; Franklin et al., 2005; Shaughnessy, 2003). As Richard Scheaffer, past president of the American Statistics Association notes:

Mathematics is about numbers and their operations, generalizations and abstractions; it is about spatial configurations and their measurement, transformations, and abstractions. . . . Statistics is also about numbers—but numbers in context: these are called data. Statistics is about variables and cases, distribution and variation, purposeful design or studies, and the role of randomness in the design of studies, and the interpretation of results. (Scheaffer, 2006, pp. 310–311)

Statistical literacy is needed by all students to interpret the world. This chapter describes some of the big ideas and essential knowledge regarding statistics and explains a general process for doing statistics. Each of the four steps in the process is used as a major section in the organization of this chapter.

Is It Statistics or Is It Mathematics?

Statistics and mathematics are two different fields; however, statistical questions are often asked in assessments with questions that are mathematical in nature rather than statistical. The risk in this is that students are not focusing on statistical reasoning, as shown by the following excellent exemplars from Scheaffer (2006).

Stop and Reflect

Read the questions that follow and label each as "doing mathematics" or "doing statistics."

1. The average weight of 50 prize-winning tomatoes is 2.36 pounds. What is the combined weight, in pounds, of these 50 tomatoes? (NAEP sample question)

   a. 0.0472   b. 11.8   c. 52.36   d. 59   e. 118

2. The following table gives the times each girl has recorded for seven trials of the 100-meter dash this year. Only one girl may compete in the upcoming track meet. Which girl would you select for the meet and why?

Runner	Race						
	1	**2**	**3**	**4**	**5**	**6**	**7**
Suzie	15.2	14.8	15.0	14.7	14.3	14.5	14.5
Tanisha	15.8	15.7	15.4	15.0	14.8	14.6	14.5
Dara	15.6	15.5	14.8	15.1	14.5	14.7	14.5

Which of these problems involves statistical reasoning? Both? Neither? As explained by Schaeffer, only the second one is statistical in nature. The first requires computing with multiplication—mathematical thinking, not statistical thinking. The second question is statistical in nature because the situation requires analysis—graphs or averages might be used to determine a solution. The mathematics here is basic; the focus is on statistics. Notice that the context is central to responding to the question, which is an indication that it is statistical reasoning.

In statistics, the context is essential to analyzing and interpreting the data (Franklin & Garfield, 2006; Franklin et al., 2005; Langrall, Nisbet, Mooney, & Jansem, 2011; Scheaffer, 2006). Looking at the spread, or shape, of data and considering the meaning of unusual data points (outliers) are determined based on the context.

Figure 18.1

Graphs help us consider the shape of the data.

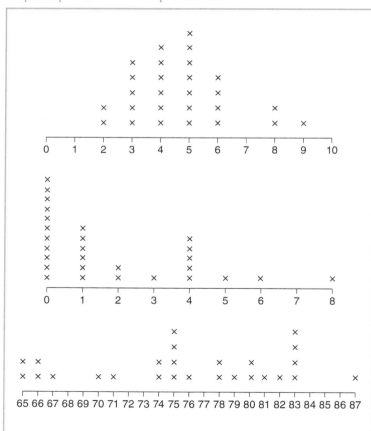

The Shape of Data

A big conceptual idea in data interpretation can be referred to as the *shape of data:* a sense of how data are spread out or grouped, what characteristics about the data set as a whole can be described, and what the data tell us in a global way about the population from which they are taken. Across the elementary curricula, students begin looking at the shape of data by examining various graphs. Different graphing techniques or types of graphs can provide a different snapshot of the data as a whole. For example, bar graphs and circle graphs (percentage graphs) each show how the data cluster in different categories. The circle graph focuses more on the relative values of the clusters, whereas the bar graph adds a dimension of quantity. The choices of which graph and how many categories to use in a graph will cause different shapes to emerge.

Part of understanding the shape of data is being aware of how spread out or clustered the data are. In grades 3 through 5, this can be discussed informally by looking at almost any graph (see Figure 18.1).

What questions could these three graphs be responding to?

The Process of Doing Statistics

To engage students meaningfully in learning and doing statistics, they should be involved in the full process, from asking and defining questions to interpreting results. This broad approach provides a framework and purpose under which students learn a variety of ways how to collect data, create graphs and analyze data. This chapter is organized around this process, which is presented in Figure 18.2.

Figure 18.2

The process of doing statistics.

1. Develop Statistical Questions
   - Use interesting, relevant questions for the students to explore
   - Engage students in generating questions that can be answered using statistics
   - Focus on questions that include variability
   - Consider what data will answer the question:
     - Include questions that generate numerical data
     - Include data that can be gathered within the classroom or school
2. Gather and Organize Data
   - Decide who will be asked the question(s) or what source(s) will be used for gathering data
   - Outline a plan for collecting the data
   - Choose the best way to record the data
   - Carry out the data collection plan
3. Choose a Data Analysis Plan
   - Decide which representation will best tell the story related to your question(s)
   - Prepare those data displays (by hand or using technology)
   - Select ways to interpret the data (combining or comparing)
   - Carry out the analysis plan
4. Interpret the Findings
   - Use representations from #3 to answer the question(s) from #1
   - Look at the shape of the data if in a graphical representation
   - Explore questions such as:
     - What does our data tell us about our class? And, what doesn't it tell us?
     - What might we infer?
     - What new questions might we have?
   - Look for factual information as well as inferences that go beyond the data

Formulating Questions

Statistics is about more than making graphs and analyzing data. It includes both asking and answering questions about our world. Data collection should be for a purpose, to answer a question. Then the analysis of data actually adds information about some aspect of our world, just as political pollsters, advertising agencies, market researchers, census takers, wildlife managers, medical researchers, and hosts of others gather data to answer questions and make informed decisions.

Students should be given opportunities to generate their own questions, decide on appropriate data to help answer these questions, and determine methods of collecting the data (CCSSO, 2010: NCTM, 2006). Whether the question is teacher initiated or student initiated, students should engage in conversations about how well-defined the question is. For example, if the teacher asks, "How many brothers and sisters do you have?" there may be a need to discuss half siblings. When students formulate the questions the data they gather become more meaningful.

Often the need to gather data will come from the class naturally in the course of discussion or from questions arising in other content areas. Science, of course, is full of measurements and, thus, abounds in data analysis possibilities. Social studies is also full of opportunities to pose questions requiring data collection. The next few sections suggest some additional ideas.

Classroom Questions

Students want to learn about themselves (what does the "typical" student look like or what is she interested in?), their families and pets, measures such as arm span or time to get to school, their likes and dislikes, and so on. The easiest questions to begin with are those that can be answered by each class member contributing one piece of data. Here are a few ideas:

- *Favorites:* TV shows, games, movies, ice cream, video games, sports teams, music
- *Numbers:* Number of pets, siblings; hours watching TV or hours of sleep; bedtime; time spent on the computer
- *Measures:* Height, arm span, area of foot, long-jump distance, shadow length, seconds to run around the track, minutes spent traveling to school

Teaching Tip

When there are lots of possibilities, start by restricting the number of choices. Give a "forced" choice of the top-five TV shows after taking a quick poll.

Beyond One Classroom

The questions in the previous section are designed for students to contribute data about themselves. These questions can be expanded by asking, "How would this compare to another class?" Comparison questions are a good way to help students focus on the data they have collected and the variability within that data (Russell, 2006). As students get older, they can begin to think about various populations and differences between them. For example, how are fifth graders similar to or different from middle school students? Students might examine questions where they compare responses of boys versus girls, or adults/teachers versus students. These situations involve issues of sampling and making generalizations and comparisons. In addition, students can ask questions about things beyond the classroom. Discussions about communities provide a good way to integrate social studies and mathematics. Here is an example followed by an activity.

Tally the number of cars (or the number of people) that pass your home from 4:30 to 5:30 p.m. Compare your data to your classmates. How busy is your street? How would you classify your neighborhood into a grouping such as urban, suburban, or rural?

Activity 18.1

CCSS-M: 3.MD.B.3

Find Me

Have students go to a site such as Google Earth to find the school's neighborhood, their neighborhood, or another area of your choice (maybe a location you are studying). Zoom down to locate approximately a one-block area. Decide in advance items to tally such as number of cars, garages, sheds, pools, play equipment, and so forth. See what you can identify. Then select another neighborhood and compare. "Ask, what do you notice? What can you tell about the neighborhood from knowing the number of backyard pools? Trees? Cars?"

Science is an area in which questions can be asked and data gathered. Some activities can also dovetail with school science fairs:

- What is the width of leaves that fall to the ground? Can you identify the tree by knowing the width of the leaf?
- How many times do different types of balls bounce when each ball is dropped from the same height?
- How many days does it take for different types of bean, squash, and pea seeds to germinate when kept in moist paper towels? What is the height of the plants every three days once they sprout?
- How many plastic bottles or aluminum cans are placed in the school's recycling bins over a week?

A distinguishing feature of statistics is that the context is front and center. Therefore, it is particularly important that the context be culturally meaningful. Culturally meaningful and relevant contexts create a supportive classroom environment (McGlone, 2008). This can be as simple as asking about favorite family meal or game, or can include an exploration of family customs. The key to having such questions lead to a supportive classroom environment is sharing the results in a way that helps others in the class appreciate the unique lives of their classmates as in the next activity.

Activity 18.2

CCSS-M: 3.MD.B.3; 4.MD.A.4

What Can We Learn about Our Community?

This activity plays out over several days. First, ask students to turn in an index card with three statistical questions they would like to investigate during the year. This could be assigned as homework, with students' families helping to brainstorm ideas. Collect these ideas. When you have time to start the investigation, take one question from the set. As a class, refine the question to one that can be answered using statistics. Examples of questions include:

(continued)

- How many different kinds of restaurants or stores are in our community (fast food restaurants versus "sit-down" restaurants; Chinese, Indian, Italian, Mexican, or American; convenience stores, grocery stores, clothing stores, variety stores)?
- How many different kinds of trees are in our neighborhood?
- How many different kinds of houses are in the community (one story, two story, three story, apartment houses)?

Discuss ways to gather the data. Set up a plan and deadline for gathering the data. When students bring in the data, encourage students to select and use data displays (e.g., scaled pictograph graph, scaled bar graphs, line plot, etc.). Invite students to suggest ways to interpret the data. Return to the question and ask, "What does our data tell us about _____?" Consider how the different data displays communicate the answer to this question.

Data Collection

There are two main types of data—*categorical* and *numerical*. NCTM suggests that by the sixth grade students should be able to sort these two data types (NCTM, 2000), making the time frame of grades 3 through 5 important in that process. Categorical data refer to information that can be collected about such things that can be grouped by labels, such as favorite vacation sites, colors of cars in the school parking lot, and the most popular suggestion for a name to give the class guinea pig. Categorical data may not have any order—the bars in a bar graph could be put in any arrangement or they could be in an order when you rank something on a scale from 1 to 10. Numerical data, by contrast, counts things or measures on a continuous scale. Numerical data are ordered numerically, like a number line, and can include fractions and decimals. This kind of data can include how many miles to school, the temperature in your town over a one-week period, or the weight of the students' backpacks.

How students organize the data and the techniques for interpreting them or analyzing them have a purpose. But gathering data without a plan is not easy for students. After receiving a question for which they need to collect data, eager students can't just ask others their question and record answers. They may want to start by just hand raising, using a tally, or by a ballot using both limited (narrowing the range of possible answers) or unlimited response options (Hudson, Shupe, Vasquez, & Miller, 2008). The problem is that they typically have no idea whom they have asked more than once or whom they have not asked at all. This provides an excellent entry into a discussion about how statisticians gather data. Ask your students to brainstorm ways to gather the data in an organized manner from their classmates.

Teaching Tip

Note that the word *data* is plural, hence the use of "data are." The singular is *datum*.

Gathering data also must take into consideration *variability*. Students can understand that asking a group of first graders their favorite TV show will produce different answers from a group of fifth graders or a group of teachers. Answers also may vary based on the day the question is asked or whether a particular show has been recently discussed.

Data can also be collected through observation. This creates a shared context for students, in that they will all be a part of observing phenomena. For example, set up a bird feeder outside the classroom window and collect data at different times during the day to either count the number or type of birds, which can be recorded on a line plot. Students can also collect observational data on fieldtrips, such as the zoo, where they can record frequencies of animal behaviors such as preening, eating, or playing (Mokros & Wright, 2009). They can also report on data from evening, weekend, or vacation activities with their families.

As you plan to collect data, make sure to include gathering data from more than one classroom to seek a more representative sample, or even use random sampling. In fact, as an extension for some students, it is important that they engage in the whole process including designing an experiment in which most variables are kept the same (controlled) so that one variable can be analyzed (plant growth under a variety of conditions such as feeding the plant water, soda, or milk).

Using Existing Data Sources

Data do not have to be collected by survey; existing data abound in various places, such as the following sources of print and Web data.

Print Resources

Newspapers, almanacs, sports record books, maps, and various government publications are possible sources of data that may be used to answer student questions. Children's literature is also an excellent and engaging resource. Nonfiction literature can be a source of data, especially for older students. For example, the *Book of Lists: Fun Facts, Weird Trivia, and Amazing Lists on Nearly Everything You Need to Know!* (Buckley & Stremme, 2006) reports on various statistics and includes surveys at the end of every section. Books on sports, such as *A Negro League Scrapbook* (Weatherform, 2005), can have very interesting statistics about historic periods that students can explore and compare.

Web Resources

The Internet provides seemingly limitless data that are often accessed by typing the related question into a search. Students may be interested in facts about another country as a result of a social studies unit or a country in the news. Olympic records in various events over the years or data related to environmental issues are other examples of topics around which student questions may be formulated. For these and hundreds of other questions, data can be found on the Web. Below are several websites with a lot of interesting data.

- The **USDA Economic Research Service Food Consumption** site offers wonderful data sets on the availability and consumption of hundreds of foods. Annual per capita estimates often go back to 1909.
- **Google Public Data Explorer** makes large datasets available to explore, visualize, and interpret.
- **NCTM Illuminations State Data Map** is a source that displays state data on population, land area, political representation, gasoline use, and so on.
- **The Central Intelligence Agency (CIA) World Fact Book** provides demographic information for every nation in the world, including population, age distributions, death and birth rates, and information on the economy, government, transportation, and geography.
- **U.S. Census Bureau** website contains copious statistical information by state, county, or voting district.

Data Analysis: Classification

Standards for
Mathematical Practice

1 Make sense of problems and persevere in solving them.

Classification involves making decisions about how to categorize things, a basic activity that is fundamental to data analysis. In order to formulate questions and decide how to represent data that have been gathered, decisions must be made about how things might be categorized based on some attribute or characteristic of the data.

Attribute activities start in as early as kindergarten, yet the reasoning involved can be expanded as students move to grades 3 through 5. At least initially, attribute activities are best done in an area where all students can see and have access to the materials to be sorted in Venn diagrams.

Activity 18.3

CCSS-M: MP 2 Reason abstractly and quantitatively

What about "Both"?

Give students two large loops of string (as Venn diagrams) and attribute pieces (these are usually blocks of two dimensional shapes that are red, blue, or yellow, large or small, and sometimes thick or thin). Direct them that the rule for the one string is that only red pieces can go inside and the rule for the other is that only triangles can go inside. Let the students place pieces in each and try to resolve the difficulty of what to do with red triangles. When the notion of overlapping the strings to create an area common to both loops is clear, more challenging activities can be explored. Students with disabilities will need to use written labels of the rule on each loop of string. As shown in Figure 18.3, the labels need not be restricted to single attributes. If a piece does not fit in any region, it is placed outside all of the loops.

As students progress, it is important to introduce labels for negative attributes such as "not red" or "not small." Also important is the eventual use of *and* and *or* connectives to form two-value rules such as "red and square" or "big or happy." This use of *and, or,* and *not* significantly widens students' classification schemes.

Figure 18.3

A Venn diagram activity with attribute pieces. A rule is written on each card.

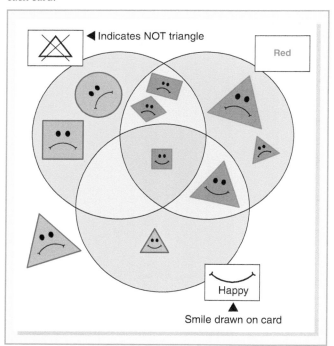

An engaging and challenging activity is to infer how things have been classified when the loops are not labeled. The following activities require students to make and test conjectures about how things are being classified.

Activity 18.4

Hidden Labels

Use attribute blocks, Woozle Cards, or illustrations of geometric figures as in the Geometry Necklace Cards. Create label cards for the loops of string used to make the Venn diagram. Select two of the label cards and place the cards face down with one next to each of the two circles of the Venn diagram. Ask students to select an attribute piece (or card) for you to place. For ELLs and students with disabilities, provide a list of the possible hidden labels with pictures and/or translations for each as a reference. Begin to sort the attribute pieces according to the hidden rules. As you sort, have students try to determine what the labels are for each of the loops. Let students who think they have guessed the labels try to place a piece in the proper loop, but avoid having them guess the labels aloud. Students who think they know the labels can also be asked to "play teacher" and respond to the guesses of the others. Point out that one way to test an idea about the labels is to select a piece that you think might go in a particular section. Wait to turn the cards up until most students have figured out the rule. Then hide the rules for three Venn areas!

"Hidden Labels" can and should be repeated with real-world materials connected to other content areas and to students' experiences. For example, if you were doing a unit on habitats, you can use pictures of different environments to sort by relevant attributes. Students can also bring in things they can recycle and these objects can be sorted by type (English, 2013). Additionally, when studying geographic regions, a resource or land feature (such as mountains) can be the rule and cuts outs of the states can be placed in the appropriate part of the Venn diagram.

Data Analysis: Graphical Representations

Graphs summarize the data that were collected. How these data are organized should be directly related to the question that caused you to collect the data in the first place. For example, suppose students want to know how many siblings their classmates have. Data collection involves each student counting his or her own family members.

> **Stop and Reflect**   500 ◗,²⁵⁰   ⸮ 3⚡ ▱ʃ♭♀ ∞◠ ⤳ 2.5
>
> If your third-grade class had collected these data, what methods might you suggest they use for organizing and graphing them? Which methods work best for these data?

A bar graph with one bar per student will certainly tell how many siblings each student has. However, is it the best way to showcase the data to interpret it and answer the question? If the data were categorized by number of siblings, then a line plot showing the number of students with no siblings, one sibling, two siblings, and so on will easily show which number of siblings is most common and how the number of siblings varies across the class.

Once students have made the display, they can discuss its meaning. If, for example, a line plot has seven sticky notes above the five, students may think that five people have seven siblings or seven people have five siblings. How can this be remedied? Interpreting data that are numerical (number of siblings) versus categorical (color of hair) is an added challenge for students as they struggle to make sense of the graphs (Russell, 2006).

Creating Graphs

Students should be involved in deciding how they want to represent their data. However, for students lacking experience with the various methods of organizing data, you will need to introduce options and present the constraints as to when each display can and cannot be used.

The goal is to help students see that graphs and charts tell information and that different types of representations tell different things about the same data. The value of having students actually construct their own graphs is not so much that they learn the techniques, but that they are personally invested in the data and that they learn how a graph conveys information. Once a graph is constructed, the most important activity is discussing what it tells the people who see it, especially those who were not involved in making the graph. Discussions about graphs of real data that the students have themselves been involved in gathering will help them analyze and interpret other graphs and charts that they see in real world settings.

What we should *not* do is only concentrate on the details of graph construction (Monterio & Ainley, 2010). Your objectives should focus on the issues of interpreting the information and communicating the results! In the real world, technology will take care of details.

The Internet also offers opportunities to explore different graphs. Create a Graph (NCES Kids Zone) provides tools for creating five different graphical displays. Illuminations Data Grapher and Advanced Data Grapher allow students to enter data, select which set(s) to display, and choose the type of representation (e.g., bar graph, circle graph etc.).

Bar Graphs

Bar graphs are some of the first ways to group and present data. In third grade, students should be able to create their own displays (CCSSO, 2010). Initially, bar graphs should be made so that each bar consists of countable parts such as squares (could be sticky notes), actual objects, or same-sized pictures of objects (also called picture graphs or pictographs). Then students move to scaled bar graphs in which a picture or symbol represents a "many-to-one" relationship—for example, one star represents five books that a student has read. The bars are separated by an equal space and represent a bar of information that, unlike numerical data, could be moved from one place to another. The scale of a bar graph (located on the axis without the bars) is merely a measuring tool like a ruler—sometimes labeled with nonstandard units and other times linking to standard units as in the next activity.

▶ Activity 18.5   CCSS-M: 3.MD.B.4; 4.MD.B.4; 5.MD.B.2

Storm Chaser

This activity involves students collecting data over time about the amount of rainfall (or snowfall) right outside their classroom. Install a rain (or snow) gauge where it can be easily accessed or collect information about your area from the Internet. After a heavy rain (or snow) storm, send a pair of students outside with a piece of cash register tape. Their task is to cut the tape as long as the height of the rain on the scale (and empty the gauge). Then they should mark the tape with the date of the storm. Place the strips chronologically on a base line labeled with the month and day. These strips form a bar graph that can be added to and analyzed over the year. For example, if it rained 2 inches on October 5, $\frac{1}{2}$ inch on October 10, and 1 inch on October 23, there would be three bars with the indicated heights (2 inches, $\frac{1}{2}$ inch, 1 inch), each labeled with the corresponding date. If the storm occurred over the weekend, the students can problem solve how they want to record that observation (one strip of paper for the whole weekend if it is one storm, cut the piece in half if there are two storms [average], or consult the news for approximate rain or snow falls). Again, the important components are combining and comparing the data: How does the storm total in October compare to the total in April? Note that this paper strip to bar graph approach can also be used with monitoring plant growth, and other measurable things.

Once a graph has been constructed, engage the class in a discussion of what information the graph tells or conveys. Students' conceptual ability to analyze data and draw conclusions and interpretations is often weak (Tarr & Shaughnessy, 2007). Ask questions such as, "What can you tell about how you cared for the plants or our classroom conditions by looking at this plant growth graph? Where was the best location to put our plants?" Graphs convey factual information (students with their plants regularly fertilized had greater growth than any other variable) and also provide opportunities to make inferences that are not directly observable in the graph (placing the plant next to the window was not as important for growth as fertilizer).

The difference between actual facts and the inferences that go beyond the data is an important idea in graph construction. Students can examine graphs found in newspapers or magazines and discuss the *facts* in the graphs and the *message* that may have been intended by the person who made the graph. The ability to recognize graph components and interpret the information is called *graph sense* (Friel, Curcio, & Bright, 2001). An effective graph allows the reader to see patterns that would otherwise remain hidden. For some situations, a graph is one of the most effective communication devices!

Standards for
Mathematical Practice

2 **Reason abstractly and quantitatively.**

Circle Graphs

Typically, we think of circle graphs (sometimes called pie charts) as showing percentages and fractional parts. As such, these are well suited for students in the intermediate grades even though circle graphs are not explicitly mentioned in the CCSS-M. But, notice that the circle graph shows information that is not as easily available from other graphs. In Figure 18.4, the two graphs show the percentages of students with different numbers of siblings. One graph is based on classroom data and the other on schoolwide data. Because circle graphs display proportions rather than quantities, the small set of class data can be easily compared to the large set of school data, which could not as easily be done with bar graphs.

Easily Constructed Circle Graphs

There are several fun and simple ways to construct a circle graph. First, use students. Suppose, for example, that each student picked his or her favorite basketball team in the NCAA tournament's Final Four. Line up all of the students in the room so that students favoring the same team are together. Now form the entire group into a circle of students. Tape the ends of four long strings to the floor in the

Figure 18.4

Circle graphs show ratios of part to whole.

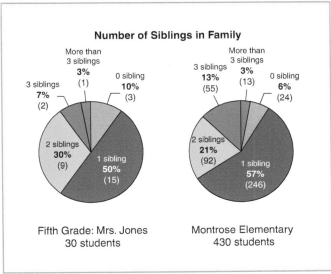

Figure 18.5

A human circle graph: Students are arranged in a circle, with strings stretched from the center to show divisions.

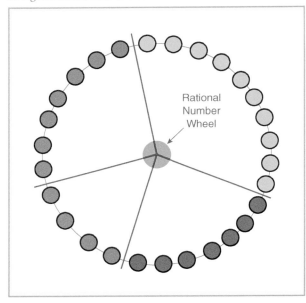

center of the circle, and extend them to the circle at each point where the teams change. Voila! A life-sized circle graph with no measuring and no percentages to calculate. If you copy and cut out a **Rational Number Wheel** and place it on the center of the circle, the area between the strings will show approximate percentages for each section of your graph (see Figure 18.5).

Alternatively, students can convert bar graphs into a circle graph by cutting out the bars and taping them together end to end into a single strip. Next, tape the two ends of the strip together to form a circular loop. Trace around the loop onto chart paper. Estimate where the center of the circle is and draw lines from the center point to the points where different bars meet. You can estimate percentages using the rational number wheel or percent necklace as described in Chapter 14. See the **Expanded Lesson: Bar Graphs to Circle Graphs** for more information on this activity.

Determining Percentages

If students have experienced the methods just described, using their own calculations to make circle graphs will make more sense. The numbers in each category are added to form the total or whole. (That's the same as taping all of the bar graphs together into a strip or lining up all the students.) By dividing each of the parts by the whole, students will find the decimals and multiplying by 100 can generate the percentages. It is an interesting proportional problem for students to convert between percents and degrees (considering the angle measure), because one unit is based on a whole of 100 and the other unit is based on a whole of 360. Start students with obvious values that can be visualized from looking at the circle, like 50 percent ($\frac{1}{2}$), 25 percent ($\frac{1}{4}$), and 33 percent ($\frac{1}{3}$), before moving to more difficult values. A table with one column for percent and one column for degrees can serve as an important tool to help students reason about the conversions.

Standards for Mathematical Practice

▶ **1 Make sense of problems and persevere in solving them.**

Percent	Degrees
25	90
50	180
60	?
10	?

 Formative Assessment Note

Students should write in a **journal** about their graphs, explaining what the graph tells and why they selected that type of graph to illustrate the data. As you evaluate students' responses, focus on whether they chose an appropriate representation and have provided a good rationale for its selection that connects back to their question (step 1 in the process of doing statistics).

Continuous Data Graphs

Bar graphs or picture graphs are useful for illustrating categories of data that have no numeric ordering—for example, favorite musical performers or video games. By contrast, when data are grouped along a continuous scale, they should be ordered along a number line. Examples of such information include temperatures that occur over time, height or weight, and numbers of test takers scoring in different intervals along the scale of possible scores.

Line Plot

Line plots (this will transition to *dot plots* in the middle grades) are counts of things along a numeric scale. To make a line plot, a number line is drawn and an X (or other mark) is made above the corresponding value on the line for every corresponding data element. One advantage of a line plot is that every piece of data is shown on the graph. It is also a very easy type of graph for students to make. It is essentially a bar graph arranged along a continuous scale with a potential bar for every indicated value on the horizontal scale. An example is shown in Figure 18.6.

The line plot is central to the curriculum in grades 3 through 5. You can go back to activities like the Storm Chaser activity and put it on a line plot instead (as it is numerical data) or look at the following activities to develop this representation of numerical information.

Figure 18.6

Line plot of temperatures.

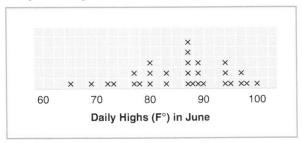

Having students be "in the graph" is an important experience that will enable them to better understand the more abstract representation.

Activity 18.6

CCSS-M: 3.MD.B.4

Stand by Me

Use painter's tape to create a line plot on the floor of the classroom. Label it with numbers ranging from 2 minutes to 20 minutes (or whatever is appropriate for your students). Have students write on a sticky note how many minutes it takes them to travel to school by walking, car, or bus. Then they are to stand on the location above that number on the line. Use the small sticky notes to recreate the line plot above a long piece of cash register tape or on the whiteboard (labeled with the same range of minutes). If there is great variability in the transportation times, you may need to cluster the times into intervals such as 1 to 3 minutes, 4 to 6 minutes, and so on. Ask students questions about their data such as "What is the combined number of minutes our bus riders take to come to school?" or "How much more time is spent by walkers than the group riding in cars? What is the total of the five longest trips? How long does Emma travel over the five days during the school week (back and forth)?" Use the data to create multi-step word problems that involve all of the four operations.

Activity 18.7

CCSS-M: 3.MD.B.4; 4.MD.B.4; 5.MD.B.2

Comparing Cubits

A cubit is an ancient measure of the length of the forearm from the crook of the elbow to the end of the fingertips. Students should use a tape measure to find the length of their cubit to the nearest half or quarter inch. Then using a cash register tape or a whiteboard with measures to the half or quarter inch labeled (and spaced far enough apart to allow for the width of a small sticky note), have students mark the location of their measurement on the line plot. Send students to other classes to get measures of other students' cubits from different grades. Use a different color sticky note to mark the measures from other classes. What patterns do students notice? Can they predict the grade levels for each of the "mystery" students? Can they broadly state if a particular mystery student is in a grade above or below their grade? Can students find the differences between two values (using fractional measures)?

Standards for Mathematical Practice

◀ **2** **Reason abstractly and quantitatively.**

 *Teaching Tip*

Note that when you are trying to find appropriate data for use in a line plot, select data with numerical values that are similar so that the range of numbers on the scale is reasonable.

Activity 18.8

CCSS-M: 3.MD.B.4; 4.MD.B.4; 5.MD.B.2

Gross!

Collect data from the Web or a nonfiction book about a topic of interest to the students, such as the length of insects (especially large ones). Again, you want data with a tightly packed range—not the lengths of mice to elephants! Use a field guide about insects to collect data (which is likely to be in a decimal form, such as the largest cockroach, which is 8.3 cm). Then create a line plot to record these lengths, asking students to round to the nearest 0.5 cm. Again, create word problems so that the students can engage in using the data to answer questions that require them to add, subtract, multiply, and divide decimals.

Activity 18.9

CCSS-M: 3.MD.B.4; 4.MD.B.4; 5.MD.B.2

Test Anxiety

Standards for Mathematical Practice

3 Construct viable arguments and critique the reasoning of others.

Show students this line plot of a set of fictitious quiz scores (a perfect score was 20) (see Figure 18.7). Have students make decisions from the data asking such questions as: Was this a surprise pop quiz? Was this a quiz at the end of a series of lessons on the topic? What can you conjecture about the data? Which students may need extra help? How can you justify your responses?

Figure 18.7

Line plot of students' quiz scores.

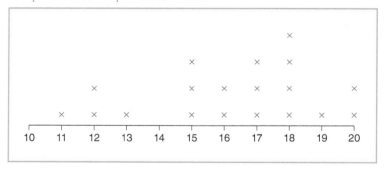

Line Graphs

A *line graph* is used to represent two related pieces of continuous data, and a line is drawn to connect the points. For example, a line graph might be used to show the length of a flagpole shadow as it changed from one hour to the next during the day. The horizontal scale would be time, and the vertical scale would be the length of the shadow. Data can be gathered at specific points in time (e.g., every 15 minutes), and these points can be plotted. A line can be drawn to connect these points because time is continuous and data points do exist between the plotted points.

Although line graphs are not the focus in grades 3 through 5, we bring them up here as they frequently are misused. Because a line graph is often a choice on a computer graphing program, elementary students can mistakenly choose this format. In fact, line graphs need to be used for identifying trends over time, such as growth in height, an increasing bank account, or temperature change. The assumption is that the points on the line between the identified values are real and that at some timeframe between those values those points were feasible (for example, those temperatures were passed through on the way to the heat wave). That doesn't work for some data (like categorical data), and students need to learn which graphs are best to display different kinds of data.

🎵 Teaching Tip

Have students explicitly note the difference between a line plot and a line graph. A line plot uses a set of points representing amounts and labels the frequency of the occurrence of that amount directly above the point on the scale. A line graph shows the relationship between two variables on two axes.

Computer programs can provide a variety of graphical displays. Use the time saved by technology to focus on the discussions about the information that each display provides. Students can make their own selections among different graphs and justify their choice based on their own intended purposes. The Internet offers opportunities to explore different graphs as discussed in the Technology Note earlier in this chapter.

Interpreting Results

Interpretation is the fourth step in the process of doing statistics. As seen in the sample test items shown in the Stop and Reflect at the beginning of the chapter, sometimes questions focus on mathematical ideas rather than statistical ideas. Although it is helpful to ask mathematical questions, it is essential to ask questions that are statistical in nature. That means the questions focus on the context of the situation and seeing what can be learned or inferred from the data. During interpretation, students might want to loop back and create a different data display to get another look at the data, or gather data from a different population to see if their results are representative.

There are three ways that students comprehend the data (Curcio, 1987): (1) reading the data; (2) reading between the data; and (3) reading beyond the data. In grades 3 through 5 we expect students to move their level of interpretation further than merely answering questions where the answer is directly in the graph or table such as "Which is most?" or "Which is least?" Instead students need to move to understanding the units which includes interpreting the scale of the graph and finding relationships in the data including situations where they must use reasoning and critically evaluate the information.

Standards for
Mathematical Practice

◀ 5 Use appropriate tools strategically.

Different researchers have recommended questions that focus on statistical thinking (Franklin et al., 2005; Friel, O'Conner, & Mamer, 2006; Russell, 2006; Shaughnessy, 2006). Here are some ideas based on their thinking to get you started on having meaningful discussions about interpreting data:

- What do the numbers (symbols) tell us about our class (or other population)?
- If we gathered data on the same question from another class (population), how would the data look? What if we asked a larger group, how would the data look?
- How do the numbers in this graph (population) *compare* to this graph (population)?
- Where are the data "clustering"? Where are the data that are not in the cluster? About what percent is or is not in the cluster?
- Would the results be different if . . . [change of sample, population, or setting]? (Example: Would gathered data on word length in a third-grade book be different from a fifth-grade book? Would a science book give different results from a reading book?)
- What does the graph *not* tell us?
- What new questions arise from these data?
- What is the maker of the graph trying to tell us?

These prompts apply across many data displays and interpretation certainly should be a major focus of your instruction. Consider it the *After* phase of your lesson, although some of these questions will be integrated in the *During* phase as well. The emphasis of the questions in this phase is on getting students to notice differences in the data and provide possible reasons for those differences (Franklin & Mewborn, 2008).

Our world is inundated with data, from descriptive statistics to different graphs. It is essential that we prepare students to be literate about what can be interpreted from data and what cannot be interpreted from data, what is important to pay attention to and what can be discarded as misleading or poorly designed. This is important for success in school, as well as for being a mathematically literate citizen.

Table 18.4. Common errors and misconceptions in representing and interpreting data and how to help.

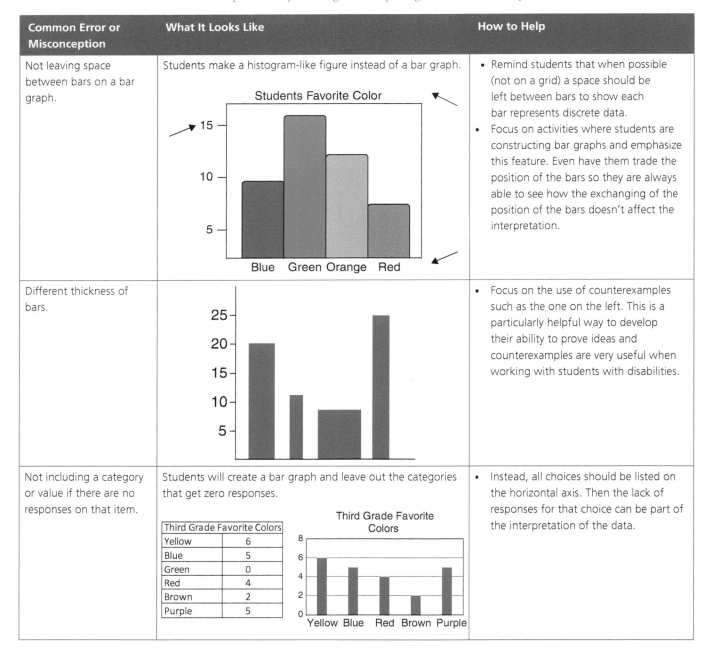

Common Error or Misconception	What It Looks Like	How to Help
Not leaving space between bars on a bar graph.	Students make a histogram-like figure instead of a bar graph. **Students Favorite Color** (bar graph: Blue ~10, Green ~16, Orange ~12, Red ~7)	• Remind students that when possible (not on a grid) a space should be left between bars to show each bar represents discrete data. • Focus on activities where students are constructing bar graphs and emphasize this feature. Even have them trade the position of the bars so they are always able to see how the exchanging of the position of the bars doesn't affect the interpretation.
Different thickness of bars.	(bar graph: bars of values ~20, ~11, ~9, 25 with differing thicknesses)	• Focus on the use of counterexamples such as the one on the left. This is a particularly helpful way to develop their ability to prove ideas and counterexamples are very useful when working with students with disabilities.
Not including a category or value if there are no responses on that item.	Students will create a bar graph and leave out the categories that get zero responses. Third Grade Favorite Colors: Yellow 6, Blue 5, Green 0, Red 4, Brown 2, Purple 5 **Third Grade Favorite Colors** (bar graph: Yellow 6, Blue 5, Red 4, Brown 2, Purple 5)	• Instead, all choices should be listed on the horizontal axis. Then the lack of responses for that choice can be part of the interpretation of the data.

Table 18.4. Common errors and misconceptions in representing and interpreting data and how to help.

Common Error or Misconception	What It Looks Like	How to Help
Confusion about the scale of the graph.	Students may not attend to the size of the symbol in a picture graph. Key — Dog, Cat, Horse, Other (50 people each) Dog Cat Horse Other	• This is a perfect opportunity to show students examples of "bad graphs" and have them discuss why the information presented is confusing as in the example to the left where the values for the pictures are the same but the size of the representations tell another story.
Not including 0 as the origin on axes.	Students will construct graphs like: 130 / 125 / 120 / 115 / 110 Dan　Heidi　Emily	• Initially, students should start their graphs at zero to help them fully interpret the correct proportion of the data. Later they might start at another point to illustrate a small difference; however, care should be taken that this representation does not distort the meaning of the data.
Challenged by the difference between categorical and continuous data.	Students are unclear as to which graphs are the best representations for different data types.	• Students need to sort questions and data into two groupings: categorical and continuous data. This activity will help them discuss the differences between these kinds of data.
Using a line graph for discrete data.	Students will make a line graph for a representation of favorites for example. 6 / 5 / 4 / 3 / 2 / 1 Red　Blue　Green　Yellow	• There is no logical connection between data points on categorical data like there is on numerical data. Show students examples of incorrect graphs made by graphing programs on the computer to explain why those are not appropriate.

Appendix A

Common Core State Standards

Standards for Mathematical Practice

The Standards for Mathematical Practice describe varieties of expertise that mathematics educators at all levels should seek to develop in their students. These practices rest on important "processes and proficiencies" with long-standing importance in mathematics education. The first of these are the NCTM process standards of problem solving, reasoning and proof, communication, representation, and connections. The second are the strands of mathematical proficiency specified in the National Research Council's report *Adding It Up*: adaptive reasoning, strategic competence, conceptual understanding (comprehension of mathematical concepts, operations, and relations), procedural fluency (skill in carrying out procedures flexibly, accurately, efficiently, and appropriately), and productive disposition (habitual inclination to see mathematics as sensible, useful, and worthwhile, coupled with a belief in diligence and one's own efficacy).

Source: Common Core State Standards for Mathematics was developed by the Council of Chief State School Officers. Copies may be downloaded at http://www.ccsso.org/.

1   Make sense of problems and persevere in solving them.

Mathematically proficient students start by explaining to themselves the meaning of a problem and looking for entry points to its solution. They analyze givens, constraints, relationships, and goals. They make conjectures about the form and meaning of the solution and plan a solution pathway rather than simply jumping into a solution attempt. They consider analogous problems, and try special cases and simpler forms of the original problem in order to gain insight into its solution. They monitor and evaluate their progress and change course if necessary. Older students might, depending on the context of the problem, transform algebraic expressions or change the viewing window on their graphing calculator to get the information they need. Mathematically proficient students can explain correspondences between equations, verbal descriptions, tables, and graphs or draw diagrams of important features and relationships, graph data, and search for regularity or trends. Younger students might rely on using concrete objects or pictures to help conceptualize and solve a problem. Mathematically proficient students check their answers to problems using a different method, and they continually ask themselves, "Does this make sense?" They can understand the approaches of others to solving complex problems and identify correspondences between different approaches.

2   Reason abstractly and quantitatively.

Mathematically proficient students make sense of quantities and their relationships in problem situations. They bring two complementary abilities to bear on problems involving quantitative relationships: the ability to *decontextualize*—to abstract a given situation and represent it symbolically and manipulate the representing symbols as if they have a life of their own, without necessarily attending to their referents—and the ability to *contextualize*, to pause as needed during the manipulation process in order to probe into the referents for the symbols involved. Quantitative reasoning entails habits of creating a coherent representation of the problem at hand; considering the units involved; attending to the meaning of quantities, not just how to compute them; and knowing and flexibly using different properties of operations and objects.

3   Construct viable arguments and critique the reasoning of others.

Mathematically proficient students understand and use stated assumptions, definitions, and previously established results in constructing arguments. They make conjectures and build a logical progression of statements to explore the truth of their conjectures. They are able to analyze situations by breaking them into cases, and can recognize and use counterexamples. They justify their conclusions, communicate them to others, and respond to the arguments of others. They reason inductively about data, making plausible arguments that take into account the context from which the data arose.

Mathematically proficient students are also able to compare the effectiveness of two plausible arguments, distinguish correct logic or reasoning from that which is flawed, and—if there is a flaw in an argument—explain what it is. Elementary students can construct arguments using concrete referents such as objects, drawings, diagrams, and actions. Such arguments can make sense and be correct, even though they are not generalized or made formal until later grades. Later, students learn to determine domains to which an argument applies. Students at all grades can listen or read the arguments of others, decide whether they make sense, and ask useful questions to clarify or improve the arguments.

4 Model with mathematics.

Mathematically proficient students can apply the mathematics they know to solve problems arising in everyday life, society, and the workplace. In early grades, this might be as simple as writing an addition equation to describe a situation. In middle grades, a student might apply proportional reasoning to plan a school event or analyze a problem in the community. By high school, a student might use geometry to solve a design problem or use a function to describe how one quantity of interest depends on another. Mathematically proficient students who can apply what they know are comfortable making assumptions and approximations to simplify a complicated situation, realizing that these may need revision later. They are able to identify important quantities in a practical situation and map their relationships using such tools as diagrams, two-way tables, graphs, flowcharts, and formulas. They can analyze those relationships mathematically to draw conclusions. They routinely interpret their mathematical results in the context of the situation and reflect on whether the results make sense, possibly improving the model if it has not served its purpose.

5 Use appropriate tools strategically.

Mathematically proficient students consider the available tools when solving a mathematical problem. These tools might include pencil and paper, concrete models, a ruler, a protractor, a calculator, a spreadsheet, a computer algebra system, a statistical package, or dynamic geometry software. Proficient students are sufficiently familiar with tools appropriate for their grade or course to make sound decisions about when each of these tools might be helpful, recognizing both the insight to be gained and their limitations. For example, mathematically proficient high school students analyze graphs of functions and solutions generated using a graphing calculator. They detect possible errors by strategically using estimation and other mathematical knowledge. When making mathematical models, they know that technology can enable them to visualize the results of varying assumptions, explore consequences, and compare predictions with data. Mathematically proficient students at various grade levels are able to identify relevant external mathematical resources, such as digital content located on a website, and use them to pose or solve problems. They are able to use technological tools to explore and deepen their understanding of concepts.

6   Attend to precision.

Mathematically proficient students try to communicate precisely to others. They try to use clear definitions in discussion with others and in their own reasoning. They state the meaning of the symbols they choose, including using the equal sign consistently and appropriately. They are careful about specifying units of measure, and labeling axes to clarify the correspondence with quantities in a problem. They calculate accurately and efficiently, express numerical answers with a degree of precision appropriate for the problem context. In the elementary grades, students give carefully formulated explanations to each other. By the time they reach high school they have learned to examine claims and make explicit use of definitions.

7   Look for and make use of structure.

Mathematically proficient students look closely to discern a pattern or structure. Young students, for example, might notice that three and seven more is the same amount as seven and three more, or they may sort a collection of shapes according to how many sides the shapes have. Later, students will see 7×8 equals the well remembered $7 \times 5 + 7 \times 3$, in preparation for learning about the distributive property. In the expression $x^2 + 9x + 14$, older students can see the 14 as 2×7 and the 9 as $2 + 7$. They recognize the significance of an existing line in a geometric figure and can use the strategy of drawing an auxiliary line for solving problems. They also can step back for an overview and shift perspective. They can see complicated things, such as some algebraic expressions, as single objects or as being composed of several objects. For example, they can see $5 - 3(x - y)^2$ as 5 minus a positive number times a square and use that to realize that its value cannot be more than 5 for any real numbers x and y.

8   Look for and express regularity in repeated reasoning.

Mathematically proficient students notice if calculations are repeated, and look both for general methods and for shortcuts. Upper elementary students might notice when dividing 25 by 11 that they are repeating the same calculations over and over again, and conclude they have a repeating decimal. By paying attention to the calculation of slope as they repeatedly check whether points are on the line through (1, 2) with slope 3, middle school students might abstract the equation $(y - 2)/(x - 1) = 3$. Noticing the regularity in the way terms cancel when expanding $(x - 1)(x + 1)$, $(x - 1)(x^2 + x + 1)$, and $(x - 1)(x^3 + x^2 + x + 1)$ might lead them to the general formula for the sum of a geometric series. As they work to solve a problem, mathematically proficient students maintain oversight of the process, while attending to the details. They continually evaluate the reasonableness of their intermediate results.

Connecting the Standards for Mathematical Practice to the Standards for Mathematical Content

The Standards for Mathematical Practice describe ways in which developing student practitioners of the discipline of mathematics increasingly ought to engage with the subject matter as they grow in mathematical maturity and expertise throughout the elementary, middle, and high school years. Designers of curricula, assessments, and professional development should all attend to the need to connect the mathematical practices to mathematical content in mathematics instruction.

The Standards for Mathematical Content are a balanced combination of procedure and understanding. Expectations that begin with the word "understand" are often especially good opportunities to connect the practices to the content. Students who lack understanding of a topic may rely on procedures too heavily. Without a flexible base from which to work, they may be less likely to consider analogous problems, represent problems coherently, justify conclusions, apply the mathematics to practical situations, use technology mindfully to work with the mathematics, explain the mathematics accurately to other students, step back for an overview, or deviate from a known procedure to find a shortcut. In short, a lack of understanding effectively prevents a student from engaging in the mathematical practices.

In this respect, those content standards which set an expectation of understanding are potential "points of intersection" between the Standards for Mathematical Content and the Standards for Mathematical Practice. These points of intersection are intended to be weighted toward central and generative concepts in the school mathematics curriculum that most merit the time, resources, innovative energies, and focus necessary to qualitatively improve the curriculum, instruction, assessment, professional development, and student achievement in mathematics.

Appendix B

Common Core State Standards

Grades 3–5 Critical Content Areas and Overviews

CCSS Mathematics | Grade 3
Critical Areas

In Grade 3, instructional time should focus on four critical areas:

1. developing understanding of multiplication and division and strategies for multiplication and division within 100;

2. developing understanding of fractions, especially unit fractions (fractions with numerator 1);

3. developing understanding of the structure of rectangular arrays and of area; and

4. describing and analyzing two-dimensional shapes.

Source: Common Core State Standards for Mathematics was developed by the Council of Chief State School Officers. Copies may be downloaded at http://www.ccsso.org/.

1. *Students develop an understanding of the meanings of multiplication and division of whole numbers through activities and problems involving equal-sized groups, arrays, and area models; multiplication is finding an unknown product, and division is finding an unknown factor in these situations.* For equal-sized group situations, division can require finding the unknown number of groups or the unknown group size. Students use properties of operations to calculate products of whole numbers, using increasingly sophisticated strategies based on these properties to solve multiplication and division problems involving single-digit factors. By comparing a variety of solution strategies, students learn the relationship between multiplication and division.

2. *Students develop an understanding of fractions, beginning with unit fractions.* Students view fractions in general as being built out of unit fractions, and they use fractions along with visual fraction models to represent parts of a whole. Students understand that the size of a fractional part is relative to the size of the whole. For example, $\frac{1}{2}$ of the paint in a small bucket could be less paint than $\frac{1}{3}$ of the paint in a larger bucket, but $\frac{1}{3}$ of a ribbon is longer than $\frac{1}{5}$ of the same ribbon because when the ribbon is divided into 3 equal parts, the parts are longer than when the ribbon is divided into 5 equal parts. Students are able to use fractions to represent numbers equal to, less than, and greater than one. They solve problems that involve comparing fractions by using visual fraction models and strategies based on noticing equal numerators or denominators.

3. *Students recognize area as an attribute of two-dimensional regions.* They measure the area of a shape by finding the total number of same-size units of area required to cover the shape without gaps or overlaps, a square with sides of unit length being the standard unit for measuring area. Students understand that rectangular arrays can be decomposed into identical rows or into identical columns. By decomposing rectangles into rectangular arrays of squares, students connect area to multiplication, and justify using multiplication to determine the area of a rectangle.

4. *Students describe, analyze, and compare properties of two-dimensional shapes.* They compare and classify shapes by their sides and angles, and connect these with definitions of shapes. Students also relate their fraction work to geometry by expressing the area of part of a shape as a unit fraction of the whole.

Grade 3 Overview

Operations and Algebraic Thinking

- Represent and solve problems involving multiplication and division.
- Understand properties of multiplication and the relationship between multiplication and division.
- Multiply and divide within 100.
- Solve problems involving the four operations, and identify and explain patterns in arithmetic.

Number and Operations in Base-Ten

- Use place value understanding and properties of operations to perform multidigit arithmetic.

Measurement and Data

- Solve problems involving measurement and estimation of intervals of time, liquid volumes, and masses of objects.
- Represent and interpret data.
- Geometric measurement: understand concepts of area and relate area to multiplication and to addition.
- Geometric measurement: recognize perimeter as an attribute of plane figures and distinguish between linear and area measures.

Geometry

- Reason with shapes and their attributes.

CCSS Mathematics | Grade 4 Critical Areas

In Grade 4, instructional time should focus on three critical areas:

1. developing understanding and fluency with multidigit multiplication, and developing understanding of dividing to find quotients involving multidigit dividends;

2. developing an understanding of fraction equivalence, addition and subtraction of fractions with like denominators, and multiplication of fractions by whole numbers; and

3. understanding that geometric figures can be analyzed and classified based on their properties, such as having parallel sides, perpendicular sides, particular angle measures, and symmetry.

1. ***Students generalize their understanding of place value to 1,000,000, understanding the relative sizes of numbers in each place.***   They apply their understanding of models for multiplication (equal-sized groups, arrays, area models), place value, and properties of operations, in particular the distributive property, as they develop, discuss, and use efficient, accurate, and generalizable methods to compute products of multidigit whole numbers. Depending on the numbers and the context, they select and accurately apply appropriate methods to estimate or mentally calculate products. They develop fluency with efficient procedures for multiplying whole numbers; understand and explain why the procedures work based on place value and properties of operations; and use them to solve problems. Students apply their understanding of models for division, place value, properties of operations, and the relationship of division to multiplication as they develop, discuss, and use efficient, accurate, and generalizable procedures to find quotients involving multidigit dividends. They select and accurately apply appropriate methods to estimate and mentally calculate quotients, and interpret remainders based upon the context.

2. ***Students develop understanding of fraction equivalence and operations with fractions.***   They recognize that two different fractions can be equal (e.g., $\frac{15}{9} = \frac{5}{3}$), and they develop methods for generating and recognizing equivalent fractions. Students extend previous understandings about how fractions are built from unit fractions, composing fractions from unit fractions, decomposing fractions into unit fractions, and using the meaning of fractions and the meaning of multiplication to multiply a fraction by a whole number.

3. ***Students describe, analyze, compare, and classify two-dimensional shapes.***   Through building, drawing, and analyzing two-dimensional shapes, students deepen their understanding of properties of two-dimensional objects and the use of them to solve problems involving symmetry.

Grade 4 Overview

Operations and Algebraic Thinking

- Use the four operations with whole numbers to solve problems.
- Gain familiarity with factors and multiples.
- Generate and analyze patterns.

Number and Operations in Base-Ten

- Generalize place value understanding for multidigit whole numbers.
- Use place value understanding and properties of operations to perform multidigit arithmetic.

Number and Operations—Fractions

- Extend understanding of fraction equivalence and ordering.
- Build fractions from unit fractions by applying and extending previous understandings of operations on whole numbers.
- Understand decimal notation for fractions, and compare decimal fractions.

Measurement and Data

- Solve problems involving measurement and conversion of measurements from a larger unit to a smaller unit.
- Represent and interpret data.
- Geometric measurement: understand concepts of angle and measure angles.

Geometry

- Draw and identify lines and angles, and classify shapes by properties of their lines and angles.

CCSS Mathematics | Grade 5 Critical Areas

In Grade 5, instructional time should focus on three critical areas:

1. developing fluency with addition and subtraction of fractions, and developing understanding of the multiplication of fractions and of division of fractions in limited cases (unit fractions divided by whole numbers and whole numbers divided by unit fractions);

2. extending division to 2-digit divisors, integrating decimal fractions into the place value system and developing understanding of operations with decimals to hundredths, and developing fluency with whole number and decimal operations; and

3. developing understanding of volume.

1. *Students apply their understanding of fractions and fraction models to represent the addition and subtraction of fractions with unlike denominators as equivalent calculations with like denominators.* They develop fluency in calculating sums and differences of fractions, and make reasonable estimates of them. Students also use the meaning of fractions, of multiplication and division, and the relationship between multiplication and division to understand and explain why the procedures for multiplying and dividing fractions make sense. (Note: this is limited to the case of dividing unit fractions by whole numbers and whole numbers by unit fractions.)

2. *Students develop understanding of why division procedures work based on the meaning of base-ten numerals and properties of operations.* They finalize fluency with multi-digit addition, subtraction, multiplication, and division. They apply their understandings of models for decimals, decimal notation, and properties of operations to add and subtract decimals to hundredths. They develop fluency in these computations, and make reasonable estimates of their results. Students use the relationship between decimals and fractions, as well as the relationship between finite decimals and whole numbers (i.e., a finite decimal multiplied by an appropriate power of 10 is a whole number), to understand and explain why the procedures for multiplying and dividing finite decimals make sense. They compute products and quotients of decimals to hundredths efficiently and accurately.

3. *Students recognize volume as an attribute of three-dimensional space.* They understand that volume can be measured by finding the total number of same-size units of volume required to fill the space without gaps or overlaps. They understand that a 1-unit by 1-unit by 1-unit cube is the standard unit for measuring volume. They select appropriate units, strategies, and tools for solving problems that involve estimating and measuring volume. They decompose three-dimensional shapes and find volumes of right rectangular prisms by viewing them as decomposed into layers of arrays of cubes. They measure necessary attributes of shapes in order to determine volumes to solve real world and mathematical problems.

Grade 5 Overview

Operations and Algebraic Thinking

- Write and interpret numerical expressions.
- Analyze patterns and relationships.

Number and Operations in Base-Ten

- Understand the place value system.
- Perform operations with multidigit whole numbers and with decimals to hundredths.

Number and Operations—Fractions

- Use equivalent fractions as a strategy to add and subtract fractions.
- Apply and extend previous understandings of multiplication and division to multiply and divide fractions.

Measurement and Data

- Convert like measurement units within a given measurement system.
- Represent and interpret data.
- Geometric measurement: understand concepts of volume and relate volume to multiplication and to addition.

Geometry

- Graph points on the coordinate plane to solve real-world and mathematical problems.
- Classify two-dimensional figures into categories based on their properties.

Appendix C
Mathematics Teaching Practices

NCTM Principles to Actions (2014)

Establish mathematics goals to focus learning.

Effective teaching of mathematics establishes clear goals for the mathematics that students are learning, situates goals within learning progressions, and uses the goals to guide instructional decisions.

Source: Republished with permission of National Council for Teachers of Mathematics (NCTM), from NCTM Mathematics Teaching Practices from Principles to Actions © 2014; permission conveyed through Copyright Clearance Center, Inc.

Implement tasks that promote reasoning and problem solving.

Effective teaching of mathematics engages students in solving and discussing tasks that promote mathematical reasoning and problem solving and allow multiple entry points and varied solution strategies.

Use and connect mathematical representations.

Effective teaching of mathematics engages students in making connections among mathematical representations to deepen understanding of mathematics concepts and procedures and as tools for problem solving.

Facilitate meaningful mathematical discourse.

Effective teaching of mathematics facilitates discourse among students to build shared understanding of mathematical ideas by analyzing and comparing student approaches and arguments.

Pose purposeful questions.

Effective teaching of mathematics uses purposeful questions to assess and advance students' reasoning and sense making about important mathematical ideas and relationships.

Build procedural fluency from conceptual understanding.

Effective teaching of mathematics builds fluency with procedures on a foundation of conceptual understanding so that students, over time, become skillful in using procedures flexibly as they solve contextual and mathematical problems.

Support productive struggle in learning mathematics.

Effective teaching of mathematics consistently provides students, individually and collectively, with opportunities and supports to engage in productive struggle as they grapple with mathematical ideas and relationships.

Elicit and use evidence of student thinking.

Effective teaching of mathematics uses evidence of student thinking to assess progress toward mathematical understanding and to adjust instruction continually in ways that support and extend learning.

Appendix D
Activities at a Glance

Volume II

This table lists the named and numbered activities in Part 2 of the book. In addition to providing an easy way to find an activity, the table provides the mathematics content of the text stated as succinctly as possible, as well as the related *Common Core State Standards*. Remember though, this is a book about teaching mathematics, not a book of activities. Every activity should be seen as an integral part of the text that surround it. It is extremely important not to take any activity as a suggestion for instruction without reading the full text in which it is embedded.

Chapter 8 Exploring number and operation sense.

Activity		Mathematical Content	CCSS-M	Page
8.1	Factor Quest*	Develop the connection between multiplication and division	4.OA.B.4	129
8.2	Factor Patterns*	Develop patterns between arrays and factors	4.OA.B.4	130
8.3	Divide and Conquer*	Develop measurement and partition concepts of division	3.OA.A.2	131
8.4	The Broken Division Key	Develop division as repeated subtraction and missing factor	4.NBT.B.6	132
8.5	Divide It Up*	Develop the distributive property	3.OA.B.5; 5.OA.A.1	134

Chapter 9 Developing basic fact fluency.

Activity		Mathematical Content	CCSS-M	Page
9.1	One More Than and Two More Than with Dice and Spinners*	Practice addition facts for +1 and +2	2.OA.B.2	147
9.2	Move It, Move It*	Develop Making 10 strategy	2.OA.B.2	148
9.3	Frames and Facts*	Develop Making 10 strategy	2.OA.B.2	148
9.4	On the Double!*	Practice near-doubles addition facts	2.OA.B.2	149
9.5	Clock Facts*	Develop minute intervals on the clock as a strategy for fives multiplication facts	3.OA.A.1; 3.OA.C.7	152
9.6	Strive to Derive*	Using known facts to determine unknown facts	3.OA.A.1; 3.OA.B.5; 3.OA.C.7	154
9.7	How Close Can You Get?	Using near facts in multiplication	3.OA.A.2; 3.OA.A.4; 3.OA.B.6	156
9.8	What's under my Thumb?*	Connect addition and subtraction facts or multiplication and division facts	2.OA.B.2; 3.OA.B.5; 3.OA.B.6; 3.OA.C.7	157
9.9	Bowl a Fact*	Practice creating equations in addition, subtraction, multiplication, and division.	2.OA.B.2; 3.OA.C.7; 5.OA.A.1	158
9.10	Salute!	Identify the missing addend or factor	2.OA.B.2; 3.OA.B.5; 3.OA.B.6; 3.OA.C.7	158

Chapter 10 Developing whole-number place-value concepts.

Activity		Mathematical Content	CCSS-M	Page
10.1	Who Am I?	Develop relative magnitude of numbers to 1000	2.NBT.A.1; 2.NBT.A.2; 2.NBT.A.4; 3.NBT.A.2	166

* Activity titles with an asterisk include a downloadable Activity Page, Expanded Lesson, or Blackline Master.

Activity		Mathematical Content	CCSS-M	Page
10.2	Close, Far, and In-Between	Explore relative differences between three-digit numbers	2.NBT.A.1; 2.NBT.A.2; 2.NBT.A.4; 3.NBT.A.2; 4.NBT.A.2	166
10.3	Too Many to Count?	Estimate and group quantities into thousands, hundreds, tens, and ones. Write and read the number	2.NBT.A.1; 4.NBT.A.1; 4.NBT.A.2	172
10.4	Three Other Ways	Develop alternative groupings of hundreds and tens to represent a number	2.NBT.A.1; 2.NBT.A.3; 3.NBT.A.2	173
10.5	Base-Ten Riddles*	Develop alternative groupings of tens and hundreds to represent a number	2.NBT.A.1; 2.NBT.A.3; 3.NBT.A.2	173
10.6	Say It/Press It	Connect oral and symbolic names for numbers to physical representation	2.NBT.A.1a, b; 2.NBT.A.3; 3.NBT.A.2	175
10.7	Digit Change	Apply place value concepts to symbolic representations	2.NBT.A.1; 2.NBT.A.3; 2.NBT.B.5; 2.NBT.B.8; 3.NBT.A.2	175
10.8	The Thousands Chart*	Extend patterns for 1 to 100 to patterns to 1000	2.NBT.A.1; 2.NBT.A.2; 2.NBT.A.3; 2.NBT.B.8; 3.NBT.A.2	176
10.9	200 and Some More	Develop 200 as a part of numbers using place value and the inverse relationship between addition and subtraction	3.NBT.A.2	176
10.10	Calculator Challenge Counting	Develop mental addition strategies through skip counting	3.NBT.A.2	177
10.11	What Comes Next?*	Develop the continuing pattern in the place-value system	4.NBT.A.1; 4.NBT.A.3; 5.NBT.A.1	177
10.12	Collecting 1,000,000	Develop an understanding of the size of large numbers	4.NBT.A.1; 4.NBT.A.3; 5.NBT.A.1	179
10.13	How Long?/How Far?	Develop an understanding of the size of large numbers	4.NBT.A.1; 4.NBT.A.3; 5.NBT.A.1	179
10.14	A Long Time	Connect units of time to large numbers	4.NBT.A.1; 4.NBT.A.3; 5.NBT.A.1	180
10.15	Really Large Quantities	Develop ability to estimate large quantities	2.MD.A.3; 3.MD.A.1; 3.MD.C.5	180

* Activity titles with an asterisk include a downloadable Activity Page, Expanded Lesson, or Blackline Master.

Chapter 11 Building strategies for whole number computation.

Activity		Mathematical Content	CCSS-M	Page
11.1	Build It and Break It*	Develop the distributive property	4.NBT.B.5	200
11.2	Make It Easy	Develop the standard algorithm for multiplication	4.NBT.B.5	201
11.3	Left Overs*	Develop the concept of remainders	4.NBT.B.6	206
11.4	Double, Double—No Toil or Trouble!	Develop a division strategy through doubling	5.NBT.B.6	211
11.5	Over or Under?*	Develop estimates of double digit by single digit multiplication	4.NBT.A.3; 4.NBT.B.5	212
11.6	That's Good Enough	Develop estimates of multiplication situations	4.OA.A.3	213
11.7	High or Low?*	Develop estimates of multidigit multiplication	4.NBT.B.5; 5.NBT.B.5	213

Chapter 12 Exploring fraction concepts.

Activity		Mathematical Content	CCSS-M	Page
12.1	Playground Fractions*	Develop concepts of equal shares using an area model	2.G.A.3; 3.NF.A.1	222
12.2	Who Is Winning?*	Develop fractional concepts using a linear model	3.NF.A.2a, b; 3.NF.A.3a, b, d	224
12.3	Class Fractions	Develop concepts of fractions using a set model	3.NF.A.1; 3.NF.A.3b	225
12.4	Fourths or Not Fourths?*	Develop understanding of fractional parts through partitioning	2.G.A.3; 3.NF.A.1	228
12.5	How Far Did Nicole Go?*	Determine shaded region on number strips where not all partitions are shown	3.NF.A.1; 3.NF.A.2a, b	229
12.6	A Whole Lot of Fun*	Partition and iterate to determine lengths of paper strips	3.NF.A.1; 3.NF.A.2a, b	232
12.7	More, Less, or Equal to One Whole*	Develop understanding of fractional parts	3.NF.A.1; 3.NF.A.2a, b	234
12.8	Pitchers and Cups	Solve word problems involving iterations of fractions – (leads to multiplication and division of fractions)	4.NF.B.3b; 4.NF.B.4a; 4.NF.B.4c; 5.NF.B.6; 5.NF.B.7a	237
12.9	On the Line*	Locate fractions on a number line	3.NF.A.2a; 3.NF.A.2b; 3.NF.A.3a	238
12.10	Zero, One-Half, or One*	Use benchmark fractions to reason about their size and make comparisons	3.NF.A.3d; 4.NF.A.2	238
12.11	Close Fractions*	Finding fractions that are between other fractions through comparison	3.NF.A.3d; 4.NF.A.2	239
12.12	Different Fillers*	Find equivalent fractions through using area models	3.NF.A.3d; 4.NF.A.2	240
12.13	Dot-Paper Equivalencies*	Develop an understanding of the concept of equivalent fractions	3.NF.A.1; 3.NF.3a, b, c	241

* Activity titles with an asterisk include a downloadable Activity Page, Expanded Lesson, or Blackline Master.

Activity		Mathematical Content	CCSS-M	Page
12.14	Apples and Bananas*	Explore equivalence using a set model.	3.NF.A.1; 3.NF.3a, b, c	242
12.15	Missing-Number Equivalencies*	Explore fraction equivalencies	3.NF.A.3a, b, c; 4.NF.A.1	242
12.16	Garden Plots*	Explore fraction equivalencies with an area model	3.NF.A.3b; 4.NF.A.1	244
12.17	Ordering Unit Fractions*	Place fractions in order from least to greatest	3.NF.A.3d; 4.NF.A.2	247

Chapter 13 Building strategies for fraction computation.

Activity		Mathematical Content	CCSS-M	Page
13.1	The Gold Prize	Explore equivalent fractions and subtraction of fractions using an area model	4.NF.B.3a, b, c; 5.NF.A.1	255
13.2	Gardening Together*	Explore addition and subtraction of fractions in an area model	4.NF.B.3a, d; 5.NF.A.1; 5.NF.A.2	256
13.3	Jumps on the Ruler*	Explore addition and subtraction of fractions in a linear model	4.NF.B.3a, d; 5.NF.A.1; 5.NF.A.2	257
13.4	More Than or Less Than One?*	Develop estimation of sums and differences of fractions.	4.NF.B.3a; 5.NF.A.2	258
13.5	Common Multiple Cards*	Practice finding common multiples	4.OA.B.4; 5.NF.A.1	261
13.6	How Big Is the Banner?	Explore multiplication of a whole number by a fraction (e.g., $12 \times \frac{1}{2}$)	5.NF.B.4a, b; 5.NF.B.4a, b	263
13.7	Fractions Divided by Whole Numbers Stories*	Explore division of fractions with areas, linear, and set models	5.NF.B.7a, c	270
13.8	Sandwich Servings	Develop the concept of estimating using division	5.NF.B.7b, c	271
13.9	The Size Is Right: Division*	Explore fractions divided by whole numbers and whole numbers divided by fractions	5.NF.B.7a, b, c; 6.NS.A.1	273

Chapter 14 Developing decimal and percent concepts and decimal computation.

Activity		Mathematical Content	CCSS-M	Page
14.1	The Decimal Point Names the Unit	Develop an understanding of the purpose of the decimal point	4.NF.C.6; 5.NBT.A.3a	280
14.2	Shifting Units*	Practice shifting the unit in place value	4.NF.C.6; 5.NBT.A.1; 5.NBT.A.2; 5.NBT.A.3a	283
14.3	Decimal Roll and Cover*	Explore the size of decimals using an area model	4.NF.C.5; 4.NF.C.6; 5.NBT.A.1; 5.NBT.A.3a	285
14.4	Build It, Name It*	Practice connecting the decimal notation to a physical model	4.NF.C.6; 5.NBT.A.1	286
14.5	Calculator Decimal Counting	Develop an understanding of the patterns in decimal notation	4.NF.C.6; 5.NBT.A.1	286

(continued)

* Activity titles with an asterisk include a downloadable Activity Page, Expanded Lesson, or Blackline Master.

Chapter 14 Developing decimal and percent concepts and decimal computation. (*continued*)

Activity		Mathematical Content	CCSS-M	Page
14.6	Familiar Fractions to Decimals*	Develop a conceptual connection between fractions and decimal notations	4.NF.C.7	287
14.7	Estimate, Then Verify*	Develop a conceptual connection between fractions and decimal notations	4.NF.C.7	288
14.8	Decimals and Fractions on a Double Number Line	Develop a conceptual connection between fractions and decimal notations	4.NF.C.6	289
14.9	Best Match*	Practice estimation of decimal numbers with simple fractions	4.NF.C.6	290
14.10	Line 'Em Up*	Develop an understanding of the way that decimal numbers are ordered	4.NF.C.6; 4.NF.C.7; 5.NBT.A.1; 5.NBT.A.3a; 5.NBT.A.3b	292
14.11	Close Decimals	Develop an understanding of the relative size of decimal numbers	5.NBT.A.3b	293
14.12	Zoom*	Explore the density of decimals	5.NBT.C3b; 6.NS.C.6	293
14.13	Representing Sums and Differences*	Build the connection between computation, models, and context	5.NBT.B.7	296
14.14	Hit the Target: Continuous Input	Estimate for any of the four operations	5.NBT.B.7; 6.NS.B.3	297
14.15	Where Does the Decimal Go? Multiplication	Use estimation to place the decimal point in multiplication	5.NBT.B.7; 6.NS.B.3	299
14.16	Where Does the Decimal Go? Division*	Use estimation to place the decimal point in division	5.NBT.B.7; 6.NS.B.3	301
14.17	Percent Memory Match*	Explore the relationship between percents and circle graphs	6.RP.A.3c	303

Chapter 15 Promoting algebraic thinking.

Activity		Mathematical Content	CCSS-M	Page
15.1.	One Up and One Down: Multiplication	Explore patterns with multiplication to develop a generalization	3.OA.A.1; 3.OA.D.9	311
15.2	Don't Push the Point	Explore patterns with decimal multiplication to develop a generalization	5.NBT.B.7	312
15.3	Diagonal Sums*	Explore place-value relationships and generalize patterns	3.OA.D.9	313
15.4	The Border Tiles Problem*	Explore a pattern to develop a generalization	4.OA.B.4	315
15.5	Equal to the Challenge*	Develop the concept of the equal sign through equivalent equations	3.OA.A.1; 3.OA.A.2	317
15.6	Seesaw Students	Develop the concept of the equal sign as a balance	3.OA.A.1; 3.OA.A.2	317
15.7	Tilt or Balance?*	Develop understanding of the equal sign and the less-than and greater-than symbols	4.NBT.A.1; 5.NBT.A.3a, b	318
15.8	True or False?	Explore the meaning of the equal sign	3.OA.B.5; 4.NBT.B.5; 5.NF.A.1	320

* Activity titles with an asterisk include a downloadable Activity Page, Expanded Lesson, or Blackline Master.

Activity		Mathematical Content	CCSS-M	Page
15.9	What's Missing?*	Explore the meaning of the equal sign	3.OA.A.4; 4.NF.B3b; 5.OA.A.2,	320
15.10	Make a Statement!	Develop true/false and open sentences	3.OA.A.4; 4.NF.B.3a; 5.OA.A.2	322
15.11	Story Translations	Develop equations that model situations	3.OA.D.8; 4.OA.A.3	323
15.12	Solving the Mystery*	Explore the meaning of variables in an equation as a way to generalize	5.OA.A.2	324
15.13	What's True for All Numbers?*	Explore patterns through properties and relational thinking	3.OA.B.5; 4.NF.A.3a	326
15.14	Broken Calculator: Can You Fix It?	Explore properties of odd and even numbers.	3.OA.D.9	330
15.15	Convince Me Conjectures	Make and test generalizations about whole-number operations (and properties)	3.OA.B.5; 5.OA.A.1	330
15.16	Predict down the Line	Explore the structure of repeating patterns	4.OA.B.4	332
15.17	Hurricane Names	Explore the structure of repeating patterns analytically	4.OA.A.3; 4.OA.B.4; 5.OA.B.3	332
15.18	Predict How Many*	Develop functional relationships in growing patterns	5.OA.B.3	334
15.19	Two of Everything*	Develop functional relationships in an input/output situation	4.OA.C.5	335
15.20	In and Out Machine	Develop functional relationships in an input/output situation	4.OA.C.5	336
15.21	Perimeter Patterns*	Generalize and graph geometric growing patterns (functions)	5.OA.B.3	336

Chapter 16 Building measurement concepts.

Activity		Mathematical Content	CCSS-M	Page
16.1	Familiar Measures	Explore ways to measure using a variety of units	3.MD.B.4	344
16.2	Personal Benchmarks	Explore useful benchmarks using body lengths	3.MD.B.4; 4.MD.B.4	344
16.3	Guess the Type of Measurement*	Develop the concept of categories of measures	3.MD.A.2; 3.MD.C.5; 4.MD.A.1; 5.MD.C.3	344
16.4	Estimation Scavenger Hunt*	Practice measurement estimation in real contexts	2.MD.A.1; 2.MD.A.3; 4.MD.A.1	348
16.5	Changing Units	Explore the inverse relationship between unit size and measure	4.MD.A.1; 5.MD.A.1	349
16.6	Conversion Please*	Develop the concept of converting from a larger unit to a smaller unit in the same system	4.MD.A.1; 5.MD.A.1	350
16.7	Two-Piece Shapes*	Develop an understanding of area; equivalent areas with different shapes	3.MD.C.5	351
16.8	Tangram Areas*	Develop the concept of area	3.MD.C.5; 3.MD.C.6	352
16.9	Cover and Compare*	Develop an understanding of units to measure area	3.MD.C.5; 3.MD.C.6	353
16.10	Rectangle Comparison—Square Units*	Develop an understanding of units to measure area; readiness for rectangle area formula	3.MD.C.5; 3.MD.C.6; 3.MD.C.7	354
16.11	What's the Rim?*	Develop the concept of perimeter	3.MD.D.8	355

(continued)

* Activity titles with an asterisk include a downloadable Activity Page, Expanded Lesson, or Blackline Master.

Chapter 16 Building measurement concepts. (*continued*)

Activity		Mathematical Content	CCSS-M	Page
16.12	Fixed Perimeters*	Explore the relationship between area and perimeter of rectangles when the perimeter is constant	3.MD.D.8; 4.MD.A.3	356
16.13	Fixed Areas*	Explore the relationship between area and perimeter of rectangles when the area is constant	3.MD.C.6; 3.MD.C.7; 4.MD.A.3	356
16.14	Sorting Areas and Perimeters	Explore the relationship between area and perimeter	3.MD.C.6; 3.MD.C.7; 4.MD.A.3	356
16.15	Capacity Sort*	Develop the concept of capacity	3.MD.A.2; 5.MD.C.3	359
16.16	Which Silo Holds More?	Explore the concept of capacity and volume with non-standard units	3.MD.A.2; 5.MD.C.3; 6.G.A.4	360
16.17	Fixed Volume: Comparing Prisms*	Explore the relationship between volume and surface area of prisms when the volume is constant	5.MD.C.3; 5.MD.C.4; 5.MD.C.5; 6.G.A.2; 6.G.A.4	360
16.18	Box Comparison—Cubic Units	Develop the concept of volume; readiness for volume formula for prisms	5.MD.C.3; 5.MD.C.4; 5.MD.C.5	361
16.19	That's Cool	Develop estimation with units of liquid capacity	3.MD.A.2	362
16.20	Squeeze Play	Develop estimation with units of liquid capacity	3.MD.A.2	362
16.21	A Unit Angle*	Develop an understanding of how units are used to measure angle size	4.MD.C.5	364
16.22	Just a Minute!!	Explore time as the duration of an event	3.MD.A.1	366
16.23	Hundred Chart Money Count*	Explore a strategy for counting money	2.MD.C.8; 4.MD.A.2	368

Chapter 17 Developing geometric thinking and concepts.

Activity		Mathematical Content	CCSS-M	Page
17.1	Shape Sorts*	Develop ways that two-dimensional shapes are alike and different	3.G.A.1	375
17.2	Property Lists for Quadrilaterals*	Explore all properties attributable to special classes of quadrilaterals	3.G.A.1; 4.G.A.2; 4.G.A.3	376
17.3	Minimal Defining Lists	Develop logic and reasoning to minimally define shapes	4.G.A.2; 5.G.B.3	378
17.4	What's My Shape?*	Develop oral descriptions of shapes	3.G.A.1; 4.G.A.2	381
17.5	Can You Make It?*	Practice representation of shapes	3.G.A.1; 4.G.A.1; 4.G.A.2; 4.G.A.3	382
17.6	Tangram Puzzles*	Practice composing shapes	3.G.A.1; 3.MD.C.5	383
17.7	Mosaic Puzzle*	Explore properties of two-dimensional shapes and compose and decompose shapes	3.G.A.1; 4.G.A.2	383

* Activity titles with an asterisk include a downloadable Activity Page, Expanded Lesson, or Blackline Master.

Activity		Mathematical Content	CCSS-M	Page
17.8	Geoboard Copy*	Create representations of shapes	4.G.A.1; 4.G.A.2; 4.G.A.3	384
17.9	Decomposing Shapes*	Practice decomposing shapes into other shapes	3.NF.A.1; 3.G.A.2	385
17.10	Constructing Three-Dimensional Shapes	Explore the construction of three-dimensional shapes	3.G.A.1; 4.G.A.1; 4.G.A.2; 5.MD.C.4	390
17.11	Mystery Definition*	Develop defining properties of special classes of shapes	3.G.A.2; 4.G.A.2	392
17.12	Triangle Sort*	Develop defining properties of triangles	3.G.A.2; 4.G.A.2; 5.G.B.3; 5.G.B.4	393
17.13	Diagonals of Quadrilaterals*	Explore the relationships between diagonals of classes of quadrilaterals	4.G.A.2; 5.G.B.3; 5.G.B.4	394
17.14	True or False?*	Explore informal deductive statements concerning properties of shapes	4.G.A.2; 5.G.B.3; 5.G.B.4	395
17.15	Pattern Block Mirror Symmetry	Develop the concept of line symmetry	4.G.A.3	397
17.16	Dot Grid Line Symmetry*	Explore relationship between line symmetry and reflection	4.G.A.3	397
17.17	Hidden Positions*	Develop a readiness for coordinates	5.G.A.1	399
17.18	What's the Point?*	Locating points on a coordinate grid	5.G.A.1	400
17.19	Step Right Up*	Writing the coordinates for points on a coordinate grid	5.G.A.1	400
17.20	Paths*	Explore the concept of location using coordinates on a grid	5.G.A.1; 5.G.A.2	400
17.21	Pentominoes*	Develop spatial visualization skills	3.G.A.1	401
17.22	Face Matching*	Explore solids in terms of their faces or sides	3.G.A.1; 4.G.A.2	402
17.23	Geometry Necklaces*	Develop visualization of geometric figures and terms	3.G.A.1; 4.G.A.1; 5.G.B.3	402

Chapter 18 Representing and interpreting data.

Activity		Mathematical Content	CCSS-M	Page
18.1	Find Me	Gather and analyze data about neighborhoods	3.MD.B.3	409
18.2	What Can We Learn about Our Community?	Students generate questions about the community, gather data, and analyze it	3.MD.B.3; 4.MD.A.4	409
18.3	What about "Both"?	Classify shapes by attributes on a Venn diagram	MP2	412
18.4	Hidden Labels*	Make and test conjectures about how things are being classified	MP2	413

(continued)

* Activity titles with an asterisk include a downloadable Activity Page, Expanded Lesson, or Blackline Master.

Chapter 18 Representing and interpreting data. *(continued)*

Activity		Mathematical Content	CCSS-M	Page
18.5	Storm Chaser	Explore line plots using real world data	3.MD.B.4; 4.MD.B.4; 5.MD.B.2	414
18.6	Stand by Me	Explore line plots using real world data	3.MD.B.3	417
18.7	Comparing Cubits	Create a line plot from measurement data	3.MD.B.4; 4.MD.B.4; 5.MD.B.2	417
18.8	Gross!	Create a line plot for data in decimal or fractional form	3.MD.B.4; 4.MD.B.4; 5.MD.B.2	418
18.9	Test Anxiety	Interpret data from a line plot	3.MD.B.4; 4.MD.B.4; 5.MD.B.2	418

* Activity titles with an asterisk include a downloadable Activity Page, Expanded Lesson, or Blackline Master.

Appendix E
Guide to
Blackline Masters

This Appendix has images of all 33 Blackline Masters (BLM) that you and your students will find useful to engage in many math activities. You can create full-sized masters from these images, print them from point of use pop-ups throughout the text or from the contents listing in the navigation bar of your eText.

Blackline Master	Number
0.5-Centimeter Grid Paper	7
10 × 10 Grids	25
10 × 10 Multiplication Array	16
10,000 Grid Paper	19
1-Centimeter Dot Paper	8
1-Centimeter Grid Paper	6
1-Centimeter Isometric Dot Paper	10
1-Centimeter Square/Diagonal Grid Paper	11
2-Centimeter Isometric Grid Paper	9
2-Centimeter Grid Paper	5
Addition and Subtraction Recording Sheets	20
Base-Ten Grid Paper	18
Base-Ten Materials	32
Blank Hundreds Chart	2
Clock Faces	31
Coordinate Grid—4 Quadrants	23
Coordinate Grid—Quadrant I	22

Blackline Master	Number
Degrees and Wedges	30
Double Ten-Frame	15
Five-Frame	12
Four Small Hundreds Charts	4
Geoboard Pattern (10 by 10)	28
Geoboard Pattern (5 by 5)	26
Geoboard Recording Sheets (10 by 10)	29
Geoboard Recording Sheets (5 by 5)	27
Hundreds Chart	3
Multiplication and Division Recording Sheets	21
Number Cards 0–10	1
Observation Checklist	33
Place-Value Mat (with Ten-Frames)	17
Rational Number Wheel	24
Ten-Frame (Horizontal)	14
Ten-Frame	13

Suggestions for Use and Construction of Materials

Card Stock Materials

A good way to have many materials made quickly and easily for students is to have them duplicated on card stock, laminated, and then cut into smaller pieces if desired. Once cut, materials are best kept in clear freezer bags with zip-type closures. Punch a hole near the top of the bag so that you do not store air.

The following list is a suggestion for materials that can be made from card stock using the masters in this section. Quantity suggestions are also given.

Five-Frames and Ten-Frames—12–14

Five-frames and ten-frames are best duplicated on light-colored card stock. Do not laminate; if you do, the mats will curl and counters will slide around.

10 × 10 Multiplication Array—16

Make one per student in any color. Lamination is suggested. Provide each student with an L-shaped piece of card stock to frame the array.

Base-Ten Materials—32

Run copies on white card stock. One sheet will make 4 hundreds and 10 tens or 4 hundreds and 100 ones. Cut into pieces with a paper cutter. It is recommended that you not laminate the base-ten pieces. A kit consisting of 10 hundreds, 30 tens, and 30 ones is adequate for each student or pair of students.

Place-Value Mat (with Ten-Frames)—17

Mats can be duplicated on any pastel card stock. It is recommended that you not laminate these because they tend to curl and counters slide around. Make one for every student.

Rational Number Wheel—24

These disks should be made on card stock. Duplicate the master on two contrasting colors. Laminate and cut the circles and also the slot on the dotted line. Make a set for each student.

Many masters lend themselves to demonstration purposes. The 10 × 10 array, the blank hundreds board, and the large geoboard are examples. The place-value mat can be used with strips and squares or with counters and cups directly on the document camera. The missing-part blank and the record blanks for the four algorithms are pages that you may wish to write on as a demonstration.

The 10,000 grid is the easiest way there is to show 10,000 or to model four-place decimal numbers.

The degrees and wedges page is the very best way to illustrate what a degree is and also to help explain protractors.

All of the line and dot grids are useful for modeling. You may find it a good idea to have several copies of each easily available.

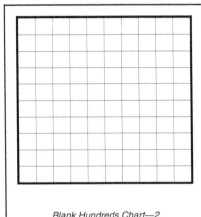

Number Cards 0–10—1

Blank Hundreds Chart—2

Hundreds Chart—3

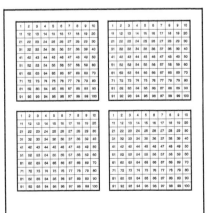

Four Small Hundreds Charts—4

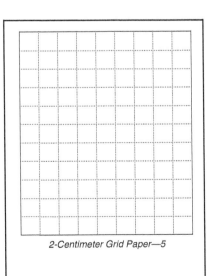

2-Centimeter Grid Paper—5

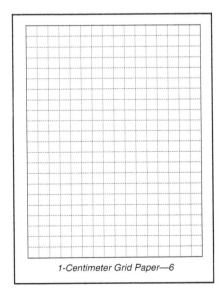

1-Centimeter Grid Paper—6

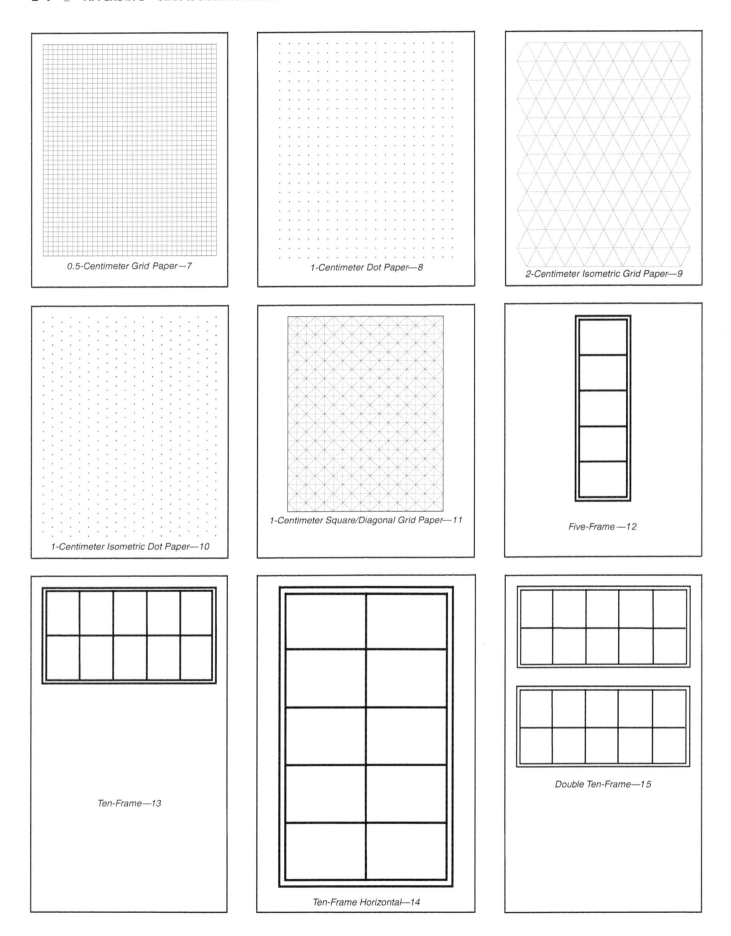

0.5-Centimeter Grid Paper—7

1-Centimeter Dot Paper—8

2-Centimeter Isometric Grid Paper—9

1-Centimeter Isometric Dot Paper—10

1-Centimeter Square/Diagonal Grid Paper—11

Five-Frame—12

Ten-Frame—13

Ten-Frame Horizontal—14

Double Ten-Frame—15

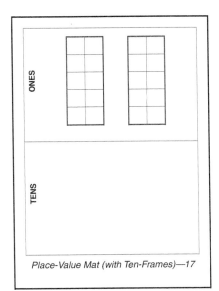

10 × 10 Multiplication Array—16

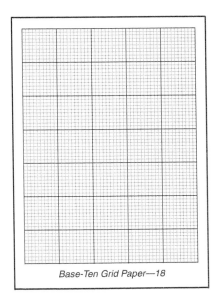

Place-Value Mat (with Ten-Frames)—17

Base-Ten Grid Paper—18

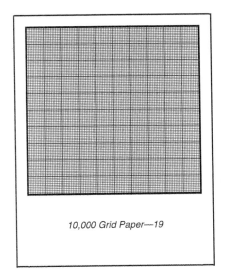

10,000 Grid Paper—19

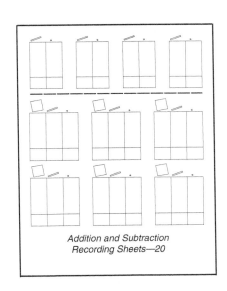

Addition and Subtraction
Recording Sheets—20

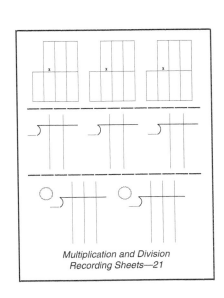

Multiplication and Division
Recording Sheets—21

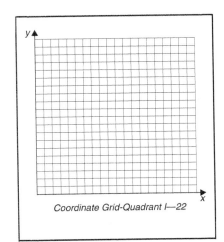

Coordinate Grid-Quadrant I—22

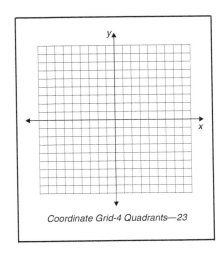

Coordinate Grid-4 Quadrants—23

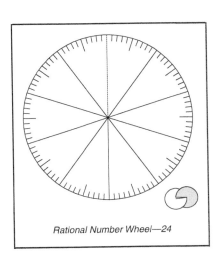

Rational Number Wheel—24

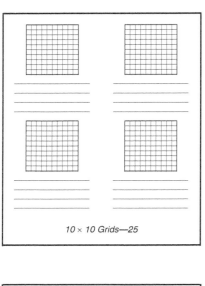

10 × 10 Grids—25

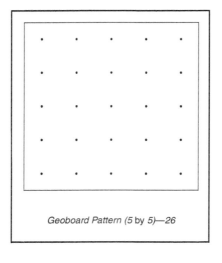

Geoboard Pattern (5 by 5)—26

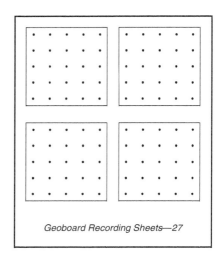

Geoboard Recording Sheets—27

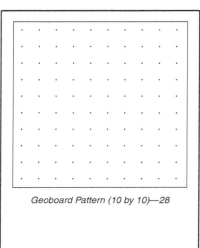

Geoboard Pattern (10 by 10)—28

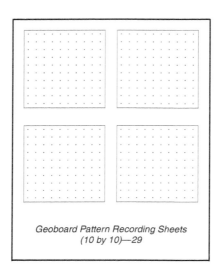

Geoboard Pattern Recording Sheets (10 by 10)—29

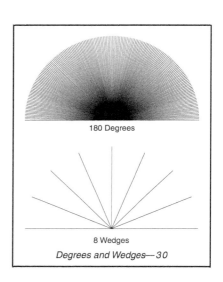

180 Degrees

8 Wedges

Degrees and Wedges—30

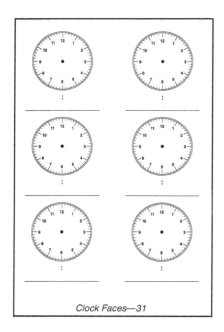

Clock Faces—31

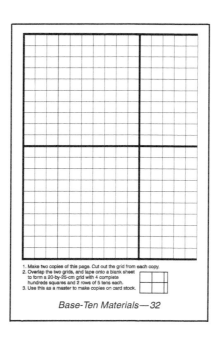

1. Make two copies of this page. Cut out the grid from each copy.
2. Overlap the two grids, and tape onto a blank sheet to form a 20-by-25-cm grid with 4 complete hundreds squares and 2 rows of 5 tens each.
3. Use this as a master to make copies on card stock.

Base-Ten Materials—32

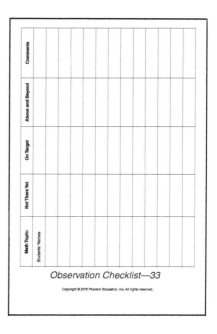

Observation Checklist—33

References

Chapter 1

Ambrose, R. (2002). Are we overemphasizing manipulatives in the primary grades to the detriment of girls? *Teaching Children Mathematics, 9*(1), 16–21.

Bleiler, S., Baxter, W., Stephens, C., & Barlow, A. (2015). Constructing meaning: Standards for mathematical practice. *Teaching Children Mathematics, 21*(6), 336–344.

Council of Chief State School Officers. (2010). *Common Core State Standards*. Washington, DC.

Claessens, A., Duncan, G., & Engel, M. (2009). Kindergarten skills and fifth-grade achievement: Evidence from the ECLS-K. *Economics of Education Review, 28*, 415–427.

Friedman, T. (2007). *The world is flat 3.0: A brief history of the twenty-first century*. New York: Picador.

NCTM (National Council of Teachers of Mathematics). (2000). *Principles and standards for school mathematics*. Reston, VA: NCTM.

NCTM (National Council of Teachers of Mathematics). (2014) *Principles and actions: Ensuring mathematical success for all*. Reston, VA: NCTM.

National Research Council, Mathematics Learning Study Committee. Kilpatrick, J., Swafford, J., & Findell, B. (Eds.). (2001). *Adding it up: Helping children learn mathematics*. Washington, DC: The National Academies Press.

Norton, A., & D'Ambrosio, B. S. (2008). ZPC and ZPD: Zones of teaching and learning. *Journal for research in mathematics education 39*(3), 220–246.

Piaget, J. (1976). *The child's conception of the world*. Totowa, NJ: Littlefield, Adams.

Schoenfeld, A. H., Floden, R. E., & the Algebra Teaching Study and Mathematics Assessment Project. (2014). *An introduction to the TRU Math Dimensions*. Berkeley, CA and E. Lansing, MI: Graduate School of Education, University of California, Berkeley & College of Education, Michigan State University.

Retrieved from: http://ats.berkeley.edu/tools.html and/or http://map.mathshell.org/materials/pd.php.

Steen, L. A. (Ed.). (1997). *Why numbers count: Quantitative literacy for tomorrow's America*. New York: The College Board.

von Glasersfeld, E. (1995). *Radical constructivism: A way of knowing and learning*. London: Falmer Press.

Vygotsky, L. S. (1978). *Mind and society*. Cambridge, MA: Harvard University Press.

Watts, T., Duncan, G., Siegler, R., & Davis-Kean, P. (2014). What's past is prologue: Relations between early mathematics knowledge and high school achievement. *Educational Researcher, 43*(7), 352–360.

Wiggins, G., & McTighe, J. (2005). *Understanding by design* (2nd ed.). Alexandria, VA: Association for Supervision and Curriculum Development.

Wood, T., & Turner-Vorbeck, T. (2001). Extending the conception of mathematics teaching. In T. Wood, B. S. Nelson, & J. Warfield (Eds.), *Beyond classical pedagogy: Teaching elementary school mathematics* (pp. 185–208). Mahwah, NJ: Erlbaum.

Chapter 2

Anderson, L.W., & Krathwohl, D. R. (Eds.) (2001). *A taxonomy for learning, teaching, and assessing: A revision of Bloom's Taxonomy of educational objectives: Complete Edition*. New York: Addison Wesley, Longman.

Ball, D. L. (1992). Magical hopes: Manipulatives and the reform of math education. *American Educator, 16*(2), 14–18, 46–47.

Boaler, J. (2016). *Mathematical mindsets*. San Francisco: Jossey-Bass.

Boaler, J. (2013). Ability and mathematics: The mindset revolution that is reshaping education. *FORUM, 55*(1), 143–152.

Bray, W. S. (2013). How to leverage the potential of mathematical errors. *Teaching Children Mathematics, 19*(7), 425–431.

Breyfogle, M., & Williams, L., (2008–2009). Designing and implementing worthwhile tasks. *Teaching Children Mathematics, 15*(5), 276–280.

Carter, S. (2008). Disequilibrium & questioning in the primary classroom: Establishing routines that help students learn. *Teaching Children Mathematics, 15*(3), 134–137.

Council of Chief State School Officers. (2010). *Common Core State Standards*. Washington, DC.

Chapin, S., O'Conner, C., & Anderson, N. (2009). *Classroom discussions: Using math talk to help students learn* (2nd ed.). Sausalito, CA: Math Solutions.

Clement, L. (2004). A model for understanding, using, and connecting representations. *Teaching Children Mathematics, 11*(2), 97–102.

Davis, B., Sumara, D., & Luce-Kapler, R. (2008). *Engaging minds: Changing teaching in complex times*. New York: Routledge.

Dweck, C. (2006). *Mindset: The new psychology of success*. New York: Random House.

Fosnot, C., & Dolk, M. (2001). *Young mathematicians at work: Constructing number sense, addition, and subtraction*. Portsmouth, NH: Heinemann.

Green, E. (2014, February). Why do Americans stink at math? *New York Times Magazine*. Retrieved from http://www.nytimes .com/2014/07/27/magazine/why-do-americans-stink-at-math .html?_r=0.

Green, E. (2015). *Building a better teacher: How teaching works*. New York: W.W. Norton.

Herbel-Eisenmann, B. A., & Breyfogle, M. L. (2005). Questioning our patterns of questioning. *Mathematics Teaching in the Middle School, 10*(9), 484–489.

Hiebert, J., Carpenter, T. P., Fennema, E., Fuson, K., Wearne, D., Murray, H., Olivier, A., & Human, P. (1997). *Making sense: Teaching and learning mathematics with understanding*. Portsmouth, NH: Heinemann.

Hiebert, J., & Grouws, D. A. (2007). The effects of classroom mathematics teaching on students' learning. In F. K. Lester (Ed.), *Second handbook of research on mathematics teaching and learning* (pp. 371–404). Charlotte, NC: Information Age Publishing.

Humphreys, C., & Parker, R. (2015). *Making number talks matter*. Portland, ME: Stenhouse.

Hunt, A., Nipper, K., & Nash, L. (2011). Virtual vs. concrete manipulatives in mathematics teacher education: Is one type more effective than the other? *Current Issues in Middle Level Education, 16*(2), 1–6.

Jacobs, V. R., & Ambrose, R. C. (2008). Making the most of story problems. *Teaching Children Mathematics, 15*(5), 260–266.

Jacobs, V. R., Lamb, L. L. C., & Philipp, R. A. (2010). Professional noticing of children's mathematical thinking. *Journal for Research in Mathematics Education, 41*(2), 169–202.

Jacobs, V. R., Martin, H. A., Ambrose, R. C., & Philipp, R. A. (2014). Warning signs! *Teaching Children Mathematics 21*(2), 107–113.

Kilic, H., Cross, D. I., Ersoz, F. A., Mewborn, D. S., Swanagan, D., & Kim, J. (2010). Techniques for small-group discourse. *Teaching Children Mathematics, 16*(6), 350–357.

Lesh, R. A., Cramer, K., Doerr, H., Post, T., & Zawojewski, J. (2003). Model development sequences. In R. A. Lesh & H. Doerr (Eds.), *Beyond constructivism: A models and modeling perspective on mathematics teaching, learning, and problem solving* (pp. 35–58). Mahwah, NJ: Lawrence Erlbaum.

Lim, K. H. (2014). Error-eliciting problems: Fostering understanding and thinking. *Mathematics Teaching in the Middle School, 20*(2), 106–114.

McCoy, A., Barnett, J., & Combs, E. (2013). *High-yield routines: Grades K-8*. Reston, VA: NCTM.

Moschkovich, J. N. (1998). Supporting the participation of English language learners in mathematical discussions. *For the Learning of Mathematics, 19*(1), 11–19.

Murrey, D. L. (2008). Differentiating instruction in mathematics for the English language learner. *Mathematics Teaching in the Middle School, 14*(3), 146–153.

NCTM (National Council of Teachers of Mathematics). (2014). *Principles to Action: Ensuring Mathematical Success of All*. Reston, VA: NCTM.

Parrish, S. (2011). Number talks build numerical reasoning. *Teaching Children Mathematics, 18*(3), 198–206.

Parrish, S. (2014). *Number talks: Helping children develop mental math and computation strategies, grades K-5*. Sausalito, CA: Math Solutions.

Pesek, D., & Kirshner, D. (2002). Interference of instrumental instruction in subsequent relational learning. In J. Sowder & B. P. Schappelle (Eds.), *Lessons learned from research* (pp. 101–107). Reston, VA: NCTM.

Philipp, R., & Vincent, C. (2003). Reflecting on learning fractions without understanding. *OnMath, 2*(7). Available to NCTM members at http://my.nctm.org/eresources/view_article .asp?article_id=6430

Rasmussen, C., Yackel, E., & King, K. (2003). Social and sociomathematical norms in the mathematics classroom. In H. L. Schoen & R. I. Charles (Eds.), *Teaching mathematics through problem solving: Grades 6–12* (pp. 143–154). Reston, VA: NCTM.

Rowling, J. K. (1998). *Harry Potter and the sorcerer's stone*. New York, NY: A. A. Levine Books.

Simpson, A., Mokalled, S., Ellenburg, L., & Che, S. M. (2014/2015). A tool for rethinking questioning. *Mathematics Teaching in the Middle School, 20*(5), 294–302.

Smith, M., Hughes, E., Engle, R., & Stein, M. (2009). Orchestrating discussions. *Mathematics Teaching in the Middle School, 14*(9), 548–556.

Smith, M. S., & Stein, M. K. (1998). Selecting and creating mathematical tasks: From research to practice. *Mathematics Teaching in the Middle School, 3*(5), 344–350.

Smith, M. S., & Stein, M. K. (2011). *5 Practices for orchestrating productive mathematics discussions*. Thousand Oaks, CA: Corwin Press.

Stein, M. K., & Bovalino, J. W. (2001). Manipulatives: One piece of the puzzle. *Teaching Children Mathematics, 6*(6), 356–359.

Stephan M., & Whitenack, J. (2003). Establishing classroom social and sociomathematical norms for problem solving. In F. K. Lester, Jr., & R. I. Charles (Eds.), *Teaching mathematics through problem solving: Grades pre-K-6* (pp. 149–162). Reston, VA: NCTM.

Thompson, P. W. (1994). Concrete materials and teaching for mathematical understanding. *Arithmetic Teacher, 41*(9), 556–558.

Wagganer, E. L. (2015). Creating math talk communities. *Teaching Children Mathematics, 22*(4), 248–254.

Wallace, A. (2007). Anticipating student responses to improve problem solving. *Mathematics Teaching in the Middle School, 12*(9), 504–511.

Wiggins, G. (2013, May 5). Letter to the Editor. *New York Times*, p. 2.

Wood, T., Williams, G., & McNeal, B. (2006). Children's mathematical thinking in different classroom cultures. *Journal for Research in Mathematics Education, 37*(3), 222–255.

Yackel, E., & Cobb, P. (1996). Sociomathematical norms, argumentation, and autonomy in mathematics. *Journal for Research in Mathematics Education, 27*(4), 458–477.

Chapter 3

Association of Mathematics Teacher Educators, & National Council of Supervisors of Mathematics (n.d.). *Improving student achievement in mathematics through formative assessment in instruction.* Joint position paper, http://amte.net/sites/default/files/overview_amte_ncsm_position_paper_formative_assessment.pdf.

Barlow, A. T., & McCrory, M. (2011). Strategies for promoting math disagreements. *Teaching Children Mathematics, 17*(3), 530–539.

Bray, W., & Santagata, R. (2014). Making mathematical errors: Springboards for learning. In K. Karp & A. Roth McDuffie (Eds.), *Using research to improve instruction* (pp. 239–248). Reston, VA: NCTM.

Council of Chief State School Officers. (2010). *Common Core State Standards.* Washington, DC.

Daro, P., Mosher, F., & Corcoran, T. (2011). *Learning trajectories in mathematics: A foundation for standards, curriculum assessment and instruction.* Philadelphia, PA: Consortium for Policy Research in Education.

Fennell, F., Kobett, B. M., & Wray, J. A. (2014). Fractions are numbers too! *Mathematics Teaching in the Middle School, 19*(8), 486–493.

Frayer, D. A., Fredrick, W. C., & Klausmeier, H. J. (April 1969). *A schema for testing the level of concept mastery* (Working Paper No. 16), University of Wisconsin Center for Educational Research.

Griffin, L., & Lavelle, L. (2010). *Assessing mathematical understanding: Using one-on-one mathematics interviews with K–2 students.* Presentation given at the Annual Conference of the National Council of Supervisors of Mathematics, San Diego, CA.

Hattie, J. (2009). *Visible learning: A synthesis of over 800 meta-analyses relating to achievement.* New York, NY: Routledge.

Hattie, J. (2015, October). The effective use of testing: What the research says. *Education Week, 35*(10), 23, 28.

Jacob, V. R., Lamb, L., & Philipp, R. A. (2010). Professional noticing of children's mathematical thinking. *Journal for Research in Mathematics Education 41*(2), 169–202.

Lepak, J. (2014). Enhancing students' written mathematical arguments. *Mathematics Teaching in the Middle School 20*(4), 212–219.

NCTM (National Council of Teachers of Mathematics). (2014). *Principles and actions: Ensuring mathematical success for all.* Reston, VA: NCTM.

Nyquist, J. B. (2003). *The benefits of reconstruing feedback as a larger system of formative assessment: A meta-analysis.* Unpublished master's thesis. Vanderbilt University, Nashville, TN.

Parker, R., & Breyfogle, L. (2011). Learning to write about mathematics. *Teaching Children Mathematics, 18*(2), 90–99.

Petit, M., & Bouck, M. (2015). The essence of formative assessment in practice: Classroom examples. *NCSM Journal of Mathematics Education Leadership, 16*(1), 19–27.

Pintrick, P. R. (2003). A motivational science perspective on the role of student motivation in learning and teaching contexts. *Journal of Educational Psychology, 95*(4), 667–686.

Popham, W. J. (2008). *Transformative assessment.* Alexandria, VA: Association for Supervision and Curriculum Development.

Rigelman, N., & Petrick, K. (2014). Student mathematicians developed through formative assessment cycles. In K. Karp and A. Roth McDuffie (Eds.), *Annual Perspectives in Mathematics Education: Using Research to Improve Instruction.* Reston, VA: NCTM.

Simpson, A., Mokalled, S, Ellenburg, L. A., & Che, S. M. (2014/2015). A tool for rethinking teachers' questioning. *Mathematics Teaching in the Middle School, 20*(45), 294–302.

Smith, M. S., & Stein, M. K. (2011). *5 Practices for orchestrating productive mathematics discussions.* Thousand Oaks, CA: Corwin Press.

Stephan, M., McManus, G., & Dehlinger, R. (2014). Using research to inform formative assessment techniques In K. Karp & A. Roth McDuffie (Eds.), *Annual perspectives in mathematics education: Using research to improve instruction* (pp. 229–238). Reston, VA: NCTM.

Stiggins, R. (2009). Assessment for learning in upper elementary grades. *Phi Delta Kappan, 90*(6), 419–421.

Webb, N. L. (2002, April). *An analysis of the alignment between mathematics standards and assessments for three states.* Paper presented at the Annual Meeting of the American Educational Research Association, New Orleans, LA. Retrieved from http://facstaff.wceruw.org/normw/AERA 2002/Alignment Analysis three states Math Final 31502.pdf.

Wieser, E. T. (2008). Students control their own learning: A metacognitive approach. *Teaching Children Mathematics, 15*(2), 90–95.

Wiliam, D. (2007). Content the process: Teacher learning communities in the service of formative assessment. In D.B. Reeves (Ed.), *Ahead of the curve: The power of assessment to transform teaching and learning* (pp. 183–204). Bloomington, IN: Solution Tree.

Wiliam, D. (2010). *Practical techniques for formative assessment.* Presentation given in Boras, Sweden, September 2010. Retrieved June 11, 2011, from www.slideshare.net/BLoPP/dylan-wiliam-bors-2010.

Wiliam, D., & Leahy, S. (2015). *Embedding formative assessment: Practical techniques for K-12 classrooms.* West Palm Beach, FL: Learning Sciences International.

Wilson, L. D., & Kenney, P. A. (2003). Classroom and large-scale assessment. In J. Kilpatrick, W. G. Martin, & D. Schifter (Eds.), A research companion to *Principles and standards for school mathematics* (pp. 53–67). Reston, VA: NCTM.

Chapter 4

Bray, W. S. (2009). The power of choice. *Teaching Children Mathematics, 16*(3), 178–184.

Cassone, J. D. (2009). Differentiating mathematics by using task difficulty. In D. Y. White & J. S. Spitzer (Eds.), *Mathematics for every student: Responding to diversity, grades pre-K–5* (pp. 89–98). Reston, VA: NCTM.

Council of Chief State School Officers. (2010). *Common Core State Standards.* Washington, DC.

Gilbert, M. C., & Musu, L. E. (2008). Using TARGETTS to create learning environments that support mathematical understanding and adaptive motivation. *Teaching Children Mathematics, 15*(3), 138–143.

Kingore, B. (2006, Winter). Tiered instruction: Beginning the process. *Teaching for High Potential,* 5–6. Retrieved from http://www.bertiekingore.com/tieredinstruct.htm.

Murray, M., & Jorgensen, J. (2007). *The differentiated math classroom: A guide for teachers, K–8.* Portsmouth, NH: Heinemann.

NCTM (National Council of Teachers of Mathematics). (2000). *Principles and standards for school mathematics.* Reston, VA: NCTM

Nebesniak, A. L., & Heaton, R. M. (2010). Student confidence & student involvement. *Mathematics Teaching in the Middle School, 16*(2), 97–103.

Skemp, R. (1978). Relational understanding and instrumental understanding. *Arithmetic Teacher, 26*(3), 9–15.

Small, M. (2012). *Good questions: Great ways to differentiate mathematics instruction.* Reston, VA: NCTM.

Storeygard, J. (2010). *My kids can: Making math accessible to all learners, K–5.* Portsmouth, NH: Heinemann.

Sousa, D., & Tomlinson, C. (2011). Differentiation and the brain: How neuroscience supports the learner-friendly classroom. Bloomington, IN: Solution Tree Press.

Sullivan, P., & Lilburn, P. (2002). *Good questions for math teaching: Why ask them and what to ask, K-6.* Sausalito, CA: Math Solutions.

Tomlinson, C. (1999). Mapping a route towards differentiated instruction. *Educational Leadership 57*(1), 12–16.

Tomlinson, C. (2003). *Fulfilling the promise of the differentiated classroom: Strategies and tools for responsive teaching.* Alexandria, VA: Association of Supervision and Curriculum Development.

Chapter 5

Aguirre, J. M., & del Rosario Zavala, M. (2013). Making culturally responsive mathematics teaching explicit: a lesson analysis tool. *Pedagogies: An International Journal, 8*(2), 163–190

Annie E. Casey Foundation. (2014). *Kids count: 2014 data book.* Baltimore, MD: Author. Retrieved May 18, 2016 from http://www.aecf.org/m/resourcedoc/aecf-2014kidscountdatabook-2014.pdf.

Averill, R., Anderson, D., Easton, H., Te Maro, P., Smith, D., & Hynds, A. (2009). Culturally responsive teaching of mathematics: Three models from linked studies. *Journal for Research in Mathematics Education, 40* (2), 157–186.

Baker, S., Lesaux, N., Jayanthi, M., Dimino, J., Proctor, C. P., Morris, J., Gersten, R., Haymond, K., Kieffer, M. J., Linan-Thompson, S., & Newman-Gonchar, R. (2014). *Teaching academic content and literacy to English learners in elementary and middle school* (NCEE 2014–4012). Washington, DC: National Center for Education Evaluation and Regional Assistance (NCEE), Institute of Education Sciences, U.S. Department of Education. Retrieved from the NCEE website: http://ies.ed.gov/ncee/wwc/publications_reviews.aspx.

Boaler, J. (2008, April). Promoting "relational equity" and high mathematics achievement through an innovative mixed ability approach. *British Educational Research Journal, 34,* 167–194.

Boaler, J., & Staples, M. E. (2014). "Creating mathematical futures through an equitable teaching approach: The case of Railside School. In N. S. Nasir, C. Cabano, B. Shreve, E. Woodbury, & N. Louie (Eds.), *Mathematics for equity: A framework for successful practice.* New York: Teachers College Press.

Council of Chief State School Officers. (2010). *Common Core State Standards.* Washington, DC.

Celedón-Pattichis, S. (2009). What does that mean? Drawing on Latino and Latina student's language and culture to make mathematical meaning. In M. W. Ellis (Ed.), *Responding to diversity: Grades 6–8* (pp. 59–74). Reston, VA: NCTM.

Celedón-Pattichis, S., & Ramirez, N. G. (2012). Beyond good teaching: *Advancing mathematics education for ELLs.* Reston, VA: NCTM.

Choppin, J. (2014). Situating expansions of students' explanations in discourse contexts. In K. Karp & A. Roth McDuffie (Eds.), *Annual perspectives in mathematics education 2014: Using research to improve instruction* (pp. 119–128) Reston, VA: NCTM.

Chval, K. B., & Pinnow, R. (2010). Preservice teachers' assumptions about Latino/a English language learners. *Journal of Teaching for Excellence and Equity in Mathematics, 2*(1), 6–12.

Cirillo, M., Steele, M., Otten, S, Herbel-Eisenmann, B.A., McAneny, K. & Riser, J. Q. (2014). Teacher discourse moves: Supporting productive and powerful discourse. In K. Karp & A. Roth McDuffie (Eds.), *Annual perspectives in mathematics education 2014: Using research to improve instruction* (pp. 141–150). Reston, VA: NCTM.

Cobb, P., Gresalfi, M., & Hodge, L. (2009). An interpretative scheme for analyzing the identities that students develop in mathematics classrooms. *Journal for Research in Mathematics Education, 40*(1), 40–68.

Cummins, J. (1994). Primary language instruction and the education of language minority students. In C. F. Leyba (Ed.), *Schooling and language minority students: A theoretical framework* (pp. 3–46). Los Angeles, CA: California State University, National Evaluation, Dissemination and Assessment Center.

Drake, C., Land, T. J., Bartell, T. G., Aguirre, J. M., Foote, M. Q., McDuffie, A. R., & Turner, E. E. (2015). Three strategies for opening curriculum spaces. *Teaching Children Mathematics, 21*(6), 346–353.

Dunleavy, T. K. (2015). Delegating mathematical authority as a means to strive toward equity. *Journal of Urban Mathematics Education, 8*(1), 62–82.

Echevarria, J. J., Vogt, M. J., & Short, D. J. (2008). *Making content comprehensible for English learners: The SIOP model* (3rd ed.). Boston, MA: Allyn & Bacon.

Echevarria, J. J., Vogt, M. J., & Short, D. J. (2012). *Making content comprehensible for English Learners: The SIOP model* (4th ed.). New York: Pearson.

Fernandez A., Anhalt, C., & Civil, M. (2009). Mathematical interviews to assess Latino students. *Teaching Children Mathematics, 16*(3), 162–169.

Garrison, L. (1997). Making the NCTM's Standards work for emergent English speakers. *Teaching Children Mathematics, 4*(3), 132–138.

Gomez, C. L. (2010). Teaching with cognates. *Teaching Children Mathematics, 16*(8), 470–474.

Gresalfi, M. S., & Cobb, P. (2006). Cultivating students' discipline-specific dispositions as a critical goal for pedagogy and equity. *Pedagogies: An International Journal, 1*(1), 49–57.

Gutiérrez, R. (2009). Embracing the inherent tensions in teaching mathematics from an equity stance. *Democracy and Education, 18*(3), 9–16.

Gutiérrez, R. (2015). HOLA: Hunt for opportunities–learn–act. *Mathematics Teacher, 109*(4), 270–277.

Haas, E., & Gort, M. (2009). Demanding more: Legal standards and best practices for English language learners. *Bilingual Research Journal, 32,* 115–135.

Janzen, J. (2008). Teaching English language learners in the content areas. *Review of Educational Research, 78*(4), 1010–1038.

Kena, G., Musu-Gillette, L., Robinson, J., Wang, X., Rathbun, A., Zhang, J., Wilkinson-Flicker, S., Barmer, A., & Dunlop Velez, E. (2015). *The Condition of Education 2015* (NCES 2015–144). U.S. Department of Education, National Center for Education Statistics. Washington, DC. Retrieved May 18, 2016 from http://nces.ed.gov/pubsearch.

Khisty, L. L. (1997). Making mathematics accessible to Latino students: Rethinking instructional practice. In M. Kenney & J. Trentacosta (Eds.), *Multicultural and gender equity in the mathematics classroom: The gift of diversity* (pp. 92–101). Reston, VA: NCTM.

Kersaint, G., Thompson, D. R., & Petkova, M. (2009). *Teaching mathematics to English language learners.* New York, NY: Routledge.

Kisker, E. E., Lipka, J., Adams, B. L., Rickard, A., Andrew-Ihrke, D., Yanez, E. E., & Millard, A. (2012). The potential of a culturally based supplemental mathematics curriculum to improve the mathematics performance of Alaska native and other students. *Journal for Research in Mathematics Education, 43*(1), 75–113.

Livers, S. D., & Bay-Williams, J. M. (2014). Timing vocabulary support: Constructing (not Obstructing) Meaning. *Mathematics Teaching in the Middle School, 10*(3), 153–159.

Mathis, S. B. (1986). *The hundred penny box.* New York, NY: Puffin Books.

Midobuche, E. (2001). Building cultural bridges between home and the mathematics classroom. *Teaching Children Mathematics, 7*(9), 500–502.

Moschkovich, J. N. (2009, March). *How do students use two languages when learning mathematics? Using two languages during conversations: NCTM Research Clip.* Reston, VA: NCTM.

Murrey, D. L. (2008). Differentiating instruction in mathematics for the English language learner. *Mathematics Teaching in the Middle School, 14*(3), 146–153.

National Research Council. (2001). *Adding it up: Helping children learn mathematics.* Washington, DC: National Academy Press.

NCTM (National Council of Teachers of Mathematics). (2014). *Access and equity in mathematics education: A position of the National Council of Teachers of Mathematics.* Retrieved from http://www.nctm.org/uploadedFiles/Standards_and_Positions/Position_Statements/Access_and_Equity.pdf.

Neumann, M. D. (2005). Freedom quilts: Mathematics on the underground railroad. *Teaching Children Mathematics, 11*(6), 316–321.

Perkins, I., & Flores, A. (2002). Mathematical notations and procedures of recent immigrant students. *Mathematics Teaching in the Middle School, 7*(6), 346–351.

Robinson, J. P. (2010). The effects of test translation on young English learners' mathematics performance. *Educational Researcher, 39*(8), 582–590.

Secada, W. G. (1983). *The educational background of limited-English proficient students: Implications for the arithmetic classroom.* Arlington Heights, IL: Bilingual Education Service Center. (ERIC Document Reproduction Service No. ED 237318).

Setati, M. (2005). Teaching mathematics in a primary multilingual classroom. *Journal for Research in Mathematics Education, 36*(5), 447–466.

Shein, P. P. (2012). Seeing with two eyes: A teacher's use of gestures in questioning and revoicing to engage English language learners in the repair of mathematical errors. *Journal for Research in Mathematics Education, 43*(2), 182–222.

Simic-Muller, K. (2015). Social justice and proportional reasoning. *Mathematics Teaching in the Middle School, 21*(3), 162–168.

Tomaz, V. S., & David, M. M. (2015). How students' everyday situations modify classroom mathematical activity: The case of water consumption. *Journal for Research in Mathematics Education, 46*(4), 455–496.

Turner, E. E., Celedón-Pattichis, S., Marshall, M., & Tennison, A. (2009). "Fijense amorcitos, les voy a contra una historia": The power of story to support solving and discussing mathematical problems among Latino and Latina kindergarten students. In D. Y. White & J. S. Spitzer (Eds.), *Responding to diversity: Grades pre-K–5* (pp. 23–42). Reston, VA: NCTM.

Vollmer, G. (2000). Praise and stigma: Teachers' constructions of the typical ESL student. *Journal of Intercultural Studies, 21*(1), 53–66.

Wager, A. (2012). Incorporating out-of-school mathematics: From cultural context to embedded practice. *Journal of Mathematics Teacher Education, 15*(1), 9–23.

Whiteford, T. (2009/2010). Is mathematics a universal language? *Teaching Children Mathematics, 16*(5), 276–283.

Yoon, B. (2008). Uninvited guests: The influence of teachers' roles and pedagogies on the positioning of English language learners in the classroom. *American Educational Research Journal, 45*, 495–522.

Zike, D. (n.d.). *Dinah Zike's teaching mathematics with foldables.* Columbus, OH: Glencoe McGraw-Hill.

Chapter 6

Assouline, S. G., & Lupkowski-Shoplik, A. (2011). *Developing math talent: A comprehensive guide to math education for gifted students in elementary and middle school* (2nd ed.). Waco, TX: Prufrock Press.

Baroody, A. J. (2011). Learning; A framework. In F. Fennell (Ed.), *Achieving fluency in special education and mathematics* (pp. 15–58). Reston, VA: NCTM.

Berch, D. B., & Mazzocco, M. M. M. (Eds.). (2007). *Why is math so hard for some children? The nature and origins of mathematical learning difficulties and disabilities.* Baltimore, MD: Brookes.

Bruner, J. S., & Kenney, H. J. (1965). Representation and mathematics learning. *Monographs of the Society for Research in Child Development, 30*(1), 50–59.

Bush, S., Karp, K., & Nadler, J. (2015). Artist? Mathematician? Developing both enhances learning! *Teaching Children Mathematics, 22*(2), 61–63.

Council of Chief State School Officers. (2010). *Common Core State Standards.* Washington, DC.

Flores, M., Hinton, V., & Strozier, S. (2014). Teaching subtraction and multiplication with regrouping using the concrete-representational-abstract sequence and strategic instruction model. *Learning Disabilities Research and Practice, 29*(2), 75–88.

Fuchs, L. S., & Fuchs, D. (2001). Principles for the prevention and intervention of mathematics difficulties. *Learning Disabilities Research and Practice, 16*(2), 85–95.

Dobbins, A., Gagnon, J. C., & Ulrich, T. (2014). Teaching geometry to students with math difficulties using graduated and peer-mediated instruction in a response-to-intervention model. *Preventing School Failure: Alternative Education for Children and Youth, 58*(1), 17–25.

Gagnon, J., & Maccini, P. (2001). Preparing students with disabilities for algebra. *Teaching Exceptional Children, 34*(1), 8–15.

Gavin, M. K., & Sheffield, L. J. (2010). Using curriculum to develop mathematical promise in the middle grades. In M. Saul, S. Assouline, & L. J. Sheffield (Eds.), *The peak in the middle: Developing mathematically gifted students in the middle grades* (pp. 51–76). Reston, VA: NCTM, National Association of Gifted Children, & National Middle School Association.

Griffin, C. C., Jossi, M. H., & van Garderen, D. (2014). Effective mathematics instruction in inclusive schools. In J. McLeskey, N. L. Waldron, F. Spooner, & B. Algozzine (Eds.), *Handbook of effective inclusive schools: Research and practice* (pp. 261–274). New York: Routledge.

Heddens, J. (1964). *Today's mathematics: A guide to concepts and methods in elementary school mathematics.* Chicago, IL: Science Research Associates.

Hodges, T. E., Rose, T. D., & Hicks, A. D. (2013). Interviews as RtI Tools. *Teaching Children Mathematics, 19*(1), 30–37.

Hunter, A. E., Bush, S. B., & Karp, K. (2014). Systematic interventions for teaching ratios. *Mathematics Teaching in the Middle School, 19*(6), 360–367.

Johnsen, S. K., Assouline, S., & Ryser, G. R. (2013). *Teacher's guide to using the common core state standards with mathematically gifted and advanced learners.* Waco, TX: Prufrock Press.

Karp, K., & Howell, P. (2004). Building responsibility for learning in students with special needs. *Teaching Children Mathematics, 11*(3), 118–126.

Lewis, K. (2014). Difference not deficit: Reconceptualizing mathematical learning disabilities. *Journal for Research in Mathematics Education, 45*(3), 351–396.

Mack, N. K. (2011). Enriching number knowledge. *Teaching Children Mathematics, 18*(2), 101–109.

Mancl, D. B., Miller, S. P., & Kennedy, M. (2012). Using the concrete-representational-abstract sequence with integrated strategy instruction to teach subtraction with regrouping to students with learning disabilities. *Learning Disabilities Research and Practice, 27*(4), 152–166.

Mazzocco, M. M. M., Devlin, K. T., & McKenney, S. J. (2008). Is it a fact? Timed arithmetic performance of children with mathematical learning disabilities (MLD) varies as a function of how MLD is defined. *Developmental Neuropsychology, 33*(3), 318–344.

McMaster, K. L., & Fuchs, D. (2016). Classwide intervention using peer-assisted learning strategies. In, S. Jimerson, M. Burns, & A. VanDerHeyden (Eds.) *Handbook of response to intervention* (pp. 253–268). New York: Springer.

Miller, S. P., & Kaffar, B. J. (2011). Developing addition with regrouping competence among second graders with mathematics difficulties. *Investigations in Mathematics Learning, 4*(1), 24–49.

NCTM (National Council of Teachers of Mathematics). (2007b). Research brief: Effective strategies for teaching students with difficulties in mathematics. Retrieved from www.nctm.org/news/content.aspx?id=8452.

NCTM (National Council of Teachers of Mathematics). (2011a, March). Position statement on interventions. Retrieved June 5, 2011, from www.nctm.org/about/content.aspx?id=30506.

Rakow, S. (2012). Helping gifted learners soar. *Educational Leadership, 69*(5), 34–40.

Read, J. (2014). Who rises to the top? *Peabody Reflector, 83*(1), 19–22.

Reis, S., & Renzulli, J. S. (2005). *Curriculum compacting: An easy start to differentiating for high potential students.* Waco, TX: Prufrock Press.

Rotigel, J., & Fellow, S. (2005). Mathematically gifted students: How can we meet their needs? *Gifted Child Today, 27*(4), 46–65.

Sadler, P., & Tai, R. (2007). The two pillars supporting college science. *Science, 317*(5837), 457–458.

Sheffield, L. J. (Ed.). (1999). *Developing mathematically promising students.* Reston, VA: NCTM.

Storeygard, J. (2010). *My kids can: Making math accessible to all learners, K–5.* Portsmouth, NH: Heinemann.

Torgesen, J. K. (2002). The prevention of reading difficulties. *Journal of School Psychology, 40*(1), 7–26.

Van Tassel-Baska, J., & Brown, E. F. (2007). Toward best practice: An analysis of the efficacy of curriculum models in gifted education. *Gifted Child Quarterly, 51*(4), 342–358.

Ysseldyke, J. (2002). Response to "Learning Disabilities: Historical Perspectives." In R. Bradley, L. Danielson, & D. Hallahan (Eds.), *Identification of learning disabilities: Research to practice* (pp. 89–98). Mahwah, NJ: Erlbaum.

Woodward, J. (2006). Developing automaticity in multiplication facts: Integrating strategy instruction with timed practice drills. *Learning Disability Quarterly, 29*(4), 269–289.

Chapter 7

Aspiazu, G. G., Bauer, S. C., & Spillett, M. D. (1998). Improving the academic performance of Hispanic youth: A community education model. *Bilingual Research Journal, 22*(2), 1–20.

Barnard, W. M. (2004). Parent involvement in elementary school and educational attainment. *Children and Youth Services Review, 26*(1), 39–62.

Bay, J. M., Reys, B. J., & Reys, R. E. (1999). The top 10 elements that must be in place to implement standards-based mathematics curricula. *Phi Delta Kappan, 80*(7), 503–506.

Bay-Williams, J. M., & Meyer, M. R. (2003). What parents want to know about standards-based mathematics curricula. *Principal Leadership, 3*(7), 54–60.

Bay-Williams, J. M. (2010). Influences on student outcomes: Teachers' classroom practices. In D. Lambdin (Ed.), *Teaching and learning mathematics: Translating research for elementary school teachers* (pp. 31–36). Reston, VA: NCTM.

Boaler, J. (2009). *What's math got to do with it? How parents and teachers can help children learn to love their least favorite subject.* New York: Penguin Books.

Britt, B. A. (2015). *Mastering basic math skills: Games for third through fifth grade.* Reston, VA: NCTM.

Civil, M., & Menéndez, J. M. (2010). NCTM *research brief:* Involving Latino and Latina parents in their children's mathematics education. Retrieved from www.nctm.org/uploadedFiles/Research_News_and_Advocacy/Research/Clips_and_Briefs/Research_brief_17-civil.pdf

Coates, G. D., & Mayfield, K. (2009). Families ask: Cooperative learning. *Mathematics Teaching in the Middle School, 15*(4), 244–245.

CCSSI. (n.d.) Myths and Facts. Accessed at http://www.corestandards.org/about-the-standards/myths-vs-facts/.

Council of Chief State School Officers. (2010). *Common Core State Standards.* Washington, DC.

Cooper, H. (2007). *The battle over homework: Common ground for administrators, teachers, and parents* (3rd ed.). Thousand Oaks, CA: Corwin Press.

Else-Quest, N. M., Hyde, J. S., & Hejmadi, A. (2008). Mother and child emotions during mathematics homework. *Mathematical Thinking and Learning, 10,* 5–35.

Ernst, K., & Ryan, S. (2014). *Success from the start: Your first years teaching elementary school.* Reston, VA: NCTM.

Henderson, A. T., Mapp, K. L., Jordan, C., Orozco, E., Averett, A., Donnelly, D., Buttram, J., Wood, L., Fowler, M., & Myers, M. (2002). *A new wave of evidence: The impact of school, family, and community connections on student achievement.* Austin, TX: Southwest Education Development Laboratory.

Hildebrandt, M. E., Biglan, B., & Budd, L. (2013). Let's take a road trip. *Teaching Children Mathematics, 19*(9), 548–553.

Hiebert, J., & Grouws, D. A. (2007). The effects of classroom mathematics teaching on students' learning. In F. K. Lester (Ed.), *Second handbook of research on mathematics teaching and learning* (pp. 371–404). Charlotte, NC: Information Age Publishing.

Jaschik, S. (2014). Evolving ACT. *Inside Higher Ed*. Accessed June 2, 2016 at https://www.insidehighered.com/news/2014/06/06/act-unveils-changes-reporting-and-some-parts-its-test.

Kliman, M. (1999). Beyond helping with homework: Parents and children doing mathematics at home. *Teaching Children Mathematics, 6*(3), 140–146.

Knapp, A. K., Jefferson, V M., & Landers, R. (2013). Learning together. *Teaching Children Mathematics, 19*(7), 432–439.

Lee, J., & Bowen, N. K. (2006). Parent involvement, cultural capital, and the achievement gap among elementary school children. *American Educational Research Journal, 43*(2), 193–218.

Legnard, D., & Austin, S. (2014). The math promise: Celebrating at home and school. *Teaching Children Mathematics, 21*(3), 178–184.

McNeil, N. M., Fyfe, E. R., Petersen, L. A., Dunwiddie, A. E., & Brletic-Shipley, H. (2011). Benefits of practicing 4 = 2 + 2: Nontraditional problem formats facilitate children's understanding of mathematical equivalence. *Child Development, 82*(5), 1620–1633.

Meyer, M., & Arbaugh, F. (2008). Professional development for administrators: What they need to know to support curriculum adoption and implementation. In M. Meyer, C. Langrall, F. Arbaugh, D. Webb, & M. Hoover (Eds.), *A decade of middle school mathematics curriculum implementation: Lessons learned from the Show-Me Project* (pp. 201–210). Charlotte, NC: Information Age Publishing.

Mistretta, R. M. (2013). "We *do* care," say parents. *Teaching Children Mathematics, 19*(9), 572–580.

Patall, E. A., Cooper, H., & Robinson, J. C. (2008). Parent involvement in homework: A research synthesis. *Review of Educational Research, 78*(4), 1039–1101.

Peterson's. (2015). *A Brief History of the SAT and How It Changes.* Accessed https://www.petersons.com/college-search/sat-scores-changes-test.aspx.

Rodríguez-Brown, F. V. (2010). Latino families: Culture and schooling. In E. G. Murillo, Jr., S. A. Villenas, R. T. Galvan, J. S. Muñoz, C. Martínez, & M. Machaldo-Casas (Eds.), *Handbook of Latinos and education: Theory, research, and practice* (pp. 350–360). New York, NY: Routledge.

Seeley, C. L. (2009). *Faster isn't smarter: Messages about math, teaching, and learning in the 21st century.* Sausalito, CA: Math Solutions.

Whitenack, J. W., Cavey, L. O., & Henney, C. (2015). *It's elementary: A parent's guide to K-5 mathematics.* Reston, VA: NCTM.

Wieman, R., & Arbaugh, F. (2014). Making homework more meaningful. *Mathematics Teaching in the Middle School, 20*(3), 160–165.

Chapter 8

Beckmann, S. (2004). Solving algebra and other story problems with simple diagrams: A method demonstrated in grade 4–6 texts used in Singapore. *The Mathematics Educator, 14*(1), 42–46.

Blote, A., Lieffering, L., & Ouwehand, K. (2006). The development of many-to-one counting in 4-year-old children. *Cognitive Development, 21*(3), 332–348.

Caldwell, J., Kobett, B., & Karp, K. (2014). *Essential understanding of addition and subtraction in practice, grades K–2.* Reston, VA: NCTM.

Carpenter, T. P., Fennema, E., Franke, M. L., Levi, L., & Empson, S. B. (2014). *Children's mathematics: Cognitively guided instruction* (2nd ed.). Portsmouth, NH: Heinemann.

Council of Chief State School Officers. (2010). *Common Core State Standards.* Washington, DC.

Champagne, Z. M., Schoen, R., & Riddell, C. (2014). Variations in both-addends unknown problems. *Teaching Children Mathematics, 21*(2), 114–121.

Clark, F. B., & Kamii, C. (1996). Identification of multiplicative thinking in children in grades 1–5. *Journal for Research in Mathematics Education, 27*(1), 41–51.

Clement, L., & Bernhard, J. (2005). A problem-solving alternative to using key words. *Mathematics Teaching in the Middle School, 10*(7), 360–365.

Crespo, S., & Nicol, C. (2006). Challenging preservice teachers' mathematical understanding: The case of division by zero. *School Science and Mathematics, 106*(2), 84–97.

Ding, M. (2016). Opportunities to learn: Inverse relations in U.S. and Chinese textbooks. *Mathematical Thinking and Learning, 18*(1), 45–68.

Ding, M., & Li, X. (2014) Transition from concrete to abstract representations: The distributive property in a Chinese textbook series. *Educational Studies in Mathematics: An International Journal, 87*(1), 103–121.

Ding, M., Li, X., Capraro, M. M., & Capraro, R. M. (2012). Supporting meaningful initial learning of the associative property: Cross-cultural differences in textbook presentations. *International Journal for Studies in Mathematics Education, 5*(1), 114–130.

Dougherty, B. (2008). Measure up: A quantitative view of early algebra. In J. Kaput, D. Carraher, & M. Blanton (Eds.), *Algebra in the early grades* (pp. 389–412). New York, NY: Erlbaum.

Drake, J., & Barlow, A. (2007). Assessing students' level of understanding multiplication through problem writing. *Teaching Children Mathematics, 14*(5), 272–277.

Fagnant, A., & Vlassis, J. (2013). Schematic representations in arithmetical problem solving: Analysis of their impact on grade 4 students. *Education Studies in Mathematics, 84*, 149–168. doi: 10.1007/s10649-013-9476-4.

Fosnot, C. T., & Dolk, M. (2001). *Young mathematicians at work: Constructing multiplication and division.* Portsmouth, NH: Heinemann.

Fuchs, L. S., Fuchs, D., Prentice, K., Hamlett, C. L., Finelli, R., & Courey, S. J. (2004). Enhancing mathematical problem solving among third-grade students with schema-based instruction. *Journal of Educational Psychology, 96*(4), 635–647.

Heng, M. A., & Sudarshan, A. (2013). "Bigger number means you plus!" Teachers learning to use clinical interviews to understand students' mathematical thinking. *Education Studies in Mathematics, 83*, 471–485.

Holbert, S., & Barlow, A. (2012/2013). Engaging reluctant problem solvers. *Teaching Children Mathematics, 19*(5), 310–315.

Hord, C., & Marita, S. (2014). Students with learning disabilities tackle multistep problems. *Mathematics Teaching in the Middle School 19*(9), 548–555.

Huinker, D. (1994, April). *Multi-step word problems: A strategy for empowering students.* Presented at the annual meeting of the National Council of Teachers of Mathematics, Indianapolis, IN.

Jong, C., & Magruder, R. (2014). Beyond cookies: Understanding various division models. *Teaching Children Mathematics, 20*(6), 367–373.

Karp, K., Bush, S., & Dougherty, B. (2014). 13 rules that expire. *Teaching Children Mathematics, 21*(2), 18–25.

National Research Council Committee. (2009). *Mathematics learning in early childhood: Paths toward excellence and equity.* Washington, DC: The National Academies Press.

Kinda, S. (2013). Generating scenarios of division as sharing and grouping: A study of Japanese elementary and university students. *Mathematical Thinking and Learning, 15,* 190–200.

Lannin, J., Chval, K., & Jones, D. (2013). *Putting essential understanding of multiplication and division into practices in grades 3–5.* Reston, VA: NCTM.

Matney, G. T., & Daugherty, B. N. (2013). Seeing spots and developing multiplicative sense making. *Mathematics Teaching in the Middle School, 19*(3), 148–155.

McElligott, M. (2007). *Bean thirteen.* New York, NY: Putnam Juvenile.

Murata, A. (2008). Mathematics teaching and learning as a mediating process: The case of tape diagrams. *Mathematical Thinking and Learning, 10,* 374–406.

NCTM (National Council of Teachers of Mathematics). (2000). *Principles and standards for school mathematics.* Reston, VA: NCTM.

Quinn, R., Lamberg, T., & Perrin, J. (2008). Teacher perceptions of division by zero. *Clearing House, 81*(3), 101–104.

Schwartz, S. (2013). *Implementing the Common Core State Standards through mathematical problem solving kindergarten–Grade 2* Reston, VA: NCTM.

Sowder, L. (1988). Children's solutions of story problems. *Journal of Mathematical Behavior, 7*(3), 227–238.

Sulentic-Dowell, M. M., Beal, G., & Capraro, R. (2006). How do literacy experiences affect the teaching propensities of elementary pre-service teachers? *Journal of Reading Psychology, 27*(2–3), 235–255.

Verschaffel, L., Greer, B., & DeCorte, E. (2007). Whole number concepts and operations. In F. K. Lester (Ed.), *Second handbook of research on mathematics teaching and learning* (pp. 557–628). Charlotte, NC: Information Age Publishing.

Whitin, P., & Whitin, D. (2008). Learning to solve problems in the primary grades. *Teaching Children Mathematics, 14*(7), 426–432.

Xin, Y. P., Jitendra, A. K., & Deatline-Buchman, A. D. (2005). Effects of mathematical word problem-solving instruction on middle school students with learning problems. *Journal of Special Education, 39*(3), 181–192.

Chapter 9

Ashcraft, M. H., & Christy, K. S. (1995). The frequency of arithmetic facts in elementary texts: Addition and multiplication in grades 1–6. *Journal for Research in Mathematics Education, 26*(5), 396–421.

Barney, L. (1970, April). Your fingers can multiply! *Instructor,* 129–130.

Baroody, A. J. (1985). Mastery of the basic number combinations: Internalization of relationships or facts? *Journal for Research in Mathematics Education, 16*(2), 83–98.

Baroody, A. J. (2003). The development of adaptive expertise and flexibility: The integration of conceptual and procedural knowledge. In A. J. Baroody & A. Dowker (Eds.), *The development of arithmetic concepts and skills: Constructing adaptive expertise* (pp. 1–34). Mahwah, NJ: Erlbaum.

Baroody, A. J. (2006). Why children have difficulties mastering the basic number combinations and how to help them. *Teaching Children Mathematics, 13*(1), 22–31.

Baroody, A. J., Bajwa, N. P., & Eiland, M. (2009). *Why can't Johnny remember the basic facts? Developmental Disabilities Research Reviews, 15,* 69–79.

Bay-Williams, J.M., & Kling, G. (2014). Enriching addition and subtraction fact mastery through games. *Teaching Children Mathematics, 21*(4), 239–247.

Bley, N. S., & Thornton, C. A. (1995). *Teaching mathematics to students with learning disabilities* (3rd ed.). Austin, TX: Pro-Ed.

Boaler, J. (2012, July 3). Timed tests and the development of math anxiety. *Education Week.* Retrieved from http://www.edweek .org/ew/articles/2012/07/03/36boaler.h31.html.

Boaler, J. (2014). Research suggests that timed tests cause math anxiety. *Teaching Children Mathematics, 20*(8), 469–474.

Brownell, W., & Chazal, C. (1935). The effects of premature drill in third grade arithmetic. *Journal of Educational Research, 29*(1), 17–28.

Carpenter, T. P., & Moser, J. M. (1984). The acquisition of addition and subtraction concepts in grades one through three. *Journal for Research in Mathematics Education, 15*(3), 179–202.

Council of Chief State School Officers. (2010). *Common Core State Standards.* Washington, DC.

Flowers, J. M., & Rubenstein, R. N. (2010–2011). Multiplication fact fluency using doubles. *Mathematics Teaching in the Middle School, 16*(5), 296–301.

Forbringer, L., & Fahsl, A. J. (2010). Differentiating practice to help students master basic facts. In D. Y. White & J. S. Spitzer (Eds.), *Responding to diversity: Grades pre-K–5* (pp. 7–22). Reston, VA: NCTM.

Fuson, K. C. (1984). More complexities in subtraction. *Journal for Research in Mathematics Education, 15*(3), 214–225.

Fuson, K. C. (1992). Research on whole number addition and subtraction. In D. A. Grouws (Ed.), *Handbook of research on mathematics teaching and learning* (pp. 243–275). New York, NY: Macmillan.

Fuson, K. C., & Kwon, Y. (1992). Korean children's single-digit addition and subtraction: Numbers structured by ten. *Journal for Research in Mathematics Education, 23*(2), 148–165.

Garza-Kling, G. (2011). Fluency with basic addition. *Teaching Children Mathematics, 18*(2), 81–88.

Gravemeijer, K., & van Galen, F. (2003). Facts and algorithms as products of students' own mathematical activity. In J. Kilpatrick, W. G. Martin, & D. Schifter (Eds.), *A research companion to Principles and Standards for School Mathematics* (pp. 114–122). Reston, VA: NCTM.

Henry, V. J., & Brown, R. S. (2008). First grade basic facts: An investigation into teaching and learning of an accelerated, high demand memorization standard. *Journal for Research in Mathematics Education, 39*(2), 153–183.

Hong, L. T. (1993). *Two of everything: A Chinese folktale.* New York, NY: Albert Whitman.

Jordan, N. C., Kaplan, D., Locuniak, M. N., & Ramineni, C. (2007). Predicting first grade math achievement from developmental number sense trajectories. *Learning Disabilities Research & Practice, 22*(1), 36–46.

Kamii, C. K., & Anderson, C. (2003). Multiplication games: How we made and used them. *Teaching Children Mathematics, 10*(3), 135–141.

Kling, G. (2011). Fluency with basic addition. *Teaching Children Mathematics, 18*(2), 80–88.

Kling, G., & Bay-Williams, J. M. (2014). Assessing basic fact fluency. *Teaching Children Mathematics, 20*(8), 488–497.

Lewis, T. (2005). Facts + fun = fluency. *Teaching Children Mathematics, 12*(1), 8–11.

Locuniak, M. N., & Jordan, N. C. (2008). Using kindergarten number sense to predict calculation fluency in second grade. *Journal of Learning Disabilities, 41*(5), 451–459.

Mazzocco, M. M. M., & Thompson, R. E. (2005). Kindergarten predictors of math learning disability. *Learning Disabilities Research & Practice, 20*(3), 142–155.

Mazzocco, M. M. M., Devlin, K. T., & McKenney, S. J. (2008). Is it a fact? Timed arithmetic performance of children with mathematical learning disabilities (MLD) varies as a function of how MLD is defined. *Developmental Neuropsychology, 33*(3), 318–344.

National Research Council. (2001). *Adding it up: Helping children learn mathematics.* Washington, DC: National Academy Press.

Peltenburg, M., van den Heuvel-Panhuizen, M., & Robitzsch, A. (2012). Special education students' use of indirect addition in solving subtraction problems up to 100: A proof of the didactical potential. Of an ignored procedure. *Education Studies in Mathematics, 79*(3), 351–369.

Ramirez, G., Gunderson, E. A., Levine, S. C., & Beilock, S. L. (2013). Math anxiety, working memory, and math achievement in early elementary school. *Journal of Cognition and Development, 14*(2), 187–202.

Rathmell, E. C. (1978). Using thinking strategies to teach the basic skills. In M. N. Suydam (Ed.), *Developing computational skills* (pp. 13–38). Reston, VA: NCTM.

Sarama, J., & Clements, D. H. (2009). *Early childhood mathematics education research: Learning trajectories for young children.* New York, NY: Routledge.

Shoecraft, P. (1982). Bowl-A-Fact: A game for reviewing the number facts. *Arithmetic Teacher, 29*(8), 24–25.

Wallace, A. H., & Gurganus, S. P. (2005). Teaching for mastery of multiplication. *Teaching Children Mathematics, 12*(1), 26–33.

Chapter 10

Burris, J. T. (2013). Virtual place value. *Teaching Children Mathematics, 20*(4), 228–236.

Byrge, L., Smith, L. B., & Mix, K. (2013). Beginnings of place value: How preschoolers write three digit numbers. *Child Development, 85*(2), 437–443.

Cayton, G. A., & Brizuela, B. M. (2007). First graders' strategies for numerical notation, number reading and the number concept. In J. H. Woo, H. C. Lew, K. S. Park, & D. Y. Seo (Eds.), *Proceedings of the 31st conference of the international group for the psychology of mathematics education* (Vol. 2, pp. 81–88). Seoul, South Korea: Psychology of Mathematics Education.

Council of Chief State School Officers. (2010). *Common Core State Standards.* Washington, DC.

Chan, B. M. Y., & Ho, C. S. H. (2010). The cognitive profile of Chinese children with mathematics difficulties. *Journal of Experimental Child Psychology, 107,* 260–279.

Dougherty, B., Flores, A., Louis, E., & Sophian, C. (2010). *Developing essential understanding of number and numeration for teaching mathematics in prekindergarten–grade 2.* Reston, VA: NCTM.

Geary, D. C., & Hoard, M. K. (2005). Learning disabilities in arithmetic and mathematics: Theoretical and empirical perspectives. In J. Campbell (Ed.), *Handbook of mathematical cognition* (pp. 253–267). New York, NY: Psychology Press.

Kamii, C. K. (1985). *Young children reinvent arithmetic.* New York: Teachers College Press.

Labinowicz, E. (1985). *Learning from children: New beginning for teaching numerical thinking.* Menlo Park, CA: AWL Supplemental.

Mix, K. S., Prather, R. S., Smith, L. B., & Stockton, J. D. (2014). Young children's interpretation of multidigit number names: From emerging competence to mastery. *Child Development, 85*(3), 1306–1319.

Moeller, K., Martignon, L., Wessolowski, S., Engel, J., & Nuerk, H. C. (2011). Effects of finger counting on numerical development: The opposing views of neuro-cognition and mathematics education. *Frontiers in Psychology, 2,* 328.

Ross, S. H. (1986). *The development of children's place-value numeration concepts in grades two through five.* Presented at the annual meeting of the American Educational Research Association, San Francisco, CA.

Ross, S. R. (2002). Place value: Problem solving and written assessment. *Teaching Children Mathematics, 8*(7), 419–423.

Schwartz, D. M. (1985). *How much is a million?* New York, NY: Lothrop, Lee & Shepard.

Thomas, N. (2004). The development of structure in the number system. In M. J. Hoines & A. B. Fuglestad (Eds.), *28th conference of the International Group for the Psychology of Mathematics Education* (pp. 305–312). Bergen, Norway: Bergen University College Press.

Chapter 11

Ambrose, R., Baek, J., & Carpenter, T. P. (2003). Children's invention of multidigit multiplication and division algorithms. In A. J. Baroody & A. Dowker (Eds.), *The development of arithmetic concepts and skills: Constructing adaptive expertise* (pp. 305–336). Mahwah, NJ: Erlbaum.

Baek, J. M. (2006). Children's mathematical understanding and invented strategies for multidigit multiplication. *Teaching Children Mathematics, 12*(5), 242–247.

Barker, L. (2009). Ten is the magic number! *Teaching Children Mathematics, 15*(6), 336–345

Barmby, P., Harries, T., Higgins, S., & Suggate, J. (2009). The array representation and primary children's understanding and reasoning in multiplication. *Educational Studies in Mathematics, 70,* 217–241.

Benson, C. C., Wall, J. J., & Malm, C. (2013). The distributive property in grade 3? *Teaching Children Mathematics, 19*(8), 498–506.

Biddlecomb, B., & Carr, M. (2011). A longitudinal study of the development of mathematics strategies and underlying counting schemes. *International Journal of Science and Mathematics Education, 9,* 1–24.

Caldwell, J., Kobett, B., & Karp, K. (2014). *Essential understanding of addition and subtraction in practice, grades K–2.* Reston, VA: NCTM.

Campbell, P. F., Rowan, T.E., & Suarez, A. R. (1998). What criteria for student-invented algorithms? In L. J. Morrow (Ed.), *The teaching and learning of algorithms in school mathematics* (pp. 49–55). Reston, VA: NCTM.

Carpenter, T. P., Franke, M. L., Jacobs, V. R., Fennema, E., & Empson, S. B. (1998). A longitudinal study of invention and understanding in children's multi digit addition and subtraction. *Journal for Research in Mathematics Education*, *29*(1), 3–20.

Council of Chief State School Officers. (2010). *Common Core State Standards*. Washington, DC.

Csikos, F. (2016). Strategies and performance in elementary students' three-digit mental addition. *Educational Studies in Mathematics*, 91, 123–139.

Confrey, J. (2008). *Student and teacher reasoning on rational numbers, multiplicative structures, and related topics.* Presentation at ICME-11, Monterrey, Mexico.

Devlin, K. (2011). *What exactly is multiplication?* Mathematical Association of America. Retrieved from www.maa.org/devlin/devlin_01_11.html.

Fan, L., & Bokhove, C. (2014). Rethinking the role of algorithms in school mathematics: a conceptual model with focus on cognitive development. *ZDM Mathematics Education*, 46, 481–492.

Fleischman, H. L., Hopstock, P. J., Pelczar, M. P., & Shelley, B. E. (2010). *Highlights from PISA 2009: Performance of U.S. 15-Year-Old Students in Reading, Mathematics, and Science Literacy in an International Context* (NCES 2011–004). Washington, DC: U.S. Government Printing Office.

Flowers, J.M., & Rubenstein, R. N. (2010–2011). Multiplication fact fluency using doubles. *Mathematics Teaching in the Middle School*, *16*(5), 296–301.

Fosnot, C., & Dolk, M. (2001). *Young mathematicians at work: Constructing number sense, addition, and subtraction.* Portsmouth, NH: Heinemann.

Fuson, K. C. (2003). Developing mathematical power in whole number operations. In J. Kilpatrick, W. G. Martin, & D. Schifter (Eds.), *A research companion to Principles and Standards in School Mathematics* (pp. 68–94). Reston, VA: NCTM.

Gravemeijer, K., & van Galen, F. (2003). Facts and algorithms as products of students' own mathematical activity. In J. Kilpatrick, W. G. Martin, & D. Schifter (Eds.), *A research companion to Principles and Standards for School Mathematics* (pp. 114–122). Reston, VA: NCTM.

Hanson, S. A., & Hogan, T. P. (2000). Computational estimation skill of college students. *Journal for Research in Mathematics Education*, 31(4), 483–499.

Hartnett, J. (2007). Categorisation of mental computation strategies to support teaching and to encourage classroom dialogue. In J. Watson & K. Beswick (Eds.), *Mathematics: Essential research, essential practice: Proceedings of the 30th annual conference of the Mathematics Education Research Group of Australasia* (pp. 345–352). Hobart, Tasmania, Australia: MERGA.

Heibert, J., & Grouws, D. A. (2007). The effects of classroom mathematics teaching on students' learning. In F. K. Lester (Ed.), *Second handbook of research on mathematics teaching and learning* (pp. 371–404). Charlotte, NC: Information Age Publishing.

Kamii, C. K., & Dominick, A. (1998). The harmful effects of algorithms in grades 1–4. In L. J. Morrow (Ed.), *The teaching and learning of algorithms in school mathematics* (pp. 130–140). Reston, VA: NCTM.

Keiser, J. M. (2010). Shifting our computational focus. Mathematics *Teaching in the Middle School*, *16*(4), 216–223.

Keiser, J. (2012). Students' strategies can take us off guard. *Mathematics Teaching in the Middle School*, *17*(7), 418–425.

Kinzer, C., & Stanford, T. (2013/2014). Distributive property: The core of multiplication. *Teaching Children Mathematics*, *20*(5), 303–308.

Lannin, J., Chval, K., & Jones, D. (2013). *Putting essential understanding of multiplication and division into practice in grades 3–5.* Reston, VA: NCTM.

Lee, J. (2014). Deciphering multiplication algorithms with the area model. *Mathematics Teaching in the Middle School*, *19*(9), 557–556.

Lynch, K., & Star, J. (2014). Views of struggling students on instruction incorporating multiple strategies in algebra I: An exploratory study. *Journal for Research in Mathematics Education*, *45*(1), 6–18.

Martin, J. F. (2009). The goal of long division. *Teaching Children Mathematics*, 15(8), 482–487.

NCTM (National Council of Teachers of Mathematics). (2014). *Position statement on access and equity in mathematics education.* Reston, VA: NCTM.

Peltenburg, M., van den Heuvel-Panhuizen, M., & Robitzsch, A. (2012). Special education students' use of indirect addition in solving subtraction problems up to 100: A proof of the didactical potential of an ignored procedure. *Educational Studies in Mathematics*, *79*(3), 351–369.

Perkins, I., & Flores, A. (2002). Mathematical notations and procedures of recent immigrant students. *Mathematics Teaching in the Middle School*, 7(6), 346–351.

Petit, M. (2009). *OGAP (Vermont mathematics partnership ongoing assessment project) multiplicative reasoning framework.* Communication with the author (September 2009).

Reinhart, S. (2000). Never say anything a kid can say. *Mathematics Teaching in the Middle School*, 5(8), 478–483.

Rittle-Johnson, B., Star J. R., & Durkin, K. (2010, April) *Developing procedural flexibility: When should multiple solution methods be introduced?* Paper presented at the Annual Conference of the American Educational Research Association, Denver, CO.

Robinson, K., & LeFevre, J. (2012). The inverse relationship between multiplication and division: Concepts, procedures and a cognitive framework. *Education Studies in Mathematics*, *79*(3), 409–428.

Torbeyns, J., De Smedt, B., Ghesquiere, P., & Verschaffel, L. (2009). Acquisition and use of shortcut strategies by traditionally schooled children. *Educational Studies in Mathematics*, 71, 1–17.

van Putten, C. M., van den Brom-Snijders, P., & Beishuizen, M. (2005). Progressive mathematization of long division in Dutch primary schools. *Journal for Research in Mathematics Education*, *36*(1), 44–73.

Verschaffel, L., Greer, B., & DeCorte, E. (2007). Whole number concepts and operations. In F. K. Lester (Ed.), *Second handbook of research on mathematics teaching and learning* (pp. 557–628). Charlotte, NC: Information Age Publishing.

Chapter 12

Bailey, D. H., Hoard, M. K., Nugent, L., & Geary, D. C. (2012). Competence with fractions predicts gains in mathematics achievement. *Journal of Experimental Child Psychology, 113,* 447–455.

Bamberger, H. J., Oberdorf, C., & Schultz-Ferrell, K. (2010). *Math misconceptions: From misunderstanding to deep understanding.* Portsmouth, NH: Heinemann.

Bay-Williams, J. M., & Martinie, S. L. (2003). Thinking rationally about number in the middle school. *Mathematics Teaching in the Middle School, 8*(6), 282–287.

Barnett-Clarke, C., Fisher, W., Marks, R., & Ross, S. (2010). *Developing essential understanding of rational numbers*: Grades 3–5. Reston, VA: NCTM.

Behr, M. J., Lesh, R., Post, T. R., & Silver, E. A. (1983). Rational number concepts. In R. Lesh & M. Landau (Eds.), *Acquisition of mathematics concepts and processes* (pp. 91–126). New York: Academic Press.

Bray, W. S., & Abreu-Sanchez, L. (2010). Using number sense to compare fractions. *Teaching Children Mathematics, 17*(2), 90–97.

Bright, G. W., Behr, M. J., Post, T. R., & Wachsmuth, I. (1988). Identifying fractions on number lines. *Journal for Research in Mathematics Education, 19*(3), 215–232.

Burns, M. (1999). *Making sense of mathematics: A look toward the twenty-first century.* Presentation at the annual meeting of the National Council of Teachers of Mathematics, San Francisco.

Council of Chief State School Officers. (2010). *Common Core State Standards.* Washington, DC.

Chick, C., Tierney, C., & Storeygard, J. (2007). Seeing students' knowledge of fractions: Candace's inclusive classroom. *Teaching Children Mathematics, 14*(1), 52–57.

Clarke, D., Roche, A., & Mitchell, A. (2008). 10 practical tips for making fractions come alive and make sense. *Mathematics Teaching in the Middle School, 13*(7), 373–380.

Cramer, K., & Henry, A. (2002). Using manipulative models to build number sense for addition of fractions. In B. Litwiller (Ed.), *Making sense of fractions, ratios, and proportions* (pp. 41–48). Reston, VA: NCTM.

Cramer, K., & Whitney, S. (2010). Learning rational number concepts and skills in elementary school classrooms. In D. V. Lambdin & F. K. Lester, Jr. (Eds.), *Teaching and learning mathematics: Translating research for elementary school teachers* (pp. 15–22). Reston, VA: NCTM.

Cramer, K., Wyberg, T., & Leavitt, S. (2008). The role of representations in the fraction addition and subtraction. *Mathematics Teaching in the Middle School, 13*(8), 490–496.

Dougherty, B., Flores, A., Louis, E., & Sophian, C. (2010). *Developing essential understanding of number and numeration for teaching mathematics in prekindergarten–grade 2.* Reston, VA: NCTM.

Empson, S. B., & Levi, L. (2011). *Extending children's mathematics—fractions and decimals.* Portsmouth, NH: Heinemann.

Empson, S. B. (2002). Organizing diversity in early fraction thinking. In B. Litwiller (Ed.), *Making sense of fractions, ratios, and proportions* (pp. 29–40). Reston, VA: NCTM.

Fennell, F., Kobett, B. M., & Wray, J. A. (2014). Fractions are numbers too! *Mathematics Teaching in the Middle School, 19*(8), 486–493.

Flores, A., Samson, J., & Yanik, H. B. (2006). Quotient and measurement interpretations of rational numbers. *Teaching Children Mathematics, 13*(1), 34–39.

Harvey, R. (2012). Stretching student teachers' understanding of fractions. *Mathematics Education Research Journal, 24,* 493–511.

Hodges, T. E., Cady, J., & Collins, R. L. (2008). Fraction representation: The not-so-common denominator among textbooks. *Mathematics Teaching in the Middle School, 14*(2), 78–84.

Hutchins, P. (1986). *The doorbell rang.* New York: Greenwillow.

Johanning, D. I. (2008). Learning to use fractions: Examining middle school students' emerging fraction literacy. *Journal for Research in Mathematics Education, 39*(3), 281–310.

Johanning, D. J. (2011). Estimation's role in calculations with fractions. *Mathematics Teaching in the Middle School, 17*(2), 96–102.

Kloosterman, P., Warfield, J., Wearne, D., Koc, Y., Martin, W. G., & Strutchens, M. (2004). Fourth-grade students' knowledge of mathematics and perceptions of learning mathematics. In P. Kloosterman & F. K. Lester, Jr. (Eds.), *Results and interpretations of the 1990–2000 mathematics assessments of the National Assessment of Educational Progress* (pp. 71–103). Reston, VA: NCTM.

Kouba, V. L., Brown, C. A., Carpenter, T. P., Lindquist, M. M., Silver, E. A., & Swafford, J. O. (1988). Results of the fourth NAEP assessment of mathematics: Number, operations and word problems. *Arithmetic Teacher, 35*(8), 14–19.

Lamon, S. (2012). *Teaching fractions and ratios for understanding: Essential content knowledge and instructional strategies.* New York: Routledge.

Lewis, R. M., Gibbons, L. K., Kazemi, E., & Lind, T. (2015). Unwrapping students' ideas about fractions. *Teaching Children Mathematics, 22*(3), 158–168.

Mack, N. K. (2004). Connecting to develop computational fluency with fractions. *Teaching Children Mathematics, 11*(4), 226–232.

Martinie, S. L. (2007). *Middle school rational number knowledge* (Unpublished doctoral dissertation). Kansas State University.

McNamara, J., & Shaughnessy, M. M. (2015). *Beyond pizzas & pies.* Sausalito, CA: Math Solutions.

National Mathematics Advisory Panel. (2008). *Foundations for success.* Jessup, MD: U.S. Department of Education.

Moyer-Packenham, P. S., Ulmer, L. A., & Anderson, K. L. (2012). Examining pictorial models and virtual manipulatives for third-grade fraction instruction. *Journal of Interactive Online Learning, 11*(3), 103–120.

Neumer, C. (2007). Mixed numbers made easy: Building and converting mixed numbers and improper fractions. *Teaching Children Mathematics, 13*(9), 488–492.

Pantziara, M., & Philippou, G. (2012). Levels of students' "conception" of fractions. *Education Studies in Mathematics, 79,* 69–83.

Petit, M., Laird, R. E., & Marsden, E. L. (2010). *A focus on fractions: Bringing research to the classroom.* New York, NY: Taylor & Francis.

Post, T. R., Wachsmuth, I., Lesh, R. A., & Behr, M. J. (1985). Order and equivalence of rational numbers: A cognitive analysis. *Journal for Research in Mathematics Education, 16*(1), 18–36.

Rampey, B. D., Dion, G. S., & Donahue, P. L. (2009). *NAEP 2008 trends in academic progress (NCES 2009–479).* Washington, DC: National Center for Education Statistics, Institute of Education Sciences, U.S. Department of Education.

Roddick, C., & Silvas-Centeno, C. (2007). Developing understanding of fractions through pattern blocks and fair trade. *Teaching Children Mathematics, 14*(3), 140–145.

Shaughnessy, M. M. (2011). Identify fractions and decimals on a number line. *Teaching Children Mathematics, 17*(7), 428–434.

Sarazen, D. N. (2012). Fractions: Thinking beyond the lines. *Teaching Children Mathematics, 19*(3), 208.

Siebert, D., & Gaskin, N. (2006). Creating, naming, and justifying fractions. *Teaching Children Mathematics, 12*(8), 394–400.

Siegler, R. S., Carpenter, T., Fennell, F., Geary, D., Lewis, J., Okamoto, Y., et al. (2010). *Developing effective fractions instruction for kindergarten through 8th grade: A practice guide* (NCEE 2010-4039). Retrieved fromwww.whatworks.ed.gov/publications/practiceguides.

Siegler, R. S., Duncan, G. J., Davis-Kean, P. E., Duckworth, K., Claessens, A., Engel, M., Susperreguy, M. I., & Chen, M. (2012). Early predictors of high school mathematics achievement, *Psychological Science, 23*, 691–697.

Smith, J. P., III. (2002). The development of students' knowledge of fractions and ratios. In B. Litwiller (Ed.), *Making sense of fractions, ratios, and proportions* (pp. 3–17). Reston, VA: NCTM.

Sowder, J. T., Wearne, D., Martin, W. G., & Strutchens, M. (2004). What do 8th-grade students know about mathematics? Changes over a decade. In P. Kloosterman & F. K. Lester, Jr., *Results and interpretations of the 1990–2000 mathematics assessments of the National Assessment of Educational Progress* (pp. 105–143). Reston, VA: NCTM.

Tzur, R. (1999). An integrated study of children's construction of improper fractions and the teacher's role in promoting learning. *Journal for Research in Mathematics Education, 30*(4), 390–416.

Tzur, R., & Hunt, J. (2015). Iteration: Unit fraction knowledge and the French fry tasks. *Teaching Children Mathematics, 22*(3), 148–157.

Usiskin, Z. (2007). Some thoughts about fractions. *Mathematics Teaching in the Middle School, 12*(7), 370–373.

Williams, L. (2008). Tiering and scaffolding: Two strategies for providing access to important mathematics. *Teaching Children Mathematics, 14*(6), 324–330.

Zhang, X., Clements, M. A. & Ellerton, N. F. (2015). Engaging students with multiple models of fractions. *Teaching Children Mathematics, 22*(3), 138–147.

Chapter 13

Barnett-Clarke, C., Fisher, W., Marks, R., & Ross, S. (2010). *Developing essential understanding of rational numbers: Grades 3–5.* Reston, VA: NCTM.

Carr, J., Carroll, C., Cremer, S., Gale, M., Lagunoff, R., & Sexton, U. (2009). *Making mathematics accessible to English learners, grades 6–12.* San Francisco, CA: WestEd.

Cavey, L. O., & Kinzel, M. T. (2014). From whole numbers to invert and multiply. *Teaching Children Mathematics, 20*(6), 375–383.

Council of Chief State School Officers. (2010). *Common Core State Standards.* Washington, DC.

Chval, K., Lannin, J., & Jones, D. (2013). *Putting essential understanding of fractions into practice: Grades 3–5.* Reston, VA: NCTM.

Cramer, K., Monson, D., Whitney, S., Leavitt, S., & Wyberg, T. (2010). Dividing fractions and problem solving. *Mathematics Teaching in the Middle School, 15*(6), 338–346.

Cramer, K., Wyberg, T., & Leavitt, S. (2008). The role of representations in fraction addition and subtraction. *Mathematics Teaching in the Middle School, 13*(8), 490–496.

Dixon, J. K., & Tobias, J. M. (2013). The whole story: Understanding fraction computation. *Mathematics Teaching in the Middle School, 19*(3), 156–163.

Flores, A., & Priewe, M. D. (2013/2014). Orange you glad I did say "fraction division"? *Mathematics Teaching in the Middle School, 19*(5), 288–293.

George, L. (2010). *Civil war recipes: Adding and subtracting simple fractions.* New York, NY: Rosen Publishing Group.

Gregg, J., & Gregg, D. U. (2007). Measurement and fair-sharing models for dividing fractions. *Mathematics Teaching in the Middle School, 12*(9), 490–496.

Hecht, S., Vagi, K., & Torgesen, J. (2007). Fraction skills and proportional reasoning. In D. Berch & M. Mazzocco (Eds.), *Why is math so hard for some children? The nature and origins of mathematical learning difficulties and disabilities* (pp. 121–132). New York, NY: Brookes Publishing.

Huinker, D. (2002). Examining dimensions of fraction operation sense. In B. Litwiller (Ed.), *Making sense of fractions, ratios, and proportions.* (pp. 72–78). Reston, VA: NCTM.

Izsák, A. (2008). Mathematical knowledge for teaching fraction multiplication. *Cognition and Instruction, 26*(1), 85–143.

Izsák, A., Tillema, E., & Tunc-Pekkam, Z. (2008). Teaching and learning fraction addition on number lines. *Journal for Research in Mathematics Education, 39*(1), 33–62.

Johanning, D. J. (2011). Estimation's role in calculations with fractions. *Mathematics Teaching in the Middle School, 17*(2), 96–102.

Kribs-Zaleta, C. (2008). Oranges, posters, ribbons, and lemonade: Concrete computational strategies for dividing fractions. *Mathematics Teaching in the Middle School, 13*(8), 453–457.

Lamon, S. J. (2012). *Teaching fractions and ratios for understanding: Essential content knowledge and instructional strategies for teachers.* New York, NY: Routledge.

Mack, N. K. (2004). Connecting to develop computational fluency with fractions. *Teaching Children Mathematics, 11*(4), 226–232.

McAnallen, R., & Frye, E. (1995). *Action fractions with hexadrons and pattern blocks.* Boston, MA: Koplow Games, Incorporated.

National Mathematics Advisory Panel. (2008). *Foundations for success.* Jessup, MD: U.S. Department of Education.

Petit, M., Laird, R. E., & Marsden, E. L. (2010). *A focus on fractions: Bringing research to the classroom.* New York, NY: Taylor & Francis.

Philipp, R. A., & Hawthorne, C. (2015). Unpacking referent units in fraction operations. *Teaching Children Mathematics, 22*(4), 240–247.

Prediger, S. (2011). Why Johnny can't apply multiplication? Revisiting the choice of operations with fractions. *International Electronic Journal of Mathematics Education, 6*(2), 65–88.

Sharp, J., & Welder, R. M. (2014). Reveal limitations through fraction division problem posing. *Mathematics Teaching in the Middle School, 19*(9), 541–547.

Schifter, D., Bastable, V., & Russell, S. J. (1999). *Developing mathematical understanding: Numbers and operations, part 2: Making meaning for operations (Casebook).* Parsippany, NJ: Dale Seymour Publications.

Siebert, D. & Gaskin, N. (2006). Creating, naming, and justifying fraction. *Teaching Children Mathematics, 12*(8), 394–400.

Siegler, R. S., Carpenter, T., Fennell, F., Geary, D., Lewis, J., Okamoto, Y., et al. (2010). *Developing effective fractions instruction for kindergarten through 8th grade: A practice guide* (NCEE 2010-4039). Retrieved fromwww.whatworks.ed.gov/publications/practiceguides.

Son, J., & Senk, S. (2010). How reform curricula in the USA and Korea present multiplication and division of fractions. *Educational Studies in Mathematics, 74*, 117–142.

Witherspoon, T. F. (2014). Using constructed knowledge to multiply fractions. *Teaching Children Mathematics, 20*(7), 444–451.

Yeong, J., Dougherty, B. J., & Berkaliev, Z. (2015). Units matter: The meat and potatoes of fraction multiplication is the change of units. *Teaching Children Mathematics, 22*(3), 170–176.

Chapter 14

Council of Chief State School Officers. (2010). *Common Core State Standards*. Washington, DC.

Cramer, K. A., (2003). Using a translation model for curriculum development and classroom instruction. In R. Lesh and K. Doerr (Eds.) *Beyond Constructivism: Models and Modeling Perspectives on Mathematics Problem Solving, Learning and Teaching* (pp. 449–464). Mahwah, NJ: Lawrence Erlbaum Associates.

Cramer, K. A., Monson, D., Ahrendt, S., Colum, K., Wiley, B., & Wyberg, T. (2015). 5 indicators of decimal understandings. *Teaching Children Mathematics, 22*(3): 186–195.

Cramer, K., & Whitney, S. (2010). Learning rational number concepts and skills in elementary school classrooms. In D. V. Lambdin & F. K. Lester, Jr. (Eds.), *Teaching and learning mathematics: Translating research for elementary school teachers* (pp. 15–22). Reston, VA: NCTM.

Cramer, K. A., Wyberg, T., & Leavitt, S. (2009). *Rational number project: Fraction operations and initial decimal ideas*. http://www.cehd.umn.edu/ci/rationalnumberproject/rnp2.html.

Depaepe, F., Torbeyns, J., Vermeersch, N., Janssens, D., Janssen, R., Kelchtermans, G., Verschaffel, L., & Van Dooren, W. (2015). Teachers' content and pedagogical content knowledge on rational numbers: A comparison of prospective elementary and lower secondary school teachers. *Teaching and Teacher Education, 47*, 82–92.

Desmet, L., Gregoire, J., & Mussolin, C. (2010). Developmental changes in the comparison of decimal fractions. *Learning and Instruction, 20*, 521–532.

Durkin, K., & Rittle-Johnson, B. (2015). Diagnosing misconceptions: Revealing changing decimal fraction knowledge. *Learning and Instruction, 37*, 1–9.

Jenkins, S. (2011a). *Actual size*. Boston, MA: Houghton Mifflin.

Jenkins, S. (2011b). *Just a second*. New York, NY: Houghton Mifflin.

Lo, J. J., & Ko, Y. Y. (2013). A bargain price for teaching about percentage. *Mathematics Teaching in the Middle School, 19*(2): 108–115.

Kouba, V. L., Zawojewski, J. S., & Strutchens, M. E. (1997). What do students know about numbers and operations? In P. A. Kenney & E. Silver (Eds.), *Results from the sixth mathematics assessment of the National Assessment of Educational Progress* (pp. 87–140). Reston, VA: NCTM.

Kloosterman, P. (2010). Mathematics skills of 17-year-olds in the United States: 1978 to 2004. *Journal for Research in Mathematics Education, 41*(1), 20–51.

Lortie-Forgues, H., Tian, J., & Siegler, R. S. (2015). Why is learning fraction and decimal arithmetic so difficult? *Developmental Review, 38*, 201–221.

Martinie, S. L., & Bay-Williams, J. M. (2003). Investigating students' conceptual understanding of decimal fractions using multiple representations. *Mathematics Teaching in the Middle School, 8*(5), 244–247.

Martinie, S. L. (2007). *Middle school rational number knowledge.* (Unpublished doctoral dissertation, Kansas State University.)

Martinie, S. L. (2014). Decimal fractions: An important point. *Mathematics Teaching in the Middle School, 19*(7), 420–429.

Olson, M., Zengami, F., & Slovin, H. (2010). The percent predicament. *Mathematics Teaching in the Middle School, 15*(7): 374–376.

Parker, M., (2004). Reasoning and working proportionally with percent. *Mathematics Teaching in the Middle School, 9*(6), 326–330.

Rathouz, M. (2011). 3 ways that promote student reasoning. *Teaching Children Mathematics, 18*(3), 182–189.

Siegler, R. S., Thompson, C. A., & Schneider, M. (2011). An integrated theory of whole number and fractions development. *Cognitive Psychology, 62*, 273–296.

Stacey, K., Helme, S., Steinle, V., Baturo, A., Irwin, K., & Bana, J. (2001). Preservice teachers' knowledge of difficulties in decimal numeration. *Journal of Mathematics Teacher Education, 4*, 205–225.

Steinle, V., & Stacey, K. (2004a). Persistence of decimal misconceptions and readiness to move to expertise. *Proceedings of the 28th conference of the International Groups for the Psychology of Mathematics Education, 4*, 225–232.

Steinle, V., & Stacey, K. (2004b). A longitudinal study of students' understanding of decimal notation: An overview and refined results. In I. Putt, R. Faragher, & M. McLean (Eds.), *Proceedings of the 27th Annual Conference of the Mathematics Education Research Group of Australasia, 2*, 541–548.

Ubuz, B., & Yayan, B. (2010). Primary teachers' subject matter knowledge: Decimals. *International Journal of Mathematical Education in Science and Technology, 41*(6), 787–804.

Vamvakoussi, X., Van Dooren, W., & Verschaffel, L. (2012). Naturally biased? In search for reaction time evidence for a natural number bias in adults. *The Journal of Mathematical Behavior, 31*(3): 344–355.

Whitin, D. J., & Whitin, P. (2012). Making sense of fractions and percentages. *Teaching Children Mathematics, 18*(8): 490–496.

Wyberg, T., Whitney, S. R., Cramer, K. A., Monson, D. S., & Leavitt, S. (2011). Unfolding fraction multiplication. *Mathematics Teaching in the Middle School, 17*, 288–294.

Zambo, R. (2008). Percents can make sense. *Mathematics Teaching in the Middle School, 13*(7), 418–422.

Chapter 15

Ball, D. L., & Bass, H. (2003). Making mathematics reasonable in school. In J. Kilpatrick, W. G. Martin, & D. Schifter (Eds.), *A research companion to Principles and Standards for School Mathematics* (pp. 27–44). Reston, VA: NCTM.

Bay-Williams, J. M., & Martinie, S. L. (2004). What does algebraic thinking look like? *Mathematics Teaching in the Middle School, 10*(4), 198–199.

Blanton, M. L. (2008). *Algebra in the elementary classroom: Transforming thinking, transforming practice*. Portsmouth, NH: Heinemann.

Blanton, M. L., & Kaput, J. (2011). Developing algebraic thinking in the context of arithmetic. In J. Cai & E. Knuth (Eds.), *Early algebraization: A global dialogue from multiple perspectives* (pp. 5–24). New York, NY: Springer.

Blanton, M., Levi, L., Crites, T. W., & Dougherty, B. J. (2011). *Developing essential understanding of algebraic thinking for teaching mathematics in grades 3–5*. Essential Understanding Series. Reston, VA: NCTM.

Boaler, J., & Humphreys, C. (2005). *Connecting mathematical ideas: Middle school video cases to support teaching and learning.* Portsmouth, NH: Heinemann.

Booth, L. R. (1988). Children's difficulties in beginning algebra. In A. F. Coxford & A. P. Shulte (Eds.), *The ideas of algebra, K-12* (pp. 20–32). Reston, VA: NCTM.

Burns, M., & McLaughlin, C. (1990). *A collection of math lessons from grades 6 through 8.* Sausalito, CA: Math Solutions Publications.

Byrd-Hornburg, C., McNeil, N., Chesney, D., & Matthews, P. (2015). A specific misconception of the equal sign acts as a barrier to children's learning of early algebra, *Learning and Individual Differences, 38,* 61–67.

Cai, J., Ng, S. F., & Moyer, J. (2011). Developing students' algebraic thinking in earlier grades: Lessons from China and Singapore. In J. Cai & E. Knuth (Eds.), *Early algebraization: A global dialogue from multiple perspectives* (pp. 25–42). New York, NY: Springer.

Canadas, M. C., Brizuela, B. M., & Blanton, M. (2016). Second graders articulating ideas about linear functional relationships. *Journal of Mathematical Behavior, 41,* 8–103.

Carpenter, T. P., Franke, M. L., & Levi, L. (2003). *Thinking mathematically: Integrating arithmetic and algebra in elementary school.* Portsmouth, NH: Heinemann.

Council of Chief State School Officers. (2010). *Common Core State Standards.* Washington, DC.

Cuyler, M. (2010). *Guinea pigs add up.* New York, NY: Walker.

Driver, M. K., & Powell, S. R. (2015). Symbolic and nonsymbolic equivalence tasks: The influence of symbols on students with mathematics difficulty. *Learning Disabilities Research & Practice, 30*(3), 127–134.

Empson, S. B., Levi, L., & Carpenter, T. P. (2011). The algebraic nature of fractions: Developing relational thinking in elementary school. In J. Cai & E. Knuth (Eds.), *Early algebraization: A global dialogue from multiple perspectives* (pp. 409–428). New York, NY: Springer.

Falkner, K. P., Levi, L., & Carpenter, T. P. (1999). Children's understanding of equality: A foundation for algebra. *Teaching Children Mathematics, 6*(4), 232–236.

Fosnot, C. T., & Jacob, B. (2010). *Young mathematicians at work: Constructing algebra.* Reston, VA: NCTM.

Friel, S. N., & Markworth, K. A. (2009). A framework for analyzing geometric pattern tasks. *Mathematics Teaching in the Middle School, 15*(1), 24–33.

Goldenberg, E. P., Mark, J., & Cuoco, A. (2010). An algebraic-habits-of-mind perspective on elementary school. *Teaching Children Mathematics, 16*(9), 548–556.

Hong, L. T. (1993). *Two of everything: A Chinese folktale.* New York, NY: Albert Whitman.

Kaput, J. J. (2008). What is algebra? What is algebraic reasoning? In J. J. Kaput, D. W. Carraher, & M. L. Blanton (Eds.), *Algebra in the early grades.* Reston, VA: NCTM.

Kieran, C. (2007). Learning and teaching algebra at the middle school through college levels: Building meaning for symbols and their manipulation. In F. K. Lester (Ed.), *Second handbook of research on mathematics teaching and learning* (pp. 707–762). Charlotte, NC: Information Age Publishing.

Knuth, E., Stephens, A., Blanton, M., & Gardiner, A. (2016). Build an early foundation for algebra success. *Phi Delta Kappan, 97*(6), 65–68.

Küchmann, D. (1981). Algebra. In K. M. Hart (Ed.), *Children's understanding of mathematics: 11–16* (pp. 102–119). London: John Murray.

Leavy, A., Hourigan, M., & McMahon, A. (2013). Early understanding of equality. *Teaching Children Mathematics, 20*(4), 246–252.

Mark, J., Cuoco, A., Goldenberg, E. P., & Sword, S. (2010). Developing mathematical habits of mind. *Mathematics Teaching in the Middle School, 15*(9), 505–509.

McNeil, N. M., & Alibali, M. W. (2005). Knowledge change as a function of mathematics experience: All contexts are not created equal. *Journal of Cognition and Development, 6,* 285–306.

McNeil, N. M., Grandau, L., Knuth, E. J., Alibali, M. W., Stephens, A. C., Hattikudur, S., & Krill, D. E. (2006). Middle school students' understanding of the equal sign: The books they read can't help. *Cognition & Instruction, 24*(3), 367–385.

Molina, M., & Ambrose, R. C. (2006). Fostering relational thinking while negotiating the meaning of the equals sign. *Teaching Children Mathematics, 13*(2), 111–117.

Powell, S. R., Kearns, D. M., & Driver, M. K. (2016, February 22). Exploring the connection between arithmetic and prealgebraic reasoning at first and second grade. *Journal of Educational Psychology.* Advance online publication DOI: 10.1037/edu000012.

Russell, S. J., Schifter, D., & Bastable, V. (2011). Developing algebraic thinking in the context of arithmetic. In J. Cai & E. Knuth (Eds.), *Early algebraization: A global dialogue from multiple perspectives* (pp. 43–70). New York, NY: Springer.

Schifter, D., Monk, G. S., Russell, S. J., & Bastable, V. (2007). Early algebra: What does understanding the laws of arithmetic mean in the elementary grades? In J. Kaput, D. Carraher, & M. Blanton (Eds.), *Algebra in the early grades.* Mahwah, NJ: Erlbaum.

Schifter, D., Russell, S. J., & Bastable, V. (2009). Early algebra to reach the range of learners. *Teaching Children Mathematics, 16*(4), 230–237.

Stephens, A., Blanton, M., Knuth, E., Isler, I., & Gardiner, A. (2015). Just say yes to early algebra! *Teaching Children Mathematics, 22*(2), 92–101.

Stephens, A. C., Knuth, E. J., Blanton, M. L., Isler, I., Gardiner, A. M., & Marum, T. (2013). Equation structure and the meaning of the equal sign: The impact of task selection in eliciting elementary students' understandings. *The Journal of Mathematical Behavior, 32,* 173–182.

Chapter 16

Amore, B., & Pinilla, M. (2006). Relationships between area and perimeter: Beliefs of teachers and students. *Mediterranean Journal for Research in Mathematics Education, 5*(2), 1–29.

Battista, M. T. (2003). Understanding students' thinking about area and volume measurement. In D. H. Clements (Ed.), *Learning and teaching measurement* (pp. 122–142). Reston, VA: NCTM.

Better Homes and Gardens. (2012). *Better Homes and Gardens new junior cookbook.* New York, NY: Wiley and Sons.

Blume, G., Galindo, E., & Walcott, C. (2007). Performance in measurement and geometry from the viewpoint of *Principles and Standards for School Mathematics.* In P. Kloosterman & F. Lester, Jr. (Eds.), *Results and interpretations of the 2003 mathematics assessment of the National Assessment of Educational Progress* (pp. 95–138). Reston, VA: NCTM.

Cass, M., Cates, D., Jackson, C. W., & Smith, M. (2002). Facilitating adolescents with disabilities' understanding of area and perimeter concepts via manipulative instruction. *Annual National Conference Proceedings of the American Council on Rural Special Education*. Reno, NV.

Council of Chief State School Officers. (2010). *Common Core State Standards*. Washington, DC.

Dietiker, L. C., Gonulates, F., & Smith, J. P., III (2011). Understanding linear measure. *Teaching Children Mathematics, 18*(4), 252–259.

Dixon, J. (2008). Tracking time: Representing elapsed time on an open timeline. *Teaching Children Mathematics, 15*(1), 18–24.

Jenkins, S. (2011). *Just a second*. New York: HMH Books for Children.

Joram, E. (2003). Benchmarks as tools for developing measurement sense. In D. H. Clements (Ed.), *Learning and teaching measurement* (pp. 57–67). Reston, VA: NCTM.

Kloosterman, P., Rutledge, Z., & Kenney, P. (2009). Exploring the results of the NAEP: 1980s to the present. *Mathematics Teaching in the Middle School, 14*(6), 357–365.

Kurz, T. (2012). A super way to soak in linear measurement, *Teaching Children Mathematics, 18*(9), 535–541.

Leedy, L. (2000). *Measuring penny*. New York, NY: Henry Holt and Company.

Livy, S., Muir, T., & Maher, N. (2012). How do they measure up? Primary pre-service teachers' mathematical knowledge of area and perimeter. *Mathematics Teacher Education and Development, 14*(2), 91–112.

Muir, T. (2005). When near enough is good enough. *Australian Primary Mathematics Classroom, 20*(2), 9–14.

Mullis, I. V. S., Martin, M. O., Gonzalez, E. J., & Chrostowski, S. J. (2004). *TIMSS 2003 international mathematics report: Findings from IEA's trends in international mathematics and science study at the fourth and eighth grades*. Chestnut Hill, MA: TIMSS & PIRLS International Study Center, Boston College.

Munier, V., Devichi, C., & Merle, H. (2008). A physical situation as a way to teach angle. *Teaching Children Mathematics, 14*(7), 402–407.

National Center for Education Statistics. (2014). Retrieved from http://nces.ed.gov/nationsreportcard/itmrlsx/search.aspx?subject=mathematics

NCTM (National Council of Teachers of Mathematics). (2015). *Position statement on the metric system*. Reston, VA: NCTM.

Outhred, L., & Mitchelmore, M. (2004). Students' structuring of rectangular arrays. In M. J. Hoines & A. B. Fuglestad (Eds.), *Proceedings of the 28th PME International Conference, 3*, 465–472.

Parmar, R., Garrison, R., Clements, D., & Sarama, J. (2011). Measurement. In F. Fennell (Ed.), *Achieving fluency in special education and mathematics* (pp. 197–216) Reston, VA: NCTM.

Perie, M., Moran, R., & Lutkus, A. (2005). *NAEP 2004 trends in academic progress: Three decades of student performance in reading and mathematics*. Washington, DC: National Center for Education Statistics.

Preston, R., & Thompson, T. (2004). Integrating measurement across the curriculum. *Mathematics Teaching in the Middle School, 9*(8), 436–441.

Putrawangsa, S., Lukito, A., Amin, S. M., & Wijers, M. (2013). Educational design research: Developing students' understanding of area as the number of measurement units covering a surface. In Z. Zulkardi (Ed.), *Proceedings of the First South East Asia Design/Development Research (SEA-DR) International Conference,* (pp. 416–426). Palembang, Indonesia.

Reeder, S. (2012). Cleared for takeoff: Paper airplanes in flight. *Mathematics Teaching in the Middle School, 17*(7), 402–409.

Thompson, T. D., & Preston, R. V. (2004). Measurement in the middle grades: Insights from NAEP and TIMSS. *Mathematics Teaching in the Middle School, 9*(9), 514–519.

Tompert, A. (1997). *Grandfather Tang's story*. New York, NY: Dragonfly Books.

Towers, J., & Hunter, K. (2010). An ecological reading of mathematical language in a grade 3 classroom: A case of learning and teaching measurement estimation. *The Journal of Mathematical Behavior, 29*, 25–40.

Zacharos, K. (2006). Prevailing educational practices for area measurement and students' failure in measuring areas. *Journal of Mathematics Behavior, 25*(3), 224–239.

Zwillinger, D. (Ed.). (2011). *Standard mathematical tables and formulae* (32nd ed.). Boca Raton, FL: CRC Press.

Chapter 17

Battista, M. T. (2007). The development of geometric and spatial thinking. In F. K. Lester (Ed.), *Second handbook of research on mathematics teaching and learning* (pp. 843–908). Reston, VA: NCTM.

Common Core Standards Writing Team. (2013, September 19). *Progressions for the Common Core State Standards in Mathematics (draft). Grades K–5, Geometry*. Tucson: Institute for Mathematics and Education, University of Arizona.

Council of Chief State School Officers. (2010). *Common Core State Standards*. Washington, DC.

Kell, H. J., Lubinski, D., Benbow, C. P., & Steiger, J. H. (2013). Creativity and technical innovation: spatial ability's unique role. *Psychological Science, 24*, 1831–1836.

Manizade, A., & Mason, M. (2014). Developing the area of a trapezoid. *Mathematics Teacher, 107*(7), 508–514.

Sarama, J., & Clements, D. H. (2009). *Early childhood mathematics education research: Learning trajectories for young children*. New York: Routledge.

Sowder, J. T., & Wearne, D. (2006). What do we know about eighth-grade student achievement? *Mathematics Teaching in the Middle School, 11*(6), 285–293.

van Hiele, P. M. (1986). *Structure and insight: A theory of mathematics education*. Orlando, FL: Academic Press.

van Hiele, P. M. (1999). Developing geometric thinking through activities that begin with play. *Teaching Children Mathematics, 5*(6), 310–316.

Yu, P., Barrett, J., & Presmeg, N. (2009). Prototypes and categorical reasoning: A perspective to explain how children learn about interactive geometry objects. In T. Craine & R. Rubenstein (Eds.), *Understanding geometry for a changing world* (pp. 109–126). Reston, VA: NCTM.

Wai, J., Lubinski, D., & Benbow, C. (2009). Spatial ability for STEM domains: Aligning over 50 years of cumulative psychological knowledge solidifies its importance. *Journal of Educational Psychology, 101*(4), 817–835. http://dx.doi.org/10.1037/a0016127.

Zwillinger, D. (Ed.). (2011). *Standard mathematical tables and formulae* (32nd ed.). Boca Raton, FL: CRC Press.

Chapter 18

Buckley, J., Jr., & Stremme, R. (2006). *Book of lists: Fun facts, weird trivia, and amazing lists on nearly everything you need to know!* Santa Barbara, CA: Scholastic.

Burrill, G. F., & Elliot, P. (2006). *Thinking and reasoning with data and chance: 68th NCTM yearbook.* Reston, VA: NCTM.

Council of Chief State School Officers. (2010). *Common Core State Standards.* Washington, DC.

Curcio, F. R. (1987). Comprehension of mathematical relationships expressed in graphs. *Journal for Research in Mathematics Education, 18*(5), 382–393.

English, L. (2013). Surviving an avalanche of data. *Teaching Children Mathematics, 19*(6), 364–372.

Franklin, C. A., & Garfield, J. B. (2006). The GAISE Project: Developing statistics education guidelines for grades PreK–12 and college courses. In G. F. Burrill & P. C. Elliott (Eds.), *Thinking and reasoning with data and chance: 68th NCTM yearbook* (pp. 345–376). Reston, VA: NCTM.

Franklin, C. A., Kader, G., Mewborn, D., Moreno, J., Peck, R., Perry, M., & Scheaffer, R. (2005). *Guidelines for assessment and instruction in statistics education (GAISE) report.* Alexandria, VA: American Statistical Association.

Franklin, C. A., & Mewborn, D. S. (2008). Statistics in the elementary grades: Exploring distribution of data. *Teaching Children Mathematics, 15*(1), 10–16.

Friel, S., Curcio, F., & Bright, G. (2001). Making sense of graphs: Critical factors influencing comprehension and instructional implications. *Journal for Research in Mathematics Education, 32*(2), 124–158.

Friel, S. N., O'Conner, W., & Mamer, J. D. (2006). More than "meanmedianmode" and a bar graph: What's needed to have a statistical conversation? In G. F. Burrill & P. C. Elliott (Eds.), *Thinking and reasoning with data and chance: 68th NCTM yearbook* (pp. 117–138). Reston, VA: NCTM.

Hudson, P. J., Shupe, M., Vasquez, E., & Miller, S. P. (2008). Teaching data analysis to elementary students with mild disabilities. *TEACHING Exceptional Children Plus, 4*(3), Article 5. Retrieved from http://escholarship.bc.edu/education/tecplus/vol4/iss3/art5.

Langrall, C., Nisbet, S., Mooney, E., & Jansem, S. (2011). The role of context expertise when comparing data. *Mathematical Thinking and Learning, 13*, 47–67.

McGlone, C. (2008, July). *The role of culturally-based mathematics in the general mathematics curriculum.* Paper presented at the Eleventh International Congress on Mathematics Education, Monterrey, Mexico.

Mokros, J., & Wright, T. (2009). Zoos, aquariums and expanding students' data literacy. *Teaching Children Mathematics, 15*(9), 524–530.

Monteiro, C., & Ainley, J. (2010). The interpretation of graphs: Reflecting on contextual aspects. *Alexandria, 3*(2), 17–30.

NCTM (National Council of Teachers of Mathematics). (2006). *Curriculum focal points for prekindergarten through grade 8 mathematics: A quest for coherence.* Reston, VA: NCTM.

NCTM (National Council of Teachers of Mathematics). (2000). *Principles and standards for school mathematics.* Reston, VA: NCTM.

Russell, S. J. (2006). What does it mean that "5 has a lot"? From the world to data and back. In G. F. Burrill & P. C. Elliott (Eds.), *Thinking and reasoning about data and chance: 68th NCTM yearbook* (pp. 17–30). Reston VA: NCTM.

Scheaffer, R. L. (2006). Statistics and mathematics: On making a happy marriage. In G. F. Burrill & P. C. Elliott (Eds.), *Thinking and reasoning about data and chance: Sixty-eighth yearbook* (pp. 309–322). Reston, VA: NCTM.

Schaeffer, R. L., and Jacobbe, T. (2014), Statistics education in the K-12 schools of the United States: A brief history. *Journal of Statistics Education, 22* (2). http://www.amstat.org/publications/jse/v22n2/scheaffer.pdf.

Schield, M. (2010). Assessing Statistical Literacy: Take CARE. In P. Bidgood, N. Hunt, & F. Jolliffe (Eds.) *Assessment Methods in Statistical Education: An International Perspective* (pp. 133–152). Chichester, UK: John Wiley & Sons Ltd.

Shaughnessy, J. M. (2003). Research on students' understanding of probability. In J. Kilpatrick, W. G. Martin, & D. Schifter (Eds.), *A research companion to Principles and Standards for School Mathematics* (pp. 216–226). Reston, VA: NCTM.

Shaughnessy, J. M. (2006). Research on students' understanding of some big concepts in statistics. In G. F. Burrill & P. C. Elliott (Eds.), *Thinking and reasoning about data and chance: 68th NCTM yearbook* (pp. 77–98). Reston, VA: NCTM.

Shaughnessy, J. M. (2007). Research on statistics learning and reasoning. In F. K. Lester (Ed.), *Second handbook of research on mathematics teaching and learning* (pp. 957–1010). Reston, VA: NCTM.

Tarr, J. E., & Shaughnessy, J. M. (2007). *Data and chance. Results from the 2003 National Assessment of Educational Process.* Reston, VA: NCTM.

Weatherform, C. B. (2005). *A Negro league scrapbook.* Honesdale, PA: Boyds Mills Press.

Index

Abstract reasoning, 3
Academic language instruction for ELLs
  assessment considerations, 81–82
  building background knowledge, 78
  comprehensible input in, 78
  content and language objectives, 76
  discourse reflecting language needs, engaging children in, 78–79
  effective learning opportunities for, creating, 73–74
  focusing on, 75–77
  groups to support language development, 79–81
  intentional vocabulary instruction and, 76–77
  linguistic load, limiting, 82
  native language, honoring, 76
  standards, 74
  student participation during, 77–81
Acceleration, for gifted children, 95
Accommodations
  in constructivism, 6
  defined, 6
  for diverse learners, 85
  for ELLs, providing, 82–83
Achievement gaps, 84
Action situations, 122
Adapting tasks, 22–23
Adaptive reasoning, 2
Adding It Up (NRC), 2, 3
Addition. *See also* Addition facts, reasoning strategies for; Addition of decimals; Addition of fractions; Computational estimation
  adding a group in multiplication, 155
  adding zeros in multiplication, 152–153
  change problems, 118, 119–120
  compare problems, 118, 119–120
  contextual problems, 120–121
  decimals, 294–296
  developmental process for basic fact mastery for, 142
  equal addition, 188–189
  invented strategies for, 189–193
  model-based problems, 121–123
  of multidigit numbers, 190–192
  part-part-whole problems, 118, 119
  problem difficulty, 120
  problem structures, 117–120
  standard algorithms for, 193
  standards, 116–117
  teaching, 120–123
  teaching for relational understanding, 7–9
  in teaching instrumental understanding, 9–10
  teaching-through-problem-solving experience, 109–110
  understanding of, 7–11
Addition facts, reasoning strategies for, 145–149
  combinations of 10, 147
  doubles, 148–149
  making 10, 147–148
  near-doubles, 148–149
  one more than and two more than, 146–147
Addition of decimals, 294–296
  algorithms, developing, 295–296
  estimating sums, 294–295
  formative assessment, 296
  Representing Sums and Differences activity, 296
  standards, 294
Addition of fractions, 252–261
  algorithms, developing, 258–259
  common errors and misconceptions, 260–261
  Common Multiple Cards activity, 261

contextual problems, 252–253
  estimation, 257–258
  formative assessment note, 253, 256, 259
  Gardening Together activity, 256
  Gold Prize activity, 255
  greater than one, 259–260
  invented strategies, 257–258
  Jumps on the Ruler activity, 257
  like denominators, 258
  mixed numbers, difficulty with, 261
  models, 254–257
  More Than or Less Than One activity, 258
  unlike denominators, 259
Add to problems, 118, 119
Administrator engagement and support, 106–107
After phase of lesson, 32, 33, 35–36
Agame Monkey Math Balance, 319
Agency, mathematical, 12
Algebraic thinking, 307–338
  common errors and misconceptions, 338
  functional thinking, 335–338
  generalizations, 308–314
  number system, explicit structure in, 326–331
  patterns, 331–338
  standards, 308
  strands of, 308
  symbols, meaningful use of, 314–326
Algorithms. *See* Standard algorithms
Alike and Different (routine), 35
AMTE (Association of Mathematics Teacher Educators), 38
Analysis
  data, 411–419
  in van Hiele levels of geometric thought, 374, 376–377, 379–380
Anecdotal notes, 40
Angles, 364–366
  comparison activities, 364
  physical models of, using, 364
  protractors, 365–366
  standards, 364
  A Unit Angle activity, 364
Anticipating, for orchestrating productive discussions, 24
Approximate language, in measurement estimation, 346
Approximate numbers, 167
Area, 351–359
  comparison activities, 351–352
  Cover and Compare activity, 353
  defined, 351
  Fixed Areas activity, 356
  formulas for, 357–358
  perimeter and, relationship between, 355–356
  physical models of, using, 352–354
  problems, 124, 126
  Rectangle Comparison-Square Units activity, 354
  of rectangles, 358–359
  Sorting Areas and Perimeters activity, 356
  standards, 352
  Tangram Areas activity, 352
  Two-Piece Shapes activity, 351
Area models
  for addition of fractions, 254–256
  base-ten materials, 282, 283, 284, 286–288, 289
  Decimal Roll and Cover activity, 285
  for division of fractions, 270, 271
  for equivalent fractions, 241
  for fractions, 221–223

for fraction-to-decimal connections, 282–285
  for iterating, 233
  in multiplication algorithm, 199–200
  for multiplication of fractions, 266
  for partitioning, 227–228
  rational number wheel, 282, 283, 284, 288, 302, 303
  Shifting Units activity, 283
  standards, 266
  for subtraction of fractions, 254–256
  10 x 10 grid, 282, 283, 285, 287–288, 289, 302
Array
  defined, 129
  model, 130, 133
  open, 200–201
  problems, 124, 126
"Ask-before-tell" approach, 112
Assessment
  of basic fact fluency, 145, 146
  of basic facts, 145
  of children with learning disabilities, 91–94
  creating, for learning, 38–52
  diagnostic interviews, 81
  for ELLs, 81–83
  formative. *See* Formative assessments
  linguistic load and, limiting, 82
  overview of, 12
  providing accommodations, for ELLs, 82–83
  rubrics in, 49–52
  summative, 39, 46
  of tasks, 22
  tasks with multiple entry/exit points, for ELLs, 81
  timed tests, 145
Assimilation, 6
Associative property of multiplication, 132–133, 195
Authority, mathematical, 12

Background knowledge, building, 78
Balance, equal sign as, 317–319
Bar diagrams, 122, 132, 190
Bar graphs, 414–415
Barriers for children with disabilities, removing, 92
Base-ten blocks, 30
Base-ten concepts
  Base-Ten Riddles activity, 173
  electronic versions of base-ten manipulatives, 172
  equivalent representations, 172–173
  formative assessment note, 169
  grouping activities, 171–172
  integrating with counting by ones, 168
  integrating with place-value notation, 170
  integrating with words, 168–170
  Three Other Ways activity, 173
  Too Many to Count? activity, 172
Base-ten materials, 170, 282, 283, 284, 286–288, 289
Base-ten models for place value, 170–171
  groupable models, 170
  nonproprtional models, 171
  pregrouped models, 170–171
Basic fact fluency, 141–162
  addition facts, reasoning strategies for, 145–149
  approaches to teaching, 143–144
  assessing, 145, 146
  combinations, developmental phases for learning, 142
  common errors and misconceptions, 162
  contextual problems for teaching, 144

Basic fact fluency (*continued*)
 defined, 141
 developing, 141–162
 division facts, reasoning strategies for, 156
 effective teaching of, 144–145
 explicitly teach reasoning strategies for, 145
 multiplication facts, reasoning strategies for,
  151–155
 standards, 142
 subtraction facts, reasoning strategies for, 149–151
 teaching, do's and don'ts for, 160–162
Basic fact mastery
 drill, 159
 fact remediation, 159–160
 games to support, 156–158
 reinforcing, 156–160
Before phase of lesson, 32, 33–34, 35–36
Benchmarks
 angles, 365
 in estimation, 267
 in measurement estimation, 340, 346–347
 numbers in computations, relationships with, 176
 in standard units, 344, 345
 time, 367
Better Homes and Gardens New Junior Cookbook
  (Better Homes and Gardens), 361
*Book of Lists: Fun Facts, Weird Trivia, and Amazing
  Lists on Nearly Everything You Need to Know!*
  (Buckley and Stremme), 411
Borrowing, 193
Broken Calculators apps, 132
Building A Better Teacher (Green), 36

Calculators, 30
Capacity, 359–361
 Capacity Sort activity, 359
 comparison activities, 359–360
 defined, 359
 instruments for measuring, 361
 physical models of, using, 360–361
 standard units of, 359
Carrying, 193
Categorical data, 405, 410, 418
CCSS-M. *See Common Core State Standards for
  Mathematics* (CCSS-M)
Center for Applied Special Technology (CAST), 94
Central Intelligence Agency (CIA) World Fact
  Book, 411
Change amount, 119
Change problems, 118, 119–120
 compare problems, 118, 119–120
 join/add to problems, 118, 119
 part-part-whole problems, 118, 119
 separate/take from problems, 118, 119
 standards, 119
Changes in mathematics curriculum
 CCSS-M and, 100–101
 content changes, 99–101
 evidence for change, 100
 reasons for, 99–100
 resistance to, 99–101
Change unknown problems, using join with, 192
Checklists, 40–41
Children as individuals, recognizing, 55–56
Children with exceptionalities. *See* Diverse learners
Chunking, 347
Circle graphs, 415–416
 easily constructed, 415–416
 percentages, determining, 416
Circular Fraction Pieces, 221–222, 233
Clarity, for children with disabilities, 92
Classification, 411–413
 Hidden Labels activity, 413
 Venn diagram, 412–413
 What about "Both"? activity, 412
Classroom discourse, orchestrating, 17, 23–29
 classroom discussions in, 24–26
 how much to tell and not to tell, 27–28
 mistakes and misconceptions to enhance learning,
  28–29

questioning in, aspects of, 26–27
 recommendations for promoting, based on
  research, 25–26
Classrooms
 dimensions of productive, 12–13
 to support invented strategies, 185
 that promote understanding, 12–13
 types of teaching in, 13
Classroom visits, 110
Clearly defined tasks, 17
Clocks, reading, 366–367
Cluster problems
 in division, 204–205
 in multiplication, 198
Coaching, 13
Cognitive demand
 level of, 18–19
 in open questions, 60–61
 overview if, 12
Combination problems, 124, 126
Commas, cultural differences in using, 69
Common Core State Standards for Mathematics
  (CCSS-M)
 active nature required in developing, 5
 addition, 116–117
 administrators' understanding of, 106–107
 algebra, 308
 area, 352
 area models, 266
 calculators and manipulatives as tools for doing
  mathematics, 30
 change problems, 119
 children with moderate/severe disabilities, 94
 compare problems, 119
 computational estimation, 211, 213
 computational fluency, 183
 computation with decimals, 294
 conjectures, 331
 conversions, 349
 coordinate graphs, 337
 decimals, 278, 281, 294
 denominators, 258
 distributive property, 198
 division, 124
 equal sign, 316
 fluency, developing, 142
 fraction concepts, 217–218, 223, 236
 fraction operations, 251, 258, 262, 263, 266
 functions, 332
 geometry, 371, 372
 improvised units, 340
 invented strategies, 185, 189
 know from memory, 156
 location, 398
 mass, 363
 measurement, 340, 345
 measurement estimation, 346
 multiplication, 124
 multiplication of fractions, 262, 263
 myths related, 100–101
 NCTM's process standards connected to, 5
 opposition to, 99
 partitioning, 228
 part-part-whole problems, 119
 patterns, 332
 perimeter, 355
 properties, 331
 protractors, 365–366
 purpose of, 2–3
 representing and interpreting data, 405
 resources for parents, 105
 standard algorithms, 187, 188, 189, 205
 Standards for Mathematical Practice, 3–5, 16, 38,
  57, 105–106
 subtraction, 116–117
 subtraction of decimals, 294
 three-dimensional shapes, 388
 time measurement, 367
 transformations, 396
 two-digit divisors, 209
 two-step word problems, 137
 variables, 323–324

volume, 359
 weight, 363
 whole-number place-value concepts, 164
Common-denominator algorithm, 274, 275
Communication, 3, 98–115. *See also* Parental
  concerns
 with administrators, 106–107
 with families, 107–111
 homework practices and parent coaching,
  111–115
 process standard of, 57
 with stakeholders, 98–106
 technology, use of, 103
Commutative property of multiplication, 132–133
Compare problems, 118, 119–120
Comparison of decimals, 291–294
 Close Decimals activity, 293
 common errors and misconceptions, 292
 density of decimals, 293–294
 on empty number line, 293
 Line 'Em Up activity, 292
 Zoom activity, 293
Comparison problems, 124, 125, 132
Comparisons, 341, 342
 angles, 364
 area, 351–352
 capacity, 359–360
 mass, 363
 time, 366
 volume, 359–360
 weight, 363
Compatible numbers, in estimation, 214, 215, 267
Compensation strategy, 189
Complete-number strategies, 194–195, 197
Complexity, raising the level for gifted children,
  95–96
Composing and decomposing shapes, 382–385
 Decomposing Shapes activity, 385
 Geoboard Copy activity, 384
 geoboards, 382, 384–385
 materials for, 382
 Mosaic Puzzle activity, 383
 mosaic puzzles, 382, 383
 subdividing shapes, 385
 tangram puzzles, 383, 384
 Tangram Puzzles activity, 383
Comprehensible input, in academic language
  instruction for ELLs, 78
Computational estimation, 211–215
 compatible numbers strategy, 214, 215
 front-end strategy, 214
 High or Low? activity, 213
 Over or Under activity, 212–213
 rounding strategy, 214, 215
 standards, 211, 213
 strategies, 213–215
 teaching, 212–213
 That's Good Enough activity, 213
Computational fluency, 183–189
 direct modeling, 184
 invented strategies, 184–187
 standard algorithms, 187–189
 standards, 183
Computational strategies, 182–216
 common errors and misconceptions, 215–216
 computational estimation, 211–215
 invented strategies for addition and subtraction,
  189–193
 invented strategies for division, 203–211
 invented strategies for multiplication, 193–202
 toward computational fluency, 183–189
Computation with decimals. *See* Decimals
Computers
 independent enrichment on, for gifted children,
  97
 in math stations, 36
Conceptua Fractions, 225
Conceptual understanding, 2, 17–18
Concerns of parents. *See* Parental concerns
Concrete, semi-concrete, abstract (CSA)
  intervention, 89–90
Cones, 388, 389

Conjectures, 394–395
Conjectures based on properties, 329–331
  Broken Calculator: Can You Fix It? activity, 330
  Convince Me Conjectures activity, 330
  standards, 331
Connecting, for orchestrating productive discussions, 24
Connections, 3
Constructivism, 5–6, 13
Content
  adapting, for mathematically gifted children, 94–97
  changes in, resistance to, 99–101
  connecting with learners, 56–58
  differentiating in terms of depth and breadth, 56–57
  how children engage in thinking about, 57–58
  learning environment and, 58
  objectives, in academic language instruction for ELLs, 76
  parental concerns over, 103–104
  relevant, in culturally responsive instruction, 71–72
  ways for children to demonstrate understanding of, 58
Content areas, 408, 413
Contexts
  in computational estimation, 212
  connections, in culturally responsive instruction, 71–72
  relevant and well-designed, 21
Contextual problems
  addition, 120–121
  addition of fractions, 252–253
  analyzing, 134–137
  direct modeling, 184
  division, 127–129
  division of fractions, 269–273
  formative assessment note, 127, 135, 139
  invented strategies, 185, 190, 193, 203
  key words strategy, avoiding, 136–137
  lessons built on, 121
  multiplication, 127–129
  multiplication of fractions, 262–266
  multistep word problems, 137–140
  numbers for, choosing, 121, 128
  remainders, 128–129
  representations, 193
  simpler-problem strategy, 136
  strategies for solving, 134–137
  subtraction, 120–121
  subtraction of fractions, 252–253
  symbolism for multiplication and division, 127–128
  for teaching basic facts, 144
  teaching operations through, 117
  thinking about answer before solving, 135
Continuous data graphs, 416–418
Conventions, 236
Conversions, 349–350
  Changing Units activity, 349
  Conversion Please activity, 350
  standards, 349
Cooperative groups, 102–103
Coordinate graphs, 337–338
Counters to model problems, 263, 265–266
Counting strategies, in process of learning facts, 142
Create a Graph (NCES Kids Zone), 414
Creativity, for gifted children, 96
CSA (concrete, semi-concrete, abstract) intervention, 89–90
Cubes, 376, 388
Cuisenaire rods, 223, 226, 227, 234, 242
Culturally and linguistically diverse children, 67–82.
  See also English language learners (ELLs);
    Mathematics instruction, culturally responsive
  assessment considerations for, 81–82
  cultural differences in algorithms, 68–69
  funds of knowledge, 67–68
  involving all families, 68
  language issues, 68–69
  teaching strategies that support, 73–81

Curriculum
  changes in, 99–101
  Curriculum Focal Points, parents' concerns with, 109
  parental concerns, 107
  principal's role in implementing, 106–107
Curriculum Focal Points (NCTM), 2, 109
Cyberchase (PBS), 225
Cylinders, 362, 388, 389

Data, 404–421. See also Data analysis; Statistics
  categorical, 405, 410, 418
  classification, in data analysis, 411–413
  collecting, 410–411
  common errors and misconceptions, 420–421
  graphical representations, in data analysis, 413–419
  numerical, 405, 410, 413, 414, 417
  print resources, 411
  questions, formulating, 408–410
  results, interpreting, 419–420
  shape of, 406
  standards, 405
  statistical literacy, 405
  Web resources, 411
Data analysis, 411–419
  classification in, 411–413
  graphical representations in, 413–419
Decimal points
  adding and subtracting decimals, 294, 296
  The Decimal Point Names the Unit, 280–281
  dividing decimals, 301
  errors and misconceptions, 292
  measurement and monetary units, 281
  metric system, 281
  multiplying decimals, 296, 299–300
  percents, 302, 303–304, 305
  place value, 279
  role of, 279–281
  Where Does the Decimal Go? Division activity, 301
Decimals, 278–282. See also Decimal points;
    Fraction-to-decimal connections
  addition, 294–296
  Build It, Name It activity, 286
  Calculator Decimal Counting activity, 286–287
  comparing and ordering, 291–294
  computation with, 294–301
  The Decimal Point Names the Unit activity, 280–281
  Decimals and Fractions on a Double Number Line activity, 289
  density of, 293–294
  division, 300–301
  equivalent fractions and, 288–289
  estimation with, 294–295, 297–300, 300–301
  Familiar Fractions to Decimals activity, 287–288
  formative assessment, 289, 290–291
  measurement and monetary units, 281–282
  multiplication, 296–300
  names and formats, 285–287
  number sense, 287–294
  regrouping, 279
  say decimals correctly, 282
  standards, 278, 281
  subtraction, 294–296
  visual models for decimals, 282–285
  Where Does the Decimal Go? activity, 299, 301
Decomposing a factor, 153–154
Decomposing numbers, 166
Decomposing shapes. See Composing and decomposing shapes
Decomposition strategy, 189
Deduction, in van Hiele levels of geometric thought, 374, 378
Denominators
  common-denominator algorithm, 274, 275
  common errors and misconceptions, 220
  in equivalent fractions, 240, 242–243, 244, 245

fraction notation, 236
iterating, 231–232
like, in addition and subtraction of fractions, 258
multiplication of fractions, 268–269
multiplying by one, 246
Ordering Unit Fractions activity, 247
standards, 258
unlike, in addition and subtraction of fractions, 259
writing fractions in simplest terms, 246
Zero, One-Half, or One activity, 238
Density of fractions, 239
Depth, for gifted children, 95
Diagnostic interviews, 42–45
  for assessing ELLs, 81
  benefits of, 45
  conducting, 42
  example of, 43
  flexibility in planning and structuring, 44
  planning or structuring, 44
  purpose of, 42
  questions, 44
  tasks in, 43
Differentiating instruction, 53–66
  classroom elements in, 56–58
  content in, 56–57
  flexible grouping in, 65–66
  learning centers in, 58
  learning environment for, 58
  open questions in, 60–62
  parallel tasks in, 58–60
  process in, 57–58
  product in, 58
  recognizing children as individuals, 55–56
  through problem solving, 53–55
  tiered lessons in, 61–65
  for whole-class instruction, 58–62
Digit Correspondence Task, 169
Direct instruction, 13
Direct modeling, 184
Discussions in classroom, 24–26
  talk moves for supporting, 25
  teacher actions for orchestrating discussions, 24–25
Disequilibrium, 6, 13
Distributed-content approach, 112
Distributive property of multiplication, 195, 198, 328, 329
Distributive property of multiplication over addition, 133, 317, 326
Diverse learners, 84–97. See also Interventions for diverse learners
  accommodations and modifications for, 85
  achievement gaps and, 84
  explicit instruction for, 88–89
  instructional principles for, 84–88
  learning disabilities, 91–94
  mathematically gifted, 94–97
  multitiered prevention model, 85–88
  NCTM research-based strategies for teaching, 88–91
  prevention models, 85–88
  teaching for equity, 84–85
Division. See also Division of decimals; Division of fractions
  cluster problems, 204–205
  contextual problems, 127–129
  equal-group problems, 123, 125, 130
  facts, reasoning strategies for, 156
  formative assessment note, 211
  fractions connected to, 219
  invented strategies for, 203–211
  missing-factor strategies, 204–205
  model-based problems, 129–132
  operation sense, developing, 123
  problem structures, 123–126
  remainders, 128–129
  standard algorithms for, 205–211
  standards, 124
  strategies for solving, 134–137
  symbolism for, 127–128
  teaching, 126–132
  two-digit divisors, 209–211
  by zero, 134

Division of decimals, 300–301
  algorithms, developing, 301
  estimating quotients, 300–301
  Where Does the Decimal Go? Division activity, 301
Division of fractions, 269–276
  common errors and misconceptions, 276
  contextual problems, 269–273
  fraction divided by whole number, 270–271
  fractions divided by fractions, 272–273
  Fractions Divided by Whole Number Stories activity, 270
  iterating, 269
  models, 269–273
  partitioning, 269, 270, 272, 275
  Sandwich Servings activity, 271–272
  The Size Is Right: Division activity, 273–274
  whole number divided by whole number, 269–270
  whole numbers divided by fractions, 271–272
Division Recording sheets, 207
"Do-as-I-show-you" approach, 14–15
Doing mathematics
  family math nights and, 109
  at home, 114
  processes of, 3, 69
Doorbell Rang, The (Hutchins), 230
Dot grids, 397–398
Dot plot, 417
Double-minus-one facts. See Near-doubles
Doubles, 148–149
Doubles-plus-one facts. See Near-doubles
Doubling, 154–155, 194–195
Down Under 10, 150–151
Drawings, to represent and illustrate mathematical concepts, 31
Drill, 159
During phase of lesson, 32, 33, 34, 35–36

Elaborating, for supporting classroom discussions, 25
Empty number line, 190
English language learners (ELLs)
  academic language, focusing on, 75–77
  assessment considerations for, 81–82
  choice of strategies to lower anxiety of, 20
  contextual problems and, 121
  involving in discussions, 26
  reflective questions for planning and teaching mathematics lessons for, 74–75
  revoicing for, 25
  teaching strategies that support, 73–81
  think-pair-share for, 35
Entry points, in tasks, 19–20
Equal addition, 188–189
Equal-group problems, 123, 125, 130, 271
Equal sign, 316–326
  as balance, conceptualizing, 317–319
  Equal to the Challenge activity, 317
  formative assessment note, 318
  inequality sign, 316
  misconceptions, 316
  open sentences, 320–322
  relational thinking, 321–322
  Seesaw Students activity, 317–318
  standards, 316
  Tilt or Balance? activity, 318
  true/false sentences, 320–322
  understanding, 316–317
Equivalent-fraction algorithm, 244–246
Equivalent representations, 164–165, 172–173, 217–218
  Base-Ten Riddles activity, 173
  Three Other Ways activity, 173
Estimation
  addition of fractions, 257–258
  benchmarks in, 176, 267
  compatible numbers in, 267
  decimal sums and differences, 294–295
  language, 212
  measurement. See Measurement estimation

  multiplication of fractions, 267, 268
  percents, 305–306
  relative size of unit fractions, 267
  subtraction of fractions, 257–258
Evaluating tasks, 22–23
Examples, in computational estimation, 212
Exit points, in tasks, 19–20
Exit slips, 48
Expectation gaps, 84
Explicit instruction
  of basic facts, 143
  for diverse learners, 88–89
  of reasoning strategies, 143
  vocabulary, for ELLs, 76–77
Explicit-trade method, 207, 208
"Exploring Properties of Rectangles and Parallelograms," 36

Facilitative methods of teaching, 13
Factor, decomposing, 153–154
Fact remediation, 159–160
Fair share model, 206
Fair-sharing problems, 125, 128
Families. See also Homework practices and parent coaching; Parental concerns
  classroom visits, 110
  communication with, 107–111
  family math nights, 108–110
  involving all families, 110–111
  Math Promise, 114
  resources for, 113–114
Family math nights, 108–110
Faster isn't Smarter (Seeley), 105
Feedback, children's performance improved by, 43
Fives, in multiplication, 152
Fixed Factor War (game), 113
Flexible grouping, 65–66
Fluency
  basic facts for developing. See Basic fact fluency
  computational, 183–189
  procedural, 2, 12, 17, 18
Formative assessments
  children's self-assessment and reflection in, 48–49
  interviews, 42–45
  key processes in, 39
  observations in, 40–41
  position statements on, 38
  purpose of, 39
  questions, 42
  streaming video compared to, 39
  of tasks, 20
  tasks in, 45–48
Four-point rubric, 50
Fractional parts of units, measuring, 350–351
Fraction concepts. See also Denominators; Fraction equivalencies; Fraction operations; Fraction-to-decimal connections; Numerators
  area models for, 221–223
  Class Fractions activity, 225
  Close Fractions activity, 239
  common errors and misconceptions, 220
  comparing, 246–249
  correct way of referring to parts of, 219
  density of, 239
  difficult nature of, 219
  division connected to, 219
  equivalent. See Fraction equivalencies
  formative assessment note, 226
  interpretations, 218–219
  iterating, 231–235
  length models for, 221, 223–224
  On the Line activity, 238
  magnitude of, 237–239
  meanings of, 218–220
  measurement, 219
  models for, 221–226
  multiplying by one, 246
  notation, 236–237
  number line for, 223–224
  operations indicated by, 219

  Ordering Unit Fractions activity, 247
  partitioning, 227–231
  part-whole, 218
  Pitchers and Cups activity, 237
  Playground Fractions activity, 222–223
  ratios connected to, 219
  remainders expressed as, 128–129
  set models for, 221, 242–225
  size of, 226
  standards, 217–218, 223, 236
  symbols, 217, 225, 227, 232, 236–237
  teaching considerations for, 249
  unit, 231, 247
  Who Is Winning? activity, 224
  writing in simplest terms, 246
  Zero, One-Half, or One activity, 238
Fraction equivalencies, 239–246
  Apples and Bananas activity, 243
  area models for, 241
  to compare fractions, 248–249
  conceptual focus on, 239–240
  Different Fillers activity, 240
  Dot-Paper Equivalences activity, 241
  equivalent-fraction algorithm, 244–246
  equivalent-fraction models, 240–244
  formative assessment note, 244
  Garden Plots activity, 244–245
  length models for, 242
  Missing-Number Equivalences activity, 242–243
  multiplying by one, 246
  unitizing, 241
  writing in simplest terms, 246
Fraction notation, 236–237
Fraction operations, 250–276
  addition, 252–261
  division, 269–276
  multiplication, 262–269
  problem-based, number sense approach to, 251–252
  remainders, 276
  standards, 251
  steps to effective fraction computation instruction, 251–252
  subtraction, 252–261
  understanding, 250–252
Fraction-to-decimal connections, 282–291
  approximation with compatible, 289–290
  Best Match activity, 290
  comparing and ordering, 291
  Decimals and Fractions on a Double Number Line activity, 289
  Estimate, Then Verify activity, 288
  familiar fractions connected to decimals, 287–291
  Familiar Fractions to Decimals activity, 287–288
  formative assessment note, 289, 290–291
  models for, 282–285
  names and formats, 285–287
  other fraction-decimal equivalents, 291
  say decimals correctly, 282
Front-end strategy, 214
Functional thinking, 335–338
  In and Out Machine activity, 336
  standards, 332
  Two of Everything activity, 335
Funds of knowledge, 67–68

Games for homework, 113
Generalizations, 308–314
  with algorithms, 307, 308–309, 315, 327, 329
  behavior of operations, 312–313
  Diagonal Sums activity, 313–314
  Don't Push the Point activity, 312
  formative assessment note, 309, 313
  with numbers and operations, 308–314
  One Up and One Down: Multiplication activity, 311
  place value relationships and, 313–314
  with symbols, 309–310
Generic rubrics, 50

Geoboards, 382, 384–385
  Decomposing Shapes activity, 385
  electronic (NCTM), 385
  Geoboard Copy activity, 384
  shapes on, 384
Geometric reasoning, 373. *See also* The van Hiele
    levels of geometric thought
Geometry, 371–403
  common errors and misconceptions, 403
  defined, 371
  dynamic geometry programs, 391–392
  geometric content, 372
  geometric thinking, developing, 373. *See also* The
    van Hiele levels of geometric thought
  goals, 372–373
  location, 398–401
  shapes and properties, 380–396
  spatial sense, 372
  standards, 371, 372
  transformations, 396–398
  visualizations, 401–402
Giftedness. *See* Mathematically gifted children
Google Earth, 409
Google Earth's Measuring Tools, 350–351
Google Public Data Explorer, 411
Graphical representations, 413–419
  bar graphs, 414–415
  circle graphs, 415–416
  Comparing Cubits activity, 417
  computer programs, 419
  continuous data graphs, 416–418
  creating graphs, 414
  in data analysis, 413–419
  formative assessment note, 416
  Gross! activity, 418
  line graphs, 418
  line plots, 417
  object graphs, 414
  picture graphs, 414
  Stand by Me activity, 417
  Storm Chaser activity, 414–415
  Test Anxiety activity, 418
Groupable models, 170, 211
Grouping activities, base-ten, 171–172
  formative assessment note, 169
  integration with place-value notation, 170
Groups/groupings
  cooperative, 102–103
  cooperative/interdependent, to support language
    development, 79–81
  flexible, 65–66
  individual accountability in, 65–66
Growing patterns, 333–335
  analyzing, 333
  coordinate graphs, 337–338
  geometric, 333
  numeric components, 333
  Predict How Many activity, 334
Guided invention, 144
Guinea Pigs Add Up (Cuyler), 309

Halving, 154–155
High-level, cognitively demanding tasks, 19
Homework practices and parent coaching, 111–115
  "ask-before-tell" approach, 112
  distributed-content approach, 112
  games and interactives, 113
  questioning prompts for parents, 112, 113
  resources for families, 113–114
  seeing and doing mathematics at home, 114–15
  teaching parents how to help their children,
    111–113
  three-phase lesson model, 111
Hundreds chart, 175–176

Ideas
  new, constructing, 6
  understanding children's, 11–12
Identity, mathematical, 12, 72–73

Identity property of multiplication, 133
Illuminations website (NCTM), 30, 37
  Equivalent Fractions tool, 246
  "Exploring Properties of Rectangles and
    Parallelograms," 36
  Fraction Models, 225, 303
  Fun with Fractions, 244
  Hiding Ladybug, 37
  manipulatives, 30
  Mirror Tool, 396
  Pan Balance-Numbers or Pan Balance-
    Expressions, 319
  Quotient Café, 209
  State Data Map, 411
Improvised units, 340, 342
Inequality sign, 316
Informal deduction, in van Hiele levels of geometric
    thought, 374, 377–378, 379–380
Initiation-response-feedback (IRF) pattern, 27
Inquiry, learning through. *See* Teaching *through*
    problem solving
Institute of Education Sciences, 218
Instructional gaps, 84
Instrumental understanding, 9–10
  addition in, 9–10
  children's ideas in, 11–12
  explained, 7
  teaching for, 9–10
Interactive number line, 123
Interactives for homework, 113
Interactive whiteboards, in math stations, 36
Interests, 55
Interventions for diverse learners, 88–91
  CSA intervention, 89–90
  explicit strategy instruction, 88–89
  NCTM research-based strategies, 88–91
  peer-assisted learning, 90
  think-alouds, 90–91
Interviews, in formative assessments, 42–45. *See also*
    Diagnostic interviews
Invented strategies, 121
  for addition, 189–193
  for addition and subtraction of fractions, 257–258
  benefits of, 186–187
  computational fluency, 184–187
  contrasts with standard algorithms, 186
  defined, 184
  for division, 203–211
  environment for, 185
  formative assessment note, 192
  jump strategy, 189
  mental computation and, 187
  missing-factor strategies, 204–205
  models to support, 189–190
  for multiplication, 193–202
  for multiplication of fractions, 267
  representations, 193–194
  shortcut strategy, 189, 190, 191
  split strategy, 189
  standard algorithms for addition and subtraction,
    193
  standards, 185, 189
  for subtraction, 189–193
Invert-and-multiply algorithm, 275–276
Iterate units, 347
Iterating, 231–235
  area models for, 233
  Counting Counters: Find the Part activity, 234
  Counting Counters: Find the Whole activity,
    234, 235
  division of fractions, 269
  formative assessment note, 234
  length models for, 232
  in measurement, 342
  More, Less, or Equal to One Whole activity, 234
  multiplication of fractions, 262, 263
  set models for, 234
  A Whole Lot of Fun activity, 232
It's Elementary: A Parent's Guide to K-5 Mathematics
    (Whitenack, Cavey, and Henney), 114
iTunes Store, 122
"I-we-you" approach, 14, 32

Join/add to problems, 118, 119
Journals, 48
Jump strategy, 189, 247, 248
Just a Second (Jenkins), 366

Key word strategy
  avoiding, 136–137
  multiplication of fractions, 269
Knowledge
  background, building, 78
  funds of, 67–68

Language
  instruction for ELLs. *See* Academic language
    instruction for ELLs
  issues, 68–69
  mathematics as, 68–69
  native, honoring, 76
  proficiency, flexible groups based on, 55
Large numbers. *See* Number relations, extending to
    larger numbers; Numbers beyond 1000
Large skeletal structures, 390
Lattice multiplication, 202
Learner-centered classrooms, 7
Learning basic facts, 142
Learning centers, 58
Learning differences, parental concerns of, 101–103
Learning disabilities, children with
  homework, approach to, 113
  moderate/severe disabilities, 94
  questions for planning instruction for, 92
  structured tasks for, 62
  stumbling blocks for, 91
  support, suggestions for offering, 92–94
  teaching and assessing, 91–94
  think-pair-share for, 35
Learning environment
  for children with disabilities, 92
  for differentiating instruction, 58
Learning outcomes, parental concerns of, 105–106
Learning profile
  defined, 55
  flexible groups based on, 55
  inventory, 56
Learning theories, 5–6
  constructivism, 5–6
  sociocultural theory, 6
Learning through inquiry. *See* Teaching *through*
    problem solving
Length, 348–351
  conversions, 349–350
  formative assessment note, 349, 350
  fractional parts of units, 350–351
Length models. *See also* Number lines
  for addition of fractions, 257
  for division of fractions, 270, 271
  for equivalent fractions, 242
  for fractions, 221, 223–224
  for fraction-to-decimal connections, 285
  How Far Did Nicole Go? activity, 229
  for iterating, 232
  for partitioning, 228–229
  for subtraction of fractions, 257
Life-long learning, 36–37
Like denominators, 258
Line graphs, 418
Line plots, 417
Line symmetry, 376, 396–398
Linguistic load, limiting, 82
Liquid volume. *See* Capacity
Little ten-frames, 164, 165, 171
Location, 398–401
  Hidden Positions activity, 399
  Paths activity, 400–401
  standards, 398
  Step Right Up activity, 400
  What's the Point? activity, 400
Lower-level tasks, 18
Low-level cognitively demanding tasks, 19

Magnitude of fractions, 237–239
Making ten, 147–148
Manipulatives
    choices for, 30
    misuse of, 31
    physical, 30
    to represent and illustrate mathematical concepts, 30–31
    virtual, 30, 225
Mass, 363
    comparison activities, 363
    defined, 363
    physical models of, using, 363
    standards, 363
Mastery, in process of learning facts, 142
Mathematically gifted children, 94–97
    acceleration and pacing, 95
    complexity, 96
    creativity, 96
    depth, 95
    strategies to avoid, 96–97
Mathematical understanding
    of addition, 7–11
    children's ideas, 11–12
    classrooms that promote, 12–13
    continuum of, 7
    instrumental, 9–10
    relational, 7–9
    teaching for, 7–11
Mathematics
    changes in, resistance to, 99–101
    classrooms that promote understanding, 12–13
    conventions, 27
    as a language, 68–69
    learning theories, 5–6
    modeling, 4
    perseverance in, importance of, 105–106
    processes of doing, 3, 69
    proficiency, strands of, 2
    Standards for Mathematical Practice, 3–5
    statistics differentiated from, 405–406
    strands of mathematical proficiency, 2
    teaching for understanding, 7–11
Mathematics instruction, culturally responsive, 69–73
    aspects of, 70
    context connections in, 71–72
    high expectations, communicating, 70–71
    interrelated mathematical ideas in, 71
    mathematical identity and, 72–73
    relevant content in, 71–72
    shared power in, 73
Math Forum@NCTM, 113–114
Math Learning Center, 123
Math Playground, 122, 336
Math Playground Fraction Bars, 225
Math Promise, 114
Math stations, 35–36
Measurement, 339–370
    angles, 364–366
    area, 351–359
    attributes, 340, 341
    capacity, 340, 359, 360, 361
    common errors and misconceptions, 369–370
    comparisons, 341, 342
    concepts and skills, 341–343
    decimal point with measurement units, 281–282
    defined, 340
    division, 123, 124, 125
    ELLs and, 78
    estimation, 345–348
    fractions, 219
    grade-level goals, 340
    length, 348–351
    mass, 363
    meaning and process of, 340–345
    measuring instruments, using, 341, 342–343
    measuring units, physical models of, 341, 342
    metric system, 281, 345
    money, 368
    nonstandard units, 343
    overview of, 339–340

standards, 340, 345
standard units, 343–345
steps in, 340
time, 366–368
volume, 359–363
weight, 363
Measurement estimation, 345–348
    activities, 348
    approximate language in, 346
    benchmarks or referents for, 340, 346–347
    chunking for, 347
    Estimation Scavenger Hunt activity, 348
    formative assessment note, 348
    iterate units for, 347
    reasons for including, 346
    standards, 346
    strategies for, 346–347
    teaching, tips for, 347–348
Measuring instruments, using, 341, 342–343
Measuring Penny (Leedy), 344
Measuring units, physical models of. *See* Physical models of measuring units
Memorization
    approaches to teaching, 143
    in low-level cognitively demanding tasks, 19
    mnemonics (memory aids) for, 92
    support for children with disabilities, 92
Mental computation strategy, 187
Methods
    alternative, telling children about, 27
    children's, clarification or formalization of, 27
Metric system, 345
Mini-lessons, 35
Minimal defining list (MDL), 378, 394–395
Misconceptions, leveraging to enhance learning, 28–29
Missing-factor strategies, 204–205
Missing-part problems, using join with, 192
Mistakes, leveraging to enhance learning, 28–29
Mixed numbers, in addition and subtraction of fractions, 261
Mnemonics (memory aids), 92
Model-based problems
    addition, 121–123
    bar diagrams, 122, 132
    Broken Division Key activity, 132
    Divide and Conquer activity, 131
    division, 129–132
    for equal-group multiplication, 130
    Factor Patterns activity, 130–131
    Factor Quest activity, 129
    multiplication, 129–132
    number line, 121–123
    subtraction, 121–123
Models. *See also* Area models; Length models; Model-based problems; Set models
    for addition of fractions, 254–257
    area models, 282–285
    bar diagrams, 190
    base-ten, for place value, 170–171
    in division algorithm, 205–209
    for division of fractions, 269–273
    empty number line, 190
    equivalent-fraction, 240–244
    for fractions, 221–226
    for fraction-to-decimal connections, 282–285
    length models, 285
    mathematic, 4
    of measuring units. *See* Physical models of measuring units
    in multiplication algorithm, 199–202
    open array, 200–201
    partial quotients using visual model, 206–207
    partition or fair share model, 206
    set models, 285
    in subtraction algorithm, 205–209
    for subtraction of fractions, 254–257
    to support invented strategies, 189–190
    written record, 201, 207–209
Moderate/severe disabilities (MSD), children with, 94
Modifications, for diverse learners, 85

Monetary units, 281–282, 368
Monitoring, for orchestrating productive discussions, 24
Mosaic puzzles, 382, 383
Multidigit numbers
    benchmark numbers, 176
    cluster problems, 198
    Digit Change Sped Icon Calc Icon activity, 175
    hundreds chart, 175–176
    Hundreds Chart, 175–176
    multiplication of, 196–198
    patterns and relationships with, 174–176
    Say It/Press It activity, 175
    Thousands Chart activity, 176
    200 and Some More activity, 176
Multiplication. *See also* Multiplication facts, reasoning strategies for; Multiplication of decimals; Multiplication of fractions
    area problems, 124, 126
    array problems, 124, 126
    associative property of, 132–133, 195
    combination problems, 124, 126
    commutative property of, 132–133
    comparison problems, 124, 125, 132
    compensation strategies, 195–196
    contextual problems, 127–129
    decimals, 296–300
    distributive property of, 195, 198, 328, 329
    distributive property of, over addition, 133, 317, 326
    equal-group problems, 123, 125, 130
    invented strategies for, 193–202
    lattice, 202
    model-based problems, 129–132
    of multidigit numbers, 196–198
    by one-digit multiplier, 194–196
    operation sense, developing, 123
    problem structures, 123–126
    representations, 193–194
    rounding, 214, 215
    standard algorithms for, 198–202
    standards, 124
    strategies for solving, 134–137
    symbolism for, 127–128
    teaching, 126–132
    zero and identity properties of, 133
Multiplication facts, reasoning strategies for, 151–155
    adding or subtracting a group, 155
    Clock Facts activity, 152
    decomposing a factor, 153–154
    derived, 153–155
    doubling, 154–155
    fives, 152
    formative assessment note, 155
    halving, 154–155
    nines, 153
    ones, 152–153
    twos, 151–152
    zeros, adding, 152–153
Multiplication of decimals, 296–300
    algorithms, developing, 297–300
    estimating products, 297
    Hit the Target activity, 297
    number line to illustrate, 298
    Where Does the Decimal Go? Multiplication activity, 299
Multiplication of fractions, 262–269
    algorithms, developing, 267
    area models, 266
    common errors and misconceptions, 268–269
    contextual problems, 262–266
    counters to model problems, 263, 265–266
    denominator in, 268–269
    estimation, 267, 268
    factors greater than one, 267–268
    fractions of fractions, subdividing unit parts, 265–266
    fractions of fractions, without subdivision, 264–265
    How Big Is the Banner? activity, 263–264
    invented strategies, 267

iterating, 262, 263
key word strategy, 269
matching multiplication situations with multiplication, 266–269
multiply fractions by whole numbers, 262–263
multiply whole numbers by fractions, 263–264
partitioning, 262, 263, 264, 265, 266, 267
scaling, 262, 263
standards, 262, 263
Multiplication Recording sheets, 201, 207
Multiplication situation, 125
Multistep word problems, 137–138, 137–140
Multitiered prevention model, 85–88
Multitiered system of support (MTSS), 85. *See also* Response to intervention (RtI)

Names for numbers, oral and written, 173–174
three-digit number names, 173–174
written symbols, 174
National Assessment of Educational Progress (NAEP), 232, 237, 287, 289, 302, 303, 342, 351, 357
National Council of Teachers of Mathematics (NCTM). *See also* Illuminations website (NCTM); *Principles to Actions* (NCTM)
academic language instruction for ELLs, standards for, 74
active nature required in developing, 5
CCSS-M's mathematical practices connected to, 5
Curriculum Focal Points, 2
e-Example, 246, 400
Figure This! Math Challenges for Families, 113
fraction game, 246
Math Forum@NCTM, 113–114
position statement on Access and Equity in Mathematics Education, 84
position statement on formative assessment, 38
position statement on metric system, 345
Principles and Standards for School Mathematics, 193–194
process standards, 3, 16, 38, 57, 106–107
research-based strategies for teaching diverse learners, 88–91
National Library of Virtual Manipulatives (NLVM), 30, 114, 225
activities for fraction addition and subtraction, 260
"Base Blocks-Decimals," 283
base-ten blocks, 172, 201
Diffy, 260
electronic geoboard, 385
Fraction Bars, 260
Fractions-Adding, 260
input-output machine investigations, 336
"Rectangle Division," 131
Tangrams, 352
What Time Will It Be?, 368
National Research Council (NRC)
Adding It Up, 2, 3
Operations Core, 116–117
Native language, honoring, 76
NCSM (National Council of Supervisors of Mathematics), 38
NCTM. *See* National Council of Teachers of Mathematics (NCTM)
Near-doubles, 148–149
Near facts, 156
Negro League Scrapbook, A (Weatherford), 411
Nines, in multiplication, 153
No-action situations, 122
Nonstandard units, 340, 343
NRICH project, 223
Number lines, 121–123
comparison of decimals on, 293
for fractions, 223–224
model-based problems on, 121–123
for multiplying decimals, 298
Number relations, extending to larger numbers, 164–167. *See also* Numbers beyond 1000
approximate numbers and rounding, 167

Close, Far, and In-Between activity, 166
decomposing numbers, 166
equivalent representations, 164–165
little ten-frames, 164, 165
part-part-whole relationships, 165–166
real-world ideas connected to, 167
relative magnitude, 166
Who Am I? activity, 166
Numbers
approximate, 167
for contextual problems, choosing, 121, 128
cultural differences in using, 69
multidigit, patterns and relationships with, 174–176
Numbers beyond 1000, 176–180
Calculator Challenge Counting activity, 177
Collecting 1,000,000? activity, 179
conceptualizing large numbers, 179–180
How Long?/How Far? activity, 179
A Long Time activity, 180
Really Large Quantities activity, 180
triples system for naming large numbers, 178
What Comes Next? activity, 177
Number sense
to compare fractions, 247–248
decimal, 287–294
Decimals and Fractions on a Double Number Line activity, 289
Estimate, Then Verify activity, 288
Familiar Fractions to Decimals activity, 287–288
formative assessment note, 289
Number system
generalizations, 308–314
properties, 327–329
structure in, 326–331
Number Talks (routine), 35
Numerators
common errors and misconceptions, 220
in equivalent fractions, 240, 242–243, 244, 245
fraction notation, 236
iterating, 231–232
multiplying by one, 246
Ordering Unit Fractions activity, 247
writing fractions in simplest terms, 246
Zero, One-Half, or One activity, 238
Numerical data, 405, 410, 413, 414, 417

Object graphs, 414
Objectives, in academic language instruction for ELLs, 76
Objects of thought, 373, 374, 376, 377, 378
Observations
anecdotal notes in, 40–41
checklists in, 40–41
in formative assessments, 40–41
One
addition and subtraction of fractions greater than, 259–260
in multiplication, 152–153
multiplication of fractions greater than, 267–268
One-digit multiplier, multiplication by, 194–196
complete-number strategies (including doubling), 194–195, 197
partitioning strategies, 195
One more than and two more than, 146–147
Online bar diagram tools, 122
Open array, 200–201
Open-ended tasks, 17
Open questions, in differentiating instruction, 60–62
Open sentences, 320–322
equal sign, 320–322
examples, 322
Make a Statement! activity, 322
relational thinking, 321–322
What's Missing? activity, 320
Operations
addition and subtraction problem structures, 117–120
common errors and misconceptions, 139–140

contextual problems for multiplication and division, 134–139
multiplication and division problem structures, 123–126
properties of multiplication and division, 132–134
teaching addition and subtraction, 120–123
teaching multiplication and division, 126–132
Operations Core (NRC), 116–117
Operation sense, 117
Ordering, decimals, 291–294

Pacing, for gifted children, 95
Parallel tasks, in differentiating instruction, 58–60
Parental concerns
changes in mathematics, 99–101
college and career preparation, 105
content, 103–104
cooperative groups, 102–103
curriculum, 107
struggling child, 105–106
student learning and outcome, 105–106
teacher as facilitator, 102
teaching and learning differences, 101–103
technology, use of, 103
Partial products, 202
Partial quotients using visual model, 206–207
Partitioning, 227–231
area models for, 227–228
defined, 227
division of fractions, 269, 270, 272, 275
formative assessment note, 228
Fourths or Not Fourths? activity, 228
length models for, 228–229
multiplication of fractions, 262, 263, 264, 265, 266, 267
set models for, 229–231
standards, 228
into three or six equal parts, 316–317
tiered lessons, 317–318
Partitioning strategies, 195
Partition model, 206
Partition problems, 125, 128
Part-part-whole problems, 118, 119
Part-whole fractions, 218
Pattern blocks, 382, 397, 399
Pattern Blocks, 30
Pattern of questioning, 27
Patterns, 331–338
coordinate graphs, 337–338
formative assessment note, 337
growing, 333–335
Perimeter Patterns activity, 336
repeating, 331–333
standards, 332
variables to represent, 325–326
PBS Kids Cyberchase, 319, 352
Peer-assisted learning, 90
Pentominoes, 401
Percentages, determining, 416
Percents, 301–306
bar diagrams to solve percent problems, 305
contextual problems, 304–305
estimation, 305–306
formative assessment, 305
linking fractions to, 302
models and terminology, 302–304
part-whole fraction exercises translated into, 304
Percent Memory Match activity, 303
Performance indicators, on rubrics, 49, 50, 51, 52
Perimeter
area and, relationship between, 355–356
Fixed Perimeters activity, 356
formulas for, 357
Sorting Areas and Perimeters activity, 356
standards, 355
What's the Rim? activity, 355
Periods, cultural differences in using, 69
Perseverance, importance of, 105–106
Physical manipulatives, 30

Physical models of measuring units, 341, 342
  angles, 364
  area, 352–354
  capacity, 360–361
  mass, 363
  volume, 360–361
  weight, 363
Picture graphs, 414
Place value
  decimal point in, 279–281
  extending to decimals, 278–279
  formative assessment note, 192
  generalizations and, 313–314
  instrumental understanding and, 9
  invented strategies, 184, 185, 186, 189
  measurement and monetary units, 281–282
  metric system, 281
  multiplication by one-digit multiplier, 195
  multiplication of multidigit numbers, 196, 197, 198
  open array, 201
  regrouping, 279
  standard algorithms, 188, 193
  10-to-1 relationship, 278–279
  two-digit divisors, 209, 210
Place-value notation, integration of base-ten
    grouping with, 170
Polygons, 386, 387, 388
Polyhedron, 388
Position statements on formative assessment, 38
Practice, for children with disabilities, 93
Precision, 4
Preferences of children, knowing, 55–56
Pregrouped models, 170–171, 212–213
Prevention models, 85–88
  progress monitoring, 87–88
  response to intervention, 85–87
Principles and Standards for School Mathematics
    (NCTM), 193–194
Principles to Actions (NCTM), 5, 16–17
  build procedural fluency from conceptual
    understanding, 17, 18
  elicit and use evidence of student thinking, 17, 24
  establish mathematics goals to focus learning,
    16, 32
  facilitate meaningful mathematical discourse, 17,
    23–29
  implement tasks that promote reasoning and
    problem solving, 16, 17
  incorporating evidence of child thinking into
    instruction, 38
  pose purposeful questions, 17, 24–27
  support productive struggle in learning
    mathematics, 17, 18, 19, 23, 27, 28
  use and connect mathematical representations, 17,
    29–32. *See also* Representations
Print resources, 411
Prisms, 389
Prisms, volume of, 362–363
Problematic tasks, 17, 18
Problem-based classroom, lessons in, 32–36
  three-phase lesson format, 32–36
Problem-based tasks, 45–46, 49, 51
Problem difficulty, 120
Problem solving. *See also* Teaching *through* problem
    solving
  differentiating instruction through, 53–55
  in mathematical proficiency, 3
  tools, 4
Procedural fluency, 2, 12, 17, 18
Procedures with/without connections, 19
Process
  complexity of, in tiered lessons, 62
  in differentiating instruction, 57–58
  standards, 57
Product, in differentiating instruction, 58
Productive disposition, 2
Products of thought, 373, 374, 375, 376, 378, 379
Professional noticing, 40
Progress monitoring, 87–88
Proof, reasoning and, 3
Properties. *See also* Shapes
  conjectures based on, 329–331
  generalizations with, 307, 314

making sense of, 327–329
  of operations, 328–329
  sets of tasks used to focus on, 327
  standards, 331
  understanding, 326–327
Properties of multiplication, 132–134
  associative property, 132–133
  commutative property, 132–133
  distributive property, 133
  Divide It Up activity, 134
  zero and identity properties, 133
Providing accommodations, 82
Pull-out opportunities, gifted, 96
Put together problems, 118, 119
Pyramids, 389

Quadrilaterals, 393–394, 395
Quantitative reasoning, 3
Quantities that vary, variables as, 326
Question probes, 42
Questions
  answers to, responding to, 27
  beyond one classroom, 408–410
  classroom, 408
  in diagnostic interviews, 44
  to engage all children, 27
  for families to help their children with homework,
    112, 113
  Fine Me activity, 409
  in formative assessments, 42
  formulating, 408–410
  level of, 26
  open, in differentiating instruction, 60–62
  in orchestrating classroom discourse, aspects of,
    26–27
  pattern of questioning, 27
  for planning instruction for children with special
    needs, 92
  reflective, for planning and teaching mathematics
    lessons for, 74–75
  reflective, to use in selecting tasks, 22
  understanding targeted by, 26
  What Can We Learn About Our Community?
    activity, 409–410

Range, in computational estimation, 212
Rate problems, 125
Rational number wheel, 282, 283, 284, 288, 302, 303
Ratios, fractions connected to, 219
Readiness
  defined, 55
  flexible groups based on, 65
Reasoning
  abstract and quantitative, 3
  critique reasoning of others, 4
  precision in, 4
  proof and, 3
  repeated, regularity in, 4–5
  for supporting classroom discussions, 25
Reasoning strategies, 110
  for addition facts, 145–149
  for division facts, 156
  explicit instruction on, 143
  formative assessment note, 142
  for multiplication facts, 151–155
  in process of learning facts, 142
  for subtraction facts, 149–151
Referents, for measurement estimation, 340,
    346–347
Reflection (children's) in formative assessments,
    46–47
Reflective questions
  for planning and teaching mathematics lessons
    for, 74–75
  to use in selecting tasks, 22
Reflective thought, 5, 6
Regrouping, 193
Relational thinking, 321–322
  formative assessment note, 321

Make a Statement! activity, 322
  open sentences, 321–322
  standards, 321
  true/false sentences, 321–322
Relational understanding
  addition in, 7–9
  children's ideas in, 11–12
  explained, 7
  instructional approach to teaching, 13
  instructional objectives for teaching, 8
  representations for teaching, 29, 31
  solution strategies for teaching, 8–9
  teaching for, 7–9
Relative magnitude, 166
Reluctant talkers/learners
  think-pair-share for, 35
  writing tasks and, 48
Remainders, 128–129, 276
Repeated addition problems, 125
Repeated subtraction, 125, 207, 209, 253, 271, 274
Repeated Subtraction Recording Sheet, 207
Repeating patterns, 331–333
  examples of, 331
  Hurricane Names activity, 332–333
  Predict Down the Line activity, 332
  standards, 332
Rephrasing, for supporting classroom discussions, 25
Representations, 3, 29–32
  process standard of, 57
  rules of thumb for using in classroom, 31–32
  tools, exploring with, 30–31
  Web of Representations, 29
Resources for families, 113–114
Response to intervention (RtI), 85–87
  defined, 86
  tiers in, 86–87
  tiers in, distinguished from tiered lessons in
    differentiation, 64–65
Result amount, 119
Revoicing, for supporting classroom discussions, 25
Rigor, in van Hiele levels of geometric thought
    (level 4), 374, 378–379
Rounding, 167
  multiplication, 214, 215
  two-digit divisors, 209–210
Routine problems, 17, 18
Routine tasks, 18
Rubrics
  in assessments, 49–52
  criteria and performance indicators on, 49, 50,
    51, 52
  four-point, 50
  functions of, 49
  generic, 50
  task-specific, 50–52
Rulers, 340
  area rulers, 354
  formative assessment note, 350
  subdivision marks on, 350
  using, 342–343

Scalene, 386, 387, 393
Scaling, 262, 263, 384
Selecting, for orchestrating productive discussions,
    24
Self-assessment (children's) in formative
    assessments, 46–47
Separate/take from problems, 118, 119
Sequences, 333. *See also* Growing patterns
Sequencing, for orchestrating productive
    discussions, 24
Set models, 312–313
  for division of fractions, 270, 271
  for fractions, 221, 242–225
  for fraction-to-decimal connections, 285
  for iterating, 234
  for multiplication of fractions, 263, 265–266
  for partitioning, 229–231
Shapes, 380–396
  Can You Make It? activity, 382
  classifying, 380–382

composing, 382–385
conjectures, 394–395
construction activities, 390–394
cylinders, 388, 389
decomposing, 382–385
Diagonals of Quadrilaterals activity, 394
in dynamic geometry programs, 391–392
formative assessment note, 381, 396
formulas for volumes of, 362–363
Geoboard Copy activity, 384
investigations, 394–395
Minimal Defining Lists activity, 394–395
mosaic puzzles, 382, 383
Mystery Definition activity, 392
polygons, 386, 387, 388
prisms, 389
proof, development of, 394–395
Property Lists for Quadrilaterals activity, 376–377, 378, 393, 394
pyramids, 389
quadrilaterals, 393–394, 395
sorting, 380–382
tangram puzzles, 383, 384
Tangram Puzzles activity, 383
three-dimensional shapes, 381, 388–389, 390
triangles, 375, 379, 380, 385, 386, 387, 393, 401
Triangle Sort activity, 393
True or False? activity, 395
two-dimensional shapes, 385–387
What's My Shape? activity, 381
Shodor's Project Interactivate, 336, 357
Shortcut strategy, 189, 190, 191, 247, 249, 252
Simpler-problem strategy, 136
Singapore mathematics, 122
Sociocultural theory, 6
Spatial sense, 372
Split strategy, 189, 247
Standard algorithms, 187–189
    addition, 295–296
    for addition, 193
    addition of fractions, 258–259
    common-denominator algorithm, 274, 275
    contrasts with invented strategies, 186
    cultural differences in, 188–189
    delay in teaching, 188
    division, 301
    for division, 205–211
    equivalent-fraction, 244–246
    generalizations with, 307, 308–309, 315, 327, 329
    invented strategies and, 186
    invert-and-multiply algorithm, 275–276
    multiplication, 297–300
    for multiplication, 198–202
    multiplication of fractions, 267
    standards, 187, 188, 189, 205
    subtraction, 295–296
    for subtraction, 193, 259–261
    subtraction of fractions, 258–259
    understanding, 188
Standards for Mathematical Practice (CCSS-M), 3–5
Standard units, 343–345
    appropriate units, choosing, 344
    Familiar Measures activity, 344
    Guess the Type of Measurement activity, 344
    important standard units and relationships, 345
    Personal Benchmarks activity, 344
    teaching, goals of, 343
    unit familiarity, developing, 344
Start amount, 119
Statistical literacy, 405
Statistics, 405–407
    analyze data, 411–419
    collect data, 410–411
    formulating questions, 408–410
    interpret results, 419–420
    mathematics distinguished from, 405–406
Story problems. See Contextual problems
Strands of algebraic thinking, 308
Strategic competence, 2
Strategies for solving problems, 134–137
Structure, 4

Subtraction. See also Subtraction facts, reasoning strategies for; Subtraction of decimals; Subtraction of fractions
    algorithms from around the world, 68–69
    change problems, 118, 119–120
    compare problems, 118, 119–120
    contextual problems, 120–121
    developmental process for basic fact mastery for, 142
    invented strategies for, 189–193
    model-based problems, 121–123
    part-part-whole problems, 118, 119
    problem difficulty, 120
    problem structures, 117–120
    repeated, 253, 271, 274
    standard algorithms for, 193
    standards, 116–117
    subtracting a group in multiplication, 155
    take-away, 192
    teaching, 120–123
Subtraction facts, reasoning strategies for, 149–151
    Down Under 10, 150–151
    take from 10, 151
    think-addition, 149–150
Subtraction of decimals, 294–296
    algorithms, developing, 295–296
    estimating differences, 294–295
    formative assessment, 296
    Representing Sums and Differences activity, 296
    standards, 294
Subtraction of fractions, 252–261
    algorithms, developing, 258–259
    common errors and misconceptions, 260–261
    Common Multiple Cards activity, 261
    contextual problems, 252–253
    estimation, 257–258
    formative assessment note, 253, 256, 259
    Gardening Together activity, 256
    Gold Prize activity, 255
    greater than one, 259–260
    invented strategies, 257–258
    Jumps on the Ruler activity, 257
    like denominators, 258
    mixed numbers, difficulty with, 261
    models, 254–257
    More Than or Less Than One activity, 258
    unlike denominators, 259
Summary, for children with disabilities, 93
Summative assessments, 39, 46
Symbols. See also Equal sign; Variables
    The Border Tiles Problem activity, 315
    connecting drawings to, 31
    for division, 127–128
    for fraction, 217, 225, 227, 232, 236–237
    generalizations with, 309–310
    as mathematical convention, 27
    meaningful use of, 314–326
    for multiplication, 127–128
    reinforcing, in after phase of lesson, 34–35
    in Web of Representations, 29
    written, 174
Take apart problems, 119
Take-away subtraction, 192
Take from 10, 151
Take from problems, 119
Talk moves for supporting classroom discussions, 25
Tangrams, 352, 383, 384
Task cards, 63–64
Tasks
    clearly defined, 17
    cognitive demand in, 18–19
    complexity of, 62
    contexts, relevant and well-designed, 21
    entry points and exit points in, 19–20
    evaluating and adapting, 22–23
    evaluation and selection guide, 22
    in formative assessments, 45–48
    forms of, 17
    ineffective, 23
    with multiple entry/exit points, for ELLs, 81
    open-ended, 17
    parallel, 58–60
    problematic, 17, 18

problem-based, 45–46, 49, 51
    routine, 18
    structure of, 62
    suggestions for adapting to increase potential for learning, 22–23
    support for children with disabilities, 92
    in teaching through problem solving, 17–23
    that develop procedural fluency and conceptual understanding, 17, 18
    in tiered lessons, 62–64
    translation, 46–47
    understanding vocabulary used in, 64
    writing, 48

Task-specific rubrics, 50–52
Teacher as facilitator, concerns of, 102
Teaching differences, parental concerns of, 101–103
Teaching for understanding, 7–13
    addition in, 7–11
    instructional approach to, 13
    instrumental understanding, 9–10
    key to, 13
    relational understanding, 7–9
    types of teaching in, 13
Teaching practices
    identified in Principles to Actions (NCTM), 16–17
    in teaching through problem solving, 16–17
Teaching through problem solving, 14–37, 49
    classroom discourse and, orchestrating, 23–29
    lessons in problem-based classroom, 32–37
    for life-long learning, 36–37
    mathematical concepts learned through, 16–17
    paradigm shift in, 16
    representations for, 29–32
    tasks in, 17–23
    teaching for problem solving compared to, 14–15
    teaching practices, 16–17
    upside down approach to, 14–16
Technology, parental concerns of using, 103
Ten
    combinations of, 147
    Frames and Facts activity, 148
    How Many More to Equal 10? activity, 147
    little ten-frames, 164, 165
    making, 147–148
    Move It, Move It activity, 148
    ten-frame, 147, 148
10 x 10 grid, 282, 283, 285, 287–288, 289, 302
Ten-frame, 147, 148
10,000 Grid Paper, 179, 285, 292
Terminology
    as mathematical convention, 27
    reinforcing, in after phase of lesson, 33, 34–35
Think-addition, 149–150, 192
Think-alouds, 90–91
Thinking Blocks, 122
Think-pair-share, 35
Three-digit number names, 173–174
Three-dimensional shapes, 388–389, 401–402
    categories of, 388–389
    classifications of, 381
    Constructing-Three Dimensional Shapes activity, 390
    Face Matching activity, 402
    formative assessment note, 381
    Geometry Necklaces activity, 402
    matching face cards with solid shapes, 402
    standards, 388
Three-phase lesson model, 32–35
    after phase, 33, 34–35, 111
    for helping parents help their child, 111
    overview of, 32–33
    before phase, 33–34, 111
    during phase, 33, 34, 111
    variations of, 35–36
Tiered lessons, 62–65
    aspects of, 62
    based on structure, 64
    characteristics of, 62
    in differentiation, distinguished from tiers in RtI, 64–65

Tiered lessons (*continued*)
examples of, 62–63
modifying original task to change level of challenge, 62–64
task cards, 63–64
Tiling, 342
Timed tests, 145
Time measurement, 366–368
comparison activities, 366
elapsed time, 367
Just a Minute!! activity, 366
reading clocks, 366–367
standards, 367
Today's Date (activity), 114
Tools
calculators, 30
defined, 30
drawings, 31–32
exploring representations with, 30–32
manipulatives, 30–31
problem-solving, 4
Trading, 193
Traits, recognizing children as individuals based on, 55–56
Transformations, 396–398
defined, 396
Dot Grid Line Symmetry activity, 397
line symmetry, 376, 396–398
Pattern Block Mirror Symmetry activity, 397
standards, 396
Translation tasks, 46–47
Translation task template, 47
Triangles, 375, 379, 380, 385, 386, 387, 393, 401
Triples system for naming large numbers, 178
True/false sentences, 320–322
equal sign, 320–322
examples, 322
Make a Statement! activity, 322
relational thinking, 321–322
True or False activity, 320
Two-digit divisors, 209–211
Double, Double-No Toil or Trouble! activity, 211
intuitive idea, 209–210
low-stress approach, 210–211
rounding, 209–210
scaffolding, 210–211
standards, 209
Two-dimensional shapes, 385–387
categories of, 385–386
classifications of, 387
Two more than. *See* One more than and two more than
Twos, in multiplication, 151–152
Two-step word problems, 137

Understanding. *See* Mathematical understanding
U.S. Census Bureau, 411
Unit fractions, 231, 247
Unitizing, 241

Universal design for learning (UDL), 94
Unknown values, variables as, 323–325
Unlike denominators, 259
Upside down approach, 14–16
USDA Economic Research Service Food Consumption, 411

van Hiele levels of geometric thought
characteristics of, 374
formative assessment note, 379
implications for instruction, 379
level 0: visualization, 374–376, 379
level 1: analysis, 374, 376–377, 379–380
level 2: informal deduction, 374, 377–378, 379–380
level 3: deduction, 374, 378
level 4: rigor, 374, 378–379
Minimal Defining Lists activity, 378
moving from level 0 to level 1, 379
moving from level 1 to level 2, 379–380
objects of thought, 373, 374, 376, 377, 378
overview of, 373–374
products of thought, 373, 374, 375, 376, 378, 379
Property Lists for Quadrilaterals activity, 377–378
Shape Sorts activity, 375
Variables, 322–326
meaning of, 322–323
as quantities that change together, 326
to represent patterns, 325–326
Solving the Mystery activity, 324–325
standards, 323–324
Story Translations activity, 323
as unknown values, 323–325
What's True for All Numbers? activity, 326
Venn diagram, 412–413
Virtual manipulatives, 30
Visual displays, for children with disabilities, 92
Visualizations, 401–402
Face Matching activity, 402
Geometry Necklaces activity, 402
Pentominoes activity, 401
three-dimensional imagery, 401–402
two-dimensional imagery, 401–402
in van Hiele levels of geometric thought, 374–376, 379
Vocabulary support for children with disabilities, 92
Volume, 359–363
Box Comparison-Cubic Units activity, 361
comparison activities, 359–360
defined, 359
Fixed Volume: Comparing Prisms activity, 360
formulas for, 362–363
liquid. *See* Capacity
physical models of, using, 360–361
of prisms, 362–363
Squeeze Play activity, 362
standards, 359

That's Cool! activity, 362
Which Silos Holds More? activity, 360

Waiting, for supporting classroom discussions, 25
Web of Representations, 29
Web resources, 411
Weight, 363
comparison activities, 363
defined, 363
physical models of, using, 363
standards, 363
What's Math Got to Do with It? How Parents and Teachers Can Help Children Learn to Love Their Least Favorite Subject (Boaler), 114
Whole-number computation. *See* Computational strategies
Whole-number place-value concepts, 163–181
base-ten concepts, extending, 171–173
base-ten grouping, integrating with counting by ones, 168
base-ten models for place value, 170–171
common errors and misconceptions, 180–181
diagnostic tasks, 169–170
extending number relations to larger numbers, 164–167
important place-value concepts, 167–171
levels of understanding, 169
multidigit numbers, patterns and relationships with, 174–176
names for numbers, oral and written, 173–174
numbers beyond 1000, 176–180
real-world ideas connected to, 167
standards, 164
Whole numbers
divided by fractions, 271–272
divided by whole numbers, 269–270
fractions divided by, 270–271
multiplied by fractions, 263–264
multiply fractions by, 262–263
Why Do Americans Stink at Math? (Green), 14
World Is Flat, The (Friedman), 1
Writing tasks, 48
Written record, 201, 207–209
developing, steps in, 207
in division algorithm, 207–209
explicit-trade method, 207, 208
lattice multiplication, 202
in multiplication algorithm, 201–202
Multiplication Recording sheets, 201, 207
partial products, 202
repeated subtraction, 207, 209
Repeated Subtraction Recording Sheet, 207
Written symbols, 174

Zero
adding, in multiplication, 152–153
division by, 134
Zero property of multiplication, 133
Zone of proximal development, 6